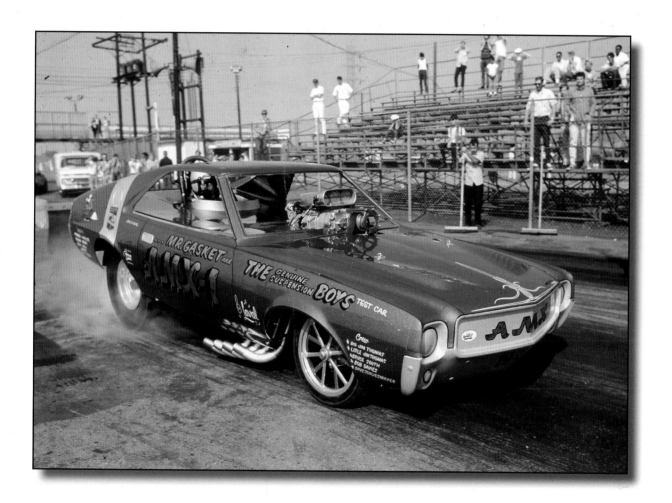

DRAG RACING
IN THE 1960s

Car Tech®

DOUG BOYCE

THE EVOLUTION IN RACE CAR TECHNOLOGY

CarTech®

CarTech®, Inc.
838 Lake Street South
Forest Lake, MN 55025
Phone: 651-277-1200 or 800-551-4754
Fax: 651-277-1203
www.cartechbooks.com

CarTech books may be purchased at a discounted rate in bulk for resale, events, corporate gifts, or educational purposes. Special editions may also be created to specification. For details, contact Special Sales at 838 Lake Street S., Forest Lake, MN 55025 or by email at sales@cartechbooks.com.

Edit by Bob Wilson
Layout by Connie DeFlorin

ISBN 978-1-61325-582-7
Item No. CT674

Library of Congress Cataloging-in-Publication Data Available

Written, edited, and designed in the U.S.A.
Printed in China
10 9 8 7 6 5 4 3 2 1

PUBLISHER'S NOTE: In reporting history, the images required to tell the tale will vary greatly in quality, especially by modern photographic standards. While some images in this volume are not up to those digital standards, we have included them, as we feel they are an important element in telling the story.

DISTRIBUTION BY:

Europe
PGUK
63 Hatton Garden
London EC1N 8LE, England
Phone: 020 7061 1980 • Fax: 020 7242 3725
www.pguk.co.uk

Australia
Renniks Publications Ltd.
3/37-39 Green Street
Banksmeadow, NSW 2109, Australia
Phone: 2 9695 7055 • Fax: 2 9695 7355
www.renniks.com

Canada
Login Canada
300 Saulteaux Crescent
Winnipeg, MB, R3J 3T2 Canada
Phone: 800 665 1148 • Fax: 800 665 0103
www.lb.ca

Table of Contents

Acknowledgments

Like any project of this magnitude, it took plenty of helping hands to see it through. Listed below are all those who graciously contributed to this project.

First and foremost, I have to thank the crew at CarTech Books: Bob Wilson and the editors who made sense of the work I submitted. A good rapport is essential, and Bob and I communicated quite a bit through this one. This book was a bit of a struggle, as it forced me into a writing style that was a bit outside of my comfort zone. I think the CarTech crew has done a great job of making sense of it all.

I have to give special thanks to a few gentlemen who have helped with previous projects and who went above and beyond any request that I made.

Forrest Bond, a contributor to *Drag Sport Illustrated*, *National Dragster*, and *Popular Hot Rodding* among other fine publications, made this project thoroughly enjoyable. He shared many of his trackside stories and spent a countless amount of time scanning negatives from his vast collection so that I was able to include the images here. The majority of these images are now being seen for the first time. When it comes to my appreciation, a simple thank-you falls far short.

James Handy has been a contributor to all my books, going back to the first one, *Grumpy's Toys*. Jim, a fine writer himself, has shared numerous backstories and graciously opened up his vast photo library to me. A big thanks, my friend.

Steve Reyes. Calling Steve a photojournalist is an understatement. His images take a backseat to no one, and the stories that this guy has are second to none. Many of those stories show up here, and many others were just too risqué to publish. We discussed tell-all book projects, but neither of us are prepared to spend the rest of our lives in witness protection.

Additional thanks goes to the following people who contributed to this project: Ed Aigner, Phil Bellomy, Ernst Blofeld, Bob Boudreau, Darren Boyce, Jim Cecil, Gordon Collett, Ken Crawford, Dennis Doubleday, John Foster Jr., John Gabrial, Robert Genat, Ed Grist, Ken Gunning, Dave Hales, Jim Hall, John Hellmuth, David Huff, Vance Hunt, Tommy Ivo, Paul Johnson, Stephen Justice, Brian Kennedy, Scott Krueger, Jim McFarland, Richard Kinstry, George Montgomery, Charles Morris, Bennie Osborn, Bill Pitts, Don Prieto, Rob Potter, Michael Pottie, Trey Ragsdale, Clare Sanders, Bill Scharing, Bob Snyder, Mike Strickler, Ray Sullins, Bill Truby, Hugh Tucker, John Vanderpryt, Gordy Waldhauser, and R. C. Williams.

Credit must also be given to the websites I used while compiling information: Twotogo.homstead.com, hotrod.com, cacklefest.com, wediditforlove.com, competitionplus.com, nhra.com, garlits.com, racingjunk.com, and hemmings.com. And I can't forget old titles and publishers such as *Drag News*, *National Dragster*, *Drag Sport Illustrated*, *Drag World*, Petersen Publishing, Argus, and Magnum.

And finally, to my wife, Laura. Without her belief, support, and patience, I wouldn't have written a single book, let alone eight of them. You're my pillar of strength, my world—and baby, you're the ginchiest.

Introduction

In another time, the old adage, *You've Come a Long Way, Baby* just might have been a fitting title of this book.

From racing jalopies down main street USA in the 1930s to the professionalism we see in the sport today, no decade in between saw more advancement than what was witnessed during the 1960s. It was like a modern-day industrial revolution wrapped up in a 10-year period. That may have been an exaggeration, but the level of progress made by the men and women of the sport during that period was undeniable. This was a group of people who never heard of the word *can't*. It just wasn't in their vocabulary. What did the NHRA call it? Ingenuity in action. And that it was. It began in the 1950s and exploded in the 1960s.

This book is written in recognition of the 10-year period that fell between 1961 and 1970. Follow the evolution of drag racing's key categories and the rise of many of the sport's top names. It's a double entendre to say that things moved fast. From AA/FD to Stock Eliminator, follow along as we show you just *how* fast.

Swamp Rat III-A *is seen at the AHRA Nationals at Green Valley on Labor Day weekend in 1961. Don Garlits came out of retirement prior to the NASCAR Winter Nationals in 1961, where he set top speed of 165 mph while driving his brother Ed's blown dragster. Connie Swingle reportedly drove the* Swamp Rat *to a best of 7.88 in 1962. (Photo Courtesy Forrest Bond)*

Chapter One
1961
. . . And Away We Go

There were 10 categories in 4 eliminator brackets to start the NHRA's 1961 season. Excluding the Stock classes, there were a total of 36 classes in which to compete. The most popular with the fans was Top Eliminator; the emerging Gassers were a close second. As far as participation went, nothing beat the entry-level Stockers.

It was there that Detroit's Big Three showed much of their own interest. Each manufacturer released performance packages in 1961 that individuals grabbed ahold of and modified to the extent of the rules and then some. It's time to hold onto your hats, folks, it's the start of a new decade with plenty to look forward to.

A Quick Study in Chassis Evolution

The decade began with mostly home-built cars that would have been equally at home in the 1950s, where many of them were initially built and raced. These cars often followed chassis designs that were available commercially. Some were inventive enough to pioneer new designs, manufacturing techniques, and materials (aluminum chassis). Bobby Joe Rutledge's car (pictured below) is a prime example of an owner-fabricated car that was competing early in the decade: large-diameter rails, a stock beam front axle, and a short wheelbase.

By the middle of the decade, chassis had grown in length to the neighborhood of 140 inches, as builders and racers looked for improved weight transfer and increased stability. There were many commercial chassis builders by this point in the decade: Frank Huszar (Race Car Specialties), George Britting, Roy Fjasted, and Woody Gilmore (Race Car Engineering).

Gilmore was responsible for the "flexy flyer" concept, a design meant to address the previously mentioned areas. Samples of his design (early and later) are shown here. In the upper photo is Paul Sutherland's *Charger*. The engine was solidly bolted to the upper frame rail, there was an upright at the engine mount, and all uprights were welded in place, top and bottom.

In the lower photo (Warren-Coburn) the engine mounts were unbolted, the engine-mount upright was absent, and the forward upright was only welded to the top rail. Characteristic of most Gilmore cars, Warren's

Paul Southerland (top) and Warren-Coburn (bottom).

had only a single radius rod on each side.

The last major innovation in chassis placed the driver ahead of the engine. While many tried the concept, Woody Gilmore and Pat Foster perfected it. After watching John Mulligan's fateful front-engine crash in 1969, Gilmore was determined to not see it happen again. In December 1969, he tested the pair's first rear-engine car.

Although the car crashed during an early outing, Gilmore was undeterred and went to work on a second car. Dwane Ong debuted the new car, which featured a 223-inch wheelbase in February 1970.

Bobby Joe Rutledge.

Dwane Ong.

Top Eliminator

There were six Dragster classes in 1961, the top dog AA/D through to D/D and finally the low-end, 4-cylinder-powered X/Dragsters. Drawing the most attention was the AA/Dragsters. They were the quickest cars on the track and mesmerized fans with their 8-second times; full-length, tire-smoking runs; and wheels-up launches. Technical advances usually began here and trickled down through the remaining classes.

To take a clear look at Top Eliminator in the early 1960s, we'll step back to the 1950s. Changes were coming fast in the latter part of the decade. The use of OEM frame rails that were standard early on was replaced by chassis manufactured by the likes of Scotty Fenn, Dragmaster, and the Logghe brothers (Ron and Gene). Weak OEM transmissions that stymied performance gains were shelved in favor of direct-drive and lock-up clutches. Getting the power to the ground meant more power could be built into the engine. Replacing multiple carburetion atop GMC blowers was 2- or 4-port injection. Although tire technology lagged, hampering performance gains, improvements came in time.

The alternate fuel, nitromethane, was introduced to drag racing back in 1949 by Vic Edelbrock. Fran Hernandez, an employee of Edelbrock at the time (and later with Mercury), took his 1932 Ford out to Santa Ana and cleaned house, running a 20-percent load.

A short study in the composition of nitro tells us that it contains more than 50 percent oxygen, so it needs very little air to combust. It's difficult to ignite, so a minimal amount of alcohol, or methanol, was added to help it along. To control the burn, 1 or 2 percent of benzene was added. Depending on the percentage used, nitro could double a reliable engine's output. By 1957, speeds had increased to the point where NHRA president Wally Parks felt that they had reached a dangerous level.

To curtail the increasing speeds, a ban on the use of nitro was implemented. The ban was first activated on February 10, 1957, at Santa Ana by track manager C. J. "Pappy" Hart. The reasons Pappy stated for the ban included overall safety, skyrocketing costs, a lack of sufficient stopping distance, and the desire of a number of participants to return to gasoline.

It seems that Emery Cook's record run of 166.97 mph at Lions on February 3 forced the decision. It is interesting to note that Cook's speed was just short of what scientists back in 1955 thought was the theoretical quarter-mile maximum speed. Going beyond 167 mph, scientists believed that the g-forces would cause a person to black out.

The NHRA's all-out nitro ban commenced with the Nationals in Oklahoma at the end of August 1957. The ban gave rise to individual meets, such as the U.S. Fuel and Gas Championship at Bakersfield, and helped grow the AHRA, as it never supported the fuel ban. Many West Coast racers, along with Don Garlits, Chris Karamesines, Bob Sullivan, Lou Cangalose, Dick Belfatti, and other Midwest and Eastern racers didn't want to give up nitro. AHRA president Jim Tice, foremost a businessman, pounced on

Mickey Thompson's X/Dragster was powered by a Hilborn-injected, GMC 3-71–blown Pontiac 4-cylinder measuring 220 ci. The car was a winner at the Nationals in 1961 and a record holder at 11.27 at 125.96 mph. Thompson was a busy man, running at least five cars under his umbrella in 1961, from Stock to a four-wheel-drive AA/Dragster powered by twin Pontiacs. Few were as innovative as Thompson. (Photo Courtesy Lou Hart)

Mike Willis can take credit for building one of the first twin-engine rails, having pieced together this twin flathead–powered, four-wheel-drive car as early as 1949. It was primitive, but such were the beginning days of organized drag racing. Tires are salt flat originals.

Eddie Hill's twin-engine, four-slick homegrown dragster left its mark at Indy in 1961. The following season, Hill used the twin, 422-ci, Pontiac-powered rail to become the first to break 200 mph on gas when he ran a 202.70 mph at Hobbs, New Mexico. (Photo Courtesy Richard Kinstry)

the opportunity to make money and sanctioned tracks that gave the fuel racers more places to run.

The NHRA ban saw many Top Eliminator dragsters going the twin-engine route to compensate for the loss of power that nitro had provided. Of course, running twins was not a new concept. Mike Willis ran a twin flathead–

powered rail in 1949. The Bean Bandits saw success in 1951, as did the team of Kenz & Leslie in 1955. Howards Cams *Twin Bears* and Tommy Ivo's twin Buick were two tough leaders after the ban. In 1959, Ivo ran twin Buicks measuring 464 inches each, and it was the first twin to crack 170 mph. He followed in 1961 with his four-engine

This maiden voyage photo of Tommy Ivo's Showboat in April 1961 provides good perspective on the size of the dragster. The four Buick engines were mounted in a Kent Fuller chassis. The two left-side engines drove the front wheels, and the two right-side engines drove the rear wheels. The power of the four Nailheads couldn't overcome the 4,000-pound weight of the vehicle, and it never ET'd well. The NHRA shunned the setup and told Ivo he could only run it as an exhibition car. (Photo Courtesy Tommy Ivo)

Lefty Mudersbach in the twin, 402-ci, gas-powered Howard Cam Special opened the 1961 season by winning Top Eliminator at the AHRA Winternationals with a record 8.63. He followed with wins at the US Fuel and Gas Championship and at the AHRA Nationals later in the year. Lefty was a prominent name well into the decade. (Photo Courtesy Forrest Bond)

After winning Top Eliminator at the NHRA Winternationals, turning an 8.99, Jack Chrisman took the Howards Cams Twin Bears AA/D on a cross-country tour. He accumulated enough points to be crowned overall world champion. Weight bias for the 1,350-pound rail was 30-70. (Photo Courtesy Richard Kinstry)

Proving the value of a single-engine Chevy, Pete Robinson won the Nationals in 1961. Some say the Chevys had the advantage off the line. They got ahold of the track quicker, thus usually getting the jump on the competition. After that, it was just a matter of holding off the bigger engines. Robinson's 352-ci Chevy lightweight had little trouble doing so. (Photo Courtesy Richard Kinstry)

Showboat, assuming that if two was good, four was better.

The team of Chet Herbert (Herbert Cams) and Zane Shubert started 1961 off right by winning the AHRA Winter meet with their twin, Chevy-powered AA/FD dragster. Chet modified the twin Chevys, which were supplied to him by Chevrolet's own Zora Arkus-Duntov by increasing the bore and stroke to 4.125 x 4.25, giving 454 ci. Herbert and Shubert met up with Ed Garlits at the AHRA Championship Drags at Green Valley, Texas, where Shubert defeated Big Daddy's little brother in the Top Eliminator final.

The twins were out in force in 1961. The most unusual may have been Eddie Hill's twin-blown Pontiac-powered dragster. When designing the car, Eddie made the 422-ci engines an integral part of the chassis with rails bolting directly to the engines. Out back, the rear end–mounted, four 8-inch slicks literally tore up the asphalt.

Taking the Top Eliminator win at Indy was the Howards Cams *Twin Bears* driven by Jack Chrisman. The car was built by Phil Johnson and Howard Johansen in 1958 and was the first successful side-by-side twin. The 310-ci engines were nestled in a fabricated chassis and were meshed at the flywheel with the left engine built to run counterclockwise.

After a crash in 1960, the 100-inch-wheelbase car was sidelined briefly. When it reappeared, Chrisman was the

new driver. He won Top Eliminator at the 1961 NHRA Winternationals with the low ET of the meet at 8.99. Taking top speed was Hayden Proffitt in the more conventional Bayer-Freitas inline, twin-blown Chevy with a 176.81 mph. Proffitt, probably best remembered for his time running Stockers, was behind the wheel of a Mickey Thompson Super Stock Pontiac by May. Chrisman, in the Jerry Johansen–crewed *Twin Bears,* closed the season amassing 540 points to win the NHRA Championship.

As for the single-engine AA/Dragsters, at the 1961 NHRA Nationals no one questioned the clocks when the Tom McEwen and Gene Adams 475-ci blown Olds dragster (driven by McEwen) laid down low ET with a 9.01 at 170.45 mph. But when unknown Pete Robinson rolled off the trailer with a 352-ci blown and injected Chevy and dropped low ET with an 8.68, the ET seemed so far out of the realm that the tower initially refused to broadcast it.

"I was pretty burned because they wouldn't show me my times for two days, but they weighed me five times," Robinson said.

Up in the tower, NHRA Executive Jack Hart had no choice but to relent and show Pete the numbers, as his clockings were just too consistent to be incorrect.

Pete opened class eliminations on Sunday with an eye-opening 8.52 and proceeded to trailer the twin-engined cars of Jack Chrisman and Eddie Hill on his way to a final face-off against McEwen. It was a close race until half-track, when Robinson opened up with a slight lead. He took the win with an 8.86 at 170.77 mph to an 8.90 at 168.55. In the Top Eliminator final, Robinson defeated Dode Martin in the Dragmaster's twin Chevy.

In an interview afterward, Robinson recounted that he had blown his engine about a week prior to the Nationals.

"I had gone through something like five engines that year and had only been out of state once," he said. "I was pretty much unknown when we headed to Indy with junk, and I mean junk."

Not only had Robinson won Indy with a junk engine, he had only been in the 8s once before. His high-revving Chevy could beat the bigger-engine cars off the line, and the light weight of the car held them off. That was his advantage, as his Dragmaster car weighed as much as 500 pounds less than his competitors.

As for speed secrets, Robinson said "put in a lot of compression and pick the right rear-end gear." Helping keep the Chevy together was water injection, something Robinson installed to help keep the Chevy from detonating and destroying itself. He ran without it after tech inspection threatened to toss him if he didn't remove it.

Although times slowed slightly, the final results showed the Chevy survived just fine without it. Robinson debuted a new Dragmaster car at the 1962 NHRA Winternationals. The car made use of the same 352-ci Chevy but featured a longer wheelbase and was said to weigh 200 pounds less than his old car.

Mid-Eliminators

The Mid-Eliminator categories were a crowded place in the 1960s. There you found the greatest variety of cars: Altereds, Comp cars, Gassers, Roadsters, Sports Production, and the lower-end Dragsters. Although many ideas born in Top Eliminator trickled down to the lower ranks, individual ingenuity in the Mid-Eliminators was alive and well.

In the Roadsters' ranks of Little Eliminator, Dick Manz (in Larry Sanchez's car) won category honors at the NHRA Winternationals, while Division 4 standout Willis Ragsdale was the Little Eliminator winner at Indy.

Ragsdale, a millwright by trade, built his 1927 Ford in 1958. For power, his *Raunchy* relied on a punched-out 283 that housed a Racer Brown camshaft and four 2-barrel carburetors on a Weiand manifold. Backing the 302-ci engine was a 50-pound flywheel (to get off the line in a hurry) and a second-and-third-gear-only 1939

Don Prudhomme's first rail came courtesy of Tommy Ivo, who sold him his Buick-powered Kent Fuller car early in 1960. Prudhomme replaced the Buick with a Dave Zeuschel blown Hemi in 1961 and was hitting 180 mph on fuel in the mid-8s. (Photo Courtesy Bill Scharing)

Two Bad *was the name of Eldon Dye and Don Hampton's Competition Coupe. With twin bored and stroked 283 Chevys, you can bet the Fiat was tough on the competition. In 1968, Hampton swapped the body for a Corvette shell. Hampton and his blowers were a popular sell in the blown ranks through the decade. (Photo Courtesy Phil Bellomy)*

Willis Ragsdale started racing in late 1958 with his homebuilt 1927 T. He ran modified versions of the car until 1978, using both Chevy power as well as a Chrysler Hemi. Over the years, he ran the car in B/Roadster, B/Altered, A/Street Roadster, and B/Street Roadster, setting class records five times. Besides winning Little Eliminator at the 1961 Nationals, Willis also won the Little Eliminator title at the 1964 AHRA World Championship. A multitude of wins at points meets followed. (Photo Courtesy Trey Ragsdale)

Ford transmission. These transmissions were known to be pretty tough parts at the time, but as horsepower increased, they became less reliable. At Indy, Ragsdale's B/Roadster defeated Sam Parriot's blown Caddy-powered A/MSP Kurtis with an 11.55 at 122.44 mph. Ragsdale set his first class record at that race, where he ran a 123.62 mph during eliminations. Ongoing refinements helped Ragsdale compete with the car well into the 1970s.

Altereds

Back when there were fewer than a handful of national events each year, there were few repeat winners. Racers built a reputation by dominating regional races. Looking at the 1950s Altereds (and Roadsters in a similar vein), early Fords (often dry lake refugees) initially dominated the categories. The heavy, wide bodies pushed a lot of wind, and drivers quickly learned that to be successful, they needed to go smaller.

Thanks to the success of people like the Brissette brothers, "Jazzy" Jim Nelson, and Walter Knoch, by the

Bob and Jim Brissette's Bantam, driven by Howard "Ike" Eichenhofer, relied upon a blown 354 Hemi to run over 160 mph in 1960. More than any other, this car wrung the death knell for the early Fords that had dominated the Roadster classes up until that point. With its fiberglass body and Chassis Research tube rails, it may be an understatement to call this car evolutionary. (Photo Courtesy Bill Scharing)

There's plenty to see in this photo of SoCal's Nick Cirino and Frank Groves's 445-ci Olds-powered A/Roadster. The five blower belts and individual chrome pipes made for some great tunes. Check out the injector ram tubes atop the GMC 6-71. (Photo Courtesy Ken Crawford)

late 1950s, compact Bantams and Fiat Topolinos dominated the Altered category. And, just as we saw in Top Eliminator during the later 1950s, injection replaced carburetion as a means to go quicker and faster. A natural progression was to add a dose of nitromethane to the

tank. Although banned by the NHRA, the AHRA welcomed the fuel burners with open arms, and over the next few years, the Altered Coupes, Sedans, and Roadsters morphed into what became known as Fuel Altereds.

An early standout in the fuel ranks was the 1934 Ford of Mooneyham & Sharp. The A/Fuel Coupe was undoubtedly the most famous fuel sedan of the period. The car was originally built in the mid-1950s and competed on the dry lakes. With Larry Faust behind the wheel and a setback 390-ci Hemi under the cowl, the full-fendered car managed a best of 133.60 mph. It was converted to run the quarter-mile in the late 1950s, and as a Fuel Coupe, it was considered quite innovative.

With its enclosed body, setback engine, 75- to 80-percent fuel load, center steering, and the rear position of the driver, many have referred to the car as the grandfather of today's Funny Car. In 1960, the Ford was the first Fuel Coupe to break 150 mph when Faust ran a 152.02 mph. By the end of 1963, the car had run its best of 8.98 at 170 mph.

At the NHRA Nationals in 1961, Michigan's Walter Knoch Jr. was an odds-on favorite in Mid-Eliminator. His blown Hemi-powered A/A Fiat, christened *Walt's Puffer II*, got the attention of the masses by lay-

"Jazzy" Jim Nelson built this Fiat on 1934 Ford rails and ran it in Competition Coupe with a bored and stroked flathead. The car was then sold to Ewell & Stecker, who campaigned it with a fuel-burning Hemi. (Photo Courtesy Connell Miller/Rudy Perez)

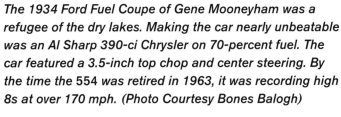

The 1934 Ford Fuel Coupe of Gene Mooneyham was a refugee of the dry lakes. Making the car nearly unbeatable was an Al Sharp 390-ci Chrysler on 70-percent fuel. The car featured a 3.5-inch top chop and center steering. By the time the 554 was retired in 1963, it was recording high 8s at over 170 mph. (Photo Courtesy Bones Balogh)

The Ratican, Jackson, and Stearns Fiat was a leader in Altered. Don Ratican built the 430-ci Olds that carried a Reath Automotive stroker crank. Bill Jackson was the chassis guy, and Ron Stearns was the man behind the wheel. The best time for the gas-powered Fiat was a 9.54 at 157 mph. (Photo Courtesy Bill Scharing)

Walt Knoch's A/Altered 1939 Fiat was the first Altered to top 150 mph, accomplishing the feat on Thanksgiving Day in 1959. A winner from the get-go, the Fiat's first pass at the Nationals in 1959 set the class record at 138.67 mph. Knoch was runner-up at the Nationals in 1960 and 1961 before winning class in 1962. Backing the 454-ci Hemi was direct drive and a quick-change rear. (Photo Courtesy Robert Genat)

ing down 10-second ETs approaching 160 mph. Walt Sr. himself had been racing since 1956, when he built his first Hemi car using his son's 1937 Ford. Walt Jr. came home from school one day to find his car gone. Asking his mom if she knew what happened to it, she told him that his dad had it in the shop. While Junior was at school, Walt Sr. wheeled the car into the garage, pulled the flathead, and placed a Hemi between the frame rails.

The Knochs' first trip to the Nationals in the Fiat came in 1959, when Junior set the class record at 137.67 mph. In what must have been a disappointment, at the 1961 Nationals, Walt lost class for the second year in a row to the blown 430-ci Olds-powered Fiat of Don Ratican, Bill Jackson, and Ron Stearns. Not to go home empty handed, Walt stormed back with his A/Roadster, *Walt's Puffer Too* to win Middle Eliminator.

Junior got himself into a heap of trouble with the NHRA in 1963, when the sanctioning body realigned its divisions. Michigan was moved from Division 2 to Division 3, which was a move that young Knoch had a real problem with. The Knochs' cars had always carried the classification number 285, in reference to Division 2, and a scale model had been produced of the Fiat with that number on it. Junior refused to change the number, and when Indy rolled around, the NHRA tossed him. The ensuing stink had the NHRA banning Junior from ever competing in the NHRA again.

The team of Ratican, Jackson, and Stearns kicked off the year by winning the AHRA Winternationals in February with its A/A Fiat, setting the class record with a 10.30 at 146.10 mph. It must have seemed like déjà vu for the team, as it repeated its 1960 wins at Cordova's World Series of Drag Racing and, of course, the Nationals. The team was short lived. Having formed in 1959, it split when the Fiat was sold at the end of the 1961 season. Don, who built the Olds, returned to building engines for competitors, while Bill returned to the business of building race-ready chassis. Ron and Don paired once more in 1962 and won class at the NHRA Winternationals in an A/SR car borrowed from Wayne Ferguson.

Gassers

Outside of the Top Eliminator Dragsters, the Supercharged Gassers held the most fan appeal. By the start of the decade, racers had gotten smart and were trading in their larger Chevys and Oldsmobile sedans for smaller and lighter Willys. The so-called Gasser Wars were just heating up in 1961, and leading the way in A/GS was "Ohio" George Montgomery and his Chevy-powered 1933 Willys.

Montgomery was a toolmaker by trade and worked in GM's Delco division. He advanced to the Gas classes in 1959 after campaigning a dual-purpose 1934 Ford, a car he had taken to Bonneville in 1952 and clocked at 118 mph. He hit the quarter-mile tracks after installing a 391-ci Cadillac mill and adding a McCulloch blower. He swapped the Ford for the now-famous Willys in 1959. A GMC blower replaced the McCulloch, and as Montgomery relayed, he had to fabricate everything to mount the blower on the Cadillac. His efforts paid off with a Little Eliminator win at the Nationals in 1959.

Montgomery hooked up with Pete Robinson around late 1961 to discuss the issues he was having with galling within his GMC 6-71. To solve the problem, the pair developed and marketed magnesium blower cases and gear drives, and a company in Oregon produced the parts. Montgomery referred to the cases as a godsend that enabled them to close the gap between the rollers and casing.

In B/GS, the California-based pair of Fred Stone and Tim Woods reigned supreme with engine builder John Edwards and driver K. S. Pittman. They debuted their 1941 Willys in 1960 after a highway towing accident destroyed their blown Olds-powered Studebaker. Prior to the Nationals in 1961, Edwards and Pittman left the team to focus their attention on their own C/GS Willys. In their place stepped Doug "Cookie" Cook.

At the Nationals, Cook won his class the tough way, having to go through the engine a few times. The Stone, Woods, & Cook (SWC) Willys met its demise in a similar destructive fashion with their Studebaker while returning home after the Nationals, which forced the build of a new Willys during the winter.

Old teammates Pittman and Edwards won class at the Nationals and billed their Willys as the world's fastest C/GS. Of course, the claim could be disputed, as Bones Balogh recorded 10.90s while driving the Mallicoat brothers' C/GS Willys.

The exploding Gasser Wars were made even more entertaining thanks to the cam grinders, whose advertisements laid it on thick, such as the Ed Iskenderian ad that hyped the

"Ohio" George Montgomery's 1933 Willys made its debut at the 1959 Nationals, where Montgomery and the GMC-blown Cadillac-powered car won A/GS class and Little Eliminator. Seen here at the Nationals in 1961, the Willys was a record holder that year with a 10.82 at 131.77 mph. (Photo Courtesy Richard Kinstry)

The team of Pittman and Edwards backed up their C/Gas NHRA Winternationals win by taking class honors at the Nationals. Power came by way of a blown Olds. (Photo Courtesy Richard Kinstry)

One of the more dominant teams in the decade's Gasser Wars, Fred Stone, Leonard Woods, and Doug Cook, came together just prior to the Nationals in 1961. Their B/GS 1941 Willys, labeled Swindler II, *was previously driven by K. S. Pittman. A blown Olds initially powered the car. (Photo Courtesy Richard Kinstry)*

Bones Balogh stated that he won more races with his 1949 Chevy than in any other car. Bones was an employee of Ed Iskenderian and stated that "everything I learned was on the Isky dyno." With multiple carbs perched on a GMC 6-71 blower, the Chevy topped out at 114 mph. Rules in the late 1950s didn't allow blown cars to run D/Gas, so Bones was forced to run C/Gas. Helping get the power to the ground were short recap slicks and a spare tire well filled with Ready-Mix. The torque tube rear end housed a strong set of 1953 Buick 4.44 gears. (Photo Courtesy Bones Balogh)

Mallicoat brothers' 1940 Willys. The car made use of the blown Chevy engine that had previously powered Bones Balogh's D/G 1949 Chevy. The ad boasted: "Powered by a loaded 283 Chevy using an Isky RR 7000T Roller Cam and Kit and the Isky Forced Induction Kit, the J&J Muffler–sponsored Willys eliminated all the competition." According to the ad, the Long Beach race was so lopsided that the competition failed to show for the top eliminator final, instead choosing to default.

Bones won five eliminator brackets in a row, taking events at Lions, San Fernando, San Gabriel, Fontana, and Pomona. Of course, Bones also laid claim to owning the fastest C/GS car and challenged everyone "regardless of the class they run." It was a subtle challenge to Pittman and Edwards, who ran an Engle cam and equipment.

The Isky ad never mentioned it, but Bones was an employee of the company. He worked for Isky from 1959 into 1966,

We all have to start somewhere. For future world champ Joe Pisano, it was with this meticulous 1929 Model A. Pisano ran the car in conjunction with his brother Frank, and the pair tore up Southern California tracks. The Chevy-powered A/Gas was a record holder with an 11.98 at 118.40 mph. (Photo Courtesy Bones Balogh)

Not the greatest shot of Mike Marinoff's 1955 Chevy, but the C/Gasser is well worth recognizing. Bill Reeves could often be found behind the wheel of the Milwaukee-based car. A 6-71 blower and Hilborn 2-port injection topped the Chevy mill, backed by a 4-speed transmission that propelled the Chevy to average 12.70 times. (Photo Courtesy Michael Pottie)

operating the dyno and developing new cam profiles. Initially, Bones raced his Chevy on Iskenderian's dime, being a paid field rep and lending assistance to other Isky racers. Bones was expected to pass any knowledge gained on the dyno to fellow racers who were running Isky equipment. One of the things Bones picked up on was that they gained 75 hp by going from 6A nozzles on a Hilborn-injected Chevy to larger 7A nozzles designed for large-displacement Oldsmobile and Cadillac engines.

In Street Eliminator, where the lower Gas cars battled it out, Johnny Loper and his B/G Willys was the cream of the crop. Loper first made an impression in 1959 when he won E/G at the Nationals at Detroit while driving a 1959 Chevy. He followed up in 1960 by winning B/G in his Oldsmobile-powered Willys named *Ole Hoss*.

In 1961, Loper won the Street category by beating the Modified Sports Production Corvette of John Mazmanian in the final. Loper was a self-made man who did all the work on his cars himself out of his Loper Performance shop in Arizona. He was a threat in Gas throughout the decade, won class in the Willys at the NHRA winter meet in 1962 and 1963, and repeated his 1960 Nationals win in 1962.

"Big" John Mazmanian, a man who measured 6 foot 4 inches in height, started racing seriously with a factory supercharged 1957 Ford. His desire to drive ended after he went through the horrors of a clutch explosion. Remember, these were the days before mandatory scattershields, and an exploding clutch could do grave damage to car and driver. Mazmanian bought his renowned 1961 Corvette new in late 1960 and put his eager nephew Rich Siroonian in the seat. With a relatively stock fuel-injected 283 under the hood, Rich won C/MSP class at the Winternationals.

It would be an insult not to mention at least a few of the year's outstanding performers, such as Junior Garrison, who won the Street Eliminator category at the NHRA Nationals. In what was typical of the day, Garrison rescued his 1940 Willys from a junkyard, rebuilt it from the ground up, and added an injected Chevy engine to compete in B/Gas. After taking class, Garrison overcame a strong field of Street Roadsters and Modified Sports cars to win the category with a 12.42 at 112.60 mph. Garrison's win, his one and only national-event victory, was backed with the class top speed award, having recorded a 122.42 mph.

Stock Eliminator

While the greatest participation in Stock was in the lower ranks (B/S through K/S), it was the latest high-performance offerings from Detroit in Super Stock and A/S that drew the most attention. The Winternationals, or the *Big Go West* as it was called, kicked off at Pomona with time trials on Friday, February 17.

The cars to beat included the factory-supported 389 Pontiac of Mickey Thompson, which was driven by Pete Petrey. This was the quickest of the Pontiacs in the program. Fords to watch included the 390-ci cars of Les Ritchey, Pete McCarroll, and Bud Harris. McCarroll was running the recently released 3x2-barrel setup, giving the Ford a 375-hp rating. "Dyno" Don Nicholson made haste building a 409 Impala that he finished the day before the meet. The only other 409 car on site was the Biscayne of Frank Sanders.

Nicholson laid down the quick time of the meet when he ran a 13.25 at 108.94, just ahead of Ritchey's Performance Associates Ford. The final round in Super Stock boiled down to the two Chevys and saw Sanders defeating Nicholson on a holeshot with a 13.63 at 105.26 mph.

The 50 fastest Stockers returned on Sunday for the Mr. Stock Eliminator crown. The runoff consisted of S/S stick and S/S automatic cars as well as A/S and B/S cars. It was nothing short of factory wars with Chevy, Ford, Pontiac, and Chrysler well represented. The Chevys and Pontiacs with their 4-speed transmissions seemed to lead the way over the weaker 3-speed-equipped Fords and Mopars. And wouldn't you know it, the final round once again boiled down to the Chevys of Nicholson and Sanders. Nicholson came out on top this time with a 13.59 at 105.88 mph.

Bruce Morgan was Stock points champ in 1961. His grand prize was this 1961 Pontiac that was presented to him by George Hurst at Indy. Morgan's fuel-injected B/Stocker went undefeated through the year, an amazing feat considering he drove his Chevy to every meet.

At the 1961 Nationals, "Dyno" Don Nicholson was initially crowned Stock champ. Upon teardown, he was disqualified on a technicality. Nicholson's string of Chevys campaigned between 1961 and 1963 birthed a winning reputation that ran close to 50 years. (Photo Courtesy Richard Nicholson)

At the NHRA Nationals in September, the Stockers ran Saturday afternoon. Stealing the show were the cars in Optional Super Stock (O/SS): 421-powered Pontiacs, 409 Chevys, and 390 Fords. The class was created and designed specifically for limited-production cars or cars featuring high-performance parts made available by Detroit's Big Three after June 1.

It was Bob Tasca who coined the phrase "Race on Sunday, sell on Monday," and by mid-1961, Ford sales were through the roof. The Tri-Power, 401 hp, 390-ci engine kept the competition on its toes. Each Holley carburetor flowed 300 cfm. (Photo Courtesy Richard Kinstry)

Leading the charge in O/SS was the 368-hp Pontiac of Mickey Thompson that was driven by Hayden Proffitt. Proffitt held the low ET and top speed with a 13.07 at 112.21 mph. Close behind was Nicholson with a 13.25 at 110.29 mph. In the eliminations, Proffitt defeated Dave Strickler's Biscayne for class honors. Proffitt ran a best of 12.55 during the meet and walked in to Sunday's 50-car Mr. Stock Eliminator runoff as the favorite.

In an unorthodox semifinal-round move that was precipitated by a burning desire to defeat his opponent (Al Eckstrand in the Ramchargers' Dodge), Thompson replaced Hayden Proffitt behind the wheel of his Pontiac. The Pontiac faithful's hopes were dashed when Thompson's Pontiac got hung up in gear. The same thing happened to Eckstrand when the 3-speed in his Dodge failed against Nicholson.

You've got to give the Ramchargers props. The team of Chrysler engineers formed in 1958 and took aim at the world of drag racing as a means to change the stodgy image that Chrysler held at the time. Initially, the team received no factory backing, but things changed as the decade proceeded. The Ramchargers developed and tested new products for the manufacturer that were passed on to factory-supported racers.

The final round for Mr. Stock Eliminator boiled down to the O/SS cars of Dyno Don Nicholson and Arnie "the Farmer" Beswick. Because of Al Eckstrand's failed gear the previous round, Nicholson and Beswick agreed that the overall winner would come back to run a best-of-three grudge race against the 413 Dodge.

At the flag, Nicholson and Beswick left bumper to bumper. On the top end, it was Nicholson inching ahead for the win with a 13.37 at 108.69 mph. In the proceeding grudge race, Nicholson lost the first round but came back to take the next two. As was customary, after the final race, the winning car was torn down for inspection, and Nicholson's Chevy was found to have numerous rule infractions.

The factory wars really kicked off in 1961, and right in the thick of things was the Super Duty Pontiac. Stan Antlocer drove this Tri-Power 389-ci-powered Poncho for Packer Pontiac. Helping the Pontiac to more than respectable times in the 12.90s was a 4-speed and 4.33 rear gears. Stan drove the car to a runner-up finish in S/S at Indy in 1962.

Dave Strickler drove the Bill Jenkins–tuned 409-powered Biscayne to a class win at the Nationals and held Optional Super Stock's first ET record with a 13.29. The primitive air-grabbing hood scoop was allowed on O/SS cars. (Photo Courtesy Mike Strickler)

Nicholson felt these were fabricated. He said, "They started picking on stuff. They pulled the valve springs off my heads. Took the shims from underneath and checked them in their little tester. They checked the springs at minimum height. I showed them how to check them at the stock height. The springs were actually down on pressure because as the runs went on, they went away. The car started missing on me a little bit in the lights and was getting a little worse with each run. I was sure it was the valve springs going away. When we checked them, there were no problems.

"Then, they started miking the heads of the valves," he continued. "I had never miked a head of a valve unless I was making a valve for something. I just pulled the valves out of the Chevrolet boxes and put them in the heads. There were some they found a few thousandths over size. I was arguing with Farmer Dismuke, the tech inspector, that Chevrolet didn't say $1^{11}/_{16}$ plus or minus 10 or 15 thousandths like Chrysler, Pontiac, and most others did. They just had the size, no plus or minus. We got that squared away, and then they said the intake (ports) was matched. The factory or whoever made the castings for them had used a die grinder to clean off the burrs as opposed to using a hand scraper. I told them it wasn't matched as it was out a quarter inch in spots."

It all got very ridiculous with Farmer Dismuke arguing that Nicholson had received special parts. Chevrolet's Paul Prior, who was attending the race, got involved in arguing the point. In the end, the disqualification stood with no real reason given and no discussion allowed. Nicholson considered legal action but dropped the matter and moved on.

GMC Blower

Without going into the *full blown* history of the GMC blower, racers have used the unit since the late 1940s, when Barney Navarro first slipped a 3-71 on a flathead Ford.

From drag racing's beginning, Top Eliminator, Gas, and Altered cars have been using the GMC blower. Simplified, the GMC blower is an air pump that increases power by forcing a greater amount of air into each cylinder. More air allows for more fuel, which equates to more power.

To increase the amount of air entering the engine, racers would "overdrive" the blower (spin it quicker than crank speed) by using a smaller blower pulley or a larger crank pulley.

Of course, too much overdrive, or boost, could have a detrimental effect and lead to detonation and destroyed engines.

As racers adapted (and learned along the way), quarter-mile times went on a downward spiral. Helping the engines survive was an aftermarket that went into the production of specific parts for the blown engines: bottom-end girdles, aluminum rods, and pistons.

Dean Lowe and his beautiful 1929 Roadster won B/SR at the NHRA Winternationals with a 11.77, a record time, which was backed by a 11.69 when his mentor, Dyno Don Nicholson, hopped behind the wheel. The injected 301-inch Chevy moved the Roadster to a best ET of 11.06 (minus the 140 pounds of ballast) at 123.87 mph. A BorgWarner 4-speed and 5.38:1 gears in a Halibrand quick change completed the drivetrain. (Photo Courtesy Don Prieto)

Chapter Two

1962
Variety: The Spice of Life

The cool thing about the early 1960s was the variety in the classes, cars, and combinations. Pretty much anything went, and if the NHRA didn't have a place for you to run, then more than likely the AHRA did. Keeping us entertained was everything from flathead-powered Stockers to straight-8-powered dragsters to Hemi-powered foreign jobs in Competition Coupe.

At one end of the spectrum stood the Top Eliminator dragsters dominated by Chrysler, Chevrolet, Oldsmobile, and Pontiac power. At the opposite end were the cars of Stock. Interest was exploding, thanks in part to Detroit's Big Three manufacturers, whose performance offerings were just what the exploding Baby Boomer market craved.

Top Eliminator

Looking back on 1962, it's tough to say what the biggest story of the year was. Was it the emergence of Don "the Snake" Prudhomme, or was it Tommy Ivo breaking the 8-second barrier late in the year? Prudhomme, who at one point was pegged with the title of "drag racing's most natural driver," started the year teamed with chassis builder Kent Fuller and engine man Dave Zeuschel. Prudhomme proved his worth by winning Bakersfield over a field of 87 Top Fuel cars. The team split shortly after; Zeuschel left to open his own engine-building business. At Fuller's suggestion, Tom Greer and Keith Black picked up Prudhomme to drive for them.

Prudhomme started his long and very successful career in the world of hot rodding by painting cars in his father's San Fernando body shop. He was a member of the Road Kings car club along with Tommy Ivo, and he soon took up with Ivo in campaigning his Top Eliminator car. Prudhomme's first driving job was in a dragster that he purchased from Rod Peppmuller.

In 1960, he campaigned a Kent Fuller car he bought from Ivo and did some driving of Ivo's twin rail. He'd later take over driving Ivo's four-engine *Showboat*, as the insurance people in Hollywood frowned upon "TV" Tommy driving himself. In late 1961, Prudhomme first teamed with Dave Zeuschel and had him build a 392 for the ex-Ivo car. Prudhomme's first major event win came at Bakersfield.

Keith Black, the man with the magic hands, was the undisputed leading engine builder of the time. Black's rise to fame began in the world of speedboats in the 1940s. Few paid attention to detail the way Black did, and this attention led to reliable, record-setting national and international boats. Black took in his first drag race back in the mid-1950s, and by the end of the decade, he opened Keith Black Race Engines south of Los Angeles.

At the insistence of his friend Cliff Collins, Black became involved with an underachieving dragster that Collins, Chuck Gireth, and Dave Carpenter were campaigning. Black went through the 354-ci Hemi, tightening tolerances and generally focusing on the details that many builders generally overlooked. The results of Black's work paid off with improved performance, reliability, and consistency.

In 1961, Tom Greer, proprietor of a successful nearby machine shop, approached Keith with a dream of running a Fuel Dragster. With Greer's seemingly bottomless pockets and a Keith Black Hemi, the pair ran the Gireth car with Gireth himself behind the wheel. Unable to make the combo work, Greer and Black ditched both Gireth and the car and moved on.

Looking for a new chassis, the pair found a Kent Fuller car early in 1961 that had briefly been campaigned by Rod Stuckey. Stuckey was burned badly in the car at Half Moon Bay and sold it to Lou Senter. By the time the AHRA Winternationals rolled around in 1962, Stuckey was healed enough to drive the car for Senter. He won Top Eliminator at the meet, and it was not long after that Greer and Black purchased the car. Stuckey would drive the car (with a Keith Black Hemi) for Greer and Black until Prudhomme was persuaded to take over.

Prior to Prudhomme taking the seat, the car was returned to Fuller's shop to clean up some work that Stuckey had previously done. Wayne Ewing formed a shell for the car before Prudhomme himself laid on the yellow paint. At the car's Pomona debut

Don Prudhomme's first major event win came at Bakersfield in 1962. Seen here (left to right) are chassis builder Kent Fuller, the honorary trophy girl, Prudhomme, and engine builder Dave Zeuschel. Prudhomme set low ET and top speed of the meet with an 8.21 at 185.36. The wheelbase of the Fuller chassis was 116 inches.

Tommy Ivo's Barnstormer had a 464-ci engine and was the first car to run a 7-second time. Run? Boy did it ever. But as Tommy recalled, "It was a bear to twinkle toes it down the track, especially when it was slippery." (Photo Courtesy Tommy Ivo)

tires and smoking the clutch at the same time. He said it [the clutch] wore down a little faster but didn't realize it was the reason we broke the 7-second barrier."

Helping further was the fact that Ivo weighed probably 100 pounds less than the average competitor. This alone gave him about a tenth up on the competition. The 7-second time was made with a 50-percent load of nitro running through the Hemi, as the inadequate tires of the day couldn't handle much more.

In between Prudhomme and Ivo fell a countless number of noteworthy performers, all pushing the envelope to advance the sport: Karamesines, Mudersbach, Hunt, Hobbs and Hirata, and Davis and Moody all put up big numbers in 1962.

Vance Hunt witnessed the dying days of the flathead when, in 1958, he

in June, Prudhomme won AA/FD, set the top speed, and ran low ET of the meet with an 8.73 at 177.51 mph while defeating Lefty Mudersbach in the twin Chevy Herbert Cam Special. Greer, Black, and Prudhomme went on a tear with the car, racking up a reported streak of 200 wins against 7 losses through 1963.

Tommy Ivo raised more than a few eyebrows when he broke the 8-second barrier with a 7.99 at 183.66 mph at San Gabriel on October 27. He backed it up with an 8.10, blowing the 464-ci Dave Zeuschel engine in the process. Ivo attributed the 7-second clocking to a number of factors, one being the chassis of his own design.

"I gave up on Kent Fuller building my chassis because it was such a fight to get him to do what I wanted," Ivo said. "So, I opened my own chassis shop [Tom's Hobby Shop] and built a dozen cars through 1963. Secondly, Dave was trying to get rid of reciprocating weight and put a 10-inch clutch in, instead of an 11 inch, and he didn't realize it was smoking the

teamed with a buddy who ran a home-fabricated dragster. Out came the Ford and in its place went a 354-ci Hemi that Hunt had been running in Gas. In 1960, he graduated to running AHRA Fuel Dragster. Hunt faced a seemingly uphill battle racing against the twin dragsters, and in 1962, he came up with a unique idea to combat

The AHRA Nationals champ Vance Hunt and driver J. L. Payne made use of a 140-inch Don Garlits chassis and a Howards Cams–equipped 392 to record 8.40 times. Hunt was a tough competitor who did all his own engine building. (Photo Courtesy Vance Hunt)

In 1962, Hunt came up with his own spin on the twin engine dragster when he bolted a nitro-burning kart engine to the front of his 392. It worked, but AHRA President Jim Tice would not allow it. (Photo Courtesy Vance Hunt)

them. His initial thought was to build a twin of his own. However, a month or so before the Labor Day Nationals, a friend who ran fuel-burning go-karts approached him with a novel idea of bolting one of his kart engines to the 392-ci engine that Hunt was now running.

"He told me they made a lot of power and he would loan me a good one just to see it go fast," Hunt recalled. "AHRA rules regarding twin-engine cars said they had to run on the same fuel, have their own shut off, and be connected to the drivetrain. So, I mounted it on a plate attached to the top frame rails and used blower pulleys on the kart engine and an extra pulley on the blower to connect the systems together. It passed tech with flying

colors. Then, I covered it up and headed for home so as not to expose this trick until the big race. Not many people noticed the kart engine until we made a very strong run to qualify. Shortly after returning to the pit, AHRA President Jim Tice came roaring up. Without any other talk he said, 'Take it off.'

"I told him that it was built to match his rule book to the letter and I intended to race it at that race. His answer to me was, 'You will never make it past the first round without getting a redlight.' Those of us who knew Tice did not question that he would do it. So, I removed the extra engine, went on to make 11 strong passes, and won the AHRA Championship, outrunning Greer-Black-Prudhomme twice."

Although the general consensus in Top Eliminator was that the Chrysler Hemi made the most power, its hefty 750-pound weight, in a class where weight meant everything, was a measured disadvantage. The Chevys, weighing in at less than 550 pounds, and even Buicks and Oldsmobiles gave the Hemis a good run for the money. Jim Nelson and Dode Martin chose a lighter Chrysler B-series wedge as opposed to the Hemi, placing a 413 crank in a 383 (426 ci) to win the NHRA Winternationals.

Meanwhile, Gene Adams made the Oldsmobile engine come alive—and understandably, considering he had been toying with them since the early 1950s when he first hopped up his parents' Rocket 88. In 1957, Adams took the same Olds, now owned by him and powered by a blown 371-ci engine, to the Nationals, where he ran B/Gas and set class record at 111.25 mph. Dragsters were

Few AA/Gas Dragsters were as feared as the shark car of Gene Adams and Tom McEwen. With Adams's potent blown Olds and McEwen's quick reflexes, the car (here at Half Moon Bay) was near unbeatable.

Mickey Thompson developed these hemi heads for the Pontiac engine in 1962. Jack Chrisman drove Thompson's 450-ci Pontiac to an AA/D class win at the Nationals. The heads alone ran $1,000 per pair. In 1964, Thompson developed similar heads for the 427 Ford wedge engine. (Photo Courtesy John Hellmuth)

the next step for Adams, whose Oldsmobile engine found its way into a Ron Scrima–owned, Scotty Fenn chassis that would be driven by Leonard Harris. Running Gas, the car broke track records around Southern California through 1960, running 9.30 times, and at one point it held the NHRA record.

Ron Scrima modified the chassis before a 6-71 blower and 4-port Hilborn injection were bolted on to a new big-inch Adams-built Olds. The team went on to win 18 consecutive Top Eliminator brackets at Lions Dragstrip through the end of the summer. Adams picked up a job at Hilborn and received a helping hand from both them and his cam supplier, Engle. Incredible ETs came by way of near smokeless runs, as Harris rode the clutch to perfection. The team won A/D class at the NHRA Nationals at Detroit in 1960 and took Top Eliminator honors, defeating Jim "Red" Dyer in the A/MR *Tennessee Bo-Weevil* with a low ET of the meet: 9.25.

McEwen got his big break when he bought out Scrima shortly after

Harris was killed while driving another team's car. The Fenn car lasted another few months before being replaced with a lighter Kent Fuller car in 1962. Nicknamed *the shark* due to the shape of the rear body, McEwen drove the car to the finals at the NHRA Winternationals, where he fell to the *Dragmaster Dodge* of Jim Nelson.

McEwen convinced Adams to run fuel at Bakersfield, and he did so with not-so-favorable results. After beating Garlits (as he had in 1961) in round one, McEwen fell in the second. The race turned McEwen on to running Fuel Dragster. At the end of the season, he split with Adams and headed out on his own in a Hemi-powered car.

The shark enjoyed great success, running 8.40 times at well over 180 mph, but the writing was on the wall for the Oldsmobile engines. As performance demands increased, Oldsmobile, with its weak bottom end and inferior breathing, couldn't compete with the Chrysler Hemi. One could easily say the same for the Nailhead Buick. The vertical valves and horizontal ports were just a bad combination. Pontiac suffered as well, further hin-

Swamp Rat V was built by Don Garlits and Connie Swingle. It was a lightweight, 120-inch wheelbase car built to run Gas Dragster but later ran Fuel. Garlits added a wing over the engine prior to the 1963 Winternationals and credits it for helping him to win his first NHRA national event. (Photo Courtesy Phil Bellomy)

The NHRA fuel ban of 1957 to 1963 contributed to an increase in popularity of the unordinary. Ashland, Ohio–based Lee Pendleton's Allison-powered Spitfire, seen here at Green Valley Raceway, was said to produce 2,700 hp. Due to its weight, the car never ET'ed well but recorded a best of 185 mph while running AA/D at Lions in 1962. (Photo Courtesy David Huff)

dered by its conjoined center exhaust ports and a weak block that suffered under increased loads of nitro.

Mickey Thompson was without a doubt one of the sport's true innovators. He had been under contract with Pontiac since 1959 and set a number of records for the

manufacturer at Bonneville and on the quarter-mile. By 1962, Mickey Thompson Equipment Company was in full swing, manufacturing everything from blower kits to stroker kits to magnesium third members. Further, he created his own aluminum hemi cylinder heads for Pontiac.

The heads were similar to its Chrysler counterpart but featured taller intake ports and larger exhaust ports. They bolted onto a poked-and-stroked aluminum block (Harvey Aluminum formed a reported half dozen blocks for Pontiac) that was said to measure 450 inches and produce 1,000 hp. Bolting the engine into an AA/D Dragmaster chassis yielded a Top Eliminator win at the Nationals for Thompson's driver, Jack Chrisman. In the final, Chrisman defeated Don Garlits with a time of 8.76 at 171.75 mph, giving Pontiac its one and only NHRA Top Eliminator win.

Garlits never dabbled with anything but Chrysler Hemis and the occasional wedge. He was a busy man in 1962, building chassis for other competitors while campaigning a Hemi-powered fuel dragster, a wedge-powered gas dragster, and a Plymouth Stocker. Garlits fabricator Connie Swingle drove the fuel-burning *Swamp Rat III* (Garlits's first chrome-moly car) while Garlits drove the gas-burning number *IV*. According to Garlits's website, the wedge-powered *Swamp Rat* went together in the spring of 1962 at the request of Chrysler's Frank Wylie.

"It was a lightweight car that went together fairly quick," he said. [Author: To whom should this quote be attributed? Garlits's website or Frank Wylie?]

It earned Garlits his runner-up finish at Indy. No doubt the car was competitive. In a match race against Gordon "the Collector" Collett in October, Garlits defeated the Collector with a best of 8.56.

During the early part of the 1960s, racers had two options when it came to running a blower: a top-mounted case driven by V-belts or a chain, or the front-mounted blower running off the crank through a Potvin drive. The downside of running the front-mounted blower was the fact it continuously ran at crank speed, so the drive ratio couldn't be adjusted. The advent of the Gilmer belt spelled the end of the Potvin drive. (Photo Courtesy Richard Kinstry)

Mid-Eliminators

Although the Mid-Eliminator brackets played second fiddle to the headline-grabbing cars in Top Eliminator, outside of Stock, the category saw the greatest participation. You can't ignore participants such as Raymond Goodman and his A/Modified Roaster, the *Tennessee Bo-Weevil*.

Goodman had visions of driving his own race cars, but that ended when he received wounds in Korea in 1951 that left him paralyzed. At the Nationals in 1961, Jim "Red" Dyer drove Goodman's Roadster to a class win with a record-setting 9.51 at 160.71 mph. Supporting a Chevy mill was a Scotty Fenn TE-440 chassis. Goodman returned in 1962 with a new Dragmaster car to run A/MR once again. With Harrison Jacobs behind the wheel, they won Mid-Eliminator honors. A true dyed-in-the-wool supporter of the Nationals, Goodman competed at Indy for 25 consecutive years as a competitor in everything from Modified to Top Fuel.

Altereds

In spite of being outlawed by the NHRA, Fuel Altereds

In 1960 and 1961, Jim "Red" Dyer drove this A/C Chassis Research car for Raymond Goodman, winning the Nationals in 1960. Goodman sold the car and began campaigning a Dragmaster-chassis machine that Harrison Jacobs took to Mid-Eliminator honors at the 1962 Nationals. The pair was a standout in 1962, finishing second in overall points. (Photo Courtesy Richard Kinstry)

saw a boost in popularity with the emergence of the team of Harrell, Reynolds, and Borsch. The team debuted its famed 1925 T at the NHRA Winternationals in 1961, winning A/Roadster class with a Jim Harrell–built 354 Hemi

The decade's headline-grabbing 1925 T Fuel Altered of Nick Harrell, Don Reynolds, and Willie Borsch went together in 1961. By the time this photo was snapped in 1964, a roof spoiler had been added and the fiberglass Cal Automotive body and rear end were narrowed, all for the purpose of improving high-end stability. These short-wheelbase Fuel Altereds ran the same engines as their Top Fuel brothers and were a handful. (Photo Courtesy Paul Johnson)

and recording 10.50 times in the process. The desire to run quicker saw them make the switch to Fuel in 1962.

"Wild" Willie Borsch earned his nickname because he often steered with one hand and hung on to the body (seemingly for dear life) with the other. Yes, these cars were a handful; yes, they were squirrely. Rarely did they cut a straight line to the finish. And yes, the fans loved them for it.

Gassers

There was no cooling the Gassers, as their popularity engulfed the nation. By 1962, the Willys of 1933–1941 vintage had taken over the upper echelons of the category, while the Tri-Five Chevys were increasingly the favorite in the lower classes. Drawing attention away from the West Coast Gassers was an increasing presence of cars hailing from points east: Illinois offered C/GS standout Sam Jones, Pennsylvania had Charlie Hill and Horace "Porky" Zartman running C/Gas, and Ohio had Jim Rodriguez down in E/Gas. These were just a few rac-

Through the early 1960s, Chevys were a popular choice in both the upper and lower Gas classes. Sam Jones and his 1937 Chevy took C/GS at the Nationals in 1962 and set the class record shortly after with a 12.05. A 327 and B&M hydro got the job done. (Photo Courtesy Richard Kinstry)

ers finding success on a national level.

Ohio George Montgomery, 1961's A/GS Nationals winner, was still running his Cadillac mill (up to 432 ci). He sat out much of the 1962 season after having a falling out with the NHRA. It seems that Montgomery made some unfavorable comments about the sanctioning body that it didn't agree with. To save face and limit gossip, they both agreed to state that Montgomery had retired. The decision didn't keep Montgomery from match racing his Willys, which was something he did with regular success.

The team of Stone, Woods, & Cook was in such demand that a second Willys was built in 1962. Running a larger, 467-ci Olds engine, the new car was painted a silver blue to match the team's other Willys, and it was christened *Swindler A*, as in A/GS. The existing car became the *Swindler B* and ran B/GS. The team won A/GS class at the NHRA Winternationals and dropped the class record in July with a 10.25 at 140.84 mph. They'd return to the Nationals in September, when they repeated last year's A/GS win.

A Nationals win was always big news and garnered plenty of ink, but the real money was being made on any given weekend where match races between rivals was drawing the crowds. In a bit of hyperbole, Woods claimed that the team hadn't been beaten in class in four years. The aftermarket finally caught on to the Willys's popularity and was producing all kinds of light fiberglass parts for the 1933 to 1941 models.

As the old adage goes, removing weight is like adding horsepower, and SWC (and pretty much every other team competing) made use of the new panels. At San Gabriel on October 27, 1962, the same weekend that Ivo ran his 7.99, the SWC team brought out its lighter A/GS Willys and proceeded to stun the crowd by running a 10.04. Cook solidified his reputation as one of the best behind a Hydra-matic transmission when he ran a backup time of 9.96 at over 141 mph! The days of 9-second Gassers was upon us. By the end of the year, 9.70 times were being realized. These are phenomenal numbers considering the amount of of air these highboys were pushing.

Little Eliminator

In the Little Eliminator category, everyone was following Hugh Tucker's A/SR 1928 Chevy and the two Modified Sports Production Corvettes of John Mazmanian and Bones Balogh. Tucker's Chevy evolved right along with the NHRA. He began by winning Little Eliminator in 1962 and carried on to Junior Eliminator in 1963, Street Eliminator in 1965, and Super Eliminator in 1966.

Tucker began gathering parts to build his Roadster in the late 1950s. He rescued the body from a salvage yard, and the 1934 Ford chassis and 4.40-gear-equipped 2-speed Columbia rear end came courtesy of a friend. Tucker's own 1949 Ford gave up the 402-ci Oldsmobile engine, which was derived from a bored-and-stroked 303. It was a healthy motor and featured six Stromberg carburetors and an Engle camshaft. Backing the Olds was a LaSalle gearbox, an item that at the time was considered the way to go. In a marathon three-day thrash, Tucker and a few friends brought all the pieces together.

With high hopes, Tucker hauled the Roadster to Indy for the 1961 NHRA Nationals, where he was soundly defeated. Tucker recalled, "Our Strombergs didn't stand a chance against the supercharged cars in class."

Tucker then partnered with Dave Stolls, who offered

Sadly, we don't see many cars like Hugh Tucker's 1928 Chevy on the track these days. Tucker won A/SR at the NHRA Winternationals in 1962, 1963, and 1964 with a blown Olds, and he repeated here in 1966 with a Hemi. Tucker's win list at major events is long and includes Indy in 1962 and 1963, Bakersfield in 1964, and the Hot Rod *magazine meet in 1967. (Photo Courtesy Forrest Bond)*

Here is proof that you didn't need a Hemi to win in 1962. This is the Olds engine that propelled Hugh Tucker's Street Roadster to a best of 9.70s at 155 mph. A 5/8 CT stroker crank gave it 476 ci and featured Hilborn 4-port injection, a GMC 6-71, a Tom Beatty blower drive, an Engle flat-tappet cam, M/T pistons and rods, and a Milodon bottom-end support.

up the 6-71 blown Olds engine that had been powering his speed boat. Stolls also contributed a B&M Hydro-Stick transmission to replace the aging LaSalle box. Bob Spar and Mort Schuman formed B&M back in 1953, and their Hydro-Stick transmissions (based upon the 1953–1957 GM Hydra-matic) were standard dragstrip fare by the early 1960s. The new transmission was a brute and could easily withstand the newfound power in front of it, and with a 4:1 first gear, nothing beat it out of the hole.

With the new combo running mid-10-second times approaching 130 mph, Tucker felt it best to swap out the Columbia rear for something more reliable. Racers couldn't do any better than a mid-1950s Oldsmobile rear end. The rear featured a stout 9.3 ring gear and proved to be bulletproof behind the blown cars in Top Eliminator. Prior to the 1962 Winternationals, Tucker swapped in the rear along with quarter elliptic springs and fabricated ladder bars.

At the Winternationals, Tucker defeated Cassiday & Sons' Chrysler-powered Roadster to win his first of three Winternationals titles. Gasser stalwart Junior Thompson was a major player in the Cassiday's drag racing effort, having built its Hemi and shared seat time in the Roadster.

Tucker followed with a class win at Indy but not before having to hunt down a blacksmith in town to

Your recipe as to how to build an unbeatable B/MSP Corvette is to take one showroom-fresh 1961 Corvette and add a Bones Balogh blown motor. Bones drove Big John Mazmanian's Corvette to record times and national event victories. (Photo Courtesy James Handy)

build him a new set of radius rods. Tucker had built his own rods out of aluminum, and every time he hit the brakes, the front axle would twist. Eventually, this twisting motion buckled the lightweight rods. The blacksmith bent up a new set of rods out of black iron. Class finalist Conway and Woodhouse screamed foul: "They can't be safe!" But officials saw nothing wrong with the new rods and let the race proceed. Tucker won, going away with an 11.08 at 127.29 mph.

At the 1962 NHRA Winternationals, John Mazmanian and driver Rich Siroonian repeated their 1961 C/MSP class win with a record-setting 12.11 at 114.84 mph. The Corvette went through a quick evolution as Mazmanian, like most drag racers, wanted to go faster. The Corvette received a 1/2-inch Crankshaft Company stroke and 0.030 bore to give 316 ci. An Isky cam lifted the valves, while a 4-71 blower and Hilborn 2-port injection fed the air/fuel.

The changes moved the Corvette into B/MSP, where Siroonian regularly butted heads with Bones Balogh, who was competing with the 1959 Corvette of Nick Marshall. More often than not, Siroonian came out on the short end of their matches. As Bones recalled, "It got to the point where Mazmanian refused to go to Indy, figuring it was futile, as I would just beat him again."

To power the Marshall Corvette, Bones installed the 328-ci (3/8 stroked 283) blown Chevy and B&M Hydro transmission that had previously powered his 1949 Chevy and the Mallicoats' Willys. Bones won class at Indy and held the class record most of the year, settling on an 11.62 at 124.82 mph late in the season. He followed Indy with big wins at Detroit and Aquasco before heading home to California.

After a rare loss in a match race against Mazmanian's Corvette, Bones discovered he had burnt one of his Venolia pistons while running at Aquasco. Bones said he never lost to Mazmanian.

"With a 6-71 to his 4-71, he didn't have the power," Bones said. "We were under-driving the 6-71, so it took less horsepower to operate but made more power. When I lost to him, I knew something was wrong."

Back in the pits, Bones discovered the telltale aluminum on the spark plug. After belittling Bones's Corvette, Mazmanian asked if he'd be interested in driving his candy red Corvette. Siroonian was heading off to serve Uncle Sam, and Mazmanian needed a driver. But Bones

Bones Balogh dropped his blown Chevy into Nick Marshall's 1958 Corvette and won B/MSP class at the Nationals in 1962. For the worlds quickest Corvette, times in the 10.80s were the norm. A 0.030 bore and 3/8 stroke gave 328 ci. (Photo Courtesy Richard Kinstry)

Mike Soskin, owner of the famed J&J Muffler Company, campaigned this injected B/A Bantam through the early 1960s. Ed Weddle built the chassis while Bones Balogh, who drove the car in 1962, built the 302-ci Chevy. The Bantam won class at the Winternationals three years running as well as a class win at Indy in 1962. Weddle took over driving and won the Hot Rod magazine meet in 1964. Ed netted the B/Altered a best of 10.65 at 128.31. (Photo Courtesy Forrest Bond)

had no interest in driving a 4-speed car, not after going through a transmission explosion in the Mallicoats' Willys.

Mazmanian asked what it would take to buy Bones's motor and hydro transmission. As Bones had most of the stuff given to him, including the B&M transmission, he told Mazmanian that $500 would do it. Mazmanian, the owner of one of Los Angeles's largest waste disposal companies and never short on funds, pulled a wad of bills from his pocket and counted out $500, stating, "Now we're partners." By the end of October, the engine and transmission transplant was complete.

Bones was a busy man in 1962 and 1963, as he also wheeled a B/Altered Olds-powered Fiat for Don Long. Long was an Inglewood neighbor of Bones, and the pair met when Bones stopped by one day after seeing sparks flying from Long's garage. It was humble beginnings for Long, who would go on to build a couple hundred Top Fuel and Funny Car chassis. The Altered was his first build, and when Bones inquired as to who was going to

Bob Tindle's Altered Orange Crate was a showstopper capable of running low 10–second times on alcohol. The beautiful Naples orange Ford won Best Competition Coupe at Oakland in 1961, 1962, and 1963. In 1962, it graced the cover of Hot Rod, and in 1963, Revell produced a scale kit. Innovative features included a 6-inch chopped, tilt body (Funny Car style) that was channeled 5 inches over a Keith Randol tube chassis. A 417 Olds carried a front-mounted Potvin blower. The suspension consisted of sprint car parts front and rear. (Photo Courtesy Michael Pottie)

drive, he stated that he had no idea and offered Bones the job.

The Altered battled it out in the short-lived Junior Eliminator at the NHRA Winternationals in 1962 and at both National events in 1963. Bones won the category at the car's Winternationals debut with a 10.69 at 128.61 mph. At the same meet, Bones also drove Mike Soskin's J&J Muffler B/Roadster, an injected Chevy-powered Bantam, to class honors. Bones went on to win B/A class at Indy and again in 1963 at the Winternationals.

Stock Eliminator

While the lower-class Stock cars battled it out for class, the factory hot cars battled it out in Super/Super Stock Eliminator. The class was reserved for Detroit's latest top-of-the-line, showroom-available performance offerings: 406-ci Fords, 421 Pontiacs, 409 Chevys, and 413-powered Plymouths and Dodges. With a push from Chrysler rep Frank Wylie, Don Garlits tried his hand in a Super Stock Dodge, although he quickly discovered a winning Top Eliminator car did not make a winning Super Stocker. With the issues Don Nicholson had at Indy in 1961, he miked everything in his 409 Chevy to ensure clearances were well within the rules. Coming off of an AHRA Winternationals loss to the Dodge of Bill "Maverick" Golden, Garlits found competition just as tough at the NHRA winter meet.

After hitting the West Coast, the Pennsylvania-based team of Strickler and Jenkins's first stop was a lead-up race at San Gabriel prior to the Winternationals. Luck would have it that on the first pass, the Chevy puked the motor. Being 2,600 miles from home, finding new parts proved no easy task. Jenkins recalled in a previous interview that after finding parts he "had to belt sand the new pistons down to size, as they were too large" and that "the car ran pretty good, considering the mess it was going together."

At the Winternationals, Strickler's *Old Reliable II* eliminated Nicholson during Saturday's class runoffs in the too-close-to-call semifinal match. Strickler then faced Hayden Proffitt's 409 Chevy in the final and lost to a quicker 12.52. Returning for Sunday's 50-car Mr. Stock Eliminator runoff, Nicholson defeated the Fords of Les Ritchey, Gas Ronda, and the S/SA Pontiac of Whittier, California's Carol Cox, before meeting Strickler in the final. With the twin Ermine white Chevys lined up ready to go, the flag came up and away they went. Dyno took a slight lead and held off Strickler's hard-charging 12.55 with a 12.84 at 109.22 mph.

At the Nationals, 50,000 fans watched Dave Strickler's *Old Reliable II* down Hayden Proffitt in SS/S with a 12.97. Chrysler dominated SS/S Automatic, and in the class final, the 413-ci Dodge of Al Eckstrand defeated Bud Faubel's Dodge. Stock eliminator had the 50 fastest Stockers battling it out to see who would be crowned the king of the hill. At the end of the day and after many hard-fought battles, the final came down to Hayden Proffitt's Cones Chevrolet–sponsored Bel-Air against Jim Thornton in the Ramchargers' Dodge.

Proffitt made quick work of the Dodge, sending

Dyno Don Nicolson made the move from Southern California to Atlanta, Georgia, in the spring of 1962 to head the performance division of Nalley Chevrolet. He made big money match racing his Chevy in the East, where they paid out $600 or more for a three rounder. Compare that to the West Coast tracks that paid $25 in war bonds (worth $17, according to Don) to the Stockers. (Photo Courtesy Robert Genat)

You race what you know, and Ted Harbit knew Studebakers. His 232-ci-powered 1953 model took Stock class wins at the Nationals seven times during the 1960s, starting with a K/S win in 1962 with a 16.90. By the end of the decade, the Chicken Hawk *was recording 15.40s. With a limited aftermarket, Harbit had to rely heavily on his own ingenuity to get the job done.*

in 1962, one of which was a 421-ci A/FX Tempest. Now, as car buffs know, the only way you could get a Tempest in 1962 was with a 4-cylinder engine and a Corvair-inspired transaxle. Mickey Thompson immediately saw the possibilities: a compact car, some 900 pounds lighter than a full-size Pontiac, and an engine bay large enough to house a V-8 . . . this spelled *instant winner.*

With Pontiac support, Thompson put employee Hayden Proffitt to work measuring and cutting and cutting and measuring until there was little left of the original car. A coil-spring rear suspension was designed to replace the transaxle, floorboards were fabricated to make room for the BorgWarner transmission, and, of course, motor mounts, linkage, and headers needed to be fabricated as well. Buttoned up and ready for action, the car was an immediate success. At the Winternationals, Proffitt won A/FX with a 12.37 at 116.27 mph time. At the Nationals in September, Lloyd Cox drove Thompson's Tempest to another A/FX class win, defeating the similar Tempest running out of Royal Pontiac in Michigan.

Thornton packing with a 12.83 at 113.92 mph to a losing 13.12 at 111.52. Proffitt was on top of his game and knew how to interpret the rule book. He ran his Chevy at the class legal shipping weight, as opposed to curb weight that many racers were still using. The difference was worth a couple hundred pounds, or approximately two-tenths of a second.

Factory Experimental

Optional Super Stock had a life span all of six months and was gone in 1962, replaced by the new Factory Experimental category. The new category consisted of classes A, B, and C and followed the same basic premise as the previous year's Optional Super Stock. Unlike the Stockers, which were classified by a weight-to-horsepower division, the Factory Experimental cars were classified by weight to cubic inches.

Dominant combinations were compacts stuffed with the largest engine possible: 413-powered Lancers; 421-powered Tempests; and Corvette-powered, fuel-injected Chevy IIs. Mickey Thompson had four Pontiacs running under his umbrella

Ford entered the factory lightweight game in 1962 when it produced 11 406-powered Galaxies for its Drag Council members. Weighing approximately 3,400 pounds, the cars were received prior to the NHRA Nationals but proved to be too heavy for A/FX. Dick Brannan dropped a 380-incher in his car and ran B/FX. In total, Brannan won more than 65 events and set 22 track records with his Galaxie. His efforts contributed to a 50-percent increase in performance and specialty car sales for Ford through the last quarter of the year. (Photo Courtesy Steve Reyes)

With Factory Experimental rules limiting tire width to 7 inches, Dyno Don took advantage of the station wagon's favorable weight distribution. He drove his injected Chevy II to B/FX class honors at the 1962 NHRA Winternationals. (Photo Courtesy Richard Nicholson)

A 421-ci Pontiac in a lightweight Tempest proved to be an instant winner for Mickey Thompson. Hayden Proffitt won A/FX at the NHRA Winternationals, and Lloyd Cox drove the same car to an A/FX win at the proceeding Nationals on Labor Day weekend.

Powered by a mid-mounted 392, the **Speed Sport** *was pegged as the world's fastest Roadster in 1963, having clocked 187 mph. The 1927 Ford T originally went together in 1956, and by 1963, the Modified Roadster had won Bakersfield four of the previous five years. (Photo Courtesy Ken Crawford)*

Chapter Three

1963
The Times They Are a-Changin'

The winds of change were blowing at the NHRA, as for the first time in five years, nitro dragsters were welcome to run in competition. It wasn't a complete lift, though, as fuel was only run at the Winternationals. The nitro cars couldn't compete in the newly implemented points-gathering program, nor were they run at Indy.

Lifting the nitro veil further, rule changes in August required that all drivers running nitro at NHRA tracks must wear approved fire suits. While displacement was reaching the 480- to 500-ci range in some categories, the NHRA looked to put the brakes on the factory hot rods in Stock. Following the lead of NASCAR and the USAC, the NHRA introduced a displacement limit of 7 liters (427.2 ci).

Top Eliminator

You knew it was going to be quite the year when on January 20 Don Prudhomme in the Greer, Black, Prudhomme AA/FD stopped the clocks with an astounding 7.77 at San Gabriel. Sure, we had Tommy Ivo crank a 7.99 late in 1962, but a 7.77? It was unheard of at the time. Heck, most fuel cars were still in the 8.10 to 8.20 range. As a case in point, at the NHRA Winternationals, the NHRA teased a hint of things to come by running an eight-car AA/Fuel Dragster program. Don Garlits took top honors over Art Malone with an 8.26 clocking.

Prudhomme explained the secret to the 7.77 run nicely in a Hemmings.com blog: "Back in 1963, the accepted logic in Top Fuel racing was that the more you smoked the tires during the run, especially with one of those big C&T stroker nitro engines, the better you got down the track. Keith, however, disagreed. We ran a stock-stroke 392 Hemi in the car, and Keith set it up so that it would slip the clutch going down the track and hardly smoke the slicks at all. With most dragsters, you kept some foot pressure on the pedal as you left the line to start the run so the clutch would slip a little. It was inconsistent and could be extremely dangerous if the clutch exploded. What Keith ultimately did was to figure out a way where I could get off the clutch at the start—just sidestep it, really—and drive the car on down the track. There'd be a counterweight on the clutch that would cause it to engage gradually as the engine's RPM built up."

Above: As one of the sport's most successful dragsters, the Greer, Black, Prudhomme car should be on everyone's top-10 list. Kent Fuller was responsible for the 112-inch chassis, Wayne Ewing formed the body, and Don Prudhomme laid on the paint.

Below: In the final run at the AHRA Nationals in August, Buddy Cortines (B/FD winner, CKC Racing) got the jump on A/FD winner Art Malone and held the lead for about three-quarters of the race before the engine swallowed a valve. Malone sailed past to take Top Eliminator. Malone raced nine times that weekend: five times for class, twice for Top Fuel, and twice for Top Eliminator. His top times for the meet were 8.16 at 200.88 mph. It was a great year for Malone who previously won the AHRA Winternationals and Bakersfield. (Photo Courtesy Forrest Bond)

There's just no comparing Art Malone's setup to the spoils of today's Top Fuel teams. Working on a single-axle trailer and out of the back of Malone's Chevy Suburban wasn't unusual. Many teams operated in similar fashion. Note the positive caster dialed into the front axle of the short-wheelbase (135-inch) dragster. This aided tracking and steering. (Photo Courtesy Forrest Bond)

Back to the Winternationals, Don Garlits was wheeling his short-wheelbase (120 inches) *Swamp Rat V* and was finding traction hard to come by, so he bolted a wing above his early Hemi and reportedly picked up a couple tenths. The move gave him the added bite he was looking for and aided in high-speed stability. In the final run, Malone took a holeshot lead on his old boss but couldn't hold it. Garlits passed Malone on the top end to earn his first NHRA national event victory. Returning to Florida after his western swing, Don and fabricator Connie Swingle went to work building a longer 140-inch chassis, all in the name of improving stability and bite.

Over at the AHRA winter meet, held for the first time at the all-new Bee Line Dragway outside of Arizona, Bob Sullivan in the *Pandemonium IV* was crowned A/FD class winner. The Rod Stuckey–chassis, 392-powered car set the class record in the process with a 196.06 mph. Sul-livan was to meet the Steinegger-Eshenbaugh team in the class final, but while going through the push start, the parachute of the S-E rail caught on the push truck and unraveled. Sullivan had already fired and was waved to shut off by the starting line crew.

AHRA President Jim Tice signaled for him to make the run, even though the S-E crew, push car, and rail were still on the track. This escalated to the point where Albert Eshenbaugh and Tice exchanged blows. When things finally settled, Sullivan made his solo run. Sullivan would split overall Top Eliminator with Dan Ongais in the Dragmaster Dart (which won Top Gas) when the final was called due to darkness. A toss of the coin saw the Dragmaster team take home the 4-foot trophy.

Malone left his home in Florida in February with his wife, daughter, and crewman Jim Strickland in tow, heading out on a two-month tour of the West. He kicked off

Here in the Top Fuel final at Indy, Don Garlits has a slight lead over Bobby Vodnik in the Kenny Hirata, Phil Hobbs car, but Vodnik came around to take the win. Vodnik was brought in to drive after engine builder Hirata and driver Hobbs were injured in a highway accident. Hobbs returned to the seat in 1964 and in 1965 won Top Gas at the Nationals. In 1966, Hobbs won Top Gas at Bakersfield. Note the zoomie headers; in 1964, almost everyone would be running them. (Photo Courtesy Forrest Bond)

the tour with a big win at Bakersfield, where he defeated Tom McEwen in the final. Reliability being what it was in 1963, Malone had a tough battle of it, making repairs to his 392 after each round.

He'd follow up by winning Fremont's fourth-annual West Coast Championship by beating Chris Karamesines's *Chizler*. Heading back East, he stopped in Arizona to defeat Bob Langley at a major AHRA event. Malone won Top Fuel at the AHRA Nationals on August 31, defeating Connie Swingle. Malone's top time was an 8.16 at 200.88 mph, an impressive clocking that some were questioning. This led officials to double-check the recording equipment and measure the track to confirm the times were legitimate. *Fast tracks* were a concern dating back to the 1950s with people questioning the length of some. Other fast tracks were on a noticeable downhill slope.

It's interesting to note that both Malone and Swingle had driven for Don Garlits and would again. Malone had come a long way since 1959, when he was known as the *green kid* on Garlits's crew. He took over the reins of the *Swamp Rat* while Garlits recovered from burns received in an on-track incident. Malone's previous race experience included driving jalopies and circle track cars.

Art Malone was the first to crack 180 mph on Daytona's 2.5-mile oval, doing so in August 1961 in a Hemi-powered Kurtis. The feat allowed him to pocket the $10,000 prize that NASCAR president Bill Frances offered to the first person to break 180.

In an interview, Malone reflected on how the Kurtis carried two air foils and had been wind tunnel tested.

"There was no guessing on the track," Malone said. "That kind of foil setup would help dragsters. It's just a matter of time until someone wind tunnels them to find out how."

On his own dragster, Malone dropped the 30 pounds of deadweight from the front axle and added an inverted wing that helped hold the car to the track. Capping Malone's oval track race experience were trips to the Indy 500 in 1963 and 1964, where he drove Novi cars for Andy Granatelli.

The NHRA Top Eliminator class reverted to an all Gas show at the Nationals, where Pete Robinson raised more than a few eyebrows when he qualified his B/GD Chevy with an 8.58. Robinson incorporated a jack system that raised the rear of his car on the start line to get the tires spinning. Before the last amber bulb on the Christmas tree turned green, he dropped the car and was gone. Although the NHRA rules said nothing regarding the use of hydraulic jacks, tech officials refused to let Robinson run them after receiving numerous complaints from other racers.

In November, Garlits penned a letter to the NHRA magazine, the *National Dragster,* voicing his displeasure with the jacks. Wally Parks agreed and banned their use. It seemed to make no difference to Robinson at the Nationals, when he repeated his 8.58 without them. Nor did he need them when he ran a class record of 8.22 at 179.28 mph (or a 7.94 at 185 mph on fuel). As a comparison of times, in one of the sport's biggest upsets, Bobby Vodnik, a relatively unknown 19-year-old from Chicago won Top Eliminator at the Nationals when he drove the Hirata-Hobbs entry past a redlighting Garlits. Vodnik's winning time was 8.62 at 174.75 mph.

Top Gas

In Top Gas, twin-engine cars seemed to be gaining in popularity, due in large part to the success of John Peters and Nye Frank's *Freight Train.* The pair built their first twin-engine rail in 1959, using a pair of Chevy engines breathing through a crank-mounted blower. By 1963, each engine carried its own top-mounted blower. The two blowers were connected via a *driveshaft* with the front blower driving the rear blower. This way, there was only one power-robbing blower belt, and it allowed Peters to couple the two engines closer together.

The car picked up its first major win in 1962, taking top honors at Bakersfield. Another Top Gas legend, Gordon Collett, earned his first major title by winning Top Gas at Bakersfield in 1963. Collett, whose status grew as the decade unfolded, suffered some serious burns late in 1963 after blowing the engine in his rail. At the time of the fire, fire suits weren't mandatory equipment in Top Gas, but they soon would be.

The *Freight Train* won Top Gas at the NHRA Winternationals in 1963 with driver Bob Muravez defeating Connie Kalitta's Chevy-powered dragster with an 8.82 at 178.21 mph. The story of Bob Muravez, aka Floyd Lippencott Jr., is an interesting one. Muravez came from a well-to-do family that frowned heavily upon his interest in drag racing. His parents were downright shocked to hear of his involvement and forbid him from driving. To avoid disownment, Muravez relinquished the driver's seat of the *Freight Train* and stood on the sidelines as driver after driver failed to match his record.

According to John Peters, the car went from top qualifier to non-qualifier in five short months. In Peters's eyes, there was only one way of rectifying the situation: get Muravez back in the seat. To keep it a secret from his family, Muravez initially raced under Peters's name to avoid recognition. When the team took Top Gas at the Winternationals, it was Peters who was credited as the winning driver.

Muravez was given the moniker Floyd Lippencott Jr. one night at San Gabriel by track announcer Mel Reck and track manager Steve Gibbs. It has been reported that the alias was made up on the spot with the name Lip-

The Freight Train *of John Peters with Bob Muravez at the wheel was the car to beat in Top Gas. A 161-inch wheelbase chassis by Peters and Nye Frank, an estimated 1,200 hp from the twin Chevys, and a total weight of 1,575 helped make winning look easy. (Photo Courtesy Forrest Bond)*

In March 1963, Tony Nancy stepped up to A/GD. Times reported in the 8.30 range were the norm for the 482-ci Chrysler wedge–powered silver/grey beauty. For a good part of the season, Tony held the No. 1 position on the Drag News top-10 list. (Photo Courtesy Michael Pottie)

The headline screamed Junior Fuel Dragster Makes Hay! Kenny Crawford proved you could have a lot of fun running a rail on a limited budget. His Kenz Muffler C/FD made use of an injected 301-ci Chevy and Kent Fuller chassis to record mid-10-second times. (Photo Courtesy Kenny Crawford)

pencott being borrowed from Gibbs's college professor. Floyd, I mean Bob, would explain his family situation to photographers, announcers, and competitors at each track he raced, and all agreed to keep his secret.

Mid-Eliminators

The NHRA shuffled its Mid-Eliminator brackets in 1963, which now consisted of Competition, Middle, Little, and Junior Eliminators. Joining Little Eliminator would be the cars of A and B/FX. These cars continued to move further away from production stock, and many were beginning to ask where it would end.

The Pure Hell AA/Fuel Altered debuted in 1963. A few drivers came and went before Dale "the Snail" Emery took over and proved to be just what the doctor ordered. Emery is caught here boiling the hides at Bakersfield in 1966. (Photo Courtesy Forrest Bond)

Altereds

Class-legal Altereds had nothing on the Outlawed Fuel Altereds and Roadsters. Although limited for the most part to the Southwest, the fan base and participation was growing. Rich Guasco debuted his *Pure Hell* in the summer of 1963, and from the get-go, the B/FR was capable of recording 8-second times.

Guasco got the bug to build a Fuel Roadster after crashing his dragster at Fremont in 1961, which put an end to his driving days. The fitting *Pure Hell* name was coined by painter Tony Del Rio, who felt it reflected Guasco's temperament. Pete Ogden built the 92-inch-wheelbase chassis that carried a high-mounted blown Chevy. The theory of the day being that the high center of gravity aided in weight transfer to the suffering slicks out back. The car scared the wits out of a couple drivers before Dale Emery took hold of the beast and made it one of the decade's more dominant Fuel Altereds.

Gassers

The ever-popular A/GS category became a real battleground in 1963 between the likes of Ohio George Montgomery and the team of Stone,

During the early 1960s, the M&H Racemaster slick was the No. 1 choice when it came to facing traction demands. Although, realistically, the 10-inch M&H pie crust slicks were just inadequate. Soft-compound rubber and wrinkle walls were still in the future, so racers made do. The slick got its pie crust *nickname from the sidewall design. As the width of the mold was narrower than the cap, supports were added to the sidewall, which gave it a pie crust look.*

RACEMASTER DRAGSTER

THE BEST DRAG TIRE MONEY CAN BUY!

This is the new M & H RACEMASTER 1000/16 ... it has no equal for bite, stability, and consistent high speed performance. 10" wide tread, exclusive M & H rubber compound.

Details on complete line of M & H RACEMASTER tires — yours for the asking. Enclose 10c for decal.

M & H TIRE CO.
433 Main Street
Watertown 72
Mass.

Woods, & Cook. Doug Cook kicked off the year by winning class at the NHRA Winternationals before moving on to the Mid-Eliminator final, where he defeated the AA/A Fiat of Jim Dunn.

At the NHRA Nationals in September, Montgomery and Cook came face to face in the class final. Such was the popularity of these cars that few people were in their seats when the two pulled to the line. It was a battle to the end with Montgomery and his now-Chevy-powered Willys coming out on top.

In the anticlimactic Mid-Eliminator final, Montgomery was to face Hugh Tucker and his AA/SR, but it didn't quite work out that way. When it came time to fire the cars, Montgomery's Chevy wouldn't go, so Tucker was asked by the starter to shut off while Montgomery worked on firing his Willys. When the car finally fired, it was Tucker's turn. His Olds wouldn't fire. When the allotted time passed and still no fire, Montgomery was sent off solo to win.

With tire technology lagging, Montgomery stated that his Chevy mill had more power than he could get to the ground. Backing the Chevy was a B&M-prepped Hydra-matic transmission and a torque-tube rear end. Supporting the rear initially were coilovers before Montgomery made the switch to leaf springs. The springs had shackles on one end and a slot on the other that allowed the springs to spread out when the car rose. His torque tube setup worked well enough that Montgomery used it on his proceeding Mustangs.

Supercharged Gas saw a new

John Mazmanian supplied the 1941 Willys, and Bones Balogh supplied the Chevy mill that dominated B/GS through 1963. By this point of the decade, the aftermarket was on a feeding frenzy, stepping up with replacement fiberglass panels for the Gassers. (Photo Courtesy Bones Balogh)

threat emerge in 1963 when Big John Mazmanian, tired of beating on everyone in the Modified Sports Production category with his Corvette, stepped up to B/GS. Mazmanian bought a 1940 Willys, installed the engine from the Corvette, and went hunting Oldsmobiles and Hemis. Bones Balogh debuted the car at Lions in June, running it for six months in B/GS before Mazmanian bit the bullet in December and stepped up to A/GS. The Chevy mill was replaced by a Bones-built 467-ci Hemi, which was derived by boring a 392-ci 0.030 and adding a 5/8 stroked crank. On the Isky dyno, the new mill produced 820 hp.

Dick Bourgeois grabbed A/G at the 1963 NHRA Winternationals in the Bourgeois and Earl Wade 374-ci injected Chevy–powered 1940 Willys. Here, Dick is on the verge of defeating the Grist brothers' Willys in the class final, running an 11.19 time. Both Bourgeois and Wade were prominent names through the decade.

The category known as Little Eliminator is where the unblown Gassers did battle. The competition was just as fierce as in the supercharged classes and just as diverse. Ohio's Gene Altizer (Anglia), Pennsylvania's Lutz & Lundberg (Anglia), Arizona's Johnny Loper (Willys), and California's Marrs brothers (Willys) were class winners and/or record holders.

Just as in the supercharged classes, competitors seemed to agree that the Willys was the best bet as far as body choice went. Drivetrains varied. The injected Chevy was seemingly the engine of choice while transmissions ranged from 4-speeds to Hydra-matics. Third members were generally the rugged mid-1950s Pontiac-Oldsmobile housings or the Ford 9 inch, mounted on leaf springs, coil springs, or quarter elliptic springs. Such were the possibilities that the A/G final at the NHRA Winternationals saw Dick Bourgeois in his A/G Chevy-powered Willys run an 11.58 to defeat the Grist brothers' Lincoln-powered Willys.

The Grist brothers (Floyd and Ralph Grist) won class at the 1961 Winternationals with their Willys, which awarded them the Lincoln engine that powered the Willys in 1963. A Reath stroker crank brought the 430 engine to 501 ci. This engine earned the Willys the title of the *world's fastest unblown coupe* at 10.92 at 129.98 mph.

The brothers were always experimenting with the car and a GM Hydra-matic transmission was adapted and backed by a locked Ford 9-inch rear. They finally settled on quarter elliptic rear springs out back. The springs were popular through the decade, as they helped plant the tires much better because spring windup was nonexistent.

The Willys had received a beautiful chopped top by a previous owner in the late 1950s and may have been

Bill Traylor's Animal, *dubbed the* world's fastest coupe, *featured an aluminum chassis of Traylor's own making and the body and candy red paint by Dave Stuckey. Shot here at Green Valley (Labor Day meet), the coupe ran an 8.34 at 187 mph. Traylor owned Traylor Engineering in Palatine, Illinois, and later built himself a Fuel Dragster. (Photo Courtesy Forrest Bond)*

Sam Parriot's national event wins go back to 1958 in a Caddy-powered Kurtis. Adhering to the diversity that Modified Sport Production allowed, Parriot debuted a new Kurtis at Indy in 1963, where he took A/MSP honors. Powered by a blown Ford, Parriot followed up with a class win at the Winternationals 1964, running 10.30 times. Parriot's 9-to-5 job was as a councilman for the City of Industry, California. (Photo Courtesy Richard Kinstry)

the first Willys drag car to have its lid lowered. The long-forgotten executioner sectioned the roof, added modified doors from a 4-door Willys, and brought it all together by shortening the body behind the doors. The Willys rear window was replaced with one from a 1946 Ford. The brothers retired the Willys in 1964, figuring they had gone as far as they could with it.

Stock Eliminator

At the NHRA Winternationals, Tom Grove in the *Color Me Gone* Plymouth led the all-Mopar Super Stock category by taking low ET with a 12.50 time. The Ramchargers (who had nothing but problems with the A239, 3-speed standard transmission in 1962) found happiness with the 727 TorqueFlite automatic transmission in 1963. Driver Al Eckstrand won Top Stock with the team's A/SA Dodge by defeating the newly formed Plymouth team of the Golden Commandos. Both Eckstrand and the Golden Commandos' driver, Bill Shirey, ran identical 12.44 times.

It was Eckstrand's final race as a member of the Ramcharger group. According to the Dave Rockwell book *We Were the Ramchargers: Inside Drag Racing's Legendary Team*, Eckstrand upset the group when he had a sponsor name (Stanford Bros Inc.) painted on each side of the Dodge without the Ramchargers' prior approval. The final straw was when word got back to the group that Eckstrand was taking all the credit for the Winternationals win. By the time Indy rolled around, Eckstrand was gone, and Herman Mozer was behind the wheel. Ironically, the two met in the Top Stock final with Mozer squeezing out the win with a 12.22 at 116.73 mph to a losing 12.23 at 114.94.

On any given weekend at any given track, fans were drawn to match race battles that involved cars from Detroit's Big Three. This only added to the growing appeal of the Stock and Factory Experimental cars. There were no rules when it came to match racing, except for those agreed upon between the combatants. Southern-style match racing took on a different perspective all together with no rules and no holds barred. The days of "run whatcha brung and hope you brought enough" match racing was upon us, and everyone who was anyone was jumping on board: Top Eliminator, Gassers, Altereds . . . It was where the money was made and where most of the experimenting with new combinations took place.

Factory Experimental

Factory Experimental continued its move away from Stock in 1963, as each of Detroit's manufacturers offered a limited run of all-out drag cars.

Chevy offered the lightweight Z11 Impala pack-age that featured a new *W* motor of 427 ci, which was wrapped in aluminum parts: fenders, inner fenders, hood, and bumpers.

Pontiac offered a similar lightweight package but took it a step further when it *Swiss cheesed* the chassis, drilling holes to further lighten the car. With a Super Duty 421 for power, these Catalina's fell into B/FX. Returning to A/FX was the 421-powered compact Tempest.

Ford countered with lightweight, twin 4-barrel 427 Galaxies.

Chrysler had its new-for-1963 426-ci Max Wedge engine, which was available in both 415- and 425-hp form and was wrapped in steel or lightweight aluminum panels.

Season-to-season improvement in quarter-mile times were helped along by the continued development taking place by aftermarket manufacturers and engine builders. Under the hood, greater attention was being placed on porting, ring seal, and camshafts. Harnessing the power

Pontiac ad man Jim Wangers drove the Ace Wilson B/FX Pontiac to a runner-up finish in Little Eliminator at the NHRA Nationals, falling to the Old Reliable A/FX Chevy of Dave Strickler. Pontiac built 14 of these 421 Super Duty–powered Swiss cheese Catalinas, lowering the overall weight by drilling approximately 130 holes in the frame and replacing body panels with lighter aluminum parts. (Photo Courtesy Robert Genat)

Before the Mopars and before the Mercury Comet, Ronnie Sox and Buddy Martin campaigned a line of Chevys. Their Z11 Impala was one of the most-feared cars on the East Coast. Coming hard off the line, the Chevy got as much weight as possible on the rear wheels, thanks to stiff springs up front and soft springs in the rear. (Photo Courtesy Michael Pottie)

Factory involvement helped steer the direction of drag racing Stockers. Ford Special Vehicles and Dearborn Steel Tubing teamed up to build this Thunderbolt prototype in 1963. Bill Humphries drove the car at the Nationals, losing out to the Z11 Impala of Don Kimball after missing a shift. Bill Lawton grabbed the A/FX top speed record with the car in Connecticut in October, running a 12.15 at 121.29 mph. (Photo Courtesy Richard Kinstry)

It was smiles all around after Dave Strickler and master tuner Bill "Jiggs" Jenkins took Little Eliminator at the Nationals. The limited run of lightweight Impalas in 1963 was Chevy's last kick at direct factory involvement in the sport. (Photo Courtesy Mike Strickler)

Gas Ronda, a charter member of Ford's Drag Council, and his 1963 lightweight Galaxie, a rebodied 1962 lightweight, made use of a Les Ritchey–prepped 427 to record competition-squashing 12.20 times. (Photo Courtesy Paul Johnson)

Nationals staple Bob Beezer (the Native American rain dancer) stands by as Greenwood, Indiana's Otis Isom and his 1963 Ford blasts off the line at Indy. In 1963, there was no eliminator program for the lower-class Stock cars.

The Ramchargers and the Golden Commandos were two teams consisting of Chrysler engineers. Al Eckstrand won the NHRA Winternationals for the Ramchargers, and Herman Mozer won Indy for them. Forrest Pitcock in the Golden Commandos' No. 1 car ran an 11.97 at Indy, which was said to be the first legal 11-second pass by a Stocker. (Photo Courtesy Jim Hall/Golden Commandos Collection)

were new 10-inch slicks produced by M&H. Although not class legal, the tires were being used in match race competition and allowed for 11.30 times by the end of the season.

By 1963, the factory wars were in full bloom. Here "Wild" Bill Flynn and Bill Lawton prepare to match race with their lightweight Super Stockers. Flynn ran a Max Wedge 426, while Lawton used a 427 in the Tasca Ford. Both were heavy hitters through the evolution of Stock to Funny Car. Check out Flynn's long traction arm. The racer put many theories into practice. (Photo Courtesy Richard Kinstry)

At the NHRA Winternationals, the Z11 Impalas, lightweight Pontiacs, and Fords were forced to run Limited Production as opposed to Super Stock due to the limited number produced. Although the Chevys were initially approved by NHRA Tech Director Bill "the Farmer" Dismuke to run Super Stock, it appears that those at Chrysler, the race's sponsor, disagreed, stating that the required number of cars had yet to be built; thus, they were ineligible to run Super Stock. The NHRA track officials agreed, and the cars in question were moved to Limited Production, a class created just for this race for these cars.

Frank Sanders of S&S Headers drove his Impala to class honors but was disqualified on a technicality. At the Nationals, the NHRA chose to place the A/FX and B/FX cars in Junior Eliminator, where the A/FX Chevy of Dave Strickler defeated the B/FX Pontiac of Jim Wangers in the category final.

You don't get much prettier than Dave Rudy's A/SR 1932 Ford. At the NHRA Nationals in 1964, Rudy fell in the class final but took solace in going home with Best Appearing Car honors. Powering the highboy to 11.55 times was a 364-ci Chevy, Olds Hydra-matic transmission, and a 5.14:1 Chevy rear. (Photo Courtesy Richard Kinstry)

Chapter Four

1964
Fueling the Fire

There's an old saying that goes, "Gas is for cleaning parts; nitro is for drag racing." In 1964, the NHRA rescinded its ban on the use of nitromethane. Many racers screamed that it was about time.

Jack Chrisman hinted at things to come when he bolted a blown, nitro-fed 427 engine into his 1964 Comet, creating the first Exhibition Stocker. The cars in lower Stock, or Junior Stocks as they came to be called, received their own eliminator program beginning at the NHRA Nationals in 1964. Pete Chisolm, a member of the well-organized, Detroit-based Chevair Racing Team, took the eliminator win with his 1964 Chevy Bel-Air wagon. One could say Stock's climb out of relative obscurity was complete. By the end of the decade, it was one of drag racing's most popular categories.

Connie Kalitta and his Bounty Hunter *cleaned house at Bakersfield, defeating Don Garlits in the final and bringing Goodyear its first major win. Kalitta qualified No. 1 here at Indy with a 7.86 at 200 mph, and he met Garlits in the final. Garlits took the win this time, recording a 7.77 at 198.22 mph. The* Bounty Hunter *featured a 145-inch Logghe chassis. (Photo Courtesy Don Prieto)*

Fuel Dragster

With the NHRA lifting the ban on nitromethane, Top Eliminator was now a category dedicated to the Fuel Dragsters, which ran classes AA/FD through B/FD. Gas Dragster (though following the same fundamental rules as the Fuel Dragster) was cut loose and given a category of its own. Classes ran AA/D through D/D. The difference in quarter-mile times between an AA/FD and an AA/D was six- to seven-tenths of a second and about 15 mph.

Helping move ETs along and produce a growing number of 200-mph runs was the tire battle brewing between M&H and Goodyear, which introduced its first drag slick in 1964. The initial 16x10 tire was said to be worth as much as two-tenths of a sec-

Ron Winkel (right) discusses the virtues of drag racing with an oh-so-tentative model. The Kent Fuller rail wasn't a big winner, but at the time, it was quite the innovative piece. Fuller was one of the best! (Photo Courtesy Bill Pitts)

ond over the M&H tire. Connie Kalitta proved them in March by winning Bakersfield. Late in the year, Don Garlits, who had been running and testing for M&H, bolted on a set of new Goodyear 16x11 test tires and reportedly ran three-tenths of a second quicker than his record 7.78. As the tire companies improved their product, it enabled

owners to build more power into their cars. The stories of rigged clocks abound, but by midseason, 200-mph runs were becoming commonplace, even on the most suspect tracks.

Twin-disc slider clutches were on their way in as racers and manufacturers struggled to find a way to harness

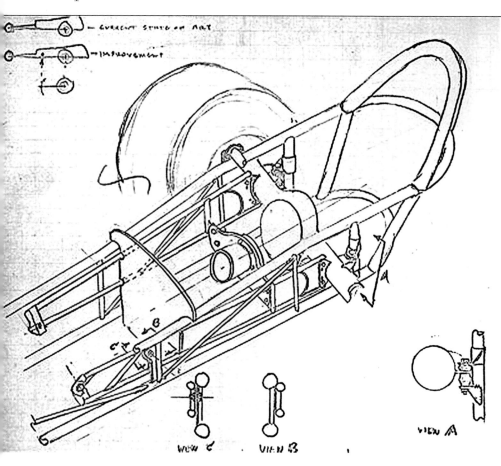

This drawing shows the ladder bar rear suspension setup that Kent Fuller designed to support the Magicar's engine and driveline. The ladder bar's pivot points were located mid-chassis. Upon acceleration, the engine would lift back to help plant the slicks. (Photo Courtesy Bill Pitts)

expectations, its uniqueness made it an instant standout and a key piece in the evolution of the dragster.

Starting at the rear, the *Magicar* rode on coil springs, unlike most dragsters of the day that relied upon a solid-mounted rear end. The rear end and remainder of the drivetrain rode on a ladder bar–style subframe that bolted to the main chassis toward the rear of the engine. Under acceleration, the engine would lift back (pivot), aiding to load the slicks. Up front, the suspension incorporated rubber biscuits in place of leaf springs or torsion bars that were typically used in dragster construction. When it came to steering, the main link passed from the steering box along the right side of the car, hooked to a tie-rod that passed across the nose piece, and bolted to a single radius rod.

At the car's San Fernando debut in October, the area surrounding the starting line resembled a chassis builder's convention. Woody Gilmore of Race Car Engineering, Roy Steen of Race Car Specialties, and Kent Fuller himself watched in anticipation. After all the hype and publicity that the car garnered (Trapp worked for *Drag News*), the debut proved a little anticlimactic. The *Magicar* performed well but failed to meet the unrealistic expectations.

Gary Casaday was the first of three drivers. Jeep Hampshire took over shortly after the car's debut. Hampshire laid down the car's best of 7.62 at 204.08 mph. With the speed in which dragsters were evolving, the *Magicar* was back in Fuller's shop by the end of 1965, collecting dust.

Emerging from Gas Dragster was Roland Leong, who chose 1964 to step up to AA/FD. Leong had been terrorizing Hawaii since 1959 with his Dragmaster car powered by a Chevy with a Potvin front-mounted blower. Leong

the newfound power. Bob and Don Spar at B&M figured they could do one better by eliminating the clutch altogether, introducing their Tork Master converter for Top Fuel cars. It was trialed by Gary Cagle and others, including Don Ratican, Don Gaide, and Kenny Safford; and the team of Don Moody, Kent Fuller, and Dave Zeuschel.

Don Prudhomme signed with B&M in 1966, taking over the Safford deal. The Tork Master was a simple torus member, an input and output turbine wheel with a pressurized fluid coupling that took the place of a clutch. Unlike a conventional torque converter, the Tork Master had no stator to multiply torque. It was said to have worked well on slippery tracks with the tires of the day but not so well on good tracks. Although it initially seemed like a viable concept, the torus was found to absorb too much power, costing valuable time. Within a couple years, it faded into history.

Chassis continued to evolve and led to some interesting designs, all in hopes of getting more power to the ground. The chassis of the Kent Fuller, Ron Winkel, and Kaye Trapp's *Magicar* that debuted in October 1964 was truly an innovative piece. Fuller, a prominent name in chassis design through the 1960s, built his first chassis in 1956. Although the *Magicar* failed to meet performance

Don Prudhomme started the year driving the Greer, Black, and Prudhomme extended-nose car before hooking up with Roland Leong. Possibly the most successful Top Eliminator car ever, Prudhomme went something like 200 matches with little more than a handful of losses. Seen in this photo are Black and Prudhomme. (Photo Courtesy Don Prieto)

One of the most anticipated match races of the year saw Tom McEwen in Lou Baney's Yeakel Plymouth Special dragster defeat Prudhomme at Lions in three rounds. The chassis came out of the shop of Woody Gilmore and featured a 392-ci Hemi tuned and built by two of the best: Vince Rossi and John Garrison. The car reappeared in 1966 as the Brand Ford Special when Baney switched affiliation. (Photo Courtesy Forrest Bond)

made the occasional trip to the mainland, and in 1962, he won both the long distance and best appearing crew awards at the Winternationals. It was Don Prudhomme who visited the track in Oahu and suggested that Leong follow his dream, which led to AA/FD. Leong was bankrolled by his mother, who raised funds by running a speed shop and agreed to give her blessing—but only if Keith Black would mentor him.

With Black onboard and Prudhomme by his side, Leong debuted his Kent Fuller *Hawaiian* at Lions late in the season. His tenure behind the wheel of the fuel burner lasted all of one hair-raising run that Leong miraculously survived. He crashed the car going 190 mph and bent it up pretty good. Track manager C. J. Hart was so worried that Leong would kill himself that he immediately revoked Leong's license. Keith Black was so shaken that he told Leong that he didn't think he could race with him anymore.

The Greer, Black, and Prudhomme venture was winding down, so Black suggested that Leong allow Prudhomme to take over driving the *Hawaiian*. As a taste of things to come, Prudhomme took the seat in November to defeat McEwen in the *Yeakel Plymouth Special* in a best of three at Pomona. The 354-ci powered *Hawaiian* ran a best of 202.24 mph that day to join the 200-mph club.

Tom McEwen was on everyone's radar in 1964, having won big at Lions, Pomona, and pretty much everywhere else through the Southwest, including a 32-car UDRA race at Drag City Fontana in October. On the match race front, he was beating everyone who dared to step up, including the nearly unstoppable team of Greer, Black, and Prudhomme, which he defeated in two straight at Lions in September.

In the match race against Prudhomme that has been said to have ignited the pair's career-long rivalry, McEwen had Chris "the Greek" Karamesines fly in from Chicago to do the tuning on his Ed Donovan Hemi. McEwen ran a best of 8.19 that day, a tad behind Prudhomme's best of 8.14. Both ran a shade over 194 mph. It was around this time that McEwen adopted the *Mongoose* nickname. Why Mongoose? Well, in the wild, the mongoose is known to devour venomous snakes. Seems fitting.

Here's an early 1964 match race between NHRA Nationals winner Don Garlits and AHRA Nationals winner Bob Langley. If you look through Garlits's right front wheel, you can see a piece of rubber hanging down from the lower frame rail. It kept the light beam broken at launch so Garlits could cheat the Christmas tree. It was spotted by CKC's J. E. Kristek, who told Langley about it after noticing it in this first round. Langley told Don that either that comes off or there would be no round 2 or 3. Garlits removed it and beat Langley anyway with times in the 7.60s. Garlits is running the all-new Goodyear 10-inch slicks here. He switched from running M&H, for which he tested Racemasters. The Goodyears were distinguished by their lack of a pie crust edge. (Photo Courtesy Forrest Bond)

Although not often mentioned, dragsters did have weight breaks. For instance, a blown Chrysler Hemi car had to weigh a minimum of 1,300 pounds, and a blown Chevy, 1,150 pounds. Helping keep the weight in check was emerging lightweight aftermarket parts. Magnesium third members, magnesium steering, bellhousings, and blowers all became standard wear.

Through pure strength and numbers, the Chrysler Hemi ran roughshod through Fuel Dragster. Gar-

lits, who was having his best year on record, surprised everyone with a record-setting 7.78 at 201.34 mph in New Jersey. He capped the year by winning the biggest race of the season, the Nationals, and credited the new M&H soft compound tires he was running.

The Michigan-based Ramchargers emerged at the Nationals as a genuine AA/FD threat. Not content run-

The Ramchargers joined AA/FD at the Nationals in 1964 with Don Westerdale at the helm of their 426-ci-powered Dan Knapp–designed car. It was the national debut for the new Hemi, and Westerdale made believers of many after laying down 7.60 times at over 205 mph. (Photo Courtesy Richard Kinstry)

The Surfers—what can you say. From inception in 1964 through to disbanding after Indy in 1965, these guys rarely lost. Mike Sorokin was a natural behind the wheel. Note the lack of idler pulley for the blower belt. The weight-conscious Surfers had no use for deadweight. Sadly, we lost Mike in 1967 while he was driving another team's car. (Photo Courtesy Forrest Bond)

Zoomies

Zoomie headers, which replaced the traditional weed burners, were not given credit that they deserved for the increase in speed that they provided.

The first set of zoomie headers appeared in 1964. Drag racing historian Don Prieto said it was Chet Herbert who put the idea to Jim Ward, crew chief on the Yeakel Special. According to Don, Chet suggested that someone should point the headers up and back to clear the tire smoke and take advantage of the thrust. It was Jim himself who partnered with Paul Sutherland at Race Car Engineering to build the first set of zoomies.

In September, they bolted the headers on Frank Cannon's *Hustler V* and headed to Lions to try them out. That weekend, Cannon recorded the first 200-mph run (200.88) on the West Coast. The zoomies were said to be worth 3 to 4 mph, and within weeks it seemed as if everyone was running them.

Credit for the *zoomie* name goes to Jim Ward. According to Don, "Jim applied the name to anything he thought was neat or better than what was available."

Photographer/historian Forrest Bond said, "There were almost as many ideas about what zoomies did [and how they worked] as there were people who ran them. With tire smoke blown up and away, drivers no longer got "smoked in" coming off the line. Shredded tire "gumballs" were largely blown away, leaving the tread surface cleaner for better traction. Zoomies were also believed to heat the tire tread, which improved traction." Note the angle of the rear tube on this 1965 Ronnie Hampshire shot.

ning roughshod through Top Stock Automatic, the team debuted its Dan Knapp Fuel Dragster at Detroit a week before the Nationals. Making use of the new-for-1964 426-ci Hemi, it was necessary for the Ramchargers to fabricate numerous parts, including the blower manifold, blower drive, and related parts.

The new Hemi had many doubters, those who believed there was nothing better than the old 392. At the Nationals, driver Dan Westerdale made believers of them by running a best of 7.95 at 194 mph on a cautious 50-percent load. He'd make it to the semifinals before falling to Garlits after the car failed to fire.

Gas Dragster

With the NHRA welcoming back the fuel dragster, Gas Dragster was now playing second fiddle. Hindsight tells us what we should have predicted: As the 1960s progressed, both participation and interest in the category dwindled. In the meantime, Gas Dragster gave rise to its own stars and made some interesting advancements.

Mickey Thompson signed on with Ford after General Motors pulled out of racing in 1963. He developed alu-

minum hemi heads for his Ford high-riser and used the combination to win A/GD at the Winternationals with an 8.64 at 180 mph.

The Thompson castings, similar to the hemi heads he developed and marketed for Pontiac's V-8, shared a few

Gordon Collett really came into his own in 1965, when he kicked the year off by winning the AHRA Winternationals. He followed with a win at the NHRA Springnationals. He closed the season by winning the division 3 points championship for the second year in a row. (Photo Courtesy Connell Miller)

Mr. Eliminator, Gordon Collett, started out with this Scotty Fenn kit dragster that was welded up at a friend's home because it had the flattest driveway. Collett earned the nickname Collecting Collett *in this car due to the number of eliminations he won. (Photo Courtesy Mark Collett)*

Collett won the Gatornationals in 1970, his last national event win. Come October, he joined the twin-engine crowd when he debuted his new car at the National Dragster Open held at Columbus. (Photo Courtesy Steve Reyes)

parts with the Chrysler Hemi, including intake rocker arms and valve covers. Unique to Thompson's hemi Ford were its three-piece pushrods, which were necessary to clear the parts. Thompson's enterprises also marketed aluminum heads for the Chrysler. They listed at $725 per pair while the Pontiac and Ford heads listed for $900, which was not cheap by anyone's standards.

There were a number of performance standouts this year: Dan "the Mangler" Ongais set out on his own after coming over from the islands with Roland Leong, Hobbs and Hirata out of the Midwest, and George Bolthoff, who ran a Chevy through 1963 before finding happiness with an early Hemi. A combination of low compression, lots of overdrive, and lots of cam made him a winner.

Gordon Collett managed to stand out above the crowd by winning Bakersfield for the second year in a row. It proved to be a great season for the Collector, who followed up with a win at the Nationals, winning the Division 5 title, and setting the class record with an 8.35 and 185.28 mph.

Collett had been racing since the 1950s, starting out behind the wheel of a mail-order Scotty Fenn car. The disassembled chassis arrived in a box and was welded together by Collett in a friend's driveway. Powered by a 392, Gordon raced the car through the spring of 1963 before building a new Rod Stuckey car.

"Stuckey offered to deliver the chassis for the same price the guys on the coast wanted just to build it," Collet recalled. "About a month later, Stuckey and his buddies rolled up in an old Caddy with the chassis on the top."

Gordon saved a ton of dough by stripping the parts from the Fenn car to use on the new one. He stuck with parts that worked and proved reliable: an Isky cam, Isky blower drive, 4-port injectors, a Schiefer clutch, and a Ford 9-inch rear end.

Late in 1963, Collett was laid up for 13 weeks after getting badly burned when his Hemi threw a rod. The Stuckey car served Collett well, closing the decade having earned more national event wins than any other Top Gas car.

"I didn't pay much attention to what others were doing," Collett said. "I knew what I had to do to win."

After his Gatornationals win in 1970, where he borrowed a transmission from D. A. Santucci and then proceeded to beat him in the final with it, Collett recalled that after the first round, his was the only single-engine car remaining. That prompted him to make the switch to a twin, using a new Stuckey chassis. The twin Hemis measured out to 465-ci each thanks to a bore and Reath stroker crank. Overdrive on the blowers was between 30 and 40 percent.

"It was getting to the point where a good twin-engine car could almost beat a Top Fueler," Collett said. "Top Fuel and Funny Car technology continued to find its way into Top Gas. In the now-famous moment at Ontario in 1970 where Gordon lost the right slick, the wheels and tires had been borrowed from the Funny Car of Jim Dunn. At the proceeding Springnationals at Dallas, the two Hemis came apart between the engines. It would be Collett's final Top Gas race.

There were plenty of Fuel and Gas teams out to prove that the Chevy wasn't dead yet, including teams such as Warren, Coburn, and Warren (WCW); Mike Snively; Lefty Mudersbach; and Zane Shubert. Shubert ran straight alcohol through his 4x4 Chevy (4-inch bore x 4-inch stroke) to produce 194-mph times. Shubert and WCW hyped their cars as the world's fastest Chevy and offered to race any Chrysler that ran a reported 200 mph.

The secret behind Shubert's record times was to "Run lots of inches and lots of compression [8.5:1 in his case]. A Moldex billet crank, 'practically' unbreakable rods, and 4-bolt mains to help hold the bottom end together."

Mid-Eliminators

It was a surprise to many how quickly the Factory Experimental cars progressed. By midseason, the GMC roots blower (a fairly inexpensive power booster) was showing up on these cars. Add nitro to the mix, and these cars were forced to run in the Fuel Dragster class during sanctioned competition. Just as Fuel Altereds match raced against Gas Dragsters, races between these cars and blown Gassers weren't uncommon because quarter-mile times were close to comparable.

Modified Production

Joining the long line of categories in the Mid-Eliminator brackets was Modified Production. To quote the NHRA's own rule book, the category was created for "dual-purpose cars to fill the gap between Stock automobiles

Roy Fjastad of Speed Products Engineering (SPE) briefly campaigned this A/Fuel Coupe with Dick Rabjohn and driver Pat Foster. I say briefly because Foster drove it off the end of Palmdale not long after its debut. Foster walked away, but the car was done. The Coupe looks, and ran similar to Frank Pedregon's Taco Taster, *a car well known for setting the slicks a blaze. Not much "coupe" in these cars. (Photo Courtesy Forrest Bond).*

and the Gas coupes and sedans." Classes ran A trough E initially and were based on a weight-to-cubic-inch factor. It was a popular category that gave rise to eventual World Champs Carroll Caudle and Scotto & Blevins.

Ralph Ridgeway was an early star of the category, running a 1955 Chevy sedan that he purchased as someone's discarded project. Ridgeway opened up a 283 to 301 ci, and not satisfied with the top end charge provided by the then-current aftermarket intake manifolds,

Thanks to fairly liberal rules, the Modified Production category offered up a variety of old and new. Dave Todd was a student of A/FX competitor Bill Shirey, who helped him prep this C/Modified Production Barracuda. Todd's was the only Barracuda at the 1964 NHRA Nationals. The 273-ci powered lightweight recorded respectful low-13-second times before falling in class eliminations. (Photo Courtesy John Durand)

The popularity of California's Fuel Altereds, Fuel Roadsters, and Fuel Coupes slowly but surely continued to grow outside the state, thanks to guys like San Antonio–based Ernie Lentz. Lentz's Fuel Roadster Bantam counted on a 392-ci engine for power. His cars were all easily identifiable, as they all carried the 888 number. (Photo Courtesy Forrest Bond)

fabricated his own *tunnel ram*–style manifold (in the days before the tunnel ram existed) by using a GM Rochester fuel-injection housing as a base. This gave him the top-end power he was looking for and contributed to the '55 setting more than 15 AHRA and NHRA class records over the next year.

Altereds

The Fuel Altered moniker took hold in 1964, and outside of the cars in Top Fuel and Top Gas, there were no cars quicker or faster. In NHRA Gas Altered, there were a number of honorable mentions in 1964. Jim Dunn repeated his 1963 Winternationals win when he took the (Henry) Velasco, (Dewey) Merritt, and Dunn Fiat to AA/A class honors at the Winternationals with a 9.36 time. The car featured a stroked Chevy and a chassis of Dunn's own design.

Julius Hughes and his *Zot II* won AA/A at the Nationals, turning a best of 9.60 at 155.97 mph. Hughes's Roadster ran a Dragmaster-designed chassis mounting a Chevy mill. Hughes started racing in the mid-1950s with a gas-powered dragster. A man with many hats, in 1960 he opened the Atlanta Speed Shop, the first speed shop in Georgia. By 1964, he was managing the Atlanta Speed Shop Dragway, the NHRA's first sanctioned track in the state.

Gassers

With all the categories running in the Mid-Eliminators, it was still the Supercharged Gas cars that held the most fan appeal. In A/GS, Stone, Woods, & Cook swapped out the Olds in their Willys for a Chrysler Hemi and became a consistent 9-second performer. Big John Mazmanian and Bones Balogh were right there, and Ohio George rattled the troops mid-year when he reportedly ran a 9.49 at Michigan.

Perennial B and C/GS winner K. S. Pittman stepped up to A/GS with a 1933 Willys and immediately became a top contender. Pittman's Willys was owned by Chuck Stolze of the Ohio-based S&S race team. Stolze had the Willys shipped west, where it was worked over by Pittman and the good folks at B&M, which supplied the Hydro-Stick transmission. Out back, the Willys rode on a not-so-common coil spring suspension. It was an unusual setup for a Gasser, but it sure worked for Pittman and company. Dave Zeuschel supplied the blown

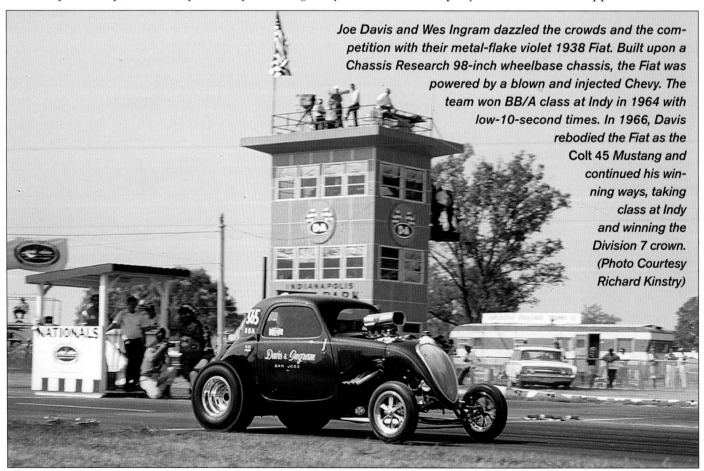

Joe Davis and Wes Ingram dazzled the crowds and the competition with their metal-flake violet 1938 Fiat. Built upon a Chassis Research 98-inch wheelbase chassis, the Fiat was powered by a blown and injected Chevy. The team won BB/A class at Indy in 1964 with low-10-second times. In 1966, Davis rebodied the Fiat as the Colt 45 Mustang and continued his winning ways, taking class at Indy and winning the Division 7 crown. (Photo Courtesy Richard Kinstry)

car are Pittman on the left and Gene Altizer, his S&S teammate. (Photo Courtesy Richard Kinstry)

420-ci Hemi that propelled the car to a class record of 9.99 at 146.10 mph. By season's end the Willys was clicking to the tune of 9.70 times at over 150 mph and held NHRA, AHRA, and *Drag News 1320* records.

In November, Pittman and Stolze took the Willys to England as part of the International Drag Racing Festival. Arranged by Dante Duce (Moon Equipment) in conjunction with Wally Parks, England's Sidney Allard, and the British Drag Racing Association, the festival saw a dozen American drag cars, drivers, and their teams go to England on a two-week excursion to wow the crowds. Upon his return, Pittman lost one of his few matches of the year to Eddie Sanzo, whose 1940 Willys pickup clobbered him in two at New York.

Sanzo, an employee of Jack Merkel Automotive, ran a 380-ci Chevy in his chopped A/Gasser backed by a Hydra-matic transmission prepped by up-and-comer Vincent Tarantola. Tarantola's Vitar transmissions and high-stall convertors were a contributing factor in lower ETs in a number of categories well into the next decade.

Revisiting their standing rivalry on February 2 were Bones Balogh and Doug Cook. Bones dropped Cook in three at Lions, recording a best of 9.97. Cook returned the favor at the Winternationals, defeating Bones in the class final, where a standing crowd witnessed a close one:

The Gasser Wars were in full bloom when this photo was snapped at the 1964 NHRA Winternationals. It was the A/GS class final that saw Doug Cook in the near lane defeat Bones Balogh with a 10.03.

10.03 to a losing 10.01. Earlier in the meet, Bones had recorded the first legal A/GS 9-second time, producing a 9.99 at 149 mph. The pair met up again in May with Cook again defeating Bones.

Big John Mazmanian was graceful in his defeat (as he would be again in June, losing to SWC in two at Rockford), but gazing into his crystal ball, Mazmanian could see the future and raised the concern that drag racing was getting away from the hot rod trend. He warned that soon all you would see would be dragsters and A/FX cars.

Bones dropped a number of jaws in March at Bakersfield when he recorded a 9.77. He credited the phenomenal time to the new M&H slicks they were using. The

John Mazmanian never had a bad-looking car. With its fresh coat of candy red, his 1941 Willys may have been the best looking of them all. Bones Balogh drove the Willys until June 1964, when Dick Bourgeois took over. Giving the car stance were a Don Long front end and a Pontiac rear with disk brakes mounted on quarter elliptic springs. (Photo Courtesy John Foster Jr.)

The Bones Balogh–built Hemi measured 467 ci and featured the best parts available: a Reath Automotive crank, Venolia pistons, and Mondello heads. Ensuring reliability was a Milodon bottom end support. There was no cutting corners here, as the Hemi produced a little more than 820 hp on the Isky dyno. (Photo Courtesy John Foster Jr.)

tires had a tread width of 11 inches and softer compound, originally destined for Art Malone's AA/FD.

"Everyone thought they'd never work," Bones said. "We walked away with a huge trophy for outstanding performance of the meet."

Hugh Tucker took over the reins of Big John's Willys in June after Bones and Mazmanian had a falling out. Regarding the change, Tucker recalled, "I defeated Bones at the Bakersfield meet in March with my Street Roadster and then won the Eliminator bracket. There were a lot of giant egos in the Gasser ranks, and knowing Big John as I did, I suspect he was upset my Oldsmobile-powered Roadster beat him. My guess was firing Bones was a knee-jerk reaction. Talk about shooting yourself in the foot. They were on the path to become the dominate Gasser of that time period."

Factory Experimental

You could say Big John's prediction regarding the Dragsters and A/FX cars

Ollie Olson and his A/G 1940 Willys took home the Best Engineered Car award at the 1964 NHRA Nationals. The Florida-based injected Chevy–powered Willys was driven by Bob Dwyer and featured owner-built independent rear suspension, headers, and other parts. Dwyer made it to the class final, where he lost to the Anglia of Lutz & Lundberg. (Photo Courtesy Richard Kinstry)

The Junior Thompson, Skip Poole Chevy–powered 1941 Willys initially ran C/GS before stepping up to B/GS in 1964. Racers often added weight or dropped weight to fit a higher or lower class, thus increasing their chance to pick up some pocket dough and another trophy for the mantle. More importantly it earned them ink in papers, such as **Drag News,** *which in turn helped when it came to booking matches. (Photo Courtesy Richard Kinstry)*

Following the similar build pattern as the Fairlane, modifications to fit the 427 to the Comets included trimming the shock towers and relocating the upper control arm mounting points. Rules of the day also required that the stock tread width be retained. To do so, the upper and lower control arms were modified. The highly modified 427s featured twin 780-cfm Holley carbs, cross-bolt mains, and a steel crank. Air/fuel flowed through 2.19 intake, 1.73-inch exhaust valves to forged pistons that squeezed out a high-octane 14:1 compression. A Toploader 4-speed was the only option when it came to transmission, as was the bulletproof 9-inch rear end.

The Comets made their first appearance at the AHRA Winternationals in Arizona (February 7–9), where Dyno Don and the lone wagon unleashed an 11.48 time. The Mopar contingency immediately protested the wagon, screaming that the car's 109-inch wheelbase didn't meet the 114-inch requirement. The AHRA crew running the show could only agree and refused to allow the wagon to run.

was fairly accurate. Action in Factory Experimental was really heating up, and the fans were relating. Plymouth, Dodge, Ford, and now Mercury were throwing their full support into the category.

Although limited to a budget that was only 10 percent of Ford's budget, Mercury's Fran Hernandez spent wisely. While Ford built 50-plus hi-rise 427-powered Fairlane Thunderbolts for Super Stock, Mercury's budget allowed for only 11 Comets (10 hardtops and a wagon) that were powered by the same hi-rise engine. The limited numbers forced the Comets into A/FX.

Mercury hired the best drivers, picking up Ronnie Sox and Don Nicholson, who each abandoned their Chevys when General Motors pulled out of racing. The Comets, like their Fairlane counterparts, were built by Dearborn Steel Tubing, an outside operation that Ford relied upon to assemble such specialty vehicles.

Feeding off the success he had with his Chevy II wagon, Don Nicholson chose the 427-ci wagon when he joined Mercury in 1964. It was Mercury's first year at the drags, and it was a roaring success. A Caliente hardtop replaced the wagon in May because Mercury team drivers cried unfair advantage. (Photo Courtesy Randy Hernandez)

Sachs & Sons campaigned two Comets in 1964: the more familiar blown car and this one, which Bill Shrewsberry drove to A/FX wins at the NHRA Winternationals and Bakersfield. (Photo Courtesy Randy Hernandez)

Mercury's Al Turner was in attendance, and he protested loudly that he had a verbal agreement with AHRA President Jim Tice that the wagon could run. Turner and Nicholson failed to convince the track officials, and the expulsion stood. Dyno was out. In protest, the remainder of factory-supported Fords and Mercurys in attendance were pulled from the race. It became pretty much an all-Chrysler

Bill "Grumpy" Jenkins, the master builder/tuner half of the Dodge Boys, proved he could make a Mopar run just as well as a Chevy when Dave Strickler repeated his 1963 A/FX win at the Nationals by defeating Tom Grove in the Melrose Missile IV with an 11.04. Here Strickler takes on the wedge-powered Comet of Dyno Don in a match race held at the famed Cecil County Drag-O-Way in Maryland. (Photo Courtesy John Durand)

show, with the lone Ford of Phil Bonner (the 1963 AHRA World Champ) left to battle.

Phil Bonner, who was cutting 10-second times with his *Georgia Peach* Falcon by season's end, scared the Mopars with the quickest time on the first day with an 11.70. Bonner was put out of contention overnight when someone sabotaged the Ford by pouring screws down the carburetors. Tommy Grove set the low ET for the Chryslers with his *Melrose Missile* recording an 11.76. Grove lost in Top Stock Eliminator to Dave Strickler in the Dodge Boys' lightweight Polara. Mr. Stock Eliminator honors the following day went to Hayden Proffitt in his *Yeakel Plymouth*. At the NHRA Winternationals, where the A/FX cars ran their own category of Factory Stock, Ronnie Sox's Comet came out on top, defeating Nicholson's wagon with an 11.78 at 120.16 mph.

Strickler's Polara was one of 50 lightweight Chryslers built featuring thin-gauge fenders, hood, doors, decklid, bumper, and brackets. The 4-speed-equipped car produced times in the high-11-second range. Come April, Dave would be one of the four recipients of the new Hemi-powered Altered Wheelbase cars released by Chrysler. The other recipients would be Tommy Grove, the Ramchargers, and their Plymouth counterparts, the Golden Commandos.

The four cars, two Dodges and two Plymouths, have come to be known as 2-percent cars due to a shuffling of their wheelbase. The Plymouths and their shorter 116-inch wheelbase had the front suspension moved forward 3 inches, while the Dodges, with their longer 11-inch wheelbase, had the front moved 3 inches and the rear suspension moved up an additional 3 inches. Although

Hayden Proffitt's career ran the gambit from Stockers to Jet Cars. His Yeakel Plymouth in 1964 held the No. 1 spot on the Drag News top 10 list. In this November 1 shot at Houston, Proffitt faced and defeated Dick Landy in three. An exhibition run using rosin netted Proffitt a 10.95 at 126.58 mph. (Photo Courtesy Forrest Bond)

the wheelbase was shifted forward, the length remained within the variance that NHRA rules allowed.

The shuffling placed greater weight (52 percent) on the required 9-inch cheater slicks. The Strickler-Jenkins team successfully campaigned three different Dodges through 1964. Their Altered Wheelbase Hemi-powered Dodge won A/FX at Indy with an 11.04. As a comparison, Strickler's Indy-winning A/FX ET in 1963 was a 12.17. He'd close the 1964 season at Cecil County in November by running a record 10.66 with the A/FXer.

The Hemi, Chrysler's ace in the whole, reappeared after a five-year hiatus in 1964. Ten months in the making, the 426-ci engine made its debut in February at NAS-CAR's Daytona 500, where Plymouths powered by the new mill finished first, second, and third.

Bugs prevented the Hemi from making its dragstrip debut at the NHRA Winternationals. Pre-Pomona testing at Lions showed the cars were suffering fuel delivery issues, so back to Detroit they went. A change in OEM Carter carburetors to Holleys rotated 180 degrees solved the problem. The Ramchargers debuted the new Hemi on April 26 at the Martin US-131 season opener. With Roger Lindamood behind the wheel, the car cranked an A/FX record-setting 11.22 at 125.17 mph. It appears that the added 67 pounds of Hemi heads up front failed to have the detrimental effect many thought it would.

With Chevy out of racing, many of those loyal to the brand went match racing by taking the previous year's Z11 427 engine out of their Impalas and placing them into the lighter Chevelles, or a Chevy II. Class rules stating the engines had to be of the current year prevented these cars from running Factory Experimental. Dick Harrell, Malcolm Durham, Tom Sturm, and Kelly Chadwick

Richard Petty and a few other roundy round boys took a turn at drag racing when NASCAR booted the Hemi. Petty was quite active match racing the Hemi Barracuda and won B/Altered at the inaugural NHRA Springnationals in 1965. Times in the 10.40s were recorded early on. NAS-CAR got serious about drag racing in 1965, running events in the East through 1967. (Photo Courtesy Jim Hall/Golden Commandos Collection)

are just a few who found happiness match racing their Chevys every week for pots of gold—money they could only dream of making running class cars. Many match racers were building dedicated cars that featured setback engines and bodies that were slid back on the chassis, all in the name of improving bite.

If you liked Factory Experimental, you loved the blown cars of Supercharged Factory Experimental (S/FX). Chrysler got the ball rolling in this imaginary category in March, when they debuted three candy red, white, and blue blown Dodge Chargers.

The lightweight 330 model sedans were prepared by Dragmaster in Carlsbad, California, and were powered

In 1964, Chrysler commissioned Jim Nelson and Dode Martin of Dragmaster to build three supercharged Dodge 330 sedans. With their 480-ci nitro wedge engines, some feel that this is where to look when searching for the begining of the Funny Car. Jim Nelson, Jim Johnson, and Jimmy Nix drove the exhibition cars. Customizer Dean Jeffries formed the front and rear rolled aluminum pans, radiused rear wheel openings, and painted the cars. (Photos Courtesy John Foster Jr.)

by blown and injected Max Wedge engines that were bored and stroked to 480 ci. Out of the gate, drivers Jim Johnson and Jimmy Nix were able to record times in the 10s at 134 mph. Widely recognized as the precursor of today's Funny Car, the Chargers were generally booked into major events and performed side-by-side exhibition runs.

Jack Chrisman and Arnie Beswick joined S/FX shortly after. Chrisman debuted a direct-drive, blown 427

Jack Chrisman entered his blown Comet in the NHRA Nationals, where he was forced to run B/Fuel Dragster. The 2,800-pound Comet cut low-10-second times at 150 mph but was no match for Harry Havis, who took Chrisman in class with a 9.40 at 154.90 mph. (Photo Courtesy Randy Hernandez)

Comet; added a pinch of nitro; and proceeded to run smoky quarter-mile times in the 10.40s. And how did the Comet perform against the S/FX Dodge Chargers? We never found out, as the good folks at Chrysler refused to allow their drivers to go up against the Comet.

In August, Chrysler recalled the Chargers and retired them. Jimmy Nix hoped to retain his ride and started tearing into it, removing weight, setting the engine back, and increasing fuel loads in preparation of beating Chrisman to the 150-mph mark, a speed yet to be obtained by a stock body car. Chrisman blasted through the barrier on August 23 at Aquasco, Maryland. By "tipping the can," he obtained a top speed of 154.10 in 10.13 seconds.

Beswick, a tough Pontiac proponent, was one of the few top performers who stuck with the Chief brand after General Motors pulled the plug. He purchased his *Mystery Tornado* GTO new from Knafel Pontiac with just 16 miles on the odometer and set out to build a match race stocker.

It's a loosely kept secret that Pontiac had big plans for a lightweight 1964 LeMans before General Motors pulled the plug on racing. Beswick stated that for him, factory support never really

Phil Bonner was on fire through the summer of 1964, match racing his 427 Falcon without a loss and taking Stock at the AHRA Nationals with 11.40 times. Here he battles to catch up to Beswick's blown GTO. Beswick's Goat would record 9.50 times before he retired the car in 1966. (Photo Courtesy Forrest Bond)

went away. His GTO arrived sans options and sound deadener, and—according to Beswick— it had an aluminum front end.

Beswick visited a local scrapyard and pulled a GMC 6-71 blower from an old bus. Having brought it up to spec, he bolted it atop the Super Duty 421 that had previously powered his 1963 *Passionate Poncho*. In the 3,200-pound GTO, the blown mill produced high 10-, low 11-second times. Beswick raced the car with and without the blower.

Remember that Beswick had two bullets to choose from. His naturally aspired 421-powered Tempest wagon could also cut the competition down. You never knew with which he'd show up with, according to Dyno Don.

Stock Eliminator

While Tri-Five Chevys and McKellar-cammed Pontiacs ruled the day in lower Stock, Top Stock belonged to Ford and Chrysler. Ford, which had been hammered by Chrysler's lighter Max Wedge cars in 1963, pulled out all the stops in 1964 by taking its 427 that had been powering its Galaxies in 1963 and placing it in the lighter, midsized Fairlane to create the Thunderbolt.

Of course, Chrysler escalated the game when it countered with the Hemi head 426 in a lightened package. And just like in 1963, the Super Stock Dodges used rear springs that located the rear wheels 1 inch forward of their Stock locations, thus equaling the wheelbase of their Plymouth counterpart. And just for good measure, they snuck them up another inch in 1964.

Dick Landy gave the new Hemi its first major quarter-mile victory when he won the *Hot Rod* magazine meet

Ford's Thunderbolt dominated Super Stock action in 1964. Here northwest heavy hitters Bill Ireland and Jim Price battle it out in their Thunderbolts at Arlington. Ireland enjoyed factory support through the later 1960s.

Mary Ann Foss ran her D/SA 1958 Pontiac through 1965 (when this photo was shot) before making the switch to Dodge. At the Nationals in 1964, she won class with the Black Magic, running a 14.24 at 98.68 mph. (Photo Courtesy Forrest Bond)

Dick Landy was running Ford Stockers when he opened Automotive Research in 1962. It took just one ride in a Max Wedge Mopar for him to change direction. In 1964, Landy competed in SS/A with the Dodge pictured here. Late in October, he pushed the front wheels forward 6 inches when he added a straight axle. Later, the rear suspension was modified to allow 8 inches of adjustment. The Altered Wheelbase, Exhibition Stock game was on. (Photo Courtesy Forrest Bond)

at Riverside in May with his aluminum nose Dodge. Dick headed the march to Exhibition Stock in October, when he tore into his S/SA legal car and created one funny-looking match racer. Landy stripped out the torsion bar suspension and installed a weight-saving straight axle, mounting it 6 inches forward of the stock suspension location. It's interesting to note that the axle carried a Chrysler part number, making the setup NHRA legal.

Additional mods to the Dodge were made to the rear, which allowed the suspension to be moved 8 inches forward. SoCal track records were set by Landy's Dodge in S/SA, A/Gas, and A/MP. Landy match raced the Altered car extensively through the end of the season and reportedly was the first Stocker to crack 130 mph, doing the deed at San Fernando in November running 130.68.

In the Super Stock stick classes, the Thunderbolt Fairlane reigned supreme with Gas Ronda defeating Butch Leal in the Mickey Thompson Thunderbolt at the NHRA Winter meet. Leal took his revenge by winning the Nationals. At the end of the season, Ronda held the class record with an 11.23, while Bill Lawton and the boys at TASCA were running 10.80s match racing their Thunderbolt.

In S/SA, it was an all Chrysler show at the NHRA Winternationals with Rich Rogers in the Town & Country Plymouth defeating the Ramchargers, 11.83 to an ever so close 11.86. Jim Thornton and the Ramchargers won class at the Nationals but fell in the Top Stock eliminator final to the equally impressive, *Color Me Gone* Dodge driven by Roger Lindamood. It's interesting to note that come 1965, all the top performers in Top Stock, Super Stock abandoned the category and moved into Factory Experimental.

Don Gay's 421-powered 1962 Pontiac was a class winner at both the NHRA Winternationals and the Nationals in 1964. Gay held the NHRA record with a 12.58 at 114.58 through mid-1964. Not bad for a 16-year-old "kid." (Photo Courtesy Forrest Bond)

Bob Sullivan's exhibition Barracuda was powered by the nitro-fed 392 that had previously powered his Top Fuel car to 200-mph times. The not-so-stock Barracuda retained its stock wheelbase, and all the lights and both windshield wipers worked. Inadequate tires limited the 3,700-pound car to times in the 9.70s at 160 mph. Ralph Suman did most of construction, building it with direct drive and an Olds rear end. In 1966, weight was dropped, and the front was extended 18 inches. Times improved to 9.40s at over 175 mph. (Photo Courtesy Richard Kinstry)

Chapter Five

1965
What's so Funny?

Interest in drag racing continued to grow, and it was now heralded as the world's fastest-growing sport. Joining the AHRA and the NHRA sanctioning bodies was NASCAR, which introduced a drag racing division in 1965. NASCAR focused its drags east of the Mississippi and ran through the 1967 season.

Outside of Factory Experimental classes, which ran down through J/FX, NASCAR rules closely mimicked those of the NHRA. As speeds increased across the board, so did safety. The NHRA rules now required all cars running over 150 mph to have a parachute. What wouldn't even have been thought of just a year ago, the emerging *funny*-looking Exhibition Stockers were now approaching those speeds.

Fuel Dragster

The year in national events kicked off with Tom Hoover defeating Turk Cox in Top Fuel at the AHRA Winternationals. Although Hoover went on to numerous wins in Funny Car, this was his only national event win in a dragster. The significance of this race was that it was the AHRA's first all-200-mph Top Fuel show. It was a tough field where Chris "the Greek" Karamesines used a twin-disk clutch and soft Goodyears to harness the power of his Hemi and earn top qualifying time of 7.42.

Connie Kalitta debuted his new Logghe car, which carried Ford's much-anticipated single-overhead cam 427. Connie qualified with an off the trailer 7.67 at 200.08 mph. The "Cammer," as it came to be known, was originally pegged for Ford's NASCAR teams to combat Chrysler's Hemi. Chrysler dominated NASCAR action in 1964, and Ford wasn't about to sit back and watch it happen again. Well, the Cammer was to be the great equalizer, but when NASCAR president Bill France reneged on his approval, the engines went to Ford drag teams.

The Cammer went from Ford's drawing board to completion in 90 days. To keep costs to a minimum, the engineering team, led by Norm Faustyn, built the engine using the existing 427 as its base. To handle the increased power of the twin cams, the bottom end of the side oiler was beefed up with cross-bolt mains, a forged crank, and improved oiling.

The cast-iron Cammer heads featured gargantuan 2.25-inch hollow-stem intake valves and 1.90-inch sodium-filled exhaust valves, all as a means to keep the valvetrain weight down and RPM up. Cast-iron rockers mounted on a hardened steel shaft actuated the valves. The empty cam space within the block was filled with a dummy shaft that operated the oil pump and dual point distributor. A separate chain ran the shaft off the crank. Covering the maze of gears and chain was a two-piece aluminum cover with removable access plates.

Showing the level of factory involvement, Kalitta's weekend finished early after his Cammer threw a rod. To ensure his car was up and running for the NHRA Winternationals a week later, Ford shipped him a new short-block. The Cammer had its growing pains and initially chewed up main bearings. According to Mercury's Al Turner, the problem was solved by reducing the crankshaft journals down to the size of Chrysler's 392 Hemi and running their bearings.

Then, there was the 6-foot chain that ran the cams. Although it was cheaper to manufacture and use, the chain stretched and threw off the timing. Some, including Dyno Don, solved the problem by going to outside sources. Don went to Germany to have a high-tensile chain made that wouldn't stretch so much.

At the NHRA Winternationals, Kalitta and his new Cammer made it as far as the third round before

NHRA World Champion Maynard Rupp in the **Prussian** *took the title, defeating a redlighting Buddy Cortines with an 8.01. Roy Steffey and Maynard Rupp previously won the Springnationals, defeating Connie Kalitta. Both Steffey and Rupp worked at Logghe chassis, later forming Rupp-Steffey Enterprises. (Photo Courtesy Forrest Bond)*

Connie Kalitta's new **Bounty Hunter** *spent a little time in Ford's wind tunnel. Whatever mods were made paid off. At Indy, he qualified No. 1. Competing at this level was not cheap; Nitro was $5 a gallon, and a Cammer or Hemi could use 3 gallons per run. Slicks cost around $80 a set and lasted 8 runs on average. (Photo Courtesy Forrest Bond)*

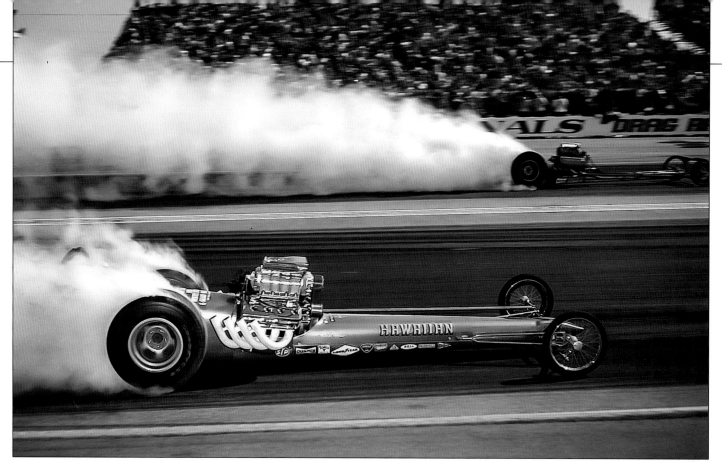

The NHRA Winternationals–winning Hawaiian of Roland Leong ran a Keith Black Hemi nestled in a 136-inch Kent Fuller chassis, wrapped in a Wayne Ewing body. As the decade progressed, chassis length grew in the name of improved stability. With Prudhomme at the helm, the Hawaiian *averaged 7.40s at around 204 mph. Airheart brakes and a Deist chute brought the car to a safe stop. (Photo Courtesy Stephen Justice)*

It was a tough year for Big Daddy Don Garlits, seen here in Swamp Rat VIII *at Indy with a new-era 426. His day ended early. Garlits moved from Florida to Detroit, and it never really worked out. (Photo Courtesy Forrest Bond)*

disappearing. In the first showdown between a 426 Hemi and the Cammer, Kalitta defeated Don Yates in the Ramchargers' rail in the second round with a 7.75. Don Prudhomme proved that it was the right move by Leong to put him behind the wheel of the Hawaiian, when he qualified with a 7.80 before improving to a 7.75.

Eliminating the competition on the other side of the ladder was Bill Alexander in the Brisette-Alexander-Herbert car, who made a bye run in the fourth. Rightly, the final round came down to the two quickest cars: Prudhomme versus Alexander. The Snake took the lead off the line and never looked back, recording a 7.76 at 201.34 mph to defeat Alexander and win his first national event.

Don Garlits, who was coming off his best year on record, was having one of his worst in 1965. It didn't help that he relocated from Florida to Detroit. Though Detroit was more central and brought him closer to Chrysler and fabricator/builder Dick Branstner, whom he admired, the move proved a disaster. Unlike Florida, where tracks are open year-round (and Garlits could test new ideas through the offseason), in Detroit snow kept the tracks closed for 4 to 5 months.

Garlits had a stable of three cars running out of his shop in 1965, with Connie Swingle starting the year in the 426-powered *Swamp Rat VIII* and Marvin Schwartz driving the *Garlits Chassis Special*. Garlits's one big win of the season came at Bakersfield, where he drove the *Swamp Rat VI-B* and shook the jinx by winning Saturday's eliminations over Mike Snively-Ed Pink, then defeated teammate Schwartz in Sunday's final.

Garlits crashed his *Swamp Rat* while racing Ron Goodsell's *Frantic 4* at Island Dragway in April after the chute failed to open. He escaped unscathed, but the car was totaled. In his haste, Garlits decided to quit racing and hired 22-year-old Carl Schiefer to drive for the remainder of the season. Well, we all know that didn't last long, and within a couple weeks Garlits was back behind the wheel.

At the Nationals, Garlits fell early in eliminations to Bobby Vodnik. This eased some pressure off of Don Prudhomme, who marched to the class final and defeated Jimmy Nix. This allowed Prudhomme to wait for the winner of the low 16 to run in the final on Monday. And the low-16 winner was Tommy Ivo, who only made the program after Bobby Levitt dropped out.

Prudhomme defeated Ivo in the final, and in doing so, set the low ET of the meet with a 7.505 while clocking a 207.33 mph. Don Westerdale and the Ramchargers held top speed with a 210.76. The Ramchargers found new power in their Hemi by feeding it more spark advance. Unlike the early 392s that were comfortable around 30 to 35 degrees, the new Hemi came alive at 55 to 60 degrees.

What a difference a year makes. In 1964, we had only a handful of Fuel Dragsters capable of cracking 200 mph. Thanks to advancements in a number of areas, we were

The Top Fuel final at the Nationals was an all-California affair that saw Don Prudhomme defeat Tommy Ivo. Prudhomme ran a 7.505 in the final for low ET of the meet. He headed home after completing his Eastern tour, where he set track records near everywhere he ran, hitting a best of 215 mph at Great Lakes Dragway. (Photo Courtesy Forrest Bond)

What would have been impossible just a year before was to gather enough cars for an all-200-mph field. In November, 52 cars converged on Fontana for Mickey Thompson's first "200 mph club" race. Connie Swingle driving Ed Pink's Old Master took the win over a redlighting Don Garlits with a 7.80 at 207.84 mph. (Photo Courtesy Forrest Bond)

Many spectators considered the push start part of the show and were disappointed when the Safety Start rollers appeared in 1964. Paul Sutherland in his Woody Gilmore–chassis car is seen here on the Pomona rollers, which were installed for the start of the 1966 season. The rollers were used through 1974, by which point remote starters were in vogue. Simpson provided Sutherland's hood, which filtered out the nitro fumes. (Photo Courtesy Forrest Bond)

Danny Ongais came from the islands as a crewman for Roland Leong. By 1964, he was making a name for himself and picked up the nickname the Mangler while driving the old Adams-McEwen shark car. (Photo Courtesy Forrest Bond)

now knocking on the 220-mph door with Jim Brisette and driver Paul Sutherland coming closest with a 219.50-mph run.

Enabling the increase in speed was a number of factors, including fuel pumps flowing 175 to 200 gph, which fed into recently incorporated port injectors. The injectors enabled builders to regulate fuel to each cylinder, which no doubt saved more than a few pistons from melting and blower explosions. Rotor tips within the blower now carried replaceable Teflon inserts, which saved blower cases and the rotors themselves from being destroyed. The inserts allowed builders to run tighter tolerances, and when the inserts wore down, they were simply and inexpensively replaced. Helping to harness the newfound power was ongoing advancements in tire and clutch design.

Streamliner

With speeds now in excess of 200 mph and horsepower peaking around 1,400, racers went looking for other ways to increase quarter-mile times. To some, cutting a cleaner path through the air was a natural progression. Robert "Jocko" Johnson was one of the first to take streamlining seriously.

With the help of eight carbs and 60-percent nitro through an early Hemi, his full-body streamliner recorded an eye-opening 7.36 elapsed time back in 1958. It was an impressive feat for a car that was deemed too heavy to overcome the aerodynamic advantages that the body provided. And in 1965, the handicap was still too much to overcome, but it didn't stop guys from trying.

Drag racers began to take a serious look at streamlining in the 1950s. They first added wings and spoilers to their Top Eliminator cars and then body panels. No one looked harder at cheating the wind than Jocko Johnson. (Photo Courtesy James Handy)

A study in aerodynamics by Tony Nancy produced this rear-engined Hemi car in 1964. Nancy wrecked the car at Sandusky, Ohio, in July 1964 and rebuilt it as the Wedge II. A blown Oldsmobile replaced the Hemi, and a solid rear axle replaced the original independent setup. Times in the low 8s approaching 200 were common for the gas burner. The wheelbase of the Roy Steen chassis was 135 inches. (Photo Courtesy Michael Pottie)

Nye Frank's *Pulsator was a fine example of the experimentation in aerodynamics that was taking place in the mid-1960s. Powering the AA/FD to 200-mph times were twin 300-ci injected Chevys. Bob Muravez ran the car at the NHRA Winternationals, where it won the Best Appearing Car award. The weight of the fiberglass body canceled out any aerodynamic advantage. (Photo Courtesy Don Prieto)*

The Scrimaliner *was designed and built by Ronnie Scrima with assistance from George Bacilek. Bob Sorrell did the aluminum body, and Joe Anderson laid the metal-flake paint. The wheelbase measured out to 133 inches. As a safety measure, Scrima chose to leave the Milodon 392 exposed. Total weight of the rail was 1,500 pounds. (Photo Courtesy Don Prieto)*

Tommy Ivo's Video Liner *rode on an RCS chassis and was designed by Tommy and Steve Swaja. The* Video Liner *ran right around 200 mph in the high 7s but was aerodynamically wrong. As Ivo described, "It was like we were running a teardrop backward, and it wanted to turn around in the lights." Ivo abandoned the car in short order and RCS had him in a new car six days later. (Photo Courtesy Forrest Bond)*

Gas Dragster

Though overshadowed by Top Fuel, Top Gas never failed to offer an entertaining program. And 1965 was no exception, not with names such as Gordon Collett, George Bolthoff, Pete Robinson, and Jimmy Nix in the lineup. Nix won the Winternationals before making the move to AA/FD. Collett won the inaugural Springnationals, defeating Pete Robinson's SOHC Ford in the final.

At the Labor Day Nationals, Collett showed true sportsmanship when he gave up his spare engine to Kenny Hirata prior to the semifinals. Wouldn't you know it, Collett blew his engine and spent the night in the hotel parking lot rebuilding it before the finals. Collett won Sunday's eliminations and faced Phil Hobbs on Monday. Hobbs took a holeshot lead on Collett and held on for the win with an 8.25 at 185.94 mph.

Pete Robinson surprised many when he swapped his Chevy mill for a punched-out 289 Ford in 1963. Always conscious of weight, Robinson couldn't resist the move after discovering the Ford weighed 50 pounds less than the Chevy. He solved the Ford's oiling issue by opening up oil passages, directing more crude to the bottom end, and installing a high-volume oil pump. By the spring of 1965, Robinson had the Ford running a 7.92 at 187 mph on gas and 7.86 at 197 on a shot of nitro. He replaced the small-block Ford with a SOHC 427 not long after defeating George Bolthoff in Top Gas at Bakersfield.

Pete Robinson's 125-inch Woody Gilmore/Race Car Engineering chassis was built for a small-block Chevy or Ford, thus it has small-diameter tubing. Robinson was a weight fanatic; note the very small parachute. Rules said you had to have one, they didn't specify the size. Robinson had the magnesium blower housing, drive, and manifold manufactured. (Photo Courtesy Forrest Bond)

The 1965 Top Gas World Champion was Jim Minnick of Nitro, West Virginia, whose one-person crew consisted of his wife. Minnick was one of the first to make use of the late-model Hemi and laid down low ET at Tulsa with an 8.19. Rod Stuckey is given credit for building the chassis.

Mid-Eliminators

While we generally focus on the Hemis, Cammers, and big-block Chevys that dominated the upper classes, pre-1960 engines (flatheads, straight-8s, and inline sixes) were hanging in there, running in D/Dragster, G/G, H/G, D/A, and C/SR. Props to those who ran these engines, as they were generally passed over by the aftermarket, and racers were forced to fabricate their own go-fast goodies. Vehicle weight restrictions based on the engine and configuration (blown, twin engine, etc.) helped keep the class competitive.

Altereds

Those wicked Fuel Altereds really seemed to be struggling for a foothold. The NHRA held no class for the Fuelers, and rumors swirled that the AHRA was on the verge of dumping them. It seems hard to believe, but some tracks outside of the Southwest had no interest in the cars and actually banned them. Gil Hayward and Ron McKibben, who campaigned the Monkey Motion Altered, and Les Hawkins of the Bad News Coupe looked to do something about the lack of respect by forming the Altereds, Coupes, and Roadsters Association. Their idea was to put together some favorable meets and match races. Their first bash was a 20-car show on January 17 at Lions.

The Beebe brothers, Harrell-Borsch-Muse, and Leon Fitzgerald were just a few to make the inaugural event.

Bill Henderson's 1941 Willys, Fantasia, *was obviously not your typical Fuel Altered. Warren Robbin built the 102-inch-wheelbase chassis that housed a 400-ci Hemi. The chassis initially featured a unique hinged quarter elliptic front suspension that allowed 10 inches of lift. Separate frame rails cradled the engine and allowed up to 3 inches more of lift, all in the name of weight transfer. John Lee attempted to tame the car, but it proved just too squirrely and he was never able to make a full pass. Chuck Finders offered his services and finally got the car straightened out enough that it recorded a best of high 8s at 160 mph. Ingenuity or an exercise in futility? Call it what you will but it sure was a sight. (Photo Courtesy Forrest Bond)*

Pure Heaven *was the first car to fly the Anaheim Speed Engineers's colors and ran in the high 7s at 168 mph. Gobs of power, a short wheelbase, and a high center of gravity helped to make these Altereds a handful but a joy to watch. (Photo Courtesy Forrest Bond)*

Not all Altereds ran a fire-breathing Hemi or a big-block Chevy. This class-legal BB/Altered Fiat of Cleveland Policeman Steve Suhajcik ran a blown 327 Chevy. Built during the early 1960s, the chassis and roll bar design are a prime example as to how primitive these cars were during that period. The Fiat is seen here at Indy in 1965, where it was runner-up in class. NASCAR and AHRA records would follow. The Fiat ran a 9.44 at 148 mph for the NASCAR mark. (Photo Courtesy Forrest Bond)

There were 11 cars entered in A/GS class at the 1965 NHRA Nationals. In the final, Dick Bourgeois, driving for John Mazmanian, lost on the line when he fouled against Doug Cook. Both cars were Chrysler powered and had been clicking off high 9s at around 150 mph. In a show at Lions in December, the SWC Willys ran a 9.30 with the help of alcohol in the tank and rosin on the track. (Photo Courtesy Forrest Bond)

Low ET went to Borsch, who ran a 9.27, launching his 6-71 blower off the top of his 398-ci Hemi in the process. By the end of the 1965 season, 8-second times were the norm. Problem was there were too few programs for these cars to run and the payout wasn't that good. Often, they found themselves racing against Fuel or Gas Dragsters.

For example, in June, Rich Guasco entered his *Pure Hell* in a Top Gas show at San Fernando. In the final, he defeated the *Freight Train* driven by Roy "Goob" Tuller with the low ET of the meet of 8.44 at 184.80 mph. At Sacramento the same month, he qualified the car for a Top Fuel show with an 8.38.

Gassers

Contributing to the Willys's dominance in the NHRA Supercharged Gas was the minimum wheelbase rule of 92 inches. This canceled out the 90-inch wheelbase 1948 to 1952 Austins and Anglias, cars that (due to their compact size) were showing up in increasing numbers in the non-Supercharged Gas classes. The AHRA Supercharged classes were more liberal and had no wheelbase minimum.

In the non-Supercharged NHRA Gas classes, Shores & Hess and the Kohler brothers' Anglias were the cream of the crop. The Kohlers' A/G Anglia ran an injected 388-ci Chevy and a Cal-Hydro to win Bakersfield with 10.80 times. A switch to an Art Carr–prepped TorqueFlite with its better gearing dropped ETs down to the 10.30s.

With the small-block/TorqueFlite combo, the Anglia would "crawl" out of the hole until they figured out the neutral start. With the push-button TorqueFlite transmission controls in the Anglia, it was easy. They staged the

The Kohler brothers debuted their Anglia in 1964 with an injected 388-ci Chevy before switching to a 427 (454 inches) Chevy late in 1965. King Kong ran in both the NHRA and the AHRA in AA/A and A/GS. The Anglia was reported to be the first Gasser to make use of the Art Carr TorqueFlite. Tire technology being what it was, the transmission's tall first gear helped minimize wheel spin. The brothers campaigned the car through 1968 and rarely lost. (Photo Courtesy Carlos Cedeno)

In May, K. S. Pittman stopped in his hometown of Mineral Wells, Texas, for a match race against Stone, Woods, & Cook, and it didn't end well. The only injuries Pittman received from the wreck of his Willys were small cuts and bruising, which is surprising considering the damage and the use of a single hoop roll bar. (Photo Courtesy Dave Hales)

Forget your Hemi-head Mopars, Fords and Pontiacs. How about a set of Leo Lyons Hemi heads for the small-block Chevy? Leo's heads were modeled after the early Ardun Hemi heads that were produced in the later 1940s for the flathead Ford. According to Bones, the other gentleman in the photo with Leo, "[The heads] never made any more power, and I never saw the engine again after this day." Reportedly the 301-ci engine made 638 hp on alcohol. (Photo Courtesy Bones Balogh)

Bones Balogh recalled that the quickest car he ever drove was the Joe Pisano Hemi-powered 1933 Willys that recorded a 9.01. The Willys was given the name Chizler Too in reference to friend, Chris Karamesines. One day, Balogh mentioned to Karamesines how he always liked the scoop that was mounted atop the 4-port Hilborn injectors on Karamesines's Chizler dragster. Well, it was Bones's lucky day, Karamesines was just switching to a new Enderle bug catcher injector. He passed the scoop to Bones who mounted it on the Willys, thus the Chizler Too name. (Photo Courtesy Don Prieto)

At the Nationals, Jack Merkel defeated the odds-on favorite A/GS 1933 Willys of Ohio George Montgomery in the first round of eliminations. Merkel's Willys was a lightweight screamer that counted on a supercharged 364-ci small-block Chevy to record a best of 9.53 at 134 mph. (Photo Courtesy Forrest Bond)

car, put it in neutral, brought the revs up, and hit the first gear button on the last yellow light.

The TorqueFlites were built by Carr with heavy-duty OEM parts, including the torque convertor. Due to the abuse the transmissions were taking, the number of runs on them was kept track of to prevent crucial failure. Neutral starts wreaked havoc on a transmission, and after one too many transmission explosions, the practice was banned. When the Kohlers made the switch to a blown big-block Chevy late in the season, they no longer needed a neutral start to get out of the hole in a hurry, as

the new engine provided that much more power.

In A/GS, K. S. Pittman kicked the year off by winning class at the AHRA Winternationals with his 1933 Willys (100-inch wheelbase) and followed up by defeating Stone, Woods, & Cook with a 9.85 at the NHRA Winternationals. The fans received their money's worth in the semifinals when they witnessed Doug Cook repeat the previous year's final round win by defeating Dick Bourgeois in Big John's Willys.

Mickey Thompson, expanding his empire, saw Cook try out the new sticky M/T slicks at Lions in March and netted a 9.88 at 150 mph for a new track record. Cook faced Bourgeois at Indy and defeated him once again after Bourgeois drew a redlight.

Back to Pittman, he made it three in a row by

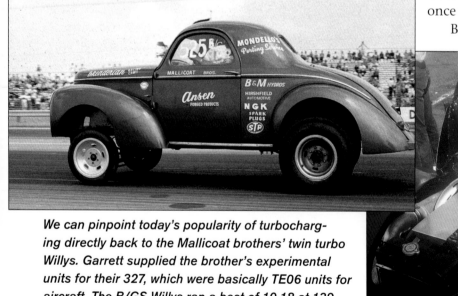

We can pinpoint today's popularity of turbocharging directly back to the Mallicoat brothers' twin turbo Willys. Garrett supplied the brother's experimental units for their 327, which were basically TE06 units for aircraft. The B/GS Willys ran a best of 10.18 at 139 mph. (Photo Courtesy Forrest Bond)

winning the UDRA winter meet at Long Beach. Sadly, the dominant S&S Willys met its end in May at a match race in Pittman's hometown of Mineral Wells, Texas. Traveling at 150 mph, the Willys ran out of racetrack and came to rest on a public highway. Pittman miraculously escaped with minor scrapes, but the Willys was a loss.

Pittman returned to California immediately after the wreck to get his old 1941 Willys out of mothballs and installed the running gear from the '33. It wasn't a good stretch for 1933 Willys, as a month later Bones Balogh lost a wheel, destroying the Bones & Dubach car.

The NHRA Modified Sport Production classes were killed off at the end of 1967, but not before producing some real oddities, like Pete Arend's Hemi-powered 1963 Corvette. Pete is seen here taking B/MSP class at the 1965 NHRA Nationals. The Corvette also took home the best engineered car award. Arend set the AA/MSP class record with the car in 1966 with a 10.16 and held the BB/MSP speed record at 133.72 mph. (Photo Courtesy Forrest Bond)

By his own admittance, George Montgomery stayed with the Chevy engine too long, and in his opinion, it cost him Indy. It didn't help that he was facing Jack Merkel, a man on a mission. Merkel graduated from B/GS in 1965 and built a lightweight 1933 Willys with the thought of dethroning Ohio George. Montgomery was being hounded by Chrysler, which was trying to lure

him with a factory deal, a deal he had no interest in.

"All my competitors on the West Coast were running Chryslers," George said. "Anything they were doing, I was going to do the opposite."

And that, he did. He signed on with Ford at the end of the season.

The scourge of B/GS were the Mallicoat brothers, Jerry

In Comp Eliminator, the year pretty much belonged to Pete Shadinger and his straight-8 Buick-powered D/Dragster. "Little Daddy" was a winner at the Springnationals and the Nationals, and his 10.38 came within a whisker of defeating the dual purpose Willys of Virgil Cates at the World Finals. With a flair for the unique, Shadinger won his first national event: the NHRA Nationals way back in 1962 with a flathead-powered dragster. (Photo Courtesy Forrest Bond)

and Gary, and their twin-turbocharged Chevy-powered 1940 Willys. They may not have been the first to bring turbocharging to the sport, but they were the first to run them with any real success. At the NHRA Winternationals, they defeated the Stone, Woods, & Cook *Swindler B* Willys driven by Hugh Tucker for class.

The brothers first started toying with turbos late in 1964. Jerry worked for Isky Cams part-time and recalled the day Bill Edwards from Cragar Industries rolled in with his twin-turbo 231-ci Chevy. The turbos piqued Jerry's interest and set the wheels in motion.

The Mallicoats reached out to Al Williams of Scientific Engineering, who put them in touch with Duke Hallock, an engineer with Garrett. Garrett got on board with the project and supplied the brothers with a pair of experimental TEO6 turbos for their 327. Williams himself fabricated the stainless steel exhaust headers and modified the Chevy Fuel Injection intake manifold for the engine.

Fuel to the twin turbos came by way of twin Carter AFB carbs. On initial outings with the new setup, the brothers had trouble getting the boost up, so they contacted Bob Spar at B&M. Spar made mods to the Hydro's torus members, which raised the stall speed to 4,000 rpm. In a comparison on the Isky dyno between their

previous GMC-6-71 engine and the twin turbo engine, the turbo setup produced 720 hp, 130 more than the blown engine. Each engine ran equal 19 pounds of boost.

Stock Eliminator

To make sense of the NHRA's ever-evolving Stock Eliminator program, let's start with the rule book, which stated that "no car will be accepted for Stock Eliminator with a weight to cubic inch factor lower than eight." This placed the following class cars in Top Stock after the Winternationals: A/FX, S/S, S/SA, AA/S, and AA/SA.

After the Winternationals, the handicap program was instituted, and each car ran off the class record. Now, I say after the Winternationals because at the winter meet, the A/FX cars ran their own eliminator, which was referred to as Factory Stock. As in previous years, A/FX was limited to current-year models only. The C/FX cars initially ran Junior Stock before being moved into Street Eliminator, where the B/FX cars competed.

Top Stock at the NHRA Winternationals was an all-Mopar show, literally, with S/SA winner Grumpy Jenkins taking all the marbles on Sunday by defeating Dick Housey with an 11.39. Having split with Dave Strickler at the end of 1964, Jenkins prepared a 1965 A990 Plymouth for New York resident, Doc Burgess. The A990 des-

Marshall Ford service manager Bud Shellenberger flat towed his 427-powered Galaxie to Indy and copped Top Stock honors. Part of Bud's winnings was a new Barracuda, which he sold back to the dealer with 4 miles on the odometer. He used the money to build a match race Ranchero powered by a Holman-Moody 427 that he received as part of his Indy winnings. Here Bud faces the similar Galaxie of Paul Moody. Moody's Ford had previously been campaigned by Paul Harvey. (Photo Courtesy Forrest Bond)

ignation referred to the specially built Hemi engine that powered these cars. In total there were 101 Dodges and 102 A990 Plymouth's built. Upgrades over the base Hemi included aluminum heads, a revised camshaft, a magnesium intake manifold with a pair of Holley 4-barrel carburetors, and tubular headers. Horsepower for these beasts was estimated to be in the 550 range. Little was required in preparing these cars for the quarter-mile, as factory modifications included lightweight bucket seats and thin-gauge fenders, hoods, doors, bumpers, and radiator supports. Side and rear glass was cut from lightweight Chemcor with the quarter windows being in a fixed position.

Of course, anything deemed unnecessary to drag racing was removed, including the radio, the heater, and the insulation. Although the 4-speed transmission was available, Jenkins's *Black Arrow* was equipped with the TorqueFlite transmission. An 8¾ rear end carried 4.56:1 gears and was supported by leaf springs that shortened the wheelbase by 1 inch.

Outside of the factory wars in upper Stock, building a Junior Stocker was becoming a science dominated by Eastern racers. The Chevair race team out of Michigan, led by Dick Griffith, were back again in 1965 after winning numerous classes in 1964. Strict attention to detail and choosing a car that fell closest to the low end of the class weight break made all the difference in the world.

Jenkins Competition out in Pennsylvania pushed the envelope when it came to building Junior Stock Chevys. Jenkins's stable car, the *Monster Mash* '55 Chevy belonging to Bill and Andy Spanakos, was the ultimate with the body slid back on the chassis for optimal weight bias, modified control arms to maintain front end geometry, blueprinted camshaft, and modified carb, valves, and ports all getting by the tech inspectors. Running off of an I/S record of 14.19, the *Monster Mash* was capable of 13.30 times.

There was a real battle brewing in C/FX through 1965 with Sylvia Hoefer's 289-ci Galaxie swapping class record with Dave Koffel's 273-ci Plymouth. The best time for the Ford was turned by Hoefer here at Half Moon Bay in October, when she recorded a 13.17 time. Both the Koffel and the Hoefer cars were running Weber carbs by midseason. (Photo Courtesy Forrest Bond)

At the NHRA Winternationals, Bill Jenkins marched to the elimination final, where he defeated Dick Housey with an 11.39 at 126.05 mph. Jenkins hoped a factory Chrysler deal was in the cards after the win, but according to Chrysler's Bob Cahill, "by that time we had all our factory drivers signed and there was nothing we could do." (Photo Courtesy John Durand)

The Stock Eliminator final at the Nationals boiled down to a pair of Chevys: the K/S 1959 Biscayne of Jon Callender and the I/S 1955 business coupe of Bill Spanakos. The final had to be run twice (a first in NHRA national event history), as the wrong handicap had been dialed into the tree, favoring the higher-class Monster Mash. *Callender won the rematch with a 15.29. (Photo Courtesy Forrest Bond)*

Factory Experimental

Ford and Mercury had a stranglehold on the category in 1965. Their Cammer-powered Mustangs and Comets ruled A/FX, while their Weber-carbureted 289 Comets and Galaxies were dominant in B and C/FX. The NHRA rule book now clearly stated, "Axles may be relocated on FX cars a maximum of 2 percent of the total wheelbase, per original stock location."

Referring back to 1964, Chrysler products were already one step ahead of the game. Ford had Holman-Moody build the 10 Cammer-powered Mustangs, while Mercury went to Dearborn Steel Tubing to modify a handful of Comets. The cars were winners from the get-go with Bill Lawton in the TASCA Mustang taking Factory Stock at the NHRA Winternationals and Dyno Don holding the class record midseason with a 10.56.

Meanwhile, Chrysler seemed to be through playing by the rules. It handed Amblewagon of Troy, Michigan (best known for its station wagon-to-ambulance conversions), five Belvederes and six Coronets with instructions to move the front suspension forward 10 inches and rear forward 15 inches. These cars were complete packages consisting of an acid-dipped main body, stainless steel K-member, and fiberglass fenders, hood, scoop, front bumper, dashboard, and trunk lid.

Initially, the cars relied upon carbureted Hemis running pump gas or high-octane aviation fuel. Transmission choice was either the rock-solid A-833 4-speed or the heavy-duty 727 TorqueFlite automatic. Although initially rejected by the NHRA, the AHRA welcomed the cars with open arms.

At the AHRA Winternationals, Bud Faubel drove his *Hemi Honker* Dodge to a Mr. Stock Eliminator win, recording 10.90 times. The NHRA buckled to demand and welcomed the cars at the Springnationals, where Dave Strickler took the Funny Car eliminator. By then, Hilborn fuel injection was the way to go, and both the factory cars and the independents moved away from carburetors, with gasoline being replaced by alcohol and nitro. Initial results of these changes showed increases in speed of up to 2.5 mph.

When it came to match racing these *funny* cars, Chrysler found the Fords and Mercurys were backing out. A bulletin was released from Leo Beebe, a Ford Special Vehicle Manager, shortly after Dick Landy's Dodge ran a 10.26 at Bakersfield. The memo read "All Ford

Dyno Don's Comet was one of 1965's most feared cars. Starting out as a mid-10-second A/FX'er, by season's end he had transformed the car into a 9-second-flat match basher. (Photo Courtesy Randy Hernandez)

This is Gas Ronda's second A/FX legal Mustang that he ran in 1965, having crashed the first one during a match at Lions in May when an axle broke. Ronda used this same Les Ritchey–prepped Mustang to win the AHRA Super Stock world title in September and set the NHRA class record in October with a 10.43 at 134.73 mph. (Photo Courtesy Larry Knapp)

Les Ritchey swapped ill-performing Weber carbs for Holleys and won A/FX at the Nationals. In the final, he defeated the similarly equipped Mustang of Gas Ronda, a car Ritchey helped prepare. Though laying down impressive 10.60 times, Ritchey and the Mustang fell in the first round of Top Stock eliminations to the Flying Carpet Dodge of Bill Harrop. Note the rule-mandated exhaust system. (Photo Courtesy Forrest Bond)

Bill Shirey, late of the Golden Commandos, ran this A990 Plymouth through 1965. Shirey added injectors to the Hemi after the Nationals, altered the wheelbase, and joined the funny crowd. In 1967, he turned his attention to NASCAR, where he competed through 1973. (Photo Courtesy Forrest Bond)

Ronnie Sox poses proudly with his Altered Wheelbase Plymouth at Cecil County, "the Nation's Traction Capital." The twin 735 Holleys on his Hemi quickly gave way to Hilborn injection. Subframe connectors came in vogue after Sox nearly folded his Plymouth in half during an early outing.

Mustang A/FX cars have been built according to safety standards and specs of NHRA. We have asked our A/FX drivers (including Mercury) not to compete against cars that do not conform to these specs."

Ford drag council boss Dick Brannan seemed to be the exception. In April, he and Charlie Gray had two Altered Wheelbase Mustangs built. One for testing and one with which Brannan used to compete. He debuted his *Bronco* with an injected Cammer at the AHRA Summernationals and won the meet, defeating the Mustang of Gas Ronda in the final. At the NHRA Nationals, where he was forced to run B/Altered, Brannan lost in the class final due to a blown head gasket. Stability issues above 150 mph led to Holman-Moody building Ford a new batch of Mustangs late in the season that would debut in 1966.

Dyno Don Nicholson abandoned A/FX class racing and defied Ford's orders by modifying his Comet to take on the Mopars. As Dyno said, "Mercury wasn't paying me a salary, and I couldn't afford not to race." By mid-July, his Comet had gone full Funny, sporting injectors, running alcohol, and using a straight-axle front suspension. To get the weight on the rear, the front suspension was moved 5 inches forward, and the rear moved up 10 inches. The changes paid off for Don, as he recorded a 90-percent win record through the remainder of the year.

In November, Nicholson ran a match race against the Ramchargers at Capital Raceway in Maryland, where he won the best of five, recording a time of 9.36 at 150.10 mph. At the time, it was reported in the *Drag News* and *Super Stock & Drag Illustrated* magazine that this was the first time an unblown door car had cracked 150.

Charlie Allen, the all-American boy, enjoyed success through the 1960s with a fine line of Dodges. His 1965 9-second match racer started out as an A-990 Super Stock. As was common practice by 1965 for these match racers, Allen ran alcohol and nitro through his Hemi. (Photo Courtesy Forrest Bond)

Al "the Flying Dutchman" Vanderwoude ran a new car in Top Stock every year since 1957. As a stock wheelbase Dodge, this 1964 hit 10.80s before Vanderwoude turned it into a much-feared Altered Wheelbase match racer. The shortened wheelbase measured 96 inches, the weight of the car was 2,300 pounds, and displacement was 510 ci. (Photo Courtesy John Foster Jr.)

B/Altered was an odd place to find match bash cars, but at the Nationals on Labor Day weekend it was the best suite for the Fords of Dyno Don and Dick Brannan. Brannan defeated Dyno before losing class to the Lil Screamer of Jack Ditmars. The previous weekend, Brannan won Mr. Stock Eliminator at the AHRA Nationals, where he recorded 10.0 times. Other "Stockers" running B/A were Hayden Proffitt and the Falcon of Phil Bonner. (Photo Courtesy Forrest Bond)

Jack Chrisman's Sachs & Sons Comet debuted at Oswego and turned a 10.18 at 157.89 mph on 30-percent nitro. The 25-percent setback Cammer and direct drive were important steps in the evolution of Stock to all out Funny Car. (Photo Courtesy Randy Hernandez)

Well worth mentioning is the number of match race battles taking place around the country involving these funny Stockers. No gathering epitomized the popularity of these cars more than the Super Stock Nationals held August 7 at Pennsylvania's York US-30. The brainchild of Jim Davis and John "Monk" Reynolds of *Super Stock & Drag Illustrated* magazine in conjunction with track manager Bill Holz, the one-day race drew an official 21,650 fans. Unofficially, it's believed as many as 40,000 fans found their way through the gate and over fences to watch 86 of the nation's best door cars do battle.

Categories were broken down by vehicle weight, carb or injected, and cubic inches. The quickest cars ran in Ultra Stock, which was considered an unlimited class with no cubic inch or weight limits. All the cars in this class, which was dominated by Chryslers, ran injectors and either alcohol or nitro. The event ran well into the early hours of the morning, by which point the crowd had hopped over barriers and were crowding the track. In the Ultra Stock final, Bob Harrop, runner-up to Strickler at the NHRA Springnationals, defeated the *Hemi Honker* of Bud Faubel with a 9.32 at 146.57 mph.

Outside of the factory efforts, a number of independents were building cars. Chevys, Fords, Pontiacs, and

Bill Flynn's Yankee Peddler burns through the rosin at New York's Dover Dragstrip prior to a run against Dick Landy. Injectors and lots of rosin was the look of match race Stockers during the summer of 1965. (Photo Courtesy doverdragstrip.com)

Adding weight to the rear of a car to gain traction seemed detrimental to going faster, so what did Chrysler do? It acid dipped its cars and slid the front and rear suspension forward, thus placing greater vehicle weight (55 percent) on the rear. Note the full roll cage Strickler ran in his Dodge. It helped stiffen up the too thin car. (Photo Courtesy Michael Pottie)

Chrysler were coming out of the proverbial woodwork. Chrysler expanded its footprint by offering blueprints and parts to anyone who wanted to build their own Altered Wheelbase match racer. With General Motors no longer supporting racing, it was left up to the individual to carry the flag. Arnie Beswick, Ron and Don Gay, Dick Harrell, Pete Seaton, and Tom Sturm did an admirable job against seemingly increasing odds.

Though opening up the bores and stroking the new Chevy "Semi-Hemi" gave them a fighting chance, the mills never had the breathing capability of the Chrysler Hemi or Ford Cammer, or the reliability of a good bottom end. This became more prevalent as nitro loads increased and blowers became the norm.

Though many of the top match racers were making the switch to the GMC blower, the Ramchargers was one team that stuck it out with injectors. By July, the team was running 30-percent nitro through its Hilborns to a long stroke 472-ci Hemi. Thornton crashed the Dodge that month, doing extensive damage but managing to

Doug Thorley's square-tube chassis Chevy II was a state-of-the-art "Funny Car" in the summer of 1965. Though Chevy was out of racing, its cars were right in the thick of the battle thanks to the efforts of guys like Thorley, Malcolm Durham, Pete Seaton, and Tom Sturm, who were all running Chevy's new-for-1965 Mark IV big-block engine. (Photo Courtesy Stephen Justice)

The easily identifiable Exhibition Stockers were sucking the wind out of the AA/FD sails in 1965. Though your street Chevy may not be able to perform like Dick Harrell's Chevy II, at least it looked the part. Harrell ran a Z11 Chevy in his Chevy II before switching to a Mark IV 427. (Photo Courtesy Stephen Justice)

bang it out enough to make a match against the GTO of Harold Ramsey a couple weeks later.

Thornton and the less-than-appealing Dodge became the first exhibition Stocker, or Funny Car (as they were coming to be known), to run an 8-second time. As reported in *Drag News*, right off the trailer with no warmup run and no traction-enhancing rosin, the big-inch Hemi, running a reported 50-percent load of nitro, blasted out a phenomenal 8.91 to leave Ramsey in its wake! The unbelievable ET had photographers and track officials clamoring to the Cecil County tower to confirm the timers.

Late in the season, Gary Dyer, who was wheeling Roger Lindamood's old *Color Me Gone* Dodge for Chicago's Grand Spaulding, proved the worth of mounting a 6-71 blower when he ran an 8.63 at Lions. The Ramchargers, boosting the load on its long arm Hemi to 80 percent (and climbing), followed with an 8.59. Getting the power to the ground were the new 10-inch Goodyear wrinkle wall slicks. Introduced late in the season, the soft compound tire gave a huge footprint and enormous bite off the line. Farther down track as speed increased, the tire grew taller (unwrinkled), allowing for a greater top end charge.

The NHRA had no idea what to do with these Exhibition Stockers. At the Nationals, the cars of Don Gay, Jack Chrisman, Bob Sullivan, Steve Bovan, and Preston Honea were placed in B/FD. First round competition saw Jack Chrisman in his SOHC Comet facing Don Gay's 421-powered GTO. It was a lose-lose situation, as Chrisman fouled on the line and Gay blew the bottom end out of the 421. Gay had previously run a 9.37. The class was won by the dragster of Dan Slitten, who ran 9 seconds flat at 160 mph. (Photo Courtesy Forrest Bond)

Could this have been the launching pad for AMC's drag racing effort? Blair's Speed Shop did the chassis work on this Marlin for Bill Kraft while Preston Honea built the injected Hemi and drove the car. To help lighten the load, the fenders and hood were replaced with fiberglass parts and the doors were acid dipped in a backyard pit. Best times were in the 9s at 140 mph. (Photo Courtesy Forrest Bond)

The Ramchargers' Jim Thornton warms up the Dodge prior to a match at Aquasco against the Falcon of Hubert Platt. Thornton swept the match, running a best of 9.27 at 157 mph. The Ramchargers ran numerous tests with injectors, varying throttle bore size and tube length before settling on $2^7/_{16}$ bores and $15^5/_8$ tubes. (Photo Courtesy Wayne Langford)

The California Flash, Butch Leal, signed on with Plymouth in 1965 and did not disappoint while running an Altered Wheelbase car for them. Here at the 1966 NHRA Winternationals, the Flash used his lightweight Plymouth to win S/S with an 11.50 at 127.11 mph. (Photo Courtesy Stephen Justice)

Chapter Six

1966
Flip, Flop, and Fly

What a year it was! There was a phenomenal number of cars competing in AA/FD. More than 100 fuel cars showed up for the U.S. Fuel and Gas Championship at Bakersfield. Never again would so many AA/FD cars appear for one show. The all-fiberglass flip-up Mercury Comets took Exhibition Stock by storm.

So remarkable were these tube chassis cars that their basic design is still with us today. Increased speeds were realized across the board as 1966 progressed, thanks to further advancement in tires, clutches, and overall inventiveness of the racers.

Top Dragster

The Top Fuel highlight of 1966 was Mike Snively driving the *Hawaiian* to wins at both the NHRA Winternationals and Indy. Car owner Roland Leong and partner Keith Black saw repeat wins as Don Prudhomme had accomplished the same deed in 1965 in the same car. The 22-year-old Snively had taken over driving the *Hawaiian* after Prudhomme accepted an offer from Don Spar at B&M to run the Torkmaster AA/FD.

Snively, green to Top Fuel, received his license at Lions on January 22, just three weeks before the Winternationals. Prudhomme, who had been given carte blanche from B&M, was realizing how tough it was to run your own program. A Dave Zeuschel Hemi powered the car and gave Don wins at the UDRA Springnationals and Cordova's World Series of Drag Racing.

Prudhomme's arch rival, Tom McEwen, was still making time in the Exhibition Stock Hemi 'Cuda, running a best of 8.88 in the car before losing to Gas Ronda at Bakersfield. Shortly after McEwen teamed with Lou Baney and the old master, Ed Pink, in campaigning the *Brand Ford Special* AA/FD. A Ford Cammer replaced the Hemi early on and propelled the Don Long car to a win at the *Hot Rod* magazine meet. Pink, considered one of the top engine builders in the nation, fabricated a number of his own parts when building the Cammer.

In the largest gathering of Fuelers ever, more than 100 cars from across the nation made the trip to Bakers-

Tom McEwen, behind the wheel of Lou Baney's Brand Ford Special *AA/FD, tears a strip off the 11x16 Goodyears to the delight of the fans. The Ed Pink Cammer ran 23-percent overdrive on the Neil Lefler–prepared 6-71 blower and fed on a 75-percent load of nitro. By the end of the season, McEwen was recording low 7s in the Woody Gilmore chassis car. In 1967, Prudhomme took over the driving for Baney. (Photo Courtesy Forrest Bond)*

Bakersfield drew more than 100 cars for AA/FD in 1966. Never before or since have so many fuel cars gathered in one place. Sunday's final saw the Surfers' Mike Sorokin (near lane) defeat a redlighting James Warren with a 7.74 at 196.06 mph. Mike had previously set low ET of the meet with a 7.34. (Photo Courtesy Forrest Bond)

This photo of Jimmy Nix and Don Prudhomme at Bakersfield illustrates the rapid change in Dragster wheelbase. Nix's Kent Fuller chassis was state-of-the-art in late 1965 when it was built, but by early 1966 Prudhomme's Don Long chassis was typical of the new standard. Oh, and Prud-homme won this Sunday match, 7.92 to an 8.13. (Photo Courtesy Forrest Bond)

The team of Gene Adams, Jack Wayre, and John Mulligan were a formidable trio in 1966, winning a lot more than they lost. Driver John Mulligan's star continued to rise when he took the seat of the Beebe & Sixt car in 1967. (Photo Courtesy Forrest Bond)

field in March for the eighth running of the U.S. Fuel and Gas Championship. Sixty-four cars qualified on Saturday and saw Mike Sorokin of the Surfers set low ET of the meet with a record 7.34.

Sorokin marched to the final, where he faced Winternationals runner-up Jim Dunn, defeating the world's fastest fireman with a 7.56. The win gave Sorokin the right to sit out Sunday's 32-car eliminations to face the winner of that field, which was the Ridge Route Terror, James Warren. Warren had defeated Snively in the preceding round but destroyed his engine in the process. So before facing Sorokin, the mad dash was on to swap the engine from the Warren-Crowes car into the Warren-Coburn car.

With little time to spare, Warren was ready to face Sorokin, or at least as ready as he was going to be. Running a less-than-perfect mill, Warren took a chance on the tree and lost, drawing a redlight and allowing Sorokin to take the win with an easy 7.74. What makes the Surfers' win that much more impressive was the fact that outside of basic maintenance, not once during the meet did they tear into the engine.

The Surfers (Sorokin, Tom Jobe, and Bob Skinner) weren't really surfers at all; it was a name they were tagged with by their peers due to their laid-back attitudes. Calm, cool, collected, and methodical would probably best describe this trio. While the rest of the field thrashed between rounds and took themselves a little too seri-ously, the Surfers relaxed by cruising the pits and watching the action on the track.

If there was a leader of the group, it was Jobe, who studied as a mechanical engineer at Santa Monica. He focused his studies on nitromethane and managed to design a fuel feed system that allowed them to run close to a 100-percent load through their early Hemi, without grenading it.

In a much-anticipated meeting of what were considered the top two cars in the nation, the Surfers and the *Hawaiian* met on March 27 at Irwindale for a three-round match race. It wasn't much of a match as Sorokin, playing Mr. Consistency, made quick of the *Hawaiian* by taking the first two rounds with 7.57 and 7.56 times. Sorokin came back to make a third run to test some new Goodyears, but prior to doing so, Keith Black approached

Jack Williams in the Warren-Crowe car (sans full body) is seen here head-on at Lions in 1966. Williams ran two cars through the season with James Warren running low ET at the NHRA Winternationals with a 7.51 in the second car. Tom McEwen can be seen plugging his ears. (Photo Courtesy Forrest Bond)

Don Garlits kicked off the year by defeating Prudhomme in a best of five match held at Half Moon Bay in January. Garlits was driving his new red car, which was literally an extension of Swamp Rat VIII with the wheelbase growing from 140 inches to 175. Garlits was running the new 426-ci Hemi, and it took him a good part of the year to sort it out. Here at the AHRA Winternationals, he failed to make it past the first round. (Photo Courtesy Forrest Bond)

the Surfers and asked if they'd mind if the *Hawaiian* lined up alongside them to make a run. "No problem," said Jobe, as long as they made it clear to those attending that this wasn't part of the match race. I guess maybe the *Hawaiian* crew was looking for a bit of consolation if they won. Well, it didn't quite work out the way they hoped because Sorokin smoked the new Goodyears and beat Snively with another 7.57.

The tire wars raged between M&H, which had its Silver Stripe, and Goodyear, which had its soft-compound six-ply then four-ply tire (183s). End-of-the-season results between the two manufacturers showed Goodyear taking the most wins, while M&H had the quicker times. Pete Robinson was riding on a pair of those M&H tires at the World Finals when he defeated Dave Beebe with a 7.27 to earn the championship. Pete had previously run a sub-record 7.19 for low ET of the meet.

The Surfers split after their mill failed them at Indy. Jobes and Skinner, figuring they accomplished all they set out to do, moved on to different ventures while Sorokin caught the wave and carried on as a hired gun.

With California being the nation's Top Fuel hotbed, you can imagine the effort it took to stand head and shoulders above the crowd. Two rising teams managed to do it: John Mulligan and his partners Jack Wayre and Gene Adams along with the team of the Beebe brothers,

Tim and Dave, with Sam Vinson and Lee Sixt.

Mulligan and Tim Beebe had previously teamed in campaigning the J&S Speed Center–sponsored Altered. Mulligan left the Fiat behind in 1964 when he went to work for Jack Wayre, pushing used cars. At the time, Wayre was partnered with Glen Ward in campaigning not one but two Top Fuel cars. One was Chrysler powered and driven by Ward, while the other, driven by Mulligan, was a Chevy.

By early 1966, Ward was out, and Gene Adams was in. Along with Gene came a new Hemi-powered Woody Gilmore car. The wins followed almost immediately. The car is credited with being the first Fuel Dragster into the 6s after Mulligan ran a 6.95 at Carlsbad in October. It was a great year for the new team that saw them pocket $30,000 running local tracks.

Tim Beebe moved from running the J&S Altered in 1965 into AA/FD. Through 1966, the team of Beebe-Vinson-Sixt racked up wins at all the Southern California tracks. With Dave Beebe manning the wheel, the team won the UDRA Nationals at Lions as well as major events at Carlsbad, Sacramento, and Irwindale.

The two teams finally came face to face after crisscrossing the state through the summer, avoiding each other until the inevitable meeting came in August at Irwindale. When it was over, Mulligan (aka the Zoo Keeper) took

Les Westenberger and Dick Bell out of Long Beach had their share of success running this 301-ci Chevy-powered Jr. Fueler. The car featured a 108-inch wheelbase, homemade chrome-moly chassis. Caught here in action at Lions, times in the 8.10s in the 177-mph range were common. (Photo Courtesy Forrest Bond)

home the glory with a best of 7.49. The names Beebe and Mulligan remained prominent through the remainder of the decade. Mulligan hopped into Beebe's car late in the year and recorded a 6.83. In 1967, the two friendly combatants joined forces.

Gas Dragster

The category was diverse in its national event winners, from Tom Larkin, who won the AHRA Summernationals and Cordova, to NHRA Nationals winner Jim Minnick. Props go to Gordon Collett, who kicked the year off by winning the NHRA Winternationals and

closed the season runner-up at the World Finals to Ohio's Dick Padar.

Relative unknown Mark Pieri won Top Gas at the NHRA Springnationals even though he drew a redlight against low qualifier, Dick Vest. At the weigh-in after the race, Vest was found to have two lead bars stashed under his seat. Safety taking the forefront, he was disqualified for carrying loose ballast and the win was given to Pieri. Pieri's best time for the weekend was an 8.25 at 187 mph.

At the World Finals, relatively unknown Dick Padar and his 426-powered Heathian defeated Gordon Collett in the final with an 8.12 at 183.66 mph.

Two of the nation's top AA/Gas Dragsters in 1966 were George Bolthoff and John Peters's Freight Train, driven here at Bakersfield by Goob Tuller. Bolthoff was a much-feared Top Gas driver through the mid-1960s, having won a few AHRA events, set class records, and played runner-up here at Bakersfield twice. A bored and stroked 392 took Bolthoff to bottom 8-second times before he retired at the end of the season. (Photo Courtesy Don Prieto)

Mid-Eliminators

The NHRA did some shuffling in 1966 and came up with the Super Eliminator category. Encompassing all the blown cars (outside of Top Eliminator and Top Gas), the eliminator rounds could and did see BB/FD, AA/SR, AA/MSP, and the blown Gassers and Altereds butting heads.

Along with bending tin for a countless number of drag cars, Al Bergler campaigned the Aggravation *and* More Aggravation *Competition Coupes. The cars were one and the same with* More Aggravation *debuting in 1966. An early Hemi and a Don Logghe chassis took Bergler to a Super Eliminator win at the NHRA Springnationals. Bergler also won the Division 3 Super Eliminator points championship. (Photo Courtesy Rob Potter)*

Altereds

In Fuel Altered, Joe Mondello, producer of those famously prepped cylinder heads that every top eliminator winner seemed to be using, teamed with Sush

Matsubara in 1965 after Matsubara purchased an Ed Weddle–built Fiat. With a Mondello-built 327-ci running a mix of methanol and nitro, the car recorded a best of 9.32 at 154 mph. The two won their share of Comp races and matches around Southern California before replacing the small-block with a 427 in 1966.

By the end of the 1967 season, the Fiat was capable of 7.90 times. These elapsed times didn't come easy, as the team ran through a number of combinations: injected on gas, injected on alcohol, blown gas, blown alcohol, and finally, blown nitro. A new Exhibition Engineering chassis was built for 1969 and, equipped with their existing nitro engine, recorded Fuel Altereds' first 200-mph run.

In an interview, Mondello was asked what made the car so quick. One thing he mentioned was the open chamber heads he had developed, a design which he referred to as "monoflow."

At the opposite end of Fuel Altered was El Monte fireman Kay Sissel and his 292-ci Chevy-powered D/A. The car was a record holder with a 10.45 at 131.96 mph and is seen here at the NHRA Springnationals, where it won its class. Sissel followed up the Altered with a twin Chevy six powered D/Dragster. (Photo Courtesy Stephen Justice)

A blown 427 Chevy made the Fiat of Joe Mondello and Sush Matsubara one of the most feared Altereds in the nation. The pair ran this Roy Fjastad (SPE)–built car through 1968, first on gas, then methanol, and finally nitro. It would be the first Fuel Altered Fiat to run in the 8s and the first to run in the 7s. (Photo Courtesy Forrest Bond)

The Hyder & McCloud 1934 Ford was one fine-looking Fuel Altered, but by 1966 its best days were behind it. The 392 propelled the all-steel five window to a best of 10.08 at 155.17 mph, well off the pace run by the smaller, lighter fiberglass cars of the day. (Photo Courtesy Stephen Justice)

At the 1966 AHRA Winternationals in Irwindale, rookie Ray "Cookie" Cook wheeled the Stone, Woods, & Cook Swindler B Willys, while his brother Doug drove the team's Swindler A Willys. Ray continued to drive the Willys into 1967, while Doug drove the team's new Mustang Funny Car. (Photo Courtesy Stephen Justice)

A 9.60 at 154.87 mph won Junior Thompson AA/G class at Bakersfield. By summer, he was into the low 9s. Thompson credited his C&O Hydro, his Isky cam, and the Funny Car slicks he was using. His winning ways go back to the NHRA Nationals in 1958, where he won Little Eliminator with his B/Gas Chevy-powered Studebaker. (Photo Courtesy Michael Pottie)

The heads had extremely large open combustion chambers, and the intake valves were taken from 2.19 down to 2.00, equal in size to the exhaust valves. At the 1969 NHRA Nationals, Matsubara set the AA/FA record with a stunning 7.24 at 213 mph. To put that into perspective, the low ET in Funny Car at the event was a 7.22 recorded by the Barracuda of Don Schumacher.

Gassers

The NHRA controversy regarding the short wheelbase Anglias in A/GS boiled to the point where Division 7 head Bernie Partridge revised the division rules, allowing Anglia racers to run A/GS if they extended their wheelbase to meet the 94-inch class requirement. Some of those running Willys screamed unfair, especially after the Kohler brothers' *King Kong* Anglia ran a 9.23 in April during a match against the Chevy II of Steve Bovan. Their argument held no water though, not after Chuck Finders and later Ohio George ran comparative 9.30 times in their Willys.

Supercharged Gasser speeds kept climbing as the year progressed, and in July, Gene Ciambella ran a 9.04 in the C&O Austin pickup to win A/GS at the AHRA Nationals. The NHRA finally put the wheelbase issue to rest at the end of the season, when it changed the class rule to a 92-inch minimum. At the same time, it lowered the minimum weight from 6 pounds per cubic inch to 5. Remember, dropping weight is the same as adding horsepower, and improved times followed.

Ohio George Montgomery debuted his Cammer-powered Willys at Detroit in May. Ford had been bugging

One of the more successful Anglias running in 1966 was the 1949 model of Jim Shores and Skip Hess. They debuted the car in 1965 with an injected 375-ci small-block Chevy running A/G. By the end of the season, they had made the switch to a big-block Chevy and were running AHRA A/GS. (Photo Courtesy Michael Pottie)

One of George Montgomery's final appearances in his 1933 Willys was here at the 1967 NHRA Winternationals, where he defeated the debuting 1933 Willys of K. S. Pittman for class. (Photo Courtesy Michael Pottie)

Montgomery for a while, so he called up Charlie Gray, who gladly signed him to a contract with Mercury. Gray wanted to stick him with a 289 initially, but Montgomery held out for a Cammer. With the Cammer being in short supply, Ford sent him the engine in parts as they came available.

Backing the Cammer was a Ford-prepped C-6 that shifted automatically at 8,800 rpm, allowing Montgomery to literally stab and steer. It's interesting to note that the Willys was the first drag car to be placed in Ford's wind tunnel. The car created 600 pounds of lift in the rear, causing it to nearly slide off the pedestal. The Cammer Willys was a winner from the get-go, taking class at the NHRA Springnationals in June and at the Nationals on Labor Day, where it ran a 9.34.

Outside of George Montgomery, the state of Ohio gave more than its share of competitive Gassers. Blame it on the clean air or a solid work ethic (more than likely), but it all seemed to start with Montgomery winning the Nationals back in 1959. Eddie Schartman got his big break in an injected 1955 Chevy.

From AA/Gas down to E/Gas, Ohio-based Gassers had it all covered. Between 1960 and 1969, they had 48 class wins at Indy. Here, Jay Rambo in his H/Gas 1955 Chevy watches as fellow Ohio resident Dave Hales and his C/Gas Willys disappear down the track. (Photo Courtesy Forrest Bond)

Bolting on dragster-size slicks and a tall gear, Schartman set the B/G record by pounding the 4-speed to the tune of 12.48 at 116.27 mph. By 1966, the category was stacked with Ohio Gassers and saw four class winners at the Nationals, a number that was maintained through the decade thanks to Bob Riffle, Dick Shroyer, and the team of Rodriguez, Jarosz, and Ploma. Following behind was Virgil Cates, Fred Hurst, Dave Hales, Gene Altizer, and the rest of the boys of the S&S Race Team.

Two Cammer Fords battle it out in eliminations at the Springnationals. Bill Coon, winner of B/MSP, faces Ed Terry and his class-winning C/FX Galaxie. Terry won here and also won class at the Winternationals and Indy. (Photo Courtesy Michael Pottie)

Factory Experimental

Sharing the Street Eliminator category with the non-supercharged Gassers were the cars of Factory Experimental and lower Experimental Stock. This was the final season for Factory Experimental, which had been steadily losing ground to the emerging Funny Cars.

Jerry Harvey in his C/XS Mustang beat Mike Schmitt in the all-Ford final of the NHRA Winternationals. Schmitt returned the favor at the following Springnationals. Ed Terry, another of those racing on the factory dime, took his C/FX Cammer-powered 1966 Galaxie to class wins at the NHRA Winternationals, Springnationals, and Indy Nationals. You got to give props to the Ford racers, as they really had to work for their wins.

Ford used five different V-8 engine designs between 1961 and 1970, and rarely did parts interchange. The lack of continuity more than likely contributed to lagging car sales and a lack of on-track saturation.

The 1964 NHRA points champion, Mike Schmitt, won his category at the 1966 NHRA Springnationals for the second year in a row. The previous year, it was Stock; this year, he did the deed in Street Eliminator with this SOHC-powered B/FX Galaxie. In the final, he defeated the Mustang of Al Joniec with an 11.51. Schmitt's lightweight 1964 Galaxie (behind) fell to Jere Stahl in the Top Stock final. (Photo Courtesy James Handy)

Experimental Stock/Funny Car

The Funny Car field was getting pretty crowded with new cars seemingly debuting weekly. In sanctioned competition, the Funny Cars started the year running Comp Eliminator (CC/FD for blown, C/FD for injected), but by the spring, the NHRA had seen its way to create a separate category for the cars. Experimental Stock (XS) consisted of five classes initially, A through E, with a Supercharged/Experimental Stock class added later. Nitro was permitted in S and A/XS, as were tube chassis (100-inch minimum) while in the remaining classes both were a no-no. There was no cubic inch limit in the two upper classes, but the lower classes were limited to 430 ci and carburetion. The B through E classes competed in Street

*Two of Chevy's finest butt heads at Bakersfield: Kelly Chadwick and Del Heinelt in **Seaton's Shaker**. Chadwick had a fine career, running through 1974. Heinelt was killed at the Nationals in 1967 while driving the Mustang of Gary Coleman. (Photo Courtesy Forrest Bond)*

Eliminator. Minimum weight for the S/XS car was set at 2,000 pounds.

Ford one-upped the competition late in 1965 when it commissioned Holman & Moody to build a half dozen longnosed Mustangs. The wheelbase was shuffled north and extended from the stock 108 inches to 112. This was accomplished by extending the front 18 inches and moving the rear suspension forward 10 inches. A 2x3 chrome alloy chassis was fabricated along with a unique twisted quarter elliptic leaf sprung front suspension. At 2,400 pounds, the Mustangs were approximately 1,000 pounds lighter than 1965 A/FX Mustangs.

Gas Ronda won Unlimited Gas at the AHRA Winternationals before winning C/FD class at the proceeding NHRA Winternationals. At the Smokers meet in Bakersfield, Ronda's Mustang became the first class-legal

Here's a late 1965 Holman & Moody construction photo showing the fiberglass longnose Mustangs going together. In true Funny Car fashion, there is 15 inches between the engine and the front spindle center line. Note the space between the fenders where inches needed to be added and also the rectangular tube chassis.

Following a 2-percent Mustang "Daddy Warbucks" Phil Bonner had Holman & Moody piece together this 427 Falcon for him. Rosin was not limited to match racing, as all sanctioning bodies outside of the NHRA used it in national events at one time or another. (Photo Courtesy Michael Pottie)

Gas Ronda's ties with Ford put him behind the wheel of a SOHC-powered longnose Mustang in 1966. Topping the 427 were 13-inch-long Hilborn injector stacks that fed a healthy dose of nitro. A C-6 automatic replaced the 4-speed midseason and was shifted at 8,000 rpm. (Photo Courtesy Ed Aigner)

This is the car that set the world of Exhibition Stockers on its ear. Don Nicholson's Eliminator I Comet so dominated the scene that even the emerging blown cars didn't stand a chance. Just 6 months after Ronda recorded the first legal 8-second Funny Car time, Nicholson recorded its first 7-second time with a 7.96 at 175 mph at US 131. (Photo Courtesy Forrest Bond)

unblown Funny Car to turn in an 8-second time when he defeated the Barracuda of Sox & Martin with an 8.96 at 155.97 mph.

To produce these magical numbers, Ronda relied upon Les Ritchey's Performance Associates to prepare the injected 427. Ritchey had opened the doors of his Performance Associates in 1955 and focused his attention on building winning Fords. He caught the attention of the manufacturer in 1962 and was instrumental in prepping its lightweight 1963 Galaxies. Ronda had his best days driving cars prepared by Ritchey. Few were hurt more than Ronda when Ritchey died on May 1, 1966, behind the wheel of his own A/FX Mustang.

I doubt anybody was prepared for what Lincoln-Mercury unleashed at the AHRA Winternationals. Drag racing's first all-fiberglass, one-piece, flip-up Funny Car. Forget the OEM chassis and the drilled square tubing, the Comets featured specially designed Logghe brothers full tube chassis. To say the Comets (there were four of them) were light-years ahead of the competition may be an understatement.

Mercury's Al Turner dreamed up the idea of a flip-up Stocker back in 1964 while discussing Chrysler's Altered Wheelbase cars

The Logghe brothers' stage 1 chassis first appeared under the flip-up 1966 Mercury Comets. Logghe was one of the decade's leading chassis builders and debuted new designs in 1969 (stage 2) and 1971 (narrow stage 3 chassis). The chassis pictured here belonged to the Dyno Don Comet. (Photo Courtesy Randy Hernandez)

Jack Chrisman debuted his topless Comet in April. Unlike Nicholson's Comet, Chrisman carried a blower atop his Cammer and ran direct drive. Many Funny Cars went the topless route in 1966, all in the name of dropping weight and improving aerodynamics. Chrisman's Comet met its fate at Cecil County, where it ran off the end of the track and burnt to the ground. (Photo Courtesy John Foster Jr.)

Sox & Martin's Bacarruda was a purpose-built match racer. All bolt-on panels were fiberglass while the glass was lightweight Lexan. The front and rear suspension were moved forward 8 inches while the 426 engine was setback 10 inches. Later in the season, the 4-speed was replaced with an automatic and the front end was extended, all in the name of improving consistency and stability as speeds approached 160 mph. (Photo Courtesy Forrest Bond)

its 25-percent-setback engine and direct drive, was the stepping stone between the original idea and the flip-up Comets of 1966.

Not to lose sight of the fact that it was all about selling cars, Lincoln-Mercury general manager Paul Lorenz let Project Managers Fran Hernandez and Al Turner know that "if the cars were going to look like the Altered Wheelbase Chryslers and not the cars we are selling then we're not going to be in drag racing." To showcase his idea, Turner built a scale model using basil wood for a chassis with a Mattel body on top and presented it to management, telling them that this is what they planned to build. With a green light from Lorenz, work immediately got under way. The lucky recipients of the four flip-top Comets were Jack Chrisman, Don Nicholson, the newly formed team of Roy Steffey and Ed Schartman, and the Colorado-based team of Kenz & Leslie.

While the Logghe brothers went about building the 116-inch-wheelbase chassis, Plastigauge of Jackson, Michigan, formed the fiberglass bodies by using a design plug provided by Mercury. The initial plans called for the Comets to have lift-off bodies, but they returned from Plastigauge heavier than expected. It was Ron Logghe who came up with the idea of hinging the bodies at the rear. Thus, creating the flip-up Funny Car.

According to Al Turner, when it came to the chassis, the Logghes were sworn to secrecy. They guaranteed Mercury that it would have an exclusive one-year deal that prevented them from building and selling the design to others. Don Nicholson tested the first Comet at West Palm Beach, Florida, with a 4-speed transmission but found shifting too cumbersome. Between missed gears and over revving, the 4-speed just wasn't going to work in the new car. A beefed-up C-6 automatic was swapped in before testing of the car was completed.

with Jack Chrisman and Gene Mooneyham. Mooneyham's 1934 Ford Fuel Coupe, 554, with its setback Hemi and center steering was nearly unbeatable through the early 1960s. Turner thought, "What if we [took a Comet and] set the engine back 25 percent with a tube chassis and a fiberglass body on it, we would kick their ass!" Chrisman's 1965 Comet, with

Landy's fairly stock–appearing Dart hid a liberally drilled 2x3 square tube chassis, a Woody Gilmore straight axle, and a quick-change rear end. Thin-gauge aluminum replaced the stock floorboards. The rear suspension was bumped up 10 inches while the front was bumped up 11 inches. Landy extended the front end in May and opened up the rear wheel wells for larger tires. By late in the year, Landy had the fastest TorqueFlite car in the nation, turning 8.30 times. An exploding transmission sidelined Landy briefly with burns, which helped with his and Chrysler's decision to say goodbye to the Funnies. (Photo Courtesy Forrest Bond)

Builders started to put a little more thought into aerodynamics, as air dams and spoilers began to make an appearance. Cars were getting closer to the ground, out of the air, and a few racers, including Hayden Proffitt and Cecil Yother went the route of chopping the roof off their cars. This not only dropped weight but also improved top end stability. Garlits went to the extreme and built a topless stretched Dodge Dart riding on one of his dragster chassis. For many racers, that was going too far, and they refused to race the Dart.

It would be remiss to forget the brands under General Motors, namely Chevy and Pontiac. The compact Corvair was proving a popular choice with new cars coming from Tom Sturm, Malcolm Durham, Pete Seaton, and Hayden Proffitt.

Proffitt was trading his Comet after finishing what he deemed to be his worst year on record. Breakage was a major problem, and he never sorted the car out. Bruce Larson's *USA-1* Chevelle took credit as the first all-fiberglass Funny Car,

It seemed as if the 4-speed was becoming obsolete in the Funny Car class, being replaced by automatics or (in the odd case of Jack Chrisman's Comet and Steve Bovan's Chevy II) direct drive. Drivers were finding that the 4-speed transmissions and clutches just couldn't live behind engines that now produced about 1,000 hp. It was too difficult to control these cars while attempting to power shift through the gears.

Ronnie Sox, who had the reputation of being the best man behind a 4-speed, swapped the transmission in his Barracuda in May for a TorqueFlite. Sox said, "There was no time to search for gears in the modern match race car, and the automatic really does the job." To further help tame these cars (without slowing them down) and enhance top end stability, many drivers went the longnose Mustang route and extended the wheelbase.

This 1933 Willys is the only drag car to ever set national records in two different NHRA classes at a national event in one day. Mansfield, Ohio's Virgil Cates was solely responsible for causing the NHRA to change the rules, limiting cars to competing in a single class at any given event. (Photo Courtesy Michael Pottie)

Emery Cook took Don Garlits's Dart 2 to Funny Car's first 200-mph time when he recorded 200.44 at Petersburg, Florida, in October. Controversy surrounds the run because many feel the Dart didn't meet the 1966 description of a Funny Car.

debuting the car in the fall of 1965. Jungle Jim Liberman saw a little double duty, driving Lew Arrington's *Brutus* GTO and his own Chevy II. From the get-go, Liberman ran a blower atop his Rat motor.

In what may have been the first successful hybrid Funny Car, Maynard Rupp debuted a Hemi-powered, mid-engine Chevelle, opening more than a few eyes of those loyal to the brand. When it came to Pontiac, there were still a few who would rather fight than switch. Arnie Beswick and Roy and Don Gay won their share but were finding it tougher to keep their Pontiac mills together under the increasing loads of nitro and life under a blower. Lew Arrington had *Brutus* running 8.50 times after swamping his Mickey Thompson Hemi–headed Pontiac for a 392-inch Chrysler.

By midseason, blowers had become common place in Experimental Stock. Racers pushed through a learning curve, where blower explosions and transmission failures

Blown match race Stockers were the rage by mid-1966, as many swapped out their Hilborns. Mr. Norm's Dodge, driven by Gary Dyer (left), was one of the first to make the switch, and it proved to be one of the quickest. (Photo Courtesy John Foster Jr.)

The first set of injectors Hilborn made for the rat motor Chevy went to Dick Harrell. By the way that the Chevy II is wheels up here at Lions, I assume Harrell was quite satisfied with the power increase provided by Hilborn. (Photo Courtesy Michael Pottie)

were not uncommon. Drivers were suffering the consequences, as hot exhaust ignited the fuel and fluids. Thank goodness for fire retardant suits and recently developed breathing masks that protected the face and neck.

Manufacturers, such as Art Carr, were making advancements in bellhousings, protective blankets for transmissions, and blowers to contain explosions. Adding to the heightened level of danger were the few daring

Jim Thornton designed the 120-inch wheelbase chassis for the Ramchargers' Dart, and Woody Gilmore welded it up. A modern-day Hemi stroked to 472-ci with a dose of hydrazine took the car to 8.40 times. (Photo Courtesy Scott Krueger)

Doc Burgess's Black Arrow *was a study in the evolution of Stock to Ultra Stock/Experimental Stock. Note the altered wheelbase, injector stacks, and grille-mounted alcohol tank in this 1966 shot. Grumpy Jenkins won Top Stock in the same car at the 1965 NHRA Winternationals. The Plymouth featured an adjustable rear suspension.*

Gene Snow was the C/FD class record holder early in 1966 with his injected Rambunctious *Dart, recording a 9.30 at 152.80 mph. Power for the Don Hardy–chassis car came by way of a Ted Detar Hemi. Snow captured Comp Eliminator honors here at the Nationals in 1966, defeating John Dellafior of the Golden Commandos. Snow returned in 1967 to win Super Eliminator. At the 1968 Winternationals, he ran the aging steel-bodied Dart in D/Altered, thus avoiding the new fuel Funny Cars and winning Comp Eliminator. (Photo Courtesy Ed Aigner)*

Running CC/FD at the 1966 NHRA Winternationals, Tom McEwen in the mid-engine Hemi 'Cuda ran top time for the so-called Funny Cars, hitting a speed of 170.48. Fred Goeske took over the car later in the season. (Photo Courtesy Stephen Justice)

You Wanna Play, You Gotta Pay

Jim Liberman honed his skills driving for Lew Arrington before building himself his 427-powered Chevy II in 1966. The car was built at sponsor Richard Guess's Goodies Speed Shop in San Jose. Liberman and a few other local Funny Car guys had a good thing going with a Goodies counterman who helped ease their financial pain. The young man was in a relationship with a rich 60-plus-year-old woman and was helping himself to her bank account, buying goods for himself (including a sports car) and engines and parts for his Funny Car friends. Liberman happened to be the main receiver of this young man's generosity.

When the counterman was arrested for theft of funds, the police went looking for his partners in crime. Rich Abate, owner of the *Samson* Dart, had his shop raided, as was the shop of Don Williamson (*Hairy Canary*). Lew Arrington was also questioned. Liberman got word of the bust and literally drove off into the sunset with the free parts, taking his Chevy II out on a tour East with Williamson. After all was said and done, the older woman dropped the charges and smoothed things over with her plaything.

Jim Liberman drove the match race Pontiac of Lew Arrington for approximately a year before he finally got around to building this match race Chevy II of his own. Liberman fabricated the chassis and blown 427 for the car, which was built at Richard Guess's Goodies Speed Shop. (Photo Courtesy Forrest Bond)

souls who introduced hydrazine into their fuel mix. The highly unstable "performance enhancer" was first used by the Nazi's during World War II as a rocket propellant. The Ramchargers were one group that used it regularly.

According to Dave Rockwell in his book *We Were the Ramchargers*, the team added 10 ounces of the fuel to a 90-percent load of nitro. The damage hydrazine could cause to car, track, life, and limb was too much for the sanctioning bodies to bear. The AHRA banned its use in 1966, and the NHRA followed suit in 1967. Of course, this didn't prevent racers from using it in match races.

Just as the Comets were the cars to beat at the start of the season, they remained the car to beat at the close of it. In just one season, Funny Car elapsed times had dropped dramatically. In December, Dyno Don was down into the 7.90s, unblown. Now, compare that to the times turned by the blown Top Gas dragsters that were still running in the 8s. Commenting on the popularity of the Funny Car, Top Fuel pilot Art Malone said, "Funny Cars are where the money is because that's what the people want to see." Malone traded in his AA/Fuel Dragster in 1967 for a Mustang Funny Car.

Stock Eliminator

Top Stock in 1966 boiled down to the battle of two A/S cars: Jere Stahl's Hemi Belvedere and Bill Jenkins's 327-powered Chevy II. Stahl won three of the four NHRA national events this year with Jenkins playing runner-up at all three. Stahl's Plymouth wasn't quite ready for the season-opening Winternationals, which left Jenkins a favorite to win. A redlight by the Grump killed any hope he had and left the door open for Shirley Shahan, the *Drag-On-Lady*, who earned the category crown with her S/SA 1965 Plymouth by defeating Ken Heimann with a 11.26 at 126.76 mph.

Shahan had been racing since the mid-1950s and won Super Stock at the first Bakersfield meet in 1959 driving a 1958 Chevy. She jumped at the chance to race for Chrysler in 1964, and the deal carried her through 1968. Her Winternationals win gave Shirley the honor of being the first woman to win a major national event.

Anyone who planned on running an A/S street Hemi were recom-mended to write Chrysler's Domestic Product Planning in Michigan for a free 14-page booklet on how to set their car up for competition. I doubt Jere Stahl needed much help. Race fans became familiar with the Stahl name after he bombed class records in Junior Stock with his 1956 and 1957 Chevys. Late in 1965, he tested a 1966 Hemi Plymouth for *Super Stock* magazine and liked it so much he contacted Dick Maxwell at Chrysler.

He said, "I called Dick, who worked for Bob Cahill, and asked him if I bought a car would they give me a parts deal."

When Dick called back with an agreement, Stahl told him that he now had to find a way to get a car. So, Bill Stiles (Dave Strickler's mechanic in 1965) and Bunny Stone each agreed to become one-third owners with Stahl in a Hemi-powered 1966 Plymouth Belvedere sedan.

"So, I ordered the car, but when it arrived, both Stiles and Stone backed out," Stahl said.

Fortunately for Stahl, he was able to get a local bank to finance the entire car.

"Since I had no place to work on the car, Stiles agreed to keep it at his shop, and we used his pickup and a trailer borrowed from Strickler to tow with," Stahl said. "We worked out a financial deal, which I wrote down and put in letter form to him."

To say it was a good year for Stahl was putting it mildly.

"The best engine of all was the one that we honed upside down with the heads torqued on and had the 'new' NHRA compression spec that I came up with," he said.

Winning Stock Eliminator at the NHRA Winternationals put Shirley Shahan and husband H.L. on the map. Shahan and company later converted the S/SA car to run match bashes by adding injectors and moving the rear suspension forward. (Photo Courtesy Forrest Bond)

Traction at the NHRA World Finals was nil due to the fact that the Tulsa track had been scraped clean the week before. To help get off the line, Jere Stahl dropped the tire pressure on his M&H slicks and trialed both 2.14 and 2.38 first gear transmissions. His strategy worked, as he made it to the final, where he defeated a red-lighting Grumpy Jenkins.

The first in the line of Grumpy's Toys was Bill Jenkins's giant-killer 327-powered Chevy II. With each NHRA Stock class being based on the weight to horsepower ratio, Jenkins's 3,000-pound Chevy II had an approximate 800-pound advantage over the Hemi Chryslers and 427 Fords in A/Stock. (Photo Courtesy Stephen Justice)

It wasn't all Chevy in Stock. Dave Kempton won more than his share with his 1962 Plymouth Sport Fury. Kempton took a rare trip outside of Division 7 in 1966 to win Stock Eliminator at Indy. Power came by way of a 305-hp 361-ci backed by an Art Carr–prepped TorqueFlite and 4.88:1 gears.

That engine ran 12.5:1 compression and went over 126 mph at Cecil County two weeks before Stahl won the World Finals at Tulsa.

Incorporating every trick in the book, Stahl did a bunch of aerodynamic work on the underside of the car. Some of that work consisted of thin aluminum panels screwed to the floor and strategically placed aluminum adhesive tape. Fellow racer Arlen Vanke took a look at the bottom side and could see something wasn't right. He took his concerns to the NHRA, which had a look themselves. They couldn't figure out what was going on under the speckled paint Stahl had painted the underside with.

"So the NHRA tells me, 'We don't know what you've done, but whatever it is you better remove it. Your previous qualifying runs do not count, and time trials are over in 40 minutes,'" Stahl said. "So, we jacked up the car in the pits and recruited everyone we could get under the car to pull off tape and unscrew panels. When all the stuff was removed, it was easy to see where the work was done because of the speckled paint."

Meanwhile, Jenkins was doing his best to make Chrysler regret not wrapping him up in a factory deal back in 1965. His giant killer *Chevy II*, factory rated at 350 hp, produced an estimated 425 and gave all (but Stahl's) Chryslers and Fords in A/S fits. The *Chevy II*'s output was limited by the rules, which dictated the OEM carburetor, which in this case flowed 585 cfm.

Though we know Jenkins was quite secretive when it came to carb mods, we do know he went to larger needle and seats, ran varied size jets, and tried the old air leak test (leaving vacuum ports open and installing washers under the carb to lift it off the base). No doubt Jenkins tried other things, but he never let the cat out of the bag. The *Chevy II* shared the class record of 11.11 with Stahl and managed off-the-record high 10s early in 1967.

The Cossey, Casler, and Hooker Connection

Wiley Cossey, one of drag racing's unsung heroes, hailed from the Bakersfield area and made the move to Pomona around 1960. There, he went to work for Bill Casler, manufacturer of the recap cheater slick that was so popular with those running Stock. With a growing reputation and the exploding popularity of the category, Casler moved to a larger building in Orange. This is where the tie-in between Casler and Hooker Headers comes in.

Gerry Hooker and Gill George founded Hooker Headers and set up shop in Orange. Things were going great until the building they were situated in burned to the ground. Having to start from scratch with orders to fill, they moved into a small shop next to Casler. With a serious lack of capital to work with, Casler stepped in.

Casler put up the needed funds and became 51-percent owner of Hooker Headers. Business continued to grow to the point where a new, larger building was

Wiley Cossey won Junior Stock at the NHRA Winternationals, wheeling this 427-ci, 425-hp 1966 Biscayne of Bill Casler. The body and engine combo was a popular choice for Chevy racers through the decade. Not so much for Cossey though, as he found himself driving Mopars after 1966. (Photo Courtesy Forrest Bond)

erected just across the street (Brook St). Meanwhile, Casler saw his cheater slick business lose ground to the onslaught of Goodyear and Firestone. Around 1968, he sold his business to Hurst. Wiley Cossey, meanwhile, went to work for Hooker and ran manufacturing for them into the late 1960s.

Richard Maskin had to be different, successfully campaigning this 1955 Canadian Pontiac in C/MP. The Pontiacs built in Oshawa and destined for the Canadian market rode on the shorter wheelbase Chevy chassis and featured Chevy drivelines. (Photo Courtesy Richard Kinstry)

Chapter Seven

1967
A Groovy Situation

In 1967, it seems that in one form or another, the young and young at heart were tuning in. A good number of people followed the sport of drag racing and watched it change (like the world around them) immensely as the year progressed. The wrinkle-wall slicks, first made popular on Factory Experimental cars, found their way in to Top Fuel. Between the tires and slipper clutches, near smokeless runs made for record-smashing performance.

Match bashes seemed to outnumber match races as multicar shows, whether they were Top Fuel, Stock, or anything in between. Junior Stock became its own category when the NHRA created the new Super Stock category. At the end of the season, the NHRA dumped

In the far lane is Connie Kalitta, on his way to winning Fuel Dragster honors at the 1967 NHRA Winternationals over Gene Goleman in the Bob Creitz & Ed Greer car. Sadly, we lost Goleman later in the year in an on track incident at Great Lakes Dragway. Kalitta, Detroit Dragway's Man of the Year in 1966, debuted this new car prior to the 1967 AHRA Winternationals and went on to win the meet. A week later, he won here at Pomona with a 7.17. A trip to Florida immediately after saw him win the NASCAR winter meet. (Photo Courtesy Forrest Bond)

Modified Sport Production due to a lack of interest. As a means of simplifying the sport and making it easier to understand, the NHRA continued to eliminate classes into the next decade.

Fuel Dragster

Connie Kalitta was named Detroit Dragway's 1966 Man of the Year after surviving a high-speed wreck in the *Bounty Hunter* late in the year. While recouping from injuries, a new Cammer-powered Logghe car was being built. Debuting in fine fashion, the new *Bounty Hunter* carried Kalitta to wins at all three season-opening winter national events: AHRA, NHRA, and NASCAR.

It was a good year for Cammer-powered cars, which numbered six now. Prudhomme, who took over driving the *Brand Ford Special* from McEwen, won the Springnationals, defeating Pete Robinson in the final. At the World Finals, Prudhomme lost a close one to the Hemi car of Tim Beebe.

Those tire wars were in full bloom at the Springnationals, where both M&H and Goodyear debuted their latest soft compound tire. M&H had its new CCs, and Goodyear with its 335 series. Tom McEwen ran a set of 11.75x16 M&H on 8-inch rims (at 5 psi) and had the top speed of the meet with a 223.32 mph. The narrow rims gave a wider footprint, while the wrinkle wall of the Funny Car–style tire gave plenty of traction. Although McEwen recalled that they made things a little sketchy on the top end. After all, the tires were designed for a 2,000-pound car going 190 mph, not a Top Fueler weighing 1,200 pounds going 220. The added weight of a Funny Car kept the tires flat on the track. To the disappointment of many fans, the tires combined with a slipper clutch made for a near smokeless run.

As eye-opening as McEwen's performance was, it was Don Prudhomme who owned the Springnationals. Prudhomme not only won the event but he was the only competitor to break into the 6s. He did so on every full run, starting with a 6.99 at 220.04 mph against Bub Reese, and then coasted to a win against a broken Jimmy Nix. Mike Sorokin in the *Hawaiian II* was next to fall when Prudhomme hit 6.97 at 220.58 mph. In the only NHRA all-Ford Top Fuel final ever, Prudhomme defeated Sneaky Pete Robinson with a 6.92, 222.76 mph. And it could have easily been the NHRA's first side-by-side 6-second run if Robinson's blower hadn't chewed up a bearing. A month before the spring meet, he had installed a pair of new-profile Crane Cams and was knocking on the 6-second door with a record-setting 7.08.

If this photo doesn't bring on a smile, you better check your pulse. It's Leroy Goldstein in the Crower and Blair Top Fueler warming the night air. Goldstein won the 1967 AHRA Springnationals, defeating a redlighting Dave Beebe in the final. Both drivers were familiar names into the 1970s. (Photo Courtesy Forrest Bond)

The beautiful rail of Creitz and Greer was always in the thick of things, thanks to the driving of Gene Goleman. Though the added tail did nothing for performance, it enhanced the looks of many mid-1960s rails. (Photo Courtesy Don Prieto)

Robinson didn't come by his *Sneaky* nickname by chance, as he always seemed to have something inventive up his sleeve. At the Springnationals, he introduced the air starter, eliminating the need to push start his *Tinker Toy*. The starter consisted of a hub that fit over the top blower pulley and a bottle of compressed nitrogen that spun the blower to speed. Though the push start was always part of the fan appeal, just as the full quarter-mile smoky runs were, it appeared that their days were numbered.

Robinson's *Toy* didn't last long past the Springnationals. While testing tires in July, he crashed the car going approximately 220 mph. Robinson received injuries to his arms, which flailed around as the car tumbled. He put

Steve Carbone in the seat of the new *Tinker Toy* while he recouped. Robinson added restraints in the new *Tinker Toy* that kept the arms and legs within the confines of the car during a crash, another one of his creations that is still in use today.

Don Garlits, the "King of the Dragsters," was struggling out of the chute. Having failed to qualify his *Swamp Rat X* at both the NHRA Winternationals and Springnationals, Garlits decided he wasn't going to shave until he broke into the 6s. A new car was built prior to Indy, where he qualified 23rd and made rounds with 7.0 times. Saving his best for last, a final round appearance against James Warren, Garlits tripped the clocks with an unreal 6.77 to Warren's 6.95. After his end track interview with ABC, Garlits was pushed back up the track, where his wife Patty handed him a razor and shaving cream. To the approval of roaring fans, Garlits proceeded to shave off his beard.

Most stories of the meet fail to mention that not only did Garlits beat Warren in the final but he defeated Tom McEwen in the semifinals. The relevance of that was that it was McEwen who turned Garlits onto the new sticky M&H slicks prior to their run. Coburn did himself no favors when he helped Garlits set up his clutch.

It was a tough pill to swallow, but the dragster was losing flavor to the increasingly popular Funny Car. Where it really hurt the dragster owners and drivers was in the pocket book, where many were barely making money. To counter, the up-and-coming promoter Doug Kruse got together with Tom McEwen to run the United States Professional Dragsters Championship (USPDC). The pair had originally formed the United Drag Racers Association (UDRA) back in 1963 to promote competitive events and improve relations between car owners and track management.

The USPDC was an offshoot of this idea and meant to counter the number of Funny Car match bashes while

Ted Gotelli and Kenny Safford's Woody Gilmore car is looking sharp under the lights of OCIR on opening night August 5, 1967. Gotelli built the early Hemi while Safford drove the car to 6-second times. Those M&H Super Camanja tires measured 11.75 x 16. Advancement in both tires and clutches not only saw elapsed times drop immensely season to season but also changed the look of the way races were run. (Photo Courtesy Forrest Bond)

Thinking outside the box, Woody Gilmore experimented with an independent front suspension in 1967. Few were built with this one hanging on the car of Tommy Allen. The intent was to allow greater suspension travel, allowing the chassis to rise while the tires remained on the track to steer. The collection of small-diameter tubes actually reduced weight when compared to a beam axle. The best time for Allen's car was a 7.04 at 218 mph. (Photo Courtesy Forrest Bond)

helping reestablish the dragsters as the king of the sport, and hopefully lead to increased purses. The first race was held on July 15 at Lions and proved an overwhelming success with more than 120 dragsters in attendance and an enthusiast crowd of around 17,000.

Qualifying for the program were 64 Fuel cars, 32 Top Gas cars, and 16 Junior Fuelers. Prudhomme won Top Fuel by defeating John Mulligan in the final with a 7.29 at 212.26 mph. Prudhomme's efforts saw him pocket a cool $7,000. Top Gas was won by the *Freight Train*, while Tom Barres driving for Sam Rose and Don Lawson took Junior Fuel. As the season drew down, Beebe and Mulligan and their Race Car Engineering rail was knocking out 6.70 times at 230 mph and seemed to be the car to beat.

It was a bittersweet period in Top Fuel. On December 30, former Surfer Mike Sorokin was killed in an on-track accident. Sorokin was driving Tony Waters's dragster at Orange County when the clutch exploded. Just a few runs

before, Mike Snively barely escaped injury when the same thing happened in the *Hawaiian*, nearly tearing the car in half.

When it came to clutches, things had been getting hairy for a while. Snively got everyone thinking about clutches earlier in the season when he made a smokeless run at Lions that produced an eye-opening elapsed time. Seems not even Leong knew why it had happened, at least at the time. It wasn't until engine builder Keith Black heard about the events and examined how the clutch had been assembled that the reason for the smokeless run became clear. Leong had installed the clutch pack backward.

"There was a dimensional difference between the leading and trailing portions of the clutch disc hubs," said Jim McFarland, who worked for Schiefer on clutch development into 1968. "Although slight, it was sufficient to prevent total contact of the sintered iron friction faces (once the pressure plate and centrifugal levers applied the clutch's total clamping force) if either of the discs happened to be accidentally installed facing the wrong direction. Even when fully released, the clutch could not become totally compressed, resulting in a measure of uncontrolled slippage.

"Top Fuel (and Top Gas) racers assumed Leong had dropped the spring pressure in the clutches, and they proceeded to do the same. It was purely experimental. How much was enough? How much wasn't? And in the process, clutch packages quickly overheated and were short-lived.

"On more than one occasion, particularly during night racing, I saw white-hot clutch parts shoot high into the darkness. Cars were cut in half. Floaters and discs were thrown into spectator areas. Racers were injured or killed. By now, most knew what had been behind Snively's first smokeless run, but the genie was already out of the bottle. Clutch package experimentation was on the loose and leaving a trail of damage in its wake. The accident involving Mike Sorokin was the last straw."

McFarland went on to say that he received a phone call from Paul Schiefer, who was concerned they were losing too many friends and wanted to work with McFarland to solve the problem.

"During the course of the next few months, Paul committed considerable funds and time to developing a solution that would enable clutches to slip (in a controlled fashion) and stay in the cars," McFarland said. "It was a Herculean effort taken on by many, including Bruce Crower, who developed the Crowerglide. Meanwhile, Mike's death had spawned the Mike Sorokin Safety Foundation (created by the then-manager of Orange County, Mike Jones) to conduct further investigations into ways for improving racer safety. It was a delicate time in drag racing's evolution, but it turned out that those who had contributed to the problem ultimately became part of the solution."

Gas Dragster

The year's battle in Top Gas saw Gordon "the Collector" Collett defeat Division 5 champ Don Cain at the World Finals. Cain, coming off of a Nationals victory, set low ET of the meet in his loss to Collett with a 7.61. Collett had a great year on his own, winning the NHRA Winternationals, losing in the final at the Springnationals to

Don Cain and Bob Pacitto battle it out in the Top Gas final at Indy. It was Pacitto's lucky day, coming out on top with a 7.65 at 184.42 mph. (Photo Courtesy Forrest Bond)

Walt Rhoades gets the Travis, Rhoades, Eldridge Gas House Gang AA/GD up on one wheel during action at Irwindale. The early Hemi mounted in a SPE chassis moved the car to times in the mid-7s. A well-seasoned driver Rhoades later drove John Peters's Freight Train to a win at the 1971 Gatornationals. (Photo Courtesy Forrest Bond)

John Peters's *Freight Train* and winning the Olympics of Drag Racing at Union Grove.

Though a national event victory eluded the *Freight Train,* its best of 7.30 elapsed times at 207 proved untouchable. Peters's edge was that he had successfully adopted Top Fuel technology in the form of tires and clutch to the *Freight Train.* They were getting the power to the ground while others stuck in the 7.50 range struggled to adapt. Peters managed a pretty decent year, considering his *Train* saw three different drivers behind the wheel: Goob Tuller, Billy Scott, and Bob Muravez.

Pete Millar of Drag Cartoons fame campaigned his Chicken Coupe through 1967. The Don Long chassis housed a 289 Ford. Millar shipped the car to Europe at the end of the season, where it eventually disappeared. The Comp Coupe classes themselves disappeared after the 1970 season. (Photo Courtesy Forrest Bond)

NorCal racer Peter "Cheatin' Chico" Breschini picked up the name at Fremont because he won so much. His Chevy-powered C/Dragster ran a Jim Davis chassis to bottom 9-second times in 1967. (Photo Courtesy Steve Reyes)

Between 1967 and 1968, the Jewel T of Joe Davis, Wes Ingram, and Jim Walvern gathered seven class records in everything from AA/A, AA/C, and BB/D. Davis won Super Eliminator at the 1967 NHRA World Finals, defeating Walt Marrs with a 9.11. The T was unique among Altereds, reportedly one of the first into the 7s, it was also the first to run an adjustable rear suspension, a low-mounted engine, and a modern B&M automatic transmission. (Photo Courtesy James Handy)

Mid-Eliminators

The problem with the Mid-Eliminators, if you want to call it one, is the fact that there were so many winners and just not enough space to tell about them all. Guys such as Fred Hurst, and Ferd Napfel in Gas, Sam Cunningham in Modified, West Virginia's Joe Law and Peter "Cheatin' Chico" Breschini in Comp. Cheatin' Chico picked up his name at Fremont, where he raced regularly between 1965 and 1970. *Drag News*'s northern briefs columnist and sometimes Fremont announcer Al Caldwell nicknamed Breschini *the Cheater* because he won so much. Chico took it all in stride and named his car *The Cheater*. He would win the NHRA Winternationals and close the season by winning the World Finals.

Altereds

Considering the competition in Altered, be it Fuel or Gas powered, it was quite the feat to stand above the pack. The winningest Altered between 1967 and 1968 was the *Jewel T* of Joe Davis, Wes Ingram, and Jim Walvern. Davis wheeled the fiberglass *T* to seven class records, in classes running from AA/A, AA/C, and BB/D. Topping the team's accomplishments was winning the 1967 NHRA Super Eliminator world championship.

The *T* was unique among Fuel Altereds; it was also the first to run an adjustable rear suspension, a low-mounted 427 Chevy, and a modern B&M automatic transmission. Reportedly, the car would be the first Fuel Altered to run a 7-second time. Further accolades

No car on the track gave a better show than the Fuel Altereds. Rich Guasco swapped out the big-block Chevy in his *Pure Hell* for a Hemi late in 1967 and watched as Dale Emery blasted out 7.60 times. (Photo Courtesy James Handy)

In the lower Altered classes, no one dominated the mid-1960s like Jack Ditmars and his B/A 1934 Ford. In 1967, Ditmars's Lil Screamer II was powered by a big-block Chevy and B&M ClutchFlite transmission. Ditmars showed that innovative thinking was not dead when he incorporated a unique adjustable rear suspension that allowed the wheelbase to grow from 96 to 102 inches in 1-inch increments, all in the name of tuning for track conditions. The setup worked to the tune of multiple class records and 11 class wins at national events between 1963 and 1967. (Photo Courtesy Rob Potter)

for the team came in the form of awards for Best Engineered Car, Best Appearing Car, Best Appearing Crew, and Driver of the Year.

Gassers

In Supercharged Gas, Stone, Woods, & Cook, a category leader since the turn of the decade, joined the Funny Car craze in 1967 by building a Mustang to go along with their Willys. The Mustang, labeled *Dark Horse II,* ran a Ron Scrima chassis and a 426 Hemi in the 2,400-pound Funny Car class. Their success with the Mustang equaled that of their Willys. But aerodynamics being what they are, during a September match race at Alton, Illinois, air got under the Mustang and sent it sailing. Traveling at 180 mph, it was a wreck from which Cook couldn't recover. SWC would carry on, but Cook's driving days were over.

At the NHRA Springnationals, Ohio George Montgomery dropped more than a few jaws when he showed up with his AA/G 1967 Mustang. Borrowing heavily from the Funny Car, many people felt that Montgomery's *Malco Gasser,* with its lift-up body, was the beginning of the end for Gas. Within the year, Mustangs, Camaros, and Barracudas with their low silhouettes and superior aerodynamics dotted the landscape, slowly replacing fan-favored Willys and Anglias as class leaders.

Being a contract driver for Mercury, Ohio George took his cue from the manufacturer. So, in 1966, when a Ford vice president said while viewing George's Cammer-powered Willys, "Nice, but we sell Fords, don't we?" the coffin was all but sealed on the Willys. A fiberglass Cal-Automotive Mustang shell was procured, and as Gas rules at the time dictated that cars must run an OEM chassis, the Mustang was mounted on his existing 1933 Willys

Both the Ron and Don Gay's GTO and the Stone, Woods, & Cook Mustang featured a fabricated chassis and non-flip-up fiberglass bodies. SWC took the 2,400-pound Funny Car class at Bakersfield in 1967 running 8.40 times with the Dark Horse II. The icing on the cake was being awarded the Best Engineered Car. (Photo Courtesy Michael Pottie)

One of the prettiest Willys ever built was the AA/G car of Jack Merkel. The car features an all-glass shell; a raked, chopped top; and a one-piece lift-off front end. Subtle changes, such as a flush-mounted windshield, molded fenders, and a channeled body, help cheat the wind. Performance matched the looks thanks to a 427 Chevy that propelled the Willys to a best of 8.70 times at over 156 mph. (Photo Courtesy of Michael Pottie)

chassis. Montgomery stuck with his tried-and-true adjustable Delco coilover shocks on all four corners and the tube drive that he found so successful in the Willys.

When Montgomery rolled into Tulsa with the car, tech inspectors took one look and said, "No way!" The NHRA head tech, Farmer Dismuke, who had been kept abreast of the build all along, stepped in and gave the car a green light. The *Malco Gasser* went on to win class with an astounding 8.94 at 160.56 mph and followed with a class win at the Nationals.

Jack Merkel pushed the limits when it came to building his new 1933 Willys. The car featured a 3-inch top chop and an all-fiberglass shell with a one-piece lift-off front end. Subtle changes, such

Ohio George's evolutionary Mustang rode on a modified Willys chassis with a 110-inch wheelbase. George would state the Mustang rode like a Rolls Royce compared to the Willys. The Cammer-powered Mustang recorded an AA/G record-setting 8.93 at 162.16 mph. Getting the bite were Goodyears measuring 16x12. (Photos Courtesy John Vanderpryt)

John Mazmanian's 1948 Austin was nicknamed the football *due to the odd shape the Gil Ayala chop gave it.* The Austin counted on a Dave Zeuschel 398-ci Hemi and a B&M TorqueFlite to record a best of 8.52. The NHRA initially disallowed the Austin from running Supercharged Gas due to its radical chop, forcing Mazmanian and driver Richard Siroonian to run BB/Altered at the NHRA meets. The car was sold to K. S. Pittman in 1968 and won BB/A at the NHRA Nationals. Pittman campaigned the Austin through 1969 before pulling the body and installing an Opel GT shell over the Exhibition Engineering chassis. (Photo Courtesy of Michael Pottie)

Gordy and Dick Waldhauser's B/Gas Overland Express was a popular Division 5 competitor from 1964 through 1967. The brothers built the unique ride by meshing back lot rejects in the form of a 1948, 2-wheel-drive Willys Overland, and a 1958 New Yorker. Powering the Express to a best of high 10s at 130 mph was a 408-ci Hemi, push button TorqueFlite, and a 5.12:1 equipped 8¾ rear end. (Photo Courtesy John Foster Jr.)

Overshadowed by the cars of A/GS were many standouts in the lower Gas classes. Walt Marrs wheeled the Marrs Boys split window Corvette to B/GS's first 9-second run when he recorded a 9.90 at 139.10 mph in October. A 327-ci Chevy backed by a B&M Clutch-flite did the trick.

Steve Woods, a Fremont regular, was trying something a little different with his Anglia. Woods fed nitro through his Hemi and ran CC/FD. The wing was from a super modified race car, and Woods admitted that the Anglia was a handful. (Photo Courtesy Steve Reyes)

as a flush-mounted windshield, molded fenders, and a body channeling, were all incorporated to help cheat the wind.

Merkel assembled the blown 427-ci Chevy, incorporating aluminum heads and a 6-71 topped with Hilborn injection. He worked closely with Crower Cams and experimented with different profiles. Vitar built a strong Chevy Turbo Hydra-matic, which Merkel backed with 4.56 rear gears in a 1960 Oldsmobile housing. Supporting the rear were coilover shocks and a unique traction arm fabricated by Merkel and based loosely on a 1940s Jaguar design.

Prior to graduating from Pratt Institute, Merkel based his thesis on the arm and came up with a mathematical equation that worked flawlessly when put into practice: the length of torque bar/arm divided by the rear gear ratio equals the distance between the driveshaft and the tip of the torque arm. If you deviated from this theory, the bar wasn't as effective. Jere Stahl studied the arm while building headers for the Willys and marketed his version to the Junior Stock racers.

Ready to race, the Willys weighed in at a measly 2,135 pounds. Merkel made his first pass on the car in August and cranked out a 9.30 at 149 mph. By the time the Willys was retired, it was recording 8.70 times at over 156.

The cars of Butch Leal were always great-looking machines, and his Experimental Stock Barracuda was no exception. The B&N fiberglass body covered a Logghe chassis that carried an injected Hemi. According to Leal, with a 100-percent load of fuel, the Barracuda ran a best of 7.82 at 181 mph. Tommy Rodgers, who purchased Leal's 1965 Plymouth, partnered with Leal on the Barracuda. Rodgers's enclosed trailer had the Barracuda traveling in style. (Photo Courtesy Michael Pottie)

Experimental Stock/Funny Car

In NHRA competition, the Funny Car split the year between running Super Eliminator and a category of its own. Over in the AHRA, the top dogs ran Unlimited Fuel while the heavier Funny Cars (2,400-pound class) ran FX/Fuel. Dyno Don Nicholson carried on his winning ways at the AHRA Winternationals, where he defeated Ed Schartman in the final eliminations with an 8.26.

Charlie Allen defeated Gas Ronda in the 2,400-pound class. Dyno followed with a win in NHRA S/XS at the NHRA Winternationals, defeating the *Destroyer* Jeep of Roger Wolford. Yes, there were a few Jeeps running Funny Car (*Secret Weapon*, *Holy Toledo*), as rules of the day allowed for the use of pretty much any body. Another oddity was the *Bronco Buster* of Doug Nash.

Nash made the move from a B/FX Comet to Funny Car with an all-fiberglass Ford Bronco. Powered by a 289, the Bronco featured an aluminum chassis, which the NHRA frowned upon

Bob Tasca Sr. first became involved in drag racing during the early 1960s by running Stockers and continued to do so as they evolved into Funny Cars. A Logghe chassis with an injected then blown Cammer took driver Bill Lawton to a best of 201 mph in the 7.30s. (Photo Courtesy Ken Gunning)

Hardly a year went by where Jack Chrisman wasn't in the headlines, and 1967 was no exception. At Bakersfield, he won the Funny Car eliminator, recording a best of 7.60 at 191 mph. Chrisman counted on a blown Cammer and a beefed C-6 transmission to keep competition at bay. (Photo Courtesy Michael Pottie)

and wouldn't allow to run in sanctioned competition. It made no difference to Nash though, as the money was in match racing and he had plenty of competitors eager to run him.

Butch Leal cashed in his Super Stock Plymouth after witnessing Mercury's flip-up Comets in action and had Logghe build him a Barracuda for 1967. Powered by an H.L. Shahan–built injected Hemi, the Barracuda gave the Mercurys fits. For a time, it was the quickest and fastest Funny Car going, recording a best of 7.82 at 181.90 on a full load of nitro.

Leal was preparing a new blown Barracuda for the 1968 season, but after witnessing Jack Chrisman explode

a blower not once but twice, he changed his mind. He sold the car to Don Schumacher and went back to running Super Stock.

The reoccurring theme of these early Funny Cars was breakage. Transmissions, blowers, and rear ends continued to be laid to waste, and running two or three (or more) match races a week, as most of the more popular cars were doing, you can see how costs were escalating. Dyno Don was pushing fellow racers and the sanctioning bodies to format some Funny Car guidelines to improve safety and combat growing costs. Don suggested no nitro, straight alcohol with blowers, minimum weight of 2,200 pounds, stock appearing bodies, and a maximum of 430 ci. In September, Dyno Don tried on a blower for

Doug Thorley and his Chevy Corvair surprised a few when he won the Nationals in 1967. As good as the car ran, it wasn't supposed to get around the favored Cammer Fords. Powering the Corvair was a Thorley, Gary Slusser–built 482-ci Chevy that housed a Reath crank, Sig Erson cam, Venolia pistons, and Enderle injection atop a GMC 6-71. Power was transmitted through an Art Carr TorqueFlite wrapped in a Chute Metal safety blanket. The Fiberglass Trends body hid a 123-inch-wheelbase chassis designed by Thorley. (Photos Courtesy Michael Pottie)

The ever-present Arnie Beswick's Fiberglass Trends GTO housed a blown Enderle injected 428 incorporating early Super Duty heads, an Isky cam, and Mickey Thompson pistons, rods, and intake. Beswick worked close with B&M, and after going through a dozen or so transmissions due to busted main shafts and hubs, found an aircraft supplier that was able to make him bulletproof parts. Times in mid-1967 were 8.40 at 173 mph. (Photo Courtesy John Foster Jr.)

Clyde Morgan in Charlie Wilson's Vicious Vette was a real threat back when pretty much anything went in Experimental Stock/Funny Car. Powering the 1958 Corvette to high-8-second times was a Bones Balogh–built, blown 427. The Corvette was later driven by future Funny Car star, Dale Pulde. (Photo Courtesy Michael Pottie)

In 1967, American Motors put up a million bucks to spearhead their drive into the world of drag racing. Front and center was the Grant Industries fiberglass Rebel SST Funny Car that was initially driven by "Banzai" Bill Hayes. Hayden Proffitt took over the ride in August 1967. Part of Proffitt's gig with AMC was making public appearances. (Photo Courtesy Phil Bellomy)

The Flying Dutchman *Dart of Al Vanderwoude featured a steel shell with bolt-on fiberglass panels. The multitalented Vanderwoude built his own blown 426, and though he was capable of building his own chassis, Ted Brown did this 114 incher. The tinwork was also completed by Vanderwoude. (Photo Courtesy Michael Pottie)*

the first time, borrowing the 6-71 from Pete Robinson to record a rampant wheels-up 7.98.

For a while, Doug Thorley held the record as the world's fastest Funny Car when his Corvair ran a 7.86 at 184.42 mph at Lions in August. Powering the Chevy was a stroked 427 measuring 482-ci backed by an Art Carr–built TorqueFlite. Thorley's Corvair defeated Joe Lunati's 427-ci Camaro at Indy in the all-Chevy final.

Thorley accepted a factory deal from AMC shortly after the race, while Lunati wrecked the Camaro two weeks later at LaPlace. As opposed to building a new car, Lunati turned his attention to manufacturing camshafts. He began his drag racing career in the Sports Production category, where rules allowed plenty of room for experimentation. In any given engine, the greatest increase in power comes from top end modifications: induction, heads, and camshaft. Lunati focused his attention on these areas and worked closely with Howard Crane in testing camshafts of different profiles. This loose partnership contributed to Lunati winning Street Eliminator at Nationals in 1964 and 1966.

With little more than a handful of nationals events to contend with, it seems every weekend there was a match race, a circuit race, or a match bash somewhere. Orange County closed the season with one of the largest meets of the season: the first-annual Manufacturers Funny Car Championship held November 25.

Forty-five of the nation's leading Funny Cars showed up with hopes of making one of the six manufacturer teams. Chevys, Fords, Mercurys, Plymouths, Dodges, and Pontiacs were all out in force. A total of 30 cars qualified, 5 cars per team battled it out in hopes of earning the $22,000 cash prize. A sample of those on hand: Nicholson, Schartman, Chrisman, Dyer, Allen, Ronda, Grove, Thorley, Seaton, Harrell, Arrington, and Roy and Don Gay. Failing to make the cut were the Novas of Liberman and Randy Walls and the Camaro of the Pisano brothers.

At the end of the day, the winning manufacturer was determined by the team with the most points. One point was given to each team for each race won. Low ET in each round earned an additional point for the team. After three rounds of bashing it out, Ford and Chevy were tied with 9 points apiece. The tie breaker was decided by adding up each team's total ETs, the team with the lowest was deemed the winner. Chevrolet came out on top with ETs totaling 124.33 to Ford's 134.93. Overall low ET went to Eddie Schartman, who laid down a 7.87. Slightly off his best run to date of 7.85.

Super Stock Eliminator

In 1967, the NHRA separated Top Stock from Stock and created the Super Stock category. Super Stock consisted of 10 classes: SS/A through SS/E and SS/AA through SS/EA for automatic transmission cars. Rules were more liberal than Stock but could easily leave a person shaking their head.

As an example, you could run any aftermarket intake manifold but had to run the stock carburetor. You could run an aftermarket camshaft of your choice but had to run stock valves and no porting. Cars ran off of established class records, and running quicker than 0.10 under during eliminations automatically got you booted. Welcome to the world of break light racing, where the quickest car didn't necessarily win.

Factory involvement was deep with General Motors, Ford, and Chrysler all getting into the game. GM's ban on racing involvement saw the manufacturer continue

Factory involvement in Stock ran deep through the 1960s. In 1966, Oldsmobile built 54 W-30 Cutlasses to do battle in C/Stock. Stiff competition came from Mercury, which prepped a number of 390-powered Comets for class. The Cutlass was a real factory goer with a 0.474-lift cam and three 2-barrel carburetors drawing fresh air from scoops in the bumper. A change in rules saw the NHRA bump the Cutlass to SS/E in 1967. Pete Kost used his Cutlass to win C/S at the 1966 NHRA Winternationals.

to slip goodies out the back door and build limited runs of factory drag packs. Grumpy Jenkins's relationship with Chevrolet's head of performance Vince Piggins is legendary. It was through their relationship that the decision was made to produce the 375-hp 396 Camaro, specifically for the new S/S category.

Ford, meanwhile, had a number of its Drag Team members in 427-equipped Fairlanes to start the year.

Chrysler, fearing harm coming to their Funny Car drivers due to parts failure, moved them all into Super Stock. Heavy hitters Sox & Martin and Dick Landy enjoyed full factory support and campaigned multiple 426- and 440-ci powered cars. Sox & Martin's and Landy's factory deals required them to hold performance clinics throughout the nation at select Dodge and Plymouth dealerships.

Bill Jenkins started the year running his aging Chevy

The team of Sox & Martin was living the dream in 1967, campaigning two Hemi cars and a 440-powered GTX. A variety of drivers were hired, including Dave Strickler, Dave Kempton, and Butch Leal, to name a few. Sox himself won the NHRA Springnationals three years running, starting in 1967. (Photo Courtesy John Vanderpryt)

Detroit took to the new Super Stock category with models built specifically for the category. Jenkins's 375-hp Camaro and Hubert Platt's SS/B 427 Fairlane are prime examples.

The 1967 S/S world champ Ed Miller of Rochester, New York, defeated Dick Arons in the final with a 11.19 at 114.35 mph. Hey, is that lowly Rambler on the left about to lose its doors? (Photo Courtesy Steve Reyes)

II and was the favorite to win Super Stock at the NHRA Winternationals, having just come off a middle eliminator win at the AHRA winter meet. But his hopes were dashed in the first round of SS/C class runoffs when he left way early, like two lights early against the *Hot Rod* magazine Camaro entered by managing editor Don Evans.

Editor Jim McFarland recalled that they immediately withdrew the Camaro from competition and pleaded, to no avail with the NHRA, to allow Jenkins to be reinstated. McFarland states that the Camaro featured a questionable blueprinted 350. It was the end of the line for Jenkins's Chevy II, as he debuted his own Camaro at the proceeding NHRA Springnationals. In the inaugural category final, it was relative unknown Eddie Vasquez and his *Too Costly* Chevy II holding off the hard charging A-990 1965 Plymouth of Ed Miller.

Miller got his revenge at the end of the season, when he defeated the Camaro of Dick Arons for the world title. It was a hard-fought battle for Miller, who recalled, "A loss of oil pressure on a time trial run Sunday morning led to quite a thrash with a lot of help from many friends."

They traced the problem to a broken rocker arm that allowed a lifter to clear its bore.

Stock Eliminator

The unwritten rule in Stock was that the only way to be competitive was to run a Chevy. And it seemed the only way to win was to have your Chevy prepared by Jenkins Competition. The Tri-Five Chevys pretty much owned Stock's middle classes. Stiff competition came from a number of racers who, like Jenkins, realized that building a winning Stocker really took doing your homework.

The Wenzel brothers beat the odds at the Nationals when their Z28 Camaro made it through a sea of Tri-Five Chevys to win Stock Eliminator. The NHRA first took a look at factory horsepower ratings in 1967 and did some re-rating. The Z28 Camaro with its 302-ci engine was one of the first cars refactored as the sanctioning body added 30 hp to Chevy's 290 rating. (Photo Courtesy Brian Kennedy)

The 1957 Ford Legal Cheater of Larry Walker stood its ground in Junior Stock, winning class more than it ever lost. Power came by way of a factory-blown 312-ci. Ford enthusiasts will note the 1958 hood.

Graham Douglas and Ed Forys put their knowledge as aerospace engineers to good use when building their 1960 Pontiac wagon. Powered by a 318-hp 389, the pair ran the 4,000-pound wonder in 1966 and 1967. The wagon was later campaigned by Paul Longenecker in F/Gas with an injected big-block Chevy.

The supercharged Fords of Larry Walker and Parham & Payne more than held their own against the Chevys, as did Arlen Vanke, who showed up at Indy with Bill Abraham and three Pontiacs to win two classes. The old saying goes the devil was in the details. If you wanted to win in Stock, you paid attention to them.

Graham Douglas and Ed Forys, a couple of aerospace engineers, paid attention to what was happening in Stock before building their 1960 Pontiac station wagon. Like all good racers, they chose their 318-hp wagon because it fell near bang on the class weight break in H/SA, which had a break of 14 pounds per cubic inch. They chose an automatic-equipped car for consistency and had Art Carr assist with tricking out the Jetaway transmission.

They said, "We removed the fluid coupler to reduce inertia, essentially making the transmission a standard shift. The shifts were pretty harsh and not wanting to continuously spend the money on broken axles, this idea was dropped. We had two levers, one for shifting the other to change the line pressure. When it came time to race you'd pull the lever to full pressure."

Working as aerospace engineers, the guys had access to computers that allowed them to enter gathered data to determine (as an example) ideal shift points. Rear suspension modifications to the wagon included Air Lift bags and a unique traction device that they devised themselves. Essentially, it consisted of three traction arms tied into one. The launch off the line was solid and with a g meter in place to measure gravitational pull, the wagon recorded 0.7 g on the green.

The pair ran the wagon in 1966 and 1967, winning class at the NHRA Winternationals in 1966 before winning the eliminator at both the AHRA and NHRA Winternationals in 1967. "We could run 0.32 seconds below our class elapsed time record (which was 14.72 midseason), which we never bumped." Fighting an uphill battle against the onslaught of Chevy sedan deliveries, they retired the wagon in mid-1967. And wouldn't you know it, it was a Jenkins-prepared delivery that won the world championship.

Gene Adams never missed a step. Running a small inch, 305-ci DeSoto Hemi gave his A/Fuel Dragster a weight advantage over the competition. The Gilmore chassis rail became the first Junior Fueler to crack 200 mph, when on August 3, 1968, driver Don Enriquez Jr. ran a 7.53 at 201.34 mph at Lions. Hilborn never made an intake that aligned with the DeSoto Hemi ports, so Adams made his own, using a Hilborn casting. The Hemi ran a reported 50 degrees advance and a 92-percent load of fuel. (Photo Courtesy Don Prieto)

Chapter Eight

1968
The Great Escape

Between riots, assassinations, and the ongoing conflict in Vietnam, it was a tumultuous year. The great escape seemed to be drag racing, where the number of those participating in the sport was approaching a million. Although the cars of Top Fuel (formerly referred by the NHRA as Fuel Dragster) and Funny Car still gave the greatest thrill, they couldn't match the door cars when it came to actual participation.

With a built-in handicap start system, even the novice door car driver had a fighting chance, at least on the local level. Nationally, the dedicated racers of Stock, Super Stock, and Modified Production shouldn't be considered anything less than professional.

The year 1968 saw the peak in factory involvement. Chrysler unleashed Hemi-powered A-Bodies (Darts and Barracudas), and Ford provided a limited run of race-prepared Cobra Jet Mustangs. Not to be left out, both Chevy and AMC countered in 1969.

Top Fuel

In 1968, Bennie "the Wizard" Osborn became the first drag racer to win back-to-back world championships. Driving his 392-ci Woody Gilmore Fueler, Osborn had defeated Prudhomme in 1967 with a 7.03, and in 1968, he took out John Mulligan with a 7.05. To close out the season, he won the AHRA World Finals at Kansas City. The icing on the cake for the Wizard was winning a $14,000 match race against Tom McEwen at Orange County International Raceway (OCIR), which was the largest payout ever offered for one race.

In total, Osborn won six T/F eliminator titles in 1968. Not bad at all for a car that was a few years old with an aging 392 Hemi (many competitors were switching to the new 426 Hemi). Consistency was the name of the game, and the Wizard built his cars to be just that.

"I ran a stock cubic inch 392 at the time when everyone was adding a stroker, running 460 or so cubic inches and blowing up" Osborn said, speaking to the increasing costs of competing. "I couldn't afford to take the chance in blowing up because if I did, I wouldn't be running the next week."

Osborn insisted that his combination was reliable because he never really leaned on it. He'd run a 95- to

Bennie Osborn's first taste of victory came at the 1962 AHRA Nationals, where his winning prize was a twin-engine Chevy Gas Dragster. Not fast enough for him, Osborn sold the car and went Fuel racing. This led to back-to-back world titles. Here, he's caught full throttle at the 1969 NHRA Winternationals. (Photo Courtesy Don Pietro)

What made the Shelby Super Snake fly was an Ed Pink Cammer, mounting a Pete Robinson magnesium blower, backed by a Schiefer clutch and a Donovan coupler. Don Long supplied the chassis. Driver Don Prudhomme kicked off the year by winning Top Fuel at the AHRA Winternationals. "Wild" Bill Carter was responsible for the fancy paint. (Photo Courtesy James Handy)

Running out of Bakersfield, the Ridge Route Terror of Warren-Coburn-Miller earned the nickname due to the amount of winning the team did on SoCal tracks. James Warren kicked off the year by winning the NHRA Winternationals. On September 23 he recorded Lions first six run when he ran a 6.98 during the track's 13th anniversary celebration. (Photo Courtesy James Handy)

98-percent load of nitro and stuck with tried-and-true parts, including a Hampton blower running 24-percent overdrive. A Hays clutch and M&H tires ensured the power got to the ground.

Ed Pink had come a long way since the days in 1947 when he earned pocket money sweeping the floors at Lou Baney's Hot Rod Heaven. By the time he hooked up with Lou once again in 1967, the "old Master" had developed a reputation as one of the sport's most respected engine builders. In 1968, he put his innovative mind to work and came up with a three-disk adjustable clutch.

Tired of spending too much time swapping the springs in the pressure plate, which required pulling the clutch pack from the car, Ed built a clutch pack that allowed spring adjustment without having to pull the pack. No doubt the three-disk setup helped Prudhomme harness the power of Baney's *Shelby Super Snake*. Prudhomme kicked off the season by winning the season-opening AHRA Winternationals.

The Ridge Route Terrors team of Warren-Coburn-Miller won the NHRA Winternationals, its first national event victory after coming close at Indy in 1967. Based in Bakersfield, Warren and Coburn took on financial partner Marvin Miller in 1968 and debuted a 180-inch Woody Gilmore car. At the Winternationals, James Warren singled in the final after opponent Dwight Salisbury failed to make the call. Don Garlits fell victim to Warren

in the third round and once told the *LA Times* that Warren in the 392-ci powered *Terror* was the toughest driver that he ever faced. The *Ridge Route Terror* rode on a set of M&H tires, which blanketed Goodyear's new 7222s in competition through 1968.

Garlits could always be counted on to run against the grain. At the Winternationals, he ran his *Swamp Rat XII-A*, a short 137-inch-wheelbase car that he felt could work. The experiment failed to show results and was back in the shop after Garlits's West Coast tour. *Swamp Rat XII-B*, a rebuilt *XII-A* with a longer 215-inch wheelbase, took Garlits to wins at the Springnationals, where he defeated John Mulligan, and the Nationals, where he defeated Steve Carbone.

Worth mentioning was Garlits's jaw-dropping 240-mph run at Alton in July, and a backup run of 238. Cars were going faster in 1968, but not that fast. More than a few questioned Alton's recording devises. Garlits closed the season winning the PDA championship, where he recorded a top speed of 222.76 mph.

Tim Beebe and partner John Mulligan had a great season in spite of a few incidents that robbed them of a couple national event wins. At the Springnationals, Mulligan held top speed and low ET, but in the final against Garlits he had to back off a lead due to a bad vibration. Turns out helper/tire changer Tom McEwen had installed

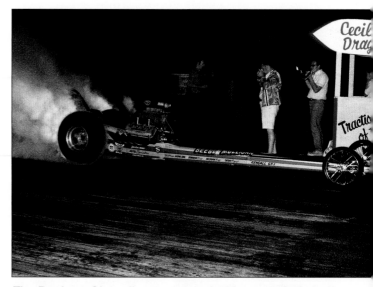

The Beebe & Sixt rail was updated with a new front half for 1968 by Race Car Specialties and reappeared as the Beebe & Mulligan car. The Zookeeper is seen here at Cecil County on June 21, where he set the track ET record with a 6.91. The team debuted a new Woody Gilmore car late in the season. (Photo Courtesy Michael Pottie)

the wrong lug nuts on a fresh set of wheels.

At the World Finals, Mulligan had a commanding lead on Osborn before his clutch went away. Before being replaced by a new Wood Gilmore car at the World Finals, the old Beebe & Sixt car, originally built in 1966, took Beebe & Mulligan to runner-up finishes at a handful of major events. At each of them, they held low ET, top speed, or both. Beebe built the ultra-reliable 392 for the car, incorporating 6:1 compression, a 23-percent overdriven blower, and the best parts from the likes of Mickey Thompson, Donovan, and Reath.

The team ran an 80-percent load of nitro. Unlike most Top Fuel teams of the day that ran 50 percent of the fuel through the blower and the other 50 percent through the port nozzles, Beebe ran 30 percent through the blower and the other 70 percent through the nozzles. Needless to say, hours were spent on the flow bench perfecting the setup. By season's end, Beebe & Mulligan had recorded 6.60 times at a NHRA record-holding 229.59 mph.

Jerry Ruth, seen here with the 204-inch Don Long Top Fueler he campaigned during 1967–1968, earned the title of King of the Northwest. By the close of the decade, he had won the Division 6 crown five times. Compare the wheelbase to what was popular at the beginning of the decade. (Photo Courtesy James Handy)

Top Gas

In Top Gas, you would be hard-pressed to pick a winner in a 16-car field because generally no more than a couple tenths separated the cars. Gary Cochran kicked the year off by winning the AHRA Winternationals, defeating

Rising Star

One of the sport's more versatile drivers, Steve Carbone, kicked off the year driving for Pete Robinson. Failing to fire in the finals of the AHRA Winternationals made it his last ride with Robinson before hooking up with John Bateman to drive his *Atlas Oil Tool Special*.

Carbone repaid Bateman the honor by winning the *Hot Rod* magazine meet. Playing musical seats, Carbone hopped in the Creitz & Donovan rail in 1969 and won the AHRA World Finals. He made one more switch before the end of 1969, when he took the seat of Larry Huff's *Soapy Sales* Fueler to win the NHRA World Championship.

Steve Carbone's star shone well into the 1970s. His career dates back to the early 1960s and is probably best remembered for the staging lane duel he held with Garlits at Indy in 1971. John Bateman is seen here in the Woody Gilmore chassis, Atlas Oil Tool Special. The car was good for 6.70 times, and a heck of a lot of local wins. (Photo Courtesy Don Prieto)

Rico Paris, caught in action here at the NHRA Winternationals, won Top Gas at Bakersfield and the NHRA Springnationals in 1968. Rico and his brother Peter also built a dominant twin-engine car in 1969. (Photo Courtesy Don Prieto)

Jack Jones. Gordon Collett won the NHRA Winternationals, defeating Jones. Schultz & Jones wouldn't be denied in 1968 though, winning the *Hot Rod* magazine meet and the NHRA Nationals by defeating Walt Rhoades.

At the AHRA finale, Bob Muravez, who was back in the *Freight Train* replacing Billy Scott, defeated Bob Noice in the final. Noice took his revenge by winning the NHRA World Finals with his early Hemi-powered car. Some would say lady luck was on Noice's side, as his invite to Tulsa came by way of a last-place finish in his Division 7 standings.

Mid-Eliminators

The Mid-Eliminator brackets saw a population explosion during 1968. Street gained competitors and ran 24 classes of cars: A/Gas through C/Street Roadster as well as Comp, which consisted of cars from A/Dragster down to E/Altered. A variation in combinations across the board was the widest, as competitors ran the gambit from destroked mills in Modified to the latest trend of running ClutchFlite transmissions in the Dragsters and the lower Altered classes.

The NHRA, which eliminated the Factory Experimental category at the end of 1967, continued its streamlining into 1968, when it eliminated the Modified Sports Production category at the end of the season due to low participation.

Altereds

The Fuel Altereds seemed to be enjoying an increase in popularity thanks to tracks such as Irwindale, which hosted the first big, all–Fuel Altered show in April. Billed as the "Roughest, Richest Roadster Riot in the History of Drag Racing," 16 of the best battled it out. The pots were still embarrassingly low for the Fuel Altereds ($300 to $500 to win compared to the $1,000 to $1,500 that Top Fuel and Funny Cars were receiving at similar events).

The Marcellus & Borsch Fuel Altered was a bear! The car weighed 1,500 pounds wet, rode on a 95-inch wheelbase, and was powered by a Marcellus-built 358. The Winged Express *made Fuel Altered's first 200-mph pass on September 23, 1967, at Irwindale, where it recorded a 200.44 mph. (Photo Courtesy Steve Reyes)*

Gabby Bleeker and his high-strung 1938 Bantam evolved with the decade and was a winner from the beginning to the end. The only car Gabby raced professionally, the Bantam started the 1960s with an Olds engine and ended with a Hemi. Winning mid-eliminator at the AHRA Nationals in 1961 was just the beginning. Gabby retired in 1968 shortly after defeating Willie Borsch in the AA/Fuel Altered final at Indy, where he ran 8.34 at 178 mph. (Photo Courtesy Steve Reyes)

Ben Christ was the promoter for the Gold Agency, and he did his best to improve the situation by arranging the first Fuel Altered National tour. The shows were so popular that they continued for the next four years, running at tracks across the United States and Canada.

Comp Eliminator is where the lower classed Altereds lived, running against everything from D class dragsters to injected Anglias. Gene Snow topped the tank of his Dart Funny Car with alcohol and ran B/A at the NHRA Winternationals. The well-worn 1966 Dodge Dart had enough oomph to win class. Carl Kirk in the Blackwood-Eckard-Kirk Anglia overcame a full 1-second handicap to win the Springnationals over the Ford 6–powered, E/A 1923 T-Roadster of Ted Kramer.

Pennsylvania motel manager Paul Luzader in his injected Chevy-powered 1932 Ford won Indy. His D/A hybrid set the class record in the process, running an 11.54. The Comp World title in 1968 belonged to Seattle's Ray Hadford driving the C/Dragster of Jim Green.

The Comp World title in 1968 belonged to Seattle's Ray Hadford driving the C/Dragster of Jim Green. A small-inch, injected Chevy was backed by a B&M ClutchFlite transmission. The combo had propelled the car to the class's first 8-second run the year before. Hadford repeated Green's 1967 Division 6 win in 1968. At the finals, Hadford defeated Canadian Bob Callahan with a 9.06 at 153.58 time.

A stroked Chevy measuring 352 ci made Harry Luzader's 1932 Ford a winner and record holder in both Gas and Altered classes. A 1937 Ford front axle, coil springs, and 4-link of Harry's own design out back gave the deuce the right stance. Backing the Chevy mill was a 4-speed and 5.38:1 rear gears. (Photo Courtesy Michael Pottie)

Powering the car was an injected small-block Chevy backed by a ClutchFlite transmission. It was a unique combo for a dragster, but it worked, propelling the car to the class's first 8-second run the year before. Hadford repeated Green's 1967 Division 6 win after taking on driving chores in 1968. At the finals, Hadford defeated Canadian Bob Callahan with a 9.06 at 153.58.

Gassers

Feeding the diehard fans' belief that Supercharged Gas was all but dead were the NHRA rule changes that now allowed the cars to use non-original equipment chassis. Further fueling the dismay was the NHRA com-bining blown Gas with blown Street Roasters. Further, the category saw a continue desertion of racers who headed for the greener (more financially lucrative) pastures of Funny Car. Big John Mazmanian was a big loss in 1968, when he gave up his football to K. S. Pittman and joined the march to the Funnies.

The NHRA Street Eliminator category was renamed *Modified Eliminator* after the Winternationals, and it was where the unblown Gas cars were found (among others). Fred Hurst and his injected Hemi 1968 Barracuda won the world title, defeating Ed Hedrick in Bill Jenkins's A/MP Camaro with a 9.45 at 147.59 mph. Hurst began racing A/G back in 1963 with his Willys, which at the time relied upon Pontiac for power. In 1965, he began an alliance with Chrysler, replacing the Pontiac engine with an injected Hemi. The following season, he picked up the A/G national record with a 9.87 at 138.89 mph. Just as was the case with Ohio George and Ford, Fred was told by Chrysler reps that they weren't selling Willys and they insisted on him running the Barracuda.

Michigan's Sam Gianino, a standout in Modified well into the 1970s, wheeled his D/G 1957 Corvette to a win at the Nationals over the A/XS Barracuda of Dave Koffel. Koffel had previously bombed his class record by 0.45. In the final against Sam, Koffel's line lock failed him and caused the Barracuda to roll through the starting beams. Koffel had previously won class at the Winternationals and

Putting a new look on the old 1948 to 1951 Austin were the Herreras, who debuted this flip-up AA/GS in 1968. The fiberglass body by Contemporary featured a 4-inch chop. Famed West Coast engine builder Jack Bayer assembled the 464-ci Hemi, which helped Manuel Herrera propel the car to 8.80 times approaching 160 mph. (Photo Courtesy Michael Pottie)

In contrast to the Herreras' Austin was the AA/GS Mustang of Skip Hess that debuted in 1968. Revell sponsored the Mustang while Ford supplied all the goods, including the SOHC 427 that Ed Pink prepared. Jim Kirby built the chassis and the famed Rollin "Molly" Sanders applied the paint. The Mustang ran a best of 8.32 at 168.75 mph on gas, and mid-7s at 180 on alcohol for the occasional Funny Car show. (Photo Courtesy of James Handy)

Street Eliminator had its variety, and few stood out like Jerry Hays's big-block Chevy-powered A/SR. Jerry initially ran a Gene Adams Oldsmobile engine in his 1928 Ford that earned him A/SR honors at the 1964 NHRA Winternationals. In 1966, he made the switch to Chevy and went on to win class at AHRA and NHRA winter meets, as well as Bakersfield and the Hot Rod *magazine race. Jerry successfully ran the Roadster into the 1970s. (Photo Courtesy Michael Pottie)*

A prominent name in 1960s Gas was John Loper. From its debut in 1963, his Chevy-powered A/G Little Hoss *Anglia dominated. Loper knew all the tricks and was a master engine builder. He'd pick up more than his share of national event victories and class records throughout the decade. (Photo Courtesy Michael Pottie)*

Springnationals with the Barracuda, which featured an acid-dipped body and a tube chassis that was designed by Chrysler engineers.

After a career that dated back to the 1950s and included a number of interesting record-setting combinations, the Barracuda was Koffel's final drag racing effort before settling into his job with Chrysler's racing program.

Sports Production

Sports Production seems to be the forgotten category of Street Eliminator. Coming out of nowhere to win Street at the NHRA Winternationals and Springnationals was Bo Laws in Bruce Behrens's D/SP 1967 Corvette. The second-generation Corvette, as aerodynamically pleasing as it was, was generally passed over by drag racers due to its weak link independent rear suspension.

A standout in the fading years of Sports Production was Bo Laws and his black-and-gold 1967 Corvette. Powered by a 390-hp 427, Laws made plenty of advancements that benefitted future Corvette racers. (Photo Courtesy Steve Reyes)

Laws was the first to work out the breakage problem (winning praise from future generations) by replacing the stock U-joints with those built for a 1-ton Chevy truck. Though an improvement, they still didn't last long. Laws discovered that when the car squatted coming off the line, it would exert too much side pressure on the needle bearings and cause them to fail. He eliminated the problem by replacing the needle bearings with brass bushings. Next, he removed the clips that retained the axles, which allowed them to slide out about a 1/4 inch when he accelerated.

The posi unit was another weak spot, and Laws could do little about it, except carry a spare. To make the R&R easier, he cut an access hole in the floorboard, allowing two people to swap out the third member in about 25 minutes. It was a busted rear end that did Laws in at Indy, leaving the door open for Sam Gianino in his Hilborn-injected Corvette to win the eliminator.

Experimental Stock /Funny Car

While the AHRA ran a separate category for the Funny Cars, the NHRA continued to lump their Supercharged Experimental Stock/Funny Cars into Super Eliminator. S/XS rules for 1968 stated the class was for cars with blowers or excessive engine relocation and allowed for a minimum weight of 2,000 pounds. The NHRA carried over A/XS from 1967 but dropped the remaining three classes.

Al Graeber's Tickle Me Pink *outfit really shows a contrast in what we see in the Funny Car pits today. Under the 1967 Charger skin lays a chassis fabricated by Graeber. The body was unique. Unlike most Funny Cars of the day (or today), where the whole body hinges at the rear, the body on Graeber's car remained stationary while the roof was hinged and the front clip was removable. (Photo Courtesy Carl Rubrecht)*

King of the Funnies, Dyno Don Nicholson gave up the seat in the fall of 1968. Dyno Don was seeing too many guys getting burnt for his liking and wanted out before the same thing happened to him. Showing no regrets about giving up the seat, Nicholson was quoted a year or so later saying, "The only thing I like about today's Funnies is that I'm not in one." (Photo Courtesy Richard Nicholson)

The Funny Car became a little funnier this year when Chrysler's Hemi started showing up more frequently in Chevys, Fords, and Pontiacs. Dick Loehr made the switch in his *Stampede* Mustang and won the AHRA World Finals. Brand loyalty being what it was, more than a few fans were up in arms.

Though a little more expensive to maintain, the overhead cam–powered Fords and Mercurys held more than their own against the Hemis. Some would argue that the Cammer could outperform a comparable Hemi due to its better breathing capabilities and its ability to reach higher RPM quicker. If there was one weakness, outside of availability (Ford ended production in 1967), it was that the engine was based upon the existing 427 wedge block. Main webbing and the existing cam hole were known weak spots where cracking would occur.

Ed Schartman's Cougar was state of the art in 1968 with its 120-inch Logghe chassis, SOHC 427, and C-6 transmission. Horsepower of the 427 was now in the range of 1,500, thanks in large part to advancements in fuel delivery. Schartman raced the car into 1969, cranking out 7.50 times at a shade over 190 miles per hour. He re-bodied the car in 1969 with a new Cougar. (Photo Courtesy Michael Pottie)

Jungle Jim Liberman started the year running a pair of Chevy IIs before making the move to a pair of new Novas late in the season. This 1967 Chevy II featured a Logghe Chassis that went under one of the Novas. A big-block Chevy and Art Carr transmission kept Jim in the winnings. You want to talk about a short ramp truck . . . (Photo Courtesy James Handy)

Dyno Don Nicholson started the year by winning OCIR's big Funny Car bash with his 1967 Comet before hopping into a SS/EA Cobra Jet Mustang for the NHRA Winternationals. It was a short weekend for Nicholson, whose 428 spun a bearing during qualifying. The car was a one-race deal for Nicholson, who was back in the Funny Car days later. In May, he put the Comet to bed and debuted his Cougar *Eliminator*, the ex-STP Funny Car of Rupp & Steffey.

Nicholson carried on his crusade to make Funny Cars safer. Exploding blowers and failed transmissions were ongoing issues that were only exasperated by the increased demands builders were putting on their drivelines. Nicholson's push gained a number of supporters who liked his idea. For the previous couple of years, racers had been watching the cost of running a Funny Car escalate. Nicholson's ideas received pushback from track operators; C. J. Hart at Lions spoke out in the trade papers, voicing the general consensus that too few people wanted to stand in the way of Funny Car progression. By the end of October, Nicholson had had his fill of the Funny Cars and relinquished the seat of his Cougar to Frank Oglesby. Nicholson's last outing was at a match race at Piedmont, where he ran a best of 7.32.

Bruce Larson showed that the Chevys could still get it done, as he had the quickest Funny Car for a while when his 427-powered *USA-1* Camaro recorded a 7.41 at the Super Stock Nationals in July. Under load, the Chevys weren't quite as reliable as the thicker, stronger Chrysler Hemi. In the process of running his 7.41, Larson watched his engine go south. He recalled having to keep the nitro load around 70 to 75 percent to prevent cracking blocks. He found they would usually break at the top of the main bearing saddle.

Larson stated that all in all, the 7.41 run was beneficial.

"It cost me a $1,000 in parts, but I got back $3,000 in publicity," he said.

It also led to an increase in match race dates. With

*The Jack Groner/Jim St. Clair **LimeFire** Barracuda was one of the nation's finest looking and running Funny Cars in 1968. Clare Sanders was the main man behind the Keith Black Hemi and beefed TorqueFlite. The Barracuda retained near stock dimensions and carried many factory trim pieces. According to Sanders, the **LimeFire** was the second Barracuda Funny Car produced and was formed by Ron Pellegrini using a Hertz rental car. (Photo Courtesy Bill Truby)*

*Feeling it to be a safer bet, Doug Thorley chose to go the mid-engine route when he built his **Javelin I**. The car debuted in May 1968, powered by an AMC mill backed by a B&M Tork Master. The AMC engine gave way to a Hemi in short order and set the record with a 207-mph blast. Wheelbase of the Woody Gilmore chassis was 122 inches. With driver Norm Weekly up against the windshield, it looks like that chassis could have used a few more inches. (Photo Courtesy Don Prieto)*

payouts in the $700 to $1,000 range and running anywhere from three to five bouts a week, the Chevy guys could afford to replace the reasonably inexpensive blocks.

Jungle Jim Liberman, no longer splitting time driving Lew Arrington's Pontiac and his own 1967 Chevy II, debuted not one but two nearly identical Nova Funny Cars in the early fall. He hired Clare Sanders out of the *LimeFire* Barracuda to run one Nova, a new Logghe car carrying Kanuika sponsorship, while Liberman himself ran a Goodies-sponsored Nova that rode on the Logghe chassis from his 1967 Chevy II.

The *LimeFire*, considered one of the era's most beautiful Funny Cars, debuted in the fall of 1967. The Barracuda reflected just how Funny Cars were built during that period, incorporating many factory trim pieces. The car featured a Logghe chassis and was the quickest Funny Car on the West Coast after recording a 7.71 at OCIR in January 1968. I digress a bit here, but it's interesting to note that Leon Fitzgerald and his *Pure Heaven II* Fuel

Altered recorded a best of 7.71 shortly before. A number of West Coast tracks took advantage of the competing times and hosted Funny Car versus Fuel Altered shows.

Clare Sanders ran the *LimeFire* through the season, match racing the wheels off of it and wearing out the thin wall chassis before hooking up with Jungle Jim. In an NHRA interview, Sanders recalled his first run in a Liberman car.

"I worked on Jim's crew while the second car was being built, and we were at a match race in Suffolk, Virginia, one night, and he caught me totally off guard when he said, 'You know, I've never seen my car make a run. Why don't you drive it tonight?'" she said. "I put on my fire suit with his helmet, goggles, and we beat Malcolm Durham (Chevy-powered Corvair) that evening with a new track record."

Chevy lost out on 1967 Nationals winner Doug Thorley when he passed his two Corvairs to Joe Pisano and Dick Bourgeois. Pisano wrecked the Nationals winner

Hayden Proffitt and the new Rebel Funny Car, seen here at its OCIR debut in March, briefly held the NHRA ET record with an 8.11. Proffitt had one of the best wrench men in the business, Amos Saterlee, helping to keep the 438-ci engine together. (Photo Courtesy Phil Bellomy)

Before riding off into the sunset, Gene Conway had a lot of success with his Hemi-powered Jeep Funny Car. In match race competition, Conway was able to coax 8.0 times out of his Destroyer. Rule changes for 1970 saw the topless cars tossed from the NHRA Funny Car. (Photo Courtesy Forrest Bond)

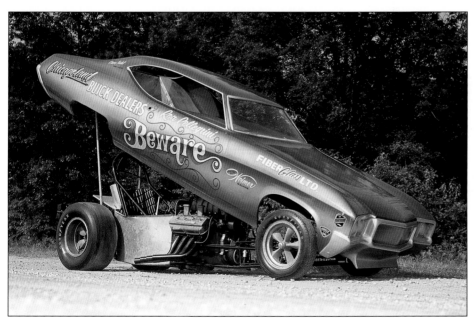

in short order, while Bourgeois, who lured mechanic Earl Wade away from Dyno Don, had a great season. Thorley, now with AMC, debuted a mid-engine AMC Javelin Funny Car in May. That gave the manufacturer two competing Funny Cars, as Hayden Proffitt campaigned the Grant Industries–sponsored Rebel SST.

Running the Rebel made Proffitt the first to race at least one car successfully from each of America's four leading auto manufacturers. Both the Proffitt and Thorley cars ran AMC mills. Proffitt's Rebel counting on a poked and stroked 343 measuring 438-ci, while Thorley's engine measured out to 449 ci. Banzai Bill Hayes initially campaigned the Grant Industries SST in 1967 but was sidelined due to a back injury. When Proffitt took over, he junked the ill-handling chassis and replaced it with a Bill Thomas chassis that he pulled from a Camaro he had planned on running prior to signing with AMC.

The Rebel was rebuilt prior to the 1968 season and received a new Logghe chassis and a red, white, and blue paint job. Though not the most competitive car, reaching low 8s at a little over 190 mph, Proffitt picked and chose his battles and won his share of races. The full potential of the AMC engine was limited by the 60- to 65-percent load it could handle.

Ron Pellegrini, owner of Fiberglass Ltd., built and campaigned this unique backward flip-up Buick Skylark in 1968. The advanced chassis was narrow and similar in design to the Top Eliminator dragsters, minus the upright rails. The lack of the extra tubing made the car flex an excessive amount, leading to poor handling. Pellegrini managed 7.70 times at 190 mph before crashing the car. (Photo Courtesy Paul Shedlik)

Anything beyond that and the poor sealing block would blow out head gaskets.

Proffitt wanted to make a switch to a Chrysler Hemi but the idea was nixed by AMC, which wanted to keep the car all AMC. Feeling he had taken the car as far as he could, Proffitt moved on to other ventures at the end of the season. Thorley swapped out his AMC mill for a Keith Black Hemi and set the class record in 1969 with a 207-mph run. The car lasted until June 1969 before being destroyed after becoming airborne at Irwindale. Thorley ran a full belly pan, and once air got under the car, well, that was it.

Super Stock Eliminator

In Super Stock it was factory war all the way. Ford challenged with six specially prepared Cobra Jet Mustangs and a string of 427 Fairlanes. Chrysler unleashed a run of Hemi Barracudas and Darts. The initial six Mustangs were specially prepared by Holman-Moody-Stroppe and debuted at the NHRA Winternationals. Modifications included a high-flow aluminum intake manifold, tube headers, forged pistons and rods, a 0.600-lift camshaft, 11:1 compression, a three-point roll bar, and a trunk-mounted battery.

The 427 ci in a Fairlane was a killer combo in either 410-hp, single 4-barrel form or as the more potent 425-hp, twin 4-barrel version. Tom Schumacher, Richard Charbonneau, Bill Ireland, and Jerry Harvey (whose 425-hp **The Quiet One** *is caught here in action) were just a few who proved the combination a winner. (Photo Courtesy Rob Potter)*

Al Joniec would run an easy 11.83 at the Winternationals with his Cobra Jet Mustang on an existing 11.93 record. Joniec recalled, "Ford engineers feared the Cobra Jet cars would run too fast, forcing the NHRA to lower the class index." As proof of the combo's reliability, Joniec noted that he never opened his hood all weekend.

As expected, the Mustangs dominated the category. The SS/EA class final boiled down to the Mustangs of Al Joniec and Hubert Platt. Well, it was Ford that decided who would win (by coin toss), and Platt lost the toss. Joniec marched on to the category final, where he beat the redlighting Mopar of Dave Wren with an easy 12.50.

Chrysler debuted its Hemi A-Bodies at the Springnationals. Few would deny that these cars were the biggest and baddest cars ever unleashed by an American manufacturer. Starting with the Hemi, right from factory the engine carried twin 650 Holleys on an aluminum intake, 12.5:1 compression, and Hooker Headers. The 70 Barracudas and 80 Darts produced were handed to Hurst-Campbell to complete the mods, which included the addition of a fiberglass hood with a 5-inch scoop, fiberglass fenders, thin steel front bumper and doors, 0.080 thin-gauge glass, lightweight Plexiglas side windows that were raised and lowered by strap (as opposed to cranks), and a trunk-mounted battery.

Cars equipped with the A833 4-speeds received the Dana 60 rear end while cars equipped with the 727 automatic transmissions received the 8.75 rear end. Rear gears were either 4.56 or 4.88. The 1968 SS/B Hemi Barracuda campaigned by Sox and Martin would hit a 10.30 time on its initial outing, a phenomenal 0.70 below the existing national record.

Arlen Vanke had one of the more successful Hemi Barracudas in 1968 and won S/S Eliminator at the Nationals that year. He returned in 1969 with new paint on the Barracuda and won the AHRA Winternationals. Here he is caught in action at the NHRA winter meet, where he set the class record with a 10.61. (Photo Courtesy Brian Kennedy)

ning time in class was below the existing class record then it became the new record, assuming the car passed inspection.

In SS/B, Sox, coming off of a category win at the Springnationals, bowed to Chrysler reps' request and reluctantly lost in the class final to Wiley Cossey. Showing his displeasure, Sox left the line on the second yellow, drawing a redlight. He refused to stop for a fuel check and instead loaded the Barracuda and left the grounds.

Grumpy Jenkins, the biggest thorn in Chrysler's side, played his hand at Indy, running his 75-pound lighter 1967 Camaro in SS/C and winning class. Dave Strickler ran Grumpy's 1968 Camaro in A/MP but had little luck. At the World Finals in October, Jenkins made a grand entrance arriving with four cars in total: two Camaros, an SS/D Nova, and the SS/F Camaro of Dave Strickler. The four-car showing paid off for Jenkins, as Strickler won Super Stock while Jenkins in his Nova was runner-up. His A/MP Camaro driven by Ed Hedrick was runner-up to Fred Hurst in Street Eliminator.

At Indy, the NHRA tried something different in hopes of dulling the pain of "break-out" racing, ending the racers' practice of jumping on their brakes in hopes of not running quicker than the class record. The thinking from the racers' perspective was to have a soft record to run against. The NHRA's revised rule saw to it that if the win-

Ron Mancini and his 440-ci Dart briefly held the SS/EA elapsed time record in the spring of 1968 with a 12.02. Considering how the Cobra Jet Mustangs dominated that year, it was quite the feat. Mancini would have greater success with his Hemi Dart that followed. (Photo Courtesy Ed Aigner)

Talk about saturation. Dick Landy was up to his neck in factory-supported cars in 1968. With his brother Mike and Bob Lambeck sharing in the driving chores, Dandy Dick campaigned seven different cars through the year, from an SS/B Hemi Dart down to D/SA 440-ci Coronet. The 440-ci Dart seen here held the SS/EA class mile per hour record with a 118.26. (Photo Courtesy Michael Pottie)

The 1968 Super Stock world champ Dave Strickler counted on this Jenkins Competition–prepped Z28 to get the job done. Strickler dropped a rat motor in the Camaro in 1969, painted it white, and made a heads-up match racer out of it.

Ed Hedrick drove Grumpy Jenkins's L78, SS/D Nova through 1968. An original 327 car, Chevy used the Nova as a test mule in Warren, Michigan, before passing it on to Jenkins. Hedrick won class at the Springnationals and recalls the best time turned for the Nova was an 11.17 recorded while qualifying at Indy.

By the end of the season, a good number of drivers were fed up with the current Super Stock "run too fast and you lose" format and approached the NHRA seeking a professional heads-up category. Buddy Martin was the spokesman on behalf of the group and presented rules that would be similar to those run at the recent Super Stock Nationals. Engines would have to be of the same manufacturer as the body and limited to a maximum of 427 ci. No blowers or injectors permitted though any carburetor, manifold, and camshaft would be acceptable. Hood scoops and lightweight body panels would also be permitted, and all cars, regardless of engine, would carry the same minimum weight of 2,800 pounds. Sounded great, but the NHRA didn't think so and balked at the idea.

Stock Eliminator

The NHRA relaxed Stock rules and allow the use of aftermarket reground camshafts. To quote the rulebook: "Stock: Regrinding to factory specifications permitted, but stock duration, overlap, and maximum lift must be maintained. No exceptions."

Note the rules said nothing about lobe angle, which would affect ramp speed, a point many racers took advantage of. The changes added greatly to the fact that class records fell on average of 0.50 seconds from the previous year. Another factor affecting the drop in elapsed times was the implementation of the no break-out rule in final round eliminations.

Hot Rod magazine editor Jim McFarland drove the Sox & Martin E/SA 340-ci Barracuda to a runner-up finish at the NHRA Winternationals. The Barracuda was one of three Sox & Martin cars in attendance at the Winternationals. Factory involvement you say? Check out the Michigan license plate. The Barracuda was a one-race car for Sox & Martin and disappeared as quickly as it appeared.

In Stock there was plenty of room for the unordinary. This 1959 Plymouth made the scene with a 361-ci engine. With 305 hp on tap, the Fury was a good fit for E/SA. Note the header collector running out of the top of the wheel well. (Photo Courtesy Rob Potter)

I don't think people realize just how involved in drag racing Oldsmobile really was. Ron Garey did his part to enlighten the masses when he won the NHRA Springnationals with his W-31-powered Cutlass.

In the mid-classes, Tri-Five Chevys with their 4-speeds and Hydra-matics retained their hold. A little over 50 percent of Stock records were held by Chevys, which shouldn't be a surprise to anyone considering the seemingly endless number of combinations available. Slowly but surely, new iron was sneaking in as factory support blossomed. Ron Garey gave Oldsmobile something to cheer about when he won the NHRA Springnationals with his 350-ci, 325-hp E/S Cutlass. No doubt Dale Smith, the gentleman who headed Oldsmobile's clandestine racing efforts, was beside himself, after all this was the manufacturer's first national event victory.

Below: The 1968 NHRA Stock World champ was Dave Boertman, whose 283-powered 1959 Biscayne defeated the 1966 427-ci Biscayne of Bill Izykowski. Both recalled the poor track condition, noting there was no traction to be had. Says Boertman, "The only reason I won was because I had a lower powered car and didn't spin the tires as much." He power-shifted the Q/Stocker to a final round 15.10. Here the Biscayne is seen at the Winternationals in 1969 where Boert-man won class. (Photo Courtesy Don Prieto)

In the world of Funny Cars, where Barracudas and Chargers were dominant, Fred Goeske's Road Runner really stood out. Fearless Fred's one big win in the Plymouth came at the Popular Hot Rodding *meet held at Martin, Michigan. Contemporary Fiberglass had the chore of laying up Funny Car's one and only Road Runner. (Photo Courtesy Don Prieto)*

Chapter Nine

1969
Move Up or Move Over

Calling 1969 the year of the Funny Car just may be an understatement. AA/FD, once the sports leader, had seen little change over the past couple of seasons, and it was costing the king his throne. In comparison, Funny Cars, which officially gained their own eliminator program in 1969, with their long, smoky burnouts, easily identifiable bodies, and continuously improving ETs, brought a new level of excitement. They were drawing the larger crowds and reaping larger match race payouts.

Even the heads-up and match race Super Stock cars were encroaching on sacred ground. So popular were these cars that the AHRA introduced a heads-up category in 1968 and crowned its first world champion in 1969. Both Chevy and AMC joined the factory wars in Super Stock. Chevy built 69 Camaros powered by its all-aluminum ZL1, 427, and AMC had Hurst Corporation prepare 50 AMXs powered by the 390-ci engine.

Top Fuel

The Winternationals have always been a great show. Adding to the excitement was the fact that teams often debuted new cars at the season opener. The 1969 Winternationals were no exception. Connie Kalitta made the first showing with Ford's new Boss 429. The engine showed promise, laying down a 7.29 at 209 mph during qualifying before melting a piston.

The Ramchargers debuted a new Woody Gilmore car at the AHRA Winternationals with new driver Leroy "the Israel Rocket" Goldstein at the wheel. It would be the Ramchargers' last year in Top Fuel, and they made it a good one. Goldstein set low elapsed time at the AHRA meet with a 6.89 and drove around a 32-car field to defeat Cliff Zink in the final. He followed with a win at the AHRA Springnationals, defeating Prudhomme in the final, then won the U.S Fuel and Gas Championship, which was at New York National Speedway. The Ramchargers team ended its stay in Top Fuel as the NHRA's Division 3 points champion and the AHRA World Champs.

Some would say that by 1969 the Funny Car had surpassed the Top Fuel Dragster as the sport's top draw. Funny Car saw an influx of a number of Top Fuel teams that chose to cash in on the Funny Car's popularity (with their increased demand and large payouts) and campaign cars in both categories. Top Fuel pilots Chris Karamesines and Tom McEwen each chose to run a Barracuda;

The Ramchargers' last year in Top Fuel was a formidable one. The team debuted its new 185-inch Woody Gilmore car at the AHRA Winternationals and won the event with a 6.89. Here at the NHRA Winternationals, Goldstein qualified third and lasted until the semifinals. (Photo Courtesy Don Prieto)

The Snake debuted his **Wynn's Winder** *late in 1968 and kicked off the new season as runner-up at the NHRA Winternationals. The car used a Don Long chassis, Hanna body, and an all-mighty Keith Black Hemi to record 7.50 times. (Photo Courtesy James Handy)*

Beebe & Mulligan took Indy by storm, setting low ET with a 6.43 in the Ramchargers' 426-ci powered car. Sadly, it was Mulligan's last race. (Photo Courtesy Steve Reyes)

Karamesines in a new Logghe car and McEwen in the old Candies & Hughes, Exhibition Engineering car. Connie Kalitta jumped into Funny Car, building a Mustang as a stablemate to his Top Fueler.

A sullen Prudhomme won Indy, defeating Kelly Brown in Leland Kolb's AA/FD. Prudhomme was one of the few who were making use of one of Leonard Abbott's Lenco Shur/Shift overdrive transmissions. Optional on the Lenco was a reverse gear. The Midwest team of Powers & Riley first introduced the reverse gear earlier in the season. It eliminated the need to physically push a car back to the line. The Lenco transmission, which really

The Newport Beach–based Smothers Brothers/Beach Boys Top Fueler was originally owned by Jim Busby before being sold to Dwight Salisbury. Hank Westmoreland took over driving from Salisbury and recorded 6.40s at a little over 230. Roy Fjastad's SPE built the chassis, while Ed Pink built the 392-ci Hemi. Westmoreland would win Top Fuel at the 1969 NHRA Springnationals with a 6.80 at 214.79 mph. Previous wins by the team included the 1966 Las Vegas Invitational and Mickey Thompson's 200-mph Championship race at Lions. (Photo Courtesy James Handy)

wasn't a transmission per se, allowed for a steeper rear gear for quicker off the line launches. A shift mid-track put the car into high gear.

One wonders what difference it may have made for John Mulligan if he had a Lenco box. Mulligan started the year off by winning his first-ever national event, the NHRA Winternationals, where he defeated Prudhomme in the final with a 6.95 at 211.38 mph. At Indy, Mulligan set low ET with a 6.43, which up until that point was the quickest time turned by a Top Fueler. No doubt Beebe & Mulligan's *Fighting Irish* was a favorite to win.

Jack Jones in the Schultz & Jones car set the class record at the World Finals with a 7.39 before defeating Norm Wilcox to capture the world title. A 460-ci Hemi got it done for Jones along with a multidisc Schiefer clutch and sticky M&H tires. (Photo Courtesy Michael Pottie)

In the first round of eliminations, the Zookeeper faced Tommy Ivo and defeated him with a 6.62 at 187.67 mph. But all hell broke loose just short of the finish line when Mulligan's clutch exploded. The explosion damaged the engine, which ignited oil and sent the burning dragster into the guardrail. Mulligan was rushed to the hospital, where he was treated for burns to his head and arms and severe cuts on both legs. Seemingly on the path to recovery, Mulligan took a turn for the worse and succumbed to his injuries a couple weeks later.

In the immediate aftermath of the Mulligan accident, SEMA, with the input of aftermarket manufacturers, recommended the following changes, which were quickly implemented.

- Aluminum direct-drive bellhousings must have a steel liner.
- A 1/4-inch steel plate must be affixed to the front of the bellhousing in a manner that will not allow shrapnel to escape even if the engine becomes disengaged from the driveline.
- It is advisable that an inspection hole in the bellhousing be provided. The hole must be on the back side, securely covered, and must not exceed the 90-degree angle of the bellhousing.

Top Gas

Jack Jones in the Schultz & Jones car was one that could never be sold short, as Jones proved in 1968. At the World Finals in 1969, he set the record with a 7.39, an ET that few could touch. A 460-ci Hemi got it done for Jack along with a multidisc Schiefer clutch and sticky M&H tires. Jones would win Indy in 1970 and come close to repeating his World Finals win. With an engine borrowed from the team of Glenn & Schultz, he'd play runner-up to Ray Motes.

By 1969, most competitors in Top Gas had adopted Top Fuel technology, which made it extra tough to name a standout. A smart man never bet against the likes of Bob Muravez, Hirata & Hobbs, Mark Pieri, Bob Noice, or Domenic (D. A.) Santucci. At the Nationals, D. A. qualified No. 1 with a 7.58. He spent a good part of the evening celebrating with fellow racers, hopping from one sponsor's suite to another, taking a nightcap, or two. By the end of the night, he was feeling no pain. Morning came too early for D. A., and he had to rush to make class runoffs.

Suffering the effects of the night before, D. A. popped in a stick of Wrigleys, which he forgot to spit out before heading for eliminations. When he nailed the throttle on the green, the gum lodged in his throat. No panic in D. A. though, as he figured when he popped the chute the gum would dislodge. Well, it didn't quite work out that way. D. A. brought the car to a quick halt and, with consciousness fading, alerted track officials that he was in dire need of assistance. An on-track official quickly loaded D. A. into an ambulance and rushed him off to hospital. By the time they arrived, D. A. had lost consciousness. Doctors removed the gum and held D. A. overnight for observation. The next day, he returned to the track to defeat Dick McFarland in the Hirata & Hobbs car with a 7.65 at 193.94 mph to win the eliminator.

Funny Car

Roland Leong left Top Fuel behind and debuted his *Hawaiian* Charger Funny Car at the 1969 NHRA Winter-

Roland Leong's **Hawaiian** *Charger, off to meet its destiny. The well-built Logghe chassis and cage protected Larry Reyes when the car became airborne. By May 30, Leong had a new mini Charger up and going. (Photo Courtesy Don Prieto)*

Big John Mazmanian towered over the competition in more ways than one. His nephew Rich Siroonian is in the background. Mazmanian's dominance in Gas carried into Funny Car. In 1969, Mazmanian added Mike Cook (former driver of Stone, Woods, & Cook) as his chief mechanic. (Photo Courtesy Don Prieto)

The **Chi-Town Hustler** *of Pat Minick (driver), John Farkonas, and Austin Coil won the UDRA Midwest Funny Car Championship in 1969. The team was credited with introducing the long, smoky burnout to Funny Car and the between round teardown. Minick stated, "The perception was that we blew up a lot but what we would do was take the preventive measure of tearing down between rounds." (Photo Courtesy James Handy)*

nationals. And what a debut it was. Larry Reyes, a veteran driver who showed nothing but success in 1968 driving the *Super Cuda* Funny Car, was hired to drive, and almost immediately raised concerns about the way the Charger was handling. He qualified the virgin car, barely making the field with an 8.33.

Reyes recalled that the car skated around, wanting to swamp ends. During qualifying, he backed off early and popped the chute to save the car from coming loose. In the first round of eliminations, Reyes had just cleared the lights after running an 8.14 against the Chevy Nova of Larry Christopherson when the real show began.

At approximately 190 mph, the Charger became airborne, swapping ends and sailing through the air upside down before coming down on its roof and rolling over onto its wheels. Miraculously, Reyes emerged unscathed, but the Charger was done. It was back to square one for Leong, who immediately ordered up a new Logghe chassis and mini Charger body.

Gene Snow was another who campaigned a mini Charger. His *Rambunctious* became the first Funny Car to crack 200 mph. Working closely with Crower in developing the Crowerglide, a four-disc clutch pack, Snow hit the mark for the first time at Dickson, Texas, in the fall of 1969. And those so called "mini" Chargers, just how mini were they? Well, NHRA rules of the day dictated that all Funnies had to be within 10 percent of the stock length and no narrower than 66 inches side to side, measured across the wheel openings. A stock 1968–1970 Charger measured 208 inches in length and 77 inches across the wheel openings.

The crew of the *Chi-Town Hustler* (Austin Coil, Pat Minnick, and John Farkonas) wasn't too concerned about the NHRA rules when building its Charger for 1969. As the guys focused their attention on match racing, UDRA, and AHRA races, they set up their car in a manner that they felt was best. The newly formed Fiberglass Ltd. body was sliced and diced to meet the dimensions the guys were after.

The location of the Ramchargers' provided 426 dictated the length of the hood and where the cockpit would be located. To lower the car, the driver was positioned to the left of the driveline as opposed to the common practice of positioning the driver over top of it. To compensate, the engine and transmission were offset to the right. John Farkonas put his trusty slide rule to work and came up with an ideal body rake of 18 degrees. This helped prevent lift on the top end, which seemed to be an issue with many Funny Cars.

The *Chi-Town Charger* is credited as being the Funny Car that introduced the long, smoky burnout. Pat Minnick perfected the smoke show during a match race against a Top Fuel car in Springfield, Illinois.

"It was done more to amuse the fans," Minnick said. "After seeing the Top Fuel car light them up, I tried it with the Funny Car, and it became a real crowd pleaser. All of a sudden, every track owner wanted the Funny Cars to be doing them."

Although the fans loved it, Austin Coil initially hated it. People were no longer interested in elapsed times and top speeds; they all wanted to see the big burnouts. Of course, a side benefit of the long burnout was improved traction, which led to quicker quarter-mile times.

After five years on the sidelines, Mickey Thompson returned to drag racing as a participant, and in a big way. Under his umbrella ran two Mustang Funny Cars and a heads-up Super Stock Mustang driven by Butch Leal. Dan Ongais piloted Thompson's *Mach I,* while Pat Foster piloted the *Mach II.*

An innovative leader from way back, Thompson proved he hadn't missed a step when he had Foster and John Buttera build the narrow Top Fuel–style chassis for the Mustangs. Buttera began his career in his native Kenosha, Wisconsin, where he teamed with Dennis Rollain to form R&B Chassis. It was Thompson who lured Buttera west to Southern California with a promise of work. Buttera's first job was helping out with Thompson's Challenger II land speed record car. Poor weather prevented

Don Schumacher was another who found happiness behind the wheel of a Plymouth Barracuda. This one was originally built for Butch Leal. Schumacher would win the AHRA Nationals in 1969 and set low ET at Indy with a 7.22. Ed Pink provided the power while the chassis was built by Logghe. The Goodyear tires were 16x12. (Photo Courtesy Don Prieto)

Mickey Thompson kicked off the year with two new Mustangs driven by Pat Foster and Danny Ongais. Ongais (driving this one) pretty much owned Funny Car in 1969. Each Mustang was powered by a Cammer and backed by a B&M-prepped C-6 transmission. As rules allowed, the top was chopped on the Mustangs by 2 inches. Oh, and those zoomie headers were a Funny Car first. (Photo Courtesy James Handy)

Yes, the Chevys were still out there and were led by Dick Harrell and Jim Liberman. Harrell kicked the year off by winning the AHRA Winternationals while "Jungle" Clare Sanders, in Liberman's second Nova won the NHRA Winternationals. Both cars were Chevy powered. (Photo Courtesy Michael Pottie)

Clare Sanders defeated the Barracuda of Ray Alley in the Funny Car final at the 1969 NHRA Winternationals, blowing off Alley with a 7.88 to Alley's lagging 8.11. Both cars featured Ron Pellegrini, Fiberglass Limited bodies. (Photo Courtesy John Prieto)

testing of the car, and the project was sidelined when Ford withdrew its support. Buttera then opened his own chassis shop in Cerritos, California. His clientele over the next decade read like a who's who of drag racing.

Both of Thompson's Mustangs featured solid-mounted engines, which went against the grain of using sliding mounts. The same went for the chassis with the only adjustments being in the four Koni coilover shocks. Foster's car featured a more flexible chassis with thinner inside diameter bottom rails, and a 5-inch longer wheelbase (121 inches). Foster's car was also 12 inches longer ahead of the windshield. Being backed by Ford, both cars counted on SOHC 427s for power.

Ongais reportedly went 55-3 through the year with the only real losses coming at the Winternationals, the United States Professional Dragsters Championship, and the World Finals. As well as all the wins, Ongais recorded Funny Car's first 6-second run when he drove the Mustang to a 6.96 on September 14 at Kansas City.

The Chevy faithful held true through 1969 with Dick Harrell and Jungle Jim Liberman kicking the year off by winning the AHRA and NHRA Winternationals. Harrell can hold claim to being the first to propel a Chevy-powered Funny Car over 200 mph when he hit the mark with his Camaro during an AHRA Grand American race at Green Valley. Further accolades came for Harrell when he was voted the AHRA's Man of the Year.

With an increase in demands though, the Chevys were running the ragged edge. Kelly Chadwick ended up with cracked cylinders while others saw the deck surface giving out. The number-2 cylinder in all the Chevys seemed to have an issue with leaning out. I'm unsure as to how other Chevy racers solved the problem, but Chadwick added a fifth fuel-feed nozzle to the right front of his Hilborn 4-port. This fed a continuous stream of fuel in the direction of the number-2 cylinder. Chadwick ran 7.5:1 to 8.5:1 compression in his cast-iron Chevy and 27-percent overdrive on the blower (42 percent at higher altitudes). He ran a 175 Hilborn pump with a Sid Waterman overdrive, and still his biggest problem was getting enough fuel into the mill.

With top-name Funny Cars now expecting $1,000 to $1,500 per match race, a lot of smaller tracks were having to say no, and they were hurting because of it. Ben Christ's Gold Agency came up with an affordable solution by teaming with Coca-Cola to present the Coca-Cola Cavalcade of Stars. Christ and his partner, Ira Lichey, offered tracks an eight-car show (of known cars) for half

Crossbred Funny Cars were pretty common by 1969, as Chrysler's Hemi showed its superiority. Jess Tyree didn't go Chrysler in his Pontiac; instead, he dropped in a Chevy. His Firebird featured an aluminum chassis fabricated by Jess himself. The Firebird was a star of the Coca-Cola Cavalcade. (Photo Courtesy Don Prieto)

the going price. The track paid half the bill while Coca-Cola picked up the other half. A 32-event series was put together and ran with great success from April through September. As reported in *Drag News*, Gary Dyer in Mr. Norm's Grand Spaulding Dodge Charger took the series crown the first year with 11 victories. The Cavalcade series would continue to fill the tracks through 1976.

This car just reeks of excitement. Originally campaigned as the Genuine Suspension Brothers AA/FA Fiat, the car was re-bodied in 1969 as the AMX-1 Funny Car in hopes of gaining sponsors. The plan worked, as Mr. Gasket took the bait. The car was said to be a handful and went through a few drivers. The best times found for the AMX-1 are a 7.35 at 193 mph. Powering the 99-inch-wheelbase car was a 354-ci Hemi. (Photo Courtesy Don Prieto)

Mid-Eliminators

Winning combinations in the Mid-Eliminators varied within each category, as the rules generally dictated. The greatest variety to be seen remained to be Super Eliminator, where the Fuel Altereds and blown Gassers resided.

The body choices varied as did drivetrain setups: solid rear axles, coil springs, quarter elliptic springs, 4-speed transmissions, 3-speed automatics, and ClutchFlites. In Comp, where the lower-class Dragsters lived, the dominant Chevy saw increased competition from the small-block Ford of all places. For example, Ken Van Cleve in C/Dragster was just one of many who used the lighter 289. Perched atop Van Cleve's engine were Gurney-Weslake heads. Ken backed the Ford with a ClutchFlite transmission, which only seemed to be gain popularity across the board.

Altereds

Leo Fitzgerald's *Pure Heaven II* was the nation's most successful AA/FA during the period of 1968 through 1971. Based out of Anaheim's Speed Engineering, the blown big-block Chevy-powered Bantam won more races during that period than any of its competition. Dave Brackett started the build of *Pure Heaven II* in 1965 but sold it to R.T. Reed and Fitzgerald when Uncle Sam came calling. With the help of chassis builder Jack Eskelson, they finished the Bantam in 1967, going from a small-block to a big-block, adding a solid rear-end and transverse front suspension. By mid-1969, the Bantam was running 7.40 times.

The northern California–based Pure Heaven II of Reed, Rockman, and Fitzgerald was built as a counterpunch to Rich Guasco's Pure Hell in the South. Pure Heaven II recorded 7.40s at over 200 mph. (Photo Courtesy Don Prieto)

Compare this photo of Mike Sullivan's Fuel Altered Fiat to others from the same period. Sullivan took into consideration the role wind plays on a car's speed and stability. Note the low silhouette and tucked-in slicks. The push truck puts into perspective just how low the Fiat was. Sullivan himself seems a tight fit within the cockpit. (Photo Courtesy Paul Johnson)

before moving up to AA/FA in 1968. In 1969, he set the class record with a 180.36 mph clocking.

Gassers

In A/Gas Supercharged Ohio George Montgomery's new 1969 Mustang cleaned house, taking Super Eliminator at the NHRA Springnationals and backing it up with a win at Indy, where he set the class record with an 8.59 at 164.23 mph in defeating the Fuel Altered of Ron Ellis. Montgomery's Mustang was just as innovative as his previous Mustang. To form the fiberglass body, a one-of-one preproduction mold was provided by Ford.

Still counting on a Cammer for motivation, the fresh engine mounted a "Montgomery" magnesium blower case and end plates that Ohio George had cast by Pacific Lightweight in Oregon. The company made about 300 cases in total for Montgomery, who sold them to competitors. A Pete Robinson gear drive was tried in place of the Cammer's 6-foot cam chain but was found to do nothing but add weight. To pick up the slack in the chain at speed, Montgomery recalls running one cam 2 degrees advance. The 427 produced 1,200 hp and was backed by a beefed C-6 transmission and 9-inch rear end, all courtesy of Ford Motor Company, of course.

Montgomery ran the Mustang through 1974, adding a twin-turbo Boss 429 in 1971. Times in the 8.40s at 175 were common. Not fully understanding turbo technology, the NHRA felt that Montgomery was holding back on power and penalized him for it by assigning a handicap. According to Montgomery, the Mustang could run a second faster than everyone else in class. He said, "I didn't dare show my full hand." His combination was eventually exiled with the NHRA telling him the car was no longer welcome.

Ron Ellis and his Trick T were the AA/A class record holder in 1968 and 1969, running a quick 8.45. Ellis played bridesmaid in Super Eliminator at the NHRA Nationals to Ohio George and at the World Finals to Jerry Gwynn. (Photo Courtesy James Handy)

Mike Sullivan brought a new dimension to Fuel Altered with his low, *low*-slung Fiat. As Sullivan describes on his webpage, when building the car "he ignored common building conventions of the day and instead built what was essentially an altered version of the dragster he had been driving [in 1966]."

All the work was done by Sullivan, including the chassis, which was closer in design to the Funny Car than the then-current crop of Fuel Altereds. The Altered was unorthodox in the sense that it threw the then-current thinking regarding weight transfer and high center of gravity out the window. It was narrow with tucked-in slicks and was built to cheat the wind. Initially, Sullivan ran the car as an injected A/FA with a direct drive 392

Supercharged Gas saw a lot of changes by the end of the decade, with one of the few constants being Ohio George winning. Here at its Indy debut, Montgomery's blown SOHC Mustang won the Super Eliminator category. (Photo Courtesy Steve Reyes)

Speaking of new Mustangs, Bones Balogh joined Stone & Woods in 1969 to campaign this hemi-powered fiberglass Shelby. Bones took it on a cross-country tour, running a four-car Gasser program with Junior Thompson, Ohio George Montgomery, and K. S. Pittman. Times in the 8.70s at over 160 were the norm for the Swindler. (Photo Courtesy John Prieto)

Proving that six in a row does go was the team of Rydell, Hope & Lang. Helping their 6-cylinder Anglia to record 10.70 G/Gas times was a cylinder head grafted from two small-block Chevy heads. (Photo Courtesy Rob Potter)

Though Gas was seeing a continued influx of Detroit's latest iron, the old fan favorite Willys and Anglias were hanging in there, winning class and setting records. Stickel & Riffle and their D/G Anglia; George Teixeira and his boys in B/G; Rydell, Hope, & Lang's *Mr. Crude* Anglia in G/G, all performed well.

Rydell, Hope, & Lang had the idea to improve the breathing of their 292-ci, 6-cylinder by fabricating a new cylinder head using a pair of small-block Chevy heads. Because the bore spacing of the six and V-8 is nearly identical, the guys found that they could lop off the end chamber from each V-8 head, bolt the two modified heads onto a 6-cylinder block, and use ni-rod to weld it up (I sure made it sound easy). The rest was pretty basic machining.

The intake for the new head came courtesy of a reworked Crower injection. The setup paid off, as the Anglia went from low 11s to 10.79 ETs and held class record for what seems like forever. At the 1969 NHRA Springnationals, their newly formed head won them the Best Engineered Car award. Of course, imitation being the sincerest form of flattery, it was just a matter of time before all the most competitive 6-cylinder cars were sporting modified V-8 heads.

Pete and Ben Hill looked to revitalize interest not only in the category but also in the old Willys and Anglias as well by creating the Blown Fuel Gasser circuit. The circuit consisted of four non-class-legal "Outlawed Gassers": Shores & Hess's 98-inch-wheelbase 1949 Anglia running

Stickel & Riffle's C/Gas Anglia, runner-up in Street Eliminator at the NHRA Winternationals, held the class record through October with a 10.42. An injected small-block Chevy got the job done. By 1969, the old Gassers (Willys, Anglias) that remained in competition had taken on a lower-to-the-ground, aerodynamic enhancing stance. (Photo Courtesy Dale Schafer)

When everyone else was running hydros and automatics, Ken Dondero surprised many when he manhandled Bob Panella's 4-speed-equipped Anglia to a Super Eliminator win at the 1969 NHRA Winternationals. Dondero followed up by taking honors at the Hot Rod magazine meet at Riverside. He returned to the Winternationals in 1970 with the 301-powered Anglia, where he was runner-up to Jack Ditmars in the new Comp Eliminator category. A 9.87 at 143.54 mph earned Dondero a win at Bakersfield before he and Panella parted company. (Photo Courtesy James Handy)

Remember the days when magazines featured project car builds? Bob Anderton's Willys was featured in a three-part Hot Rod magazine series as the "Ultimate" A/GS Willys. Built by Don Long for Don Eisner, the Willys was a trick piece that weighed in at 1,550 pounds and showcased Long's out-of-the-box thinking. Long chose the Willys and a supercharged Chevy engine to prove they could still compete against the modern Hemi cars. Anderton, who worked for metal man Tom Hanna, took over the colorful Willys and more than held his own on Southern California tracks. (Photo Courtesy Don Prieto)

Pete Hill manned the controls of this 1933 Willys while brother Bill built and tuned the 1,500-hp, 438-ci Hemi. Roger Lindamood was responsible for the bulletproof TorqueFlite. Chuck Finders, whose Fire Brew Anglia is in the background, built the 100-inch wheelbase chassis. Low 8s were the norm for these flip-body outlaw Gassers. (Photo Courtesy Carl Rubrecht)

Competing with five different cars in 1969, Landy was on fire. Sharing the driving chores were Bob Lambeck, Butch Leal, and Herb McCandless, among others. When Dick and his Dart lost A/MP to Ronnie Sox at the NHRA Winternationals, he hopped in his B/MP Charger and won Street Eliminator. (Photo Courtesy Don Prieto)

Super Stock racer Mike Fons preferred his odds in Modified Eliminator and converted his big-block Camaro to A/MP. The gamble paid off, as Fons defeated Bo Laws to capture the world title. Modified Eliminator was the fastest-growing category in the late 1960s, and its popularity continued to grow well into the 1970s. (Photo Courtesy Michael Pottie)

An oddity in the lower Gas ranks was the Top Cat 1967 Mercury Cougar of Jack and John O'Connor and Darrell Droke. The D/Gasser ran a 305-ci Gurney-Weslake engine. Dan Gurney designed the large port heads with intake ports set at a 9-degree angle. The Weber carbs were angled toward the center of the engine and fed directly into the ports. The Division 7 Cougar won Street Eliminator at Bakersfield in 1969 and held class record with an 11.11 at 126.31 mph. (Photo Courtesy Brian Kennedy)

a 460-ci Chevy, Prock & Howell's 100-inch-wheelbase 1933 Willys powered by a 488-ci Hemi, the Hill brothers' 100-inch-wheelbase 488-ci Chrysler 1933 Willys, and Chuck Finders's 98-inch-wheelbase 1949 Anglia powered by a 461-ci Hemi. Needless to say, with a combination of short wheelbase and hordes of power, the cars were a handful.

"When we cleared the top end, that is to say, after crossing the lanes a couple of times, back pedaling, and basically steering clear of each other and the wall, we usually ran in the mid to upper 8s," said Finders.

Typical of the cars, the Prock & Howell *F-Troop* was built around a Logghe Funny Car–style chassis and featured a B&N fiberglass body and tin work by Al Berger.

Mimicking what Finders had said, Jay Howell added, "At 165 mph, the fun really began as the Willys would

skate around. The Logghes came up with the solution, mounting a pair of small wings on the rear fenders. When Tom and I showed up out East for a race, we rolled the Willys out of the trailer and the Hill brothers and group cracked up. Pointing and laughing, they referred to the wings as Mickey Mouse ears. The first pass I laid down was a 178 mph! The next week, they all had the wings! The *F-Troop* pretty much dominated the circuit, running consistent 8.0s at 185 plus while pedaling it."

Super Stock Eliminator

No denying, with wins at the NHRA Springnationals (for the third year in a row), the Nationals, and the World Finals, the year belonged to the team of Sox & Martin. Sharing in driving of the team's four cars was Don Carlton. Many racers who were fed up with Super Stock's breakout rules boycotted the NHRA Winternationals or ran alternative categories. Sox & Martin and Dick Landy were two who choose to bypass S/S and ran A and B/MP instead. Their move to Modified left the door open for Don Grotheer and his SS/B Automatic Hemi Barracuda to win the category, running a healthy 10.73. The automatic-equipped Hemi cars were now running times comparative to the 4-speed cars, which was largely due to the high-stall torque converters developed by Chrysler in conjunction with B&M.

When it came to national events, the winning Mopars weren't without competition. You can't overlook Sandy Elliot's Border Bandit Fords running out of Chatham, Ontario, Canada. The team consisted of John Elliot, who wheeled the team's A/S 427 Comet, and Barrie Poole, who wrenched the cars and drove the team's SS/H Cobra Jet Mustang. Poole was runner-up to Sox at the Springnationals and World Finals. In between, he won the first *Popular Hot Rodding* meet.

It was Grumpy Jenkins who threw a wrench into Mopar's monopoly by driving his *Grumpy's Toy IV* Camaro to victory at the AHRA Springnationals. Jenkins

If looking for unique, take one lightweight 1953 MGB and add an injected big-block Chevy and you've got Ed Sigmon's AHRA and NHRA Winternationals Comp Eliminator winner. At the NHRA meet, Sigmon defeated Ray Hadford's C/Dragster in the final with a 9.51 at 143.54 mph. Into 1971, Sigmon ran a Pro Stock Camaro simultaneous to the MGB, swapping the 427 and automatic transmission from car to car. (Photo Courtesy James Handy)

A couple years before the NHRA introduced its Pro Stock category, the AHRA ran a heads-up Super Stock category, not to be confused with NHRA's handicap Super Stock. Leading the charge and winning the world title in 1969 was the Kimball brothers with Grumpy Jenkins's old Camaro. (Photo Courtesy Michael Pottie)

In heads-up Super Stock at the AHRA Winternationals, Ronnie Sox qualified the team's former SS/B Barracuda No. 1 with a 10.67. A broken clutch in round one ended their weekend early. The Barracuda was wrecked in a towing accident on its way to the NHRA Winternationals. (Photo Courtesy Steve Reyes)

Ford countered Chrysler's drag clinics with their own Drag Team seminars. Ford's West Coast team (seen here) consisted of Ed Terry and Dick Woods, while Hubert Platt and Randy Payne manned the East Coast team. The Cobra Jet–powered cars were competitive, and the seminars drew the crowds. More importantly to Ford, the publicity sold cars. (Photo Courtesy Dale Schafer)

Running heads-up Experimental Stock at the Super Stock Nationals, Grumpy Jenkins recorded Super Stock's first 9-second time. Jenkins, well known for his experience in building winning small-blocks, admitted that when it came to building big-blocks, initially there was a lot of guess-work going on. Trial and error and attention to detail made Grump a winner.

Match racing door cars was where it was at in 1969. Butch Leal teamed up with Mickey Thompson once again and did battle behind the wheel of this heads-up Boss 429-powered Mustang. Bottom-10-second times did the job. (Photo Courtesy Brian Kennedy)

proved to be Sox's fiercest rival. At the fifth-annual Super Stock Nationals held at York, Jenkins defeated Sox in the Experimental Super Stock final, recording the fastest time of the event with a 9.94 at 141.93 mph to Sox's 10.13 at 135. This was the first sub-10-second time recorded by a Super Stock car.

Jenkins chose to forgo Super Stock at the NHRA Nationals and instead ran his Camaro in B/Gas using a Chaparral aluminum 427-ci engine. Chevrolet developed the engine back in 1966 in conjunction with Jim Hall for use in his Chaparral race cars. These aluminum blocks were available to select racers through Chevrolet's Performance Group, and it's believed that Jenkins was the only one in drag racing to try it. Excluding the weight savings, Jenkins felt there was no real advantage in using the aluminum over the iron block. By the end of the season, he had his Camaro running 9.70 times.

Sometime during the NHRA Nationals, Buddy Martin took the time to speak with several of the more prominent Super Stock racers (Jenkins, Booth, Poole, and others), asking them to attend a meeting at the Holiday Inn the day after the race. There, it was proposed that the racers form a Super Stock Drivers Association. The stated purpose was to lobby the NHRA for more eliminator and class win money, fairer treatment, etc. Martin stated that Super Stock was the most popular form of racing with the

fans, and he felt they deserved better.

Super Stock racer Lance Hill attended the meeting.

"At the head table were Buddy, Ronnie, and Jenkins, among others representing Ford racers," Hill recalled. "Approximately 20 people were in attendance. We all knew the scheme had originated with Chrysler and weren't entirely sure why or what they intended, but we all agreed to join and be on a mailing and phone list. A second meeting was held at the World Finals in Dallas prior to the race. The same guys at the head table, with Buddy Martin always the spokesman.

"Between Labor Day and this juncture, we had all received a mailing or a phone call telling us that the purpose had abruptly changed. No longer was it the Super Stock Drivers Association; talks had been undertaken with the NHRA and it was resolved. We were forming an entirely new category, Pro Stock. At the meeting, it was revealed that the rules and regulations had already been decided. It was a done deal.

"Quite a few of the guys were not happy to have been blindsided with all of this and were opposed to the change. New Jersey racer Al Olster was particularly irate and vocal. What Chrysler had been up to from the get-go, as it was later revealed, was having these very discussions with the NHRA prior to the first meeting. In any event, quite a few left the meeting before its conclusion, wanting no part of the deal. I wasn't particularly pleased

AMC got into the factory Super Stock wars in 1969 when it had Hurst Performance prepare 52 390-powered AMXs. This one, campaigned by Jim Mann and Jack Farwick out of Minneapolis, recorded 10.70 times. (Photo Courtesy John Foster Jr.)

either, but I recognized it was going to happen regardless, and I do clearly remember standing at the head table and signing a document that was to be presented to the NHRA, completing the establishment of Pro Stock."

Stock Eliminator

Stock classes now reached from A through V/S. And with the weight breaks tightening up, the playing field became more balanced. It was hard to believe that for the first time since the inception of Stock Eliminator back in 1964, no Chevy won a national event.

The year kicked off with 17-year-old Mark Coletti winning Stock Eliminator in his 340-ci Barracuda, the

With the popularity of drag racing exploding in the late 1960s, the magazines went all in when it came to building and sponsoring drag race cars. Bill Shrewsberry wheeled this Car Craft magazine–sponsored Swinger in F/S at the NHRA Winternationals before presenting it to the sweepstakes winner. Keith Black built the 340, and George Barris laid on the wild paint. (Photo Courtesy Don Prieto)

With Bob Burkitt at the wheel of the Burkitt & Pratte Dart 440 wagon, the team won the NHRA World Championship in 1969 and was runner-up in 1970. A B&M TorqueFlite backed the 383-ci while rear gears varied from 4.30 to 4.88. You've got to appreciate the clean looks that added to the feel of professionalism that now encompassed Stock. As Burkitt recalled the fancy pearl white and blue paint added about 70 pounds to the car. Average times for the wagon were in the 12.60 range. (Photo Courtesy Don Prieto)

same car his father used to win class with in 1968. Bob Burkitt and John Pratte closed the season winning the World Finals with their G/SA 1962 Dodge wagon. The pair had originally bought Dave Kempton's Sport Fury to do battle in D/SA, but when Pete Kost bombed the record with his Oldsmobile, they hunted down a wagon and swapped in the Kempton drivetrain.

Adding a level of professionalism to Stock were the Smothers brothers, a popular comedy team that had backdoor support from Oldsmobile, which sponsored five Stock class Cutlasses and a pair of Top Fuel cars. The team included the Top Fuel cars of Don Garlits, Dwight Salisbury, and the Stockers of Willard Wright, Pete Kost, Ron Garey, Jim Waibel, and Lloyd Woodland driving for Berejik Olds. Oldsmobile provided the cars fresh off the assembly line sporting the Smothers brothers' chosen red and gold colors.

Pete Kost recalled the Smothers brothers' deal, stating that Oldsmobile sponsored the brothers' television show and support for the racers was funneled through the show. "We'd be at a national event and a gentleman would walk up, hand us an envelope with money, wish us luck, and be on his way." The envelopes contained $2,000 in cash. The Smothers' deal ran into 1971, when the brothers' focus moved to other interests. One could

Mark Coletti, a 17-year-old wonder kid, won Stock Eliminator at the NHRA Winternationals driving this F/SA 340-powered Barracuda. His dad won class with the same car the year before. Well into the 1970s, the northwest Colettis ran a successful business building class-winning Mopars. (Photo Courtesy Murray Chambers)

easily say that Oldsmobile received a pretty good shake on their return with multiple class wins, class records, and publicity they never would have garnered otherwise. Such were the ways of GM's racing endeavors.

The build of Joe Allread's J/S 1957 Chevy wagon was chronicled in Car Craft magazine back in 1968 and 1969 and was probably responsible for more Tri-Five Chevy builds than any one single car. Sadly, rule changes in 1970 made the Ultimate Junior Stock all but obsolete. (Photo Courtesy Michael Pottie)

The Smothers Brothers' team cars ran their own colors after 1969. Here's the new 1970 Berejik F/S Cutlass in action with Lloyd Woodland behind the wheel. The W-30-powered car was good for regular 12-flat times. (Photo Courtesy Michael Pottie)

Although national event victories eluded Jungle Jim Liberman, his forte was match racing, where he never failed to please. Liberman made the switch to red cars in 1970 before switching back to blue in 1971. That same year, he moved away from Chevy engines to the Chrysler Hemi. (Photo Courtesy John Foster Jr.)

Chapter Ten

1970
A Sweet Season

The NHRA's Super Season saw more changes, as the sanctioning body dropped more classes that suffered through low participation and lower fan appeal. By the end of season, the NHRA was running 16 categories in 8 eliminator brackets that encompassed 144 classes. Over at the AHRA, a person could get lost in the 250-odd classes that were offered.

The NHRA's new Professional Stock (Pro Stock) category was an instant hit with the fans, who easily identified with the stock-appearing (for the most part) cars. The instant green Christmas tree was tried for the first time at the season-ending Supernationals. Used for only the pro-class cars, the instant green did away with the three amber countdown bulbs. The system would be used at all NHRA national events starting in 1971.

Top Fuel

The AHRA Grand American series kicked off 1970 with a new format that saw the pro categories (T/F, F/C, S/S) at each national event run a 16-car field, with the top 8 positions held by prequalified racers. These eight were established racers and previous event winners.

Don Garlits, one of those eight in Top Fuel, kicked off the year by winning the AHRA's Winternationals with *Swamp Rat XIII*, defeating John Weibe in the final with a 6.92 at 220.40 mph. Weibe snoozed on the green and wasted a record-setting 6.74 at 227.84. It was a good start to the year for Garlits, who was trialing his new Garlits Drive transmission, a modified version of the Lenco overdrive that he had been running with great success through the latter half of 1969.

Garlits's next stop on the AHRA event trail was at Lions on March 8 for a big Grand American race, where things went unexpectedly south. Garlits had set the AA/FD class record with a 6.57 and was about to face Richard Tharp in the Creitz & Donovan car in the elimination final when the transmission let loose in an ugly way. Garlits later said that the sprag in the transmission failed as he let out the clutch, causing the engine to over-rev. This caused the transmission drum to spin backward at about three times the engine speed. The drum came apart and literally tore the car in half, taking a portion of Garlits's right foot with it.

Laid up in the hospital, Garlits put pen to paper and began planning his next *Swamp Rat*. By the time the AHRA Springnationals rolled around in June, 13 weeks

after the explosion, Garlits had recovered enough to crawl behind the wheel of the repaired *Swamp Rat* and set low ET of the meet with a 6.80 at 224 mph. Though the race was won by Tharp, I'm sure every memory centers on Garlits's return.

One of the most spectacular Top Fuel finishes of all time took place at the NHRA Nationals in 1970. Don Prudhomme, hoping to win his second Nationals in a row, faced Jim Nicoll, an all-business competitor who had trailered a redlighting Garlits in the semis to make his third final-round appearance of the year. Prudhomme, riding on a set of new super slick Goodyears, set low ET of the meet with a 6.43. He trailed Nicoll off the line, but by the 1,000-foot mark he had gained ground and had pulled even.

It was a race too close to call, but as the cars entered the timing traps at an estimated 225 mph, Nicoll's clutch let loose in a fiery explosion, sawing his dragster in half. The back half of the dragster, with Nicoll on board and chute extended, bounced off the track and over the guardrail, where it eventually came to rest. The front half of the dragster and the still-spinning Hemi slid across the track, passed Prudhomme, and came to rest in the sand traps. Miraculously, Nicoll escaped with little more than a concussion and a swollen foot. Though Prudhomme had won with a 6.45 at 230.78 mph, the incident shook him up enough that he vowed never to race again.

Those who watched the race on ABC's Wide World of Sports saw the crash, which the show used during its opening segment for years. A scene never caught by the cameras was Nicoll being loaded into the ambulance. Someone failed to latch the rear doors, and like a scene straight out of a comedy flick, when the ambulance pulled away, Nicoll went rolling out the rear doors.

It wasn't all ugliness during the 1970 NHRA season. Drag racers are the fiercest competitors on

The final round in Top Fuel at Indy was like no other. Don Prudhomme took the win after Jim Nicoll's clutch let loose and sawed the car in half. It was a miracle he survived with only minor scrapes. (Photo Courtesy Steve Reyes)

Larry Dixon Sr. kicked off the year by running a 6.80 against Tony Nancy to win the NHRA Winternationals. Dixon earned his win with an engine borrowed from the **Howards Cams Rattler** *after melting a piston the previous round. As a driver, this was Dixon's one and only national event victory. (Photo Courtesy James Handy)*

the track, but off it, they can be thick as thieves. You could say camaraderie was never lacking in the sport. Case in point, Larry Dixon took Top Fuel at the NHRA Winternationals in the SPE chassis, *Howards Cams Rattler.*

Dixon waded through the 32-car field to win his one and only national event, defeating Tony Nancy in the final with a 6.80. Dixon earned his win after melting a piston in the semis, forcing him to swap the engine before

Though he was successful in Top Gas, Tom Larkin found things a little tougher when he stepped up to Top Fuel. He never failed to be a threat with his Woody Gilmore–chassis car that relied upon an early 392 for power. Nitro-powered dragsters had started the decade running in the 8.80 range and closed it running 6.40s. (Photo Courtesy Steve Reyes)

the final. With 45 minutes to call, Dixon relied upon the helping hands of many, including a few he had beaten to get the car ready. In a *CARS* magazine interview, Larry was quoted to say, "There were people working on the car I didn't even know. Loaning things to get us back to the line."

Though Garlits is often given credit for ushering in the modern rear-engine dragster, debuting his car on December 27 at St. Petersburg, Florida, credit should really be given to Woody Gilmore and Pat Foster. After watching John Mulligan's crash at the Nationals in 1969, Gilmore was determined not to see it happen again. In December of that year, he tested the pair's first rear-engine car. The dragster crashed during an early outing, but Gilmore and Foster were undeterred and went to work on a second car.

The new car (pictured in chapter 1) featured a 223-inch wheelbase and went to Dwane Ong. Ong debuted the car at Orange County in February 1970 (10 months before Garlits's rear-engine car), where he laid down a 6.93 at 214 mph. In August 1970, Ong's rear-engine car became the first to win a national event when he took honors at the AHRA Summernationals. In the event held at Long Island, New York, Ong defeated Fred Ahrberg with a 6.82 at 217.39 mph to a 6.85 at 221.21.

Top Gas

Late in 1969, the first whispers were heard regarding the not-so-bright future of Top Gas. The class had become stagnant with little growth, which was reflected in declining interest. R.C. Williams was concerned enough that before he went ahead and replaced his single-engine car with a twin, he conferred with the NHRA, which reassured him that the class wasn't going anywhere. The NHRA told him that all was well, and to put everyone at ease it gave notice in the *National Dragster* that the class would be around for another five years. Immediately after losing to the *Freight Train* at Bakersfield, Williams headed to Mark Williams's shop in Colorado, where they set to work building the twin 484-ci Hemi car.

With Ray Motes behind the wheel, they debuted the car May 20 at Colorado's Thunder Road, where they ran 196.06 mph on the car's first pass. Motes went on to win the event and a follow-up race at South Dakota before winning the NHRA Springnationals. He closed the season by winning the World Championship, defeating the single-engine, Lenco-equipped car of Jack Jones in the final round. Williams & Motes campaigned the car for 17 months and won their division crown in 1970 and 1971 before the NHRA went back on their word and killed the category.

Funny Car

The year started on a sour note when Gas Ronda was seriously burned in his Funny Car at the AHRA Winternationals. During qualifying, the Cammer let loose in a bad way, leading to a transmission explosion. The ensuing fireball left Ronda with life-threatening burns to two-thirds of his body and ended his career. Shortly after, the sanctioning bodies mandated that all Funny Cars be fitted with fire-suppression systems. New NHRA rules for 1971 went a step further and stated that all Fuel cars and blown Gas Dragsters were to contain a 5-pound fire-suppression system.

Ronda's Mustang was rebuilt and campaigned by Amos Saterlee and Mike Pohl before being sold to Dave

At the NHRA Springnationals at Dallas, Motes & Williams defeated Walt Stevens here in the **Gas House Gang** *car before defeating Norm Wilcox in the final. The wheelbase of the Mark Williams chassis measured 210 inches. The two Hemis were mated by a (10) splined shaft at the crankshafts. Up top, the twin blowers were joined by a main shaft. Motes held the Gas record through 1970 with a 7.08 at 212.76 mph. (Photo Courtesy Steve Reyes)*

Bowman. In retirement, Ronda went to work for Foulger Ford in West Covina, California. It's said that sales of performance parts at Foulger increased by 1,000 percent when Ronda came onboard.

Fifty cars showed up for the 16-car field at the AHRA Winternationals. Mickey Thompson arrived with three cars in tow: Danny Ongais in his *Mach 1*, Johnny Wright in a white Mustang, and a John Buttera–built Maverick

Another prominent Mustang during 1969 into 1970 was the Russ Davis–sponsored car of Gas Ronda. Ronda lost the car in a fire at the AHRA Winternationals. He received extensive burns that ended his drag racing career. (Photo Courtesy James Handy)

By the end of the 1969 season, the wheels in Mickey Thompson's head were once again churning, coming up with the monocoque Mustang Funny Car. The Mustang weighed in at a measly 1,845 pounds. Development died in the spring of 1970 as factory support disappeared and the car's performance to that point was nowhere near expectations. Thompson fielded five different cars in 1970. (Photo Courtesy James Handy)

driven by Arnie Behling. Thompson's monocoque Mustang Funny Car stayed home. The unique Nye Frank design experiment combined the body and inner "tub" structure as one in an aircraft or Indy-car style. There was no chassis, per se, and all the main components tied into the inner structure. The body flipped up along the beltline for access. The car weighed in at 1,850 pounds, some 300 pounds less than Thompson's conventional Mustang. The best time found for the Boss 429–powered car was a 7.40 at 196 mph.

At the Winternationals, Johnny Wright qualified second behind the Firebird of Gordon Mineo, who clocked a 7.45. Ongais qualified further down the pack, while Behling missed the program. Other qualifiers included Don Schumacher, Larry Reyes, Candies & Hughes, and Leroy Goldstein in the Ramchargers' Dodge Challenger.

Goldstein had never been in a Funny Car, so he surprised the masses when in only his second pass in the Woody Gilmore–chassis car recorded a 7.48 at 204.08 mph for the top speed of the meet. Goldstein made it to the second round of eliminations before redlighting against Larry Reyes. Low ET went to Roy Gay, whose Hemi-powered GTO recorded a 7.23.

Roy and Don Gay were two of many going full Funny Car, choosing to run a Hemi under a non-Chrysler body. Mr. Chevrolet (Dick Harrell) was another you'd never guess would make the trade, but by the end of the season, his Camaro was running a Hemi. At the Winternationals, Gay's high hopes for the new combo disappeared in the first round of eliminations when his car broke against Gene Snow. In the second, Snow defeated Danny Ongais. In the third, he defeated Kenny Safford, who was wheeling Mr. Norm's Charger. In the other semifinal round, Larry Reyes defeated Leonard Hughes. In the anti-

By the 1970 NHRA Winternationals, Don and Ron Gay had seen the light and had switched from Pontiac power to a Keith Black Hemi. Don knocked out 7.20s with the car before the brothers re-bodied the GTO as a Firebird in the spring. (Photo Courtesy James Handy)

At the Gatornationals, Candies & Hughes owned both cars in the final round of Funny Car. Leonard Hughes ran the team's new 'Cuda, while Larry Reyes ran the 1969 Barracuda. Both parties agreed before the run that Reyes would throw the race, as Candies & Hughes were working on landing a key sponsor. (Photo Courtesy Michael Pottie)

climactic final, Reyes defeated a redlighting Snow with an easy 7.67 at 196 mph.

At the NHRA Gatornationals, Funny Car history was in the making as both cars in the category final belonged to the same team: Candies & Hughes. Pairing with Leonard Hughes to run the team's 1969 Barracuda were Winternationals winners Larry Reyes and Roland Leong. The two parties admitted later that Hughes, driving the team's new 1970 Barracuda, had asked Reyes to throw the race, as Candies & Hughes were working on landing a key sponsor. The outcome was decided before the race, and it showed in the final clocking. Hughes won the race with a 7.29 at 202.24 mph, while Reyes was on and off the gas shut-off with an oh-so-close 7.12 at 191.08.

The Ramchargers team went into the engine-building business in 1969, and its Hemis were now powering some of the quickest and fastest fuel cars in the nation. The team itself won its only NHRA national event of the year when Leroy Goldstein defeated Gene Snow at the Springnationals. Goldstein did the job on a new set of Firestone 500 slicks. Firestone released tires for the Stock and Super Stock cars in 1969 and joined M&H and Goodyear at the Springnationals in the battle for supremacy in the pro categories.

By the time Indy came around, where Candies & Hughes set low ET with a 6.80 at 214.79 mph (on M&H tires), all the top teams were well into the 6s. Advancements in tires and clutches allowed builders to step up

their combinations and feed more air/fuel and boost into their engines. Gone from Funny Car were the weak link OEM automatic transmissions. Showing favor was Lenco's overdrive transmission. Candies & Hughes adopted a combination Crowerglide clutch and B&M ClutchFlite 2-speed transmission. The transmission had an interesting box that could be run as a direct drive, 2-speed, or even 3-speed.

Drag racing in general took a huge step forward when McEwen and Prudhomme struck a sponsor deal with toy manufacturer Mattel. It was drag racing's first major sponsorship, and it brought a level of respectability to the sport that hadn't been seen before. Sure, Coke was onboard in a big way in 1969, but the Mattel deal was something special. It took a lot of leg work by McEwen, and it was helped further along by the fact that his mother worked as a secretary for Mattel while his stepfather was an attorney for the company. No doubt this helped McEwen and Prudhomme garner an audience with Art Spear, a company vice president.

It was reported that the Mattel deal was worth in the neighborhood of $250,000 and ran from 1970 through 1972. Ron Scrima's Exhibition Engineering built four chassis for the pair: two went to Top Fuel cars and the other two went under a Duster for McEwen and a 'Cuda

The Ramchargers returned to Funny Car in 1970 with Leroy Goldstein behind the wheel of the team's Challenger. They won the NHRA Springnationals and were runner-up at the Nationals after setting low ET. The Ramchargers ended the season as the AHRA World Champs. (Photo Courtesy Michael Pottie)

Fort Worth's Gene Snow won the AHRA driver of the year honors in 1970 (repeating in 1971) and was the NHRA Funny Car champion. Snow's Keith Black–powered Challenger was capable of 6.70 times by the end of the season. (Photo Courtesy James Handy)

Kenny Safford proved his worth in Top Fuel before replacing Gary Dyer behind the wheel of Mr. Norm's mini-Charger in 1969. Safford could do it all and ran Funny Car into 1977, winning numerous events before back issues ended his driving career. (Photo Courtesy James Handy)

Tom McEwen was quite possibly the greatest PR man drag racing ever had. The Mongoose took drag racing to another level when he hammered out the McEwen-Prudhomme sponsorship deal with toy manufacturer Mattel. Fans loved the Mongoose-Snake rivalry, and the kids ate up the Hot Wheels scale cars. (Photo Courtesy James Handy)

Don Prudhomme debuted his Hot Wheels 'Cuda at LaPlace, Louisiana, in April, where he was runner-up to the 1970 'Cuda of Candies & Hughes. Keith Black power helped ensure that Prudhomme remained one of the best in class. An Exhibition Engineering chassis carried a 118-inch wheelbase. (Photo Courtesy James Handy)

As well as running his Cammer-powered Top Fueler in 1969, Connie Kalitta also tried his hand in Funny Car with this Logghe chassis Mustang. The car ran the gambit from a Boss 429 to a Cammer to a Chrysler Hemi. Try as he might, major event victory eluded the Bounty Hunter. (Photo Courtesy James Handy)

Rising Star

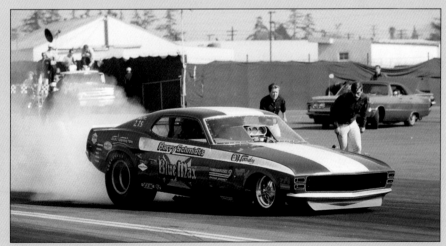

(Photo Courtesy Don Prieto)

Harry Schmidt's *Blue Max* Mustang made its debut at the NHRA Winternationals in 1970, where it set top speed of the meet with a 203.61 mph. Jake Johnston, former wrench for Gene Snow, found happiness behind the wheel of the Don Hardy car, which was powered by a Ramchargers-built Hemi. At OCIR'S annual manufacturer meet in November, Johnston recorded a 6.72 at 217.91, the quickest ET for a F/C up to that point. Johnston returned to the Snow camp shortly after, taking the wheel of Snow's second Dodge Challenger. Replacing him in the *Blue Max* was Richard Tharp, who drove the car (and the Creitz & Donovan T/F) at the season-ending Supernationals. With Raymond Beadle taking the driver's seat in 1973, the *Blue Max* became one of the 1970s most-feared Funnies.

When Tim Beebe returned to drag racing after the death of John Mulligan, he chose to campaign a Funny Car with his brother Dave. Tim Beebe pulled wrenches on the Keith Black 392 that propelled the Logghe chassis car to a best of 6.99 at 208.81 mph in 1970. (Photo Courtesy Don Prieto)

Going back to the early 1960s, Malcolm Durham ran a string of memorable Strip Blazer Chevys. With its punched out 454-ci Chevy mill, Durham's Camaro was capable of low-7-second times. (Photo Courtesy Michael Pottie)

for Prudhomme. Keith Black built the Hemis for Prudhomme while John Hogan, formerly of Chris Karamesine's crew, started the year building engines for McEwen before McEwen turned to the Ramchargers for power.

Pro Stock

The NHRA finally caved to demands and presented a heads-up, no breakout Professional Stock category in 1970. When compared to what the Super Stock drivers had initially proposed back in 1968, Pro Stock differed very little. A minimum weight of 7 pounds per cubic inch was agreed upon with a minimum car weight, minus the driver, of 2,700 pounds. Cars had to be American made and produced within the previous three years. The engine had to be of the same manufacturer as the body and could be no larger than 430 ci. Any internal engine modifications were permitted along with any transmission, rear end, or tire, as long as they fit the "stock" wheel well. Fiberglass fenders, hood, hood scoop (no taller than 7 inches in height), and decklid were also permitted. Cars of choice were the so-called compacts: Camaros, Barracudas, Dusters, and Mavericks. Being cars that fans could relate to ensured that the category took hold like wildfire.

Of the 16 (17 if you count the NHRA-sanctioned Supernationals) AHRA heads-up Super Stock and NHRA Pro Stock national events held in 1970, the team of Sox & Martin won all but five of them. Their efforts accumulated in an AHRA World title. At the season-opening AHRA Winternationals, Ronnie Sox drove the team's 1970 Hemi 'Cuda and set the tone for the year by grabbing the number-one qualifying position with a 10.07. Close behind was teammate Don Carlton, who was wheeling the Sox & Martin 1969 Barracuda.

It's been 50 years since Pro Stock looked anything like this. The cars are gathered at OCIR in February for the first Pro Stock Championship. Grumpy Jenkins's Camaro defeated Dyno Don Nicholson's Maverick in the final. Recognize many? (Photo Courtesy Richard Nicholson)

And you wonder why Pro Stock was an immediate hit with the fans. After prepping the track with rosin, John Hagen and his Hemi 'Cuda found traction more than ideal. Laying the rosin, sweeping it in, and burning through were all part of the fan appeal. Just like in the early days of Funny Car. (Photo Courtesy John Foster Jr.)

Ford-Mercury savior Dyno Don Nicholson had a dilemma. He wanted to compete in the AHRA-NHRA heads-up categories at the Winternationals but had no car. His match race Cougar Eliminator was too heavy, and his Modified Production 1966 Mustang was too old. So, with no time to spare, a donated Maverick from Foulger Ford in Covina, California, was shipped to M&S Race Cars in Azusa, where they spent the next seven days

installing a SOHC 427 and related hardware.

Dyno Don's first run on the Maverick came during time trials at the AHRA Winternationals. Things went south almost immediately as the "good" engine failed him. He spent a good part of the evening piecing together a new engine only to lose out in the first round of eliminations to the Camaro of Mike Fons. Nicholson would get it together by midseason and, with the help of top wrench Earl Wade, earned Ford its first Pro Stock National event victory by winning the AHRA's Grand American race at Epping, New England.

Handing Sox & Martin their first major loss of the season was Bill Jenkins, who defeated Sox in the final round at the NHRA Winternationals. Jenkins qualified his 430-ci 1968 Camaro in the second spot behind Sox's 10 flat with a 10.08. It was a tight field with Sam Auxier Jr. and his SOHC Maverick sitting on the bubble with a 10.49.

On his march to the final round, Jenkins disposed of Bill Hielscher with Pro Stock's first 9-second run of 9.98.

Back when you could build a Pro Stocker in a week's time, Don Nicholson and the guys at M&S Race Cars did so. Dyno's Cammer Maverick proved to be one of the few threats to Chrysler's dominance. Note the stacked carb spacers under the 660-cfm Holley carburetors. The fabricated independent runner intake came shortly after the initial build. The plenum is an Edelbrock big-block Chevy part. (Photo Courtesy Richard Nicholson)

After losing the first two meets of the inaugural NHRA Pro Stock season, Sox went on a tear, compiling a phenomenal win streak. At the summer's Super Stock National held at York US-30, he drove around a 50-car field to take the win. (Photo Courtesy James Handy)

He dropped the Camaro of Mike Fons in the second, and in the third, he defeated a redlighting Dick Landy, who was toying with new 16–spark plug Hemi heads on his Challenger. Was the extra plug per chamber worth more power? Well, as Ted Spehar noted in Geoff Stunkard's book *Chrysler's Motown Missile*, "It made the engine run smoother, idle better, but there was no real performance gain there."

The two plugs per chamber fired simultaneously and allowed for improved burn. A twin neck distributor was created to fire the plugs using a modified Hilborn drive. Each distributor head could be set to a specific advance.

In the Pro Stock final, Jenkins strapped a 9.99 on

In semifinal Pro Stock action at the NHRA Winternationals, Dick Landy and his twin-plug Hemi Challenger faced Grumpy Jenkins. Landy got a slight lead off the line, thanks to a redlight. (Photo Courtesy James Handy)

It's a toss-up as to who was "bridesmaid" more often: Arlen Vanke or Dave Wren. Vanke, seen here at the 1971 Winternationals, was runner-up at three national events in 1970 alone. He took some consolation in having won all five Division 3 points meets. (Photo Courtesy James Handy)

Ronnie Sox, who came up short with a 10.12. Jenkins's 139.55 mph on the final run proved to be the top speed of the meet. Jenkins followed up with major wins at Ontario and Detroit. In Florida at the Gatornationals, he once again defeated Sox in the final with a 9.90. Jenkins remained Chevy's No. 1 guy, killing them on the match race circuit but for all his efforts, he wouldn't see another national event win until 1972.

Pro Stock has always run tight fields, and the first year was no exception. Racers were all looking for an edge and came up with some innovative ideas. Arlen Vanke of Akron, Ohio, was working close with the folks at Chrysler and spent the early part of the year experimenting with a 180-degree crank in his Hemi. The crank was designed to keep the Hemi's number-5 and number-7 cylinders (side by side) from firing one after the other. The crank changed the firing order from 1-8-4-3-6-5-7-2 to 1-4-7-2-5-8-3-6.

On the dyno, the setup netted a reported 20-hp increase, but it did nothing to keep Vanke in the running. The best he could muster with the crank was a 10.12 at 137.73 mph. Vanke debuted a Hemi Duster in the spring and proved to be Sox & Martins biggest threat through the remainder of the season, playing runner-up at the Nationals, World Finals, and Supernationals.

Al Joniec got the most out of his SOHC-powered Maverick when he bolted on four 2-barrel carburetors. Joniec had been toying with injectors on his Cammer but Pro Stock rules dictated carburetors. He had initially tried four 500-cfm 2-barrel carburetors bolted to his modified intake, figuring the 2,000 cfm would do the job. The results were less the spectacular.

With the hood off and bringing the revs up on the Cammer, Joniec watched as the fuel fogged out of the top of the carbs. A quick call to his sponsor, Holley carbs, and a brief lesson in reversion told Joniec the problem. When the intake valve closes, a

Al Joniec looked to balance the feed on his Cammer by splitting two Holley dominator carbs. The changes took his Maverick from a bottom 10s car to high 9s. (Photo Courtesy Al Joniec)

The Motown Missile, seen here in 1971, was campaigned by a group of Chrysler engineers whose main objective in building the car was to research, develop, and test parts that would benefit Chrysler's contracted teams. Ted Spehar built the twin-plug Hemi that set the NHRA's first Pro Stock ET record with a 9.95. (Photo Courtesy Michael Pottie)

compression wave forms, which is the result of the air/fuel mixture reflecting back off the closed valve, pushing the intake runner back up. In a regular intake manifold, if the wave reaches a reflective surface, a wave of the same form is reflected back along the ports. Since an individual runner fuel injector manifold (as Joniec was using for his carbs) doesn't have any reflective area, the mixture was being pushed back out the carbs.

To solve the problem, Joniec built a bigger plenum under each carb and made an H-pattern system of 1¼-inch hoses to connect the individual plenums together. This permitted these waves to cancel each other out as well as adding to the reflective area of the much bigger surface area of a larger plenum.

"I had to use larger CFM carbs, as the individual cylinders demanded more flow than what the 500-cfm carbs could supply," Joniec said. "So, I took two Dominators, cut them in half, and mounted them. I had to add idle system passages to the rear halves. Also, by making the plenum larger, each cylinder could then pull from both throttle plates, which increased flow as well."

Joniec's inventiveness saw the Maverick go from a low-10-second performer to high 9s at 140 mph.

Dick Loehr was one of the first to jump on the "fewer the better" cubic inch bandwagon when he and mechanic John Skiba de-stroked a SOHC 427 to 393 ci for their Holman-Moody-prepped Ford Drag Team Maverick. The near 700-hp Ford cranked out a best of 10-flat times. Behind the Cammer rode a 5-speed transmis-

Dick Loehr's Stampede Maverick relied upon a de-stroked Cammer for go. Built by M&S Race Cars, Dick's Maverick later tried an injected Cleveland on for size to run Gas. (Photo Courtesy John Foster Jr.)

sion that Skiba created by mashing a pair of top loaders together. The 5-speed helped keep the SOHC within its optimal RPM range, which Loehr found to be right around 6,000.

The *Motown Missile* crewmembers, which consisted of a string of Chrysler engineers, put their heads together with the folks at B&M to create a workable Turbo-clutch transmission to use in their Hemi Challenger. The turbo-clutch, as many may recall, used a clutch to get the car off the line but was shifted automatically from gear to gear. It helped the *Missile* record compatible 9.90 times, but in the end, it proved to be too inconsistent and was swapped for a 4-speed.

Mid-Eliminators

The NHRA's streamlining continued as it did away with the Sports Production category, which eliminated five classes of cars. In total, the NHRA was down to 44 classes in the Mid-Eliminator bracket. Meanwhile, the AHRA continued to offer a class for every combination and configuration imaginable. Although it was more confusing, it left plenty of room for racers to experiment with different combinations.

Altereds

Looking back on the decade that was, AA/FA never really received the recognition or respect it deserved. I doubt any class of cars presented more bang for your buck than this class of car. Be it the low-end E/A or the AA/Fueler bad boys, these guys campaigned these cars for the love of it.

The Fuel Altereds required pretty much the same maintenance as the Top Fuel and Funny Cars but raced for pittance in comparison. Riding in a car with a 92-inch wheelbase with a nitro-fed blown Hemi or big-block Chevy upfront and turning speeds in the bottom 7s showed who had the bigger "you know whats."

The *Nanook*, driven by Dave Hough, was often referred to as the World's Fastest Altered with speeds in 1970 being a shade over 219 mph. The *Nanook* was powered by a Donovan-built Hemi and played the role of test mule in the development of Donovan's all-aluminum Hemi that debuted in 1971. Mike Sullivan laid a new patriot paint job on his unorthodox Fiat and pushed the car to a record 7.12. The king of the Fuel Altereds, Willie Borsch, debuted a new Logghe chassis *Winged Express* in July after going for a hair-raising ride and crashing the old one. In time, Borsch coaxed a best of 6.96 out of the Ford T.

Further down the Altered line, Jack Ditmars and his

AHRA's Junior Pro Stock

The AHRA GT classes, a poor man's Pro Stock category, was initiated in 1970 and consisted of three classes: GT-1 for cars weighing 8 pounds per cubic inch, GT-2 for cars weighing 9 pounds per cubic inch, and GT-3 for cars 10 pounds per cubic inch. Maximum cubic inch rules were in effect: GT-1 allowed for 401 and greater, GT-2 was 350 to 400 ci, and GT-3 was 300 to 349 ci. For the few years the category ran, it was dominated by first-generation Camaros, namely the cars of Bill Hielscher, Larry and Gary Kimball, and the team of Hiner & Miller. At the end of season one, the world champs were Gary Kimball in GT-1, David Jones driving for Bill Hielscher in GT-2, and Hiner & Miller in GT-3.

By the close of the decade, Bill Hielscher had in the neighborhood of 80 AHRA class records under his belt. He dominated with his string of Chevys, beginning in 1966 with a Corvette. Here he's caught running his 427-ci Camaro in heads-up Super Stock, the AHRA's equivalent to NHRA Pro Stock. (Photo Courtesy Michael Pottie)

Don Green's 392-powered Rat Trap was part of the Gold Agency's Fuel Altered Tour in 1970 (through 1972), by which time it was clocking mid-7-second times approaching 220 mph. Dennis Watson built the 100-inch-wheelbase chassis. The independent front suspension and friction shocks flew in the face of convention. (Photo Courtesy James Handy)

And you thought the lines between the Gassers and the Funny Cars were blurred. Jack Ditmars's flip-top Opel Kadett ran A/FA but saw action running injected Funny Car programs and Gasser events. Ditmars debuted the car at the Springnationals in 1968, where he won best appearing car and crew awards. Here, at the 1970 Winternationals, he won Comp Eliminator. Powering the Mini Brute to record 8.0 times was a 513-ci Chevy engine. (Photo Courtesy James Handy)

Dick Shroyer and his Rod Shop–sponsored D/Altered 1948 Thames were winners in Modified Eliminator at the NHRA Summernationals. Shroyer's Shaker also saw duty as a D/Gasser. An injected Chevy made the Thames a winner. Note the transverse leaf spring, drilled axle, and weight bar. Some people had less confidence in the transverse setup than a leaf spring–supported axle and steered clear. (Photo Courtesy Steve Reyes)

In 1970, the Mallicoat brothers debuted their BB/A, twin-turbo Barracuda. Air Research supplied the turbochargers, which helped propel the car to mid-8-second times at 170 mph. Exhibition Engineering built the chassis hiding under the old John Mazmanian body. (Photo Courtesy James Handy)

You'll be forgiven if you thought this was a blown Street Roadster as opposed to the supercharged Gasser that it is. In 1970, Gary Burgin's 1927 Ford was a fine example of the type of cars you could now find running in AA/GS. The days when Austins, Anglias, and Willys dominated were over. (Photo Courtesy Michael Pottie)

A/FA Opel defeated Ken Dondero in the Panella Trucking Anglia at the NHRA Winternationals, lowering the class record in the process with an 8.03 at 173.07. Jack was runner-up at the Gators and the Springnationals. The *Mini Brute* was built back in 1968 and featured a 100-inch chassis built by Dennis Rollain and John Buttera's R&B Automotive.

Gassers

The Gas category now ran all the way down to J/Gas. The low end of the category was ruled by 6-cylinder Chevys and screaming VW Bugs. The quirky little Beetle had quite the following, thanks to its popularity on the street and the efforts on the track by Dean Lowry; the Schley brothers, who held the H/G record; and Darrell Vittone, who drove the EMPI *Inch Pincher* to an I/G class record 12.33. Running in the neighborhood of 2,150 cc, an overall lightweight (1,100 pounds light!),

European Motor Products Incorporated (EMPI) was launched by Darrell Vittone in the late 1950s. His Inch Pincher VW was the scourge of J/G in 1970, running 13.30 times. Though a VW never won a national event, the cars were the cause of many headaches in Modified Eliminator. How popular were these Bugs? By 1970, annual sales of EMPI products exceeded $6 million. (Photo Courtesy Michael Pottie)

Mike Mitchell, the world's fastest hippie, had originally campaigned this colorful 1933 Willys in A/GS with a blown Chevy. Mike Vincz took over the car and campaigned it with an injected Chevy. The Willys ran in both Gas and Altered classes. Renown West Coast Gas legend Chuck Finders built this one. (Photo Courtesy Ed Aigner)

compression in the 14:1 range, a modified oiling system, and a good bottom end cradle helped to keep these Bugs flying.

Merging Supercharged Street Roadsters with Supercharged Gas in 1969 really left a person confused. Gary Burgin's AA/GS Roadster looked out of place in Gas, especially when running against someone like K. S. Pittman, who dropped the Austin "football" body and replaced it with an Opel GT shell. Ohio George Montgomery and his Mustang continued to dominate the class, holding the record with an 8.59. An obvious identity crisis within blown Gas saw fan appeal drop to a new low.

Modified Eliminator

Gaining in popularity was the NHRA's Modified Eliminator, and no wonder with the number of categories under its umbrella. It had Gas Dragsters (B/D to E/D), Altereds (B/A to F/A), Gassers (A/G to J/G), Street Roadsters (A/SR to C/SR), and Modified Production (A/MP to H/MP). With such a wide variety of classes, a handicap of

Old Chevys never died—they just became dominant Modified Production cars, right? Few were as tough as the multi-record-holding 1955 Bel Air of Carroll Caudle.

waiting on the line could be agonizing for a quicker car. At season's end, the Modified Eliminator World Champ was Division 4 points champion Carroll Caudle and his F/MP 1955 Chevy. Caudle defeated Dave Armbruster's redlighting B/Dragster with a record-setting 11.83.

Modified Production

Carroll Caudle's 1955 Bel Air was a prime example of the caliber of cars running Modified Production. The Chevy was stock in appearance and ran multiple classes with multiple small-blocks derived from boring, stroking, and de-stroking. As history has shown, the small-block Chevy is very responsive to change and lost little power when de-stroked down to sizes as low as 266 ci.

In 1970, only Stock had more entrants than Modified Production. Putting it into perspective, Modified Production had 8 classes while Stock ran 36 classes. A number of factory teams filled the upper echelons of Modified Production and stole a couple Eliminator titles. Dick Landy used his A/MP Hemi Dart to defeat the Rod Shop–sponsored C/Gas Anglia of Jim Thompson at the Winternationals. At the proceeding Gatornationals, Herb McCandless took Billy Stepp's B/MP Barracuda to a category win over Bob Pigg's Hemi-powered A/G Anglia. Go beyond A and B/MP and it was pretty well an all-Chevy show. Chevys held 14 of the 16 class records through most of the season.

Super Stock Eliminator

Just as Top Gas took a back seat to Top Fuel back in 1964, Super Stock faced the same scenario in 1970 when the category saw a mass exodus of racers heading to Pro Stock. Chrysler's Hemi Darts and Barracudas continued to dominate the top echelon of Super Stock, as they would for years to come.

Ron Mancini and his SS/AA Dart captured two national events: the NHRA Summernationals and Indy, where he ran a 10.33 to defeat the AMX of Lou Downing.

By far the most successful factory drag cars ever produced were the Hemi-powered Barracudas and Darts of 1968. Ron Mancini took his SS/AA Dart to wins at the NHRA Summernationals and Nationals in 1970 with a record time of 10.33. The record stood for two years. (Photo Courtesy Michael Pottie)

Some felt the Cobra Jet engine in a Mustang coupe was a bad combo, as traction would be hard to find. Barrie Poole proved them wrong with a category win at the Winternationals, a runner-up at the Summernationals, and a class record of 11.27. (Photo Courtesy James Handy)

John Elliot and Barrie Poole continued to steal Wallys across the border, winning the Winternationals and the Springnationals with their pair of Cobra Jet Mustangs. Ray Allen and Truppi-Kling, graduates of Stock, took their SS/EA 454-powered Chevelle ragtop to a pair of national wins, in spite of Chrysler's attempt to dethrone them. The manufacturer built a bogus 512-ci Superbird for Jack

Werst (*Mr. 5 and 50*) to face down Allen and prevent the world title from falling into Chevy hands. Their efforts failed miserably, and Allen, who had the only Chevy in Super Stock at the World Finals, took the title, defeating Dave Wren, whose SS/DA Barracuda lost the transmission on the final go.

Stock Eliminator

In a major blow to the Chevrolet fraternity, the 1955 through 1957 Chevrolet sedan deliveries that so dominated the category during the latter part of the decade lost their Corvette mills and Hydra-matic transmissions to rule changes. Considering they weren't available factory installed in the first place, the NHRA, with pressure from Detroit, closed the loophole. The largest powerplant now allowed in the 1957 model delivery was the 220-hp 283, which could only be backed by a 3-speed standard transmission or a cast-iron Powerglide.

Though Chevy wasn't the only brand to come out of the 1970 rule revisions scathed, it was the one hurt the most by them. To the delight (no doubt) of both Chevy and the NHRA, Bobby Warren won the World Finals with his 350-ci-powered 1969 Nova.

Marv Ripes of A-1 Automatic Transmission found a way to keep the cast-iron Powerglide Chevys in contention when he adapted an 8-inch Opel torque convertor to the Powerglide in his 1957 Chevy. The combination helped him win the NHRA Springnationals and the season-ending Supernationals.

To refresh the memories, Opel was a GM import that was sold through Buick dealerships starting in 1969. For a Buick dealer to be approved for an Opel franchise, it was required to stock one of every part. Drag racer Bob Lambeck, a friend of Marv's, happened to work in the parts department at Cummings Buick in Santa Monica and came across the 8-inch convertor.

Don Grotheer won SS/BA at the 1969 NHRA Winternationals and repeated here in 1970, now running SS/AA in the same Hemi Barracuda. Grotheer's class winning time was a 10.62 at 114.79 mph. (Photo Courtesy James Handy)

One of the bogus combos that the NHRA quashed at the end of 1970 was the 427 engine in a Fairlane station wagon. Richard Charbonneau ran the combo through 1970, winning the Division 5 points championship and the Winternationals, where he defeated the V/S Olds of Keith Berg with a 12.06. (Photo Courtesy John Foster Jr.)

"It was in a tiny box labeled in German, *Konverter*." Lambeck said. "I couldn't believe the size of it."

Lambeck placed a call to Ripes, who immediately saw the potential and purchased it. To make the little convertor work in the Chevy, the turbine hub, the bolt pattern, and the pilot hub all had to be modified. Now to make the cast-iron Powerglide hold up to the expected 4,000-rpm stall, Ripes increased the line pressure and installed a clutch hub designed for the 348-ci Powerglide. The 348 Powerglide transmissions featured a heavier hub, and Ripes could put five clutches in them as opposed to the standard Powerglide, which used four.

Ripes found that they would break a planetary occasionally, but generally the transmission held up pretty good behind the estimated 300 hp generated by an injected 283. With the reworked Powerglide, Ripes saw an immediate reduction in elapsed times, going from 14.50s to 14.0s. Once traction issues were resolved, the old Chevy was pushing wind to the tune of 13.80s on its own 14.50 record. A-1 had the market cornered on the high-stall convertor, and in no time, customer demand saw a backorder of approximately 400 units. It seems the Tri-Five Chevys of Stock Eliminator weren't quite dead yet.

It took Marv Ripes, proprietor of A-1 Automatic Transmissions, to show there was still hope for cast-iron Powerglide-equipped 1957 Chevys. Ripes won Stock Eliminator at the NHRA Springnationals and the Supernationals in 1970, running record 13.40 times. (Photo Courtesy Dale Schafer)

The 1970s rang in a whole new era in Top Fuel. By 1973, the front engine rail was all but dead, replaced by safer mid-engine cars. Don Garlits seemed to lead the charge with his line of **Swamp Rats**. At the NHRA World Finals in 1975, he set the ET record with a phenomenal 5.63. The record stood through mid-1982. (Photo Courtesy Don Prieto)

Chapter Eleven

Forward and Faster

A h, the 1970s. If you look past the low-performance cars, the gas crisis, and disco, it wasn't a bad decade. The sport of drag racing continued to grow in participation, and fan appeal was never stronger. In regard to evolution and technical advances, the decade pulled a close second to the 1960s.

In Top Fuel, Don Garlits ushered in a new era when he won both the AHRA and the NHRA world titles in 1971 with his mid-engine *Swamp Rat 14*. His immediate success with the new car rendered the slingshot rail all but obsolete. The final Top Fuel national event win by a front-engine dragster came at the 1972 NHRA Grand-nationals, where 23-year old Art Marshall, in Don Prud-homme's old high-back Hot Wheels car, defeated Jeb Allen.

Though Garlits had won his titles using factory cast blocks, the days of aftermarket castings were upon us. Ed Donovan debuted his aluminum 417 ci at the Superna-

*Weight breaks in 1972 made the 331-ci Vega the car to beat in Pro Stock. Bill Jenkins remained Chevy's No. 1 through the decade. His line of **Grumpy's Toys** cars won two AHRA world titles and two NHRA world titles. (Photo Courtesy Michael Pottie)*

No matter what it was, Top Fuel or Funny Car, Don Prudhomme was one of the best in class. Between 1975 and 1978, he won four straight NHRA Funny Car world titles. His Monza won 15 national events and the world title in 1975 and 1976. (Photo Courtesy Bob Boudreau)

tionals in 1971. In short order, Keith Black followed suit, and by the end of the decade, an aftermarket block was the only way to go in Top Fuel and Funny Car.

The 5-second barrier was broken in Top Fuel on October 22, 1972, when TV Tommy Ivo recorded a 5.97 at Pittsburgh. Don Prudhomme broke the barrier in Funny Car on October 12, 1975, when he propelled his Keith Black–powered Chevy Monza to a 5.98 at Ontario Motor Speedway.

Grumpy Jenkins put the Pro in Pro Stock in 1972 when he debuted his small-block-powered Vega with its yards of chrome-moly tubing. Chrysler's Hemi domination was over, as Jenkins and his 331-ci Vega owned Pro Stock that year, taking the championship after winning six of the seven national events he entered. Weight breaks took off the same year, and through the decade their fluctuation drove the racers nuts.

Chrysler boycotted the NHRA races due to what it felt was unfair weight breaks. Ford's better-breathing Cleveland-powered cars seemed to suffer with the most added weight as the NHRA attempted to maintain a level playing field. Interesting enough

Bob Glidden, a graduate of 1960s Stock and Super Stock racing, all but owned NHRA Pro Stock in the 1970s. Between 1971 and 1980, his string of Cleveland-powered Fords won five world titles. (Photo Courtesy Bob Boudreau)

though, the Fords still managed to win seven Pro Stock world titles through the 1970s.

But not all changes were good. Upsetting many was the demise of Top Gas at the end of 1971. In 1972, Stock reverted to a Pure Stock format, forcing those with modified cars to look to other categories to race. As a means to make drag racing a little less complicated to the fans, the NHRA dumped the Gas and Altered categories and merged the classes with Comp Eliminator after 1974.

Sadly, the racetrack took some of our favorites: Sneaky Pete Robinson, Dick Harrell, and Pro Stock's Don Carlton come to mind. Helping to fill the void were rising stars in Gary Beck, Bob Glidden, and Ken Veney, among others.

It was a decade full of memorable moments. A decade like the 1960s will not soon be forgotten.

What looks like an old Super Eliminator A/GS Opel was actually a CC/Altered Comp Eliminator car in the mid-1970s. Dave Kroona and Dave Sandberg with driver Phil Featherston took the old Bob Panella Opel to a Comp Eliminator win at the 1976 NHRA Winternationals, repeating Featherston's and Panella's 1975 win. A de-stroked 354 Hemi propelled the Opel to 8.30 times.

Is it any wonder that NHRA Modified Production was so popular well into the 1970s? With its vast array of door cars, high revs, and wheels-up launches, what wasn't there to like. Lee Smith's 1966 Plymouth C/MP Whackee Wagon *ran a Hemi, 4-speed combo and was a stablemate to his* Crazee 'Cuda *Pro Stocker. (Photo Courtesy Bob Martin)*

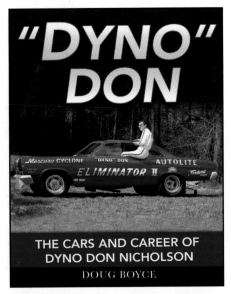
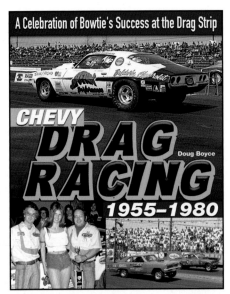

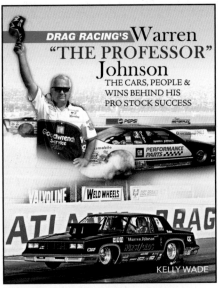

WORK AND WAGES

Natural law, politics and the eighteenth-century French trades

MICHAEL SONENSCHER

King's College, Cambridge

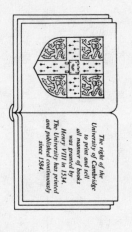

The right of the
University of Cambridge
to print and sell
all manner of books
was granted by
Henry VIII in 1534.
The University has printed
and published continuously
since 1584.

CAMBRIDGE UNIVERSITY PRESS

Cambridge
New York   New Rochelle
Melbourne   Sydney

Published by the Press Syndicate of the University of Cambridge
The Pitt Building, Trumpington Street, Cambridge CB2 1RP
32 East 57th Street, New York, NY 10022, USA
10 Stamford Road, Oakleigh, Melbourne 3166, Australia

First published 1989

Printed in Great Britain by the University Press, Cambridge

British Library cataloguing in publication data

Sonenscher, Michael
Work and wages: natural law, politics
and the eighteenth-century French trades.
1. France. Working conditions, 1700–1800
I. Title
331.2′0944

Library of Congress cataloguing in publication data

Sonenscher, Michael.
Work and wages: natural law, politics, and the eighteenth-century
French trades/Michael Sonenscher.
p. cm.
Bibliography: p.
Includes index.
ISBN 0-521-32984-1
1. Artisans–France–History–18th century. 2. Wages–France–
History–18th century. I. Title.
HD2346.F8S66 1989
331.2′944-dc 1988–27457 CIP

ISBN 0 521 32984 1

UP

MB

CONTENTS

v

vi   *Contents*

FIGURES

TABLES

I would not have been able to undertake the research upon which this book is based without the financial support of the British Academy, the Economic and Social Research Council, the Nuffield Foundation, the Pasold Fund and the Middlesex Polytechnic. I am particularly grateful to the Economic and Social Research Council for the award of a personal research grant in 1984–5. It allowed me to complete the time-consuming task of creating a machine readable data base and organise a large amount of very disparate material into something resembling a first draft of a book.

I owe a substantial debt to my former colleagues at the Middlesex Polytechnic, particularly Roger Waterhouse, Norman Levy and Jonathan Powers, for their unstinting support and willingness to accommodate my research in circumstances that were never of their making and were always unpropitious to sustained historical inquiry. Robyn Smits, Mike Bell and Steve Pickering of the Middlesex Polytechnic Computer Centre made it possible for me to use a computer. Without their help I would not have been able to write this book. Beverley Chapman and her colleagues in the Middlesex Polytechnic Library introduced me to aspects of library service that I had never previously imagined. They also responded to my interminable requests for inter-library loans with great speed, efficiency and forbearance.

I am grateful to the many archivists and librarians in Paris, Rouen, Laon, Amiens, Reims, Chalons-sur-Marne, Metz, Sedan, Troyes, Dijon, Mâcon, Chalon-sur-Saône, Lyon, Grenoble, Aix-en-Provence, Marseille, Privas, Nîmes, Montpellier, Toulouse, Bordeaux, La Rochelle, Nantes, Rennes and Le Havre who placed their expertise at my disposal during my visits to France and replied to my many letters with unfailing courtesy and thoroughness. Like so many historians who have come to France, I found much intellectual generosity and human warmth, as well as many rich and illuminating sources of information in the libraries and archives I visited.

x   *Acknowledgements*

My interest in some of the questions addressed in this book was awakened an alarmingly long time ago when I was a student at Warwick University. I owe a great deal to Edward Thompson, who, soon after I arrived in England in 1966, allowed me to join a course on industrialisation that he taught. It was a formative experience, not only for its content, but also for the intellectual honesty, rigour and exemplary care with which it was done. Some years later, Gwynne Lewis agreed, at rather short notice, to accept me as a graduate student and became the supervisor of a thesis that allowed me to find my feet in archival research in France. However distant the content of much of this book may be from their own concerns and preoccupations, it is an outcome of a dialogue in which I have participated with gratitude.

Most of the research on which this book is based took place as part of a wider project on 'Work and wages in eighteenth-century France'. The book's final title is as much a recognition of what I have omitted, or failed to address, as it is an indication of its range and content. I have sought, however, to show why the work of urban and agricultural labourers, domestic servants and women (none of them mutually exclusive categories) took place in somewhat different circumstances from those that I have addressed.

I am indebted to Lesley Miller, Jane McCleod and Carolyn Sargentson for their kindness in sending me information from Lyon, Bordeaux and Paris during their own research there. John Annette, Richard Andrews, Maxine Berg, Alain Cottereau, Arlette Farge, Andy Federer, David Garrioch, Daryl Hafter, Doug Hay, Pat Hudson, Colin Jones, Steven Kaplan, Peter Linebaugh, Tim Le Goff, Andrew Lincoln, Hans Medick, John Merrington, Jeanette Neeson, Tim Putnam, Jonathan Rée, Daniel Roche, Bill Sewell, Michael Sibalis, John Styles, David Sugarman, Miles Taylor, Cynthia Truant, Mark Whitaker and Jonathan Zeitlin have contributed to this book in so many different ways that a proper expression of gratitude would need another large volume. Elizabeth Allen set me an example of courage and determination that encouraged me to get on with it. The many remaining defects that this book contains are my own responsibility.

A.C. = Archives communales
A.D. = Archives départementales
A.N. = Archives nationales (Paris)
B.M. = Bibliothèque municipale
B.N. = Bibliothèque nationale (Paris)

The standard unit of currency in eighteenth-century France was the *livre*. One *livre* was made up of 20 *sous* and one *sou* (or *sol*) was made up of 12 *deniers*. The *écu* was worth three *livres* and the *louis* was worth six *livres*.

Unless otherwise specified, all weights are denominated in Parisian pounds and ounces. A pound in eighteenth-century Paris was equivalent to 489·5 grams. A hundred pounds (a hundredweight) was known as a *quintal*.

I have retained the original spelling, but modernised punctuation, in citations in French.

In 1791 the *philosophe*, chemist and financier Antoine-Laurent Lavoisier published an essay on the wealth, population and consumption of the city of Paris.[1] The work was one of those combinations of reasoned inference and arbitrary deduction that were a hallmark of the late eighteenth-century statistical mind. Lavoisier began by making an informed guess at the size of the city's population. He went on to produce a table of the annual amount of food and other materials needed to support that population. The table was one that Borges would have admired. It revealed that in addition to 107,000,000 pounds of bread, 90,000,000 pounds of meat and 679,000 hectolitres of wine, the 600,000 inhabitants of late eighteenth-century Paris ate and drank their way through an assortment of foodstuffs that included 75,000 pounds of shrimps, 800,000 carps, 425,000 pieces of fresh cheese, 476,000 pounds of plums, 78,000,000 eggs, 54,000 hectolitres of beer and 2,500,000 pounds of coffee.

Food was only a part of the huge array of primary goods transformed into manufactured commodities every year. The material infrastructure that supplied the capital's population with its housing, furniture, transport and clothing was represented by, among other things, an annual consumption of 1,600,000 cubic feet of timber, 3,200,000 pounds of lead, 3,717,000 strong slates, 3,700,000 pounds of hide and leather, 8,000,000 pounds of iron and 6,000,000 ells of cloth. Every year these materials were transformed into an immense variety of finished products in the course of itineraries that passed through tens of thousands of workshops, building sites, sheds and garrets whose structured inter-dependence endowed the multiple and elaborate divisions of labour of the eighteenth-century urban economy with their internal architecture and coherent form.

Exercises of a similar sort were carried out in many French towns and cities – from Lille to Nîmes and from Rennes to Grenoble – during the late

---

[1] Antoine-Laurent Lavoisier, 'Essai sur la population de la ville de Paris, sur sa richesse et ses consommations', printed in his *Œuvres* (Paris, 1893), vol. 6, pp. 429–39.

eighteenth century.[2] The results they generated are an evocation, rather than an accurate representation, of the scale of the work involved in transforming raw materials into vendible commodities in eighteenth-century France. This book is a study of the men and, insofar as it has been possible, the women who performed that work. Most of them, including the women, were artisans of one kind or another. Some of them, including some women, were also members of guilds or, as they were called in France, corporations.

The two terms – artisans and corporations – belong to an established historiographical tradition. They are most familiar in the context of studies of the relationship between artisans, radical politics and the process of industrialisation in the late eighteenth and nineteenth centuries.[3] The purpose of this book is to change that context in a number of ways. Instead of corporations, it is concerned with the law. Instead of artisans, it is concerned with the economy of the workshop. Instead of the customary world of pre-industrial society, it is concerned with markets, prices and profits. Instead of the geographical and cultural continuities associated with crafts and skills, it is concerned with the mobility and adaptability associated with different kinds of labour market and changing patterns of employment. Instead of rigid divisions between master artisans and the journeymen they employed, it is concerned with the passage of time and the fluidity of relationships between the generations that its management engendered. Instead of the culture of artisans, it is concerned with the culture of the French polity.

Much of this may read as a manifesto for a neo-classical reinterpretation of the world of eighteenth-century artisans. That is not its purpose. Markets and prices, like work and consumption, are not the same at all times and places. The aim of this book is not to transpose a variant of modern micro-economic theory to the urban trades of eighteenth-century

[2] See Jean-Claude Perrot, *L'Age d'or de la statistique régionale française (an IV-1804)* (Paris, 1977); Louis Bergeron, ed., *La Statistique en France à l'époque napoléonienne* (Brussels, 1981).

[3] The classics are E. P. Thompson, *The Making of the English Working Class* (London, 1963); E. J. Hobsbawm, *Primitive Rebels* (London, 1959) and *Labouring Men* (London, 1964); George Rudé, *The Crowd in the French Revolution* (Oxford, 1959), *The Crowd in History* (New York, 1964), *Paris and London in the Eighteenth Century* (London, 1970). More recent works include Iorwerth Prothero, *Artisans and Politics in Early Nineteenth-Century London* (London, 1979); Maxine Berg, *The Age of Manufactures 1700–1820* (London, 1985); and John Rule, *The Experience of Labour in Eighteenth-Century Industry* (London, 1981), together with his *The Labouring Classes in Early Industrial England 1750–1850* (London, 1986). Broadly similar perspectives inform recent studies of artisans in the U.S.A. – notably Paul G. Faler, *Mechanics and Manufacturers in the Early Industrial Revolution* (New York, 1981) and Sean Wilentz, *Chants Democratic. New York City and the Rise of the American Working Class, 1788–1850* (New York and Oxford, 1984) – and in France: see William H. Sewell Jnr., *Work and Revolution in France: The Language of Labor from the Old Regime to 1848* (Cambridge, 1980); William M. Reddy, *The Rise of Market Culture: The Textile Trade and French Society, 1750–1900* (Cambridge, 1984).

France; instead, its aim is to bring a fuller, more varied and more historically precise analytical vocabulary to bear upon the eighteenth-century French trades and, by implication, upon the internal dynamics of artisanal production in early modern Europe as a whole. In different guises – as artisans, the 'middling sort' or the *petite bourgeoisie* – many of the ordinary inhabitants of towns remain the least-known component of French (or British) society in the seventeenth and eighteenth centuries. This book is an attempt to explore the artisanal economy of eighteenth-century France on its own terms and, at the same time, to restore master artisans and the journeymen they employed to the place that they occupied in the institutional life of the polity as a whole.

The need to do so became increasingly clear to me in the course of the archival research upon which this book is based. That research began as an attempt to find out more about the disputes between masters and journeymen that had formed the basis of Germain Martin's *Les associations ouvrières au xviiie siècle*, published in 1900. As Martin had shown, the record of many disputes was to be found among the papers of the courts responsible for what, in eighteenth-century France, was known as the *police des arts et métiers*, or the enforcement of corporate statutes and regulations. Research in the papers of the *chambre de police* of the Châtelet of Paris, among the voluminous surviving minutes of the 48 *commissaires* of the Châtelet, and in the municipal archives of most of the major cities of eighteenth-century France produced a mass of information about some 500 disputes between journeymen and their masters.

Some of that information was remarkably rich. The records of the courts contained petitions, depositions, interrogations and memoranda that were sometimes highly coloured by well-informed and often conflicting appreciations of working arrangements in particular trades. They lent themselves very readily to the sort of close scrutiny of significant detail that is one of the keys to historical understanding.[4] Yet they also presented that information in an episodic and fragmented manner. In part this was because many of the records of the relevant courts had been destroyed or divided among several different archival series.[5] More fundamentally, however, it was because the record of disputes between journeymen and their masters was structured by the relatively invisible presence of a number of other elements.

---

[4] For an earlier example of a procedure that has given rise to some rather inflated claims in recent years, see Georges Lefebvre, 'Le Meurtre du comte de Dampierre,' in his *Etudes sur la Révolution française*, 2nd edn (Paris, 1963), pp. 393–405. Two particularly stimulating recent studies are Carlo Ginzburg, *The Cheese and the Worms: The Cosmos of a Sixteenth-Century Miller* (London, 1982), and David Warren Sabean, *Power in the Blood: Popular Culture and Village Discourse in Early Modern Germany* (Cambridge, 1984).

[5] An outline of the sources used in this study can be found in the Appendix at the end of the book.

The most obvious of these elements was the largely unknown number of masters and journeymen who did not appear in depositions or interrogations arising from disputes in particular trades. The records of the corporations themselves were of little assistance in overcoming this difficulty. For several reasons they contain little information about the ordinary arrangements and daily activities carried out in the trades they regulated. Corporations were, firstly, essentially legal institutions and their records reflect the formal character of their identity and function. Generally, they have as much (or as little) relation to the life of the trades as eighteenth-century marriage contracts have to the relationships between the men and women who signed them. Most corporations were, in the second place, composite bodies, administered by a small proportion of the total number of artisans associated with a particular trade. These corporate officials – *gardes*, *jurés*, *syndics*, *prud'hommes* or *bayles* as they were variously known in different cities – enjoyed considerable administrative discretion and little trace of their executive actions can be found in the record of corporate decisions themselves. Finally, in Paris and in most eighteenth-century cities, the great majority of master artisans and, *a fortiori*, journeymen played little active part in the decisions recorded in the formal minutes of corporate deliberations because they did not belong to the small body of people, or *bureau*, elected (or selected) to manage corporate affairs. Eighteenth-century French corporations were not, therefore, the same as the eighteenth-century French trades. Yet without some information about the many anonymous masters and journeymen whose activities informed the everyday life of the trades, it was very difficult to place the things that were said and done when disputes occurred in any precise context.

Here an accidental discovery supplied an opportunity to identify and measure that context with some degree of confidence. In some eighteenth-century French cities, disputes between masters and journeymen over what would now be called breach of contract led to the establishment of corporate labour exchanges, or *bureaux de placement*. Journeymen were required to register with these institutions before they found work, while master artisans were obliged to use them when they took on the men that they employed. The registers of three such corporate labour exchanges, established by the master tailors, wigmakers and locksmiths of the city of Rouen in the late eighteenth century, have survived.[6] Instead of the relatively small number of masters and journeymen identified in

[6] For the results of an early and limited analysis of one register, see Michael Sonenscher, 'Journeymen's Migrations and Workshop Organization in Eighteenth-Century France', in Steven L. Kaplan and Cynthia J. Koepp, eds, *Work in France: Representations, Meaning, Organization and Practice* (Ithaca, N.Y., 1986), pp. 74–96. See also chapters 4 and 5 below.

proceedings arising from disputes in the trades, the registers of registration contain information about thousands of journeymen and hundreds of the master artisans who employed them. Two other registers have also survived: one concerning journeymen in almost every trade in the town of Tours and another concerning journeymen wigmakers in the city of Nantes. Although the information they contain is not as full as in Rouen, and all five series of records cover a relatively small number of years, the records of corporate labour exchanges made it possible for me to envisage reconstructing something of the ordinary life of the eighteenth-century trades with some precision.

The information about the composition of the workforce, patterns of geographical migration, rhythms of employment and the structure of local labour markets that the registers disclosed made it possible to bring a greater degree of sensitivity to the things that were said and done in the course of disputes in the trades. Yet the record of legal proceedings was also structured in a number of other, more or less visible ways. The courts concerned with the *police des arts et métiers* were only a part of the complex hierarchy of juridical institutions of eighteenth-century France. The identities of the actors – corporations, master artisans, unincorporated artisans and journeymen – whose concerns and preoccupations filled the record of their proceedings were, I began to realise, largely defined elsewhere. In part, they were defined in the course of the daily, weekly and seasonal cycles of work, wages, production and consumption that informed the local economies of particular trades. In part, however, they were also defined within the conventions of eighteenth-century French civil jurisprudence and the legal procedures that supplied corporations with their formal regulations and statutes.

Those conventions and procedures were not established by the courts concerned with the *police des arts et métiers* and the enforcement of corporate regulation, but by the Parlements and the Royal Council, the highest courts of appeal in eighteenth-century France. Here again a series of chance discoveries in the largely unexplored riches of the papers of the Parlement of Paris served to reveal a much more elaborately structured world of legal argument and judicial process than my initial pre-suppositions about the place of artisanal production and artisanal culture in eighteenth-century French society had led me to expect.[7] As my

7 The records of the courts have been used in the main by historians of crime and the criminal law. In the context of eighteenth-century France this has led to the emergence of a consensus among historians that the law was often a last recourse in disputes that were often settled by other, infrajudicial, means: see particularly Nicole Castan, *Justice et répression en Languedoc à l'époque des Lumières* (Paris, 1980), especially pp. 13–51. The view has its merits, if only in dispelling a number of myths about the litigious character of early modern societies. At the same time, however, the criminal law was only a part of the French legal system and the civil law had a very much more substantial place in

capacity to find my way around the papers of the Parlements improved, I discovered that there were many occasions during the seventeenth and eighteenth centuries when hundreds of journeymen combined to take part in legal proceedings against master artisans over many different issues. Not only did this discovery suggest substantial revisions to my assumptions about the character of artisanal culture and associations among journeymen, it also prompted a more wide-ranging reassessment of the character of the eighteenth-century French civil law and its relationship to the life of the trades.

The combined effect of a closer acquaintance with the everyday economy of certain trades on the one hand, and the wider environment of eighteenth-century French civil jurisprudence on the other, has led me to modify many of my initial presuppositions. The full, relatively self-contained image of artisanal production with which I began my research has changed as I have become more aware of the elisions and effects of foreshortening created by too close a dependence upon the depositions, interrogations and other documents created in the course of disputes in the trades. The result, in a paradoxical way, has obliged me to move away from the now familiar otherness of the customary world of pre-industrial society and begin to understand an economy and a political culture that, in the eighteenth century, were effortlessly taken for granted. The resonances of the things that journeymen and their masters said and did in the course of disputes in the eighteenth-century French trades derived from conditions and circumstances that were left unsaid and undescribed because they were so banal. This book is an attempt to reconstruct something of that once familiar world by looking beyond the written record of words used in arguments and conflicts towards the less spectacular, but no less fundamental, ordinariness of the circumstances in which they occurred.

the making and unmaking of rights and obligations than the criminal law. Before the Revolution, much of what became 'politics' can be found in the proceedings of the civil courts: some of the reasons why this was so are outlined in chapter 2 below.

CHAPTER I

The limits of memory

Before the Revolution of 1789 many of the thousands of workshops, hangars or building sites associated with the trades of urban France fell under the formal jurisdiction of corporations. The largest number were to be found in Paris. In 1724 or 1725, according to Jacques Savary des Bruslons, the capital's 117 corporations had a total membership of some 35,000 master artisans.[1] As a centre of artisanal production, Paris was at once typical and untypical of many other large cities in eighteenth-century France. It was typical in the sense that the city's largest artisanal corporations were represented by the clothing and victualling trades; it was untypical in the way that furnishing and decoration far outstripped the size of corporations associated with textile production or the building trades (Table 1). The capital's association with high-quality, decorative artefacts undoubtedly had a long history. Yet whatever the differences between the Parisian corporations and those of Lyon, Marseille, Bordeaux, Nantes, Rouen or Lille (the largest provincial cities in early eighteenth-century France) it has been usual to emphasise their similarities. The combination of small-scale production, urban artisans and self-contained corporations has formed an abiding image of the world of the eighteenth-century French trades.

Artisans, however, produced their own images of artisanal production.

---

1 Jacques Savary des Bruslons, *Dictionnaire universel de commerce*, 2 vols (Paris, 1723). The figures come from the sixth edition (Paris, 1750), p. 1056, under 'communauté', and were derived from 'les listes que les jurés qui entrent en charge ont coutume de faire imprimer et d'où cet extrait a été tiré dans les années 1723, 1724 et 1725.' They were reproduced in the *Almanach de cabinet* (Paris, 1765) – see Archives de la ville de Paris, D⁵B⁶ 346 – and copied again by the *abbé* Expilly in his *Dictionnaire géographique, historique et politique des Gaules et de la France* (Paris, 1768), vol. 5, pp. 418–20. No other set of figures of the size of the Parisian corporations exists. The two most recent historians of the Parisian trades have avoided the problem of measuring their size by reproducing Savary's totals and proceeding to concentrate upon journeymen and labourers rather than master artisans: see Daniel Roche, *Le Peuple de Paris* (Paris, 1981), p. 72, and Jeffry Kaplow, *The Names of Kings: The Parisian Laboring Poor in the Eighteenth Century* (New York, 1972), p. 19. For fuller discussion of the size of some corporations in both Paris and the major cities of provincial France, see chapters 4 and 7 below.

1. The Parisian corporations in the early eighteenth century

Category	Total	Item	Number
Textiles	1,957		
		Woollen merchants	190
		Hosiers	540
		Ribbon-weavers	735
		Silk-weavers	318
		Dyers	35
		Wool-croppers	40
		Woollen-weavers	79
		Fullers	20
Clothing	10,277		
		Furriers	47
		Tailors	1,882
		Shoemakers	1,820
		Seamstresses	1,700
		Cobblers	1,300
		Wigmakers and barbers	805
		Dealers in old clothes	700
		Laundresses	659
		Button-makers	530
		Embroiderers	265
		Hatters	319
		Glove makers	250
Furnishing and decorating	6,068		
		Goldsmiths	500
		Painters and sculptors	967
		Joiners	895
		Carpet-weavers	627
		Gilders on leather	360
		Bronze-founders	330
		Toymakers	209
		Glaziers	300
		Locksmiths	355
		Cutlers	120
		Fanmakers	130
		Turners	29
		Makers of inlaid ware	72
		Lutemakers	102
		Engravers on metal	127
		Clock and watchmakers	180
		Enamelware-makers	130
		Musical instrument-makers	50
		Mirror-fitters	130
		Metal-polishers	240
		Potters	215
Building	1,012		
		Masons	254
		Carpenters	96
		Plumbers	43
		Roofers	197
		Pavers	35
		Sewermen	36
		Toolsmiths	170
		Nailmakers	68
		Ropemakers	113
Victualling	6,294		
		Bakers	580
		Butchers	240
		Candle-makers	269
		Fruiterers	321
		Seed merchants	260
		Pastry-cooks	243
		Roasters	307
		Market-gardeners	1,200
		Wine-sellers	1,500
		Grocers	640
		Brewers	75
		Charcutiers	132
		Cooks	207
		Vinegar-makers	320
Transport	1,440		
		Saddlers	253
		Coopers	202
		Harness-makers	200
		Spurmakers	25
		Wheelwrights	192
		Farriers	181
		Basket-makers	387
Others	3,816		
		Mercers	2,167
		Surgeons	500
		Curriers	260
		Dancing-masters	442
		Booksellers and printers	218
		Bookbinders	229
TOTAL	31,583		

Source: Jacques Savary des Bruslons, *Dictionnaire universel du commerce*, 6th edn (Paris, 1750). A.D. Ville de Paris, D⁵B⁶346. (Note that the total does not include members of such corporate bodies as the notaries, lawyers, doctors etc.)

The words they used have played a part in evocations of that world of small shops, craft skills and traditional rights often associated with the culture of artisans in the eighteenth and early nineteenth centuries. Yet the words that artisans used require careful interpretation and close attention to the contexts in which they were uttered.[2] Many of the more ordinary characteristics of the workshop economy have been rendered obscure by the selective filter of memory. Others have been disguised in more subtle ways by the ease with which artisans ignored, overlooked or merely alluded to some of the most significant and familiar aspects of the circumstances in which they lived and worked. They did so not because they wilfully chose to conceal or omit them, but because they assumed that the various audiences or interlocutors to whom their statements were addressed were as aware of these circumstances as they were themselves. Understanding artisanal culture thus calls for some familiarity with the things that artisans took for granted. The significance of what was said is best measured by what was also not said, or had been forgotten, or had been overlain by different circumstances and conditions.

A nineteenth-century example can be taken as an initial illustration. In 1879 delegates to a congress of the French hatters' union declared that men working on the finishing side of the trade had always been paid by the piece.[3] The hatters' newspaper *L'ouvrier chapelier* reiterated the claim in 1885. Piecework was, it said, best suited 'à nos moeurs et à notre indépendance'. Yet, in the eighteenth century, journeymen working on the finishing side of the hatting trade were always paid by the day. The introduction of piece-rates was the product of years of bitter conflict and protracted litigation, all of which had been long forgotten by the last quarter of the nineteenth century.[4] The independence associated with payment by the piece was the product of a complex process of historical adaptation, in which the identity of the past changed to conform to the expectations of the present.

2 This is not the place for a long methodological disquisition on a subject that has, rightly, given rise to much discussion. The work of Clifford Geertz on the one hand, and J. G. A. Pocock on the other, offers two fruitful and highly influential approaches to the question, even if they were not concerned, in their work, with eighteenth-century French artisans. See especially Clifford Geertz, *The Interpretation of Cultures* (New York, 1973) and *Local Knowledge* (New York, 1983); and J. G. A. Pocock, *Virtue, Commerce and History* (Cambridge, 1985), pp. 247–66. For some critical thoughts on similar problems see E. P. Thompson, 'Folklore, Anthropology and Social History', *Indian Historical Review*, 3 (1978), pp. 247–66; David Sabean, *Power in the Blood* (Cambridge, 1984), pp. 1–36; Steven L. Kaplan, ed., *Understanding Popular Culture* (Berlin and New York, 1984); Giovanni Levi, 'I Pericoli del Geertzismo', *Quaderni Storici*, 58 (1985), pp. 269–77; Bob Scholte, 'The Charmed Circle of Geertz's Hermeneutics', *Critique of Anthropology*, 6 (1986), pp. 5–15.

3 Jean Vial, *La Coutume chapelière* (Paris, 1941), pp. 114–15.

4 Michael Sonenscher, *The Hatters of Eighteenth-Century France* (Berkeley, California, 1987), pp. 114–15.

Amnesia of this sort was intrinsic to statements produced by artisans in France during the eighteenth century.[5] Yet the difference between what was said and what was either omitted, forgotten or taken for granted is not particularly easy to establish. To do so, it is necessary to compare statements made in several different contexts and juxtapose information from a number of different sources. The procedure is best applied to a number of autobiographical or quasi-autobiographical accounts of working lives that were written by artisans in the eighteenth and early nineteenth centuries. Three of them have survived and have recently been published. They contain accounts of the history and present circumstances of the trades with which their authors had been associated that lend themselves very readily to a timeless and universal image of artisanal production. Yet they also contain many minor details which, when taken together, modify that image in a number of fundamental ways. Close examination of these details discloses significant variations in the structure and internal organisation of different trades. It suggests that the world of the trades was a complex compound whose constituent elements – the law, the production of different commodities, the daily and seasonal cycles of work, wages and consumption, the nexus of kin, credit and clients, the accumulation and redistribution of wealth from one generation to the next – need to be identified and examined in their own right. Above all, it indicates that the things that artisans said were not a simple and unmediated reflection of the things that they did.

CATS, PRINTERS AND FOREMEN

The earliest of the three texts is a description of the customs, manners and usages of journeymen in the Parisian printing trade in the mid-eighteenth century.[6] It was written by a printer and former foreman (or *prôte*) named Nicolas Contat who, by the time the text was completed in 1762, had left the trade to become a wine merchant and part-time engraver. The text, entitled *Anecdotes typographiques*, can be interpreted in a number of ways.[7] The first, and most obvious, is as a description of the forgotten and

[5] For more wide-ranging methodological discussions, see Jack Goody, ed., *Literacy in Traditional Societies* (Cambridge, 1968), pp. 1–26; Eric Hobsbawm and Terence Ranger, eds., *The Invention of Tradition* (Cambridge, 1983); and Marshall Sahlins, *Islands of History* (Chicago, 1985).

[6] Nicolas Contat dit Lebrun, *Anecdotes typographiques où l'on voit la description des coutumes, moeurs et usages singuliers des Compagnons imprimeurs*, edited by Giles Barber (Oxford, 1980).

[7] The manuscript contains both a dedication and a reference to a fictitious publisher ('Pierre Hardy, à la Vérité') in Brussels. It is possible that the manuscript was not the only one produced. Although it did not belong to the kind of clandestine literature discussed by Margaret Jacob in *The Radical Enlightenment* (London, 1981), the difficulties faced by anyone wishing to comment publicly upon issues related to legislation affecting the Parisian trades before it became law meant that many such observations were circulated

unfamiliar rituals of artisans. The second is as a contribution to contemporary debate among master printers, booksellers and the Parisian police authorities over proposals to change the trade's corporate regulations, particularly as they applied to journeymen. Both these interpretations can be justified by explicit passages in the text and by additional information from other sources. The third interpretation is more speculative, and derives from a careful reading of the two longest parts of the text. The first is well-known: it is an account of a massacre of a master printer's cats by his apprentices.[8] The second passage is almost as long, and is a detailed description of the work carried out by a print-shop foreman. The third interpretation of Contat's manuscript requires some understanding of the relationship between these two passages.

On an initial reading, the first interpretation is closest to the text as a whole. The *Anecdotes*, as the title implies, were organised as a series of stories designed to present the Parisian printing trade to a public unacquainted with the variety and esoteric character of the customs observed by its journeymen. Contat arranged the stories into a semi-autobiographical account of an individual's passage from apprenticeship to journeywork to create a description of a young man's initiation into a world whose codes were embodied in the ceremonies and informal rituals devised and performed by the journeymen of the trade. The process of initiation consisted of a sequence of ceremonies – *prise de tablier*, *réception de quatre heures*, *droit de première banque*, *droit de chevet*, *bienvenues and conduites* – simultaneously marking the transition from apprenticeship to journeywork, the itinerary leading from childhood to manhood and the passage from technical incompetence to technical proficiency. The narrative ends with a description of a foreman's work, presented as the culmination of a journeyman's career, as it had been for Contat himself.

Contat's account is very much a description of a world apart – 'un peuple, ou plutôt une république qui vit séparé des autres nations', as he put it[9] – whose conventions and rules were created and maintained by journeymen independently of the formal prescriptions of corporate regulation and the law. Print-shops had their own informal organisations, or chapels, whose existence was tacitly accepted by master printers. Each chapel had its rules and journeymen were expected to make amends for violating them by paying a fine into a common fund: five *sous* for leaving a lighted candle unattended; five *sous* for swearing in the presence of a

8 Discussed by Robert Darnton in *The Great Cat Massacre and Other Episodes in French Cultural History* (New York, 1984), pp. 75–104.

9 Contat, *Anecdotes*, p. 31.

in manuscript. In 1776 the Conseil d'Etat prohibited five printed memoranda opposing Turgot's projected abolition of the corporations on the grounds that 'il n'a jamais été permis à aucun particulier de discuter d'avance l'objet ou les dispositions des loix' (*Gazette des Tribunaux*, 1 (1776), p. 226). As will be shown, it is likely that Contat's text belonged to this category.

woman; three *livres* for blasphemy; three *livres* for failing to wear a hat in public or any other form of impropriety; three *livres* for bringing the good name of the chapel into disrepute; a *livre* for drinking with apprentices, and so on. The *bon de chapelle*, made up of the proceeds of such fines, together with money from the books that journeymen were customarily entitled to keep, was distributed and partially consumed every year on St Martin's Day (11 November), one of the trade's two main holidays. Contat's description of the episode in which the eponymous apprentices of his narrative slaughtered all the cats belonging to the master printer to whom they had been engaged is entirely in keeping with the predominantly burlesque tone of many of the exchanges described in the *Anecdotes*.

The descriptions lend themselves readily to incorporation into established images of artisanal production. They evoke a world of symbolic exchange, where ridicule and laughter were essential components of the culture of the workshop, where journeymen identified with the particularities and distinctive values of their trades rather than the wider nexus of belief, institutions and law of the polity as a whole, where the language of class was entirely absent from conflicts between journeymen and their masters, and where corporate power both underpinned the authority of master printers and perpetuated the subordination of the journeymen they were free to engage and dismiss at will. It is important, however, to recall that Contat's description of the Parisian printing trade in the mid-eighteenth century was not written for the subsequent benefit of historical ethnographers. It had a contemporary purpose whose identity is not immediately apparent. To understand that purpose, it is necessary to place a phrase that appears in Contat's preface to the work in its contemporary context.

In his preface Contat explained that the *Anecdotes* had two objectives: the first was to describe the unusual customs of the journeymen who worked in the printing trade, and the second was to show that these customs belonged to a timeless and immutable order. The government, he wrote, *armé de toute son autorité despotique*, had sought to undermine and eliminate journeymen's associations and customary retributions, but its efforts had been in vain.[10] The descriptive intent of the work was thus subordinated to a more specific end. Contat's emphasis upon the unchanging character of the customs of the trade was designed to show that the provisions of corporate regulation prohibiting journeymen from assembling or associating were pointless. Journeymen would continue to observe their particular rules and regulations as they had done since the invention of printing.

Contat did not explain why he felt that it was necessary to make this

10 *Ibid.*, p. 30.

point. It is probable, however, that at the time that he wrote the *Anecdotes*, explanations were superfluous. The period between 1760 and 1770 was a decade of considerable turbulence in the Parisian trades: many of them experienced prolonged and substantial conflicts between masters and journeymen.[11] A large number of these conflicts were occasioned by, or resulted in, changes in corporate regulations affecting conditions of employment and the formal status of journeymen. The printing trade was not exempt from these tensions. In 1761 its officials considered the possibility of revising the corporation's regulations to bring them into line with those that had been adopted by the wigmakers' corporation in 1760.[12] These regulations reiterated a long-standing prohibition upon journeymen's assemblies, but their most notable feature was the power that they conferred upon the *syndics* of the wigmakers' corporation to order the arrest of any journeyman, including anyone found on the streets, who was not in possession of a certificate attesting to his identity, place of work and record of previous employment.[13] Nothing appears to have come of the proposal to add this power to those already enjoyed by the *gardes de l'imprimerie*, nor of a later proposal to require journeymen in the printing trade to carry printed certificates modelled on those adopted by the shoemakers' corporation in 1763.[14] Yet anyone familiar with the affairs of the printing trade who read the preface to Contat's manuscript in 1762 would have recognised the subject to which he was alluding.

It is very probable, therefore, that the text had a very precise contemporary purpose and that it was written in the context of debate over the desirability of changing the corporation's regulations to impose a wider series of obligations upon journeymen in the trade. It is also probable that anyone familiar with the trades, and the printing trade in particular, would have recognised the significance of Contat's allusions to despotic authority and the despotic authority of the government. The phrases are, at first glance, somewhat surprising. Yet they were not, as might first appear, an expression of the concerns of a proto-*sans-culotte*. Instead, they, belonged to an established rhetoric of legal argument that was widely used in disputes in the French trades, among master artisans as well as between masters and journeymen. By 'government' Contat was referring not to the

11 For further details, see below, chapter 8.

12 B.N. MS. fr. 22 064 fol. 208 (draft of a projected *arrêt du conseil*, September 1761). The essay has given rise to some (somewhat imprecise) discussion: see Roger Chartier, 'Texts, Symbols, and Frenchness', *Journal of Modern History*, 57 (1985), pp. 682–95; Robert Darnton, 'The Symbolic Element in History', *Ibid.*, 58 (1986), pp. 218–34; Dominick LaCapra, 'Chartier, Darnton and the Great Symbol Massacre', *Journal of Modern History*, 60 (1988), pp. 95–112; James Fernandez, 'Historians Tell Tales; Of Cartesian Cats and Gallic Cockfights', *Ibid.*, 60 (1988), pp. 113–27.

13 The journeymen wigmakers objected strongly to the innovation and appealed to the Parlement of Paris: see below, pp. 56–7, 73.

14 B.N. MS. fr. 22 123 fol. 92 (draft of a projected *arrêt*, 5 May 1769).

royal government, but to the government exercised by the printers and booksellers' corporation. By 'despotic authority' he was referring not to the power of the King, but to the legal powers that the corporation enjoyed.

The contemporary resonances of Contat's allusion to despotic authority are one of the keys to a fuller understanding of his text. To understand their significance it is necessary to have a clearer picture of what had happened in the Parisian printing trade before the middle of the eighteenth century.[15] For Contat's reference to despotic authority echoed a number of terms used during a long sequence of disputes between masters and journeymen in the Parisian printing trade that began at the time of the Fronde and continued until the third decade of the eighteenth century.[16] These disputes were closely related to substantial changes in both the internal organisation of the trade as a whole and in the formal status and everyday circumstances of journeymen in particular. To understand why Contat wrote the kind of text that he did, it is necessary to know how these changes affected both the circumstances of journeymen and, more importantly, the relationship between print-shop foremen and the masters and journeymen with whom they dealt. Once established, this information can be used to form the basis of a final interpretation of the *Anecdotes*.

Until the late seventeenth century, the Parisian printing trade shared many of the characteristics of the majority of the trades of urban France. It was made up of a relatively large number of small enterprises in which the division of labour involved in printing and bookselling was devolved upon many separate concerns. The majority of printing enterprises were too small to support the fixed costs of integrated production and distribution. In 1644 only 14 master printers had four or more printing presses. In all, the 183 presses in existence at the time were distributed among a total of 76 print-shops.[17] Even among the printers themselves, many of them did not have the minimum stock of fount needed to produce whole books.[18] Sub-contracted work was therefore very widespread. In 1644, for example, a selected edition of the works of Saint Augustine was

[15] Much of that picture is presented in Henri-Jean Martin, *Livre, pouvoirs et société à Paris au xviie siècle (1598–1701)* (Geneva, 1969).

[16] The disputes are described (somewhat anachronistically) by Paul Chauvet, *Les Ouvriers du livre en France, des origines à la Révolution de 1789* (Paris, 1959). The sources he used (principally in the Delamare and Anisson-Duperret collections of the Bibliothèque nationale) can be supplemented by the original rulings of the Parlement of Paris, which, on occasion, contain more information than the copies and printed *arrêts* in the Bibliothèque nationale. See A.N. X^{1a} 5742 (7 September 1650); X^{1a} 2282 fol. 30 (7 September 1650); X^{1a} 2356 fol. 706vo (14 July 1654); X^{1b} 1600 (14 July 1654); X^{1a} 5798 (14 August 1655); X^{1a} 2386 fol. 194 (18 September 1655); X^{1a} 2439 fol. 458 (13 April 1658); X^{1a} 2519 fol. 44vo (20 October 1662); *ibid.*, fol. 270vo (27 October 1662); X^{1a} 2565 fol. 613 (8 May 1665). See too X^{2a} 649 (10 July 1724); X^{1b} 3296 (15 December 1725); V^6 664 (7 November 1681); B.H.V.P. MS. CP 3997.

[17] Martin, *Livre, pouvoirs et société*, pp. 372–3.

[18] *Ibid.* p. 371.

produced on five different presses belonging to five different masters.[19] Separate but interdependent enterprises, rather than integrated processes, were the norm in the mid-seventeenth-century printing trade.

By the early eighteenth century, however, the internal architecture of the trade had changed very substantially. Formally, the change was the product of a series of legislative measures beginning in 1649 and culminating in a major revision to the trade's statutes in 1686. They fixed the number of print-shops in Paris at 36 and stipulated that each shop should have a minimum of four printing presses.[20] The measures had the obvious advantage of allowing the royal authorities greater opportunity to police the book trade at a time when religious controversies and memories of the Fronde were both sources of considerable official concern. More fundamentally, however, the measures were the product of pressure from master printers and booksellers themselves. The smaller number of print-shops made it easier to limit the possibility of piracy and maintain greater control over the contracting markets faced by the book trade during much of the latter half of the seventeenth century.[21] At the same time, the decision to fix the number of printing enterprises at 36 was a powerful incentive towards a very much higher level of integration of the previously separate functions of printing and bookselling. The artificially low limit placed upon the number of separate printing enterprises meant that integration was the best way to prevent printers from commanding the high market prices resulting from their relative monopoly position. Thus, by the late seventeenth century, almost all the leading publishers in Paris were either owners of print-shops or were former printers themselves.[22]

At the end of the reign of Louis XIV the Parisian printing trade had come to be characterised by a very much higher level of vertical and horizontal integration of the various stages of production and distribution than could be found in most of the urban trades of eighteenth-century France. The change was accompanied by, and linked to, a large number of conflicts between masters and journeymen not only in the Parisian trade but in its counterpart in Lyon as well.[23] These conflicts took the form of episodic stoppages of work and, more importantly, of a succession of legal cases presented to the Parlement of Paris and the *Conseil du Roi* between 1648 and 1724. Between 1648 and 1658, argument centred mainly upon the

[19] *Ibid.*, p. 563.
[20] *Ibid.*, pp. 682–3, 685.
[21] *Ibid.*, pp. 597–8.
[22] *Ibid.*, p. 709.
[23] Lyon fell within the jurisdiction of the Parlement of Paris, and the book trade there was subject to the same corporate provisions as its Parisian counterpart. These formal links were complemented by movements of both capital and labour between the two cities, and by a long-standing concern among journeymen to maintain wages and working conditions at comparable levels. See Natalie Z. Davis, 'A Trade Union in Sixteenth-Century France', *Economic History Review*, 2nd Series, 19 (1966), pp. 48–69, and Jacqueline Roudier, 'La Situation de l'imprimerie lyonnaise à la fin du xviie siècle', in Henri-Jean Martin, ed., *Cinq Etudes Lyonnaises* (Paris and Geneva, 1966), pp. 77–111.

length and content of the working day that printers and compositors were expected to perform. Subsequently, in 1664–5, 1671–4, 1683–9, 1699–1702 and 1720–4, it widened into protracted litigation over periods of notice and the form of the wage, over the number of apprentices that masters were entitled to employ and, by the late seventeenth century, over the right of masters to take on workers known as *alloués* who had not served an apprenticeship at all.[24]

The changes in the internal structure of the Parisian trade and the conflicts that they occasioned can be linked to Contat's *Anecdotes* in a number of ways. The first is in the choice of language used in the preface to his work. Contat's allusion to despotic authority echoed a number of terms used by journeymen printers in the legal memoranda and *factums* that they presented to the courts in the seventeenth and eighteenth centuries. In 1664, the Parisian journeymen objected to the introduction of certificates attesting to the satisfactory completion of their work because they were a 'servitude' and were therefore incompatible with their formal status and civil rights.[25] In 1700, they rejected a proposal to allow masters to take on additional men to finish work that was already in progress on the grounds that it violated the principles of the contract of employment, principles that were grounded in natural law.[26] In 1723 they opposed regulations allowing masters to employ anyone they chose, including *alloués* who had not served an apprenticeship at all, because, they claimed, the trade would fall into the hands of mercenaries 'qu'on veut réduire à la condition des esclaves'.[27] An anonymous pamphlet written in 1725, after the journeymen's legal campaign had failed, described their condition as 'une rude servitude, dont les plus vils domestiques sont exempts en France'.[28] A further memorandum, written in 1757, explained that the purpose of employing *alloués* had been to 'reduire ces misérables ouvriers [i.e. the journeymen printers] au titre de bas valets, pour s'en servir despotiquement'.[29]

[24] Chauvet, *Ouvriers du livre*, pp. 77–179, and the archival sources cited above, note 16.

[25] 'Les demandeurs sont tous apprentis de cette ville de Paris et la plus grande partie nais [sic] en ycelle; qu'ils y demeurent actuellement et y ont famille; qu'ils payent toutes les charges de la ville et de la même manière que les autres bourgeois...Ainsi l'on ne peut pas les reduire à prendre des billets des maistres qui est une servitude en laquelle l'on ne voit point que l'on y oblige aucun ouvrier des autres vacations dont le privilège est au dessous des demandeurs.' B.N. MS. fr. 22 064 fol. 83 (1664).

[26] 'Ces principes,' they stated, 'sont de Droit naturel, suivant lequel l'obligation des contractans doit être mutuelle.' B.N. MS. fr. 22 064 fol. 119.

[27] B.N. MS. fr. 22 062 fol. 175.

[28] B.H.V.P. MS. CP 4005, subsequently printed in L. Faucon, ed., *Mémoire sur les véxations qu'exercent les libraires et imprimeurs de Paris* (Paris, 1879). See also B.N. MS. fr. 21 741 fol. 127. 'Du libelle des compagnons imprimeurs contre les maitres imprimeurs et libraires de Paris' (1725).

[29] B.N. MS. fr. 22 116 fol. 347. 'Mémoire sur les abus qui si commettent au sujet des apprentifs de librairie et des compagnons imprimeurs qu'on appelle alloués' (20 April 1757).

Contat's reference to despotic authority was therefore an allusion to a rhetoric that bore the marks of the changes that had occurred within the Parisian printing trade and the conflicts to which they had given rise. Yet there were other ways in which his text bore the marks of those changes. Here, however, the contemporary resonances of a particular phrase are of little help in identifying them, for it is unlikely that Contat himself was fully aware of how profoundly the printing trade had changed since the late seventeenth century. In this sense, the text was also affected by the selective filter of memory. Paradoxically, where Contat sought to show that the despotic authority of the printers' corporation had been unable to affect the age-old customs and associations of journeymen printers, he made use of an age-old rhetoric centred upon terms like 'servitude', 'slavery' and 'natural law', to present a series of customs and forms of association that were, in fact, very much more recent in origin.

The changes that had taken place in the Parisian printing trade affected the composition of the workforce in several ways. The effects of the reduction in the number of print-shops upon the opportunity costs of entry to the trade were reinforced by a series of corporate decisions between the late seventeenth and mid-eighteenth centuries effectively restricting entry to the corporation to all but the sons or sons-in-law of established master printers. The corporation discouraged masters from taking on apprentices and, instead, promoted the employment of *alloués* who had not served an apprenticeship at all and, for this reason, had no formal right to become masters themselves. The practice was most widespread on the printing side of the trade, where physical strength, rather than the literacy and manual dexterity required of a compositor, was the most important attribute needed for that aspect of book production.[30] The use of *alloués* may have owed something to a recognition of the need to limit the number of journeymen when there were so few opportunities in Paris to become a master. It is also likely that it represented a substantial saving on wage costs at a time when the reduction in the number of print-shops meant that the number of presses in each shop was rising. Since two pressmen were usually employed to work on a single compositor's output they formed the largest component of the workforce and the largest obstacle to economies on wage costs.

By the middle of the eighteenth century, the combined effect of very limited access to full membership of the corporation (marriage was the only real possibility for a journeyman whose father was not a master printer) and widespread employment of *alloués* resulted in the emergence

---

[30] In 1688 the journeymen complained that a former packer (*emballeur*) in the Parisian Hôtel-Dieu had been taken on by the *veuve* Langlois and her son (B.N. MS. fr. 21 749 fol. 69). In 1701 a former ship's corporal complained that he had been forced to leave two employers because of the journeymen's refusal to work with him (B.N. MS. fr. 21 741 fol. 119).

of a workforce divided between young men in their teens and early twenties who had not served an apprenticeship at all (the *alloués*), and journeymen who had frequently served an apprenticeship outside Paris and whose number included a larger proportion of relatively old, often married men than was usual in the majority of the eighteenth-century French trades.[31] Only two of the 11 journeymen interrogated in the course of a raid upon a print-shop where an illegal life of the Jansenist martyr, Pâris, was being printed in 1731 were under 30 years old. Six of them were over 40.[32] Indirect evidence of a more general nature can be found in a petition that the Parisian journeymen printers addressed to the Chancellor in 1751 complaining about the number of married men working as *alloués*, although, according to them, only journeymen themselves were entitled to marry and continue to work in the trade.[33] It implies that there were many married men working in the trade at the time that Contat wrote his *Anecdotes*. In Paris, the most that they could expect to become was a print-shop foreman. In this, Contat's own career was probably typical.

It is probable that these changes in the composition of the workforce were matched by changes in patterns of employment. Here the evidence is very slim indeed, but the reduction in the number of print-shops and the emergence of a smaller number of relatively integrated publishing concerns are likely to have affected the rhythms of production in a number of ways. They meant that the Parisian labour market became more centralised and that most print-shops employed relatively substantial numbers of people.[34] It is also possible that many of these people worked for the same employer, or at least remained in Paris, for fairly long periods of time. The growth of a small number of relatively integrated firms by the middle of the eighteenth century makes it very probable that production in the printing trade was more evenly distributed throughout the year than it was in the majority of the urban trades.[35] Although print runs remained low, and the

31 See below, pp. 100–4.

32 A.N. Y 9532 (*saisi* on the premises of Jacques-Philippe-Charles Osmond).

33 B.N. MS. fr. 22 064 fol. 185.

34 The somewhat questionable declarations made to the revolutionary authorities in 1790 and 1791 (but when the abolition of the corporation in 1791 and the printing explosion in post-revolutionary Paris favoured new, and arguably smaller, entrants to the trade) reveal a total of 1,606 workers employed by 61 printers or booksellers, or an average of over 25 per employer. The figures have been calculated from F. Braesch, 'Un Essai de statistique de la population ouvrière de Paris vers 1791', *La Révolution française*, 63 (1912), pp. 289–321.

35 There is a substantial contemporary literature on theories of the firm that, despite its somewhat abstract quality, is relevant to this discussion. See, for a general overview, Louis Putterman, ed., *The Economic Nature of the Firm: A Reader* (Cambridge, 1986). For a recent survey of the literature, see Jim Tomlinson, 'Democracy inside the Black Box? Neo-Classical Theories of the Firm and Industrial Democracy', *Economy and Society*, 15 (1986), pp. 220–50. For an attempt to apply these concepts, see O. E. Williamson, 'The Organization of Work', *Journal of Economic Behaviour and Organization*, 1 (1980),

economy of the trade continued to be affected by the seasonal and liturgical calendars of its principal sources of revenue, the law courts and the church, it is probable that the episodic, batch production associated with large numbers of very small enterprises and high levels of sub-contracted work gave way to more regular output organised into what might be termed serial-batch production.[36]

Many of the ceremonies that Contat described conform to this state of affairs. Although the *droit de bienvenu* that journeymen paid when they began work at a new shop or arrived in Paris from elsewhere is indicative of the mobility that was so common in the eighteenth-century trades, the great majority of the customary obligations that journeymen printers were expected to honour could not have existed if the workforce had been dominated by young, single migrants moving frequently from shop to shop and town to town. Among the customary retributions incumbent upon journeymen printers were a *droit de chevet* that entitled a journeyman to his share of the *bon de chapelle* when it was distributed every year on the feast of St Martin; and the *bon de chapelle* itself. Neither of the latter two retributions would have been viable unless a proportion of the workforce remained in the same shop for at least the better part of a year. The rights and obligations associated with print-shop chapels were, for under-standable reasons, limited to those in relatively stable employment. A *règlement pour le bon de la Saint Martin* drawn up by the journeymen working in a Parisian print-shop in 1760 stipulated that only men who had been working in the shop for three months or more were entitled to admission to the chapel. The entry fee of four *livres* 10 *sous* was reduced by 10 *sous* for every additional month of employment.[37]

The chapels and ceremonial that Contat described were not, therefore, an unambiguous manifestation of the culture and concerns of the workforce of the trade as a whole. They were, instead, institutions

pp. 5–38; S. R. H. Jones, 'The Organization of Work. A Historical Dimension', *ibid.*, 3 (1982), pp. 117–32; and the subsequent debate in *ibid.*, 4 (1983), pp. 56–66. I am grateful to Dr Jones for referring me to this discussion.
36 The terms have been borrowed from Herman Freudenberger and Fritz Redlich, 'The Industrial Development of Europe: Reality, Symbols, Images', *Kyklos*, 17 (1964), pp. 372–403, and Stanley Chapman, 'The Textile Factory before Arkwright: A Typology of Factory Development', *Business History Review*, 48 (1974), pp. 451–78. For more recent discussion of industrial organisation and its various forms, see Charles Sabel and Jonathan Zeitlin, 'Historical Alternatives to Mass Production: Politics, Markets and Technology in Nineteenth-Century Industrialization', *Past and Present*, 108 (1985), pp. 133–76; Philip Scranton, *Proprietary Capitalism: The Textile Manufacture at Philadelphia, 1800–1885*, (New York and Cambridge, 1983); Steven Marglin, 'What Do Bosses Do?' in André Gorz, ed., *The Division of Labour* (London, 1976), and David Landes, 'What Do Bosses Really Do?' *Journal of Economic History*, 46 (1986), pp. 585–623.
37 B.N. MS. fr. 22064. In 1765, Hérissant, the printer in question, had some 45 journeymen or *alloués* working for him (Chauvet, *Ouvriers*, p. 438).

representing the concerns of a core of stably-employed journeymen whose age, marital and residential status were different from those of the relatively substantial number of itinerant journeymen and *alloués* also employed in the large, integrated printing concerns of mid-eighteenth century Paris. Contat referred to them as *ouvriers sédentaires* and pointed out that they alone benefited from the *bon de chapelle*.[38] Significantly, he also used the phrase *les anciens de la maison*, rather than *les anciens du métier*, when he referred to seniority among journeymen.[39] Sedentary workers who spent relatively long periods in the same shop were the men who maintained established working arrangements and ensured that the rules of the chapels were recognised by the workforce as a whole.

It is likely that the existence of the chapels themselves owed something to the changes that occurred within the structure of the trade between the mid-seventeenth and early eighteenth centuries. For many of the chapel's functions were analogous to those more usually associated with journeymen's confraternities. The important difference, however, was that chapels were associated with particular printing enterprises rather than with the trade as a whole. During the second half of the seventeenth century many journeymen printers had belonged to a confraternity established in the abbey of Saint-Jean-Porte-Latine near the rue Saint-Jacques, where the majority of the capital's printing and bookselling shops were located. The confraternity played a prominent part in the disputes between journeymen and their masters between 1650 and 1725 and was prohibited repeatedly by the magistrates of the Châtelet and the Parlement of Paris. Its final demise was not, however, entirely a result of the attitude of the Parisian authorities. Many journeymen's confraternities established in other Parisian trades continued to lead shadowy existences until well into the second half of the eighteenth century, despite a plethora of hostile court rulings.[40] The demise of the journeymen's confraternity in the printing trade was a result of the changes in the internal structure of the trade and the resultant transfer of many of its functions either to institutions attached to particular enterprises or to the relatively large number of supervisory workers, or *prôtes*, employed to manage the daily affairs of the capital's printshops. A confraternity was redundant when many journeymen worked in the same shop for relatively long periods of time and when most shops had foremen responsible for matching the supply of labour with the schedules of production.

[38] Contat. *Anecdotes*, p. 82.

[39] 'Monsieur Jérôme, à present Sous-prôte, est servi régulièrement par les apprentis; il a l'honneur d'assister aux buvettes des compagnons, même des anciens de la maison.' *Ibid.*, p. 66.

[40] David Garrioch and Michael Sonenscher, '*Compagnonnages*, Confraternities and Associations of Journeymen in Eighteenth-Century Paris', *European History Quarterly*, 16 (1986). pp. 25–46. See also below, chapter 3.

There are good reasons, therefore, for suspecting that many of the apparently immutable customs and retributions that Contat described were more recent in origin than he was aware. They were not, of course, particularly different from many other informal customs whose evanescent existence has been preserved by legal proceedings and court rulings in many parts of urban and rural France. Yet, if they were a variant upon a wider corpus of ceremony and ritual, including those of the church and the courts, their particular form corresponded closely to the peculiar circumstances of the mid-eighteenth century Parisian printing trade. In his depiction of those customs, Contat may have paid rather more tribute to those peculiar circumstances than he was able to recognise.

It is possible too that the story about the cat massacre was also more of a tribute to those circumstances than Contat knew. It is, in several significant respects, a strange story for a foreman to tell. For Contat had been a *prôte* and devoted a large part of his *Anecdotes* to a description of a foreman's work. His remarks contain some suggestive ambiguities. Print-shops were, he wrote, 'l'assemblage d'un grand nombre d'ouvriers dont le Prôte est le chef'.[41] Foremen were therefore identified with the journeymen they supervised. They were the heads of print-shop chapels, exacted their customary fines and retributions, and shared in the redistribution of the *bon de chapelle* every year.[42] They were also required to manage the daily affairs of a relatively large and complex organisation, a task that could include negotiating wage-rates and taking on or dismissing journeymen. A *prôte* was therefore in a particularly delicate situation: on the one hand, he was the custodian of the informal arrangements associated with the chapel; on the other, he was accountable to the master printer who employed him for the efficient conduct of the shop. Another foreman, the future *sans-culotte* Antoine-François Momoro, and the author of a treatise on the printing trade that was not dissimilar to Contat's work, was involved in a brawl when a journeyman working in a shop that was one of the sites of a long-drawn-out dispute over wage-rates in 1785 and 1786 challenged the rates he had been offered and told the other journeymen 'qu'il faloit n'avoir pas de coeur pour faire de l'ouvrage au prix proposé'. Momoro had the journeyman arrested, but did not pursue the case.[43] Foremen and journeymen did not always have the same point of view.

Contat's story is redolent of these ambiguities. It is a tale about apprentices (who killed some cats) told by a foreman to an audience of journeymen. The principal protagonists (the apprentices, the master printer, his wife) were unlikely to have been present when the story was

41 Contat, *Anecdotes*, p. 30.
42 *Ibid*, pp. 37–41, 66–7, 80–1.
43 A.N. Y 11 429 (4 September 1786). See also Y 15 012 (24 July 1785) and Chauvet, *Ouvriers*, pp. 193–203.

told, since the print-shop chapel and the convivial evenings where such stories were told were the domain of sedentary journeymen and foremen. A journeyman who drank with an apprentice was likely to find that he owed the chapel a fine. It may not be too far-fetched to see the story as an early episode in the history of workshop management. To do so is not to belittle its significance; instead, it is to place it more securely in the special context of the mid-eighteenth-century Parisian printing trade, where foremen were first among the journeymen whose loyalty they could not take for granted and last among the master printers upon whom their authority ultimately rested. Like so much that eighteenth-century artisans said and did, the story may have more to say about the teller and his times than he may have known.

THE CORPORATE WORLD AND THE ECONOMY OF THE BAZAAR

The second text – entitled *Journal de ma vie* – was the work of a Parisian master glazier named Jacques-Louis Ménétra.[44] It was written between 1764 – when Ménétra returned to Paris after seven years of work and travel as a journeyman on the *tour de France* – and 1802, when the manuscript ends. As its title implies, the text is very much more autobiographical than Contat's *Anecdotes*. Although much of the *Journal* is exaggerated or fictitious, it is also full of small pieces of information about a trade that was rather more typical of the majority of the urban trades of eighteenth-century France than the printing trade.[45] As such, it is a suitable point of departure for an examination of the ordinary circumstances of master artisans.

It is all the more appropriate because much of the information that Ménétra presented was not entirely consistent with the formal prescriptions of corporate regulations. Corporate statutes emphasised a rigid separation between the respective functions and obligations of masters, journeymen and apprentices. Masters owned and disposed of the materials and finished products of their trades, while apprentices and journeymen were expected to carry out the work appropriate to their respective positions.[46] Ménétra presented a rather different state of affairs. Some master glaziers employed other master glaziers. Journeymen frequently worked on their own account for private individuals. Masters formed partnerships with merchants, journeymen or even with their own apprentices. They employed their own relatives as well as journeymen, but

[44] Jacques-Louis Ménétra, *Journal de ma vie*, ed. Daniel Roche (Paris, 1982).
[45] In addition to the editorial discussion by Daniel Roche (Ménétra, *Journal*, pp. 287–426), see the review by Robert Darnton, 'Working Class Casanova', *New York Review of Books* (28 June 1984), pp. 32–7.
[46] Steven L. Kaplan, 'Réflexions sur la police du monde de travail, 1700–1815', *Revue historique*, 261 (1979), pp. 17–77.

paid them in the same way. They made a wide variety of different articles, ranging from the relatively predictable windows and framing glass, to street lamps, coloured lanterns, glass cases and miniature Chinese pagodas complete with live white mice.[47] They paid the people they employed in a bewilderingly wide variety of ways: by the day, the month, with meals or without meals, by the piece, or by combinations of all these modes of payment. Both the form of the wage and the character of the work were typical of a world of short-term arrangements, fleeting opportunities and brief associations, a world which has more in common with a North African or Oriental bazaar (not to mention the neo-classical economists' concept of a spot market) than with the corporate world of eighteenth-century French artisans.[48]

One reason for this discrepancy can be found in an episode that Ménétra did not mention at all. The episode was a decision by the Parisian glaziers' corporation in 1763 to change its regulations governing the journeymen of the trade. As has been mentioned, the decade between 1760 and 1770 was a period of widespread conflict between masters and journeymen in many Parisian trades. The discussions within the printers' corporation in 1761 and 1769 over the desirability of modelling its regulations upon those adopted by the wigmakers and shoemakers were only one of a number of occasions in which tension between masters and journeymen led to changes in corporate regulations. Among them were a series of disputes between masters and journeymen in the Parisian glazing trade.[49] In September 1763 the *bureau* of the glaziers' corporation was informed that journeymen in the trade had formed 'factions', held clandestine meetings and established a scale of piece-rates which they had attempted to impose upon master glaziers. The annual mass celebrated by the master glaziers' confraternity in the church of Sainte-Croix-de-la-Bretonnerie in honour of Saint Joseph L'Allemand, the trade's second patron saint, had occasioned scenes of 'scandal' and disturbances. One of the senior members of the corporation (an *ancien*) had found 'plusieurs impudicités' concerning his wife and daughters written on the wall of the room where his journeymen slept. Finally, and more substantially, Parisian journeymen had prevented men arriving from the provinces from working for

[47] Ménétra, *Journal*, pp. 145, 155–6, 158, 169, 186, 191, 198, 200, 204, 206, 216–18, 222, 244, 257. He also imported Baccarat glass from Alsace, despite a corporate prohibition. On the marketing of glass in Paris, see Warren C. Scoville, *Capitalism and French Glassmaking* (Berkeley, California, 1950), pp. 100–1, 133–6.

[48] On the bazaar economy, see Clifford Geertz, *Pedlars and Princes* (Chicago, 1963) esp. pp. 30–47; and Clifford Geertz, Hildred Geertz and Lawrence Rosen, *Meaning and Order in Moroccan Society* (Cambridge, 1979), pp. 123–244. On labour markets, see Charles F. Sabel, *Work and Politics* (Cambridge, 1982), chapter 2; for a recent presentation (and critical discussion) of neo-classical theories of markets, see Geoffrey M. Hodgson, *Economics and Institutions* (Oxford, 1988), chapters 8 and 9.

[49] A.N. X¹ᵇ 3847 (6 August 1766).

lower rates and had boycotted shops where their wage-norms had not been accepted.

Accordingly, the corporation decided to revise its regulations in order, as it put it, to restore the journeymen's subordination to their masters.[50] It ordered them to register their names, addresses and places of work with the corporate office. Journeymen engaged by the month were required to complete their term, while those employed by the day were obliged to give two weeks' notice before going to work elsewhere. Journeymen working in shops in which several men were employed were ordered to observe an interval of a month between each period of notice, while those working for widows were obliged to work an extra two weeks so that their replacements could acquaint themselves with work in progress. Finally the corporation decided to introduce a system of printed certificates which journeymen were required to carry as evidence that they had satisfied the statutory periods of notice. They were expected to pay a fee of ten *sous* each time that they registered with the corporate office.

The regulations and the disputes that occasioned them were the product of an aspect of the workshop economy that has often been ignored or misunderstood, partly because texts like Ménétra's *Journal* are so rare. It is easy to associate terms like 'subordination' or its opposite, 'licence', with work discipline or its absence. Although the terms could – and did – have these associations, they also referred to patterns of work that were more specifically related to those features of the eighteenth-century French urban trades that underpinned the activities that Ménétra described: a highly developed division of labour; a large number of separate and specialised artisanal enterprises; and a high level of sub-contracted work. 'Subordination' in this context referred as much to the many opportunities available to journeymen to undertake work on their own account as to their assiduity in following their masters' orders. In this context, the careful regulation of periods of notice, control of journeymen's identities and registration with the corporate office are indirect testimony to the scale and frequency of sub-contracted work in the glazing trade.

Two further clauses in the glaziers' regulations indicate the importance of the problem. The first referred to the seasonal character of the trade. The corporation noted that many master glaziers lost clients during the three or four months of the year when orders were most frequent and journeymen were able to take advantage of shortages of labour by taking on work themselves.[51] Accordingly, it decided to prohibit journeymen from

[50] 'De 'rétablir la subordination envers les maîtres de cette communauté de la part des compagnons' ('Avis sur la délibération de la communauté des maîtres vitriers', 13 September 1763. A.N. Y. 9500).

[51] 'Lorsque l'ouvrage abonde un peu plus qu'à l'ordinaire, ce qui arrive ordinairement trois ou quatre mois de l'année, dans ce tems la plupart des maîtres perdent la plupart de leurs

undertaking sub-contracted work, or 'travail à l'entreprise'. It also decided to change the provisions of its statutes and allow master glaziers to take on two apprentices at a time, the second half-way through the first apprentice's four-year term. Finally, journeymen who left a master were ordered to spend at least a month working outside the parish in which they had been employed.

The problem remained a serious one. In 1768, in a deliberation that was ratified in the form of Royal Letters Patent in 1772, the corporation reiterated its concern about the scale of sub-contracted work and the traffic by journeymen, unincorporated artisans, architects, masons and joiners in ready-cut glass. The effects of this unauthorised competition had, it claimed, been exacerbated by two other developments: the growing use of Bohemian glass (*verre de Bohème*), particularly in the new street lanterns (*lanternes à réverbère*) that had been introduced in the capital. The new glass was stronger and much easier to clean than the pieces of broken glass that were traditionally used in making lanterns. It had also been imported to Paris by independent entrepreneurs and a small number of master glaziers who had acquired their titles by *brevets*, rather than by the usual formalities. The combined effect of the loss of the work of cleaning and repairing lamps made of pieces of broken glass, together with the loss of the opportunity to recycle broken pieces of glass into lamps and lanterns, amounted to an annual loss of over 40,000 *livres*. In the light of these developments, the corporation requested (and was granted) a strict prohibition upon the sale of glass to anyone who was not a master glazier.[52]

Ménétra made no reference to these rulings in his *Journal de ma vie*. He presented the glaziers' corporation as no more than a distant, alien and occasionally intrusive irritation. Some of the arrangements that he made came close to violating the provisions of its regulations. He formed a partnership with a 'young man' he had taken on as an apprentice to make 120 street lanterns for another master glazier.[53] He took on his brother-in-law to work in a room on the rue Saint-Louis on another piece of sub-contracted work for a master glazier with a shop on the rue Verbois.[54] Not surprisingly, his relationship with the corporation was less than cordial. On one occasion he was involved in an argument over sub-contracted work that he had taken on for a glazier living in the *faubourg Saint-Antoine*, who, for this reason, was not entitled to have a shop in the city itself. On another, he was accused of employing a journeyman who had not registered with the corporate office.[55] Ménétra made his living in a

[52] A.N. X¹ᵃ 8796 fol. 256ᵛᵒ (15 January 1772) registering letters patent of 19 November 1770 and deliberation of 19 November 1768.

[53] Ménétra, *Journal*, pp. 145, 155.

[54] *Ibid.*, p. 191.

pratiques, parce que les compagnons se font valoir dans ces sortes de saisons encore plus que dans les autres'. A.N. X¹ᵇ 3847 (6 August 1766).

[55] *Ibid.*, pp. 186, 245.

bazaar rather than an orderly corporate world. His artless references to the arrangements made by small-scale entrepreneurs with little credit and few resources hint at the existence of an artisanal world whose rules had little in common with the norms and prescriptions of corporate statutes.

In one sense, his indifference to the provisions of corporate regulation was not surprising. There were some 260 master glaziers in Paris in 1769 and it is unlikely that more than 30 of them were directly involved in the deliberation of 1763.[56] Corporate decisions in eighteenth-century Paris were made by a small, elected body known as the *bureau*. Its membership consisted of the incumbent *jurés*, or *syndics*, responsible for the day to day administration of the corporation, together with representatives of the three classes of master artisans into which members of the Parisian corporations were divided.[57] Master artisans fell into one or other of these three classes – known as *jeunes*, *modernes* and *anciens* – according to the length of time that they had belonged to the corporation. The most junior members of a corporation, the *jeunes*, were usually ineligible for corporate office and, occasionally, were also unrepresented on its *bureau*. Corporate officials (the *jurés* or *syndics*) were selected from among the *modernes*. After they had served their period of office they became *anciens*. An eighteenth-century corporation was a composite body governed by a *bureau* in which the majority of master artisans were not directly involved. In the case of the glaziers' corporation, there was little reason why Ménétra should have been particularly concerned by the deliberation of 1763.

Yet the omission is more surprising than it may seem. For one of the master glaziers who signed the deliberation of 1763 was his own father.[58] Moreover, although the glaziers' corporation made its decision in 1763, the provisions of the new regulations were not ratified by the Parlement of Paris until August 1766. By then, Ménétra had bought a shop on the rue du Petit-Lion-Saint-Sauveur in 1765, married and established himself as a master glazier in his own right. As such, he would have been issued with a printed copy of the new regulations and been required to acquaint any of the journeymen he employed with their content. Ménétra's silence was not, therefore, entirely the product of his

[56] B.N. V 52072, Roze de Chantoiseau, *Essai sur l'almanach général d'indication d'adresse personelle et domicile fixe des six corps, arts et métiers* (Paris, 1769). Returns to 41 of the 48 *sections* in 1790 and 1791 collated by Braesch include only 25 glaziers, employing a total of 132 individuals: F. Braesch, 'Essai de statistique de la population ouvrière de Paris vers 1791', *La Révolution française*, 63 (1912), pp. 289–321.

[57] There is no full study of corporate government in eighteenth-century Paris. See, however, Emile Coornaert, *Les Corporations en France* (Paris, 1941), and, more recently, Steven L. Kaplan, 'The Character and Implications of Strife among the Masters inside the Guilds of Eighteenth-Century Paris', *Journal of Social History*, 19 (1986), pp. 631–47.

[58] His signature appears on the copy of the deliberation ratified by the Parlement of Paris in August 1766: A.N. X^{1b} 3847 (6 August 1766).

distance from, and indifference to, corporate affairs; it was also the product of his distance from his own father.

The reasons for this distance can be pieced together from Ménétra's account of his life. He had fallen out with his father – 'je savais', he finally decided, ' de quel bois se chauffait mon père '[59] – and had little to do with his uncles and cousins who were also master glaziers in Paris. He bought his own shop with the money provided by his wife's dowry and inherited nothing from his father. His circumstances, and his relationship with his father in particular, go a long way to explaining the distance and indifference to corporate affairs that is one of the most striking aspects of his *Journal*. If Ménétra made his way in a bazaar, he did so partly because his own circumstances placed him outside the orderly world of corporate life.

Yet, despite appearances to the contrary, bazaars were also orderly institutions. Unlike the order of corporate prescription, however, the order found in the bazaar-like economy of the trades of eighteenth-century Paris was as much an expression of the ordinary concerns of its members as it was a result of rules ratified by the courts of law. It was an order in which relations between kin, neighbours, patrons and clients were the ground upon which the evanescent arrangements and fleeting transactions of small-scale entrepreneurs were based, for they provided the two most important elements of the economy of the bazaar: information and workers. The two were different aspects of an economy in which a highly developed division of labour co-existed with a wide range of different kinds of sub-contracted work and a wide variety of possible clients, markets and outlets. A capacity to take advantage of the short-term opportunities that they supplied depended upon a combination of adequate information and access to labour. Both were functions of the range of acquaintances at an artisan's disposal. Ménétra's own measure of success was indicative of the fact. ' A la fin ', he wrote, recalling the difficult period that followed his marriage and purchase of a shop, ' nous commençames à faire des connaissances.'[60]

Many of these acquaintances were supplied by neighbours, kin or former work associates. The categories were often indistinguishable. Ménétra employed his brother-in-law on work that he had sub-contracted from other master glaziers. He sent his son to Beauvais to work for one of his former apprentices. He supplied his uncles with glass from a glazier he had worked for in Tours. One of the journeymen he employed subsequently went to work for his father, and married his sister. His frequent complaints about his wife's financial independence were an indirect acknowledgement of the fact that she, and not he, managed cash payments and receipts. Predictably, when he fell ill, he noted gloomily that his illness

[59] Ménétra, *Journal*, p. 204.

[60] *Ibid.*, p. 209.

had encouraged his most senior journeyman to contemplate taking his place.[61] Order in this informal world was the product of the interplay between the overlapping categories of work, kin, neighbourhood and acquaintance.

In an indirect way, the many details that Ménétra noted down as he recalled his life in Paris also throw some light on the very different conditions that he described in his account of the time he spent as a journeyman working outside Paris on the *tour de France*. There, he was known simply as *Parisien le Bienvenue*, the name given to him when he became a *compagnon du devoir* and was initiated into one of the many networks of informal association formed by itinerant journeymen.[62] The relative anonymity of the *sobriquet* was an unconscious testimony to the absence of many of the ties of kin or neighbourhood that were the basis of many of Ménétra's activities in Paris. It was also testimony to the diversity of trades associated with the *compagnonnages*. Members of the *compagnonnages* were known either by their place of birth or by some physical or personal attribute. The trades that they practised rarely entered into their nicknames.

Unlike the print-shop chapels that Contat described, membership of the *compagnonnages* was not limited to a single trade. Among the *compagnons du devoir* that Ménétra frequented were saddlers, locksmiths, carpenters, tinsmiths, cutlers, hatters, stone-cutters, joiners, tailors and roofers.[63] The diversity of occupations is initially surprising. It does not appear to be especially compatible with the particularity of the corporate world, still less with any assumptions that associations among journeymen prefigured trade or industry-wide unions. It is very much more comprehensible, however, in the light of the bazaar-like economy that Ménétra described, for the diversity of occupations associated with the *compagnonnages* mirrored the circumstances of single men in unfamiliar places.

Patterns of association among itinerant journeymen were structured by the work that they did, rather than, as in Paris, the wider range of ties formed by kin, neighbourhood or acquaintance. In an economy characterised by highly developed divisions of labour and a high degree of specialisation between different trades, information supplied by journeymen in one trade was the key to employment for journeymen in other, ancillary, trades. The patterns of association among journeymen from apparently heterogeneous trades that was one of the hallmarks of the *compagnonnages* mirrored the heterogeneity of the division of labour of the eighteenth-century trades. In unfamiliar places, single men relied heavily

[61] *Ibid.*, pp. 169, 191, 198, 213, 222, 249, 252.
[62] I have followed Daniel Roche in reproducing Ménétra's spelling of *Parisien le Bienvenue*. For a fuller discussion of the *compagnonnages*, see below, chapter 9.
[63] Ménétra, *Journal*, pp. 52–3, 57, 59, 63, 68, 71, 79, 82, 87, 89, 95, 136–7.

upon information transmitted between various parts of particular divisions of labour for the work that they undertook.[64] Whatever their other functions, the diversity and variety of the *compagnonnages* echoed the diversity and variety of trades associated with elaborate divisions of labour and complex networks of sub-contracted work.

In this sense, Ménétra's *Journal de ma vie* can be interpreted as an extended commentary upon the divisions of labour that were so characteristic a feature of the majority of the eighteenth-century urban trades. In the printing trade of mid-eighteenth-century Paris, most of those divisions of labour were incorporated into integrated enterprises. In the glazing trade, as in most others, they were devolved upon many separate enterprises. The relationship between these enterprises had many different forms, ranging from simple commercial transactions to hierarchical arrangements of varying degrees of complexity and durability. The relationship between contractors and sub-contractors cut across the particularities of trades and corporations to form elaborate networks whose interdependence endowed the bazaar-like economy of the Parisian trades with its coherent form.

Relationships between enterprises were also relationships between people. They were relationships in which bargains were struck and reputations were made or unmade. Transactions of this kind included the most intimate exchanges between fathers and sons, as well as among other groups of kin. Ménétra's *Journal* and his silence over a regulation that his father had approved but which he himself ignored are indicative of the kinds of tensions informing the ordinary circumstances of eighteenth-century artisans. The provisions of corporate prescription and legal regulation were a very distant commentary upon these smaller, more intimate dramas. The idiom in which they were couched, which was the idiom of the law, was not identical to the idiom of the bazaar, just as the corporations themselves were never identical to the trades. Ménétra's recollections are an elaborate and detailed illustration of the difference.

THE UNCERTAIN ORIGINS OF CAPITALIST ENTERPRISE

The allusions in Contat's *Anecdotes typographiques* reveal variations in the organisation of particular trades and modes of legal argument that are not often associated with artisanal production. The omissions from Ménétra's

[64] In Ménétra's case the reasons are the more obvious because the glazing trade was relatively specialised. Only 32 journeymen glaziers (less than one per cent of a total of 3,511) registered with the municipal authorities of Tours between 1782 and 1789. Representatives of most of the other trades that Ménétra frequented registered by the hundred: A.D. Indre-et-Loire E 492. It is easy to understand, in the light of these figures, why a man like Ménétra needed information from men working in other, ancillary trades.

Journal de ma vie suggest the distance between the particularities of corporate prescription and the divisions and sub-divisions of labour that structured the economy of the eighteenth-century trades. Together they indicate that the environment informing relations between journeymen and their masters in eighteenth-century France was very much more complex than might first appear to be the case. Beyond the corporate world lay the courts of law and a world of legal argument, civil jurisprudence, claims and entitlements whose terms and propositions endowed corporate regulations with their particular form; on the other side lay the world of the bazaar, with its multiple divisions of labour, variegated products and multiform markets. Beyond that world lay yet another, whose vitality was a product of relationships between kin, members of different generations, men and women, friends, neighbours, patrons and clients.

The third text, the autobiography of a Parisian turner and chairmaker named Jacques-Etienne Bédé, is an illustration of the difficulty that artisans experienced when they attempted to integrate these many different facets of the world of the trades into a single narrative.[65] It was composed during the third decade of the nineteenth century, well after the abolition of the corporations in 1791. Before then, Bédé would have been known as a journeyman. When Bédé wrote his autobiography the term had no formal status, although the work that he did was very similar to the work performed by journeymen in the eighteenth-century Parisian furniture trade. It was, in fact, very much more similar than Bédé himself was able to recognise. Many of the features of the furnishing trade that he described appear, on a first reading, to have originated in the abolition of the corporations and the restrictions upon capitalist enterprise that they represented. In fact this was not the case. What had changed was not so much the trade itself, but the legal environment in which it existed. Bédé, however, took that environment for granted.

He decided to write his account of his life to explain his involvement in a year-long dispute in a section of the Parisian furniture trade between 1819 and 1820. It occurred on the rue de Cléry, which, along with the Marais and the *faubourg* Saint-Antoine, was one of the centres of furniture production in Paris during the eighteenth and early nineteenth centuries. As Bédé described it, the dispute originated in a number of changes that had occurred in the trade in the aftermath of the Revolution, the most important being the rise of sub-contracted work and the emergence of a new type of entrepreneur, an urban putter-out or *verläger*. The two developments were complemented by the growing practice of paying workers for agreed quantities of finished articles, rather than by the day or

[65] Rémi Gossez, ed., *Un Ouvrier en 1820, manuscrit inédit de Jacques-Etienne Bédé* (Paris, 1984). What follows is an adaptation of my review in *History Workshop Journal*, 21 (1986), pp. 174–9.

the piece. According to Bédé, journeymen in the furniture trade had been previously paid by the day. The wages they earned were not, therefore, directly related to the number of articles they produced. Time spent collecting and unloading timber, or delivering and installing pieces of furniture, was not time lost from directly productive work because the wage was not a piece-rate. As sub-contracted work became more widespread and workers undertook to produce given quantities of particular goods at agreed prices, it became very much more difficult to ignore the effects of lost working time upon income. This, according to Bédé, was why he and scores of other workers had stopped work in 1819. They wished to put an end to what they called *corvées*, or unpaid labour, with all the overtones of coercion and servitude that the word implied. They did not, however, go on strike. Instead, they found work elsewhere, notably in a workshop that came to be known as the *Champ d'asyle*, where *corvées* were not required.

In fact there was nothing new about sub-contracted work and the system of payment that came to be known as *marchandage*. It was a very ordinary part of the work that Ménétra described, even though the glaziers' corporation had prohibited 'travail à l'entreprise' in 1766. It was equally widespread in the building and furnishing trades well before the early nineteenth century. In the Parisian joining trade, where over 1,000 master artisans belonged to the corporation alone in 1787, and several hundred more had shops in the *faubourg* Saint-Antoine and other privileged areas, there were considerable differences between large and small employers.[66] In a small way, these differences were acknowledged in a clause of the corporation's statutes of 1751 allowing masters with little work to lease their right to take on two apprentices to those with more substantial requirements.[67] More substantially, however, they found their expression in widespread sub-contracting.

Sub-contracted work meant that some master joiners were brokers rather than manufacturers, supplying orders and clients to other masters

[66] On the size of the corporation, see BHVP Z 214, *Tableaux de la communauté des maîtres menuisiers–ébenistes–tourneurs & layeteurs de la ville, faubourgs et banlieue de Paris* (1787 and 1789). An *état des pauvres maîtres et veuves* belonging to the corporation in 1769 can be found in A.N. Y 11 085 (7 February 1769). Some indication of the size of a small number of workshops in which journeymen were found without *livrets* in 1785 can be found in A.N. Y 14 348 (5 December 1785). Among them were 18 journeymen working in two *ateliers* in the Hôtel de Lamoignon for a royal architect. Neither of the two published accounts of the Parisian furnishing trades have much on sub-contracting: see Paule Garenc, *L'Industrie du meuble en France* (Paris, 1958) and Pierre Verlet, *L'Art du meuble à Paris au xviiie siècle* (Paris, 1968). More information can be found in S. Eriksen, *Louis Delanois, menuisier en sièges (1731–1792)* (Paris, 1968) and Françoise Raison-Jourde, *La Colonie auvergnate de Paris au xixe siècle* (Paris, 1976).

[67] A.N. X¹ᵃ 8757 fol. 391 *et seq.* (20 August 1751); see article 88. Printed copies of the statutes can be found in the B.N. and the Goldsmiths' Library of the University of London: G.L. 8611.

or journeymen, who carried some, or all, of the costs of materials and wages until they settled their accounts with the principal contractor. Many of these arrangements, like those that Ménétra made, were not entirely in keeping with the provisions of corporate regulations, even if they were perfectly consonant with the bazaar-like character of many of the eighteenth-century urban trades. Despite the risks associated with encroaching upon corporate privilege and the dangers of prosecution as *faux-ouvriers*, journeymen too acted as brokers. Prosecutions of journeymen who took on sub-contracted work in the joining and furnishing trades indicate that the practice was carried out on a substantial scale, sometimes with the connivance of the corporate officials. In some instances, as many as a dozen individuals were illegally employed by journeymen working on a sub-contracted basis.[68]

As Ménétra's *Journal* suggests, the existence of sub-contracted work created tensions between corporate officials and enterprising artisans, and between contractors and sub-contractors. In 1749 journeymen working on the rue de Cléry were prosecuted for a stoppage occasioned by a dispute over the piece-rates they were paid for making armchairs with frames (*fauteuils à chassis*) and cane chairs.[69] In 1770, two generations before Bédé composed his autobiography, a joiner named André-Jacob Roubo produced a description of the joiners' trade in which the same innovations were described and denounced in almost identical terms. According to Roubo, the practice had led to the production of shoddy goods, constant argument over the appropriate level of rates and mutual accusations of chicanery among masters and journeymen. The solution, he concluded, was a restoration of the emulation and concord associated with payment by the day.[70]

These remarks undoubtedly owed something to events in the trade at the time. Although Roubo did not say so in so many words – and a learned treatise on the joiner's art destined for publication by the *Académie des sciences* might not have been the best place to do so – 'emulation' and 'concord' were notably absent from the trade at the time that the work was composed. In 1770, the year that Roubo's work was published, the joiners' corporation decided to prohibit sub-contracted work. An assembly in March 1770 was presented with a long litany of complaints and recriminations about journeymen 'à qui les maîtres donnent des ouvrages

[68] A.N. Y 15 365 contains scores of prosecutions for this kind of activity. See also X^{1a} 4469 (6 June 1764) and X^{1a} 4503 fols. 56–111 (3 July 1765) for a long lawsuit among the corporation's members over sub-contracted work that had been put out to *faux-ouvriers* with the connivance of the *jurés*.

[69] A.N. Y 15 345 (4 October 1749); Y 9523^b (November 1749).

[70] 'Si tous les ouvriers travailloient à la journée...ces difficultés s'évanouiroient, et l'émulation et la concorde regnéroient parmi les ouvriers, et entre ces derniers et leurs maîtres': André-Jacob Roubo, *L'Art du menuisier*, 4 vols. (Paris, 1770), vol. 4, p. 1244.

à tâches et à leur pièce marchande'.[71] There had been combinations and stoppages. Journeymen had failed to give adequate notice before leaving their masters. They had refused to install furniture that had been repaired or replaced and were not prepared to do a full day's work. In short, journeymen were behaving exactly as Bédé claimed that they were entitled to behave 50 years later. Having undertaken to produce a given quantity of pieces of furniture, they were not prepared to lose time by observing a week's notice or by transporting and installing the goods they had made. As the corporation rightly put it, they assumed that 'après leurs ouvrages finis ils sont quittes de tout service'.[72]

The decision by the joiners' corporation was the product of a series of disputes and legal actions between masters and journeymen that, on the journeymen's side, have all the appearances of a carefully co-ordinated and well-funded general campaign. The legal actions themselves are an indication of how difficult it was to translate certain aspects of the economy of the bazaar into the provisions of the law. This difficulty was particularly apparent in disputes over sub-contracted work because the formal provisions of corporate statutes usually defined the respective rights and obligations of masters and journeymen in a very general way. The statutes of the joiners' corporation of 1751 had little to say about the modalities of wage-payments or the forms of redress available to either masters or journeymen in the event of disputes. This was not unusual. The details of the contract of employment were frequently left to decisions by the civil courts, whose rulings established precedents applicable to specific trades. Yet journeymen sometimes argued that such decisions did not apply to their particular trades. As has been mentioned, journeymen printers argued that their masters had no right to take on additional journeymen to finish work in progress because it was a violation of the natural law principle that all contracts, including the contract of employment, were mutually binding. In eighteenth-century France there was no general legal framework regulating the terms and conditions of the contract of employment.

The status of sub-contracted work was particularly problematic. For master artisans, it had a number of practical advantages: it enabled them to transfer some of the costs of materials, equipment and wage-payments to the journeymen to whom they put work out and, at the same time, allowed them to operate a number of workshops in different parts of the capital, even though the practice was prohibited under article 38 of the corporation's statutes of 1751.[73] Sub-contracted work also had several

[71] A.N. X¹ᵇ 3926 (23 April 1770).

[72] *Ibid.*

[73] Goldsmiths' Library, University of London: GL 8611. In 1766 the joiners of the *faubourg Saint-Antoine* appealed to the Parlement over a police sentence prohibiting them 'd'avoir chacun d'eux plus d'une établie montée de son affutage': A.N. X¹ᵇ 3856 (9 February 1767); x¹ᵃ 4559 fol. 79ᵛᵒ (24 March 1767); x¹ᵃ 8220 fol. 180 (27 November 1770).

disadvantages. The brokerage function that was intrinsic to sub-contracting could be taken on easily by sub-contractors themselves. When work was put out, and journeymen agreed to supply given quantities of chairs, window-frames, doors or other articles at negotiated prices, the space, equipment and materials that they had at their disposal created many opportunities to furnish clients on their own account. The number of possible occasions for dispute also increased considerably. The price of materials and cost of equipment had to be taken into consideration, since part of their value may have been met by masters and part by journeymen. Time had also to be measured and valued. Yet there was time spent working, time spent collecting and delivering, and the value of the finished product was not necessarily a multiple of either the one or the other. In the last analysis, sub-contracted work presented acute problems of measuring and evaluating the relative contributions of contractors and sub-contractors. The difficulty was reinforced by the absence of any clearly defined procedures for the process of valuation itself.

These problems lay at the core of the legal actions and disputes that occurred in the joining trade between 1760 and 1789. They were not confined to the furnishing trade: court rulings affecting conditions of employment in several trades in which sub-contracted work was widespread were also cited in the disputes in the joining trade. As has already been noted, the Parlement of Paris confirmed the glaziers' decision to outlaw 'travail à l'entreprise' in 1766. In 1767 it produced an important ruling in a dispute between two locksmiths over the value of 24 wrought-iron balconies and banisters that one of the two had installed in the *hôtel* belonging to the Marquis de la Tour du Pin. The sub-contractor had complained that he had not been paid in full for the balconies, although the principal contractor had given him 19 old balconies as part payment. They had agreed to refer the dispute to the *jurés experts*, a body of officials established during the reign of Louis XIV which was empowered to value disputed building work, particularly in cases in which disagreements involved ordinary members of the public and building contractors. This decision led to the intervention of the locksmiths' corporate officials in the proceedings, on the grounds that they alone were entitled to value work in disputes between masters and journeymen.[74] The Parlement ruled in favour of the corporation and dismissed the valuation made by the external assessor.

In the same year, however, the Parlement made a rather different

---

[74] 'Qu'ils fussent maintenus et gardés en leurs qualités de jurés de leur communauté dans le droit et possession d'estimer les ouvrages de serrurerie entre les maîtres et les compagnons serruriers; cette estimation faisant partie de la police intérieure de la communauté': A.N. X^{1b} 8305 (21 March 1767). The case in fact began in 1756: see X^{1a} 4224 fol. 53vo (24 February 1756).

ruling. It was the product of civil proceedings initiated by two journeymen joiners to recover the sum of 982 *livres* outstanding on the larger amount of 3,742 *livres* which, the two claimed, was owed to them by a master joiner for work done 'à la tâche ou à la pièce' between 1764 and 1766.[75] The dispute had led to contradictory rulings by the lower courts. The Consulat of Paris had ruled in favour of the master joiner who was the principal contractor. The two journeymen had presented their case to the civil division of the Châtelet and secured a ruling in their favour. On appeal to the Parlement, the master joiner was supported by the officials of his corporation, claiming, as in the locksmiths' case, that they alone were empowered to set a value on disputed work. The two journeymen were able, however, to produce a letter signed by the master joiner's wife accepting an outside valuation and thanking the *juré expert* who had done the work for his time and effort. The Parlement accordingly ruled in favour of the journeymen and ordered the master joiner to pay the outstanding amount and the costs of the case.

The ruling led to a minor explosion of legal actions in the lower courts by journeymen who had undertaken sub-contracted work and had it valued by outside assessors. This legal guerrilla warfare was the context in which the joiners' corporation decided to prohibit sub-contracted work in April 1770. By then, however, it was too late to prevent a major legal trial of strength between the corporation and the journeymen over the issue of independent valuation. Between 1770 and 1774 the Parlement of Paris was presented with appeals arising from nine separate legal actions between a dozen journeymen and ten master joiners. The case became a massive lawsuit when the officials of both the joiners' corporation and the *jurés experts* intervened as well. It ended when the Parlement, citing the locksmiths' case as a precedent, ruled against the journeymen and confirmed the officials of the joiners' corporation in their right to set a value on disputed pieces of work.[76]

The scale of the proceedings and the costs they entailed indicate that it was an organised campaign by journeymen in the trade as a whole. The joiners' corporation was in no doubt that this was the case. It referred sententiously to an earlier legal trial of strength, in 1755 and 1756, when it said, over 800 journeymen had combined to challenge a corporate decision ordering them to register with the corporate office and present certificates of good conduct before they were able to find work in the capital.[77] The action before the Parlement was, it claimed, motivated 'par

---

75 A.N. X1a 8115 fol. 234vo (3 July 1767); B.N. MS. Joly de Fleury 1879 fols. 48 *et seq.*
76 The details have been pieced together from the huge final *arrêt*: A.N. X1a 4738 fol. 111 (22 January 1774).
77 On that dispute, see A.N. X1b 3657 (25 March 1755); X1a 4193 fol. 5vo (25 March 1755); 7791 fols. 300vo and 322 (1 October 1755); 7795 fol. 298vo (11 December 1755); 4239 fol. 289 (4 August 1756); K 1031 no. 121.

le même esprit de caballe et de révolte '.[78] The magistrates of the Parlement appear to have shared the sentiment, and in their final verdict reiterated a series of legal injunctions prohibiting associations among journeymen in the trade running from 1680 to 1756, which, in their very uniformity, are indicative of the enduring character of the associations themselves.[79]

The claims that each side made centred upon the problem of valuing sub-contracted work. The officials of the joiners' corporation argued that it had enjoyed the 'droit, usage et possession' of settling disputes over valuation 'depuis un tems immémorial'. Valuations by other parties, particularly by architects owning the office of *juré expert*, were 'une innovation sans fondement' and contrary to the practice followed 'dans toutes les communautés d'arts et métiers de cette ville de Paris'.[80] This, it claimed, had been demonstrated clearly enough by the Parlement in its ruling in favour of the locksmiths. The journeymen, on the other hand, denied that the corporation's officials had ever valued sub-contracted work.[81] The most they had ever done was to convoke the parties in a dispute to the corporate office and announce that a particular piece of work was worth a certain sum.[82] They had never, in other words, assessed the respective contributions of masters and journeymen to the value of the work in question.

The arguments, and the lawsuit itself, prefigured most of the issues and the circumstances that Bédé described nearly 50 years later. Nor did the decision to prohibit sub-contracted work in 1770 and the ruling by the Parlement in 1774 put an end to the problem. In 1775, in the first phase of the Physiocratic campaign against the corporations, the ruling by the Parlement was overturned and the joiners' corporation was divested of its right to adjudicate on disputes over work carried out 'à la tâche ou à l'entreprise'. In 1780, however, after a sustained campaign in which the joiners were supported by the carpenters, farriers, iron-founders, lock-smiths, pavers, roofers and plumbers – a list that is an illustration of the ubiquity of sub-contracted work – the Royal Council restored the right.[83] The decision was followed by a ruling by the Parlement in September 1780, confirming a corporate decision entitling master joiners to have an

[78] A.N. X^{1a} 4738 (22 January 1774).

[79] In addition to the rulings cited in note 77 above, see A.N. E 1802 fols. 78 and 256, *arrêts de conseil* (9 August and 16 December 1680); X^{2a} 487 (4 January 1696); AD+ 633 (19 July 1704); B.N. MS. Joly de Fleury 1879 fol. 60, *sentence de police* (26 November 1743).

[80] On journeymen's associations in the joining trade, see below, p. 84.

[81] A.N. X^{1a} 4738 (22 January 1774).

[81] 'Ils sont dans l'impuissance d'en raporter la minute, ni le moindre vestige d'aucune', *ibid.*

[82] 'Ils ne montrent pas leur rapport aux parties …les font venir au bureau et leur disent que la totalité de l'ouvrage vaut tant', *ibid.*

[83] B.N. F 21201 (39) *arrêt du conseil* (2 February 1780).

atelier on separate premises from their shops.[84] The decision reversed the provisions of the corporation's statutes of 1751 and was clear evidence of the scale of sub-contracted work within the trade. Its importance was further underlined by an additional clause empowering the corporation's officials to serve summonses upon master joiners involved in disputes with journeymen over sub-contracted work to present the work in question for valuation. It noted that masters involved in disputes generally refused to issue the statutory certificates of good conduct to their journeymen. Journeymen were consequently prevented from finding work elsewhere until the dispute was settled, causing unnecessary delays and shortages of labour.

This final clause is an indication of how the economy of the bazaar affected the tenor of relations between journeymen and their masters during the eighteenth century. Registration, certificates of good conduct, and the rhetorical exhortations to serve and obey that frequently justified their introduction are easy to misinterpret. They appear to belong to an archaic patriarchal system where deference, subordination and corporate power governed the relationship between masters and journeymen. It is important to remember, however, that the rhetoric surrounding such devices had a legal provenance and that the purpose of the devices themselves was often very different. In the context of the furnishing trades, as in that of the glazing trade with which Jacques-Louis Ménétra was associated, their purpose was governed as much by the ubiquity of sub-contracted work as by the imperatives of an authoritarian patriarchalism that is otherwise not easy to explain. When journeymen objected to these provisions – as the journeymen joiners did in 1755 and again in 1785 – they did so as much because they played an active part in undertaking sub-contracted work as because they objected to the subordination that registration represented.

There are good reasons therefore for supposing that many of the innovations that Bédé associated with *corvées* and *marchandage* were well-established features of many of the Parisian trades before the early nineteenth century. Even André-Jacob Roubo, who wrote so strongly against the practice in 1770, was involved in a lawsuit over the valuation of sub-contracted work in 1789.[85] Yet if the problem of sub-contracted work was not a new one, the circumstances in which Bédé lived were still very different from those in which masters and journeymen had lived before the Revolution. The difference, however, was legal and institutional rather than productive or commercial. As the long sequence of argument over sub-contracted work in the joining trade has revealed, the economy of the bazaar was controlled to varying degrees by the range of powers

[84] A.N. X^{1b} 4118 (7 September 1780).

[85] A.N. X^{1b} 4340 (21 October 1789).

available to the officials of the corporations. Unless the courts ruled otherwise, they were able to set a value on disputed sub-contracted work and, through the combined effects of registration, certificates of good conduct and statutory periods of notice, prevent journeymen from becoming brokers themselves by putting materials out to other individuals or working on their own account. The power of corporations was, in this sense, a counterpoint to the ramifications of sub-contracted work.

By 1819, when Bédé and the chairmakers on the rue de Cléry stopped work to obtain payment for their *corvées*, the situation had changed in a number of respects. The provisions of corporate regulation had been replaced by the provisions of the Civil Code. The panoply of coercive powers represented by statutory periods of notice, registration and certificates had been abolished; instead, the Civil Code contained two clauses whose significance is particularly striking in the light of the long-standing problem of the status of sub-contracted work. They are, again, easy to misinterpret. Article 1781 of the Code contained the notorious provision that, in disputes over wage-payments, 'le maître est cru sur son affirmation'.[86] The phrase has connotations of despotic authority, connotations that finally led to the repeal of the offending article in 1868. It is probable that the article was used in a punitive sense, but it is equally probable that its original purpose was to fill the hiatus left by the abolition of the right of corporate officials to value sub-contracted work themselves.

Its purpose is clearer in the light of the less celebrated article that preceded it. Article 1780 of the Civil Code stipulated that a worker could not be physically constrained to complete unfinished work. In disputes involving breach of contract, 'un ouvrier ne peut être contraint par corps'.[87] Instead, an employer was limited to a civil action for damages and interest. Together, the two articles placed sub-contracted work and disputes over its value in a different context. Before the Revolution, master artisans had been able to exercise some authority in arguments over sub-contracted work because the extensive coercive powers that corporations enjoyed made it difficult for journeymen to function as brokers themselves or to undertake work at the best possible rates without infringing statutory regulations concerning periods of notice, registration and certificates of good conduct. After the Revolution, a principal contractor had no such protection. Although printed certificates acquired a general character in the form of the *livret*, employers were unable to compel workers to return

[86] For a discussion of the article and its repeal, see André Castaldo, 'L'Histoire juridique de l'article 1781 du Code Civil: "Le maître est cru sur son affirmation"'. *Revue historique de droit français et étranger*, 55 (1977), pp. 211–37. On the earlier history of labour legislation, see Michael Sonenscher, 'Journeymen, the Courts and the French Trades 1781–1791', *Past and Present*, 114 (1987), pp. 77–109.

[87] P. A. Fenet, *Receuil complet des travaux préparatoires du Code Civil*, 15 vols (Paris, 1827–36) vol. 14, p. 255. See also Guy Poulain, *La Distinction des contrats de travail à durée déterminée et indéterminée* (Paris, 1971), and chapter 2 and Conclusion, below.

to work.[88] If a worker left work in progress and took on other work, the most that an employer could do was to sue for damages and interest on the value of the uncompleted work. Article 1781 ensured that their assertions could not be challenged in disputes of this kind.

This was the context in which the dispute that Bédé described took place. The words that he used in his account of the long conflict echoed those used in earlier legal proceedings arising from disputes over sub-contracted work. Just as the officials of the joiners' corporation described valuation of disputed work by outsiders as an 'innovation' which violated a usage that they had enjoyed 'depuis un tems immémorial', so Bédé ascribed the practices of *marchandage* and *corvées* to a group of *nouveaux maîtres*, ruthlessly prepared to sacrifice usages recognised by *les anciens* in pursuit of profit. 'Aujourd'hui', he wrote, 'ce ne sont plus des honnetétés que l'on reçoit de Messieurs les nouveaux maîtres tourneurs de la rue de Cléry, c'est des vexations et des abus multipliés qui révoltent la justice et la raison.'[89] The juxtaposition of past and present that structured his narrative echoed procedures used in legal argument during the eighteenth century, but masked some of the differences between that time and his own.

The abolition of the corporations added a further difference to the situation of workers like Bédé in the early nineteenth century. It meant that there were no formal obstacles to entry to either the furnishing trades or most other branches of production in early nineteenth-century Paris. All that was needed was sufficient capital, credit and the 'connaissances' that Ménétra identified as the basis of success. Unpaid working time had an added significance in this context, particularly for a man like Bédé, for his own resources were meagre. By 1819 he was over 40 years old, an age at which many journeymen would have established themselves as masters of a corporation during the eighteenth century. Sub-contracted work was an opportunity to effect this transition. Unpaid work and lost time were major obstacles to the slow accumulation of the resources needed to effect the transformation from sub-contractor to principal contractor.

Both the issue itself and the long selective boycott that the chairmakers on the rue de Cléry imposed upon employers who insisted that *corvées* were a part of sub-contracted work owed a great deal to the events of the revolutionary decades. Yet the nature of that debt was more complex than might first appear. It had little to do with the development of sub-contracted work itself, for that was intrinsic to the economy of the eighteenth-century trades. Instead, it derived from changes in the law and

[88] On the *livret*, see the Conclusion below: Kaplan, 'Réflexions' and Charles Schmidt, *Industrie: Receuil de textes et de notes. Commission de recherche et de publication des documents relatifs à la vie économique de la Révolution* (Paris, 1910).

[89] Gossez, ed., *Bédé*, pp. 200–1.

in the legal status of employers and workers. In the eighteenth century, journeymen in the joining trade brought civil actions against employers over the value of sub-contracted work, and challenged the right of the joiners' corporation to have the last word in disputed valuations. In the nineteenth century, such actions were pointless, because the last word belonged to employers. Yet workers could no longer be forced to return to complete unfinished work. When Bédé and his fellow-workers walked out on their employers and went to work in their *Champ d'asyle* for nearly a year, they were the unconscious heirs of the Revolution in more ways than the word *corvée* implies.

VARIETIES OF ARTISANAL ENTERPRISE

The words used by artisans are not as easy to interpret as they seem. Careful reading and additional information reveal allusions, omissions or amnesia embedded in the words themselves. Once elucidated, these latent signifiers reveal unsuspected variations in the architecture of the trades, differences between the particularism of corporations and the extensive divisions of labour of the economy of the bazaar, hierarchies among journeymen as well as master artisans, and a world in which the terms master and journeyman could also mean father and son, or patron and client, or all three, in either a literal or a metaphorical sense. In different ways, Contat, Ménétra and Bédé also wrote about or alluded to legal processes and a vocabulary of legal argument in which terms like *despotisme, possession, liberté* and *droit* had precise contemporary meanings. They too require elucidation, for the words that artisans used were not unaffected by the vocabulary of public life.

There are, in other words, many different approaches to the world of the eighteenth-century French trades. The difficulty is that they converge and intersect at unexpected moments. Masters and journeymen belonged to corporations, yet members of one corporation often had more to do with members of other corporations than with their own, because the trades they exercised were part of elaborate divisions of labour and complex networks of sub-contracted work. Masters and journeymen were sometimes employers and employees, but sometimes they were patrons and clients, or fathers and sons, or fathers-in-law and sons-in-law. In different ways, each of these categories was complemented by various aspects of the civil law. There was a legal dimension to work and wages which overlapped with the material conditions in which productive activity took place.

To understand the world of the eighteenth-century French trades it is necessary to place these multiple relationships within the broadest possible context. Corporations were only a component of the wider sphere of legal provision and political institutions of eighteenth-century France. Disputes between masters and journeymen were moments within broader cycles of production, distribution, exchange and consumption that endowed the local economies of particular trades with their specific forms. The law, the multiform structures of the trades and the many different circumstances in which masters and journeymen lived and worked are the keys to a fuller understanding of the arguments and conflicts they had. The first of these, the law, is an essential point of departure because it supplied many of the terms that masters and journeymen used in the course of conflict in the trades. It also played a part in the formation of images of artisanal production that are somewhat at variance with the realities of the workshop economy.

Images of artisans

The engraving opposite is a picture of an artisan. He is, we are told, not alone. Two tiny figures reveal that the arts were a synthesis of mental and manual labour. Seated above the artisan's head is Minerva, goddess of science. The figure of industry on his left hand holds a spider's web, while a swarm of bees surrounds her head. The purposeful industriousness symbolised by the bees and the web reinforce the title beneath the engraving. In colloquial French, to pull the Devil by the tail meant to work hard to get a living. At first glance the image appears to present an allegory of human conduct: a choice between the two forms of secular behaviour symbolised by honour and profit. A more careful scrutiny, and the words beneath the image, tell a different story, for both the plumes of honour and the bag of coins in the artisan's field of vision are in the hands of the Devil. The message is clear: the goals are a chimera, the ephemeral stuff of which the world is made. So too, by implication, is the array of miniature objects and figures that fill the image. The artisan may not appear to be alone, but, like sinful humanity as a whole, he is. His duty is to attend to the salvation of his soul and find reconciliation with God, for God is the *magie bleue* which he is advised to seek.[1]

The image was produced by a Parisian engraver named Nicolas Guérard towards the end of the seventeenth century.[2] It is an indication that work, and images of work, have a long history, and that the vocabulary currently used to describe and delineate its features may not be the only possible one. In Guérard's engraving, the two tiny figures of science and

[1] On the phrase 'tirer le diable par la queue', see Antoine Jean Vincent, *Le Livre des proverbes français* 2 vols (Paris, 1859), vol. 1, p. 15. The phrase 'magie bleue' is more mysterious, but is analogous to 'sacré bleu', the better-known (and now debased) synonym for God. On the religious connotations of the colour blue, see E. Hoffmann-Krayer and Hans Bachtold-Staubli, *Handwörterbuch des Deutschen Aberglaubens* (Berlin and Leipzig, 1927), p. 1371 (s.v. 'blau'). I am grateful to Jill Kraye of the Warburg Institute Library for her help on the question.

[2] Bibliothèque nationale, Département des Estampes, *Inventaire du fonds français: graveurs du xviie siècle* (Paris, 1968), vol. 5, pp. 80–99. Guérard died in Paris in 1719, aged 71.

IL N'EST PAS SEUL

L'artisan . tire le diable par la queue .

Tirez le diable par la queue .
Artisans par vôtre industrie .
Veillez cherchiez la magie bleiu .

Pour bien profiter de la vie .
Et si vous nanaiez du bien .
C'est que les arts ny valent rien .

Se Vend a Paris chez N. Guerard Graveur rue St Jacques a la Reyne du clergé proche S. Yves . C.P.R.

But de l'artisan

honneur

profit

l'industrie

la France

Efforcez vous devenez vertueux
vous aurez par là tout les deux

arts et metiers

O ciel qui scait comme je tire .
Faits que des deux un peu j'attire .

2.1 Il n'est pas seul (author's collection).

industry are enclosed by the wider drama enacted between the artisan and the Devil. The image is a rehearsal of a familiar Christian theme – sharpened, perhaps, by the austere injunctions emanating from Port Royal. Work was Adam's curse, the price exacted from sinful humanity for its misuse of the Divine gift of free will, the daily obligation to obtain the transient goods of this world by arduous toil.

The theme was echoed in many eighteenth-century sermons. 'Qu'est-ce qu'est la terre?' asked one practitioner in a sermon composed for the second Sunday of Advent: 'Une vallée de larmes et de soupirs, un séjour de contrainte et d'esclavage…Les uns y gémissent sous le poids de l'indigence, les autres sous celui du travail.'[3] These images of work as a burden borne across the vale of life's tribulations, or a symbol of the vain pursuit of worldly goods, are at once familiar in a general way and unfamiliar in the specific context of the study of artisans. They are familiar because enough of the culture of early-modern Europe has survived to ensure that the rhetoric of Christian other-worldliness is not particularly alien. They are unfamiliar because the history of artisans has been placed within a different context.

It seems, in a sense, to have been written in advance. Artisans always appear to have belonged to a world that was already archaic, a world of small workshops, idiosyncratic customs and exotic traditions whose end was already inscribed in its beginning. From its inception, the history of the urban trades seems to have been bathed in a warm glow of autumnal retrospection.[4] Artisans invariably appear to have found themselves on the wrong side of anonymous processes whose lines had already been drawn: defending their skills, protecting their traditional rights, for ever, it would seem, looking back. At some point, those skills, those traditional rights and that incorrigible nostalgia for better days were bound to disappear. This, of course, is something of a caricature. Yet the image is founded upon much of what artisans said. Instead of assuming that it bears the mark of a distinctively artisanal culture, it is worth asking why artisans actually used this language.

The idea of artisanal production has come to be associated with a number of terms which, together, signify the difference between the world of the eighteenth-century workshop and the world of mechanised systems of commodity production. Three terms, in particular, stand out: the concept of pre-industrial society, the notion of custom and the idea of

---

[3] N. G. Papillon du Rivet (1717–82) in *Collection intégrale et universelle des orateurs sacrés* (Paris, 1844), vol. 59, p. 1179. To my knowledge, there are no studies of the sermon as a form of rhetoric and as a source of political metaphors in eighteenth-century France.

[4] Eighteenth-century engravings of artisans have come to be viewed in a similar fashion: see William H. Sewell Jr., 'Visions of Labor: Illustrations of the Mechanical Arts before, in, and after Diderot's *Encyclopédie*', in Kaplan and Koepp, *Work in France*, pp. 258–86.

popular culture.[5] Such precision as they have owes a great deal to a series of binary oppositions. Thus the concept of pre-industrial society evokes a world of small-scale, fragmented units of production in opposition to the large-scale, integrated units of production of industrial society. The notion of custom has, as its opposite, that of the market. It implies that the allocation of resources in pre-industrial societies owed something to reciprocities and arrangements that fell outside the monetary nexus of prices and profits. The notion of custom is associated with an idea of popular culture in which moral considerations and the informal power of small-scale communities formed a relatively self-contained world, set against the wider (and implicitly hostile) culture of the elite.

This process of characterisation by way of negation is itself somewhat questionable, the more so because it is predicated upon a highly simplified model of industrial society. Enough has been written about local variations in industrial organisation, differences in product and labour markets, and the multiplicity of legal and institutional inflections placed upon the value of these two conceptual monoliths as explanatory categories.[6] The concepts of pre-industrial society, custom and popular culture are, in this respect, simplified counterparts of a highly simplified idea of modernity.

There is an additional qualification. For many of the concepts associated with artisanal production were developed by British historians concerned with English conditions. They have (and this is the measure of their success) been transposed to other times and places.[7] There may, however, have been hidden disadvantages in this procedure, for, as the image of the artisan pulling the Devil by the tail in his all-too-human pursuit of honour

5 See the classic essay by E. J. Hobsbawm, 'Custom, Wages and Work-Load' in *Labouring Men* (London, 1964), pp. 405–35; George Rudé, *The Crowd in the French Revolution* (London, 1959); and E. P. Thompson, *The Making of the English Working Class* (London, 1963). More recently, see Maxine Berg, *The Age of Manufactures* (London, 1985).

6 See, for example, Charles Sabel, *Work and Politics* (Cambridge 1982); Charles Sabel and Jonathan Zeitlin, 'Historical Alternatives to Mass Production', *Past and Present*, 108 (1985), pp. 133–76; Philip Scranton, *Proprietary Capitalism, the Textile Manufacture at Philadelphia, 1800–1885* (Cambridge and New York, 1983).

7 For some examples, see Michael Hanagan, *The Logic of Solidarity: Artisans and Industrial Workers in Three French Towns, 1871–1914* (Urbana, Illinois, 1983); Alan Dawley, *Class and Community: Lynn in the Industrial Revolution* (New York, 1979); Paul G. Faler, *Mechanics and Manufacturers in the Early Industrial Revolution* (New York, 1981); John M. Merriman, ed., *Consciousness and Class Experience in Nineteenth-Century Europe* (New York, 1981); Jonathan Prude, *The Coming of Industrial Order* (New York and Cambridge, 1983); Sean Wilentz, *Chants Democratic* (New York and Oxford, 1984); Maurice Agulhon, 'Working Class and Sociability in France before 1848', in Pat Thane, Geoffrey Crossick and Roderick Floud, eds, *The Power of the Past* (Cambridge, 1984), pp. 37–66; Joan Scott and E. J. Hobsbawm, 'Political Shoemakers', *Past and Present*, 89 (1980), pp. 86–114; Mary Lynn Stewart-McDougall, *The Artisan Republic: Revolution, Reaction and Resistance in Lyon, 1848–1851* (Montreal, 1984). For some thoughts on the question of artisanal culture, see Jacques Rancière, 'The Myth of the Artisan', in Kaplan and Koepp, *Work in France*, pp. 317–34.

and profit suggests, there were differences in belief, institutions and law in the circumstances of artisans between one society and another. The concepts of pre-industrial society, custom and popular culture have, however, made it easy to overlook or minimise these differences, because they tend to limit the field of analysis to a lateral section of society, inhabited exclusively by the men, women and children involved in the trades. The wider context of belief, institutions and law to which artisans belonged – and the relationship between that context and the details of particular kinds of work – have almost disappeared from the history of the trades.

Surprisingly, we do not know a great deal about the ordinary political life of eighteenth-century France. In part, of course, this was because politics in the modern sense did not exist. Yet argument and debate about freedom and duty, rights and obligations were not unknown before the Declaration of the Rights of Man. Much of it took place in the courts.[8] The decisions they made and, more importantly, the reasons why they made those decisions, derived from assumptions and forms of argument that belonged to a distinctive political culture. Petitions, corporate deliberations, lawsuits and records of criminal proceedings were not drafted in a random way; they followed certain rules and drew upon certain rhetorical procedures. Many images of artisanal production were created in the course of drafting records of this kind. Yet there has been a blindness to the legal position of the urban trades in the public life of eighteenth-century France. Artisans have been consigned to a world beyond ordinary politics and a history in which they played no active part. As a result, it is not easy to establish the links that existed between an engraving depicting a conventional Christian theme and the things that artisans said and did in France during the eighteenth century. Yet the links existed. They did so because some of the things that artisans said and did in eighteenth-century France were closely related to images of sinful human nature, ideas of natural obligation and natural rights, and a rhetoric of divine law and Christian duty that was an intrinsic part of the ordinary life of the wider polity.

If a great deal of what took place in eighteenth-century French

8 Recent research on the history of the law has been concerned almost entirely with the criminal law. See, in particular, Nicole Castan, *Justice et répression en Languedoc à l'époque des Lumières* (Paris, 1980). The emphasis placed here upon informal means of settling disputes, while a timely corrective to many unfounded assumptions about the nature of the legal process in early modern Europe, does not give sufficient weight to the public character of much civil litigation. The point of departure for a history of the civil law in eighteenth-century France remains Michel Antoine, *Le Conseil du Roi sous le règne de Louis XV* (Geneva, 1970). See too, for one (atypical) example of how the courts were used, Darlene Gay Levy, *The Ideas and Careers of Simon Nicolas Henri Linguet* (Urbana, 1980). For a thought-provoking essay on the relationship between the law, politics and representation since the Middle Ages, see Stephen C. Yeazell, *From Medieval Group Litigation to the Modern Class Action* (New Haven, 1987).

workshops was governed by prevailing technical conditions and the opportunities supplied by the particular resources of time and place, the words that artisans used, the discussions and arguments they had, the arrangements they made and the agreements they reached were inseparable from the culture of the wider polity. For the work of making shoes, or hats, or coaches, involved recognition of rights and obligations of some kind. Work did not simply happen – it was a continuous process of negotiation.[9] Relationships between master artisans, between masters and journeymen, between men and women, adults and children were grounded upon subtle and complex reciprocities, differences, inequalities and affinities whose existence was both the outcome and the basis of endlessly changing configurations of identity and power. Some rights and obligations were formal; others were not. The division between the two was never absolute and never stable. This was why artisans played an active part in the history of their own trades.

The images that artisans presented of themselves, their circumstances and their place in the wider forums of public life, drew heavily upon the metaphorical vocabulary of eighteenth-century France. One range of metaphors can be found in Guérard's engraving, with its evocation of Christian simplicity, ascetic piety and the vanity of worldly achievement. Others can be found in the words used by artisans themselves, which were not necessarily simple or pious. Others too can be found in the words of court rulings and royal edicts. The assumptions embodied in legal rulings of this kind were echoed in the allusions to 'despotism' made by Contat in his *Anecdotes typographiques*. They were associated with a tradition of jurisprudence that had much in common with the image of sinful humanity presented in Guérard's engraving, a tradition which is usually associated with the idea of natural law.[10]

The history of the law in eighteenth-century France, and the history of

[9] Here the work of ethnographers has been particularly instructive. See especially Pierre Bourdieu, *Esquisse d'une théorie de la pratique* (Geneva, 1972), and his *Le Sens pratique* (Paris, 1983). Like many historians, I have learned much from Clifford Geertz, *The Interpretation of Cultures* (New York, 1973) and *Local Knowledge* (New York, 1983). Historians have, at times, tended to overlook some anthropologists' sensitivity to the wider forums of power and public life in *their* descriptions of 'popular culture'. For one such example, see Peter Burke, *Popular Culture in Early Modern Europe* (London, 1978).

[10] On the metaphors used in political argument in early modern France, see in particular Harro Höpfl and Martyn P. Thompson, 'The History of Contract as a Motif in Political Thought', *American Historical Review*, 84 (1979), pp. 919–44; Martyn P. Thompson, 'The History of Fundamental Law in Political Thought from the French Wars of Religion to the American Revolution', *American Historical Review*, 91 (1986), pp. 1103–28. One of the best outlines of the natural law tradition is in Duncan Forbes, *Hume's Philosophical Politics* (Cambridge, 1975), pp. 3–58. I am greatly indebted to what might be called the Cambridge school of historians of political thought in my attempts to understand eighteenth-century French legal argument. In addition to Forbes, the following works are relevant to the questions discussed below: Richard Tuck, *Natural Rights Theories* (Cambridge, 1979); James Tully, *A Discourse Concerning Property: John Locke and his Adversaries* (Cambridge, 1980); Istvan Hont and Michael Ignatieff, eds., *Wealth and*

civil jurisprudence in particular, is relatively unknown territory. In a sense it is the other face of the Enlightenment: a body of commonplace rhetoric, established doctrine and familiar platitude which formed a silent counterpoint to the programmes, projects and public manifestos produced by its enlightened critics.[11] Yet the forgotten sonorities of forms of philosophical, historical and legal argument that owed nothing to Rousseau or Helvetius also supplied artisans with a vocabulary that could be used to define or challenge the identities, rights and obligations that were brought into play in the ordinary course of the work they did. The conventions and propositions used in such argument were the products of elaborate discussions of the nature of liberty, sovereignty and absolutist rule conducted over a long period of time. These discussions and debates were not, of course, confined to France. The leading French exponents of the tradition of natural law – jurists like Domat, Burlamaqui, Barbeyrac, Prévôt de la Jannès, Réal de Courbon and, in a more limited but none the less entirely characteristic way, the so-called father of the Civil Code, R. J. Pothier – were the intellectual heirs of the Dutch jurist Hugo Grotius, the German jurist Samuel Pufendorf and, to some degree, their English counterparts, John Selden and Thomas Hobbes.[12]

The natural law tradition generated an epistemology and an ethics that were entirely compatible with the concept of Absolute Government.[13] It also contained a concept of natural rights that remained a vital component of legal argument and philosophical discourse for much of the eighteenth century. Historians have tended to overlook this concept of natural rights, partly because it is almost invisible in the work of eighteenth-century France's most celebrated legal theorist, Montesquieu, and partly because,

11 *Virtue: The Civic Tradition in the Scottish Enlightenment* (London, 1983); and John Dunn, *The Political Thought of John Locke* (Cambridge, 1969). See also James Farr, '"So Vile and Miserable an Estate", The Problem of Slavery in Locke's Political Thought', *Political Theory*, 14 (1986), pp. 263–89. Despite the recent revival of interest in the intellectual history of eighteenth-century France, there has, as yet, been no study which brings the same historical subtlety and precision to bear upon French argument and debate as can be found in the works cited above and in J. G. A. Pocock, *Politics, Language and Time* (London, 1972); *The Machiavellian Moment* (Princeton, 1975) and, most recently, *Virtue, Commerce and History* (Cambridge, 1985). For the most fruitful developments, see particularly K. M. Baker, 'On the Problem of the Ideological Origins of the French Revolution', in Dominick LaCapra and Steven L. Kaplan, eds. *Modern European Intellectual History: Reappraisals and New Perspectives* (Ithaca, 1982).

The other side of the Enlightenment – the eighteenth-century French equivalents of Locke's Filmer – has been little studied. See however, Robert Derathé, *Jean Jacques Rousseau et la science politique de son temps* (Paris, 1950).

12 There are no satisfactory studies of these writers. For bio-bibliographical information, see René Frederic Voeltzel, *Jean Domat (1625–1696), essai de reconstitution de sa philosophie juridique* (Paris, 1936); F. Funck-Brentano, 'Le Droit naturel au xviiie siècle', *Revue d'histoire diplomatique*, 1 (1887), pp. 491–511; Luc Henri Dunoyer, *Blackstone et Pothier* (Paris, 1927); Armand Piret, *La Rencontre chez Pothier des conceptions romaines et féodales de la propriété foncière* (Paris, 1937); Benvenuto Donati, *Domat e Vico, ossio del Sistema del Diretto Universale* (Macereata, 1923).

13 As demonstrated convincingly by Richard Tuck, *Natural Rights Theories*.

where it does appear (as, most famously, in Rousseau), it was used as a counterpoint to a philosophical history involving the alienation and recovery of rights whose natural identity was shrouded in ambiguity.[14] Eighteenth-century jurists used the notion of natural rights in a much simpler way. They were a logical counterpart to the natural human attributes of reason and free will (and this assumption of what was naturally human is the measure of the difference between the natural law tradition and its eighteenth-century critics). Since God had endowed humanity with the natural faculties of reason and free will, humanity was entitled to enjoy those rights that made rational choice possible. Their identity was, of course, a matter of much learned debate. They can, however, be presented schematically as natural rights to life, liberty and property.[15]

The concept of natural rights was associated with a number of other terms that, together, made it possible to produce a coherent account of the prevailing political order in terms that were compatible with both natural reason and the injunctions of divine law. Four terms, in particular, call for special comment: the notions of *droit*, *privilège*, *possession* and *esclavage*. They were not only used in high political theory but were also the core of much ordinary legal argument throughout the eighteenth century. They formed the conceptual foundations of innumerable legal memoranda, *mémoires*, *précis* and *factums* produced, and often printed for publication, in the course of civil and criminal proceedings of every hue. Together with the concept of natural rights, they had an enduring relevance in the process of naming and identifying the rights and obligations brought into play in the eighteenth-century French trades.

Since France was an absolute monarchy rather than a despotism, appeals to natural rights were more than an argument of last recourse. Although the positive law of the King and his courts was the ordinary medium in which rights and obligations were defined or modified, and positive law was difficult to transcend, appeals to natural rights were statements about the non-despotic nature of absolute government. They were a claim about the character of the polity and the rights of its members. The terms *droit*, *possession*, *privilège* and *esclavage* were, therefore, invested with a powerful rhetorical charge because of their close conceptual relationship to prevailing philosophical arguments that natural rights and absolutist government complemented, rather than contradicted, one another.

14 On the proto-historicism of much enlightened thought, see J. G. A. Pocock, *The Machiavellian Moment*, part 3.
15 On property rights as natural rights, see the works by Tuck and Tully cited above, which have done much to correct the misconceptions and errors of historical interpretation found in C. B. Macpherson, *The Political Theory of Possessive Individualism* (Oxford, 1962).

'Tous les hommes sont libres ou esclaves,' wrote Prévôt de la Jannès in his *Principes de la jurisprudence française* (1750). 'La liberté est le droit naturel que chaque personne a de faire ce qui lui plaît, à l'exception de ce qui est défendu par les loix, ou de ce que la violence empêche de faire.'[16] Liberty was a natural right (*droit*) and, like all such rights, was a right of property (*possession*). Men had property in their liberty just as they had property in their lives, and they could alienate that property either voluntarily or involuntarily. Involuntary loss of liberty was the product of violence and conquest, and amounted to slavery (*esclavage*); voluntary servitude was different, and was the conceptual basis of the notion of absolutist rule. In the natural law tradition, voluntary servitude was a contractual relationship between ruler and ruled, a freely chosen renunciation of natural liberty in return for the rules of civil conduct supplied by the sovereign power to whom absolute liberty had been surrendered. Natural liberty was thus modified and constrained (but not necessarily eliminated) by the rules of civil law supplied by the sovereign power in whom natural rights had been vested. The civil law endowed each person (whether an individual or a collectivity) with possession of rights (*droits*) that were compatible with a given identity and place in a rule-bound social order. Natural rights were curtailed or inflected by possession of the particular rights (*privilèges*) supplied by the civil law. Consequently, society was an association of persons entitled to possess the rights and privileges with which they had been vested by the law. In this sense, the law singled out certain individuals or collectivities and endowed them with an exceptional status by virtue of their possession of certain rights and privileges. Civil rights and privileges were, by their nature, exceptional in character. They were the social equivalents of the natural rights that everyone possessed.

This schematic outline of a body of argument developed over many centuries does little justice to the range of different interpretations, opinions and theories that could be attached to the concepts of *droit*, *possession*, *privilège* and *esclavage*. They were the stuff of which legal arguments were made, supplying lawyers and magistrates with a wide variety of possible usages in many different contexts and circumstances. They were also a part of the vocabulary of public life, for lawyers were obliged to consult with their clients, and the proceedings and decisions of the courts had a vital bearing upon the practical concerns of the individuals and collectivities who made up the polity of eighteenth-century

[16] Prévôt de la Jannès, *Les Principes de la jurisprudence françoise*, 2nd edn (Paris, 1770), vol. 1, p. 9. 'On prouve en *droit naturel* que tous les hommes tiennent de la nature une liberté et une indépendance qu'ils ne peuvent perdre que par leur consentement': Emmerich de Vattel, *Le Droit des gens ou principes de la loi naturelle* (Leiden and Neuchâtel, 1758), p. 38.

France. Their significance is therefore best illustrated not by synthetic summaries of treatises of jurisprudence but by the practice of the courts themselves. Here two areas of judicial practice are of particular relevance. The first concerns the legal status of slaves in the natural law tradition, and can be taken as a model of how words like *droit*, *privilège*, *possession* and *esclavage* were used in eighteenth-century France. The second, which will be discussed at greater length, is more directly relevant to the trades themselves, and concerns the rights and privileges of corporations.

Slavery was the antithesis of natural liberty. It was also incompatible with the contractual nature of absolutist rule. Slaves had not freely alienated their natural liberty in exchange for the privileges and limited rights supplied by the civil law. A slave was someone who had been divested of his or her natural rights by force. Yet citizens of France owned slaves, and many slaves continued to remain slaves even after they had been brought into the kingdom. This apparent paradox is easier to understand in the light of the arguments used in legal proceedings initiated by a number of slaves to secure their liberty during the eighteenth century. They reveal how it was possible to accommodate both the notion of natural rights, and their evident absence in the condition of slavery, within the natural law tradition. This has considerable relevance to the world of the trades. Argument over the rights of slaves indicates that the terms *droit naturel* and *droit* had a precise sense in eighteenth-century French jurisprudence, which allowed people without formal rights to challenge the rights that others claimed to possess. This had important implications for the legal status and rights of eighteenth-century journeymen.

The arguments used in the cases were very similar. Liberty was a natural right: 'ce droit imprescriptible, ce droit inaliénable et sacré de l'espèce humain', as one barrister (*avocat*) put it; 'ce bien, le seul que l'homme apporte en naissant', in the words of another.[17] It was a right that had been recognised and safeguarded in France, where 'l'air qu'on y respire est celui de la liberté ...[et] cette liberté n'est autre chose que la voix de la nature elle-même'.[18] Yet it was possible to own slaves in France because the civil law had authorised the right. None the less, the terms of the civil law were precise. A royal edict of 1716 and a declaration promulgated in 1738 both specified that any slave brought into the kingdom could be brought only after formal notification had been given to both the colonial authorities and the officials of the port authority (*greffe consulaire* or *admirauté*) at which the slave had disembarked.[19] Failure to

17 Blondel, 'Plaidoyer pour Jean Louis', *Gazette des tribunaux*, 1 (Paris, 1775), p. 82; Henrion de Pansey, 'Plaidoyer pour Roc. nègre', reprinted in *Annales du barreau français*, 6 (Paris, 1825), p. 47.
18 'Plaidoyer pour Gabriel Pampey et Antoinette Julienne', *Gazette des tribunaux*, 1 (Paris, 1775), pp. 213 and 216.
19 *Encyclopédie méthodique: Jurisprudence* (Paris, 1784), vol. 4, pp. 320–35 (under 'esclave'). As the barrister Henri Cochin argued in 1746 in a case involving a female slave donated

observe these formalities meant that the title of ownership of the slave no longer existed. A slave who belonged to no one was no longer a slave. In this way, natural rights were limited by the dispositions of royal legislation, but were able to come into their own when it could be shown that those dispositions did not apply. Slaves were no longer slaves, according to the Royal Council and the Parlement of Paris, when their owners were unable to demonstrate possession of a legal title of ownership.

Argument of this kind was grounded upon the assumption that natural rights survived where the law was silent. The words used in defining and delimiting the rights embodied in the provisions of the civil law were surrounded by the wider claims of the rights which nature had vested in everyone. Thus while the law supplied slave owners with rights of property in slaves to whom they had the prescribed titles of ownership, failure to meet the dispositions of the law meant that, in France at least, slaves reverted to their natural condition of liberty. Even in the French colonies themselves, the provisions of the *Code noir* of 1686 derived from similar assumptions about the relationship between slavery and liberty. Liberty was a natural human right whose involuntary alienation by force and conquest had created a population of black slaves. Yet where titles of ownership did not exist, as, for example, among the children of black women and white men, the Code was silent. Only the positive law of the colonial courts introduced an element of discrimination between white settlers and the free black or mixed race inhabitants of the French colonies during the eighteenth century.[20] In the natural law tradition, however, slavery had nothing to do with questions of race or colour; it was, instead, a condition that derived from the involuntary loss of natural liberty and, in France, where natural liberty had been voluntarily alienated to an absolute monarch in exchange for the rights and privileges of civil society, slavery could not exist.

This mode of argument was used in a great variety of circumstances. The maxim 'nul privilège sans titre' could be used to challenge seigneurial rights and dues. The absence of a clear entitlement enjoining the inhabitants of a particular locality to take their corn to be milled at the local seigneurial mill meant, it was argued in an appeal heard by the Parlement of Paris in 1767, that they had not surrendered possession of

by a slave-owner in Martinique to his son in France, the slave was only a slave in Martinique. If the slave-owner wished to retain his rights over his slave he was obliged to return to Martinique: Henri Cochin, *Œuvres*, 8 vols (Paris, 1821–2), vol. 1, p. 9.

[20] Yvan Debbasch, *Couleur et liberté. Le Jeu du critère ethnique dans un ordre juridique esclavagiste*, 2 vols (Paris, 1967), vol. 1, pp. 30–1. See also Robert M. Cover, *Justice Accused: Antislavery and the Judicial Process* (New Haven, 1975), pp. 8–30; Serge Daget, 'Les Mots esclave, nègre, noir et les jugements de valeur sur la traité négrière dans la littérature abolitionniste française de 1770 à 1845', *Revue d'histoire d'outre-mer*, 60 (1973), pp. 511–48.

their natural liberty to take their corn wherever they chose.[21] Argument of a similar kind was a commonplace of litigation in the eighteenth-century urban trades. Nor, as this example indicates, did such argument necessarily require the parties involved to have their own legal titles and identities. Where the law was silent, it was possible to invoke the rights of nature.

In many cases, including legal argument involving corporate bodies, matters were very much less clear than they were in argument over the rights of slaves. The wording of the law was, as it tends to be, subject to many possible interpretations. Nor, in eighteenth-century France, was it immediately obvious what the law was. In the simplest sense it was what the King decided.[22] It is well known however that the 13 Parlements, which were the highest courts of appeal, also claimed (and exercised) the right to register and publish royal decisions before they had the force of law.[23] Rulings by the Parlements themselves (*arrêts de règlement*) could also have the force of law.[24] It is also well known that, particularly among the myriad jurisdictions of rural France, a vast body of prescription and proscription existed in the form of custom and, despite the work of generations of compilers and codifiers, custom remained irreducibly heterogeneous and diverse. In these circumstances the distinction between natural rights and legal entitlement was not easy to establish. This was why litigation, including litigation involving corporations, took the form of the assertion of claims and precedents marking titles to the possession of rights. Counter-argument took the form of claims and precedents marking the point beyond which the possession of rights no longer applied. Yet in a culture in which the law conferred possession of particular rights, the absence of a clear title to that possession could, in the last analysis, allow the rights which nature had conferred upon everyone to come into their own.

The word *droit*, in other words, had a more limited sense in eighteenth-century jurisprudence than it has since acquired. In the usage of the courts, and in the wider context of the natural law tradition, it implied

21 B.N. MS. Joly de Fleury 1879.

22 Any discussion of proposed legislation was, for this reason, an infringement of absolute sovereignty. Thus the Conseil d'Etat prohibited the publication of a number of pamphlets and memoranda by the Parisian corporations objecting to their proposed abolition in 1776 on the grounds that 'il n'a jamais été permis à aucun particulier de discuter d'advance l'objet ou les dispositions des loix' (*Gazette des tribunaux*, 1 (Paris, 1776), p. 266).

23 As a result, it was also possible to initiate civil proceedings opposing the registration of Royal Letters Patent or Edicts. For one example, see below, p. 94.

24 'Les arrêts de règlement étaient aussi des actes legislatifs....Ils étaient lus et publiés....et ils avaient *force de loi* jusqu'à ce que le Monarque eut lui-même exprimé sa volonté royale par un édit, une ordonnance etc.' C. Dupin, *Dictionnaire des arrêts modernes en matière civile et criminelle* (Paris, 1814) (s.v. 'arrets').

possession of a right. In this sense, civil rights consisted of so many islands of particularity within the broader expanse of rights that nature had conferred upon everyone. The law, in this usage, was always exceptional. It marked a point at which the universal claims of nature were obliged to defer to the rights embodied in a particular form of words.

This characteristic of eighteenth-century jurisprudence requires emphasis, because many historians have equated the apparent particularism that resulted from this mode of legal argument with the wider culture of eighteenth-century France.[25] They have noticed the exceptional and particularistic character of legal rights but have not noticed the uniform and universal character of the natural rights against which they were set. Yet a rhetoric of natural rights was as much a part of legal argument as were the particular claims made by those who possessed the privileges which the law conferred. Historians have perceived only the most perceptible part of the legal landscape of eighteenth-century France.

This myopia has resulted in several misinterpretations which have been particularly significant in the context of the urban trades of eighteenth-century France. It is well known that many of the trades of the major cities and towns were organised into corporations. In legal terms a corporation was a collective body – a *personne morale* – that had been granted the right to govern its own affairs. Its powers were defined in its statutes, which constituted its title to the right to be a *personne morale*. In themselves, the statutes of a corporation had no legal status; their legal force only came into being after they had been approved by the King (by Letters Patent or a Royal Edict) and registered by one of the Parlements.[26] Corporate statutes

---

[25] Thus Pierre Goubert: 'Il faut redire que l'esprit "cartesien" est le plus souvent aux antipodes de l'esprit de l'Ancien Régime. Rien en lui, quoi qu'on ait prétendu, ne fut vraiment général. La "loi" la plus générale, c'était le privilège, *lex privata*, loi privée qui régit une province, une ville, un corps, une personne même.' P. Goubert, *L'Ancien Régime: Les Pouvoirs* (Paris, 1973), p. 15. All of which is true, but does not take the wider concerns of the natural law tradition into account. In the context of the trades, the same partiality has affected the stimulating study by William H. Sewell Jr., *Work and Revolution: The Language of Labor in France from the Old Regime to 1848* (Cambridge, 1980). Thus, corporations were an expression of 'the particularism of old-regime culture' (p. 16) and its 'pronounced degree of internal diversity' (p. 18). Again, the statements are not false, but they miss the point of the relationship between particularity which was exceptional in character and the wider sphere of natural rights against which privileges were set.

[26] 'Les fonctions attribuées à chaque profession sont de droit public. Leurs lois sont écrites dans les statuts que le souverain veut bien approuver et revêtir de son autorité. On convient que ces statuts n'acquièrent le caractère de loy publique que par l'enregistrement que se fait dans les Parlements, lors duquel sa Majesté laisse néantmoins à ces cours la faculté de faire les changements et modifications que leur prudence suggère.' A.N. E 1286° (10 April 1753). Corporate statutes were not, as Sewell states, lawful because they had been ratified by the King alone (*Work and Revolution*, p. 26). The result of this omission is to exclude the Parlements from their central place in the legal life of the eighteenth century. On the origins of corporations in the trades, see Bernard Chevalier, 'Corporations, conflits politiques et paix sociale en France aux xive et xve siècles', *Revue historique*, 268 (1982), pp. 17–44, and, on the complex relationship between

were therefore drafted by lawyers, scrutinised by magistrates, ratified by the King in his Council and registered by one of the 13 Parlements.

Just as the terms of corporate statutes conferred particular rights upon those entitled to their possession, so enforcement of their provisions belonged to those judicial authorities entitled to possession of this particular area of the law.[27] Thus, what in the eighteenth century was termed the *police des arts et métiers* was also a right which various groups of magistrates were entitled to possess. In some cities, notably Paris but also Troyes, Reims and, to some degree, Rouen, this judicial right belonged to the *lieutenants généraux de police*: a body of magistrates whose offices were attached to the local *bailliage* or *sénéchaussée* courts or, in the case of the capital, to the *Châtelet* of Paris. In most other cities, the enforcement of corporate statutes belonged to the local municipal authorities: *consuls* in Lyon, *jurats* in Bordeaux, *échevins* in Marseille and *capitouls* in Toulouse to name the best known.[28] However it was administered, the *police des arts et métiers* was a province of the law. In the context of the trades, its provisions could be challenged in the courts.[29]

In the final analysis, therefore, the Parlements were the source of most of what constituted the *police des arts et métiers* in the eighteenth century. Here, two groups of magistrates played a particularly important part in interpreting and adjudicating between claims arising from disputes in the trades. The first was made up of the councillors of the Parlements, the magistrates who, as *rapporteurs*, were assigned particular cases and whose decisions became the courts' verdicts. The frequency with which the

27   corporations, trades and local institutions, see especially Simona Cerutti, 'Du Corps au métier: la corporation des tailleurs à Turin entre xviie et xviiie siècle', *Annales E.S.C.* 43 (1988), pp. 323–52. Most of the trades of Lyon and Marseille were incorporated only in the late seventeenth century or later: see Maurice Agulhon, *Pénitents et francs-maçons de l'ancien Provence* (Paris, 1968), pp. 67–85; Maurice Garden, *Lyon et les lyonnais au xviiie siècle* (Paris, 1970), pp. 325–8. As Chevalier shows, corporations were often grafted on to established confraternities. It is regrettable that historians of eighteenth-century corporations have neglected the earlier studies by Henri Hauser, notably his 'Le Travail dans l'ancienne France', printed in his *Les Débuts du capitalisme* (Paris, 1931), pp. 80–125. See too Emile Coornaert, *Les Corporations en France* (Paris, 1941).

28   This too could be a matter of legal dispute. Public life in late eighteenth-century Nîmes, for example, was affected by a protracted conflict between the magistrates of the *Présidial* and the *consulat* over rights of jurisdiction over the textile trades: see M. Sonenscher, 'Royalists and Patriots: Nîmes and its Hinterland in the late Eighteenth Century' (unpublished Ph.D Thesis, University of Warwick, 1978). In Rouen, possession of the *police des arts et métiers* and the *police des manufactures* was divided between the municipality and the *bailliage*, with the former enforcing the *police interne* and the latter the *police externe* of the trades.

29   There has been no adequate study of these highly important local magistrates. See, for one example, Jean Marie Augustin, 'Les Capitouls, juges des causes criminelles et de police', *Annales du Midi*, 84 (1972), pp. 183–211.
    The relationship between the *police* and the courts is absent from the pioneering essay by Steven L. Kaplan, 'Réflexions sur la police du monde de travail, 1700–1815', *Revue historique*, 259 (1979), pp. 17–77.

names of certain individuals appear in litigation involving the trades – de Monthullet, Tudert, Terray and de Glatigny among the councillors of the Parlement of Paris in the second half of the eighteenth century – is an indication that this area of the law had its specialists.[30] The second group consisted of the King's own legal officers, the *procureurs* and *avocats généraux*. Their place in the political life of eighteenth-century France has been greatly overshadowed by the attention given to the Royal Intendants.[31] Yet in many respects they were figures of greater power and influence. Their decisions and recommendations (known as *avis*) played a considerable part in defining the rights and privileges that corporate bodies were entitled to enjoy.

The statutes of the corporations were, like any other title to possession of a right, exceptional in character. In this, they were no different from the exceptional rights enjoyed by other collectivities or individuals. Each amounted to a title to particularity within the wider sphere of natural rights. This dual character, in which the particular was combined with the exceptional, requires emphasis, for too close an insistence upon corporate rights, the rhetoric of corporate particularity and the informal idiom of corporate identity in the context of the eighteenth-century French trades can be somewhat misleading.[32] The corporate idiom was only the most visible part of a very much wider and broader sphere of legal argument and public rhetoric. The particularity of corporate identity represented a publicly sanctioned exception to the wider terms of reference of the natural rights and obligations to which all were entitled.

Nor, of course, were the terms of the statutes and regulations of particular corporations unique. Legal decisions made in favour of one corporation were frequently used as models by others, as when rulings by the Parlement of Paris regulating the conduct of journeymen wigmakers and shoemakers in 1760 and 1763 were used as models by the Parisian printers when they discussed the possibility of introducing new regulations

[30] Their names appear regularly in court rulings cited throughout this study. The fullest studies of the eighteenth-century French legal profession are concerned almost entirely with who lawyers were rather than what they did. See Lenard Berlanstein, *The Barristers of Toulouse in the Eighteenth Century (1740–1793)* (Baltimore, 1975); Maurice Gresset, *Gens de justice à Besançon au xviiie siècle* (Paris, 1983); Michael P. Fitzsimmons, *The Parisian Order of Barristers and the French Revolution* (Cambridge, Mass., 1987).

[31] The papers of the Joly de Fleury, *procureurs-généraux* of the most important of the Parlements, the Parlement of Paris, are the major, still relatively unused source (B.N. Fonds Joly de Fleury). Other information can be found in the papers of the *procureur général* of the Parlement of Normandy, Godard de Belbeuf, in the Archives of the Seine-Maritime (Série 16). Neither J. H. Shennan, *The Parlement of Paris* (London, 1968), nor William Doyle, *The Parlement of Bordeaux and the End of the Old Regime 1771–1790* (London, 1974), deals with the practice of the courts.

[32] Thus, it is not quite accurate to assert as Sewell (*Work and Revolution in France*) does that 'each métier formed a particular community devoted to the perfection of a particular art, and these communities of artisans had no bonds uniting them with one another' (p. 28). The wider context of law and legal argument has, as elsewhere, been lost.

for their journeymen in 1761 and 1769. Legal decisions over the valuation of sub-contracted work were cited by joiners, locksmiths, roofers, carpenters and other corporations associated with the building and furnishing trades. In 1763, during a dispute over piece-rates in the cotton trade in Rouen, the city's master weavers petitioned the Parlement of Normandy to ratify a series of regulations approved by the Parlement of Paris during a dispute between masters and journeymen in the capital's ribbon trade in 1762.[33] Locksmiths in Nantes drafted regulations governing the conduct of journeymen in their trade which were modelled upon those devised by their counterparts in Bordeaux, and shoemakers in Marseille recommended the adoption of the provisions of a Royal Declaration which had been produced to end a stoppage of work by journeymen farriers in Paris in 1786.[34] The practice was a normal part of the life of the trades. Corporations in different cities corresponded regularly with one another. They exchanged information and advice, drew upon the precedents and examples set by local courts and, in this way, ensured that legal provision governing relations in the trades remained relatively similar throughout the kingdom.

The practice was particularly widespread in trades in which local variations in working conditions were relatively unimportant. Wigmaking was one of the most striking examples of a trade whose local rhythms and schedules were governed almost entirely by a social and liturgical calendar that was common to the kingdom as a whole. Demand for wigs and opportunities for employment for journeymen followed the same seasonal pattern in every large eighteenth-century French city. Not surprisingly local corporate regulations were remarkably uniform in character. Those adopted by the Parisian wigmakers' corporation to control the movement of journeymen from shop to shop in 1760 and 1773 were replicated in Versailles, Reims, Orléans, Troyes, Lyon, Marseille, Bordeaux, Toulouse, Nantes and Rouen.[35] Traces of the huge traffic in information

33 B.N. MS. fr. 22064 fols. 208 and 215; A.D. Seine-Maritime, 1BP 15044 (28 April 1763).

34 A.C. Nantes, HH 164 (6 March 1755); A.D. Ile-et-Vilaine, 1Bf 1432 (6 March 1755). Other examples include A.C. Nantes, HH 116 (1786) (nailmakers); A.C. Nantes, HH 147 (27 January 1758 and 12 September 1781): A.D. Ile-et-Vilaine, 1Bf 1449 (27 January 1758) (joiners); A.C. Nantes, HH 91 (19 July 1764); A.D. Ile-et-Vilaine, 1Bf 1495 (13 July 1768) (wigmakers): A.C. Nantes, FF 149 (23 November 1769) (bakers). Further examples of correspondence between corporations in some of these trades can be found in Henri Hauser, *Les Compagnonnages d'arts et métiers à Dijon aux xviie et xviiie siècles* (Paris, 1907), pp. 174–83. On the use of legislation arising from the dispute among Parisian farriers in Marseille, see A.D. Bouches-du-Rhône, 240E[26] (15 May 1786).

35 On the uniformity of seasonal fluctuations in local labour markets in the wigmaking trade, see below, chapter 5. On regulations affecting journeymen in Paris, see A.N. X[1b] 3740 (12 and 23 December 1760): X[1a] 7931 fol. 131 (29 July 1761); AD XI 25 (6 September 1773). On Reims and Marseille, A.N. X[1a] 4470 fol. 425[vo] (25 June 1764). On Troyes, A.N. X[1a] 4503 fol. 477 (3 July 1765), 4525 fol. 52 (22 February 1766), 4528

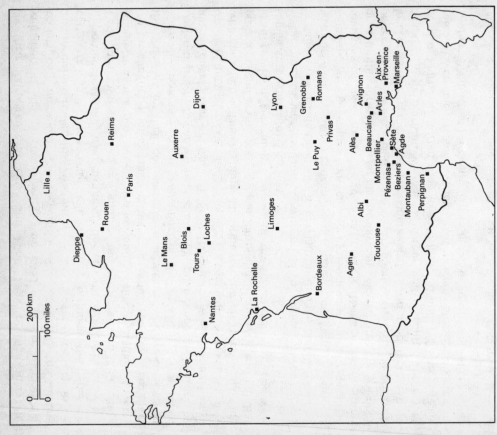

2.2 Correspondents of the wigmakers' corporation of Nîmes (1776–91). Source:
A.D. Gard, IVE 223.

underpinning this uniform body of corporate regulation can be found
among the papers of the wigmakers' corporations of Caen and Nîmes.[36]
Between 1776 and 1791 the wigmakers of Nîmes received hundreds of

fol. 207ᵛᵒ (25 March 1766). On Versailles, A.N. X¹ᵃ 4394 fol. 1 (26 February 1762),
X¹ᵇ 4185 (15 May 1783). On Lyon, A.N. X¹ᵇ 3777 (12 November 1762); X¹ᵇ 3814 (24
October 1764). On Bordeaux, A.D. Gironde, B (unclassified, 27 March 1762). On Nantes,
Rouen, Toulouse and Orléans see A.C. Nantes, HH 91 (19 July 1764 and 8 June
1768).

36 A.D. Gard, IVE 233. On the wigmakers of Caen, A.D. Calvados, 6E 21.

letters or printed circulars from corporations in cities all over France (Figure 2.2). They supplied the corporation in Nîmes with the signatures of corporate officials elsewhere, so that migrant journeymen who forged their own certificates of previous employment (*billets de congé*) could be identified and apprehended. They provided information about local corporate deliberations or the actions of individual journeymen and, in a more general way, served to maintain a body of disciplinary regulation that covered the kingdom as a whole.

Wigmaking was a relatively unusual trade. The limited range of products and services that it supplied and the uniformity of local variations in demand for labour generated by the national dimensions of the social and liturgical calender lent themselves readily to common corporate regulation. In most of the urban trades of eighteenth-century France, however, local economic circumstances prevailed over wider external pressures, and corporate regulation was therefore less easily adapted to uniform prescription. As the *procureur général* of the Parlement of Guyenne put it in 1757,

Tel est le sort des loix en matière de police; de ne pouvoir prétendre à l'immutabilité des autres loix: étant de la nature de celles qui concernent la police de se proportionner toujours aux circonstances des tems.[37]

Even where local circumstances were determinant, the statutes and regulations of the Parisian corporations occupied a special place within the many semi-formal networks of information linking corporations in different localities. They did so not only because the Parisian corporations were the largest in the kingdom, but also because masters of the Parisian corporations enjoyed rights and privileges which made the provisions of their statutes relevant throughout France. Members of the Parisian corporations were, in particular, entitled to become masters of provincial corporations without having to satisfy local requirements controlling access to a *maîtrise*. The right was confirmed by a frequently cited ruling by the Parlement of Paris in 1704, and remained in force (despite much local opposition) throughout the century.[38] It meant that the practice followed by the Parisian corporations had an exemplary character for their counterparts in provincial cities. In some cases, therefore, the corporations of provincial cities explicitly modelled their statutes upon those of the capital. The joiners of Amiens, for example, corresponded regularly with their Parisian counterparts, used the same Parisian barrister and consulted one of the Parisian corporation's former officials when they redrafted their statutes in 1744.[39]

In these circumstances, master artisans and journeymen in provincial

[37] A.D. Gironde, B. (unclassified *arrêt*, 20 September 1757).
[38] Mathieu Augéard, *Arrêts notables des différents tribunaux du royaume*, 2nd edn (Paris, 1756), vol. 1, p. 737.
[39] A.C. Amiens, HH 591.

cities were particularly aware of the norms and prevailing usages of the capital. Tailors in Marseille cited the statutes of the Parisian tailors' corporation of 1664 when they decided to prohibit payment by the piece to their journeymen in 1750.[40] Journeymen hatters in Marseille stopped work on a number of occasions between 1760 and 1790, claiming that their employers were violating what they called 'le règlement de Paris' by expecting them to make three or more hats a day.[41] Inversely, journeymen working in Paris itself were particularly aware of the need to maintain rights sanctioned by the courts. That was one reason why litigation between journeymen and their masters was so frequent in eighteenth-century Paris.

The particularity of corporate rights was, in this sense, part of a wider arena in which rights and obligations were named and challenged in the course of a continuous process of comparison: between times, places or trades. The medium of litigation was the context in which the particularities of time, place and trade were situated. At the same time, however, the rights which corporations enjoyed retained their exceptional character. Where the law was silent, or ambiguous, or could be challenged, arguments couched in other terms could be brought into play.

In a culture in which rights were property, demonstration of possession could be challenged in three ways. The first was to argue that the rights possessed by one individual or collective body were nullified by those possessed by others. This involved establishing other titles to the possession of different rights. Possession of this kind could be found in earlier legislation or by proving immemorial usage, which, it could be claimed, was a form of possession. In this way one set of rights could be nullified by proof of possession of others that were accepted as better established. Much of the argument between particular corporations took this form. Joiners could claim precedence over wheelwrights in the right to make carts by establishing proof of their title to do so in the wording of long-forgotten court rulings unearthed by diligent legal research. This was why eighteenth-century corporations kept a careful control of their archives.[42] Alternatively, argument could take the form of a denial of the relevance of the right or rights in question to the person or body upon whom they had been brought to bear. Claims to certain rights could be shown to have originated in activities and identities that were so radically different from those carried out by rival claimants that there could be no basis in

[40] A.D. Bouches-du-Rhône, 380E[236] fol. 202 (17 February 1750); B 5336 (26 August 1750).

[41] On disputes in the hatting trade and links between masters and journeymen in Paris, Lyon and Marseille, see Sonenscher, *Hatters of Eighteenth-Century France*.

[42] This was also why, when Turgot abolished the Parisian corporations in 1776 and again in 1791, their archives were sealed and confiscated by the police officials. They were, literally, their title to a public identity.

natural reason for any common obligation to recognise the rights in question. In the context of the urban trades, argument of this kind could lead to minute discussion of particular kinds of work, materials, techniques or artefacts, designed to demonstrate the essential difference between the ends and purposes (in an entirely Aristotelian sense) of the activities performed by the respective litigants. Painters could claim that they alone were entitled to make articles out of *papier-mâché*, just as goldsmiths had the sole right to use gold or pewterers to use zinc. Dealers in inlaid ware (*tabletiers*) argued, equally disingenuously, that the lathes they used to finish *papier-mâché* articles were intrinsically different from those used by painters.[43] The nature and finality of one kind of work, implement, corporate body or type of material could be shown to be so different from that of another that the rights enjoyed by the one were essentially alien to the nature of the other. In a culture in which civil rights had an exceptional character, it was always possible to claim an identity that was other than that upon which rights had been conferred.

Finally, it could be argued that rights claimed by one individual or collective body amounted to a violation of the natural rights to which everyone was entitled. There were, however, many possible definitions of a natural right, and this in turn could become the basis of further legal argument. The term 'art libéral', for example, could be taken to mean, as a sculptor from Aix-en-Provence claimed in the late seventeenth century, an art practised by free men who were not, therefore, bound by the regulations of a corporation. This, it was argued, was the sense in which it had been defined by Pliny. Alternatively, it could mean 'une occupation de l'entendement dans la connoissance de quelque perfection', as his corporate opponents (following Aristotle) claimed. In this instance the Parlement of Provence preferred Pliny to Aristotle and found in favour of the sculptor.[44] Here, the court was prepared to accept that sculptors were different from joiners because their art embodied the identity and rights of free men rather than initiation into a corporately controlled process of learning a trade.

In most circumstances, however, argument over rights involved a combination of all three forms of challenge and counter-claim. Precedent, difference and appeals to natural rights could all be invoked to demonstrate that rights that appeared to have been sanctioned were, in fact, inappropriate, irrelevant or illegal. In the context of the urban trades, the limited and exceptional character of rights, and the variety of ways in

43 A.N. X¹ᵃ 4060 fol. 70 (19 July 1749): E 1286° (10 April 1753).
44 Here too the meaning of words was susceptible to a variety of interpretations in the course of legal argument. This is why too rigid an insistence upon the distinction between the 'liberal' and 'mechanical' arts based upon citation from one legal treatise (Sewell, *Work and Revolution*, pp. 23–4) is too much of an ideal type, rather than a source of legal discussion and debate as it was in the eighteenth century.

which they could be challenged, had a number of important implications. It ensured, firstly, that corporations were juridically composite bodies. Differences among master artisans were also – or could be claimed to be – differences of a formal and legal kind. Almost every corporation housed a variety of different activities and specialities. There were retailers and wholesalers, artisans who specialised in primary processes and others who specialised in finishing and embellishing manufactured goods, specialists in different kinds of product or market. At the same time, there were more personal differences: in age or seniority in the trade; in the length of time that an individual had been a member of a corporation; and between different forms of entry into the corporations. Some members of corporations were the sons of masters; others had served a full apprenticeship and paid the full fee required to become a master of a corporation; others had been able to acquire a privilege dispensing them from the normal formalities of an apprenticeship and a *maîtrise*.

Some of these differences were carried over into the constitutions of the corporations themselves. In most corporations, particularly in Paris and in those of the largest provincial cities, some formal recognition was given to differences in age and seniority. The Parisian corporations were made up of three broad groupings: *anciens, modernes* and *jeunes*.[45] The specific rights and obligations of each group varied from one corporation to another (and there were between 117 and 120 in Paris alone until 1776, and 44 thereafter). In Paris, as in most cities, each corporation had an office or *bureau* where representatives of each grouping, together with the current officials (*jurés, syndics* or *directeurs*, according to the statutory powers vested in them), met to deal with current business. The composition of each *bureau* differed again from one corporation to another, but in general the dominant role was played by the *anciens*. Yet just as the rights of the corporations were particular and exceptional, so were the rights of corporate officials and *anciens*. They could be, and very often were, challenged by the *modernes* and *jeunes*.[46]

The inner life of the corporations was, in this respect, a continuous process of negotiation between its juridically separate components. The limited involvement of the majority of master artisans in the daily management of corporate affairs was, in some measure, matched by the claims of legal entitlement that they were able to mount in the name of their own separately defined rights. When corporations were very large – and membership of the largest Parisian corporations, like the tailors,

[45] On the internal organisation of corporations, see Emile Coornaert, *Les Corporations en France* (Paris, 1941).

[46] See, for example, A.N. Y 13 121 (26 November 1769); Y 10 784ᵃ (15 Feburary 1770); Y 10 784ᵇ; Y 13 133 (9 July 1781) and, for others, Steven L. Kaplan, 'The Character and Implications of Strife Among the Masters Inside the Guilds of Eighteenth-Century Paris', *Journal of Social History*, 19 (1986), pp. 631–47.

shoemakers, joiners or painters and decorators, was over 1,000 strong – most master artisans had little to do with decisions made by the 50 or 60 artisans who formed the corporate *bureau*.[47] They were able, however, to challenge those decisions because they themselves had their own rights and legal identities. A dispute between two groups of master bakers in late eighteenth-century Paris is a good illustration of this combination of distance and negotiation.

In 1785 six master bakers successfully petitioned the Conseil d'Etat for a reduction in the duty on the wood they used in their ovens, and, to defray the costs of their action, they organised a collection. When the *syndics* of the bakers' corporation heard of this unauthorised action they began legal proceedings. Sixteen master bakers gave evidence in the affair, saying that they had given sums of between three and six *livres* each to the collection, and had signed their names on a list. Invariably they stated that they had contributed because they had recognised the signatures of other bakers on the list. As one put it, 'ayant vu sur cette liste les noms de plusieurs confrères voisins', he had assumed that the collection was official. Another stated that 'il croiot ces particuliers être syndics de sa communauté'.[48] None of the bakers could actually recognise the *syndics* of the corporation, but they assumed that a collection to meet the costs of legal proceedings must have been sanctioned officially. The six masters who had organised the collection argued in their turn that they had done so because the corporate officials had failed to perform their proper functions. In this, as in many similar disputes, the composite juridical character of the corporation gave rise to a form of internal debate and argument in which the question of representation was relatively unimportant (it did not matter that 16 master bakers were unable to recognise their *syndics*), because rights and obligations could be challenged in the name of other rights and obligations. What mattered, therefore, was which set of rights and obligations the courts were prepared to recognise.

The limited and exceptional character of legal rights, and the variety of ways in which they could be challenged, had a second implication. Since rights were property recognised by a legal entitlement, their extent was limited by the form of that entitlement. A ruling by the Parlement of Paris over a banal dispute between two master wigmakers in the little town of Murat in the Gâtinais is a case in point.[49] One of the masters had engaged a journeyman from Paris to work for him. After a month the journeyman

[47] Figures of the size of the Parisian corporations can be found in Jacques Savary des Bruslons, *Dictionnaire universel de commerce*, 6th edn (Paris, 1750); A.D.V.P. D⁵ B⁶ 346. See also chapter 4.

[48] A.N. Y 15 397 (19 September 1785). Total membership of the corporation was over 500: see Savary des Bruslons, *Dictionnaire universel de commerce* (s.v. 'boulanger'); A.D.V.P. D⁵ B⁶ 346.

[49] *Gazette des tribunaux*, 19 (Paris, 1785), p. 305.

left and began working for the second master. His former employer, fearing for the loss of his clientele, began legal proceedings. His case rested upon one of the provisions of the statutes issued to all the wigmakers' corporations in France by Royal Letters Patent in 1725. Article 42 of these statutes prohibited masters from taking on journeymen without the written consent of their previous employers, and since no written consent had been given in this case, the issue appeared to be beyond doubt. Accordingly, the local court ruled in favour of the first master. On appeal however, the Parlement of Paris ruled that the provisions of the Letters Patent were applicable only in towns in which the trade in question had been properly incorporated. Since there were no *métiers jurés* in Murat, the provisions of the Letters Patent did not apply. Corporations had rights, but, like all rights conferred by the law, they were, in essence, finite.

This finite quality meant, in the third place, that rights possessed by corporations could be challenged not only from within the corporations themselves, or by members of other corporations, but also by artisans who did not belong to a corporation at all. There were very many artisans in this position in eighteenth-century France. In addition to the scores of tiny localities in which corporations had not been established (and there were some 800 towns with populations of 2,000 or more inhabitants in late eighteenth-century France), almost every major city contained a suburb or liberty which had its own privileges and rights.[50] The best known was, of course, the *faubourg* Saint-Antoine in Paris. There were many others: Vaise in Lyon, Saint-Sever in Rouen, the *sauvetats* of Saint André and Saint-Seurin in Bordeaux, the *faubourg* Croncels in Troyes and five other *lieux privilegiés* in Paris itself.[51] Residents of these areas could claim their own rights and challenge those which the corporations claimed to possess. At different times during the eighteenth century workers in the largest trades of the *faubourg* Saint-Antoine (and in this context the word *ouvrier* meant a small entrepreneur rather than a waged worker) brought legal actions against the Parisian corporations for violating their own rights.

A long-drawn-out lawsuit between the bakers of the *faubourg* and the bakers' corporation of Paris is an illustration of the range of argument used in litigation of this kind.[52] It centred upon two new clauses that the master

---

50 On the population of French towns, see R. Le Mée, 'Population agglomerée, population dispersée au début du xixe siècle', *Annales de démographie historique*, 7 (1971), pp. 455–510; B. Lepetit and J. F. Royer, 'Croissance et taille des villes: contribution à l'étude de l'urbanisation de la France au début du xixe siècle', *Annales E.S.C.*, 35 (1980), pp. 987–1010; and B. Lepetit, 'La Croissance urbaine dans la France pré-industrielle'. *Bulletin de l'Institut d'histoire économique et sociale de l'Université de Paris 1*, 7 (1978), pp. 1–19.

51 On the importance of the *lieux privilegiés* in eighteenth-century Paris, see A.N. F^{12} 781^{c-e}. The legal status of the *faubourg* Saint-Antoine is not discussed in Raymonde Monnier, *Le Faubourg Saint-Antoine (1789–1815)* (Paris, 1981).

52 Bibliothèque de l'Ordre des Avocats (Paris), Collection Chanlaire, vol. 102, no. 4, 'Mémoire signifié pour les boulangers-forains du fauxbourg Saint-Antoine…contre les maîtres boulangers de Paris' (Paris, 1760). For other examples of this mode

bakers had inserted into their statutes in 1746. The first placed strict limitations upon the right of bakers to deliver bread to the homes of their clients; it was designed, the Parisian bakers claimed, to ensure that bread was sold only in public places and to prevent bakers from the suburbs from selling bread wholesale to unauthorised retailers. The second clause prohibited non-members of the Parisian corporation from selling small loaves of fine white bread (known as *pain mollet*) in Paris. The bakers of the *faubourg* Saint-Antoine challenged the two clauses by combining an appeal to precedent, an assertion of difference and an invocation of natural rights. Restrictions upon the delivery of bread were 'une nouveauté dangereuse', designed to infringe 'la liberté naturelle qui tout marchand doit avoir de faire porter, si on l'exige, la marchandise qu'il a vendu à ceux qui l'ont acheté'. Bakers from the suburbs enjoyed 'une possession immémoriale' of the right to sell all kinds of white bread weighing three pounds or more in the 26 Parisian markets on Wednesdays and Saturdays. The bread named in the new clause was, moreover, a different kind of bread from that usually made by the bakers of the *faubourg*. *Pain mollet* was made with milk and salt, as well as flour and water. The bread made in the suburb contained only flour and water, and there were many legal precedents demonstrating the right of bakers to sell bread of that kind anywhere in Paris.

Argument of this kind was successful, at least in the short run. In this instance the Parlement of Paris ruled that implementation of the new clauses should be suspended until it had produced a final verdict. Not surprisingly legal actions by artisans who were not members of a corporation were relatively common. During the 1760s the Parlement of Paris heard appeals from three such groups – the cobblers (*savetiers*), joiners (*menuisiers*) and bakers (over a second dispute, concerning the registration of journeymen) – representing several hundred artisans living in the *faubourg* Saint-Antoine.[53]

The formal status of unincorporated artisans was itself a matter of argument. In 1770 the Parlement of Paris dismissed an appeal by the joiners of the *faubourg* on behalf of two of their number who had fallen foul of the Parisian corporation for employing unregistered journeymen and

53 of legal argument, see University of Toronto Library, T-10/7 (11 and 21), *Mémoire des maîtres gardes de la communauté des maîtres-ouvriers et marchands d'étoffes d'or, d'argent et de soye (de Lyon)* (Lyon, 1732), and *A Messieurs les Prevôt des Marchands et Echevins juges consulaires des arts et métiers de la ville de Lyon* (Lyon, 1777). In 1732 a proposal to change the relationship between the master weavers and master merchants within the corporation would mean, the weavers claimed, that 'ils seront dans l'esclavage des marchands' (*Mémoire*, p. 7). In 1777, the master weavers objected that the institutional reorganisation of the *Grande fabrique* would prevent them from selling their own products 'contre le droit de la nature et des gens'. The result would be that 'les nouveaux esclaves tombent bientôt dans l'opprobre et la misère' (*A Messieurs*, p. 3). A.N. X¹ᵇ 8177 (24 November 1761); X¹ᵇ 3856 (9 February 1767); X¹ᵃ 4559 fol. 79ᵛᵒ (24 March 1767); X¹ᵃ 4634 fol. 25ᵛᵒ (1 April 1769).

having more than one work-bench. In doing so, the court prohibited joiners in the suburb from any further collective legal action in the name of *les ouvriers menuisiers du faubourg Saint-Antoine* and ordered them, in future, to declare their names, addresses and legal qualities.[54] Yet artisans who were given a collective identity in the words of the law itself, as the bakers of the *faubourg* Saint-Antoine had been in the disputed articles of the Parisian bakers' statutes of 1746, were able to respond in kind. Thus even where corporate status did not exist, it was possible to challenge the terms of obligations defined in the words of the law. Since rights were exceptional in character, their scope and extent required a name. In this way, rights claimed by the corporations could be disputed by anyone named in the course of defining the extent and content of those rights.

That is the main reason why the many thousands of women who worked for wages or managed their own affairs in the eighteenth-century trades occupy so limited a place in surviving records of the trades.[55] Women were rarely given an identity in the words of the law (at least as it pertained to the trades) and, as a result, were rarely able to claim rights of their own. Where they were entitled to a corporate identity of their own – as was the case in Paris and Rouen in particular – their corporations enjoyed privileges that were entirely comparable to those possessed by the masters of other corporations.[56] Yet incorporation of this kind was limited to a small number of trades – seamstresses, embroiderers, milliners and hairdressers were the most usual – whose nature was closely related to assumptions about female nature itself. If the composition of the 80 members of the *bureau* of the Parisian seamstresses' corporation in 1762 is any guide, many of the women who belonged to these corporations were relatively prosperous minor entrepreneurs. In that trade, over half the corporation's *anciennes* and *jurées* were widows or single women, while the 37 married women were the wives of men whose titles or occupations (nearly 20 were *bourgeois de Paris*) placed them outside the world of the trades.[57]

The anonymity of the many thousands of other women who worked in the textile or clothing trades is an indirect testimony to the role of the law in defining the boundary between the public and the private. Where the words of the law did not supply a name that could be challenged, little trace of the things that women said and did could survive. The record is therefore invariably episodic and minimal: a police ruling setting the

[54] A.N. X¹ᵃ 8220 fol. 180 (27 November 1770).
[55] The forthcoming study by Daryl Hafter will throw more light on the whole question. See too Natalie Z. Davis, 'Women in the *Arts Mécaniques* in Sixteenth-Century Lyon', in *Lyon et l'Europe, hommes et sociétés* (Lyon, 1980), pp. 139–59.
[56] See, for example, N. Désessarts, *Causes célèbres, curieuses et intéressantes* (Paris, 1775), vol. 1, pp. 164–80 for a case involving the rights of the *coiffeuses de femmes* of Rouen.
[57] A.N. X¹ᵇ 3762 (12 February 1762).

wages of the women who twisted the warps used in the woollen industry of Amiens in 1786;[58] a brief glimpse of an inn, the Hostellerie de la Chasse, in Saint Quentin where the women preparing flax in the *buerie* belonging to the immensely rich Fromaget family 'iroient se divertir ordinairement',[59] a complaint by an 80-year-old woman in Reims living below the room where 14 or 15 spinners worked and made an intolerable noise, 'dansant et sautant d'une manière outrée...et ce singulièrement le jour de Saint Blaise';[60] a 'cabale terrible' by women working in a hatting enterprise in Lyon in 1780 or 1781.[61] Yet no trace of these activities reached the courts. Women had rights as wives, widows or daughters, but the work they did, perhaps because it was so closely associated with the economy of the household, did not belong to the sphere of legal argument.[62] The situation of journeymen was, in this respect, very different.

Journeymen were the largest group of people employed in the eighteenth-century French trades with no corporate status. This does not mean however, that they played no part in legal argument over rights and obligations; in fact they did for much of the eighteenth century.[63] They too engaged solicitors and barristers to argue that the rights claimed by corporate bodies were either inappropriate, irrelevant or illegal. The arguments used in such cases were very similar to those used in other circumstances: a combination of an appeal to precedent, an assertion of difference and an invocation of natural rights. Yet natural rights were individual rights. In many cases, however, hundreds of journeymen combined to undertake legal proceedings against their masters. This aspect of the relationship between masters and journeymen calls for particular comment.

Throughout the eighteenth century, large numbers of journeymen in many different trades – in Paris, above all, but also in Lyon, Marseille, Bordeaux, Rouen, Nantes and Troyes (and many other cities too) – embarked upon long, relatively costly legal actions against their masters.

58 Bibliothèque municipale, Amiens, H 3793" (7 February 1786).
59 A.D. Aisne, B 4501 (18 November 1760).
60 A.D. Marne, 18B 1349* (9 February 1781).
61 Bibliothèque municipale, Lyon, MS. 114 107, 'Lettre de Mr. Buisson à MM. les gardes et députés du corps des maîtres et marchands chapeliers de Lyon' (1781).
62 For other aspects of the legal position of women in the eighteenth century, see Arlette Farge and Michel Foucault, *Le Désordre des familles* (Paris, 1982). On the close relationship between women's work and the household economy, see William H. Sewell Jr. *Structure and Mobility: The Men and Women of Marseille, 1820–1870* (Cambridge, 1985), pp. 270–312. It is unlikely that eighteenth-century patterns were markedly different.
63 It was not the case that 'journeymen and apprentices were legally considered to be incorporated in the master's family', as Sewell (*Work and Revolution*, p. 31) puts it. Nor did they lack 'any independent juridical personality' (*ibid.*). The reason why jurists did not treat of the relationship between masters and journeymen was not, as Sewell (following Coornaert) puts it, because the latter were under the 'domestic authority' of the former, but precisely the opposite.

At times, they were accused of forming an illegal combination or, in the usual French term, a *cabale*.[64] The precise meaning of the term was sometimes a matter of argument. Master artisans and the officials of their corporations made frequent claims that legal actions brought by many hundreds of journeymen were evidence of combinations or *cabales*. The courts almost invariably prohibited journeymen from claiming any title to a collective, public identity. Yet journeymen who claimed no such title were able to mount legal actions in which their collective identity existed in all but name.

That, however, was the point. For journeymen were named in the wording of corporate statutes or corporate decisions ratified by the courts and were able to invoke and challenge that name in legal proceedings. In a paradoxical way, the collective identity that corporations conferred upon master artisans allowed journeymen a kind of collective identity too. Only when master artisans were divested of *their* collective identities were journeymen collectively unable to challenge their claims to legal entitlements in the courts. This was the significance of the Allarde and Le Chapelier Laws of 1791.[65] They marked the end of a tradition of civil jurisprudence in which rights were property, but property of a particular kind.

There was, in other words, no clear or rigid separation between a corporate world consisting of master artisans secure in the enjoyment of their rights and privileges, and an unenfranchised world of journeymen divested of any rights or privileges at all.[66] The rights which master artisans enjoyed were, in the jurisprudence of the eighteenth century, exceptional rights, and, by their nature, were limited in force and scope. For this reason, the relationship between masters and journeymen was a relationship between separate legal agents, rather than one in which the rights of the former were grounded upon the necessary subordination of the latter. Such subordination as did exist (as, of course, it did) was the product of the law and, in particular, of the manner in which the form of the wage relationship was defined in juridical terms.

Here, two aspects of the natural law tradition were particularly relevant.

[64] On *cabales* see Kaplan, 'Réflexions sur la police du monde de travail'.

[65] This indirect opportunity to challenge the terms of corporate statutes was recognised in a court ruling in 1753: 'Les loix faites par ces statuts sont irrévocables. Les cours sont indispensablement obligés de s'y conformer. Le seul cas ou ces statuts peuvent estre mitigez, et changez apres leur enregistrement c'est lorsqu' un tiers non ouy y forme opposition': A.N.E 1286ᵉ (10 April 1753). On the Allarde and Le Chapelier laws, see below, pp. 346–51.

[66] In this I have learned much from E. P. Thompson, 'The Grid of Inheritance, a Comment', in J. Goody, Joan Thirsk and E. P. Thompson, eds., *Family and Inheritance* (Cambridge, 1976), pp. 328–60.

On the one hand, work was a natural obligation, a condition which was as much a part of the natural order of things as were the obligations of parents to children or *vice versa*.

Il n'y a...point de condition, sans en excepter les plus élevées qui n'ait pour son caractère essentiel, et pour son devoir capital et indispensable, le travail pour lequel elle est établie

wrote the seventeenth-century jurist Jean Domat.

Celui qui prétend être sans engagement au travail ignore sa nature et l'usage de son esprit et de son corps; il renverse le fondement de l'ordre du monde, il viole la loi naturelle et la loi divine, et il est plus un monstre dans la nature que celui qui, étant privé de l'esprit ou de quelques membres, se trouve dans l'impuissance de travailler.[67]

On the other hand, workers had natural rights of property in their labour just as they had rights of property in their lives. When jurists discussed the wage relation in early modern France, they did so as a form of *locatio conductio operarum*, as a contract analogous to the lease of property. The term 'louage', wrote Domat, in a work that was reprinted 64 times between its first appearance in 1689 and 1777, meant 'le commerce que font les hommes en se communiquant l'usage des choses, ou de leur industrie ou de leur travail pour un certain prix'. The form of the agreement echoed the prescriptions of Roman Law.

Toutes ces espèces de conventions ont cela de commun, qu'en chacune l'un jouit de la chose de l'autre, ou use de son travail pour un certain prix, et c'est pour cette raison que dans le droit romain elles sont toutes comprises sous les noms de louage et de conduction.[68]

Formulations like this were a commonplace of eighteenth-century jurisprudence. 'Il se fait tous les jours dans le commerce de la vie des louages du travail et de l'industrie,' wrote Prévôt de la Jannès.[69] Burlamaqui, in his *Principes du droit de la nature et des gens*, echoed the definition.

Le louage donc en général est un contrat par lequel l'un donne à l'autre, moyennant un certain loyer ou un salaire, l'usage et la jouissance d'une chose, ou de son travail et de son industrie, pour un certain temps.[70]

[67] Jean Domat, 'Harangue prononcée aux assises de 1679', in his *Œuvres* (Paris, 1835 edn.), vol. 4, p. 88.

[68] Jean Domat, 'Les Lois civiles dans leur ordre naturel', in his *Œuvres* (Paris, 1835 edn.), vol. 1, pp. 199–200. René Frédéric Voeltzel, *Jean Domat (1625–1696), essai de reconstitution de sa philosophie juridique* (Paris, 1936), pp. 17–22, contains a list of successive printings.

[69] Prévôt de la Jannès, *Les Principes de la jurisprudence françoise*, 2nd edn (Paris, 1770), vol. 2, pp. 255–6.

[70] J. J. Burlamaqui, *Œuvres* (Paris, 1820 edn), vol. 3, p. 273.

The wage-relation also found its way, logically, into Pothier's *Traité du contrat de louage*, where it was examined, equally logically, under the rubric of the lease of goods and services.[71]

Ordinary usage concerning the payment of wages in eighteenth-century France derived from these formulations. The usual phrases were 'le prix de son travail', 'le prix d'une journée de travail', 'le prix de la façon', and, less currently, 'le salaire', or, finally, the word 'gages'. This last term was indicative of the difference between those employed for limited periods, who were usually journeymen or labourers, and those employed for longer periods. It was used almost exclusively in connection with payments to domestic servants. There were good reasons for this limited usage. The terms 'le prix d'une journée' or 'le prix de son travail' denoted the contractual and limited nature of the engagement. Labour was hired for a certain price for a certain duration. Eighteenth-century dictionaries of jurisprudence contain no precise definition of the wage because there was no difference in status between someone hiring out his labour and someone hiring out a coat.[72] The status of domestic servants was somewhat different, since they had engaged themselves to their masters or mistresses (and were therefore *à leurs gages*), for extended periods (of a year in usual circumstances). In addition, they worked in their employers' households (rather than a *boutique* or *atelier*) and used their possessions. The nature of their engagement was therefore more extensive.[73] The wages of servants were the price of their engagement; the wages paid to journeymen were the price of their labour.

There was, therefore, an essential difference in the natural law tradition

[71] R. J. Pothier, *Œuvres*, ed. M. Bugnet, 2nd edn (Paris, 1861). See also O. Kahn-Freund, 'Blackstone's Neglected Child: The Contract of Employment', *Law Quarterly Review*, 93 (1977), pp. 508–28. I am grateful to David Sugarman for this reference and, generally, for much helpful advice on the topic of the law.

[72] Thus in the nine editions of Dénisart's *Collection de décisions nouvelles et de notions relatives à la jurisprudence actuelle*, 9th edn (Paris, 1786) the wage appears under the rubric of *gages* on some occasions and *salaire* on others.

[73] So too, because it embraced the condition of all those living and working in a household, was the definition of domestic service itself. 'La domesticité est une sorte d'esclavage, volontaire en apparence, mais réel en effet et commandé par le besoin de vivre': *Encyclopédie méthodique: Jurisprudence* (Paris, 1789), vol. 9, p. 15 (s.v. 'abus'). 'Born free, like all other citizens, but however, obliged by the occupation they embraced to sacrifice their repose to the need, the taste, sometimes even the caprice of those to whom they devote themselves … they live in a state of veritable slavery', as a police ordinance of 1778 put it (Des Essarts, *Dictionnaire universel de Police*, vol. 3, p. 478), cited by Cissie Fairchilds, *Domestic Enemies* (Baltimore, 1983), p. 18. Servants 'are not supposed to be free, or integrated into the body of citizens' (Joseph Berthelé, ed. *Montpellier en 1768 et 1836 d'après deux manuscrits inédits*, p. 69), cited by Sara C. Maza, *Servants and Masters in Eighteenth-Century France* (Princeton, 1983), p. 109. Neither author devotes much space to an examination of the legal status of domestic servants or their place within natural law jurisprudence. The same criticism can be made of Jean-Pierre Gutton. *Domestiques et serviteurs dans la France de l'ancien régime* (Paris, 1981) and Jacqueline Sabatier, *Figaro et son maître* (Paris, 1984).

between the status of journeymen and the status of domestic servants. This difference also applied to agricultural labourers and, in particular, to the workers engaged to bring in the harvest in July and August every year. A ruling by the Parlement of Normandy in July 1721 prohibited ‘les domestiques et ouvriers de la campagne’ from combining together to raise their wages ‘dans les foires et autres endroits où ils s’assemblent pour se louer’. The identification of harvest work with domestic service was reiterated the following year and repeated in a ruling by the Parlement of Britanny in July 1722. A number of rulings by the Parlement of Paris relating to harvest work in the great cereal-producing region to the north of the capital, where conflicts between harvesters and landowners were a very frequent occurrence, specified that disputes over wages would be dealt with in summary fashion by the *maréchaussée*. In its rulings ratifying decisions made by the *bailliage* courts of Crépy en Valois, Ermonville, Brégy and Laon in 1778 and 1780 the Parlement defined harvest workers as *ouvriers forains*, who, if they refused to work for the wages set by assemblies of the principal landowners in a parish, were subject to arrest and imprisonment as vagabonds.[74] The summary justice of the *maréchaussée* was, of course, well suited to the pressurised schedules of harvest work, but was rarely used in disputes in the urban trades.

The differences between journeymen employed in the trades, agricultural labourers and domestic servants were also transposed to the criminal law. Journeymen could be prosecuted for *vol domestique*, a betrayal of their distinctive obligations to their employers.[75] The obligations of journeymen were different, because they retained rights of property in their labour which, like all natural rights, were modified and inflected by the provisions of the civil law. In this, they shared in the common situation of all those whose natural liberty had not been circumscribed by the provisions of corporate statutes or other legal titles.

In practice, this meant that where the law was silent natural rights

[74] The rulings by the Parlement of Normandy of 9 July 1721, 27 August 1721 and 26 June 1722 are printed under their dates in *Suite du nouveau receuil des édits, déclarations, lettres patentes et réglements de Sa Majesté* (Rouen, 1741); A.D. Loire-Atlantique, C 779 (*arrêt du Parlement de Bretagne*, 8 July 1722: *arrêt du Parlement de Paris*, 7 August 1780); A.N. X¹ᵇ 4068 (7 September 1778). On disputes in harvest work, see Jean-Marc Moriceau, ‘Les ‘‘Baccanals’’ ou grèves des moissonneurs en Pays de France (seconde moitié du xviiie siècle)’, in Jean Nicolas, ed., *Mouvements populaires et conscience sociale* (Paris, 1985), pp. 420–33. On the *maréchaussée* and its powers, see Iain Cameron. *Crime and Repression in the Auvergne and the Guyenne, 1720–1790* (Cambridge, 1981).

[75] *Encyclopédie méthodique: Jurisprudence* (Paris, 1787), vol. 7, pp. 297–300. See also Anne Bresson-Le Minor, ‘Le Vol domestique au xviiie siècle d’après les arrêts du Parlement de Paris’ (Thèse de droit, Université de Paris, 1978). There is, again, no reliable study of the subject. The remarks by Gérard Aubry, *La Jurisprudence criminelle du Châtelet de Paris sous le règne de Louis XVI* (Paris, 1971), pp. 129–30, are marred by an absence of sensitivity to occupational distinctions.

came into their own. A dispute between a ship's captain and his crew is a model of this state of affairs.[76] The ship had sailed from Marseille to Cayenne in 1782 but, instead of returning directly to the port, had put in at Tenerife to prepare for a second voyage. The crew refused to make the second voyage and were charged with desertion. They argued that their captain had no right to expect them to undertake another voyage. 'Un capitaine de navire…n'est pas un despote; en louant un matelot pour son service, il ne contract pas avec des esclaves.'[77] Possession of the right to engage a crew for a single voyage was not possession of the right to expect an unlimited engagement. The court accepted the argument and dismissed the charge of desertion.

The formal status of the wage-relationship was identical. Master artisans were not despots, and journeymen were not slaves. The law supplied the particular, and infinitely varied, terms upon which the labour of journeymen became, for a time, the property of their masters. These terms could be general or particular, concrete or abstract. As they were discussed or defined, argued over and redefined, the identity of the work performed in the urban trades could be modified in several ways. Words were the way in which rights and obligations crystallised into temporary configurations of identity and power.

[76] *Gazette des tribunaux*, 18 (Paris, 1784), p. 221 (where Pothier was cited to support the verdict).
[77] *Ibid.*

CHAPTER 3

Journeymen and the law

In the late summer of 1775 a journeyman shoemaker named Alexandre Voltaire was arrested by the police authorities in Bordeaux. He was accused of having taken part in three meetings called to oppose the establishment of a corporate labour exchange (*bureau d'embauchage*) in the town hall. On each occasion between 300 and 400 journeymen shoemakers had been present. They had elected six men to draw up a request to the Parlement of Bordeaux and collected the sum of 75 livres to pay for the initial costs of the appeal. Voltaire readily agreed that he had attended the meetings, and added that he had been particularly zealous to be among the first there. He explained that the journeymen had stopped work and held their assemblies to maintain their rights and free themselves from slavery (*pour soutenir leurs droits et s'afranchir* [sic] *de l'esclavage*).[1]

The words were, perhaps, particularly fitting from a journeyman named Voltaire. In a more general way, however, they are indicative of the resonances of the vocabulary of the law in the ordinary affairs of the eighteenth-century French trades. A letter sent by the journeymen wigmakers of Rouen to their counterparts in Marseille in 1773 was equally redolent of that vocabulary. It was sent to inform the journeymen of Marseille that *garçons perruquiers* in Bordeaux and Lyon planned to embark upon a co-ordinated campaign against a recently established requirement to carry printed certificates of good conduct. The campaign, the wigmakers of Rouen wrote, would shatter the yoke (*secouer le joug*) by which their masters held them in chains (*par le quelle les boujois* [sic] *nous*

1 Asked 'en quoy il fait concister [sic] les droits des garçons cordonniers et leur liberté', he replied 'qu'il conciste à ne travailler que où ils jugent à propos'. A.D. Gironde, 12B 352. interrogation of Alexandre Voltaire (23 August 1775). On the decisions surrounding the stoppages, see A.D. Gironde, C 1804 (3, 31 July, 16 August 1, 10 October 1775) and below, pp. 277–8.

73

tienne anchaîné) and revive 'notre première liberté qui nous a été sy injustement ravie'.[2]

As these examples indicate, concepts used in treatises of civil jurisprudence – 'esclavage' or 'première liberté', for example – were also used by journeymen in the ordinary course of disputes in the trades. Although they made frequent reference to the particularities of the trades to which they belonged, journeymen also made use of the wider conceptual framework of natural law and natural rights to situate and define their sense of civil entitlements and civil rights. Assertion of particularity was as much a measure of their familiarity with the rhetorical tropes of eighteenth-century legal argument as, with hindsight, it appears to denote their inability to recognise their common condition. If, in the nineteenth century (to put it crudely) that common condition found its expression in a range of terms associated with the concept of class, in the eighteenth century it found its expression in a range of terms associated with rights. Just as the language of class of the nineteenth century was made up of a body of metaphors associated with the production, distribution and ownership of wealth, so the idiom of corporate particularity of the eighteenth century was made up of body of metaphors associated with the presence, absence or ownership of rights.[3]

In eighteenth-century France, the notion of rights had a particular sense. Since civil rights were limited and exceptional in character, their presence was a permanent invitation to comparison. Inversely, however, their absence, or possible absence, was a permanent invitation to evoke those two conditions that lay beyond the law: natural liberty and slavery. The provisions of the civil law supplied the formal terms of reference governing the relationship between journeymen and their masters. Master artisans were not despots; journeymen were not slaves. Instead of despotism and slavery, the law made reference to civil liberty and civil rights, and was instrumental in defining the conditions under which liberty and rights co-existed with duties and obligations. The sense of those terms was not, of course, unequivocal because the law was neither ready-made nor immutable. It was at once heir to the gradual consolidation of royal absolutism during the sixteenth and seventeenth centuries and, more immediately, was subject to the intermittent pressures placed upon it by masters and journeymen themselves. Both the legacy of the past and the inevitably imperfect correlation between the provisions of the law and

---

[2] A.C. Marseille, FF 383 (17 January 1774).

[3] These remarks, as should be apparent, derive in part from a reading of Sewell, *Work and Revolution*, and Gareth Stedman Jones, *Languages of Class* (Cambridge, 1983), pp. 1–24, 90–178.

the circumstances of the trades meant that much of the dialogue between masters and journeymen was conducted in the courts.

In the eighteenth century, the legacy of the past was visible in the formal terms of the relationship between masters and journeymen in two ways. The first concerned the status of journeymen who had been apprenticed to master artisans belonging to particular corporations, while the second concerned the status of journeymen's confraternities within the secular conventions of the civil law. Both the rights associated with having served an apprenticeship in a particular place, and the uncertain legal status of associations whose purposes were manifestly spiritual in form (if not always in fact), meant that rights possessed by master artisans were circumscribed by those which journeymen could claim to possess. The voluntary and contractual character of civil association in the natural law tradition meant that masters and journeymen were separate legal agents. As a result, the three most common forms of argument used in eighteenth-century litigation – appeals to precedent, invocation of difference, and assertions of natural rights – could be brought to bear upon situations in which the law appeared to be ambiguous, or upon legal decisions in which journeymen could claim that they had not been heard. For much of the eighteenth century, the episodic arrangements informing the life of the trades were variations or improvisations upon the more measured and distant tones of rulings by the courts.

The act of apprenticeship was analogous to the primordial alienation of natural liberty. It implied entry into the rule-bound social existence of civil society, embodied in this instance by the statutes of particular corporations. Journeymen in the building trades of Lyon argued in an appeal to the Parlement of Paris in 1787 that they could not be expected to carry a printed record of employment (or *livret*) because they had never been apprenticed in the city. Since they were not *compagnons de la ville*, they had never contracted an engagement with the masons' corporation of Lyon or surrendered their liberty to work where they chose.[4] The contractual element that was one of the hallmarks of the natural law tradition was particularly evident in this interpretation of the act of apprenticeship. It was equally apparent in the sixteenth- and seventeenth-century statutes of the Parisian corporations, where the duties and obligations incumbent

---

[4] 'Les règlements pour la police des apprentis et compagnons de ville...ne peuvent s'appliquer aux ouvriers maçons, tailleurs de pierre et plâtriers, qui ne sont ni apprentis ni compagnons de ville, et n'ont jamais contracté aucun engagement envers la communauté...L'on ne doit rien innover de contraire à leurs droits et possession pour la *liberté* du travail et le changement de maîtres et bourgeois, suivant que cela se pratiquoit autrefois et de tout temps.' A.C. Lyon, *Imprimés*, 703. 981, *Mémoire pour les ouvriers, compagnons et manœuvres maçons, plâtriers et tailleurs de pierre de Lyon* (Lyon, 1787), p. 6.

upon apprentices were matched by recognition of the rights that apprenticeship bestowed. In the broadest and most obvious sense, completion of an apprenticeship entitled journeymen to become masters of a corporation. In addition, many of the sixteenth- and seventeenth-century statutes of the Parisian corporations contained clauses which ensured that this right was complemented by more specific entitlements to employment. Journeymen who had served an apprenticeship in the capital were given preferential rights of employment over men from elsewhere, so that continuity of employment was the practical counterpart to the right to enter a corporation and the formal equivalent to the duties and obligations incumbent upon apprentices.

Provisions of this kind existed in at least 27 of the statutes of the Parisian corporations drawn up during the sixteenth and seventeenth centuries.[5] They were not, of course, uniform – they varied from trade to trade and time to time. In some instances, journeymen from outside Paris were merely required to pay a fee (usually a small one) to the trade's confraternity before working in the capital.[6] In others, journeymen from the provinces were explicitly prohibited from working in Paris for longer

[5] This figure is based upon René de Lespinasse, *Les Métiers et corporations de Paris*, 3 vols (Paris, 1886–94). A systematic examination of the statutes themselves would undoubtedly reveal an additional number of cases, since Lespinasse was interested mainly in the names of the things which artisans made and tended to summarise or omit clauses which did not deal with that subject. Discriminatory regulations concerning journeymen from outside Paris existed in the following trades: *boulangers* (statutes, Saint Germain-des-Prés, 1659, art. 29; statutes, Paris, 1719, art. 42, Lespinasse, vol. 1, pp. 213, 225); *tireurs d'or* (statutes, 1551, art. 27, Lespinasse, vol. 2, p. 74); *paternôtriers* (statutes, 1583, art. 2, *ibid.*, p. 106); *doreurs sur métaux* (statutes, 1573, art. 19, *ibid.*, p. 139); *boutonniers-passementiers* (statutes, 1559 art. 24: statutes, 1653 art. 13, *ibid.*, pp. 149, 155); *ouvriers en draps d'or* (statutes, 1615, art. 27, *ibid.*, p. 293); *armuriers* (statutes, 1562, art. 17, *ibid.*, pp. 332–3); *arquebusiers* (statutes, 1575, art. 16, *ibid.*, p. 348); *couteliers* (statutes, 1565, art. 50, *ibid.*, p. 391); *fondeurs* (statutes, 1572, art. 13, *ibid.*, p. 421); *potiers d'étain* (statutes, 1613, art. 25, *ibid.*, p. 537); *aiguilliers* (statutes, 1599, art. 17, *ibid.*, p. 562); *paveurs* (statutes, 1502, art. 8, *ibid.*, p. 620); *couvreurs* (statutes, 1566, art. 5, *ibid.*, p. 627); *menuisiers* (statutes, 1580, art. 53, *ibid.*, p. 653); *tapissiers* (statutes, 1636, art. 4, *ibid.*, p. 710); *vanniers-quincailliers* (statutes, 1467, art. 8, *ibid.*, p. 741); *cardeurs de laine* (Lespinasse, vol. 3, p. 92); *tondeurs de drap* (arrêt, 1495, *ibid.*, p. 110); *teinturiers* (statutes, 1575, art. 13, *ibid.*, p. 127); *tailleurs d'habit* (sentence de police, 1601, *ibid.*, p. 194); *bonnetiers* (statutes, 1550, art. 4, *ibid.*, p. 249); *chapeliers* (statutes, 1480, art. 5; statutes, 1578, art. 7; sentence de police, 1700, *ibid.*, pp. 285, 287, 292); *plumassiers* (statutes, 1659, art. 34, *ibid.*, p. 301); *mégissiers* (statutes, 1517, art. 39, *ibid.*, p. 332); *cordonniers* (statutes, 1573, art. 20, *ibid.*, p. 349); *savetiers* (statutes, 1659, art. 28, *ibid.*, p. 364).

[6] Thus article 42 of the statutes of the bakers' corporation of 1719 stipulated that 'les compagnons de dehors ne pourront estre recus à travailler chez les maistres qu'après avoir donné leur nom aux jurez, et payé une fois seulement 20 sous au profit de la communauté, et ne pourront acquérir droit de maîtrise à Paris, quelque espace de tems qu'ils y demeureront chez les maistres, s'ils n'y font pas apprentissage': Lespinasse, vol. 1, p. 225.

than a specified period.[7] Rulings by the courts were also incorporated into the statutes of the trades and tended to have the same discriminatory sense. An *arrêt* by the Parlement of Paris in 1495, 'sur la demande des varlets jurés et gardes des heures' of the cloth-dressers and -croppers, for example, ordered masters to employ Parisian journeymen by the year, whether or not there was work to be done, and, if they chose to employ '*étrangers*', to apply the same terms to them too. A ruling by the Châtelet in 1701 entitled 'poor masters' and *compagnons de la campagne*, provided trade to preferential employment over *compagnons de Paris* working in the trade (there were many other *étrangers*) prompted the corporation's officials to seek the right hundred or so *compagnons de Paris* working in the trade (there were partially abandoned in 1765 when a series of stoppages by some of the wished to work in Paris. It was reiterated in 1725 and 1738 and was only relatively substantial sum of ten *livres* to the trade's confraternity if they journeymen cardmakers 'qui viendroient de la campagne' to pay the statutes were revised in 1752.[8] Another ruling, in 1648, ordered that wages were the same. It was reiterated when the corporation's to create 50 additional apprentices.[9]

In the seventeenth century, journeymen in many Parisian corporations – joiners, saddlers, gunsmiths, cutlers, iron-founders, gilders, bakers, roofers, hatters, tailors and shoemakers, to name some of the largest – who had served an apprenticeship and were domiciled in the capital were legally entitled to enjoy preferential rights of employment over men who had been apprenticed elsewhere. Rights of this kind, or claims to rights of this kind, were the basis of many legal actions by journeymen who had served an apprenticeship in the capital. In the course of the long sequence of actions that they brought before the Parlement between 1650 and 1725, journeymen in the Parisian printing trade repeatedly invoked article 32 of the Royal Letters Patent granted to the corporation in 1572 to justify their entitlement to employment over journeymen who had served an apprenticeship elsewhere. They also referred to a ruling by the Parlement in favour of the journeymen printers of Lyon in 1655 and a sentence by the *bailliage* court of Rouen in 1664 fining a master printer for employing a journeyman who had not been apprenticed to a master of the

[7] Article 5 of the roofers' statutes of 1566 stipulated that '*étrangers*' were not entitled to work in Paris for more than a week: Lespinasse, vol. 2, p. 627.

[8] Lespinasse, vol. 3, p. 110: B.N. F 44 776, *Statuts des maîtres potiers de terre, carleurs de la ville de Paris* (Paris, 1752), p. 102. It is possible that the ruling was a result of a dispute in the trade in 1700: see A.N. Y 13 047 (28 March 1700).

[9] Archives de la préfecture de police, Fonds Lamoignon, 12 fol. 924 (20 March 1648): A.N. Y 9615 (14 December 1725): B.N. F 12 918 (*Statuts des maîtres cartiers, papetiers, faiseurs de cartes, tarots, feuillets et cartons*, Paris, 1764): A.N. Y 15 463 (20 September 1764): 15 372 (12 August 1766): Y 9500 (28 August 1765): B.N. MS. Joly de Fleury, 648 (28 August 1765).

corporation.[10] In 1631 Parisian journeymen carpenters appealed to the Parlement to enjoin their masters 'd'employer les compagnons charpentiers qui auroient fait leur apprantissage et estoient domiciliez en nostre dicte ville par préférance aux compagnons estrangers du mesme metier'.[11] Despite the Parlement's rejection of the appeal, as well as a second legal action by the journeymen in 1656, the Royal Council still found it necessary to stipulate that master carpenters were entitled to emply 'tels compagnons que bon leur sembleront' in a ruling in 1697.[12]

Even when corporate statutes denied the entitlement, journeymen continued to behave as if it existed. The statutes of the plumbers' corporation of 1549 explicitly allowed masters to hire journeymen from outside Paris, yet even in 1765 the corporation found it necessary to obtain Royal Letters Patent allowing masters to employ journeymen from the provinces, 'avec defenses aux compagnons de la ville de les troubler, à peine de punition'.[13] None the less, a master plumber was still obliged to lodge a complaint against his apprentice (himself an immigrant from Normandy) in 1770 for attempting to force a provincial journeyman to leave Paris on the grounds that he had no right to work there.[14]

Preferential rights to employment were not confined to journeymen who had served an apprenticeship in Paris. Linen weavers (*ouvriers tolliers*) in seventeenth-century Rouen were able to refer to rulings by the *bailliage* court in 1635, 1637 and 1640 stipulating that men who had been apprenticed to a master of the corporation should be employed in preference to natives of the city, and, in their absence, that natives of Rouen should be given preference over journeymen from elsewhere. Similar rulings applied to the woollen trades of Elbeuf, Louviers, Orival and Darnétal.[15] Journeymen printers in Rouen, as well as in Lyon, enjoyed similar rights.[16] A ruling by the Parlement of Paris in 1662 stated that an act of apprenticeship in the printing trade of Lyon was void unless it had been signed by one of the journeymen's *syndics*. The journeymen were also empowered to visit the city's print-shops, accompanied by a clerk or a bailiff, to inspect the apprenticeship documents of both natives of, and migrants to, the city.[17] The journeymen bakers of Lyon expressed the sense

---

10 B.N. MS. fr. 22 064 fol. 83 (1664); A.N. X^{1a} 2566 fol. 613 (8 May 1665).
11 A.N. X^{1a} 399 (30 August 1631).
12 A.N. X^{1a} 2397 (17 May 1656); Archives de la préfecture de police, Fonds Lamoignon, 13, fol. 673 (17 June 1656); A.N. E 661^b fol. 101 (16 March 1697); Y 13 046 (27 February 1698).
13 B.N. MS. Joly de Fleury 648, fol. 126 (28 August 1765); A.N. Y 9500 (28 August 1765).
14 A.N. Y 12 175 (2 February 1770).
15 A.D. Seine-Maritime, 5E 775; Michael Sonenscher, 'Weavers, Wage-Rates and the Measurement of Work in Eighteenth-Century Rouen', *Textile History*, 17 (1986), pp. 7–17 (pp. 14–15).
16 A.N. X^{1a} 5798 (14 August 1655).
17 A.N. X^{1a} 2519 fol. 44v (20 October 1662).

of such entitlements particularly pithily (if not wholly accurately) in a call for 'apprentifs ou compagnons de la ville: bon pain et contentement populaire'.[18]

It is probable, however, that formal entitlements of this kind were rather more of a rarity in provincial France than in sixteenth- and seventeenth-century Paris.[19] Yet even where corporate statutes made no reference to the particular status of apprentices in cities in which they had served their time, or, as in the case of the woollen-cropper's corporation of Sedan in 1666, explicitly prohibited discrimination in favour of journeymen who had served an apprenticeship there, the ambiguous legal status of journeymen's confraternities tended to favour of men who were domiciled and in regular employment in particular localities.[20] It did so because, until the late eighteenth century, confraternities fell largely outside the sphere of the civil law. As they had been since the thirteenth and fourteenth centuries, confraternities were voluntary religious associations whose existence was sanctioned by the church. Until the mid-eighteenth century, and the complex political struggle between Jansenists and Jesuits, confraternities could be established without royal approval – all that was needed was a Papal Bull or the sanction of bishop.[21] The assimilation of confraternities into the secular world of corporate regulation was never complete. Consequently, the protracted process that led to the formation of corporations as civil institutions did little to affect the formal status of confraternities or modify their position in public life.[22]

The relationship between corporations and confraternities belongs to the relatively little-known history of relations between the church and the state in seventeenth- and eighteenth-century France.[23] It was, however, a

---

18 A.C. Lyon, HH 24.
19 The whole subject of the status of journeymen in the sixteenth and seventeenth centuries requires further study. Further research in the papers of the Parlements (particularly the Parlement of Paris) is likely to yield a great deal more information.
20 The status of journeymen in Sedan was set out in an *arrêt du conseil* of 30 September, 1666: A.N. F¹² 788: E 2298²¹⁹ (23 June 1750).
21 'Pour l'établissement des confrairies il n'est pas besoin de l'autorité du Roy; il suffit des Bulles du Pape ou de l'autorité meme des Eveques'. If, however, members were expected to pay a fee, 'en ce cas, cela regarde le temporel'. Royal Letters Patent were then needed: see Pierre Jacques Brillon, *Dictionnaire des arrêts*, 2 vols (Paris, 1727), p. 340. More generally, see Bernard Chevalier, 'Corporations, conflits politiques et paix sociale en France aux xive et xve siècles', *Revue historique*, 268 (1982), pp. 17–44 (pp. 29–30, 40). The word *compagnon* referred to a member of a confraternity and had no substantive association with work in the trades.
22 As Chevalier rightly puts it, 'La confrérie est un corps, mais, en vertu de sa destination, elle ne relève pas dans son existence de l'autorité civile' (*ibid.*, p. 30). The key problem, given the ubiquity of confraternities, is to explain the emergence of secular corporations. 'Au fond la question qu'il faudrait résoudre n'est pas celle de l'émergence des confréries professionnelles, mais plutot celle des corporations de droit public' (*ibid.*, pp. 40–1).
23 The subject has barely been studied outside the context of Jansenism and the Jesuits. See Dale Van Kley, *The Jansenists and the Expulsion of the Jesuits, 1757–65*. (New Haven,

more distant relationship than might be supposed. Although the statutes of many corporations made provision for the existence of confraternities among master artisans (to which journeymen could also belong), neither the corporations nor the courts could prevent journeymen from seeking clerical authorisation for their own associations. In Lyon in 1680, journeymen bakers who were denied the right to use their own drums, violins and oboes in the annual procession in honour of St Honoré walked off with the offering (*pain bénit*) and distributed it in a *cabaret* to the members of their own confraternity. Journeymen hatters in Marseille began legal proceedings in 1716 to safeguard their right to take part in processions and elect officials at the same time as their masters, while their counterparts in Lyon made a point of refusing to contribute to their masters' confraternity in 1741 on the grounds that to do so would have violated their established rules. Journeymen dyers petitioned the Archbishop of Rouen in 1747 for the restoration of their own confraternity because, they stated, they had no rights in their masters' association.[24]

Repeated rulings by the civil courts prohibiting journeymen's confraternities during disputes in the trades are sufficient evidence that the church was reluctant to allow the civil authorities to affect its right to allow journeymen to maintain confraternities in parish churches, convents or monasteries. Master artisans were aware of the limitations of the civil law in this context. In 1747, when the journeymen dyers of Rouen sought to re-establish their confraternity, their masters were obliged to petition the Archbishop to warn him that the association would be a source of conflict and division and remind him of a ruling by the *bailliage* court of 1720 prohibiting confraternities among journeymen.[25] Yet rulings by the secular courts did little to prevent the ecclesiastical authorities from authorising journeymen's confraternities. A journeymen joiners' confraternity established in the church of Sainte-Marie-Madeleine in Paris was twice outlawed by rulings of the Royal Council in 1680, but continued to

1975); Timothy Tackett, *Religion, Revolution and Regional Culture in Eighteenth-Century France*, (Princeton, 1986). On confraternities, see Martine Segalen, *Les Confréries dans la France contemporaine* (Paris, 1975); Maurice Agulhon, *Pénitents et francs-maçons de l'ancienne Provence* (Paris, 1968); Marc Venard, 'Les Confréries dans l'espace urbaine: l'exemple de Rouen', *Annales de Bretagne*, 90 (1982), pp. 321–32. Earlier, and ineffectual, royal legislation proscribing confraternities (including the celebrated royal ordinances of Villers-Cotterets, Orléans, Moulins and Blois of 1539, 1561, 1566 and 1579) derived partly from disputes in the printing trades of Paris and Lyon during the sixteenth century. See Henri Hauser, *Ouvriers du temps passé* (Paris, 1899), pp. 190–1; Emile Levasseur, *Histoire des classes ouvrières et de l'industrie en France* (Paris, 1901), vol. 2, pp. 131–6.

[24] They complained that they had ' pour toute prerogative qu'un bouquet et un craquelin, encore lorsqu'il s'en trouvoit de trop pour les maistres ': A.D. Seine-Maritime, G 1246, cited by Marc Venard, 'Christianiser les ouvriers en France au xviie siècle', *Actes du 109e congrès national des sociétés savantes. Section d'histoire moderne et contemporaine* (Paris, 1984), vol. 1, pp. 19–30 (p. 27). On the bakers of Lyon, see A.C. Lyon, HH 24 (3 June 1680); and on hatters, see Sonenscher, *Hatters*, pp. 81–96.

[25] Marc Venard, 'Christianiser les ouvriers', pp. 27–8.

function throughout the eighteenth century.[26] The confraternity established by the Parisian roofers (*compagnons couvreurs*) was outlawed by the Parlement in 1651, but was still in existence 100 years (and five further prohibitions) later.[27] Among the many other Parisian confraternities whose existence does not appear to have been affected by hostile rulings by the courts were those established by the journeymen carpenters, hatters, printers, framework knitters, painters and gilders.[28]

Their continued existence undoubtedly owed something to the active support of both the regular and secular clergy. The friars of the abbey of Saint-Jean-Porte-Latine intervened in legal proceedings in 1700 to uphold the journeymen printers' right to celebrate mass and maintain their confraternity, while the confraternity of journeymen shoemakers invited the Dean of Notre Dame to mediate in a dispute with their masters in 1720.[29] Attitudes outside Paris were similar, even in the late eighteenth century. In 1779 the *procureur du roi* of La Rochelle complained that the city's religious orders continued to allow journeymen to use rooms in their establishments, despite a Royal Edict in April 1777 prohibiting confraternities. In Nantes, a police official reported in 1781 that he had been unable to arrest a number of journeymen joiners affiliated to one of the *compagnonnages* because the Jacobin friars in whose convent they were meeting refused him entry. In 1788, the chaplain of the *chapelle de Malthe* in the Temple of Bordeaux informed his vestry nun that, despite a large number of court rulings, he knew nothing about any prohibition preventing journeymen joiners from celebrating a high mass on the feast day of St Anne and would continue to allow the journeymen to do so until someone told him to stop.[30]

Throughout the eighteenth century the civil authorities handled the relationship between journeymen's confraternities and the church with conspicuous circumspection. Although they regularly prohibited confraternities, they made no attempt to prosecute members of either the secular or regular clergy whose institutions housed associations which, in terms of the civil law, were illegal. A police official who was ordered to arrest two journeymen framework knitters during an assembly of their confraternity in the Picpus friars' convent in Marseille in 1781 made a point of emphasising that the sacrament was covered and that there was

[26] A.N. E 1802 fols. 78, 256 (9 August and 16 December 1680); A.N. F¹² 4280 (dossier on the *société Sainte Anne*). I am grateful to Dr Michael Sibalis for this reference.
[27] A.N. X¹ᵃ 455 (4 March 1651); David Garrioch and Michael Sonenscher, '*Compagnonnages*, Confraternities and Associations of Journeymen in Eighteenth-Century Paris', *European History Quarterly*, 16 (1986), pp. 25–45 (p. 31).
[28] *Ibid.*, pp. 41–2.
[29] B.N. MS. fr. 21 749 fol. 80 (19 June 1702); University of Chicago Library, John Crerar Collection, 1260; A.N. S 118 fol. 1 (16 October 1720).
[30] B.N. MS. Joly de Fleury 510, fol. 303 (12 January 1779); A.C. Nantes, HH 150 (18 August 1781); A.D. Gironde, 12B 385 (14 August 1788), deposition of Jeanne Tardy.

no sign of any service in progress when he entered the building. The friars were, none the less, unsympathetic to the intrusion and face was saved only when the two journeymen gave their word to make their own way to the *hôtel de ville* to be arrested.[31]

The limited purchase of the civil law in ecclesiastical affairs allowed a large number of journeymen's confraternities to survive until well into the eighteenth century. Confraternities formed by journeymen in the hatting trades of Lyon and Marseille survived until the last decade of the *ancien régime* and, particularly in Marseille, enjoyed considerable civil recognition. Those formed by journeymen in the joining trade were equally durable. In 1791 the journeymen joiners of Nantes petitioned the municipal authorities to allow them to transfer their confraternity from the now defunct Carmelite abbey to the church of Saint Pierre.[32] In cities like Lyon and Marseille, where the incorporation of the trades was both late and limited, confraternities were the most common form of collective association among both master artisans and journeymen throughout the century. Journeymen in the majority of the larger trades – shoemakers, tailors, bakers, hatters, woollen-, linen- and cotton-weavers, framework knitters, wigmakers, tanners, iron-founders, turners and coopers – were members of associations that were invariably attached to a church or one of the religious orders and, particularly in Marseille, often enjoyed recognition by the civil authorities as well as their clerical counterparts.[33]

Even in Paris and the cities of northern France, with their well-established corporate institutions, journeymen's confraternities occupied an established place in public life. A list of Parisian confraternities published in 1621 made reference to over a dozen journeymen's confraternities, including associations of tailors, shoemakers, carpenters, hosiers, coopers and tanners.[34] Weavers in most of the major centres of textile production of northern France – Amiens, Beauvais, Troyes and Rouen – all had confraternities in the early eighteenth century, as did the weavers of Paris itself. In Amiens and Rouen, journeymen dyers, hosiers

[31] A.C. Marseille, FF 391 (14 January 1781), deposition of André Guizon.

[32] 'Ils faisoient désservir dans l'église des Carmes de Nantes une confrairie de Sainte Anne: que depuis l'extinction des Carmes et la cloture de leur eglise, ils ont été à la paroisse St Nicolas pour faire désservir cette confrairie, mais comme il n'y a pas assez de prêtres à la paroisse St Nicolas pour acquitter cette confrairie, ils sont venus demander si elle ne pourroit pas l'êtres dans l'église de St Pierre.' B.M. Nantes, MS. 1016 (8 August 1791). Sonenscher, *Hatters*, chapter 7.

[33] On Marseille: A.D. Bouches-du-Rhône, 366E²⁴⁶ (17 February 1733), woollen-weavers: B unclassified (8 January 1765), bakers: B 3707 (21 June 1787), hatters and tanners: A.C. Marseille, FF 362 (28 July 1755), wigmakers: FF 379 (19 June 1770), linen- and cotton-weavers: FF 391 (14 January 1781), framework-knitters: FF 392 (26 April 1782), coopers (*caissiers*): FF 393 (28 August 1783), shoemakers: FF 394 (24 July 1784), turners; FF 397 (30 June 1787), iron-founders (*forgerons*).

[34] J. B. Le Masson, *Le Calendrier des confréries de Paris* (Paris, 1621). I have used the reprinted edition, introduced and annotated by Valentin Dufour (Paris, 1875).

and hatters were also members of confraternities, as were the wool-combers of Dieppe.[35] Only in 1760 did the Parlement of Paris issue a ruling calling upon all such associations to present their titles to the civil courts for ratification. The returns are far from complete,[36] but, together with scattered references from other sources, they indicate that between 1620 and 1760 there were at least 45 journeymen's confraternities in some 35 Parisian trades.[37] Some were very old: the journeymen shoemakers claimed that their confraternity had been found in 1379, while the carpenters twice asserted that their association had been found by King Robert in 997.[38] As this claim implies, some confraternities also had civil titles to their right to exist. The journeymen shoemakers confraternity had been found by Charles V. The joiners' confraternity of St Anne was ratified by Royal Letters Patent in 1673, while one of the hatters' confraternities was approved by the *lieutenant général de police* in the same year.[39]

Journeymen's confraternities in the eighteenth century had three main characteristics. They were usually small, with no more than 50 to a 100 members. Their membership included a relatively large number of men in their thirties or forties, including many married men. Finally, the majority of their members were settled in the cities in which they worked. In Paris,

35 A.N. Minutier central, XXX, 267 (8 September 1736) (*confrérie de Ste Anne des compagnons tisserands*): Marc Venard, 'Christianiser les ouvriers', pp. 25–8: Pierre Deyon, *Amiens, capitale provinciale: étude sur la société urbaine au xviie siècle* (Paris, 1967), pp. 218–19. A petition by the journeymen hosiers of Amiens in 1738 for the right to celebrate the *fête de Saint Louis* separately from their masters made reference to a confraternity of tailors, as well as those of the *houppiers* and *sailteurs*: A.C. Amiens, HH 835 (August 1738 and 29 July 1740).

36 B.N. MS. Joly de Fleury 1590. They cover 26 of the 48 parish churches of eighteenth-century Paris, and 43 of the 103 convents and monasteries. Returns for other cities – Amiens, Beauvais, Lyon and Troyes – are even less complete.

37 The sources are cited in Garrioch and Sonenscher, 'Compagnonnages, Confraternities', p. 42. In addition to the sources listed there, see Le Masson, *Calendrier*, pp. 75, 93, for confraternities of journeymen coopers and tailors, as well as two confraternities of journeymen tanners (p. 141): A.N. Minutier central, XXX, 267 (8 September 1736): weavers' confraternity: F12 4280: joiners' confraternity: Y 13 046 (27 February, 25 May and 15 November 1698): four confraternities of journeymen carpenters: Jean Gaston, *Les Images des confréries parisiennes avant la Révolution* (Paris, 1910), pp. 24, 40, 58, 127, 129, for confraternities of journeymen basket-makers, *rotisseurs*, woollen-croppers, pavers and mirror-makers not listed by Garrioch and Sonenscher. A report to the *société philanthropique de Paris* in 1821 lists 13 associations established before 1792 – including two societies among joiners and printers, as well as others formed by tanners, coopers, goldsmiths, and wallpaper-workers employed by Revellion and his successors Jacquemart and Bénard: B.H.V.P. 4371, *Rapport de la société philanthropique de Paris* (Paris, 1821). See also Jean Bennet, *La Mutualité française: des origines à la Révolution de 1789* (Paris, 1981).

38 Garrioch and Sonenscher, 'Compagnonnages, Confraternities', p. 30.

39 A.N. S 118: Archives de la préfecture de police, Fonds Lamoignon, 16 fol. 184: Pierre-Jacques Brillon, *Dictionnaire des arrêts, ou jurisprudence universelle des Parlements de France* (Paris, 1727), under 'confrérie': Sonenscher, *Hatters*, p. 81.

the joiners' *société de Sainte Anne* had between 60 and 150 members during the eighteenth century. A confraternity of *garçons fripiers* had 64 members, while 89 members of a confraternity of journeymen roofers signed a deliberation in 1739.[40] In Marseille, a framework knitters' confraternity had 90 to 110 members in 1781, while a turners' confraternity had a mere 24 members in 1784. Even in a very large trade like the Parisian shoemakers' trade, only 360 journeymen took part in electing the officials of their confraternity in 1759. Confraternities of weavers in Rouen in the late seventeenth century and in Troyes in the mid-eighteenth century had been 300 and 400 members.[41]

The relatively small size of journeymen's confraternities was partly a result of the small number of men who, having completed an apprenticeship, remained in the same city to work as journeymen. Marriage, or migration followed by marriage, meant that some of the men who completed an apprenticeship each year established themselves as master artisans relatively rapidly.[42] More importantly, however, the small size of confraternities made it easier to husband their resources. Although initial entry to confraternities was usually restricted to men under the age of 40 or 45, because of the demands that older men were likely to make upon their funds, the modest weekly contributions required by most associations left them exposed to the claims of a large ageing membership or to sudden increases in illnesses or accidents.[43] Nor, of course, could confraternities protect themselves very easily from the misappropriation of their funds. Legal actions against impecunious former treasurers were unlikely to lead to the return of the money.[44]

---

[40] A.N. F[12] 4280. According to this (nineteenth-century) dossier the joiners' confraternity had some 45 members between 1695 and 1745; 80–90 between 1745 and 1755; about 140 between 1755 and 1775; and 78 in 1778–9. B.N. MS. Joly de Fleury, 1590 fol. 94 (*garçons fripiers*): A.N. Minutier central, LXXXVI 601 (19 July 1739).

[41] A.C. Marseille, FF 391 (14 January 1781), framework knitters; FF 394 (24 July 1784), interrogation of Jean Ballas, turners (it is worth noting that the four officials of the confraternity were aged 45, 60, 36 and 27); A.N. S 118 fol. 18 (13 May 1759), shoemakers; Sonenscher, 'Weavers, Wage-Rates and the Measurement of Work', p. 14; A.C. Troyes, HH supplement (unclassified; July 1773).

[42] See below, chapter 4.

[43] Sonenscher, *Hatters*, chapter 7; A.D. Bouches-du-Rhône, 358E[204] fol. 118 (11 February 1768); 358E[209] fol. 275 (18 February 1773); 358E[210] fol. 162 (10 February 1774); B.N. MS. Joly de Fleury, 1590 fol. 94; Réserve. Fonds Thoisy, 9, fol. 281; Archives de la préfecture de police, Fonds Lamoignon, 16, fol. 184.

[44] The treasurer of the journeymen hatters' confraternity of Marseille was required to allow the contents of their box to be inspected every two weeks: A.D. Bouches-du-Rhône, 358E[221] fol. 55v (3 February 1785). Even so, when a treasurer died in 1779, his accounts were 218 *livres* 14 *sous* in arrears. His successor agreed to repay the deficit at the rate of 6 *livres* a month for two years, with the balance of 74 *livres* 14 *sous* due on 31 July 1781: *ibid.*, 358E[215] fol. 425 (31 May 1779). There were also abuses by members. In 1772 the confraternity noted that 'il y a eu certains confrères qui ont abusé de l'oeuvre, les uns en feignant d'être malades et ne trouvant point chez eux lorsqu'on a été porter les pacquets à eux destinés, les autres ne faisant pas difficulté d'aller prendre de l'ouvrage pour le travailler chez eux': *ibid.*, 358E[208] fol. 231 (27 February 1772).

These practicalities meant that journeymen's confraternities often
moved from one religious institution to another, while members of the
same trade sometimes established several confraternities in different
neighbourhoods. The practice was particularly marked in Paris, where
both the size of the city and the number of religious institutions favoured
a multiplicity of associations. By 1760 the location of at least a dozen of
the journeymen's confraternities in existence in the late seventeenth or
early eighteenth centuries had changed. The journeymen carpenters
appear to have had four confraternities attached to different churches or
abbeys in the late seventeenth century. The hatters had at least two, as did
the tanners and the joiners. Confraternities in the city itself were
sometimes complemented by others in the *faubourgs* or other privileged
areas, as seems to have been the case with the stocking-makers and
framework knitters.[45] Civil rulings prohibiting confraternities may have
reinforced the tendency to move from one *quartier* to another. It was,
however, a somewhat inevitable result of their small size and relatively
limited resources.

The surviving regulations of journeymen's confraternities indicate that
married men in settled and relatively regular employment made up a
substantial component of their membership. The regulations of the
Parisian joiners' confraternity of 1673 and the carpenters' *confrérie de
Saint Joseph* of 1695 both made provision for membership by journeymen's
wives. In 1726, the municipal authorities of Bordeaux explained the
absence of the *compagnonnages* from Paris in terms of the large number of
married journeymen in the capital. Nor was the phenomenon confined to
Paris. Journeymen shoemakers in Marseille informed the civil authorities
in 1783 that their confraternity was made up of a large number of married
men in settled abode, as did the nailmakers of Nantes in 1768.[46] Regular
weekly contributions and provisions for the payment of benefits over
periods of up to a year in the event of illness or accident were only possible
if the membership of confraternities was sedentary. The Parisian
shoemakers' confraternity decided that members who failed to keep up
with their contributions for six years or 'un très longtemps' would not be
able to take part in elections of the association's officials. Men elected to
be the priors or masters of journeymen's confraternities were often very
much older than the majority of men working in the trades. As a Parisian
journeyman locksmith put it in 1746, they were 'les gros d'entr'eux'.[47]

The composition and ambiguous legal status of confraternities

[45] A.N. Y 13 046 (27 February 1698); B.N. MS. Joly de Fleury, 1590 fol. 175; Garioch
and Sonenscher, '*Compagnonnages*, Confraternities'; p. 41; J. B. Le Masson, *Calendrier*, pp.
133, 141; Anne Lombard-Jourdan, 'Les Confréries parisiennes des peintres', *Bulletin de
la société d'histoire de Paris et de l'Ile-de-France*, 107 (1980), pp. 87–103.
[46] A.D. Gironde, C 1814; A.C. Marseille, FF 393 (28 August 1783); on Paris, see note 43
above.
[47] Garioch and Sonenscher, '*Compagnonnages*, Confraternities', pp. 36–7.

complemented formal entitlements to employment. They meant that in Paris and in many large provincial cities, the workforce of many trades contained a core of journeymen in their thirties and forties who lived and worked in the localities in which they had served their apprentice-ship, who expected to become master artisans, and who belonged to confraternities.[48] The combination of settled abode, marital status and the rights associated with being a *compagnon de la ville* were powerful obstacles to the rapid implementation of corporate decisions affecting conditions in the trades. The protracted legal battles between masters and journeymen in the printing trades of Paris and Lyon between 1650 and 1725 were by no means unusual.[49] Nor, as the succession of legal rulings on conditions in the printing trade suggests, were the courts prepared to meet the demands of corporations of master artisans in their entirety.

The formal dialogue between masters and journeymen was, as a result, conducted at a relatively measured pace. Journeymen named in a general way in corporate deliberations presented to the courts for ratification could claim that they had a right to be heard. In many trades, journeymen, as well as master artisans, had the resources and entitlements to enable them to engage solicitors and barristers to oppose corporate decisions and exploit the tactical and strategic opportunities supplied by the judicial system with considerable sophistication. The point was made particularly emphatically by a journeyman during a dispute in the Parisian painting and decorative trades in 1766, when he brandished the key of his confraternity's box under a master painter's nose and told him that 'il y avoit dans ledit coffre de quoi plaider et faire manger des poulets aux compagnons'.[50] The threat was not an empty one. Some confraternities could call upon funds running into hundreds of *livres* and sustain the costs of litigation over several years. Master artisans were well aware that protracted litigation was designed to promote divisions within their own ranks, and their fears were often justified.

Even when journeymen had relatively limited resources, they were prepared to go to considerable lengths to organise appeals to the Parlements. One of the officials of the Parisian journeymen locksmiths' confraternity described how, in 1746, he and his fellow officials had spent days fruitlessly seeking legal advice after they had initially persuaded a bailiff to act on their behalf. Journeymen or labourers were equally prepared to spend a great deal of time and effort on petitions to the King.

[48] On entry into the corporations and the various entitlements available to journeymen of different kinds, see below, chapter 4.

[49] See above, chapter 1.

[50] A.N. Y 9534, deposition of Jean-Jacques Prudhomme. On the costs of litigation, and the relatively substantial funds that some groups of journeymen could command, see Sonenscher, *Hatters*, pp. 116, 125. Journeymen linen-weavers in Marseille spent nearly 577 *livres* on litigation in 1770 (A.C. Marseille, FF 379, 19 June 1770).

Louis Boyer, a labourer employed in the Parisian quarries, described how he had organised a collection among his workmates to present a petition over the illegal deductions from wages that, the quarry workers claimed, had occurred after a private entrepreneur had taken over the management of the quarries from the crown. Early in June 1784 he had spent 36 sous on a memorandum drafted by a public scribe who occupied a kiosk in the courtyard of the Parlement and had walked to Versailles to present it to the King. When there was no response, he returned to the *écrivain public* and spent a further three *livres* on a second, more detailed memorandum. Porters and journeymen in the Parisian building trades presented similar petitions to the King in 1785.[51]

These petitions were not expressions of a credulous faith in royal justice. They occurred only when the trades or occupations in question fell directly under the jurisdiction of the crown or when conflicts involved disputed royal privileges. The petitions presented by workers in the Parisian quarries owed a great deal to the fact that, until 1779, the quarries fell directly under royal control. The porters and Parisian building workers who petitioned Louis XVI in 1785 did so because a disputed privilege (a title granted to a private company to transport parcels and messages in the capital) and a court ruling (by the *chambre royale des bâtiments*) implicated the crown in the issues in contention. The great majority of legal actions, however, came before the Parlements. Both because of the extent of its own territorial jurisdiction and because of the size of the capital itself, the largest number came before the Parlement of Paris.

Between 1650 and 1789 the Parlement of Paris heard appeals by at least 40 groups of Parisian journeymen in two dozen different trades.[52] Journeymen in most of the principal trades of Lyon, which fell within the Parlement's jurisdiction, also brought cases before the court in considerable numbers. At various times during the eighteenth century the Parlement of Paris dealt with cases presented by journeymen printers, hatters, stonecutters, silk-weavers, framework knitters, carpenters and dyers from Lyon. Intermittent appeals by journeymen in Marseille to the Parlement of Provence, in Nîmes to the Parlement of Toulouse, in Bordeaux to the Parlement of Guyenne, in Nantes to the Parlement of

51 A.N. Y 13 751 (7 September 1746); Y 13 693 (28 July 1784). See also Sonenscher, 'Journeymen, the Courts and the French Trades'.
52 See Appendix. For litigation of a similar character in a rural context, see Hilton Root, *Peasants and King in Burgundy* (Berkeley, California, 1987), chapter 5. Root's somewhat teleological emphasis upon the kinds of argument used in such litigation as a prefiguration of revolutionary political discourse ignores the natural law tradition outlined in chapter 2. For a recent discussion of the subtlety and range of issues that such arguments could embrace, see Istvan Hont, 'The Language of Sociability and Commerce', in Anthony Pagden, ed., *The Language of Political Theory in Early-Modern Europe* (Cambridge, 1987), pp. 253–76.

Brittany and in Rouen to that of Normandy are further testimony to the enduring significance of major test cases and legal trials of strength in the ordinary life of the eighteenth-century trades. Although appeals to the Parlements were complemented occasionally by appeals to the *conseil d'état*, so that some lawsuits lasted many years, the Parlements were entitled to ratify rulings by the council: a right that could, in its turn, become the basis of further cycles of appeals and counter-appeals. Throughout the century the Parlements remained the most important source of legal decisions affecting the trades.

Major test cases did not occur particularly often. A large corporation in which many different kinds of journeymen were employed, such as the Parisian joiners' corporation, was involved in no more than half a dozen substantial legal trials of strength between 1650 and 1789. Litigation on a comparable scale in other large Parisian trades – shoemakers, hatters, painters or saddlers, for example – was as infrequent.[53] Yet, although they were a relatively rare occurrence in the history of a single trade, lawsuits involving scores or hundreds of journeymen had a significance that outweighed their numerical infrequency. Appeals to one of the Parlements established precedents not only for the trade in question, but also for the corporate world as a whole. Appeals did more than settle episodic local disputes over wage-rates or working conditions, for these matters were the affair of the local courts responsible for the *police des arts et métiers*. They were designed to settle matters of principle and promote or prevent substantive changes to the formal relationship between masters and journeymen.

In most cases, journeymen were the appellants, but the defensive posture that they were forced to adopt did not mean that they were unsuccessful. In 1727 a number of masters in the Parisian roofing trade decided to modify the corporation's statutes of 1566 by abolishing two articles restricting the number of apprentices that masters were allowed to engage and imposing a maximum period of a week that journeymen from outside Paris could work in the capital. The decision was precipitated by a number of stoppages of work and fights between Parisian apprentices and journeymen and men from outside the capital.[54] The master roofers claimed that the Parisian apprentices and journeymen had exploited shortages of labour not only by 'exorbitant' wage-demands but by taking lead and other materials from the building sites where they worked. The journeymen appealed to the Parlement, calling upon the court to maintain the provisions of the statutes of 1566, a police sentence of 1701 and a

---

[53] For examples see Sonenscher, *Hatters*; 'Weavers, Wage-Rates and the Measurement of Work'; 'Journeymen, the Courts'.
[54] A.N. Y 14 523 (8 October 1726). Regrettably the *minutes* of the other *commissaires* who heard complaints against journeymen in the roofing trade in 1727 have not survived.

royal declaration of 1704, as well as to dismiss the insulting charge (*les termes injurieuses*) of the theft of lead. In 1729 the Parlement upheld their appeal and refused to sanction any change to the corporation's statutes.[55]

Forty years passed before the proposed changes to the corporation's statutes were finally sanctioned by the courts. The intervening period contained three major legal battles: from 1739 to 1746, 1750 to 1756, and 1763 to 1768.[56] In 1768, when the Parlement finally sanctioned all the changes that had first been proposed in 1727, the journeymen still insisted that men from the provinces were not entitled to go the Place de Grève to find work. '*C'est à tort*,' they argued, 'que les jurés couvreurs ont voulu installer les compagnons couvreurs forains en la place de Grève, qui est établie depuis cinq cens ans pour la place desdits compagnons (de Paris).'[57] The journeymen's confraternity of the Holy Trinity, attached to the abbey of Saint Denis de la Chartre, was a constant presence in the long sequence of legal campaigns. Its officials met every Sunday in an inn called *La Cave* after members of the confraternity had attended mass in the abbey. As was usual on such occasions, the offering was distributed among those present and afterwards, as one journeyman explained, 'on s'entendoit et serroit tout'.[58] In this instance, the composition and resources of a confraternity were reinforced by an almost impregnable legal position. The journeymen were able not only to invoke the provisions of the corporation's officials. The Parlement's ruling in favour of the journeymen in 1729 was based as much upon its awareness that the proposal had not been approved in due form as upon its acceptance of the legal precedents

Differences among master artisans played a part in the journeymen roofers' initial success. The proposal to change the roofers' statutes in 1727 was made by a group of master artisans, without the support of the corporation's officials. The Parlement's ruling in favour of the journeymen in 1729 was based as much upon its awareness that the proposal had not been approved in due form as upon its acceptance of the legal precedents

[55] A.N. X1a 8987 fol. 195 (21 July 1729); X1a 3547 (19 August 1729). On the theft of lead see A.N. AD+802 (6 September 1727), and below, p. 208.

[56] A.N. X1a 7505 fol. 76 (10 July 1743); E 1210b 18 (25 February 1744); X1a 3959 fol. 170 (20 August 1745); X1a 8750 fol. 216v (4 August 1746); B.N. F 21035 (*statuts des maîtres couvreurs*, pp. 49–70); MS. Joly de Fleury, 645, fol. 253; 2340 fol. 88 et seq.; Archives de la Préfecture de police, Fonds Lamoignon, 35 fol. 318; A.N. Y 11 167 (2 April 1750); X1a 4207 fol. 80v (27 August 1755); X1a 4244 (4 September 1756); A.N. Y 11 682 (26 July, 9 September 1763); Y 9466a (10 February 1764); Y 9500; AD XI 16 (31 May 1766); X1a 4528 (21 March 1766); X1a 4536 fol. 267 (20 June 1766); X1a 8087 fol. 30v (5 and 6 August 1766); X1a 4611 (1 August 1768).

[57] A.N. Y 12 768 (3 October 1768); *ibid.* (10 October 1768); Y 15 375 (11, 19 September, 21, 23 October, 7 November, 11, 12 December 1769); Y 10 899b (30 April 1770). A further series of disputes, over the length of the working day, occurred in 1779–81: A.N. AD XI 16 (19 June 1779); Y 11 020a (8 June 1779); Y 10 879b (30 April 1770); Y 13 689 (21 March 1781).

[58] A.N. Y 11 159 (18 February 1740).

[59] See particularly Bibliothèque de l'Ordre des Avocats, Paris, Fonds Gaultier-Debreil, 35 (68), *Mémoire en la cause pour Jean Chastel...et autres au nombre de quatre-vingt-six, tous compagnons couvreurs de la ville et fauxbourgs de Paris* (Paris, 1743).

that the journeymen cited. Divisions, or the absence of divisions, within corporations also contributed to journeymen's ability to mount legal campaigns. The Parisian journeymen locksmiths failed to mount an appeal to the Parlement against a decision by their corporation in 1746 requiring them to register with the corporate office, because, despite some sympathy from master locksmiths, they were unable to find anyone prepared to challenge the decision in public. In other appeals, master artisans played a more active part. Over a dozen master hatters intervened in an appeal by the Parisian journeymen against a court ruling in 1748. Opposition by some master painters and decorators repeatedly undermined corporate attempts to establish a formal system of *placement* in Paris between 1763 and 1789. In some cases, as occurred among the Parisian wheelwrights in 1766, support from master artisans came from men who were working as journeymen; in others, among painters and decorators for example, it came from employers of relatively large numbers of journeymen. In both cases, the bazaar-like economy of the trades in question generated pressures that cut across formal divisions between masters and journeymen. [60]

Yet support from master artisans was a tactical advantage rather than a strategic necessity. Even when master artisans did not intervene, journeymen were still willing to embark upon campaigns in the courts, not only because of the possibility of success, but also because litigation itself was likely to lead to divisions among master artisans and pressure to bring disputes to an end. The legal campaigns mounted by the journeymen roofers between 1739 and 1768 had no support from master artisans. Nor did those organised by Parisian journeymen joiners and hatters in 1755 and 1785 respectively. The journeymen locksmiths' attempt to organise an appeal in 1746 failed as much because their internal divisions precipitated a decision to stop work before the officials of their confraternity could find the lawyers they needed, as because of the absence of support from masters of the corporation. [61] Journeymen organised their own appeals and used the main forms of eighteenth-century legal argument – appeals to precedent, assertions of difference and invocations of natural rights – because the contractual character of the natural law tradition implied that some of them could claim a right to be heard when they were named in corporate decisions affecting their civil rights and obligations.

[60] Garrioch and Sonenscher, 'Compagnonnages, Confraternities', pp. 35–6; Sonenscher, *Hatters*, p. 92; B.H.V.P. 402 104 *Mémoire signifié pour la communauté des maîtres charrons-carossiers de la ville et faubourgs de Paris* (Paris, 1767); A.N. X^{1a} 4528 (24 March 1766); X^{1a} 8078 fol. 4548 fol. 847 (6 September 1766); 4553 fol. 132v (19 January 1767); X^{1a} 8078 fol. 282 (11 June 1766); 8079 fol. 70 (14 June 1766); 8100 fol. 345 (4 February 1767); Y 9534 (14 April 1766); 9525 (26 April 1766); 11 007^a (14 May 1766); 11 007^b (18 December 1766, 7 July 1767); 11 010 (8 and 13 May 1769); Bibliothèque de l'Arsénal, MS. Bastille 12 369. On the relationship between the economy of the trades and the interests of different kinds of master artisan, see below, chapters 4 and 7.

[61] A.N. Y 14 391 (7 August 1746); Y 13 751 (13 September 1746).

The combination of appeals to precedent, assertion of difference and invocations of natural rights occurred particularly frequently in legal campaigns against corporate decisions requiring journeymen to register with *bureaux de placement* and carry certificates attesting to the satisfactory completion of their work. Journeymen insisted that marriage and the entitlements that apprenticeship conferred set men in settled abodes apart from the peripatetic sector of the workforce of the trades. Nailmakers in Nantes argued in 1768 that regulations designed to establish 'une police raisonable [*sic*]' had been given 'une extension abusive' when they were applied to married journeymen. The requirement to register and be given work by a corporate official would endow the nailmakers' corporation with 'une sorte de jurisdiction qui ne pouroit que dégénérer en tiraisné...et qui seroit en elle [même] destructive du droit naturel'. Married men were not 'compagnons passagers' but 'citoyens'. They paid the *capitation*, performed their duties as members of the *garde* and generally fulfilled 'tous les devoirs d'habitant'. The corporation's rights were limited ones and, like all privileges, could be interpreted only in the narrowest sense, 'suivant l'axiome *odia restringende* [*sic*]. Any other construction would prejudice the natural rights of married men. The journeymen also referred to a decision by the joiners' corporation abolishing their corporate labour exchange and allowing journeymen to find work themselves, a decision that had been sanctioned by the Parlement of Brittany in February 1768.[62]

Comparison between proper regulation – 'une police raisonnable' – and despotism was a standard rhetorical procedure, used in both legal memoranda and ordinary speech. While regulation was entirely compatible with the contractual character of civil society, tyrannical authority was an invitation to appeal to natural rights. Invocation of natural rights was a frequent component of appeals against certificates and systems of registration primarily because the power vested in corporations to direct journeymen to work for masters selected by a corporate official was a flagrant violation of the natural law principle of freedom of choice. Thus, in 1755 journeymen joiners in Paris appealed to the Parlement against a corporate decision establishing a system of *placement* and called to be maintained

dans la possession et liberté où ils sont de tems immémorial de se louer à tels maîtres qu'ils jugeront à propos, sans congé, permission, ni certificat de qui que ce soit, et d'en sortir aussi librement suivant leur convention.[63]

[62] A.C. Nantes, HH 120.
[63] A.N. X^{1b} 3657 (25 March 1755); X^{1a} 4193 fol. 5v (25 March 1755); X^{1a} 7791 fol. 300v and fol. 322 (1 October 1755); X^{1a} 7795 (11 December 1755); 4239 fol. 289 (4 August 1756); K 1031 (121).

Journeymen wheelwrights described a corporate decision of 1766 (and modelled on that taken by the joiners) as the annihilation of liberty and the establishment of slavery, while journeymen harness makers and saddlers (*selliers*) claimed in 1768 'qu'ils n'ont jamais voulu, et ne veulent point vivre dans le dérèglement et le désordre, mais seulement éviter la tirainie et l'esclavage dont ils sont menacés'.[64]

Argument was not, however, confined to the semantic field of natural rights, civil obligation, slavery and tyranny. It was equally possible to assert difference, and claim that while the provisions of corporate regulation might apply to one trade or group of journeymen, they could not apply to another, because the needs, circumstances and identities of those affected were radically different. In 1769, long after the Parlement had rejected the Parisian joiners' appeal, journeymen joiners who made trellises argued that they were not bound by the obligation to register, because it applied only to journeymen who made coach bodies. They were, they said, trellis-makers and were free. They would prefer to work the land or carry water than register with the corporate office.[65] Journeymen locksmiths, faced with similar rulings, claimed that they applied only to particular sectors of the trade. In Paris, in 1746, locksmiths working on wrought iron claimed that only men making springs for coaches or the simpler sort of building materials were required to carry certificates. Journeymen locksmiths in Bordeaux made similar claims in 1785, arguing that married men, or men paid by the month, or men doing certain kinds of work were exempt from registration. The Parisian sculptors claimed that certificates were not appropriate to 'gens à talent' whose work embellished the facades of aristocratic abodes.[66] Turners in Marseille stated that they were not 'compagnons' but 'ouvriers' and could not be bound by measures that applied to the *compagnonnages*. Even journeymen working in their rooms as *chambrelans* argued that corporate officials had no right to confiscate their tools and materials on Sundays without special authorisation, because the provisions of court rulings prohibiting work at home applied only to working days.[67]

[64] 'Ils voyent dans ces arrêtés leur liberté anéantie, l'esclavage établie, un avenir qui promet les traitemens les plus barbares': B.H.V.P. 402 104 *Mémoire signifié pour la communauté des maîtres charrons-carossiers de la ville et faubourgs de Paris* (Paris, 1767); B.N. MS. Joly de Fleury 648 fol. 293. Sonenscher, 'Journeymen, the Courts', pp. 95–100.

[65] 'Disant être libres, être treillageurs et non menuisiers…qu'ils aimeroient mieux travailler à la terre et porter de l'eau.' A.N. Y 13 673 (29 April 1769).

[66] Garrioch and Sonenscher, '*Compagnonnages*, Confraternities', p. 36; A.D. Gironde, C1775 (1 March 1785): 'les uns prétendent qu'il a [sic] différence qu'on met dans les salaires qu'il [sic] retirents [sic] de leur travail les dispence de cette execution: d'autres pretende [sic] que c'et [sic] le genre de travail dont il [sic] s'occupent le plus communement qui doit les en dispencer: d'autres enfin prétendent qu'étant marié et domicilié en cette ville il [sic] ne doivent pas être soumis aux mêmes règles et la même discipline que les autres ouvriers.' See too A.N. X1a 4027 fol. 124v (28 March 1748); X1b 3578 (4 May 1748); X1a 4039 fol. 518 (26 August 1748); B.N. F 22 182 (12 March 1749).

[67] A.C. Marseille, FF 394 (24 July 1784); HH 404 (8 January 1781): *Gazette des tribunaux*, 13 (1782), p. 25.

Faced with the claims that journeymen could present to the courts, master artisans were obliged to devise arguments that met their own purposes. Although it was always possible to claim that journeymen had no right to take legal action at all because they were not members of properly constituted corporate bodies, the frequency with which the courts allowed appeals by large numbers of journeymen is evidence enough that arguments of this kind were an insufficient basis of a successful case. Appeals to the Parlement of Paris by journeymen carpenters, printers, hatters, roofers, joiners, wheelwrights, painters and saddlers were made in the names of hundreds of individuals and were all too evidently based upon the resources of collective association. There was, moreover, nothing to prevent journeymen from using their funds to support a test case by a single individual, as the journeymen carpenters of Lyon did in 1744 when a journeyman named Noel Robin appealed against a corporate decision prohibiting journeymen from finding work for one another because, he claimed, it contravened a ruling by the Parlement in 1666.[68] The contractual character of the natural law tradition implied that those named in the wording of corporate decisions were entitled to be heard. Corporations were obliged therefore to base their cases upon a more extensive repertoire of argument.

General reference to the law-bound character of civil society served as one component of that repertoire. Master artisans were as adept as journeymen in playing upon the standard rhetorical tropes of the natural law tradition in their own arguments. The master joiners of Bordeaux accused the journeymen of the trade of seeking to 'asservir les maîtres qu'ils servent au despotisme le plus affreux' by undermining the orderly stability of the rule of law. The Parisian wheelwrights' corporation argued that its decision to establish a system of registration in 1766 was designed

Reference to the utility of particular decisions in the light of prevailing circumstances and the needs of the public formed a second component of the repertoire. The Parisian roofers repeatedly argued that statutes drawn up in 1566 were entirely inappropriate to the great city that the capital had become by the eighteenth century. The wheelwrights pointed out that

une discipline générale, qui tient en équilibre les droits du maître et ceux des personnes qui s'occupent de l'art de charrons. Cette délibération frappe également sur les maîtres en boutique, sur ceux qui font le compagnonnage, sur les compagnons, sur les apprentifs; elle tient entre tous la balance de la justice et veille à leurs intérêts, à leur tranquillité, à leur sureté commune.[69]

68   A.N. X¹ᵃ 3928 fol. 327 (27 June 1744). A corporate deliberation of 27 May 1744 indicates that this was not an isolated appeal (A.D. Rhône 3E 2804, 27 May 1744).
69   A.D. Gironde, 12B 367 (20 August 1781); B.H.V.P. 402 104 *Mémoire signifié pour la communauté des maîtres charrons-carossiers de la ville et fauxbourgs de Paris* (Paris, 1767). A.N. X¹ᵇ 3854 (19 December 1766); X¹ᵃ 8101 fol. 99 (7 February 1767); X¹ᵃ 8114 (20 June 1767); X¹ᵃ 8121 (29 August 1767); X¹ᵃ 4618 fol. 185 (1 September 1768).

their trade met the universal need for transport. Comparisons with other trades were therefore irrelevant.

Chaque corps a ses règles, des usages qui lui sont propres, lesquels sont déterminés par le besoin, par ses liasons au Public, par l'intérêt général, par son intérêt particulier.[70]

Yet comparisons were, in fact, the most decisive arguments that corporations could deploy, since corporations were usually very much better placed than journeymen to cite precedents which favoured their claims.

Citation of precedent ensured that the formal history of the trades was somewhat analogous to a genealogical tree, although the line of descent from one precedent to another was more usually tangential or lateral than vertical, and ran across many different trades and cities. The Parisian joiners' decision to establish a system of registration, printed certificates of good conduct and a corporate labour exchange in 1755 was modelled upon an earlier decision by the city's locksmiths, ratified by the Parlement in 1746. The joiners' decision was used as a precedent by the saddlers in 1763 and *their* decision was cited by the wheelwrights in 1766. The two rulings were later invoked during a dispute among the painters and sculptors in 1786. Rulings made at the beginning of the century continued to be cited in the courts nearly 100 years later. A sentence by the Châtelet in 1702 was still invoked by the Parisian joiners in 1785.[71] Precedents established in one locality were transposed to the same trades in other cities: from Paris or Lyon to Dijon or Marseille, from Toulouse to Bordeaux, from Bordeaux to Nantes, and from Nantes to Rouen, in a continuous process of comparison and adaptation.[72]

Journeymen, of course, used the same procedures. The journeymen joiners of Paris challenged their corporation's regulations by questioning the legality of the decision by the locksmiths, while the journeymen wheelwrights argued that the saddlers' regulations were more appropriate to their trade than those adopted by the joiners. Journeymen painters referred in 1785 to a decision by the Parlement on the saddlery trade in the previous year, while the saddlers referred to an earlier ruling in 1766, just as, in 1766, they had cited a ruling of 1744. Litigation in the hatting

[70] *Ibid.*; B.N. MS. Joly de Fleury, 2340 fol. 93, *Mémoire pour les syndics, jurés et communauté des maîtres couvreurs de la ville de Paris* (Paris, 1743).

[71] On disputes in the painting trade, see chapter 7 below; A.N. Y 14 348 (5 December 1785); Sonenscher, 'Journeymen. the Courts', pp. 87–8. See also notes 60 and 66 above.

[72] As the master locksmiths of Toulouse informed their counterparts in Bordeaux in 1785, 'notre corps s'est enfin décidé de prendre des arrangements au sujet des compagnons...C'est pourquoy nous vous aprenons par cette présente que nous sommes tous prêts et que lorsque tout sera finy nous prendrons la liberté de vous en faire passer une exemplaire'. A.D. Gironde 6E 112 (3 August 1785). For other examples, see chapters 2 and 8.

trade invariably entailed comparison between rulings by the Parlements of Paris and Provence.[73] Throughout the eighteenth century citation of precedent was one of the pillars of legal argument and formed a continuous counterpoint to the rhetoric of corporate particularity.

Precedent could take two forms. The first was merely designed to demonstrate the similarities or differences between particular trades in order to prove or deny the exemplary character of earlier court rulings. The nailmakers of Nantes argued that it was pointless for their journeymen to refer to a ruling by the Parlement of Brittany abolishing a corporate labour exchange in the joining trade as a precedent because the trades were totally different. While a joiner's work varied from the excessively simple to the elaborately ornate, the work done by nailmakers was of a very much more uniform quality. Masters and journeymen in the nailmaking trade had no need to make a careful choice of particular kinds of work or particular kinds of skill. The Parisian wheelwrights dismissed their journeymen's invocation of regulations affecting the working day in the saddlery trade as a means of opposing a working day that began at 4 a.m. in summer and 5 a.m. in winter by referring to the difference between the trades in question. Saddlers performed useful and agreeable work, but it was not of universal necessity. A more appropriate comparison, they argued, was with the 16 hours performed by bookbinders, the 14 hours by journeymen farriers and the long hours of night-work carried out by bakers, butchers, brewers and wine-sellers. Wheelwrights met the needs of travellers. Journeymen unable to recognise the importance of those needs 'ont à se reprocher d'avoir choisir un état qui ne répond pas à la délicatesse de leur tempérament'.[74]

Legal precedents arising from disputed corporate decisions had a more precise significance. The Parlements were the final courts of appeal and, once they had produced their verdicts, it was very difficult to carry formal opposition any further. There was therefore a considerable difference between a court ruling made in response to a corporate decision (an *arrêt sur requête*) and a ruling in which journeymen had been heard (an *arrêt contradictoire*). Once journeymen had presented their case and a Parlement had heard their appeal, its verdict was final. As precedent followed precedent, and the combined effects of pressure from master artisans and the predispositions of the magistracy reverberated from trade to trade and city to city, the character of the formal relationship between masters and journeymen was gradually modified.

Court rulings sanctioning corporate decisions to establish labour

73 A.N. X[1a] 4239 (4 August 1756); B.H.V.P. 402 104; A.N. X[1b] 8720 (5 February 1785); 8734 (6 August 1785); 4243 (5 September 1785); 4247 (23 November 1785); 4253 (21 February 1786); 8716 (11 December 1784); 8076 (14 May 1766); X[2b] 997 (20 October 1745); Sonenscher, 'Journeymen, the Courts', p. 88 and *Hatters*, pp. 150–1.
74 A.C. Nantes, HH 120; B.H.V.P. 402 104.

exchanges, certificates of good conduct and systems of registration were particularly important precedents both because they were relatively easily transposed from trade to trade and place to place and because of the significance of the legal principles that they established. *Billets de congé*, or the more elaborate *livrets* of the late eighteenth century, represented a substantial departure from the contractual character of the natural law tradition. In practical terms, they appeared to allow master artisans to withhold a signature or refuse to hand over the vital document and, as a result, prevent journeymen from leaving their shops. In a more legalistic sense, they appeared to confer substantial powers upon private individuals instead of the corporations to which they belonged. Allusions to slavery and despotism had a precise meaning in this context. As the journeymen tailors of Lyon put it in 1688, an obligation to seek a master's formal consent before they went to work elsewhere was 'contre la police et la liberté'. Civil obligations were limited by the provisions of the civil law, which, in the context of the trades, applied to corporations rather than individuals. If a master artisan had the power to prevent journeymen from working where they chose, 'ils seroient proprement les esclaves des maistres'.[75]

The Parlements were undoubtedly aware of the problem and were relatively circumspect in sanctioning corporate decisions establishing labour exchanges, certificates of good conduct and compulsory periods of notice. The care taken to define the precise modalities of such systems was indicative of the legal difficulties that they engendered. The obvious tension between the power that registration appeared to confer upon private individuals and the civil rights that journeymen, particularly married men who belonged to confraternities, could claim, was a fertile source of detailed legal argument. At different times, the courts were obliged to decide whether printed certificates were to be issued free or whether journeymen should pay for them, whether they should be held by masters or remain in the possession of journeymen during periods of employment, whether registration was the responsibility of masters or men, whether journeymen should register once or whenever they changed shop, whether journeymen could register and place themselves in work, be placed by any master of a corporation or be placed only by the corporate official responsible for the *bureau de placement*.[76]

Technical decisions of this kind were an oblique acknowledgment of the formal egalitarianism inherent in the contractual character of civil society. Since journeymen were not slaves, their masters could not be despots. The

[75] A.C. Lyon HH 185 (18 December 1688). The original ruling by the *consulat* of 3 October 1688 is printed in B.N. F 26473 *Règlements des maistres tailleurs d'habits de la ville et fauxbourgs de Lyon* (Lyon, 1729), p. 38.

[76] Sonenscher, 'Journeymen, the Courts', pp. 96–100. See also below, chapter 8.

tension between formal equality and potential servility intruded into other aspects of their relationship. Although the disputed question of registration and certificates of good conduct was the major area in which the courts were forced to consider the relationship between natural rights and civil obligations, it was not the only one. Arguments over the length of the working day, or the respective rights and obligations of masters and journeymen over periods of notice, fell within the same framework of debate and definition. Even a relatively esoteric dispute in 1757 between the Parisian shoemakers' corporation and the journeymen's confraternity, over whether the confraternity's administrators were entitled to employ other journeymen during their term of office, was conducted within the same terms of reference. The journeymen asserted that they were not 'les valets des maîtres'. 'Ils travaillent pour eux dans le métier de cordonnier mais ils ne sont astreints à aucune oeuvre servile.'[77] Their confraternity was not bound by the rules of the masters' corporation and, among its titles, was the right of its officials to employ other journeymen during their term of office.

Throughout the eighteenth century, the rhetoric of natural law that was drawn upon so frequently in legal argument and formal submissions to the courts was echoed in less formal contexts. An anonymous letter addressed to a Parisian grocer's clerk (*garçon épicier*) soon after he had registered with the corporate office in 1786 informed him that

Cela est très digne de vous, c'est à dire des maîtres et des valets. Vous n'avez pas changé de sentiment. Je souaite que cela puisse continuer. Vous avez toujours été un plat, un lâche et un jean foutre.[78]

Journeymen locksmiths who registered in Paris in 1746 were 'des laquais', and, according to a locksmith in Bordeaux in 1785, 'des f...spontons. Ils faisoient comme des portefaix en se faisant numéroter.' A journeyman tailor seen working during a dispute over registration in Marseille in 1731 was 'un forçat de travailler'. The *bayles* of the joiners' corporation in Bordeaux were 'des marchands de billets' while the official of the glaziers' corporation in Nantes responsible for placing journeymen was told that he would have journeymen 'lorsqu'il naîgera et quant on lui en coulera dans un moulle'.[79]

The language of the courts was also the idiom of the *cabaret*. Master artisans and the journeymen they employed faced one another as formal equals. Unless the courts ruled otherwise, the rights of the former were not grounded upon the subordination of the latter. The limited and exceptional character of civil rights and obligations in the jurisprudence of eighteenth-

77 A.N. L 551 (42). See below, chapter 8.
78 B.N. MS. Joly de Fleury, 1732 fol. 353.
79 A.D. Gironde, 12B 376 (7 April 1785); A.C. Marseille, FF 337 (6 June 1731); A.D. Gironde, 13B 213 (25 June 1755); A.C. Nantes HH 153 (28 December 1756).

century France favoured a form of dialogue between masters and journeymen in which assertions of the particular and specific took precedence over invocations of the uniform and universal. Since the particular was exceptional, it was the particular that required the sanction of the courts. Yet assertions of particularity can all too easily mask the wider tradition of natural law to which they belonged. When a journeyman like Alexandre Voltaire talked of freeing himself from slavery, or a printer like Nicolas Contat referred to corporate regulation as despotic authority, it is apparent that the culture of eighteenth-century journeymen was more deeply rooted in the culture of the polity as a whole than too literal an interpretation of corporate particularity might suggest.

The prevailing conventions of civil jurisprudence in eighteenth-century France meant that some disputes between masters and journeymen were conducted in the courts. Others, however, were not. In some cases, this was because what was in dispute did not lend itself readily to formal litigation. In others, it was because some journeymen were unable to assert the entitlements and rights that others claimed.[80] The reason why some disputes between masters and journeymen were legal in character, while others were not, owed much to journeymen's awareness of, and ability to evoke, the rights that formal entitlements and civil distinctions supplied. Yet the law was only a component of the world of the trades. Many aspects of the relationship between masters and journeymen derived from circumstances and expectations that were not established by the courts. If the language of the law cast the relationship between masters and journeymen into a dialogue over rights and obligations, it also magnified formal differences and ignored many of the similarities that obtained between some masters and some journeymen. The clarity and durability of legal formulae mask much of the fluidity and impermanence of the workshop economy. The world beyond the courts was one in which time and money, rather than rights and obligations, occupied a more substantial and significant place.

[80] See below, chapter 9.

CHAPTER 4

The world of the trades

The formal terms of the relationship between masters and journeymen were set out in the words of the law, but what happened in eighteenth-century workshops depended upon more than legal prescription. Corporate statutes and corporate decisions were cryptic summaries of a number of more extended dialogues: between masters and journeymen, between different groups of master artisans, and between journeymen themselves. Artisans, whether they were masters of corporations or residents of privileged suburbs like the *faubourg* Saint Antoine in Paris, owned or leased workshops, sometimes formed partnerships or took on sub-contracted work, bought in materials and equipment, employed a certain number of journeymen, sought outlets for the goods that they produced and sold them to a great variety of intermediaries or final consumers. Journeymen too were not solely concerned with the work that they did and the wages they earned. Some, but not all of them, were the sons of master artisans, while others had survived the ordeal of apprenticeship. Most of them were single men who expected to marry by the age of 30 and, by one route or another, to establish themselves either as masters of a corporation, or as independent artisans.

The life of the trades was made up of several different temporal rhythms. There were the daily, weekly and seasonal cycles of work and employment; there were also the slower, but no less important, cycles of working lives which, in different ways, governed the acquisition and transmission of patrimonies in particular trades and localities. To understand the relationship between journeymen and their masters in eighteenth-century France it is necessary to have an initial sense of the significance of both these temporal processes. The world of the trades was not static: it changed as membership of the trades changed, and as local structures of employment and opportunities to enter particular sectors of production changed. The environment in which masters and journeymen defined and argued over their respective rights and obligations was shaped as much by these two factors as by the provisions of the law. What happened in

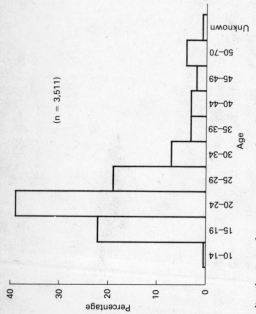

4.1 Age-distribution of journeymen employed at Tours (1782–9). Source: A.D. Indre-et-Loire, E 492.

eighteenth-century workshops was related not only to the daily and weekly cycles of work, wages and consumption, but also to the more complex economy of a working life.

The relationship between journeymen and their masters was a relationship between young men and older men. Figure 4.1, for example, is a graph of the ages of 3,511 journeymen who registered to find work in the town of Tours between 1782 and 1789. Nearly two thirds of them (61·2 per cent) were less than 25 years old. A little over a quarter (26·6 per cent) were between 25 and 34, while only a tenth (11·9 per cent) were 35 or more. The proportions were radically different from the age-composition of the male population of France as a whole during the latter half of the eighteenth century. Excluding all those aged 14 or under (who accounted for no more than 0·3 per cent of the journeymen who registered in Tours), a little over a quarter of the male population of France (25·9 per cent) was aged between 15 and 24, a little over a fifth (22·4 per cent) was aged between 25 and 34, while over half (51·7 per cent) was at least 35 years old.[1] There were over twice as many young men working as

[1] Figures of the age-composition of the male population of France aged 15 or more are based upon Louis Henry and Yves Blayo, 'La Population de la France de 1740 à 1860', *Population*, 30 (1975), pp. 71–122 (p. 102). The percentages given are those of the average male population between 1740 and 1789, less the population aged 0–14. Figures of journeymen's ages have been calculated from A.D. Indre-et-Loire, E 492 and A.D. Seine-Maritime, 5E 654 and 649. They are the only registers of registration on which the ages of journeymen were recorded. The ages of master artisans have been calculated from a wide range of sources in which the ages of witnesses in criminal

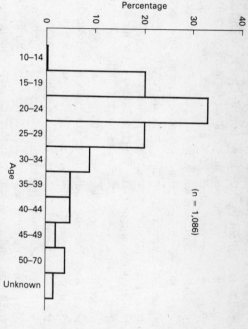

4.2 Age-distribution of journeymen locksmiths employed in Rouen (1782–91). Source: A.D. Seine-Maritime, 5E 654 and 649.

Percentage
(n = 1,086)

Age
10–14
15–19
20–24
25–29
30–34
35–39
40–44
45–49
50–70
Unknown

journeymen in Tours and less than a quarter as many men who had reached their 35th year as in the male population as a whole. It is clear, in other words, that work for wages was a temporary condition for the great majority of journeymen. By the age of 35 most of them had either become master artisans or abandoned the trades altogether.

There were, of course, minor variations among trades and between localities. The proportion of the 558 journeymen shoemakers aged 25 or more who registered in Tours was a little over 30 per cent, while just over 35 per cent of the 477 journeymen joiners (and exactly a third of the 311 journeymen locksmiths) who registered fell within the same age-group. Just over half (53·8 per cent) of the 1,086 journeymen locksmiths who registered to find work in the city of Rouen between 1782 and 1791 were aged between 15 and 24 (Figure 4.2). Their mean age was somewhat higher than that of the heterogeneous contingent of journeymen who registered for work in Tours, and the proportion of men aged 35 or more (14·6 per cent) was slightly larger. A small number of them (3·1 per cent) were married, and an even smaller number (0·7 per cent) were said to be master artisans working as journeymen. None the less, the great majority of the men who registered in both Tours and Rouen were young men. All the evidence that can be found indicates that most journeymen were

proceedings arising from disputes in the trades were recorded. They have been confirmed in a study of the ages of new members of the corporations of eighteenth-century Dijon: see Edward Shepherd, 'Social and Geographic Mobility of the Eighteenth-Century Guild Artisan: An Analysis of Guild Receptions in Dijon, 1700–1790', in Steven L. Kaplan and Cynthia J. Koepp, eds, *Work in France* (Ithaca, 1986), pp. 97–130 (pp. 126–7).

young, usually single men in their late teens and early twenties, while their masters were usually married and a dozen or more years older.

This difference was one effect of the complex process by which membership of the corporations was renewed over the generations. At any one moment in time, a given cohort of journeymen was poised between a number of possible destinies. Some of them would become master artisans and members of a corporation. Some would set themselves up in areas like the *faubourg* Saint-Antoine in Paris, which fell outside the jurisdiction of the corporations. Others would live and work in little towns or large villages where corporations did not exist. Yet others would remain journeymen all their lives, or would move gradually away from the trades with which they had been associated, into domestic service, the army, the navy or the precarious and growing world of the itinerant poor.[2] Two divisions were fundamental to the urban economy of eighteenth-century France. There was a division between those who made things and those who moved them, and there was a further division among those who made things: between those who became master artisans and those who did not. The world of the trades, and the world of the corporations in particular, was a world of relative prosperity. Beyond it lay varying degrees of penury. Yet the evidence suggests that there was a considerable gulf between the world of the trades and the labouring population as a whole. It existed because most journeymen were able to become master artisans.

A little over a tenth of the 1,086 journeymen locksmiths who registered for work in Rouen between 1782 and 1791 were at least 35 years old. The figure can be taken as a rough indication of the minimum number of men who remained journeymen all their lives. The proportion of journeymen locksmiths of over 35 admitted to the Hôtel Dieu of Nîmes during almost the same period was very similar. Between January 1777 and June 1785 a total of 151 journeymen locksmiths were admitted to the hospital.[3] The

---

[2]   Most social mobility in the eighteenth-century trades was therefore downward, rather than upward. This continued to be the case in the nineteenth century: see Jean-Claude Farcy, 'Rural Artisans in the Beauce during the Nineteenth Century', in Geoffrey Crossick and Heinz-Gerhard Haupt, eds., *Shopkeepers and Master Artisans in Nineteenth-Century Europe* (London, 1984), pp. 219–38. Census returns in late nineteenth-century Germany suggest that as many as 50 per cent of journeymen in the shoemaking trade abandoned the trade altogether: Josef Ehmer, 'Master's Household or Journeyman's Family: The Units of Artisan Outwork Production in Central Europe and England in the Mid-Nineteenth Century' (paper presented to the ESRC Workshop on Proto-Industrial Communities, University of Essex, October 1986). It is probable however that more integrated markets and competition from capital-intensive units of production played a part in this high rate of failure. On the eighteenth-century poor, see Olwen Hufton, *The Poor of Eighteenth-Century France* (Oxford, 1974).

[3]   The figures have been extracted from the unclassified registers of admissions to the Hôtel-Dieu. For a discussion of the sources, see Colin Jones and Michael Sonenscher, 'The Social Functions of the Hospital in Eighteenth-Century France: The Case of the Hôtel-Dieu of Nîmes', *French Historical Studies*, 13 (1983), pp. 172–214. Similarly, nearly half (47 per

4.3 Age-distribution of journeymen locksmiths admitted to the Hôtel Dieu of Nîmes (1777–85). Source: A.D. Gard, unclassified papers of the Hôtel Dieu of Nîmes.

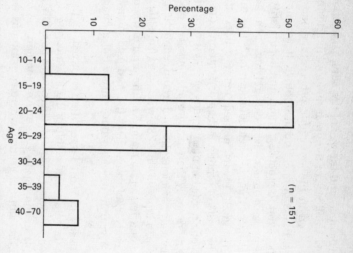

(n = 151)

majority of them (64·2 per cent) were young men, of the same age as the majority of journeymen who registered for work in Rouen (see Figure 4.3). Most of them were simply exhausted after many days of walking, or had been involved in fights or accidents at work. A little under ten per cent of them were aged 35 or more. They were the other side of the corporate world, the men who worked for wages all their lives.

The proportion is, of course, a minimum, because an indeterminate number of a given cohort of journeymen abandoned work in the trades altogether. It is impossible to measure the size of this dark figure with any real precision, since it is likely to have varied from time to time and place to place, but the steep fall in the proportion of journeymen aged 35 or more in the trades of Tours and Rouen, the substantial discrepancy between the

cent) of a sample of 780 men aged under thirty drinking in eighteenth-century Parisian *cabarets* were journeymen or unspecified artisans, while only 12 per cent of under thirty-year-old drinkers were master artisans or shopkeepers. Inversely, 27 per cent of the over thirty-year-olds belonged to the former category, but 36 per cent were master artisans or shopkeepers: Thomas Brennan, *Public Drinking and Popular Culture in Eighteenth-Century Paris* (Princeton, 1988), p. 153.

age of most journeymen and the age of the adult population as a whole, and the relatively small size of the great majority of artisanal enterprises all suggest that, even in the late eighteenth century, most journeymen became master artisans of one kind or another. It was not necessary to belong to a corporation to practise a trade, and the majority of those who did practised their trades on a modest scale, relying upon the labour of kin or employing no more than a single journeyman.[4] The suburbs of most cities and many small towns housed many trades that were not incorporated. The costs of renting a shop or acquiring the small number of fixed installations needed in most trades were not very great. Materials were invariably more costly than fixed installations. The price of what was probably a relatively spacious (it had room enough for ten chairs) shoemakers' shop in Marseille in 1786 was, apart from the rent, only 623 *livres*, and three quarters of that sum was the price of the unsold stock of shoes and leather. Nor, of course, was the sum paid in cash. Instead, the purchaser had a year to pay for what consisted of a quantity of readily saleable goods.[5]

Yet most artisans in most large cities belonged to the incorporated trades. In Paris, the total membership of the 117 incorporated trades in the early 1720s stood at some 35,000.[6] There were probably only a quarter as many artisans in the *faubourg* Saint-Antoine and the other privileged areas.[7] Even in the south of France, where corporations were established

[4] On the size of artisanal enterprises, the distribution of the workforce and the substantial hierarchies among master artisans, see chapter 5 below.

[5] A. D. Bouches-du-Rhône, 351E[1198] fol. 208v (27 April 1786). Other trades were, for obvious reasons, more capital-intensive. Some figures for the hatting trade can be found in Sonenscher, *Hatters*, pp. 41–56.

[6] The only surviving figures of membership of the Parisian corporations during the eighteenth century are printed in Jacques Savary des Bruslons, *Dictionnaire universel de commerce*, 6th edn (Paris, 1750), vol. 1, p. 1056 *et seq.* They were based upon the lists of members drawn up by the officials of the corporations in 1723, 1724 and 1725. They reappear in every subsequent publication, notably Expilly's *Dictionnaire géographique, historique et politique* (Paris, 1768), vol. 5, pp. 418–20. My initial excitement in discovering a manuscript list of the members of the corporations in 1765 (Archives de la Ville de Paris, D⁵ B⁶ 346) rapidly evaporated when it became clear that the figures there had also been copied from Savary. The few alternative figures are cited below, p. 115.

[7] At the end of the century the number of enterprises in the *faubourg* Saint-Antoine stood at some 1,826: Raymonde Monnier, *Le Faubourg Saint-Antoine (1789–1815)* (Paris, 1981), p. 305. Earlier figures can be found in A.N. F¹² 781ᶜ&ᵈ: see Steven L. Kaplan, 'Les Corporations, les "faux-ouvriers" et le faubourg Saint-Antoine au xviiie siècle', *Annales E.S.C.*, 43 (1988), pp. 453–78. The most precise figures were supplied by the corporation of curriers in 1720. They stated that there were 38 independent masters in the suburb employing a total of 183 journeymen. The shoemakers stated that there were 1,160 shoemakers in the *faubourg*, a figure that seems greatly exaggerated, as does the tailors' claim that there were 'plus du double' the number of *ouvriers sans qualité* than masters of the corporation. In 1737 it was stated that there were 317 stocking frames in the privileged areas and 428 in the area covered by the corporation (B.N. MS. Joly de Fleury 1732 fol. 215v). The inhabitants of the other suburbs fell within the jurisdiction of the corporations. On the economy of the *faubourg* Saint-Marcel, see Haim Burstin, *Le Faubourg Saint-Marcel à l'époque révolutionnaire* (Paris, 1983), pp. 90–267.

only towards the end of the seventeenth century, most artisans in large cities were members of an incorporated trade.[8] The majority of artisans who belonged to corporations did so not only because corporate officials were active in prosecuting individuals (*ouvriers sans qualité*) who practised a trade without the requisite title to do so, but also because membership of a corporation conferred certain important advantages.[9]

Three in particular stand out. Corporations acted as tax assessors for the royal government and made it possible for master artisans to exercise a degree of self-regulation in their contributions to the public revenue. Corporations also had their own solicitors, barristers and notaries and, in certain instances, were prepared to meet the costs of litigation undertaken by individual master artisans. Finally, membership of a corporation provided artisans with regulated access to the materials used in their trades. Most of these materials were not, of course, locally available – they were supplied by merchants and large commercial houses, and were sold in designated places under regulated conditions. In many cases materials were delivered to a stockyard or shed adjoining the corporate office.[10] There were, in addition, many specialised markets, such as the *halle aux cuirs* or the *halle aux vins* in Paris. In either case, the officials of the corporations were required to control both the terms upon which materials were sold and the identities of those who purchased them. Litigation between members of a corporation over the imputed failure of corporate officials to carry out these functions is indirect evidence of the

8   Here confraternities of master artisans also had an enduring public function, as the legal cases cited above (p. 80) indicate. On Marseille, see Maurice Agulhon, *Pénitents et francs-maçons de l'ancienne Provence* (Paris, 1968), pp. 68–85; on Nîmes, see the figures of the size of corporations in A.N. F¹² 780. More generally, see Emile Coornaert, *Les Corporations en France* (Paris, 1941).

9   *The minutes of the commissaires* of the Châtelet in Paris contain hundreds of confiscations of goods, materials or equipment from *ouvriers sans qualité*: see Kaplan, 'Corporations'. A survey of the *saisis* made in 1769–70 unearthed over 200. Most corporations engaged a *commissaire* to accompany their officials on their monthly visits around the city. As a result, it is unlikely that *ouvriers sans qualité* in the furnishing or building trades would have escaped attention. The clothing trades were less easy to police, because independent artisans could work in their rooms as *chambrelans*. It was, of course, always possible for corporate officials to connive in violations of corporate statutes, in exchange for a fee; see A.N. Y 13 133 (9 July 1781) for an example among the farriers, and Y 9528 and Y 9535 for other examples. Yet in either case, the problem of access to materials is likely to have meant that most illegal workers were located on the periphery of the trades.

10   On tax assessment by the corporations, see A.N. Y 9532 (12 June 1722): Y 9533 (18 September 1755): X¹ᵃ 4576 fol. 58 (20 August 1767) for a case brought by the shoemakers against a linen merchant for illegally selling leather in Paris: X¹ᵇ 3904 (5 May 1769) on the supply of membrane to card-makers: Y 11 084 (31 December 1768) on regulations in the *Halle aux cuirs* and Y 11 257 (17 August 1770) on regulations at the veal-market. Corporations also protected the ownership of designs: see the examples of the button-makers of Lyon, A.N. X¹ᵇ 3833 (25 November 1765), the bronze-founders and instrument-makers of Lyon, Paris, A.N. X¹ᵇ 3847 (30 July 1766), and the silk-weavers of Lyon, A.D. Rhône, 3E 5114 (276) (24 October 1785) and 3E 5117 (76) (5 March 1788); B.L. 27 d. 13 (83), *arrêt du conseil*, (14 July 1787).

importance that master artisans attached to these regulations.[11] Once purchased, materials could of course be resold or put out to an artisan in one of the suburbs as part of a sub-contracting arrangement. The nominal independence associated with the unincorporated trades was, at times, modified by links of subordination and credit to members of the incorporated trades.[12] Membership of a corporation transferred some of the costs and uncertainty attached to the acquisition of materials to institutional devices, which was one reason why some of the attributes of corporate life continued until well into the late nineteenth century in most large French cities.[13]

There were, in other words, good reasons why master artisans belonged to collective associations. It is likely therefore that most journeymen, faced with a choice, would have preferred to belong to a corporation rather than settle in one of the suburbs or privileged areas. Membership of a corporation allowed artisans to evade many entrepreneurial decisions.[14] The problem, of course, is whether such choices existed, for access to the incorporated trades was affected by several conditions, the best known of which were the formal regulations governing the acquisition of a *maîtrise*. Unless an individual was the son of an established master, admission to most corporations entailed a period of apprenticeship and the payment of a fee, although failure to do so did not entirely eliminate the possibility of entry. It was also possible to buy an office or obtain a special dispensation from the royal government.[15] This however, was a very much more costly procedure, as a journeyman iron-founder in Paris discovered when, after serving a six-year apprenticeship, he found, to his horror, that his former master had forgotten to register his engagement with the corporation. He

[11] On marketing arrangements in Paris, see David Garrioch, *Neighbourhood and Community in Paris, 1740–1790* (Cambridge, 1986), p. 101. For an example of a dispute over the supply of slates in the Parisian roofing trade, A.N. Y 10 784ᵇ (28 October 1770) and over the supply of calf-skins for bindings in the book trade, Ernest Thoinan, *Les Relieurs français (1500–1800)* (Paris, 1893), pp. 86–7.

[12] The legal proceedings between the Parisian bakers and their counterparts in the *faubourg Saint-Antoine*, as well as the case between the joiners of the suburb and their incorporated counterparts (see above, pp. 64–5) were the product of such arrangements. For some further examples of sub-contracting, see below, pp. 225, 228, 232.

[13] See Andrew Lincoln, 'Le Syndicalisme patronal à Paris de 1815 à 1848: une étape de la formation de la classe patronale', *Le Mouvement social*, 114 (1981), pp. 11–34.

[14] William M. Reddy, *The Rise of Market Culture: The Textile Trade and French Society, 1750–1900* (Cambridge, 1984), pp. 34–8.

[15] On the formal provisions governing admission to the Parisian corporations, see Alfred Franklin, *Dictionnaire des arts, métiers et professions* (Paris, 1906); René de Lespinasse, *Les Métiers et corporations de la ville de Paris*, 3 vols (Paris, 1886–97). Jean-Claude Perrot's caustic invitation to imagine a society in which the right to drive a car could be bought for a fee is the most appropriate comment on the level of competence needed to become a member of a corporation. We can assume that a shoemaker knew how to make a shoe. Some did so better than others, but there is no need to exaggerate the levels of skill needed to become a master artisan. See below, chapter 9, and Jean-Claude Perrot, *Genèse d'une ville moderne: Caen au xviiie siècle* (Paris, 1975), p. 340.

was faced with the prospect of spending 1,000 *livres* to obtain the appropriate dispensation instead of the usual 400 *livres* required to become a master.[16]

It is well known that many eighteenth-century critics of the corporations claimed that these regulations served to limit access to the trades.[17] In fact, it is unlikely that they did. Corporations were not self-perpetuating oligarchies. The age-composition of the workforce of a number of late eighteenth-century trades is an initial indication that only a minority of journeymen did not become master artisans of one kind or another. Furthermore, and in contradistinction to the claims made by the Physiocrats and by Turgot in 1776, recent research has established that the corporations were relatively open institutions. The destruction of the papers of the Parisian corporations in 1871 makes it difficult to say much about the trades of the capital. Records of entry into one Parisian corporation (the locksmiths) reveal that only 116 (34 per cent) of 346 new masters admitted between 1742 and 1776 were the sons of established masters. In an earlier, and partially overlapping enumeration, between 1735 and 1750, only 38 (20 per cent) of 186 new entrants were the sons of master locksmiths. A further 69 were apprentices or journeymen admitted after they had met the full panoply of statutory requirements.[18] The composition of the masons' corporation appears to have been similar. Between 1750 and 1765 its size increased from 284 to 303. Exactly half of the membership listed in 1750 had disappeared from the list of members drawn up in 1765. Of the 161 new members, only 48 (or 29·8 per cent) had the same second names as men already listed in 1750.[19] The high level of entry into the Parisian corporations in the late eighteenth century is a further indication of their relative openess. The rate at which *lettres de maîtrise* were acquired in Paris between 1785 and 1788 (an average of 1,550 a year) was far higher than simple succession from father to son could have produced.[20]

Provincial sources provide more precise information. In Dijon, under 20

16 A.N. Y 12 175 (26 June 1770). Although the use of credit in buying a *maîtrise* was prohibited (A.N. Y 9499, 18 June 1734), it was impossible to prevent the practice (see Sonenscher, *Hatters*, p. 48 and A.N. Y 18 580 for several examples in the late eighteenth century).

17 These attacks are summarised in William Sewell, *Work and Revolution*, pp. 72–7. They continue (erroneously) to find their way into standard histories of France: thus, according to Pierre Goubert, *L'Ancien Régime* (Paris, 1969), p. 205, 'toutes les maîtrises et tous les ateliers sont pratiquement héréditaires'. The phrase is repeated *verbatim* in Pierre Goubert and Daniel Roche, *Les Français et l'Ancien Régime* (Paris, 1984), p. 167.

18 H. R. D'Allemagne, *Les Anciens Maîtres serruriers et leurs meilleurs travaux*, 2 vols (Paris 1943), p. 139; Anne-Marie Bruleaux, 'Les Maîtres-Serruriers parisiens et leurs travaux de grande serrurerie', (Thèse de l'École des Chartes, n.d.), pp. 107–8.

19 A.N. AD XX^c 65 (47, 61 and 89).

20 See Haim Burstin, 'Conditionnement économique et conditionnement mental dans le monde du travail parisien à la fin de l'ancien régime', *History of European Ideas* 3 (1982),

per cent of the 7,861 *lettres de maîtrise* acquired by master artisans between 1693 and 1790 were issued to the sons of masters practising the same trade.[21] The proportion of new entrants who followed the same trades as their fathers had done fell from over 30 per cent at the beginning of the century to 12 per cent in the last years of the Old Regime. Not surprisingly, less than a half of all new masters were natives of Dijon. The relative stability of the size of the city's corporations (meaning that they grew in size at rates which matched the growth of population) was coupled with a high level of non-endogamous entry consisting largely of immigrants, rather than the native-born sons of members of different trades. The corporations in Dijon appear to have been unusually open. In Rouen, the proportion of newcomers among an admittedly incomplete total of 8,488 *lettres de maîtrise* issued during the eighteenth century was, on average, 41 per cent.[22] In Caen, however, the level of direct continuity was significantly lower: an average of only 45 per cent of the 6,189 individuals admitted to the *maîtrise* between 1730 and 1789 were the sons of masters of the same corporation. The proportion was falling before the corporations were abolished briefly by Turgot in 1776 and remained at under 40 per cent until the Revolution.[23] The same increasingly low level of dynastic continuity can be found among the architects and building entrepreneurs of late eighteenth-century Bordeaux. Under half of the membership of what was a relatively capital-intensive trade were the sons or sons-in-law of established masters.[24]

This combination of limited continuity and an increasingly diverse membership is an indication that recruitment to the corporations was a more complex process than mere succession from one generation to the next. There are obvious reasons why this was the case. Some masters died without leaving any male heirs. Others went bankrupt or, either because of their success or failure, abandoned the trades entirely. Others sent their sons to be apprenticed in other trades or towns, or arranged for them to be married to the daughters of masters in other corporations or localities. The urban population of eighteenth-century France was, as studies of Vannes and Caen have shown, highly mobile.[25] The membership of the corporations did not escape this more general pattern. Only 64 (23 per

pp. 23–9 (p. 24). The bundle A.N. Y 9490[a] contains a large number of complaints by, among others, the Parisian farriers, shoemakers, hatters, joiners, bakers, dyers and painters over the influx into the corporations after 1776.

[21] Edward J. Shepherd, 'Social and Geographic Mobility', pp. 123–6.

[22] Jean-Pierre Bardet, *Rouen aux xviie et xviiie siècles* (Paris, 1983), p. 237.

[23] Perrot, *Caen*, vol. 1, pp. 338–40.

[24] J. P. Mouilleseaux, 'Recherches sur l'activité du bâtiment à Bordeaux (1769–1790)', (T. E. R. Université de Bordeaux, 1970), vol. 1, p. 151.

[25] T. J. A. Le Goff, *Vannes and its Region: A Study of Town and Country in Eighteenth-Century France* (Oxford, 1981), pp. 49–56; Perrot, *Caen*, vol. 1, pp. 153–66.

cent) of the 284 members of the Parisian masons' corporation enumerated in 1750 were still at the same address in 1765. A further 77 (27 per cent) had moved to a different address, while 142 (50 per cent) had either died or abandoned the trade altogether. It is probable that mobility in smaller towns was (at least in relative terms) more pronounced. In 1769 the 43 master tailors of Châlons-sur-Marne borrowed the sum of 4,000 *livres*. Nine years later, a court ruling ordered the corporation to repay the sum, and a levy of ten *sous* a week was made on all its members. By then, the corporation had increased in size to 45 members, but 13 of them had been admitted since 1769. All but one of them had a different surname from those of the original 43 members. Of the 11 masters who had disappeared from the corporation between 1769 and 1778, six had died and five were said to have left the town.[26]

Membership of the corporations was thus self-depleting and was renewed by a regular injection of exogenous entrants. A proportion of this influx was supplied by apprentices born outside the localities in which they served their time. Only 167 (28·5 per cent) of the 585 apprentices engaged by master artisans in Lyon in 1746 and 1747 were natives of the city. Two thirds of the 629 apprenticeship contracts drawn up in 1786 involved immigrants to Lyon.[27] Yet only a proportion of the apprentices engaged by master artisans completed their time. In the declining linen trade of Valenciennes only a quarter of the boys taken on as apprentices during the eighteenth century were the sons of masters, although masters' sons accounted for over half the entrants to the corporation itself. The members of the 250 strong Parisian masons' corporation were each entitled to take on an apprentice every six years. Even if all the dozen or two dozen men who annually entered the corporation were men who had successfully completed an apprenticeship – and at least a quarter were, in fact, the sons of established masters and, in Paris, did not need to serve an apprenticeship – no more than ten per cent of the membership of the corporation could ever have engaged an apprentice.[28] Even if a majority of master masons did

26 A.N. XX^c 65 (47 and 61). The loan raised by the tailors of Reims had still not been repaid in 1800. By then only 18 of the 45 master tailors were still in a position to continue to repay their share. Five, who had already paid their contribution, had died, and it was impossible to recover anything from the heirs of the remaining 22, who had all left the trade. B.M. Reims, MS. 2176.

27 Maurice Garden, *Lyon et les lyonnais au xviiie siècle* (Paris, 1970), pp. 62–3, 67.

28 Philippe Guignet, *Mines, manufactures et ouvriers du Valenciennois au xviiie siècle* (New York, 1977), pp. 512–34. Rough estimates of the number of entrants to the Parisian masons' corporation derive from the lists in A.N. AD XX^c 64 and 65. For comparable figures in early nineteenth-century Sweden, see Lars Edgren, 'Crafts in Transformation? Masters, Journeymen and Apprentices in a Swedish Town, 1800–1850', *Continuity and Change*, 1 (1986), pp. 363–83. The subject awaits study in a British context. See, however, Richard Wall, 'Work, Welfare and the Family: An Illustration of the Adaptive

not, in fact, engage apprentices, the proportions suggest that as many as 30 per cent of apprentices failed to complete their time.

The trades of the large cities of eighteenth-century France drew thousands of young adolescents into apprenticeships that were never completed. Those who survived were not, however, guaranteed an unimpeded path into the corporate world. A further proportion of the new membership of corporations was supplied by journeymen who had served an apprenticeship elsewhere, but married the daughters or widows of established masters. This possibility was a source of tension between journeymen who had served an apprenticeship in a particular city and journeymen who had been apprenticed elsewhere. In either case, the social and juridical itinerary from apprenticeship to membership of a corporation was complemented by some form of geographical migration and was structured by elaborate networks of kinship and patronage.

The apparent continuities of corporate life were, therefore, the product of a complex combination of inheritance, migration, apprenticeship, further migration as a journeyman, marriage and the acquisition of a *maîtrise*. There were many possible variations within this range of alternatives. At one extreme, an individual could remain in the same locality all his life, inheriting his trade and membership of a corporation from his father; at another, a master of a corporation might have been sent from a small town to serve his apprenticeship in a larger city and then, after years of wandering, have settled in a third city and married one of his employers' daughters. Most corporations were made up of varying combinations of either type. Not all journeymen became masters in the towns in which they had been born; neither were all masters immigrants from other localities. The relative importance of inheritance and immigration in the continuities of corporate life were related closely to the circumstances of particular trades in particular localities.

An initial distinction can be made, therefore, between inheritance and immigration as routes into the corporations. They generated two possible tensions. The first was between the sons of established master artisans and journeymen from elsewhere. The second was between the total number of potential master artisans in a given locality and the number of viable enterprises that a particular trade could support. The one was not the same as the other: the first was a distinction whose existence was based entirely upon the provisions of corporate statutes, while the second existed independently of the provisions of the law. There was, however, a connection between the two. Prosperous trades in thriving cities meant,

Family Economy', in Lloyd Bonfield, Richard Smith and Keith Wrightson, eds., *A World We Have Gained* (Oxford, 1986), pp. 261–94, and his 'Leaving Home and the Process of Household Formation in Pre-Industrial England', *Continuity and Change*, 2 (1987), pp. 77–101.

on the one hand, a larger number of viable enterprises, but also meant a wider range of opportunities for employment, larger numbers of journeymen and greater competition among potential members of the corporations. At a certain point the continued influx of newcomers could become a threat to the viability of established enterprises. In 1733, for example, the master tailors of Lyon complained that the size of their corporation had grown to nearly 500 members because, they claimed, the costs of entry were much lower than in Toulouse, Bordeaux, Nantes, Clermont, Riom and other smaller towns in the vicinity. They requested the right to modify their statutes to limit the future intake of immigrants.[29]

Yet the opposite state of affairs did not eliminate the tension between indigenous and immigrant contenders for membership of the corporations. Moribund trades in decaying cities meant a declining number of viable enterprises; they also meant more incentive to attempt to limit membership of the corporations to the sons of established masters. Thus in either case there was a connection between the relative vitality of the trades, local patterns of employment, recruitment to the corporations and the provisions of the law. The significance of corporate regulation governing access to the trades is best understood in this context. Since no one could know how viable a particular enterprise or trade was likely to be, the law supplied a modicum of power in an uncertain world. It was an imperfect instrument that, on occasions, could be used to adjudicate between the competing claims of inheritance and immigration.

The respective shares of inheritance and immigration in the continuities of corporate life were, in their turn, affected by two more general features of eighteenth-century French society: the large number of small towns and the uneven distribution of the trades within urban society. Neither of these two features has been given much recognition. Yet both ensured that the circumstances of master artisans in eighteenth-century France were rather different from those of their counterparts elsewhere in Europe. They meant, in particular, that with the possible exception of Paris and a very small number of large provincial cities like Lyon, Marseille and, in the latter half of the century, Bordeaux, recruitment to the trades was closely related to complex circuits of geographical migration.

It is usual to think of eighteenth-century France as an overwhelmingly rural society. There are, of course, compelling reasons for doing so. On the eve of the Revolution only some 15 per cent of a population of 27·9 millions lived in towns.[30] Yet urban France had two distinctive

29 B.N. MS. Joly de Fleury, 181 fol. 279.
30 See, most recently, Donald Sutherland, *France 1789–1815: Revolution and Counter-revolution* (London, 1985), p. 53; Michel Vovelle, *La Chute de la Monarchie* (Paris, 1972), p. 17.

characteristics. First, although the proportion of the population living in towns was low (lower indeed than in England, the Low Countries or Italy), the number of towns was itself remarkably high. The definition of a town is, of course, somewhat elusive.[31] But by any criterion, there were more towns in eighteenth-century France than in any other territorial state in Europe.[32] Although early eighteenth-century figures are imprecise, they suggest that there were 55 localities in France with at least 10,000 inhabitants in 1700. By 1800 the figure had reached 78.[33] The comparable figures for England and Germany were 11 and 44, and 30 and 53 respectively.[34] At a somewhat lower level, there were some 286 localities with populations of at least 5,000 inhabitants in France in 1794, and 292 in 1806. A total of 867 localities had populations of 2,000 or more inhabitants in 1806.[35]

The second characteristic of urban France in the eighteenth century was its diversity. This diversity found its expression in very much more than variations in the range of occupations and activities found in different localities. It was also the product of the more complex processes by which towns of different sizes and structures grew or decayed during the eighteenth century. The little that is known about the urban demography of eighteenth-century France suggests that the aggregate urban population grew slowly, more slowly than that of rural France, so that the proportion of the population living in towns of at least 10,000 inhabitants fell slightly (from just over nine per cent to just under nine per cent) between 1700 and 1800.[36] Yet this trend masks vast changes in the distribution of the urban population, as some cities, like Bordeaux and Nîmes, almost doubled in size while others, like Dijon or Troyes barely grew at all.[37]

The implications of these two characteristics of urban society for the world of the trades were manifold. The large number of relatively tiny urban centres ensured that many trades were distributed widely over the surface of the kingdom. At the same time, because many towns were small, their capacity to support large numbers of artisans was relatively limited. Some trades were, of course, highly localised. By any measure there were very many more mathematical instrument-makers and

---

[31] The best discussion of the question is in Jan de Vries, *European Urbanization (1500–1800)* (London, 1984), pp. 3–13.

[32] See the figures in de Vries, *Urbanization*, pp. 288–304.

[33] *Ibid.*   [34] *Ibid.*, p. 29.

[35] R. Le Mée, 'Population agglomerée, population dispersée au début du xixe siècle', *Annales de démographie historique*, 7 (1971), pp. 455–510; B. LePetit and J. F. Royer, 'Croissance et taille des villes: contribution à l'étude de l'urbanisation de la France au début du xixe siècle', *Annales E. S. C.*, 35 (1980), pp. 987–1010.

[36] de Vries, *Urbanization*, p. 39.

[37] Figures and estimates of the populations of the major French towns are conveniently brought together in Daniel Roche, *Le Siècle des Lumières en Province*, 2 vols (Paris, 1978), vol. 2, pp. 357–62. On the population of Troyes, see Lynn Hunt, *Revolution and Urban Politics: Troyes and Reims, 1786–1790* (Stanford, 1978), pp. 9–10.

opticians in Paris than in Lyon, let alone Uzès or Tarbes.[38] Yet small clusters of the members of the more conventional building, furnishing or clothing trades were components of the occupational structures of many small and medium sized urban centres: four master joiners in Baugé in the mid-eighteenth century, for example; six in Châteauduloir, two in Vibray, three in Saint Calais, two in Mondoubleau, three in Besse, twelve in La Flèche, four in Sablé, two in La Suze, 28 in Laval, a dozen in Loudun – all of them little towns in the area that fell within the *généralité* of Tours.[39]

There were however, significant regional variations. Some of them are visible in the social composition of the eighteenth-century French army, where the sons of artisans were more heavily represented among soldiers from northern and north-western France than the eastern half of the kingdom.[40] The patterns are clearer (and are unlikely to have been of recent origin) in the occupations of the men conscripted into the army between 1819 and 1826.[41] The relatively large numbers of tailors from south-western and north-eastern France, shoemakers from the centre and saddlers and harness-makers from the Parisian region are indications of durable regional differences. Yet their significance should not be exaggerated. Most trades existed in most towns: what mattered was their relative size and vitality.

There were also significant geographical variations in the size of the corporations to which master artisans belonged. To take one example, the number of master joiners ranged from between 0·21 and 0·26 per cent of the total population of Nîmes in 1769 and Lyon in 1746, to 0·17 per cent of the respective populations of Marseille and Bordeaux in 1782 and 1788.[42] In practice, these variations meant a difference of between a quarter and a third as many corporate places to be filled. The figures are, of course, no more than an order of magnitude because both the difficulties of measuring urban populations and the indeterminate number of unincorporated artisans make it impossible to measure the relative sizes of trades with any precision. Yet differences of this kind affected the relative contributions of inheritance and immigration to recruitment to the corporations.

The size and distribution of most trades varied in terms of both the size

38 On these trades, see Maurice Daumas, *Les Instruments scientifiques aux xviie et xviiie siècles* (Paris, 1953).
39 A.D. Indre-et-Loire, C 147.
40 André Corvisier, *L'Armée française de la fin du xviie siècle au ministère de Choiseul: Le soldat*, 2 vols (Paris, 1964), p. 531.
41 J. P. Aron, P. Dumont and E. Le Roy Ladurie, *Anthropologie du conscrit français* (Paris, 1972), pp. 104, 106, 128.
42 Figures of the size of the corporations have been taken from: A.N. F¹² 780 (Nîmes); Bibliothèque de l'Arsénal, 8° J 4684 (Lyon); A.C. Marseille, HH 416; A.C. Bordeaux, HH 70. Population figures of the four cities have been taken from Roche, *Siècle des Lumières*, vol. 2, pp. 357–62.

of particular localities and in terms of what economic geographers have termed their potential, or their capacity to interact with all other localities within a given area or region.[43] The two were not the same. The potential of many small centres of textile production (particularly towns in the west and south-east of France, like Cholet or Alès, producing for distant markets) was substantially greater than that of comparably-sized centres of rentier expenditure, like Bayeux or Fontainebleau. Nor were such differences confined to the textile trades. Centres of production of shoes, hats and other items of clothing or furniture for the colonial trade or for large, relatively centralised markets, like the army or the navy, housed trades whose potential was different from those of identical trades in other localities.[44] It is probable that some of the size and vitality of the Parisian silk, ribbon, button-making and tailoring trades derived from military and naval commissions and the large amount of ancillary and sub-contracted work that they generated. Button-makers in the capital with large orders from the provinces were thrown into consternation in 1790 when the National Assembly decided to change the *motif* on the buttons of National Guard uniforms from *La Loi et Le Roi* to *La Nation* after thousands of buttons had been made.[45] For similar reasons, the Parisian shoemaking trade was not the same as its counterpart in Marseille, which produced large quantities of shoes for export to southern Europe and the French and Spanish colonies. The relative size of the trade in Marseille was larger than its Parisian counterpart.[46] For equally obvious reasons, ship-building and wine-shipping ensured that there were very many more opportunities for potential masters in the carpentry or coopering trades of Bordeaux in the late eighteenth century than there were in Toulouse.[47]

Neither the size nor the potential of different trades and localities was static. As a result, the differential urban capacity to support given numbers of master tailors, shoemakers, joiners or locksmiths gradually changed. This had its effects upon both the distribution of employment and upon opportunities for entry into the trades. Yet such evidence as there is

[43] de Vries, *Urbanization*, pp. 154–67.

[44] On the hatting trade, see Sonenscher, *Hatters*, chapter 4.

[45] A.N. F^{12} 652.

[46] Some indication of the size and structure of the shoemaking trade of Marseille can be gleaned from a protracted dispute in 1769. It involved conflict between masters and journeymen – and bitter acrimony among masters dealing in different markets. One of the corporation's *prieurs* testified that during the nine months of his tenure of office 'il n'a cessé d'avoir de plaintes des divers maîtres sur ce qu'ils manquent de garçons pour le service de leur boutique...tandis qu'il y a plusieurs maîtres qui travaillent tant pour la ville que pour les isles de l'amérique, dont les boutiques et les atteliers regorgent de garçons, y ayant de ces maîtres qui en ont, les uns quinze, les autres vingt, vingt cinq, trente et d'avantage, y en ayant même un nommé Paret qui en a jusques à quatre vingt': A.C. Marseille, FF 378 (29 July 1769, deposition of Jean Bernard Pèbre). See also *Ibid.* (23 February and 26 July 1769).

[47] Jean Pierre Poussou, *Bordeaux et le Sud-Ouest au xviiie siècle* (Paris, 1983), pp. 288–9.

suggests that many urban corporations (with the major exception of those branches of textile production whose size was geared to the international markets for which they produced) remained relatively stable in size over long periods of time. In Dijon the occupational distribution of the working population recorded on tax rolls in 1700 and 1790 remained practically the same.[48] In Nimes, the considerable increase in the proportion of framework knitters and silk-weavers within the active population was not matched by any substantial change in the relative size of the non-textile trades.[49] A similar continuity appears to have existed in eighteenth-century Rouen.[50] The pattern was not, however, a universal one. In Caen a minor increase in the productive population masked sharp variations between the expanding building and furnishing trades and the contracting clothing and leather trades.[51] Parisian sources are almost non-existent, but the limited information that can be found suggests that there were significant variations in the rates at which the size of many corporations changed. The size of the carpenters' corporation was relatively stable, with a minimum of 82 and a maximum of 97 members (including widows) between 1736 and 1752. The masons' corporation grew from 234 to 303 members (some 29 per cent) between 1733 and 1760. The first three decades of the eighteenth century appear to have seen a substantial increase in the number of painters, sculptors and decorators who belonged to the Académie de Saint-Luc; but membership of the joiners and cabinet-makers' corporation grew rather more modestly between 1723 and 1789.[52]

The figures are, of course, somewhat misleading. As some towns spilled beyond their boundaries during the eighteenth century, many artisans established themselves in areas which fell outside the jurisdiction of the

48 Shepherd, 'Social and Geographic Mobility', pp. 108–10, 112–14.
49 See the figures presented by Marie-Bernadette Boyer, 'Nimes au xviiie siècle' (D. E. S. Université de Montpellier, 1960) chapter 2. and the analysis of all the marriage contracts drawn up in the city in 1705–9 and 1785–9 in M. Sonenscher, 'Royalists and Patriots: Nimes and its Hinterland in the late Eighteenth Century', (unpublished Ph.D. thesis. University of Warwick, 1978).
50 Bardet, *Rouen*, pp. 185–6.
51 Perrot, *Caen*, vol. 1, p. 269.
52 Figures of membership of the carpenters' and masons' corporations can be found in the surviving printed lists of members in A.N. AD XXᶜ 64 and 65. The carpenters' corporation numbered 82 (1736), 86 (1737), 87 (1738). 93 (1740), 97 (1743), 95 (1749), 93 (1750), 91 (1751) and 92 (1752). Membership of the masons' corporation was 234 (1733), 232 (1734), 248 (1736), 275 (1739), 270 (1740), 287 (1745), 281 (1746), 284 (1749), 284 (1750), 303 (1765). According to Savary, the joiners' corporation numbered 895 masters or widows. In 1787 there were 1,062 *menuisiers–ébenistes* in the capital and in 1789, 1,142 (B.H.V.P. Z 214), an increase of 28 per cent in over 60 years. The painters and sculptors had 584 members in 1697. Savary recorded 967 in 1725, and in 1764 it was said to have 1,100 members (Bibliothèque de l'Arsénal. MSS. Bastille 10295: J. Guiffrey, *Histoire de L'Académie de Saint Luc* (Paris, 1915), p. 17). Figures of the number of master hatters show the same gradual increase (Sonenscher, *Hatters*, pp. 45–51).

corporations. In other localities (Caen and Rouen, for example), changes in the structure of different branches of production led to corporate amalgamations and functional differentiations that distorted and out-weighed the significance of simple numerical changes in corporate size. Yet the continuities of size in areas covered by the corporations suggests the existence of a tendency towards a certain homeostatic balance between the size of a corporation and the number of viable enterprises which a trade could support. Master artisans were well aware of the need for such a balance. Several corporations had regulations preventing journeymen from establishing themselves on the same street, or even the same *quartier* as their former masters. They were most frequent in trades like baking, wigmaking and other branches of the clothing trades whose viability depended upon stable local clienteles and a high level of turnover on relatively low margins.[53] On some occasions corporations took action to limit entry into a trade by raising the price of a *maîtrise* (as the master tailors of Lyon proposed to do in 1733), or, as the Parisian goldsmiths did in 1632, by restricting access to the *maîtrise* to the sons of established masters.[54] The master bakers of Lyon did likewise in 1765, when, after the size of the corporation had reached 178, and ten of them 's'étant détruits' after incurring heavy losses during the dearth of 1764, they decided not to take on any apprentices for ten years.[55] The most durable and best known of such restrictions were those established by the Parisian printers, which were introduced in 1686 and remained in force until 1776.[56]

Yet measures of this sort were relatively infrequent. The balance between the size of a corporation and the number of viable enterprises which a trade could support appears to have been struck more durably and less formally in the complex processes by which its membership was renewed over the generations. The scale of this complexity has been greatly underestimated. Any lingering vestiges of the physiocratic image of the corporations as small, self-perpetuating oligarchies are almost entirely irrelevant to the realities of their identity and composition over the course of time. At most, it would seem that only half the membership of a corporation was able to pass on its patrimony to its heirs. Continuity in the trades was bound up with questions of marriage, inheritance, local variations in opportunities for employment and, subsequently, with

[53] On corporate amalgamations, see Perrot, *Caen*, 1, pp. 327–36, and Jochen Hoock, 'Réunions de métiers et marché régional: les marchands réunis de la ville de Rouen au début du xviiie siècle', *Annales E. S. C.*, 43 (1988), pp. 301–22. On limitations on competition, see the regulations of the Parisian glove-makers of 1778 (University of Chicago Library, John Crerar Collection, 1400).

[54] See above, p. 111 and René de Lespinasse, *Les Métiers et corporations de la ville de Paris*, (Paris, 1892), vol. 2, p. 44.

[55] A.D. Rhône, 3E 3005 (27 March and 10 June 1765). The period was later reduced to six years by an *arrêt* of the Parlement of Paris.   [56] See above, chapter 1.

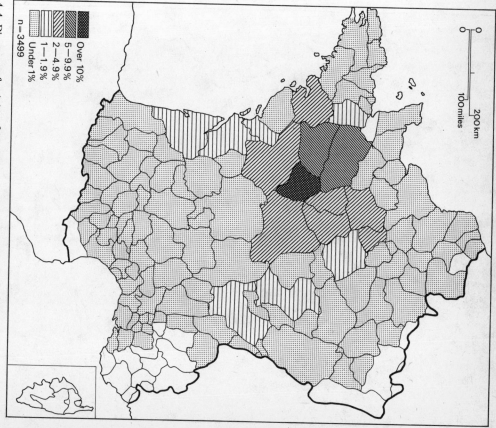

4.4 Dioceses of origin of journeymen working in Tours (1782–9). Source: A.D. Indre-et-Loire, E 492.

Legend:
- Over 10%
- 5–9.9%
- 2–4.9%
- 1—1.9%
- Under 1%
- n = 3499

adequate markets and stable clienteles. They, in their turn, were affected by gradual changes in the size and potential of different localities. Very few eighteenth-century French towns were endowed with sufficient resources to enable the corporations they housed to be self-sufficient.

For this reason, only a minority of trades in an even smaller minority of towns can be set in the context of a single locality. Most trades were part of urban systems and sub-systems rather than single towns or cities. The trades of large regional centres like Nîmes or Amiens were linked to their

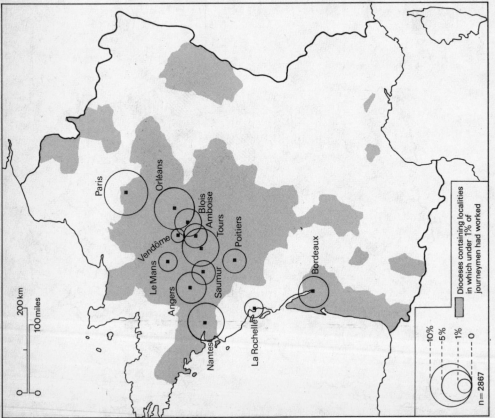

4.5 Principal places of previous employment of journeymen working in Tours (1782–9). Source: A.D. Indre-et-Loire, E 492.

counterparts in clusters of smaller towns – Uzès, Beaucaire, Aramon, Saint-Hyppolite, Le Vigan and Sommières in the case of the former; Albert, Peronne, Bapaume, Roye, Noyon, Clermont and Ham in the case of the latter – by a variety of ties arising from kinship, apprenticeship or the remarriage of widows to journeymen from other localities.[57] Migrations of some kind were inseparable from the life of the trades.

[57] On Amiens, see Pierre Deyon, *Amiens, capitale provinciale* (Paris, 1967), pp. 9–10; on Nimes, see Sonenscher, 'Royalists and Patriots' and, for a later period, Leslie Page Moch, *Paths to the City* (London, 1983), pp. 33–9.

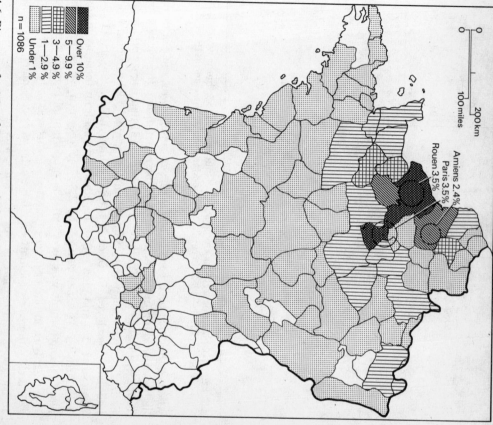

4.6 Dioceses of origin of journeymen locksmiths working in Rouen (1782–91).
Source: A.D. Seine-Maritime, 5E 654 and 649.

Over 10%
5—9.9%
3—4.9%
1—2.9%
Under 1%

n = 1086

Amiens 2.4%
Paris 3.5%
Rouen 3.5%

Yet not all master artisans were immigrants and not every journeyman was obliged to travel to become a master of a corporation. The places of birth of the 3,511 journeymen who registered for work in Tours between 1782 and 1789 suggest that there was a considerable difference between the migratory propensities of journeymen who had been born in small towns and those who were natives of large cities. Only 55 journeymen (1·5 per cent) had been born in Paris. The same number had been born in Orléans and almost as many in Nantes, Angers and Blois. The great majority were natives of very much smaller localities (see Figure 4.4). Yet

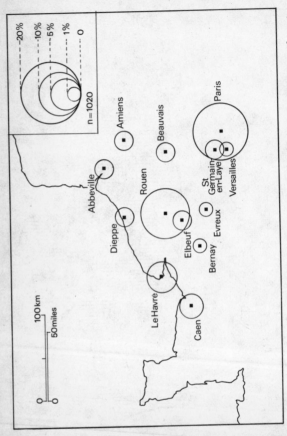

4.7 Principal places of previous employment of journeymen locksmiths working in Rouen (1782–91). Source: A.D. Seine-Maritime, 5E 654 and 649.

whether they had been born in large cities or small towns, most of them had been working in the major cities of the region before they arrived in Tours (see Figure 4.5). The largest number (313) had been working in Paris. They were followed by slightly smaller groups of journeymen who had been employed in Orléans (268), Nantes (226), Angers (155), Bordeaux (136) and Blois (103). Together, arrivals from these six towns accounted for 41·9 per cent of the 2,867 journeymen whose previous place of employment was recorded. The proportion of journeymen who had been born in one or other of these six towns was only 7·1 per cent.

It is clear therefore that natives of large cities were very much less likely to become migrants than natives of small towns and large villages. The same contrast can be found among the 1,086 journeymen locksmiths who registered for work in Rouen between 1782 and 1791. Only 38 (3·5 per cent) of them were natives of Paris (see Figure 4·6). Yet 175 (16·1 per cent) of them had come to Rouen after having worked in Paris (see Figure 4·7). The majority of the journeymen locksmiths who arrived in Rouen were natives of small towns and villages to the north and north-east of the city. The large number of these small towns in eighteenth-century France as a whole meant that migration was the usual experience of young men who learned a trade outside a large city. It was of course more marked in some trades than others. Over three quarters (76·3 per cent) of the 3,511 journeymen recorded in Tours between 1782 and 1789 belonged to ten

4.8 Trades of journeymen working in Tours (1782–9). Source: A.D. Indre-et-Loire, E 492.

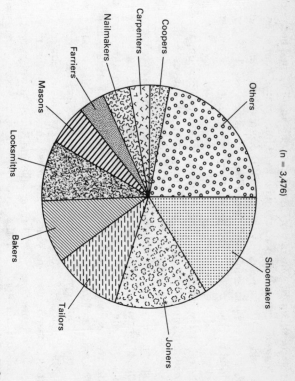

(n = 3,476)

trades (see Figure 4.8). As one would expect, journeymen bakers, shoemakers, joiners, tailors, masons and locksmiths belonged to the trades that were distributed most widely among the towns and villages of eighteenth-century France. For them, becoming a master artisan often meant leaving a small town and, by one route or another, finding a place within the corporate world of large cities. Large cities, however, were able to accommodate the sons of established masters more easily. As a result, natives of Paris, Lyon or Marseille accounted for a disproportionately small component of the peripatetic sector of the working population of eighteenth-century France.

Yet the workforce of the trades of large cities did not contain large numbers of journeymen who had been born there. Only five per cent of the journeymen tailors who registered for work in Rouen between 1777 and 1781 were natives of the city.[58] The proportion of natives of Rouen among the locksmiths who registered there between 1782 and 1791 was even lower: only 3·5 per cent. Elsewhere the proportions were a little higher, although migrants remained a substantial majority. Eighteen per cent of

---

58 The figures have been calculated from the registers of registration of journeymen tailors in the city between 1778 and 1781 in A.D. Seine-Maritime, 5E 709 and 708 running from 13 July 1778 to 14 November 1781. For a fuller discussion of the source, see chapter 5 below.

the 260 journeymen joiners working in Marseille in 1782 had been born there, and a further 10·7 per cent who were immigrants from elsewhere were said to be domiciled in the city.[59] The proportion was somewhat lower among the locksmiths of Marseille in the same year: 16·5 per cent of a total workforce of 126 journeymen were either natives or residents of the city.[60]

The relatively small proportion of natives of large cities among itinerant journeymen, and the equally small proportion of natives within the workforces of large cities, presents a difficult problem. It may be that statistics have created an illusion. If it were possible to discover the sum of all the journeymen who had been born in Paris working at a given moment in the provinces, it might transpire that emigration from the capital was as usual an occurrence in the life of young Parisians as it was for the natives of much smaller towns. Yet there were also good reasons for Parisian journeymen to remain in the capital, for, until they were reorganised after 1776, the statutes of many corporations required future masters to spend two to six years working as journeymen before they were entitled to acquire a *maîtrise*.[61] In Marseille and Rouen however, provisions like this did not apply, yet the proportion of native-born journeymen working as joiners, locksmiths or tailors in the two cities was strikingly low. Again, it can be assumed that some of them did migrate. It is also probable, however, that a further proportion did not work as journeymen at all, but married and set themselves up soon after they had completed their apprenticeship. The wide range of different trades and potential marriage partners in large cities, together with the structural character- istics of large urban markets, made it possible to meet these objectives without having to travel.

Two factors favoured a disproportionate rate of emigration by young men from small towns rather than large cities. The first was the size and composition of the markets for manufactured goods in large cities. The second was the relatively labour-intensive character of most eighteenth- century trades, which meant that there was a limit on the number of transactions that any single artisanal enterprise could conduct without increasing the size of its workforce. The two factors interacted in different ways in cities of different sizes. A marginal increase in the population of a large city was capable of generating a larger number of niches for employment (or for the establishment of additional artisanal enterprises) than a comparable rate of increase in a small town. A one per cent annual rate of increase in the population of a city of 50,000 inhabitants was comparable to a ten per cent rate of increase in a town with 5,000 inhabitants. The discrepancy was particularly significant in eighteenth-

[59] A.C. Marseille, HH 416.
[60] *Ibid.*, HH 430.
[61] Garrioch and Sonenscher, 'Compagnonnages, Confraternities', pp. 38–9.

century France. Although the rate of population growth of small towns was higher than that of large cities, high infant mortality and the practice of wet-nursing meant that much of the net increase in the population of large cities was made up of adult migrants who consumed more than the basic range of subsistence goods.

Large cities, and Paris in particular, were therefore magnets that drew in thousands of journeymen from elsewhere and, at the same time, limited the outward movement of the indigenous workforce. This process of concentration ensured that a very substantial process of selection occurred within the mainly peripatetic workforce of the trades. If most journeymen became master artisans, it does not follow that they became masters in the large cities where most of them worked. Although the costs of becoming a master were not very great, a viable enterprise was, to varying degrees, dependent upon credit, and credit, in its turn, depended upon kin, friends and patrons. One measure of the importance of credit and the chronic shortage of ready cash in the eighteenth-century trades is the huge success of the Parisian *Mont de Piété* after its establishment in 1777. It soon grew to have a staff of over 50 clerks and 40 office attendants handling some 700 to 800 items a day. In the miserable year of 1789 it made nearly 300,000 loans, worth nearly 12 million *livres*.[62] Many of its clients were artisans of one kind or another. Even in more prosperous times, credit was one of the keys to the continuity of the workshop economy.

Here, three different sources appear to have had a particular importance. There were the resources of kin, the resources supplied by friends from the same region and those supplied by former employers. Measurement of their respective contributions to the economy of the trades is impossible, because the only sources of information are heavily distorted. Inventories present master artisans at the end of their careers rather than the beginning. Bankruptcy records are, by their nature, a record of failure rather than success. Complaints to the police authorities and civil actions are the other, exceptional, side of a much larger number of more durable and successful arrangements. They do, however, suggest that becoming a master artisan often involved an initial loan from a relative, a former employer or a friend from the same region.[63] Variations in access to one or

[62] B.N. MS. Joly de Fleury, 2542 fol. 130 *et seq.*: B.H.V.P. 12834. *Tableau de la comptabilité du Mont de Piété* (Paris, 1790). See also R. Bigo, 'Aux origines du mont-de-piété parisien: bienfaisance et crédit', *Annales d'histoire économique et social,* 4 (1932), pp. 113–26: and, on Lyon, Jean-Pierre Gutton, 'Lyon et le crédit populaire sous l'ancien régime: les projects de mont-de-piété', in *Studi in Memoria di Federigo Melis,* 5 vols (Naples, 1978), vol. 4, pp. 147–54.

[63] For some examples of credit relations among kin, see A.N. Y 12 596 (15 February 1752); 13 760 (21 February 1752); 13 514 (21 July 1772); 13 283 (30 June 1781); 14 476 (23 September 1781). On connections between credit, regional origin and previous employment, see A.N. Y 12 175 (26 June 1770); 13 802 (18 April 1781). The

other of these resources was one of the differences between the sons of established master artisans, immigrants who had served an apprenticeship in a large city and other immigrants who came there to work as journeymen.

Thus even though the corporations of large cities appear to have been relatively open, they were not as open as they seem. Although it is probable that the proportion of new members who were the sons of established members of the same corporation was generally less than 50 per cent, a substantial number of the remaining places were filled by the sons of members of other corporations within the same locality. In large cities, and Paris in particular, occupational continuity from one generation to the next was less important than the continuity of the family patrimony. Master artisans (like peasants in a different context) were more concerned with the stability and continuity of the resources of the lineage than the mere succession of generations in the same trade.[64] As a result, the Physiocrats had a point. The urban trades *were* relatively closed. Yet their inaccessibility was not a direct consequence of the provisions of corporate requirements for admission to the *maîtrise*; instead, it was an indirect result of the greater opportunities available to master artisans in large cities to place their sons in other trades and form marriage alliances with other dynasties within the same locality.

While some master artisans encouraged their sons to practise the same trade, others apprenticed them to masters of comparable standing and credit in different trades. Some of these young men subsequently became master artisans by marrying the daughters of established masters in the same city or even the same *quartier* soon after they had completed their apprenticeship. This was the main reason why the age of new masters who had been born in large cities was lower than that of men who had been born elsewhere. Throughout the eighteenth century at least half of all the journeymen who had been born in Dijon had become masters by the age of 30, while the average age of new masters from outside the city was significantly higher. Between 1761 and 1790 59 per cent of them were at least 30 years old when they became masters, while the comparable figure for natives of the city was 41 per cent.[65] The division between natives of

misfortunes of a Parisian wine merchant are particularly eloquent. He came to Paris in 1755 at the age of 14 from a village in the Champagne to be apprenticed to a wine merchant. In 1767, at the age of 28, he married and borrowed money from his former employer to set himself up in the trade. After losses of various kinds he decided to become a wheelwright and set himself up in partnership with 'les nommés Champagne, ses pays': A.N. Y 18 580 (dossier Herbillon).

[64] On peasants, see Pierre Bourdieu, 'Les Stratégies matrimoniales dans le système de reproduction', *Annales, E. S. C.*, 27 (1972), pp. 1105–27. For some urban examples, see David Garrioch, *Neighbourhood and Community in Eighteenth-Century Paris* (Cambridge, 1986), pp. 62–3.

[65] Figures have been calculated from Shepherd, 'Social and Geographic Mobility', p. 126.

large and small towns which is visible in the composition of the peripatetic population was matched by a division between the range of potential marriage partners available to the sons of established masters in large cities (whatever the trade they practised) and those available to the sons of the inhabitants of small towns.

The likelihood that this is what happened is enhanced by comparing the geographical origins of men who married in a certain number of cities with the origins of journeymen who registered for work. The proportion of natives within urban populations was invariably much higher: 54 per cent of all the artisans who married in Rouen, 53 per cent of a sample of all the men who married in eighteenth-century Marseille, 48 per cent in Nîmes and 49 per cent in Caen.[66] These are much higher proportions than the three to 20 per cent of native-born journeymen found in the workforces of some of the trades of Rouen and Marseille. Clearly some of the additional number consisted of men who returned to the cities of their birth to marry and become masters of a corporation after several years on the road, but others were the sons of the masters of one trade who, after serving an apprenticeship in another, married and set out to establish themselves in their own right. Studies of marriage contracts in eighteenth-century France have been carried out mainly to establish a measure of the scale and social distribution of wealth. As a result, less attention has been paid to the legal status and family strategies of those involved. It is clear, however, that marriage was the moment when journeymen set out to establish themselves as masters in their own right. In cities in which marriage contracts were drawn up by almost every section of the population (mainly in southern France), notarial records contain a disproportionately small number of contracts involving master artisans. Most of them were widowers. Thus, in Bordeaux, only 16 of the 317 bakers represented in a sample of marriage contracts drawn up between 1737 and 1791 were masters.[67] In Nîmes, master artisans were almost entirely absent from the 1,038 and 1,728 contracts drawn up between 1705–9 and 1785–9 respectively. Over 80 per cent of the artisans involved in marriage contracts were described as journeymen.[68]

The initial opposition between the respective places of inheritance and immigration in the life of the trades thus requires modification. Access to the trades was also mediated by marriage, and, in this, the inhabitants of large cities enjoyed the great advantage of relatively stable residence in densely populated neighbourhoods and *quartiers*, and the many potential marriage partners that they could offer. Becoming a master artisan did not

---

66 The figures are summarised conveniently in Jean-Pierre Bardet, *Rouen*, pp. 211–12. On Nîmes, see Sonenscher, 'Royalists and Patriots'.

67 Poussou, *Bordeaux*, pp. 430–1.

68 Sonenscher, 'Royalists and Patriots'.

depend solely upon the relative importance of inheritance and immigration in the continuities of the trades – it also depended upon the range of lateral links that artisans in different localities were able to construct. They were the basis of inter-generational mobility between different trades and, at the same time, the key to the continuity of local patrimonies from generation to generation.

Measurement of the phenomenon is particularly difficult, because both the mobility of master artisans within cities and the bias of most of the sources available to historians make it easier to recover information concerning single households and nuclear families than extended patterns of kinship. Lateral links between brothers, cousins and brothers-in-law are very much more difficult to reconstruct. The best sources of information about the relationship between patterns of kinship and the occupations of master artisans are the councils of wardship (*conseils de tutelle*) set up to manage a patrimony when an individual died leaving a family of minors. A preliminary study of the composition of over 1,000 councils in Lyon between 1745 and 1779 has shown how substantial these lateral links were. Despite the scale of movement into and out of the city during the eighteenth century, most families of artisans could look to at least two sets of relatives of the same generation.[69] The figure is undoubtedly something of an exaggeration, since a certain number of widows with young children whose only relatives lived outside the city are likely to have returned to the towns and villages where they had been born, but it is an indication of both the importance of lateral kin groups in the life of the trades, and the degree to which large cities were able to offer the sons of indigenous master artisans a wide range of different trades in which they could serve an apprenticeship and, subsequently, a wide range of acceptable kin with whom marriage alliances could be arranged.[70]

Brothers and brothers-in-law, not to mention cousins and more distant kin, did not, of course, all follow the same trade. A Parisian metal polisher (*maître fourbisseur*) who died in 1768 had a brother and an uncle who were master shoemakers and, on his wife's side, an uncle who was a master painter. A framework knitter's kin in 1771 included a master goldsmith, an engraver and a bookseller on his wife's side.[71] As a result, if there was a division between the possibilities available to journeymen from different localities, it was not simply a division between the respective claims of inheritance and immigration – it was also a division between

[69] Maurice Garden, 'Les Relations familiales dans la France du xviiie siècle: une source, les conseils de tutelle', in Bernard Vogler, ed., *Les Actes notariés* (Strasbourg, 1979), pp. 173–86.

[70] The best (but still unexploited) source of information on the question is to be found among the ecclesiastical dispensations granted for marriages between relatives up to the fourth degree of consanguinity. See Jean-Marie Gouesse, 'Parenté, famille et mariage en Normandie aux xviie et xviiie siècles. Présentation d'une source et d'une enquête', *Annales, E.S.C.*, 27 (1972). pp. 1139–54.

[71] A.N. Z² 3668 (Actes de tutelle de la Justice de Saint-Jean de Latran).

journeymen who had been sent to serve an apprenticeship in a large city, and expected to marry a local master artisan's daughter, and the equally large number of journeymen who also came to work in large cities, but had learned their trades elsewhere.

Both groups were made up mainly of immigrants. Only a third of all the apprentices in Lyon in 1746, 1747 and 1786 were natives of the city.[72] We can assume that the majority of them became masters of one or other of the local corporations. The much larger proportion of apprentices who had been sent to the city from small towns and villages in its hinterland were left to compete for the remaining number of potentially viable enterprises with the equally large number of peripatetic journeymen who came to work in Lyon and had also been born in small localities all over France. As a result, the destinies of many natives of small towns were decided in large cities. Here, marriage was the central moment in an elaborate and diffuse process of selection and exclusion which ensured that only a proportion of the young men who were sent to serve as apprentices, or came to work as journeymen, were able to settle in the great cities of eighteenth-century France.

Becoming a master of a trade was therefore the outcome of a very complicated series of intra-generational calculations of geographical and legal advantage. Mere continuity from one generation to the next was only one mode of entry into the corporations and, present evidence suggests, was by no means the most usual. At least as many master artisans acquired their positions through a more elaborate process of migration, apprenticeship, further migration and marriage. Measurement of the scale of selection and exclusion which this process engendered is almost impossible, because the records of the corporations only contain those who, by one route or another, were selected. It is therefore not possible to measure the proportion of the combined total of apprentices and journeymen, some born in large cities and others immigrants to large cities, together with those who succeeded their fathers in the same trades, who became masters of the large urban corporations. All that can be said is that the largest proportion of the workforce of the trades of the great cities of eighteenth-century France consisted of immigrants from smaller towns and villages. Yet only a minority of that itinerant population was able to settle there and become a member of a corporation. The real cleavage in the world of the trades was the division between immigrants of different kinds. Only a minority of immigrant apprentices and migrant journeymen were able to establish themselves in the trades of the great cities.

If most journeymen became artisans (and all the evidence suggests that they did), many of them were obliged to return to the small towns and villages in which they had been born after failing to find a place within the network of more substantial urban enterprises. Here marriage, rather than corporate regulation, was the principal filter which set the course of many different destinies. Among the large number of potential contenders for the daughters of established master artisans, only a small, but imprecise, proportion were able to succeed. Precision, of course, was equally impossible for journeymen themselves. Such calculations as they may have made could only be guesses, based upon gossip and familiarity with particular localities, but the course of their lives was inextricably bound up with the outcome of such calculations. Such opportunities as there were to reduce the element of the unknown within the maze of contingent possibilities which informed the apparent stability and continuity of corporate life were therefore of considerable value.

It is easier to understand the resonances of certain characteristic terms of abuse in this context. When a Parisian master artisan said angrily that one of his creditors (a master hosier) had come to the capital wearing clogs ('il étoit venu avec des sabots à Paris') the point was the sharper because most members of the Parisian corporations undoubtedly had not.[73] When a Parisian journeyman expressed his deep desire to see his master die in a hospital, the point was also the sharper because of the scale of social failure that it implied.[74] Insults like these were an indirect and inverted acknowledgement of the care and effort that artisans lavished upon the management of the passage of time, the succession of generations and the apparently effortless continuities that ensued. They were a commentary upon the skill with which artisans applied themselves to finding sons- and daughters-in-law of comparable wealth and standing within the same locality. The phenomenon of occupational endogamy can be found in any large French city during the eighteenth century. In Rouen, for example, over 60 per cent of the sons of master tailors married the daughters of master artisans.[75] If the scale of endogamous marriage has been somewhat exaggerated (it is very much easier to measure), there is no doubt that its existence ensured that the opportunities available to immigrants were fewer than their considerable presence in the workforce of the trades might suggest. Only a minority of the thousands of journeymen tailors or locksmiths who came to work in large cities like Rouen or Marseille were able to become masters of the corporations there.

It is easier too, in this context, to understand the prevalence of idioms of a geographical sort in the everyday life of the trades, particularly the abiding interest in regional origin and rhetorical loyalty to the *pays*. Commonalities of this kind were a constituent element of the nexus of kin.

[73] A.N. Y 10 783ª (3 November 1769). More generally, see David Garrioch, 'Verbal Insults in Eighteenth-Century Paris', in Peter Burke and Roy Porter, eds., *The Social History of Language* (Cambridge, 1987), pp. 104–19.   [75] Bardet, *Rouen*, p. 234.
[72] A.N. Y 11 007ᵇ (18 December 1766).

friends and patrons which was brought into play to produce the social itinerary involved in the transition from apprentice to master. Continuity of employment – if not with the same master, at least within the same productive network – was a second, often complementary, element within the same process. As a result, such legal rights that journeymen enjoyed within particular local networks of employment had a significance which went beyond the weekly cycle of work, wages and consumption. They also affected the wider opportunities available for accomplishing the transition to full membership of a corporation.

Here, the relationship between immigrants who had served an apprenticeship in a large city and immigrants who came to large cities to work as journeymen was particularly sensitive. Many of the distinctive characteristics of the associations formed by journeymen in eighteenth-century France were an expression of the tensions which that relationship induced. So too were many of the often surprisingly varied characteristics of disputes in the trades, whose forms derived from some of the different legal identities and entitlements that existed among journeymen of different conditions. The sons of master artisans, the immigrant journey-men who had served an apprenticeship in large cities, and the itinerant journeymen who also came to work in the great cities could each claim different kinds of rights of property in the labour that they sold. These entitlements and identities were not, of course, given; they were defined in the context of legal debate and legal argument, and changed as the terms of reference of legal argument changed. They also depended upon local labour markets and patterns of employment, and the extent to which different kinds of journeymen were able to remain within particular networks of employment. Here too there were differences. For the fluid, unstable, yet finally durable physiognomy of the trades within different urban systems and sub-systems was matched by an equally fluid and unstable relationship between masters and journeymen within local labour markets and the local economies of particular trades.

CHAPTER 5

Patterns of employment: the economy of the trades and the economy of the bazaar

Patterns of migration and the varying opportunities available to migrants of different kinds played their part in the formation of the different entitlements and identities that were brought into play in the relationship between masters and journeymen. They were not, however, the only source of such differences. The long cycles informing the acquisition and transmission of artisanal patrimonies were the outcome of shorter weekly and monthly cycles of work, wages and consumption. They, in their turn, were affected by differences between various types of artisanal enterprise. There were several significant variations in the internal architecture of the trades. Some master artisans worked alone or with no more than one or two journeymen, and depended mainly upon family resources to meet additional orders or seasonal changes in levels of demand, while others regularly employed between three and several dozen individuals. Patterns of employment and the structure of labour markets varied according to the proportion of either within the local economies of particular trades.

Variations in the size of particular workshops were matched by variations in the length of time that journeymen spent with the same master and the frequency with which they moved from shop to shop. Here there were further differences in the internal organisation of the trades which affected the character of patterns of employment. In some trades the majority of master artisans produced mainly for final consumers rather than intermediaries of one kind or another, but in most trades many master artisans produced mainly for other master artisans. This difference gave rise to different forms of division of labour. In some cases, where different phases of the process of production were relatively integrated, the character of different kinds of artisanal enterprise presents analogies to the economy of the factory or proto-factory.[1] More usually, however, where

[1] For typologies of different forms of industry in the eighteenth century, see S. D. Chapman, 'The Textile Factory before Arkwright: a Typology of Factory Development', *Business History Review*, 48 (1974), pp. 451–78; H. Freudenberger and F. Redlich, 'The Industrial Development of Europe: Reality, Symbols, Images', *Kyklos*, 17 (1964), pp. 372–403. More generally, see Michael Piore and Charles Sabel, *The Second Industrial Divide* (New York, 1984); Charles Sabel and Jonathan Zeitlin, 'Historical Alternatives to Mass

different components of the productive process were devolved on a multiplicity of separate enterprises, the analogies are closer to the economy of the bazaar or a spot market.[2]

The degree to which the trades were variously integrated or dis-integrated (and therefore more or less analogous to the bazaar in their organisation) affected the quality of the relationship between masters and journeymen. In the relatively dis-integrated glazing trade of eighteenth-century Paris, masters and journeymen dealt with one another in ways that had much in common with the transactions of the bazaar. In the more integrated printing trade, relations between masters and journeymen were significantly more hierarchical in character.[3] Variations in levels of integration also affected the quality of relationships among journeymen themselves. Journeymen could be taken on and paid in different ways. Some of them remained in the same workshop for relatively long periods of time, while others moved rapidly from master to master or town to town. The proportion of each within particular local economies also played its part in the formation of the entitlements and identities that were brought into play in the work of the trades.

Sources that have long been used by social historians – tax rolls, marriage contracts, wills and inventories – disclose substantial variations in the wealth and resources of members of the same trade which were not, of course, matched by any differences in corporate titles or the wording of the law.[4] The names of the corporations themselves – joiners, hatters, locksmiths, etc. – also have a misleading simplicity. Joiners made house-hold furniture, but they also made the bodies of coaches and carriages, while others made trellises and still others made the frames of the looms and spinning-wheels used in the textile trades.[5] Locksmiths made more than locks: they also produced wrought-iron railings and balconies, door hinges and handles, shop signs, springs for coaches and the complicated arrangement of rods and needles used in making stocking frames.[6] There

[1] Production', *Past and Present*, 108 (1985), pp. 133–76, and, for a case study analysed in slightly different terms, Steven Fraser, 'Combined and Uneven Development in the Men's Clothing Industry', *Business History Review*, 57 (1983), pp. 522–47.

[2] I owe the analogy with the bazaar to Clifford Geertz, *Peddlers and Princes* (Chicago, 1963), pp. 30–47, and his 'Suq: The Bazaar Economy in Sefrou', in Clifford Geertz, Hildred Geertz and Lawrence Rosen, *Meaning and Order in Moroccan Society* (Cambridge, 1979), pp. 124–5, 219.

[3] See above, chapter 1. On the collective character of markets, see Geoffrey M. Hodgson, *Economics and Institutions* (Oxford, 1988), chapter 8.

[4] See, among many others, the studies by Maurice Garden, *Lyon et les lyonnais au xviiie siècle* (Paris, 1970), and Jean-Pierre Poussou, *Bordeaux et le Sud-Ouest au xviiie siècle* (Paris, 1983).

[5] For a dispute involving different sectors of the trade in Paris, see A.N. Y 13 673 (29 April 1769).

[6] For a dispute involving divisions between journeymen locksmiths in different sectors of the Parisian trade, see David Garrioch and Michael Sonenscher, 'Compagnonnages, Confraternities and Associations of Journeymen in Eighteenth-Century Paris', *European History Quarterly*, 16 (1986), pp. 25–45.

were shoemakers who made men's shoes, others who made women's and children's shoes, and others who made boots for the army and the navy.[7] The examples could be multiplied indefinitely. Even bakers made different kinds of bread.[8]

Differences of this order meant that the local economies of the trades were very much more complex than the wording of corporate statutes might suggest. Not only were the volume and value of the goods produced by some master artisans very much more substantial than those produced by others, but there were also wide variations in the range of products and markets encompassed by the rubrics of particular corporate titles. The textile trades are the most obvious example, but trades like the hatting and shoemaking trades also produced for many different local and international markets.[9] Corporations were only the juridical form of the trades. Viewed from a different standpoint, they were also aggregations of more or less substantial divisions of labour.

Divisions of labour can take many forms. In the context of the eighteenth-century French trades, the most obvious was the division of labour between members of different corporations. Even a master tailor presented with a piece of cloth by a customer relied upon members of other corporations for certain ancillary materials: for scissors, needles, thread, gold braid, buttons, lace or silk ribbons.[10] The process of making a coach or decorating an apartment called for more extensive co-operation between members of different corporations.[11] In this sense, each workshop was part of a wider productive network, and each master artisan was involved in a more or less substantial nexus of credit, sub-contracted work and marketing arrangements. There were many different positions within such networks. In the Parisian building trades, the apex within the hierarchy of sub-contracted work belonged to the architects and building entrepreneurs. In the furnishing trades, a great deal of sub-contracting was organised by master carpet-makers, who did not necessarily make carpets but were instead the principal contractors for the decoration and furnishing of many apartments. Their counterparts in the production of coaches and carriages were the saddlers and harness-makers, who may have made leather goods, but also put out sub-contracted work to many joiners, wheelwrights, locksmiths and decorative painters.[12] Since the master artisans within these informal networks paid one another at

---

7   See below, pp. 180–1.
8   See above, pp. 65, and Steven L. Kaplan, *Provisioning Paris* (Ithaca, 1984).
9   On the hatting trade, see Sonenscher, *Hatters*, pp. 33–4, 37.
10 For some examples of tailors' work, see A.D. Rhône, B (unclassified) Fonds de Vitry and Gayet (Liasses III, IV and V); Fonds Carret (Liasse XVIII).
11 The best known analysis of this division of labour can be found in Karl Marx, *Capital* (reprinted London, 1965), vol. 1, chapter 14, pp. 318–47.
12 For examples of sub-contracting among master artisans, see A.D. Paris D⁵ B⁶ 1661: 3653; 4171: 5342.

irregular intervals for the goods and services they supplied, transactions involving credit rapidly acquired the character of patron–client relationships.

Only a proportion of a master artisan's transactions were with a final consumer. That proportion varied between trades. One measure of this variation can be found in the demands for small coin made in Paris during the early years of the Revolution. Ninety trades are represented among the 3,781 requests for the cash needed to pay wages, yet there are no bakers or wigmakers, and only a tiny number of tailors and shoemakers among the dossiers.[13] Members of these trades also employed journeymen, but they were less affected by shortages of cash because of their direct dealings with final consumers. Although deferred payments were also a usual part of the relationship between members of the food and clothing trades and their clients, the conspicuous absence of members of these trades from the requests for small coin is evidence that liquid income from clients and customers was sufficient to meet their wage bills. In the majority of trades, however, transactions with a final consumer were the least significant proportion of a master artisan's affairs. The multiplicity of trades associated with building, furnishing and decorating are the most obvious example. There, the great majority of a master artisan's clients consisted of other master artisans.

Joiners and cabinet-makers, for example, dealt mainly with other members of the same trade – as well as with brass-founders, sculptors, gilders, varnishers, marble-cutters and producers of ceramics and chinaware. The former supplied different varieties of wood or made articles to order; the latter produced the ornamental embellishments that were added to household furniture. Invariably transactions between them involved deferred payments. Here, for example, are one Parisian cabinet-maker's dealings with a marble-cutter and polisher in the course of a year.[14] In January 1759 he owed him 72 *livres*. In February he paid him 12 *livres* and added a further 12 *livres* in April. At the same time he received a small piece of marble, worth 24 *livres*. He made three further payments of 12 *livres* each in May, June and July but then nothing at all until February 1760. In the mean time he had received several more pieces of marble worth a total of 104 *livres*, so that the accumulated debt now stood at 140 *livres*.

---

13 A.N. F^{30} 109–24, 129, 131–4, 136–60. They were first studied by F. Braesch, 'Un Essai de statistique de la population ouvrière de Paris vers 1791', *La Révolution française*, 63 (1912), pp. 289–321. They are an unreliable source of information on the trades as a whole not only because of the purpose for which they were established (which meant that trades involved directly with final consumers are virtually absent) but also because there was no reason for principal contractors i.. sub-contracting arrangements to specify whether the workers they paid had been engaged by themselves or the sub-contractor.

14 A.D. Paris, D^5 B^6 5491.

As this example indicates, cash payments were an infrequent component of transactions between master artisans. In eighteenth-century Paris and most large provincial cities promissory notes, payable at three or six months, were the usual form of deferred payments. They could be endorsed or discounted for cash. In large cities there were many possible sources of cash, willing, for a fee, to turn paper into coin. Wine merchants and inn-keepers met much small-scale demand. More prosperous holders of paper could look to notaries, who, especially in Paris, behaved like discount houses in all but name.[15] The owners of other offices with ready access to cash, and tax-collectors in particular, performed a similar function.[16] In the last resort there was the legion of pawnbrokers, usurers and, in Paris after 1777, the *Mont de Piété*.[17] The practice of endorsing and discounting fiduciary notes was a well-established and widely recognised element within the economy of the eighteenth-century trades.[18]

The ubiquity of deferred payment meant that each artisanal enterprise was a node within a kaleidoscopic undergrowth of credit. Cash payments marked the beginning and end of relationships whose normal course was filled by promissory notes, book debts, and adjustments made by transferring the ownership of materials of common utility. A cabinet-maker sold two pieces of mahogany weighing 764 pounds at 20 *livres* a hundredweight to pay for part of the 664 *livres* of goods he had received from one of his regular sub-contracting partners.[19] A Parisian master mason settled part of an outstanding debt of 6,000 *livres* by offering his creditor, a master carpenter, 800 pieces of timber he had at the *Port de la Rapée* at 520 *livres* a hundred. There was no standard scale for the price of goods like these, and the multiplicity of artisanal enterprises in most large cities ensured that no single enterprise could make the prices of most of the materials used in the trades. Master artisans bought and sold the materials they used in ways which have much in common with the procedures of the bazaar. A Parisian bronze-founder who bought some copper filings from a plumber's clerk described a typical transaction. They went to a *cabaret* and agreed on the sum of 54 *livres* plus 'six francs à manger'.[20] Even here payment was not in cash, but was deferred until a month later.

---

[15] For examples of these different sources of cash. see A.N. Y 11 439 (25 November 1786); Y 9529 (11 April 1777), where a notary discounted paper at the rate of 4 *deniers* per *livre*: Y 13 314 (9 July 1786); Y 18 580 (which contains many examples of credit relations in the trades).

[16] On office holders as sources of cash. see A.N. Y 13 711 (27 March 1756).

[17] On usurers, see A.N. Y 11 520 (Inventory of Clavel, *maître menuisier*, 1776); Y 18 580: Y 15 117 (17 January 1787). and, on the *Mont de Piété*, see above, pp. 123, and A.N. Y 13 162.

[18] For examples of the complex chains which resulted, see A.N. Y 13 760 (19 September 1752); Y 11 514ᵇ (5 July 1785); Y 13 208 (9 April 1781); Y 13 689 (16 September 1781).

[19] A.D. Paris, D⁵ Bᶜ 5491; A.N. Y 11 024 (20 September 1782).

[20] A.N. Y 12 175 (26 June 1770).

The analogy between the economy of the trades and the economy of the bazaar can be extended well beyond simple transactions like these. At different times master artisans were both buyers and sellers. These activities required both an established network of regular partners and an eye for identifying short-term commercial advantage. There was, of course, a certain tension between the two, which found its expression in the frequent allegations made by master artisans to the police authorities that their reputations and creditworthiness had been jeopardised by slanderous comment. A widow who owned a wrought-iron works on the rue du Bout-du-Monde in Paris complained that the proprietors of a rival concern in the *faubourg* Saint-Antoine had spread the alarming rumour that she used arsenic rather than sal-ammoniac to restore kitchenware. They had done so, she claimed, because a well-endowed tax official (a *receveur général des finances*) had recently transferred his custom to her.[21] A master button-maker complained that another member of his corporation had told his suppliers among the gilt and silk merchants of the capital that he had engineered a fraudulent bankruptcy.[22]

Complaints like these were the product of the need to maintain a recognised place within a circle of potential creditors and trading partners made up, in the main, of other master artisans. The division of labour between members of different corporations was matched by endless negotiation between the individuals whose interdependent needs it supplied. This was why reputations mattered. It was also why disgruntled journeymen, like disgruntled competitors, talked freely and openly about their masters' creditworthiness.[23] The fact that they could and did was a strong inducement to ensure that wages were paid in full and on time; it was also a strong inducement to avoid having to pay wages at all. Journeymen may have had their uses, but they also represented a regular demand for cash.

The local economies of the trades were variously integrated or dis-integrated. These differences in levels of integration gave rise to less obvious forms of division of labour than the division between members of different corporations. The production of certain types of commodity entailed more or less complicated technical processes. In some cases (and

21 A.N. Y 10 784ᵃ (9 March 1770). See also David Garrioch, 'Verbal Insults in Eighteenth-Century Paris', in Peter Burke and Roy Porter, eds., *The Social History of Language* (Cambridge, 1987), esp. pp. 110–11.

22 A.N. Y 15 202 (4 December 1775); see also Y 15 841 (19 November 1769) and Y 12 684 (12 February 1779) describing a dispute between a Parisian *râpeur de tabac* and a water-carrier he employed from time to time as a tobacco-grinder, where the latter threatened that 'il se transporterait chez toutes les pratiques et débitants pour lequel le comparant travail [*sic*]' to ruin his creditworthiness.

23 A.N. Y 13 760 (19 November 1752); Y 15 452 (1754); Y 14 096 (23 August 1769); Y 12 174 (22 September 1769); Y 10 899ᵇ (24 May 1770); Y 15 117 (2 August 1788). For other examples, see Brennan, *Public Drinking*, chapter 2.

the printing and hatting trades are good examples) these processes were integrated within a single establishment.[24] In others (and the textile trades are the most striking example) they were devolved on to a multiplicity of specialised sub-occupations and activities carried out in separate locations and, in some cases, associated with different corporations.[25] The economies of relatively integrated trades present analogies to the economy of the factory. The economies of dis-integrated trades present analogies to the economy of the bazaar.[26]

In eighteenth-century France integration reached its highest level in the privileged manufactories associated mainly with the production of high-quality textiles, metal goods, porcelain and ceramics.[27] The costs of integration were, however, high. The outlay on fixed installations ran into thousands of *livres* rather than the hundreds associated with even the most capital-intensive trades.[28] More importantly, large-scale enterprises were obliged to carry the heavy costs of substantial quantities of materials and a large, regularly employed workforce. The bitter conflicts that took place in the vast Van Robais woollen manufactory in the early eighteenth century were a measure of the difficulties encountered by manufacturers when orders slackened and wages still had to be paid. A remark about the weavers employed in the Van Robais works at Abbeville in 1716 that has

24 In the printing trade, compositors and pressmen were required to co-ordinate their schedules. See, for a good analysis of the process, D. F. Mackenzie, 'Printers of the Mind', *Studies in Bibliography*, 22 (1969), pp. 1–75. Similar co-ordination existed between the felting and finishing sides of the hatting trade: see Sonenscher, *Hatters*, pp. 20–5, 68–70.

25 The division of labour in the textile trades has not been given sufficient study in its own right. It is described in some detail in Jean-Michel Chaplain, *La Chambre des tisseurs, Louviers: cité drapière 1680–1840* (Paris, 1984).

26 See the works cited above, note 2 and, more generally, Louis Putterman, ed., *The Economic Nature of the Firm: A Reader* (Cambridge, 1986).

27 There is no adequate study of these establishments. For an overview, see Pierre Deyon and Philippe Guignet, 'The Royal Manufactures and Economic and Technological Progress in France before the Industrial Revolution', *Journal of European Economic History*, 9 (1980), pp. 611–32.

28 On fixed capital in the privileged manufactories, see J. K. J. Thomson, *Clermont-de-Lodève, 1633–1789* (Cambridge, 1982), pp. 154–71; and, in other integrated enterprises, see S. D. Chapman and Serge Chassagne, *European Textile Printers in the Eighteenth Century* (London, 1981), pp. 134–8; Serge Chassagne, 'La Naissance de l'industrie cotonnière en France: 1760–1840. Trois générations d'entrepreneurs' (thèse de doctorat. Ecole des Hautes Etudes en Sciences Sociales, Paris, 1986) chapters 1 and 2; J. M. Schmitt, *Aux Origines de la révolution industrielle en Alsace* (Strasbourg, 1980), pp. 212–19; Pierre Jacquet, 'La Manufacture Zuber & Cie', *Bulletin de la Société Industrielle de Mulhouse*, 793 (1984), pp. 81–6; H. Clouzot and C. Follot, *Histoire du papier peint en France* (Paris, 1935); Louis Bergeron, *Banquiers, négociants et manufacturiers parisiens du Directoire à l'Empire* (Paris, 1978), pp. 213–17; Claude Pris, *Une Grande Entreprise française sous l'ancien régime: la manufacture royale des glaces de Saint-Gobain, 1665–1830* (New York, 1981), pp. 63–153; Régine de Plinval de Guillebon, *Paris Porcelain, 1770–1850* (London, 1972), *La Porcelaine à Paris sous le Consulat et l'Empire* (Geneva and Paris, 1985), and her 'La Manufacture de porcelaine de Dihl et Guerhard, rue de Bondy et rue du Temple', *Bulletin de la société de l'histoire de Paris et de l'Ile de France*, 109 (1982), pp. 177–212.

echoed down the centuries – 'la manufacture n'est point fait pour eux mais [ils] sont faits pour la manufacture' – was the sharpest expression of the dilemma faced by the owners of huge quantities of unsold goods who were also the employers of workers with families living and working on the premises.[29]

This was why, from the fine-quality woollen manufactories established at Abbeville or Sedan in the late seventeenth century, to the calico works and wallpaper manufactories established by entrepreneurs like the Danton brothers of Angers or Jean-Baptiste Reveillon in late eighteenth-century Paris, royal privilege allowed integrated firms to transfer some of the costs of fixed capital, large installations and slow turnover time to public resources.[30] There was a further problem which privilege was able to overcome: this was the heterogeneity of the skills and trades which were brought into juxtaposition within a fine-quality textile enterprise, a calico works or a wallpaper manufactory. Since the civil law conferred exceptional rights of a finite character, a particular title was needed to cover the range of activities and occupations housed by integrated firms. The title of *manufacture royale* was also a title to govern the affairs of a large-scale, integrated enterprise as if it were another corporation. Privilege, in this sense, was identical to the privileges enjoyed by other corporate bodies. The directors of manufactories could devise their own rules and regulations just as the members of particular corporations were able to do.[31]

A high level of integration was therefore largely associated with the relatively secure markets which privilege conferred, and with the legal powers that entitled privileged entrepreneurs to govern the multiplicity of different activities housed in their own establishments.[32] They were the basis of many of the proto-factories established in eighteenth-century France.[33] Most master artisans, however, were unable to enjoy relatively secure markets, nor were they able to enjoy more than the limited rights embodied in the provisions of the statutes of their own corporations. A master tailor had no legal title to tell a master button-maker how to organise his affairs, however interdependent their activities might be. As a result, the local economies of the trades had more in common with the economy of the bazaar than with the economy of the factory. Instead of serial production, most trades made goods to order. Instead of long runs sold at relatively uniform prices, most trades made short runs of many

29 A.D. Somme, C 149. The remark, it should be said, was made by the local *sub-délégué* in a report on the dispute, rather than by Van Robais himself.
30 Serge Chassagne, *La Manufacture de toiles imprimées de Tournemine-les-Angers* (Paris, 1971), pp. 72–4.
31 B.N. MS. Joly de Fleury 805 fol. 98: 806 fol. 351 (28 January 1784).
32 See, for example, the rules of the Manufacture des Gobelins: A.N. O¹ 2047.
33 On proto-factories, see the works cited above, note 1.

different articles sold within a range of heterogeneous prices. Instead of economies of scale, most trades sought to economise on costs. Instead of durable outlets in established markets, most trades depended upon a multiplicity of constantly changing outlets in a variety of dispersed markets. Instead of integration, most trades were organised around complex networks of informally constituted co-operative arrangements involving varying combinations of partnership, patronage and clientage. Instead of a permanently employed workforce, most trades depended upon an irregular supply of labour employed for the minimum amount of time.

As a result, both time and information had a particular importance in the local economies of the trades. Calculations of the rate of amortisation of fixed assets in relation to the liquidities generated by variable levels of output at relatively stable prices were very much less important than calculations of the schedules of production needed to meet episodic changes in the level of demand. The relationship between time and work in the eighteenth-century trades was mediated not by the presence of fixed capital, but by the vagaries of short-term fluctuations in the level of demand. Some of these fluctuations were relatively constant and seasonal in nature: they were most ubiquitous in the building trades.[34] Others were equally predictable because they were tied to the major religious festivals and public holidays, which were also the periods when rents fell due, bills were paid and new cycles of activity began: they were most visible in the furnishing and clothing trades.[35] Many others, however, were the product of fleeting opportunities, additional orders and brief associations in elaborately sub-contracted undertakings. Consequently, the uses to which

[34] For the effect of seasonal fluctuations on employment and earnings in the building trades, see A.N. Y 11 376 (23 September 1769) and below, pp. 203–4.

[35] A master shoemaker in Paris could find it worth mentioning 'qu'il se trouve maintenant à la tête de sept à huit garçons qu'il occupe toute l'année': A.N. Y 12 173 (16 June 1769). On seasonal fluctuations in the Parisian painting and decorating trades, see B.N. 4° Fm 20904. (p. 61): 'presque tous les compagnons nés en province ou à l'étranger, partent au mois d'Octobre pour leur patrie et ne reviennent qu'au mois de Mars'. Some indication of the scale of turnover of labour in the Parisian trades can be deduced from the number of free *livrets* that the Parisian corporations offered after the re-establishment of the corporations in 1777 to induce journeymen to register early with corporate labour exchanges. The shoemakers offered 1,000: the glaziers, potters and *fayenciers* 200: the grocers 500: the gunsmiths, cutlers and *fourbisseurs* 20: the *charcutiers* 100: University of Chicago Library, John Crerar Collection. In 1785, the Parisian grocers estimated that its 1,000 to 1,100 members employed a total of 1,500 *garçons*. A sixth of that total (some 250 *garçons*) were newcomers; a further 500 *garçons* moved from shop to shop every year: B.N. MS. Joly de Fleury, 1732. fols. 256vo–257. In 1789, the Parisian journeymen wigmakers estimated that the 18,000 men employed in the trade changed shop three times a year: B.H.V.P. 950 771, *Trait de bienfaisance patriotique des garçons perruquiers de la ville de Paris*. On seasonal patterns of employment in early nineteenth-century Paris, see A.N. F²⁰ 434–5 and Michael Sibalis, 'The Workers of Napoleonic Paris, 1800–1815', (unpublished Ph.D. thesis, Concordia University, Montreal, 1979). I am grateful to Dr Sibalis for allowing me to read his work before its eventual publication.

time was put were largely a function of the information which master artisans had at their disposal. This was one reason why part of the life of the trades took place in *cabarets*. Master artisans met and talked because information was one of the basic requirements of their trades.[36]

The relationship between time and information also affected patterns of employment in the trades in three ways. Most obviously it affected the number of journeymen employed by individual master artisans. Changes in the level of demand were usually matched by changes in the number of individuals working in particular *boutiques* or *ateliers*. The relationship between time and information also affected the conditions at which journeymen were taken on or dismissed. Finally, it affected the conditions upon which master artisans engaged the journeymen they employed. Journeymen could be taken on by the day, the week or the month, and paid by the day, the piece or for a given quantity of finished goods. The form of the wage was, from a master artisan's point of view, a way of economising upon fixed costs when the future was always uncertain.[37] Thus, just as the economy of the bazaar is an illuminating analogy in the context of relations between master artisans, so many of its characteristics are of comparable significance in the context of relations between masters and journeymen.

Where credit was so central a component of the economy of the workshop, and where so many transactions concerned other masters rather than final consumers, there were considerable advantages in avoiding the recurrent costs associated with the payment of wages. This was one reason why certain aspects of the relationship between masters and journeymen have close similarities to transactions between master artisans. The wage-relation too could be sub-contracted out to the journeymen engaged by master artisans. The practice was most widespread in the building trades, where many journeymen masons, roofers and stone-cutters engaged and paid their own labourers. In 1776 there were rumours of a stoppage by labourers in the Parisian building trades against the journeymen who went to engage them on the place de Grève.[38] Even in other trades the line dividing an employment relationship from a sub-contracting relationship was often very fine.[39] Work

[36] On *cabarets*, see Thomas Brennan, 'Beyond the Barriers: Popular Culture and Parisian Guinguettes', *Eighteenth-Century Studies*, 18 (1984–5), pp. 153–69; and David Garrioch, *Neighbourhood and Community in Paris, 1740–1790* (Cambridge, 1986), pp. 180–91.

[37] For a fuller discussion of the wage in the eighteenth-century trades, see below, chapter 6.

[38] 'Le 13 de ce mois...il y avoit un complot formé parmi les manoeuvres pour faire le lendemain grand tapage à la Grève si les compagnons ne leur promettoient une augmentation de leurs journées'; A.N. O¹ 487 fol. 758 (17 October 1776).

[39] For other examples of journeymen as sub-contractors, see A.N. Y 9500 (20 May 1765); Y 13 675 (6 February 1770); B.N. MS. fr. 8093 (20 December 1712) and below, p. 192.

'à l'entreprise' or 'à la tâche' was an established element within the relationship between masters and journeymen (particularly in the Parisian furnishing trades) well before the nineteenth century. The difference between the kinds of sub-contracted work done by eighteenth-century Parisian journeymen and the sub-contracted work outlawed in 1848 owed more to changes in the law than to changes in the workshop economy itself.[40]

Studies of artisans have largely ignored the mobile and evanescent character of many of the ordinary transactions carried out in the eighteenth-century French trades. Instead, it has been usual to approach the economy of the workshop as a small-scale equivalent of the factory. Yet while factories were, to varying degrees, places in which many different activities were integrated and where the size of the workforce was closely related to the forms of fixed-capital installations, eighteenth-century workshops were very much less self-contained. In the context of the eighteenth-century trades, the term 'productive network' is, in many respects, a more meaningful one than the factory-based term 'productive unit'. The tendency, however, has been to examine artisanal workshops as if they were productive units rather than components of more extensive productive networks. It has been usual, therefore, to emphasise the small-scale, dispersed and static character of artisanal economies rather than the wider divisions of labour and the more fluid environment to which many workshops belonged.

This tendency has been most pronounced in studies of the size of units of production in the eighteenth-century trades. The procedure has consisted of calculating the average number of journeymen employed in particular trades by dividing the total in employment by the total number of master artisans. It was first used by the French historian F. Braesch in a study of the working population of Paris in 1790 and 1791.[41] The figures which he used and the results he obtained have, rightly, been heavily criticised.[42] Where Braesch claimed to have found an average of over 16 journeymen in each unit of production in Paris in the early years of the French Revolution, most historians would now agree that the typical unit of production contained no more than a master artisan and two journeymen.[43] Yet however reliable the sources (and those used by Braesch were not at all reliable) it is not evident that calculations of the

[40] See above, chapter 1.
[41] F. Braesch, 'Essai', cited above (note 13).
[42] George Rudé, *The Crowd in the French Revolution* (Oxford, 1959); Albert Soboul, *Les Sans-Culottes parisiens en l'An II*, (Paris, 1958). See also M. Sonenscher, 'The Parisian *Sans-Culottes* of the Year II', *Social History*, 9 (1984), pp. 301–28, and the remarks above, note 13.
[43] Rudé, *Crowd in the French Revolution*, pp. 17–20; A. Soboul, *Sans-Culottes*, pp. 433–9.

5.1 Number of journeymen employed by each master and distribution of the workforce among the locksmiths of Marseille (1782). Source: A.C. Marseille, HH 430.

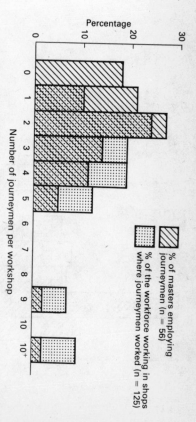

Percentage

Number of journeymen per workshop

% of masters employing journeymen (n = 56)

% of the workforce working in shops where journeymen worked (n = 125)

average number of journeymen at a single moment in time are the best approach to an understanding of the local economies of the trades.

Statistics require careful interpretation and averages more care than most. An examination of sources that are more reliable than those used by Braesch suggests that averages are, in many ways the least useful statistical representation of the structure of the eighteenth-century trades. Two lists of the journeymen and apprentices employed by the masters of two corporations in late eighteenth-century Marseille can be used to illustrate the point. The first (Figure 5.1) was drawn up by the locksmiths' corporation in 1782, and contains the names of 56 masters who employed a total of 125 journeymen or apprentices, or an average of a little over two each.[44] In fact only 15 master locksmiths employed two individuals. A dozen of them employed one journeyman and a further ten employers none at all. Inversely, almost half the total number of journeymen and apprentices (59) were working for 11 master locksmiths.

The second enumeration, made by the master joiners of Marseille in the same year, presents a very similar state of affairs (Figure 5.2).[45] The 144 masters employed some 260 individuals, or a little under two each.[46] Thirteen master joiners employed a total of 78 journeymen (or almost a third of the entire workforce), while a further 55 masters employed only a single individual. Workshops were small. Yet it is clear that averages are

44 A.C. Marseille, HH 430.
45 A.C. Marseille, HH 416.
46 The total number of journeymen is a little lower than the real figure because three master joiners refused to declare the number of journeymen they were employing. The difference does not affect the remarks made here.

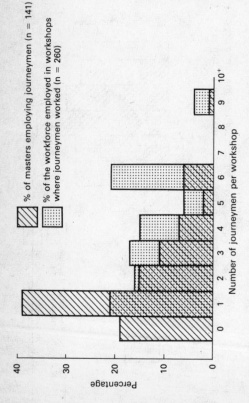

% of masters employing journeymen (n = 141)

% of the workforce employed in workshops
where journeymen worked (n = 260)

5.2 Number of journeymen employed by each master and distribution of the workforce among the joiners of Marseille (1782). Source: A.C. Marseille, HH 416.

particularly misleading in this context. Although the average number of journeymen working for each master was two, the largest proportion of the total workforce of the two trades could be found in workshops belonging to master artisans who employed five or more individuals. There was a sharp difference between a large number of master artisans who worked alone or employed no more than a single individual and a very much smaller number who employed either a large minority or the majority of the workforce. A similar pattern can be found among the locksmiths and joiners who requested small coin in Paris in 1790 and 1791 (Figure 5.3). For obvious reasons, the figures do not take individuals working alone into account, yet they too show that, while most members of the two trades employed only a small number of individuals, the majority of those employed worked for a relatively small number of large employers.[47]

This division is itself somewhat misleading, because it suggests that there was a durable polarity between the large number of master artisans who worked alone or with a single journeyman, and the much smaller number who employed between a half-dozen and a dozen individuals. In one sense there was. At any one time, local labour markets were centred upon a minority of workshops. Despite the relatively large number of master artisans belonging to corporations like the joiners or locksmiths of

[47] The two trades were selected because they are represented more fully than any others in the dossiers of requests for small coin. Calculations are based on the figures in F. Braesch, 'Essai'.

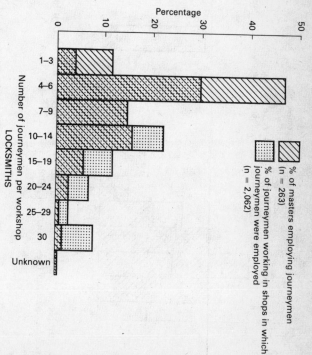

LOCKSMITHS

Number of journeymen per workshop

Percentage

% of masters employing journeymen
(n = 263)

% of journeymen working in shops in which
journeymen were employed
(n = 2,062)

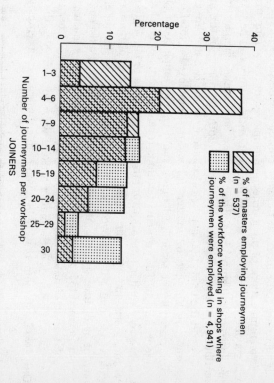

JOINERS

Number of journeymen per workshop

Percentage

% of masters employing journeymen
(n = 537)

% of the workforce working in shops where
journeymen were employed (n = 4,941)

5.3 Number of journeymen employed by each master and distribution of the
workforce among the locksmiths and joiners of Paris (1790–1). Source: F. Braesch,
'Essai'.

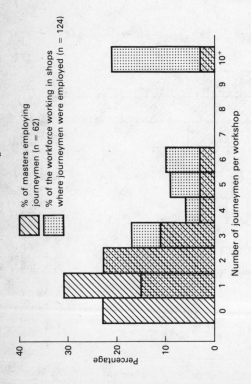

5.4 Number of journeymen employed by each master and distribution of the workforce among the joiners of Amiens (c. 1765–6). Source: A.C. Amiens, HH 591.

late eighteenth-century Paris and Marseille, journeymen tended to be concentrated among a much smaller number of *boutiques* or *ateliers*. Yet they were not to be found in the *same* cluster of workshops all the time.

Two enumerations of the journeymen employed in the joining trade of Amiens during the second half of the eighteenth century can be taken as an illustration (Figure 5.4). They disclose substantial changes in the distribution of the workforce over time.[48] Both the names of the master joiners and the totals that can be calculated from the two lists are almost the same. In the first, 62 masters (or widows) employed a total of 124 journeymen; in the second, 61 masters and widows employed a total of 116 journeymen. The two enumerations reveal patterns of employment that are very similar to those found in the same trade in late eighteenth-century Paris and Marseille. Again the largest number of masters and widows (33 and 30) employed only a single individual or did not employ anyone at all. Inversely, six master joiners named on the first list employed 38 journeymen (31 per cent of the total workforce) and five masters listed on the second enumeration employed 33 journeymen (or 28 per cent of the total). The names of the master artisans were not, however, the same. Only two master joiners were listed on both enumerations as employers of

[48] A.C. Amiens, HH 591. Neither of the lists is dated, but both the handwriting and the fact that the names of the masters and widows on the two lists are almost identical suggests that they were drawn up at very brief intervals at some time during the second half of the eighteenth century. The results are, in any event, the same as those on two enumerations of journeymen locksmiths in Rouen in 1788 and 1789 discussed below, pp. 150–2.

five journeymen or more.[49] The numbers are, of course, very low, but they are a hint of the scale and frequency with which journeymen moved from master to master, and the corresponding fluctuations in the size of an individual master's workforce.

Instead of the uniformities generated by calculations of averages, it is more helpful to envisage the local economies of the trades in terms of a central core of relatively large employers of journeymen and a larger periphery of master artisans who worked alone or, at most, employed two individuals at a time. At any one time, therefore, a large minority or a majority of journeymen were employed by a core of relatively large employers. All the evidence suggests that this pattern existed both in relatively large- and capital-intensive trades like hatting or printing (where some master artisans employed as many as 80 or 100 men and women), and in trades conducted on a very much smaller scale, such as wigmaking or tailoring, where a dozen individuals amounted to an exceptionally large workforce.[50]

The difference between large and small workshops was not, therefore, solely a function of the scale of investment in equipment, space and other forms of fixed capital. In comparison with outlays on wages, materials and sub-contracted work, fixed capital remained a relatively unimportant component of artisanal expenditure until well into the nineteenth century. Yet even in trades in which fixed installations were minimal, some artisanal enterprises became very much larger than others. They were, of course, a very tiny proportion of the total number of artisanal enterprises. The small number of relatively large employers among the joiners or locksmiths of eighteenth-century provincial cities like Amiens and Marseille is obvious. In 1836 the 269 Parisian firms employing 50 or more workers represented fewer than one per cent of the total number of industrial establishments.[51] Although a significant minority of them owed something of their size to steam power and textile machinery, the majority were firms in the entirely traditional clothing, furnishing, building and

49 The names of all the masters appear on both lists: only the numbers of journeymen they employed are different.

50 On the size of the workforce of the hatting trade, see Sonenscher, *Hatters*, pp. 41, 44–55; and, on the tailoring trade, see below, p. 166–8.

51 Maurice Daumas and Jacques Payen, eds., *Evolution de la géographie industrielle de Paris et sa proche banlieue au xixe siècle* (Conservatoire National des Arts et Métiers, Centre de documentation d'histoire des techniques, Paris, 1976), pp. 45–61. See also Gilbert Joseph Gaspard Chabrol de Volvic, *Recherches statistiques sur la ville de Paris*, 3 vols (Paris, 1823–9); Adeline Daumard, *La Bourgeoisie parisienne de 1815 à 1848* (Paris, 1963), pp. 440–77. As has recently been emphasised, few historians have given much thought to the short-term calculations and decisions that allowed some artisanal enterprises to become bigger or more successful than others: Julian Hoppit, 'Understanding the Industrial Revolution', *Historical Journal*, 30 (1987), pp. 211–24 (p. 224). For some general approaches, see Nathan Rosenberg, ed., *The Economics of Technological Change* (London, 1971), and, for one recent set of hypotheses, J. Michael Montias, 'Cost and Value in Seventeenth-Century Dutch Art', *Art History*, 10 (1987), pp. 455–65.

metallurgical trades. Large artisanal enterprises were not, in other words, entirely a product of fixed capital and new technologies.

Variations in the size of artisanal enterprises await detailed examination and explanation. It is probable, however, that large artisanal enterprises grew as much by way of product and market diversification as by way of market expansion. Large enterprises became large not simply by making more of the same thing, but by adding to the variety of their products and to the range of clients and intermediaries that they supplied. The process was most marked in textile production, where the range of cotton or silk fabrics produced in Rouen, Lyon or Nîmes doubled in size during the latter half of the eighteenth century. It was equally visible in the growing variety of objects and artefacts supplied by relatively substantial artisanal enterprises in the Parisian furnishing, painting and decorative trades. The size of the enterprises established by the cabinet-maker Bernard Van Risenbergh, whose son managed a commercial house in Lisbon, by the engravers Gabriel Huquier, Jacques Chéreau and Pierre-François Basan, whose commercial activities encompassed London, Amsterdam, Stockholm and Warsaw, by the sculptor François Leprince and by the printer and publisher Firmin Didot was complemented by a correspondingly varied range of products.[52] Increases in the size of some artisanal enterprises by way of product diversification were matched by comparable changes in the range and variety of goods supplied by wholesalers and commercial houses. Just as some artisanal enterprises increased in size because they produced a wider range of goods, so some wholesalers, including many of the Parisian *marchands merciers*, became increasingly differentiated from the mass of ordinary merchants because of their participation in a wide variety of different markets.[53]

Variations in the size of artisanal enterprises had a number of effects

---

[52] On textile diversification in Rouen, Nîmes and Lyon, see Sonenscher, 'Weavers, Wage-Rates and the Measurement of Work'; 'Royalists and Patriots'; and the forthcoming thesis by Lesley Miller of Brighton Polytechnic on silk-designers in eighteenth-century Lyon. On product diversification in the Parisian decorative trades, see A.N. MC LXVI 432 (7 January 1738), inventory. Bernard Van Risenbergh: MC XXXVI, 453 (27 April 1746), inventory François Leprince: A.N. Y 11 028 (5 October 1785), on the size of Leprince's *atelier*: Pierre Casselle, 'Pierre-François Basan, marchand d'estampes à Paris (1723–1797)', *Paris et Ile de France*, 33 (1982), pp. 99–185; Maxime Préaud, Pierre Casselle, Marianne Grivel and Corinne Le Bitouzé, *Dictionnaire des éditeurs d'estampes à Paris sous l'Ancien Régime* (Paris, 1987); Catherine Hamet, 'Les Ebenistes parisiens dans la seconde moitié du xviiie siècle (à partir des inventaires après decès)', Mémoire de maîtrise, Université de Paris X (Nanterre), 1973. See also chapter 7 below, and, on furniture, see Hector Lefuel, *Georges Jacob, ébéniste du xviiie siècle* (Paris, 1923).

[53] Hints of the activities of the Parisian *marchands merciers* can be found in Serge Grandjean, *Catalogue des tabatières, boites et étuis des xviiie et xixe siècles du musée du Louvre* (Paris, 1981); Pierre Verlet, 'Le Commerce des objets d'art et les marchands-merciers à Paris au xviiie siècle', *Annales E.S.C.*, 14 (1958), pp. 10–29, and Pierre Verlet, *Les Bronzes dorés français du xviiie siècle* (Paris, 1987).

upon the relationship between large and small workshops. It has been customary to emphasise the extent to which large enterprises were a potential threat to their smaller counterparts because of the economies of scale, greater resources of credit and lower prices that they could command. From this perspective, the periphery of smaller workshops was forced into a position of subordination because of its incapacity to survive other than by undertaking sub-contracted work at heavily discounted rates.[54] In some trades or mono-industrial towns, where a uniform range of products was supplied to a very limited range of markets, that possibility may have occurred; in most cases, however, the relationship between large and small artisanal enterprises was more complex. Many large artisanal enterprises grew in size by increasing the range of goods that they produced. In large cities, particularly in eighteenth-century Paris, the process entailed extending the range of sub-contractors responsible for supplying semi-finished materials, worked-up parts or decorative embellishments. In most cases involving product diversification, sub-contracted work was carried out by members of other trades, since it was they who were in command of the materials, tools or skills that might be needed.

The core of any particular trade was, therefore, the basis not so much of the periphery of the same trade as of segments of the peripheral parts of an indeterminate number of others. There were, of course, substantial variations in the range and shape of the networks formed by these cross-trade divisions of labour. They were very much more extensive in the furnishing or decorative trades than, for example, in printing or shoemaking. In other trades, like hatting or watchmaking, where retail and repair work were important sources of income for many tiny workshops, large and small artisanal enterprises complemented each other's contribution to the circuits through which particular products passed. Yet whatever the differences in the shape and range of cross-trade divisions of labour, their existence meant that the relationship between different-sized artisanal enterprises in any single trade was often less

[54] See, for example, Clive Behagg, 'Custom, Class and Change: The Trade Societies of Birmingham', *Social History*, 4 (1979), pp. 455–80 (pp. 464–5), and his 'Masters and Manufacturers: Social Values and the Smaller Unit of Production in Birmingham, 1800–50', in Geoffrey Crossick and Heinz-Gerhard Haupt, eds., *Shopkeepers and Master Artisans in Nineteenth-Century Europe* (London, 1984), pp. 137–54. Most discussions of *marchandage*, or the supply of quantities of finished or semi-finished goods at cut prices, which was a source of substantial conflict in the Parisian clothing and building trades in the first half of the nineteenth century, follow a similar line of argument. The whole subject is in need of further thought, if only because most of the literature concerned with *marchandage* assumes undifferentiated markets and uniform products: see, for example, Rémi Gossez, ed., *Un Ouvrier en 1820*, pp. 11–43. An alternative approach, in which the emphasis falls less on the rise of competitive sub-contracting and more on the effects of institutional change, is outlined in chapters 1 and 8.

significant than that between large and small artisanal enterprises in many different trades.

It is not easy, therefore, to explain conflict among master artisans solely in terms of the subordination of small producers to large enterprises. The cores and peripheries of the eighteenth-century trades were very much more fluid than their modern industrial counterparts. Yet the tension between corporate particularity and cross-trade networks of sub-contracted work was a recurrent source of friction among master artisans.[55] Product and market diversification meant, at times, that the concerns and interests of some master artisans became increasingly bound up with those of their clients or suppliers and increasingly detached from those of other members of their own corporations. Many disputes between *jeunes*, *modernes* and *anciens* over access to materials, the supply of labour, the modalities of tax assessment or the procedures of corporate decision-making were an expression of the heterogeneity of interests within corporations, particularly between established members and younger, recent entrants whose own preoccupations went unrecognised by corporate officials drawn from artisans whose concerns sometimes lay elsewhere.

In a more immediate sense, however, cross-trade contours linking the cores of some trades to the peripheries of others affected patterns of employment in two ways. They ensured that the boundaries separating one occupation from another were more permeable than appearances might initially suggest. They also provided many opportunities for comparisons between working conditions in trades that fell under entirely separate corporate jurisdictions. It is unlikely that the early career of the very successful Parisian engraver Johann-Georg Wille was the only instance of the resultant combination of occupational mobility and opportunistic calculation available to some journeymen. After learning the rudiments of engraving with a gunsmith near his native Königsburg, Wille arrived in Paris in 1736. His first employers in the capital were two gunsmiths, for whom he worked for periods of three and eight months respectively. He then went to work for a watchmaker, but, after several weeks making fine steel wire (*des pièces d'acier trempé de l'épaisseur d'un crin de cheval*), he came to an arrangement with an engraver on the quai de l'Ecole to produce a series of medallions of the kings of France at 20 *livres* a plate. The step from engraving medallions to engraving portraits was a small one, and portrait-engraving became the basis of his subsequent career.[56]

[55] On conflict among members of the Parisian corporations, see Kaplan, 'The Character and Implications of Strife'.

[56] Jean-Georges Wille, *Mémoires et Journal*, ed. Georges Duplessis, 2 vols (Paris, 1857), vol. 1, pp. 33–68. A complaint by Parisian journeyman bronze-founder in 1779 reveals a similar case of occupational drift. He stated that a fellow journeyman had publicly

The interplay between the cores of some trades and the peripheries of others meant that occupational fluidity and cross-trade comparison played a significant part in the determination of the norms and customary usages of particular trades. Customary practices, particularly those associated with the *compagnonnages*, owed as much to comparison and differentiation as to continuity and tradition.[57] Wage-rates, wage-differentials and customary entitlements were structured around the contours of comparison established by journeymen in ancillary trades. Repeated references to working conditions among saddlers and harness-makers, joiners, locksmiths and painters during several cycles of litigation in the eighteenth-century Parisian trades owed as much to their common involvement in coach-making as they did to the niceties of legal precedent.[58]

Yet variations in the range of products and markets that some artisans supplied engendered more than occupational mobility and cross-trade comparisons. They contributed too to differences and distinctions among journeymen. Product and market diversification did not necessarily lead to increases in the size of the workforce employed in particular artisanal enterprises. Increasingly extensive networks of sub-contracted work were as likely to result in additional employment on the peripheries of ancillary trades as in increases in the size of the workforce of core enterprises. None the less, the growing range of products supplied by some artisans meant that they were able to employ some journeymen very much more regularly than others. The difference between large and small artisanal enterprises was, therefore, measured less in terms of the size of the workforce, for that changed regularly, and more in terms of the proportion of the workforce that remained in regular employment in the same shop over relatively long periods. Differences in age, seniority and skill among journeymen were closely related to these variations in periods of employment.

Sharp temporal variations in the size of the workforce employed in any single artisanal enterprise meant that the structural division between the

58 blackened his reputation by claiming, while they were working in a master goldsmith's shop, that none of the masters for whom he had worked was prepared to give him a certificate of good conduct. 'Ce soupçon, quoique mal fondé, le prive de plusieurs boutiques qui lui seroient avantageuses': A.N. Y 12 684 (25 January 1779). On divisions of labour in the production of *bronzes-dorés* see the work by Pierre Verlet cited at note 53 above. In 1807 the Parisian Chamber of Commerce noted that 'L'habitude d'un métier rend propre à cinq ou six autres qui ont avec le sien une analogie rapprochée...Le faiseur de porteteuilles travaille à la buffleterie, le sellier fait des bottes, le peintre d'éventails s'essaie sur la porcelaine, le fabricant d'acier devient armurier, fourbisseur, ainsi du reste': cited in Bergeron, *Banquiers* (note 28 above), p. 318.

57 On the *compagnonnages*, see chapter 9 below. On wage-contours and 'orbits of coercive comparison' see John T. Dunlop, 'Wage Contours' and Arthur M. Ross, 'Orbits of Coercive Comparison', in Michael Piore, ed., *Unemployment and Inflation* (New York, 1979). I owe this reference to Jonathan Zeitlin.

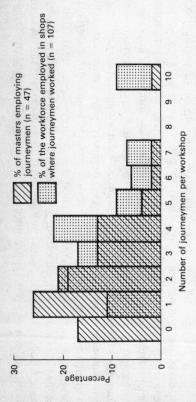

5.5 Number of journeymen employed by each master and distribution of the workforce among the locksmiths of Rouen (1782). Source: A.D. Seine-Maritime, 5E 658.

core and the periphery of the majority of the eighteenth-century French trades was not a stable one. The composition of both changed constantly as journeymen were taken on or laid off to meet the varying schedules of particular workshops. While the general pattern of uneven distribution remained relatively constant, the identity of the master artisans who employed five or more journeymen at a time did not. Two registers of all the journeymen locksmiths who arrived to work in the city of Rouen between November 1782 and April 1791 contain sufficient information to illustrate this unstable relationship between the core and the periphery of the trade with some precision.[59]

When the corporation decided to establish a formal system of registration of migrants to the city, it drew up a list of all the journeymen currently employed in the trade.[60] The 47 master locksmiths on the list employed a total of 107 journeymen, again an average of a little over two each (Figure 5.5). Six masters (12·8 percent) each had five or more journeymen working for them at that time (a total of 38 or 35·5 per cent of the workforce). Between November 1782 and April 1791 a total of 1,086 journeymen locksmiths came to work in Rouen (the registers do not record changes of employment in the city itself). A fifth of them (227 or some 20·9 per cent) went to work for one or other of the five largest employers in 1782. The largest employer in 1782 (with ten journeymen) also took on the largest number of journeymen during the whole period. Yet nothing distinguished the four other relatively large employers recorded in 1782 from a further half dozen master locksmiths who also engaged between 30 and 40 different individuals at various times between 1782 and 1791. The composition of the core of the trade changed constantly, but it was never

[59] A.D. Seine-Maritime, 5E 654 and 649.   [60] A.D. Seine-Maritime, 5E 658.

entirely interchangeable with the whole of the periphery. Only a quarter of the total membership of the trade were ever regular employers of a relatively large number of journeymen.

It is also possible to deduce something of the scale of the turnover of the labour force employed by the locksmiths of Rouen from the same source. During the 102 months covered by the registers a total of 1,086 journeymen arrived in Rouen, or a monthly average of 10·65. If the total of 107 journeymen working in the trade in November 1782 is taken as a constant over the entire 8·5-year period, so that the monthly average of new arrivals (10·65) was matched by an equivalent number of departures, some ten per cent of the labour force changed every month. After ten months the whole workforce of the trade would have been entirely different. During the 8·5 years covered by the registers, the entire labour force of the trade would have turned over no less than ten times. On average a journeyman would have remained with the same master for a little over ten months.

These are, of course, deductions based upon the erroneous assumption that the aggregate size of the workforce in the trade remained constant. Nor do they take changes of employment within the city into account. Both these additional variables meant that the average period of employment was, in fact, significantly lower. Two further enumerations made in 1788 and 1789 suggest that levels of employment in the trade fluctuated very substantially.[61] In 1788 a total of 65 masters had 166 journeymen working for them. In 1789 the size of the workforce had fallen to 148. If the highest figure is taken as a constant, the maximum length of time that the average journeyman would have remained with the same master was some six months. Yet averages conceal more than they reveal. Some journeymen undoubtedly remained with the same master for much longer periods. The registers list 35 individuals whose names and identities were recorded retrospectively, and in 16 cases they also specify the length of time that a journeyman had been working before registration. In each case, the period of employment was at least a year, and in four cases ten years or more.

It is probable that continuity of employment was more usual among journeymen working for masters employing only one or two individuals than among those working in larger shops. Only a quarter of the master locksmiths employing three or more individuals had the same number of journeymen working for them in 1789 as they had in 1788, while half of those employing one or two men had the same number in both

[61] A.D. Seine-Maritime, 5E 651. The brief periods of employment in this and the other trades discussed in this chapter were by no means a product of late eighteenth-century demographic conditions. For similar patterns in mid-seventeenth-century Paris, see Corinne Beutler, 'Bâtiment et salaires: un chantier à Saint-Germain-des-Prés de 1644 à 1646', *Annales E.S.C.*, 26 (1971), pp. 484–517.

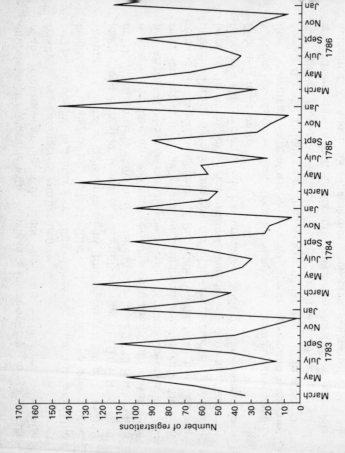

5.6 Monthly totals of registrations by journeymen wigmakers in Rouen (1783–91).
Source: A.D. Seine-Maritime, 5E 148.

years.[62] Although the size of the workforce in the trade fell by 12 per cent between 1788 and 1789, there was no uniform fall in the number of individuals employed in each workshop. Thirteen master locksmiths in fact had more journeymen working for them in 1789 than in 1788, although there were a further 21 masters whose workforces had fallen in size. Most changes in the size of the workforce took place among artisans with three or more journeymen. Relatively large workshops were the places where marginal changes in the size, composition and terms of employment of the workforce occurred.

Thus, just as the world of master artisans was divided into a core and a periphery whose constituent parts were not very stable, so the labour force of many workshops contained the same basic structure. A minority of journeymen remained with the same master for relatively long periods, while the majority moved very frequently from shop to shop. Among the

[62] It is, of course, possible that the journeymen were different, even if the number was the same. There is no reason, however, to suppose that the pattern would have been more marked among masters employing one or two individuals than those employing more. As a result, the difference is still valid.

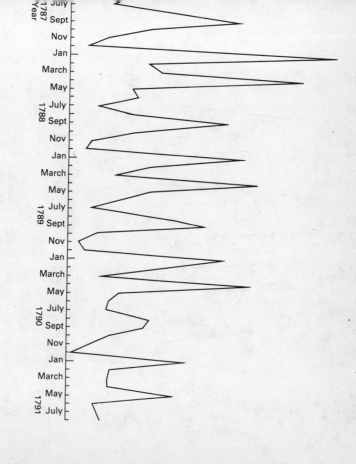

locksmiths of Rouen, it would seem that the average period of employment was between six and ten months. In fact it was lower, because the registers of registration do not record the frequency with which journeymen moved from shop to shop within the city itself. Fortunately, two further series of registers, kept by the wigmakers and tailors of Rouen respectively, record both new arrivals and changes of employment within the city, and can be used to reconstruct patterns of employment with greater precision.

The register kept by the wigmakers' corporation runs from March 1783 to August 1791.[63] During those nine years a total of 3,274 journeymen registered with the corporate office on 5,320 occasions. By linking records of individuals with the same names, places of birth, previous employer and new employer from one registration to the next, it is possible to calculate how long any journeyman who registered more than once remained with the same employer. The relatively long period covered by the register and

[63] A.D. Seine-Maritime 5E 148. I would not have been able to undertake the (laborious) work of making the calculations that follow without the help of Robyn Smits and Mike Bell of the Computer Centre at the Middlesex Polytechnic. They wrote the programmes and supplied the advice which enabled a novice in computing to work with some measure of independence. I am very grateful to them both.

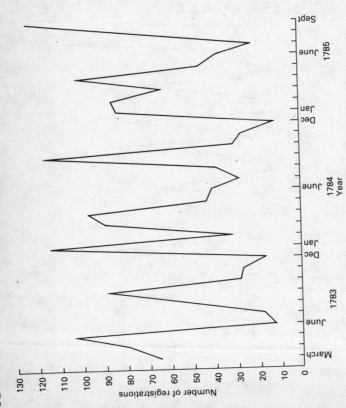

5.7 Monthly totals of registrations by journeymen wigmakers in Nantes (1783–5).
Source: A.C. Nantes, HH 101.

the large number of journeymen who registered no more than twice or three times (while only six per cent registered four times or more) make the 1,475 measurable periods of employment that it is possible to calculate a representative sample of patterns of employment in the trade as a whole. They reveal that, on average, journeymen wigmakers remained with the same master for 118 days, or four months.

The average of four months that journeymen spent working for the same master was a reflection of the highly seasonal character of the labour market in the wigmaking trade. In each of the seven full years covered by the register, the highest monthly totals of registrations occurred in January, April and September (Figure 5.6). The rhythms of movement from shop to shop and of immigration by journeymen from cities outside Rouen followed a similar pattern. In both cases, the life of the trade was governed by the cycle of the social and liturgical calendar. Only after 1789, as that cycle began to disintegrate, did the rhythm of registrations begin to change. Nor, of course, was the eighteenth-century social and liturgical calendar peculiar to Rouen. A register of journeymen kept by the wigmakers' corporation of Nantes reveals an identical pattern of

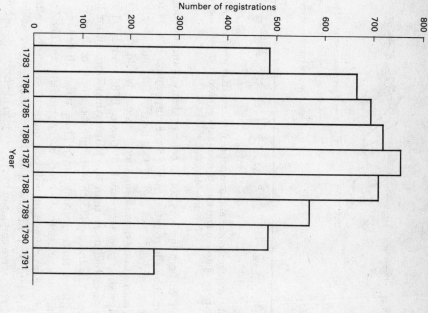

Number of registrations

Year

5.8 Annual number of registrations by journeymen wigmakers in Rouen (1783–91). Source: A.D. Seine-Maritime, 5E 148.

registrations, with annual peaks in January, April and September of each year (Figure 5.7).[64] It is probable that schedules of employment and fluctuations of demand for labour in the wigmaking trade were among the most nationally uniform of any of the eighteenth-century French trades. It is not surprising, in the light of this pattern, to find that disputes in the wigmaking trade reverberated from town to town with remarkable regularity.[65]

It is also possible to calculate how many journeymen each master employed during the period covered by the register and measure changes in the distribution of the workforce between master wigmakers who employed journeymen regularly and those who did not. Membership of the

[64] A.C. Nantes, HH 101.

[65] See above, chapter 2.

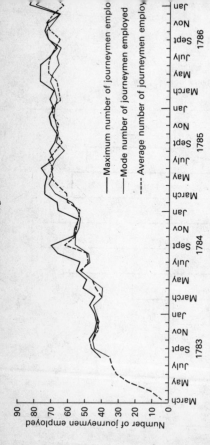

— Maximum number of journeymen emplo[yed]
— Mode number of journeymen employed
--- Average number of journeymen emplo[yed]

5.9 Monthly average, modal and maximum numbers of journeymen employed in wigmaking trade of Rouen and total of man-days worked (1783–91). Source: A.D. Seine-Maritime, 5E 148.

wigmakers' corporation was not, of course, identical throughout the nine years covered by the register. In 1788 the corporation had 94 masters or widows, but between 1783 and 1791 a total of 140 individuals employed a journeyman at one time or another.[66] As one would expect, the size of the average shop was very small. Between 1783 and 1791 no master wigmaker ever had more than five journeymen working for him at the same time, while the workforce of the great majority of shops consisted of no more than a single journeyman.[67] Thus, although between 400 and 750 journeymen registered for work every year between 1783 and 1789, the size of the workforce at any one moment was substantially lower (Figures 5.8 and 5.9). At most a total of 83 journeymen wigmakers (in January 1787) were employed by the 90 or so members of the corporation.

The relatively small size of the workforce of the trade is entirely in keeping with the average number of journeymen employed by master artisans in the clothing trades. While master joiners and locksmiths employed, on average, two journeymen each, master wigmakers barely averaged a single individual. However the average conceals substantial differences between the core and the periphery of the trade. Between 1783 and 1791 the labour force of the wigmaking trade in Rouen worked for a total of 174,224 man-days (i.e. the total number of journeymen

66 University of London Library, Institute of Historical Research. *Tableau de Rouen pour l'année 1788* (Rouen, 1788).

67 The registers record journeymen's seniority in particular shops. No journeymen was ever employed as more than 'en cinquième'. Although it it possible that some journeymen did not register at all and certain that others left Rouen after working for no more than one master (so that it is impossible to link two records of registration), the long period covered by the register makes it very unlikely that the figures of the aggregate size of the workforce (between 1784 and 1790 in particular) are far below the real totals. For a further consideration of the problem, see below. p. 165–6.

multiplied by the total number of days). Only 27 masters regularly employed a sufficient number of journeymen to generate a total of 2,000 or more man-days during the entire period. Together they represented a little under a fifth (19·3 per cent) of the total number of employers, but the journeymen they employed performed nearly half (46·5 per cent) the total number of man-days worked.

Like the locksmiths, the wigmaking trade was divided into a relatively small core and a larger periphery. The distance between the core and the periphery was, however, significantly lower. The workforce employed by master wigmakers ranged in size from one to five, while master locksmiths employed up to ten or more journeymen. The degree of overlap between membership of the core and membership of the periphery of the wigmaking trade was therefore more substantial. At different moments, a higher proportion of master wigmakers were employers of what, by the standards of the trade, were relatively large numbers of journeymen. A third of the 29 masters who employed three or more journeymen at one time or another between 1783 and 1791 were not among the 27 masters who employed a sufficient number of men to generate 2,000 or more man-days of work during the period covered by the register. Inversely a further third of the latter group never employed three journeymen for as long as a month during the whole period. Labour markets in the wigmaking trade were more decentralised than in the furnishing or hatting trades. In the wigmaking trade, competition among masters and the relatively wide range of opportunities for employment available to journeymen were one reason for the importance that corporations attached to the control of journeymen's migrations and the regulation of working conditions.[68]

[68] On disputes in the wigmaking trade, see above, chapter 2.

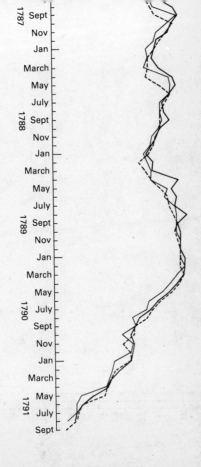

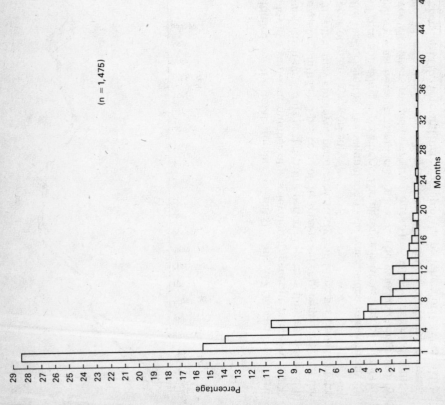

(n = 1,475)

5.10 Length of periods of employment in the wigmaking trade of Rouen (1783–91). Source: A.D. Seine-Maritime, 5E 148.

The division between the core and the periphery of the trade is also apparent in patterns of employment among journeymen. Although the average journeyman remained with the same master for 118 days, the figure was the product of a wide range of different periods of employment (Figure 5.10). Over a quarter (28·4 per cent) of the 1,475 measurable periods of employment were for less than a month. Inversely, 79 periods (5·4 per cent) were for a year or more. As was generally the case, the workforce of the wigmaking trade was divided into two relatively distinct segments, one of which was relatively sedentary, while the other was more mobile. Yet the decentralisation of the labour market ensured that there was no stable hierarchy within the workforce of the trade. The register of registration indicates that journeymen were taken on at varying levels of seniority: 'en premier', 'en deuxième', 'en troisième', and so on. Fewer than a half of them, however, were able to move from shop to shop and remain at the same level or move to a higher one than they had occupied before. The high level of turnover from shop to shop (and city to city) meant that in any particular locality, hierarchies of age, experience and seniority were fragile and temporary components of the working environment. This was one reason why legal entitlements and preferential rights of employment were a matter of such concern to journeymen. Much of the ritual and ceremony of journeymen's associations, particularly the *compagnonnages*, were an inverted acknowledgment of their absence.[69]

In the wigmaking trade of Rouen the rhythm of journeymen's movements from master to master was governed by the social and liturgical calendar: from the New Year to Lent, from Easter to Pentecost, and from All Saints to Christmas. In the tailoring trade, patterns of employment were affected by very much more episodic changes in levels of demand. On average journeymen tailors in Rouen remained with their masters for no more than five weeks. The registers kept by the tailors of Rouen are one of the fullest sources of information about patterns of employment in an eighteenth-century trade that can be found.[70] The two registers only cover a relatively brief period, from 13 July 1778 to 19 November 1781, but during those 41 months a total of 4,903 journeymen tailors registered with the corporate office and paid its clerk a fee of five *sous* to be placed in work. The registers record not only their names, place of birth and previous place of employment (either in Rouen or elsewhere), but also the addresses of the inns or furnished rooms where many of them lodged, together with the names of the masters (or widows) to whom they were sent to work. Many journeymen registered with the corporate office more than once. As a result the 4,903 registrations were made by 1,859 individuals.

The short period covered by the two registers might suggest that links between records of registration could produce a distorted image of patterns of employment. Some individuals undoubtedly registered very much more often than others. One journeyman appears on the registers no less than 30 times, while two others registered on 21 occasions each. The three of them were thus responsible for no less than 69 measurable periods of employment. The nature of the source also means that journeymen about

[69] On the *compagnonnages*, see below, chapter 9.
[70] A.D. Seine-Maritime, 5E 709 and 710. One of the two registers was used as the basis of Michael Sonenscher, 'Journeymen's Migrations and Workshop Organization in Eighteenth-Century France', in Kaplan and Koepp, eds, *Work in France*, pp. 74–96. What follows is a considerably modified version of that paper. In Paris, similar patterns of employment can be illustrated in a more impressionistic way from the inspections of journeymen's certificates carried out by the *commissaires* of the Châtelet: see A.N. Y 15 375 (11 April 1769–7 March 1775) for visits to bakers' shops and journeymen's lodging houses by the *commissaire* Serreau.

to leave Rouen in May 1778 or those who had just arrived in November 1781 only appear once. In all 939 individuals (50·5 per cent) registered on only one occasion. Fortunately the majority of the remainder (527 or 57·3 per cent of the remaining 920) registered only twice or three times. Together with the 393 journeymen who registered more than three times, they form a total that is sufficiently large to outweigh the distortions that might be caused by the frequent registration of a very small number of individuals.

The decision to establish a system of registration in the tailoring trade was not unanimous. Six master tailors were opposed to the system and appealed to the Parlement of Normandy against the decision. Yet the evidence is that virtually every master tailor and the great majority of journeymen made use of the corporate office once it had been established. The names of the masters who appealed to the Parlement in 1777 appear as frequently on the registers as those of the officials of the corporation at the time the decision was taken.[71] The tailors' corporation of Rouen was a large one, with a total membership of 274 masters in 1775.[72] The registers contain the names of some 347 master tailors who employed at least one journeyman between 1778 and 1781. The figure is substantially higher than the total membership of the corporation in 1775 not only because the normal incidence of mortality, retirement, bankruptcy and new entry meant that membership of the corporation changed from year to year, but also because some masters moved to new addresses in Rouen between 1778 and 1781. A small proportion of the total number of employers has, as a result, been counted more than once.[73] At one time or another, however, almost every master tailor or widow appears to have made use of the corporate office and registered the names of the journeymen that he or she had engaged.

Journeymen who failed to register were fined and faced the possibility of imprisonment. Enforcement of the requirement to register depended upon the corporation's officials. The registers reveal that they ordered journeymen to register retrospectively on 13 occasions, but there were undoubtedly some journeymen who refused to register. Some may simply have left Rouen and gone to work in one or other of the smaller towns of the vicinity. The registers list the names of ten individuals who refused to register or pay the fee of five *sous* to the corporation's clerk. They were all denied employment, but most of them registered at a later date. As this

[71] A.D. Seine-Maritime, 1BP 15 227 (20 November 1777).

[72] *Tableau de Rouen pour l'année 1775* (University of London Library, Institute of Historical Research), under 'tailleurs'; Marc Bouloiseau, *Cahiers de doléances du tiers état du bailliage de Rouen* (Paris, 1957), vol. 1, p. 194.

[73] Ninety-eight names appear with changes of address. Some were, of course, relatives of established master tailors who had set themselves up in their own right; others, however, were the same individuals who had moved to a different street.

Table 2 *Annual registrations by journeymen tailors of Rouen, 1778–81*

1778 (July–Dec.)	654
1779	1,148
1780	1,688
1781 (Jan.–Nov.)	1,613

suggests, it may not have been easy to find work elsewhere. On 33 occasions, mainly in the autumn of 1778, journeymen who did register were listed as being currently 'sans boutique'. Nor did masters automatically accept the journeymen supplied by the corporation's clerk. Journeymen were rejected on 41 occasions, for reasons which were not recorded. Despite this, all of them re-registered and were able to find work subsequently.

The scale of registrations (an average of 120·5 a month) is a further indication that most journeymen complied with the formality. One reason why they were prepared to do so was because the new system did not replace informal networks of finding work. Instead, it was superimposed upon established practices and, as it was intended to do, provided masters with written evidence and a source of legal redress if a journeyman walked out without completing his work. All the evidence indicates that registration became more frequent as the system became more securely established. The average number of 120·5 registrations a month is, in fact, heavily biased in favour of the consistently higher number of registrations during the last eight months of the period covered by the two registers. Almost a third of all registrations (32·9 per cent) occurred during the ten and a half months of 1781. The annual number of registrations rose constantly, although there were differences in the six-monthly rates of registration (Table 2).

These variations are more apparent in the monthly rates of registration (Figure 5.11). The graphs of the monthly rates of registration in each of the four years covered by the registers reveal a number of sharp peaks and troughs. Significantly, however, they do not coincide. Since the majority of registrations were the result of the movement of journeymen from master to master within Rouen, it is clear that there were no general factors affecting the rhythm of changes in employment in the trade. The movement of journeymen within the city was governed by the discordant rhythms of the multiple schedules of scores of different workshops. It reflected the constantly changing configuration of the relationship between the core and the periphery of the trade.

There was a very much more regular pattern in the monthly rate of new arrivals to the city. Almost a third (32·4 per cent) of the 4,903

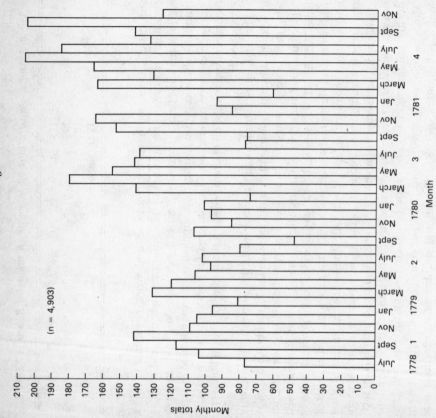

5.11 Monthly totals of registrations by journeymen tailors of Rouen (1778–81).
Source: A.D. Seine-Maritime, 5E 709–10.

registrations involved newcomers from other localities. An average of 39 journeymen from outside Rouen (or 33 per cent of the monthly average) registered with the corporate office every month. The monthly proportion of immigrants varied considerably, from 15 to 51 per cent, and followed a distinct pattern (Figure 5.12). The largest monthly proportion of newcomers (between 33 and 51 per cent) registered in April and October of each of the three full years covered by the registers.[74] In this respect, the rate of registration of new arrivals is a clearer indication of the underlying seasonal nature of the economy of the trade. They suggest that masters expected to take on additional labour immediately after Easter and just

[74] Only in December 1778, when 41 per cent of all registrations involved immigrants, was the pattern broken.

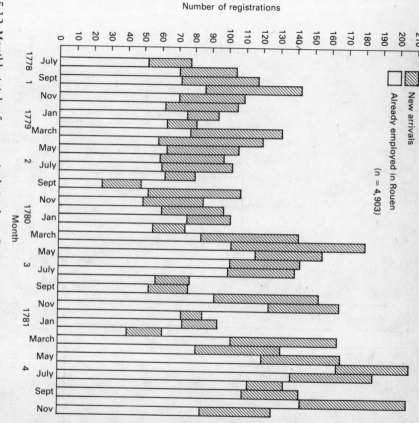

5.12 Monthly totals of new arrivals in the tailoring trade of Rouen (1778–81). Source: A.D. Seine-Maritime, 5E 709–10.

before the Feast of All Saints, and that journeymen timed their movements to coincide with the additional demand for labour. They also suggest that disputes between masters and journeymen over conditions of employment were more likely to have occurred in the spring and autumn, when the presence of relatively large numbers of newcomers made it possible for one side or the other to call previously established practices into question.

The large number of newcomers, coupled with the larger number of re-registrations by journeymen already working in Rouen, are an indication of the generally erratic rhythms of employment in the trade, reinforced by recurrent seasonal variations in the market for labour. They suggest that master artisans worked very much from week to week, taking on or dismissing journeymen when orders came in or a particular piece of work was finished. It is likely too that seasonal fluctuations were reinforced by

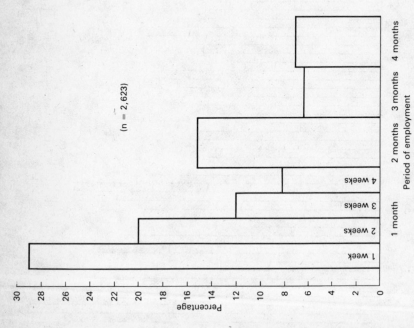

(n = 2,623)

5.13 Length of periods of employment in the tailoring trade of Rouen (1778–81).
Source: A.D. Seine-Maritime, 5E 709–10.

the immediate pressure of holidays and public festivities. The pattern was an old one. In 1688 the journeymen tailors of Lyon replied to their masters' claim that they were unwilling to work from 5 a.m. to 8 p.m. by pointing out that most of their masters expected them to work through the night on the eve of holidays, but did not pay them any additional amount.[75] It is unlikely that the pattern had changed very much in Rouen nearly 100 years later.

The links that can be made between the records of registration make it possible to measure these patterns of employment with some precision. In all, links occurred between 2,623 records of registration (or 53·5 per cent

[75] 'La pluspart des maistres qui les employent les font travailler la veille des festes toute la nuit et jusques au lendemain sept à huict heures du mattin, sans qu'ils leur payent pour cella plus grande somme que celle qui est reiglée': A.C. Lyon, HH 185 (18 December 1688).

of the total number of registrations). By adding the number of days between successive records involving the same journeyman, it is possible to calculate how long an individual remained with the same master. Overall the average period of employment (which includes Sundays and holidays) was no more than 34 days. Again, the average is misleading (Figure 5.13), because almost a half (1,283 or 48·9 per cent) of the 2,623 measurable periods of employment were for intervals of between one and fourteen days. A further 535 (20·4 per cent) were periods of between 15 and 28 days. Thus over two thirds of all the periods of employment lasted for no more than a month.

The reason why the modal period of employment was so much lower than the average was because a small but significant number of journeymen (238 or 9·1 per cent) were employed for periods of more than three months. This smaller group of journeymen employed for relatively long periods of time was distributed very widely among master tailors. At least 100 different masters employed one journeyman for more than three months. A number of tailors' shops thus consisted of one or two journeymen employed for relatively long periods of time, together with a larger number of individuals taken on for extremely short periods. The relatively stable core of the working population was surrounded by a constantly changing periphery of highly peripatetic journeymen often employed as *aides* on a single piece of work for a day or two at the most.

Despite the large number of journeymen who came to work in Rouen, the number of men employed at any one time by each master tailor and in the trade as a whole was surprisingly low. In this respect the trade was very similar to the wigmaking trade. It is possible to calculate the number of journeymen employed by each master (by adding together periods of employment which overlapped) and the total number in employment on any day during the whole period (by adding together the daily totals of journeymen employed by each master). The procedure has rather more limitations when applied to the tailoring trade than to the wigmakers because of the relatively short period covered by the tailors' registers. Journeymen who worked for only one master and then left Rouen; journeymen employed by the same master for more than three and a half years; journeymen already established with a single master before the system of registration began who then married and became masters in their own right; and journeymen whose names were recorded only at the beginning and end of the registers would not be included in the calculations. The figures that can be calculated are therefore undoubtedly an understatement, although it is unlikely that they are much of an understatement. Since the great majority of measurable periods of employment were so short, it is unlikely that the totals calculated for

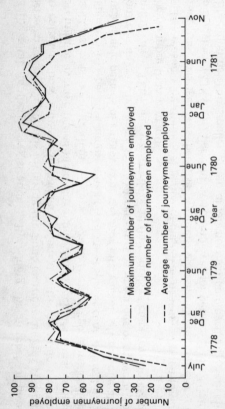

5.14 Monthly average, modal and maximum numbers of journeymen employed in the tailoring trade of Rouen (1778–81). Source: A.D. Seine-Maritime, 5E 709–10.

1779, 1780 and the first six months of 1781 are much lower than the total number of journeymen actually working in the trade.

In one instance the registers provide a static image of a master tailor's workforce. In June 1781 a master tailor named Chercheporte died. He had four journeymen working for him at the time, of whom one had been employed for three years and the others for periods of eighteen months, a year and four months.[76] The method of linking records shows that Chercheporte employed three journeymen in April 1781, or one fewer than the real number. There is, regrettably, no way of knowing whether this 25 per cent difference was generally true. Even it it were, it does not affect the general conclusions that can be drawn from an examination of the size and distribution of the workforce of the trade.

The total number of journeymen working in the trade was lower than that produced by the average of two journeymen per master among the locksmiths or joiners of Amiens, Marseille or Rouen, but comparable to the total number of journeymen employed by master wigmakers. At any one time the number of journeymen working in the tailoring trade in 1779, 1780 and the first half of 1781 was never more than 100 (Figure 5.14). There were, in other words, many more masters working in the trade than there were journeymen. Given the relatively small scale of the trade and the absence of any need for fixed installations (the least a master tailor needed to practise his trade was a room) the figures are not surprising. In Bordeaux in 1744, the 189 master tailors listed on the *capitation* roll employed a total of 161 journeymen.[77] In Rouen, the highest number of

[76] A.D. Seine-Maritime, 5E 710 fols. 123vo–124.

[77] J. Lacoste-Palisset, 'Les Tailleurs bordelais dans la seconde moitié du xviiie siècle', (T.E.R. Université de Bordeaux, 1973), part 2, chapter 1

journeymen working in the trade according to the calculations based upon the registers of employment was no more than 97 (in November 1780). Even if there were three times as many journeymen omitted from the calculations (which is unlikely) there would still have been only two dozen more journeymen than masters working in the trade.

It is apparent therefore that most master tailors did not employ journeymen in a regular way, or, when they did, they employed no more than a single individual. Only a minority of masters, and a very small one, regularly employed more than one journeyman. Thus 54 of the 97 journeymen employed on 3 November 1780 were working for 20 master tailors. One of them had six journeymen working for him while another had five. A fuller measure of the unequal distribution of employment can be made by calculating the total number of man-days worked during the whole period (87,335) and the proportion of that total filled by each master tailor (Figure 5.15).

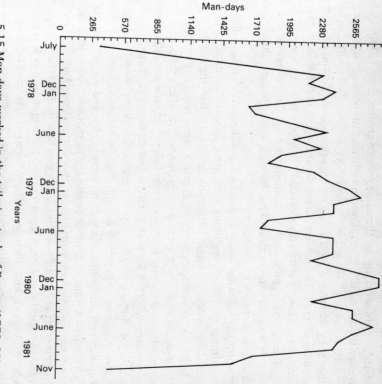

5.15 Man-days worked in the tailoring trade of Rouen (1778–81).
Source: A.D. Seine-Maritime, 5E 709–10.

On only 32 occasions was the total number of man-days which journeymen spent working for the same master greater than 1,000. Only five master tailors regularly employed a sufficient number of journeymen to produce a total of over 2,000 man-days during the entire period. Together they accounted for 16,425 or 18·8 per cent of the total number of man-days worked. The five employed almost a fifth of the total number of journeymen who registered for work in Rouen between 1778 and 1781. Three of them had opposed the establishment of the system of registration.[78] It is easy to understand why, for they were the individuals most vulnerable to disputes in the trade.

Although the tailoring trade in Rouen was a large one, it was divided into a number of distinct segments. The great majority of master tailors worked alone or with a single journeyman (but still had the resources of their families). A small minority of masters were regular employers of journeymen, most of whom were engaged for periods of less than a month. At any one time, of course, even large employers had only a small number of journeymen working for them. The largest employer of them all was a master tailor named Vandercruysse, yet although he was the largest employer of labour in the trade (accounting for some four per cent of the total number of man-days worked) he never employed more than eight journeymen at a time, according to the registers. Only one master tailor ever had ten journeymen working for him at the same time.

The pattern is very similar to those that can be found in other trades. As with the locksmiths and, to a lesser degree, the wigmakers of Rouen, the joiners of Amiens and their respective counterparts in Marseille, the market for labour was surprisingly centralised. The great majority of the 1,859 journeymen tailors who worked in Rouen between 1778 and 1781 were employed by less than three dozen master tailors. The considerable discrepancy between the large number of master tailors in the city, and the very much smaller number of regular employers of a number of journeymen, has two clear implications. It is easier to understand how journeymen maintained so clear a sense of the norms of a trade in the light of the recurrent pattern of core and periphery (however much membership of either changed) which characterised the internal structure of many local economies. The norms of a trade depended upon what happened in a very small number of workshops or *boutiques* and the behaviour of a very small number of masters. It is also easier to understand the significance of disputes and stoppages by journeymen which often appear to have been limited and partial. Since the terms of the relationship between journeymen

---

[78] The five largest employers were Bertrand, Brackmans, Couche, Duport, Vandercruysse and Zaly. Three of them (Vandercruysse, Bertrand and Brackmans) opposed the establishment of the *bureau*. Their names, as well as those of three other masters, can be found in A.D. Seine-Maritime, 1BP 15 227 (20 November 1777).

and their masters were set within the small core of the trades where most journeymen worked, apparently selective stoppages, or boycotts of particular employers, often had a significance that outweighed the relatively small number of individuals involved.

The relationship between masters and journeymen in the tailoring trade of Rouen was structured in another way which also introduced a substantial element of cohesion into the apparently fragmented and dispersed character of the local economy. Just as the structure of core and periphery meant that what happened between masters and journeymen was centred upon a relatively small number of workshops, and what happened among journeymen was centred upon the relationship between a small number of relatively long-established individuals and a larger number of journeymen employed for very brief intervals, so the supply of labour depended upon what happened in a very small number of lodging houses. The 4,903 registrations recorded by the corporate clerk between 1778 and 1781 did not occur in a random way. Master tailors recruited many of the journeymen they employed from a small number of lodging houses, each of which supplied a different segment of the labour market.

The registers of the corporate office record the names and streets of the inns or furnished rooms where journeymen tailors lodged. Where they do not, it can be assumed that journeymen lodged with their masters. In 1768 under a third of the 424 journeymen on a list of potential members of the militia (which was not, of course, confined to the tailoring trade) were housed by their masters.[79] In the tailoring trade, where the number of journeymen employed by most masters was very low, the proportion was somewhat higher and stood at a little over 50 per cent. There was a clear difference between masters who housed most of the journeymen they employed, and those whose journeymen stayed in what were termed the *logis*. As one would expect, the majority of the larger employers did not house all their journeymen themselves. Twenty-one of the 32 largest employers of labour recruited journeymen from one of three inns or *logis*, located respectively on the rue des Bons Enfants, the rue Percière and the rue Saint-Lô. The three inns accounted for 1,687 (or 34·4 per cent) of the 4,903 registrations of journeymen tailors between 1778 and 1781. Since over 50 per cent of all the journeymen who registered lodged with a master, the three inns supplied 73 per cent of the journeymen who lived in lodgings.

Eleven of the 32 largest employers of journeymen in the tailoring trade had nothing to do with the three inns: they either housed their journeymen themselves, or recruited them from other lodging houses which were not closely identified with the trade. The majority of the core of the trade

[79] Jean-Pierre Bardet, *Rouen aux xviie et xviiie siècles* (Paris, 1983), p. 239.

housed some individuals themselves but relied upon one or other of the three principal lodging houses for most of their journeymen. Most of them employed journeymen from a single lodging house. Only three of the 21 master tailors who recruited journeymen from the three main inns employed men from more than one of them. The remainder employed individuals from a single source. Thus 55 of the 101 journeymen taken on by a master tailor named Najac between 1778 and 1781 lodged *chez* Deforge (himself a master tailor) on the rue Percière. He housed the other 46 himself. A master named Brackmans, with a shop on the rue Grand Pont, recruited 96 of the journeymen he employed from the inn on the rue des Bons Enfants and housed a further 64 himself. The lodging house on the rue Saint Lô supplied 58 journeymen to a master tailor named Glasson, and he housed all the others he employed himself.

Three master tailors used more than one of the principal lodging houses. Yet they did not recruit their journeymen indiscriminately from one or the other of the three inns; instead, they relied upon a single inn for a certain length of time and then changed to one of the other two. Thus at different times between 1778 and 1781, each of the three lodging houses regularly supplied journeymen to eight master tailors. The symmetry is remarkable and is unlikely to have been an accident – instead, it suggests that a very effective informal process of selection was at work. It meant that the local labour market was relatively highly segmented, and that the lodging houses played an important part in determining conditions of work in the trades. The core of regular employers of relatively large numbers of journeymen was matched by a small cluster of inns with their own relatively stable circuits of employment. Journeymen lodging *chez* Naudin on the rue Saint-Lô worked mainly for one set of master tailors, while those lodging on the rue Percière or the rue des Bons Enfants worked for two almost entirely different circles.

The internal organisation of particular trades consisted, therefore, of very much more than a large number of tiny, dispersed units of production. There is no reason to suppose that the patterns of employment and local labour markets that existed in Rouen were particularly different from those that obtained in any large late eighteenth-century French city. They were structured in three ways: between a small core of master artisans who regularly employed two, three or more journeymen and a larger number who did not; between a minority of journeymen who remained with the same master for relatively long periods of time and a much larger majority that did not; and between journeymen lodging in the small number of lodging houses that supplied regular employers with up to three quarters of their workforce, and those who were housed by their masters, or lived with relatives or in their own lodgings elsewhere in the city. Two further characteristics of the local economies of the trades call for special comment. The first is that the divisions between different kinds of master and different kinds of journeymen were not stable. Although the general division between core and periphery was a durable one, the composition of its component parts was not. The appearance of continuity was, in other words, the product of a continuous process of negotiation: between masters over the distribution of journeymen, between journeymen over where they would work, and, where itinerant journeymen formed a significant part of the labour force, between masters and the inhabitants of particular inns over for whom they would work. The second characteristic is an obvious one, for none of this complexity found its way into the law. The provisions of corporate statutes and deliberations were a highly simplified commentary upon a process of negotiation carried out from day to day and week to week beyond the boundaries of legal provision. The law was only one of the instruments that masters and journeymen had at their disposal to define their respective rights and obligations.

The impermanent clusters of masters and journeymen at the core of the trades came to their arrangements largely outside the terms of reference of legal provision, but the very impermanence of the relationship between core and periphery generated tensions among master artisans and between masters and journeymen that precipitated recourse to the courts. These tensions found their expression in three ways. The first centred upon the daily and weekly cycles of work and wages, and the extent to which individual master artisans were able to exercise authority over the journeymen they employed. The second centred upon the contract of employment and the extent to which wage-rates and working conditions responded to the varying schedules of particular artisanal enterprises. The third centred upon the longer process by which journeymen became masters, and masters in their turn passed on their patrimonies to their sons, sons-in-law or other kin. These tensions were not confined to the relationship between masters and journeymen. The instability of the relationship between the core and the periphery of the trades meant that disputes between masters and journeymen could easily become disputes among master artisans, just as disputes between master artisans could also become disputes between masters and journeymen.

These recurrent tensions are most immediately obvious in the debates and divisions that arose among master artisans over the desirability of establishing formal systems of corporate registration themselves. Disputes over the issue were a regular occurrence in the life of the trades throughout the eighteenth century. The tailors' decision to establish a corporate office in Rouen in 1777 was opposed sufficiently strongly by six masters that they were prepared to carry their opposition to the Parlement of Normandy. It is unlikely to have been a coincidence that they were all regular employers of journeymen. Similar divisions occurred among the locksmiths of Rouen. In 1773 they decided not to require journeymen to register or present written certificates attesting to the satisfactory completion of their work when they were taken on by a new employer.[80] In 1780 however, they reversed their decision, and in 1782, following the example of their counterparts in Paris, decided to require journeymen to carry a *livret*. In this, the attitude of relatively large employers of journeymen was invariably ambiguous.[81]

The unstable division between the core and periphery of the trades also explains why it was almost impossible for the corporations to establish permanent systems of registration. Sooner or later the short-term requirements of some master artisans were bound to undermine the prescriptions of the law. For registration did not create new patterns of employment – that was not its purpose. Instead it superimposed a series of formal requirements upon an already established network of segmented labour markets, and supplied master artisans with additional legal resources against journeymen in breach of contract. On the other hand, it made it more difficult for regular employers of labour to come to their own arrangements with journeymen on occasions when sudden increases in demand made it necessary to take on additional labour. In the usual course of events these contradictory pressures cancelled one another out. Yet the relatively decentralised labour market in the wigmaking trade, the absence of any clear pattern in the rhythm of registrations among the tailors of Rouen, and the differential direction of changes in the size of the workforce among the locksmiths of the same city are all indicative of the multiplicity of different schedules kept by regular employers of journeymen. As a result, the small number of regular employers of labour were required to compete with other master artisans and negotiate with journeymen in a small number of lodging houses to find the labour needed for the brief bursts of additional work that they undertook.

The constantly changing relationship between the core and periphery meant that masters and journeymen in most urban trades conducted their informal negotiations and settled their differences within the evanescent environment of the bazaar. If, as eighteenth-century jurists put it, the wage was the price of a day's work, the structure of urban labour markets meant that it was also a bargain. Most master artisans engaged most journeymen for the time it took to meet a limited schedule of orders, and most journeymen could expect to work in the same shop for a period of weeks rather than months. Yet bargains tend to be less uniform in character than prices. Such was also the case with wages in eighteenth-century France. The unstable relationship between the core and periphery

[80] A.D. Seine-Maritime, 5E 647 (23 October 1773).
[81] A.D. Seine-Maritime, 5E 650 (14 December 1780); 5E 657 (26 October 1782).

of the trades, the relatively segmented character of local labour markets, the high level of turnover of the majority of journeymen from shop to shop, and the relatively brief periods for which most journeymen worked for wages, all combined to ensure that the average wage was as unrepresentative of wages in general as the average workshop was unrepresentative of workshops as a whole.

CHAPTER 6

Work, wages and customs

In a formal sense, the wages paid to journeymen in the eighteenth-century French trades were 'le prix de leur travail', 'le salaire de leur travail' or 'le prix d'une journée de travail'. The phrases were redolent of the contractual character of the natural law tradition. Yet the various forms of wage-payment that existed in eighteenth-century France owed more to the bazaar economy of the trades than to the prescriptions of the law. The extensive divisions of labour linking workshops in related trades, the short-term schedules of production followed by most master artisans, the rapid movement of most journeymen from shop to shop, and the durable but unstable division between the core and periphery of most urban labour markets affected systems of wage payments in several ways. They meant, in the first place, that no single workshop or unit of production was ever the locus of a particular system of wage payments. They meant too that the division between relatively sedentary and rather more mobile journeymen was matched, in the majority of urban trades, by a wide variety of different modes and rates of pay. Thirdly, they meant that continuity of employment had a significance that went beyond rates of pay and the amounts that journeymen earned, since work for wages was a temporary condition in most journeymen's lives. By the age of 30 most journeymen had either established themselves in one way or another, or had abandoned the trades altogether. Work for wages was also a matter of working to become a master artisan.

It may be convenient, therefore, to regard the wage as a cipher in which a number of different assumptions were encoded. Unlike a cipher in the literal sense, however, the wage was a cipher with more than one author. It embodied codes enscribed by many different authors, whose premises were not entirely the same. It was a cryptic summary of many different assessments of the significance of the passage of time: time to perform different kinds of work, time to collect orders, materials and money, time spent working in the same shop, time to find work elsewhere, time to find a son-in-law, or a wife and a place in a trade. The character of such assessments varied as the interplay between the work of making different products, the extent of particular markets, the development of divisions of labour, and changes in the relative sizes of the core and periphery of local labour markets affected the proportions of sedentary and peripatetic journeymen in the workforces of specific trades.

The well-established discrepancy between the long-term upward movement of prices and the lower rate of increase in wage-rates in eighteenth-century France is easier to understand in this context. It is well-known that average wage-rates (at least the daily rates that were usual in the building trades) rose by some 24 per cent, while the average wholesale price of corn rose by between 66 and 71 per cent between 1726–41 and 1785–9. Even in the Parisian roofing trade, where shortages of labour were endemic and masters sometimes claimed that they were forced to pay journeymen up to 4 *livres* 10 *sous* a day, the corporation was able to maintain an official scale of day-rates of 45 *sous* in winter and 50 *sous* in summer for nearly a generation between 1755 and 1776.[1] Long-term wage stability of this kind had its origins in the demographic structure of the workforce of the trades. The fact that most journeymen were single men aged between 15 and 25, who expected to marry and establish themselves as master artisans, meant that the rates they were paid were affected both by the need to remain in regular employment until they married and by the probability that they would receive some of their parents' and parents-in-law's property when they established themselves.

In general, wage-rates mirrored these considerations. Rates paid on a monthly or yearly basis were invariably lower than day- or piece-rates. The value of dowries, however, appears to have matched the movement of prices. In Lyon, the assets that journeymen received (or were promised) in marriage contracts drawn up between 1786 and 1789 were, on average, some 80 per cent higher than those in contracts drawn up between 1728 and 1730.[2] There were, of course, wide variations in the amounts of

[1] C. E. Labrousse, *Esquisse du mouvement des prix et des revenus en France au xviiie siècle*, 2 vols (Paris, 1933), pp. 448–95; D. M. G. Sutherland, *France 1789–1815* (London, 1985), pp. 54–5. A.N. E 1210°(18)(25 February 1744): X¹ᵃ 4244 fol. 181 (4 September 1756): X¹ᵃ 4611 (1 August 1768): Y 15 375 (11 and 12 December 1769): Y 13 689 (21 March 1781).

[2] On the value of dowries, see Maurice Garden, *Lyon et les lyonnais au xviiie siècle* (Paris, 1970), p. 339. Garden's figures are, of course, rough orders of magnitude, encompassing a wide variety of men and women at very different stages in their lives and drawn from a large number of different occupations, including the city's silk industry. On the heterogeneity of life-cycles before the late nineteenth century (at the earliest) see Michael Anderson, 'The Emergence of the Modern Life-Cycle in Britain', *Social History*, 10 (1985), pp. 69–87. Comparison of marriage contracts in the city of Nîmes in 1705–9 and 1785–9 for men who were called either *compagnons* or *garçons*, but were not involved in textile production, indicates a comparable trend to that found in Lyon. The value of the possessions listed in 200 inventories of Parisian journeymen in 1695–1715 and 1775–90 also appears to have matched the long-term movement of prices: Daniel Roche, *Le Peuple de Paris* (Paris, 1981), pp. 74–6. Matters are, of course, complicated by the

property transferred between the generations in this way, but, for those able to effect the transition, the resources available to journeymen at the end of the Old Regime were at least comparable in value to those that journeymen acquired in the early years of the reign of Louis XV.

Not all journeymen, however, were able to effect the transition. In mid-eighteenth-century Paris, the carpenters' corporation received an average of half a dozen new members every year. No more than a score of new masters were admitted annually to the masons' corporation, while the average rate of entry to the locksmiths' corporation between 1735 and 1750 was a dozen. Even a very large corporation like the 1,000-strong Parisian joiners' corporation received between 30 and 90 new entrants a year between 1778 and 1788, at a time when lower costs had reduced the difficulty of acquiring a *maîtrise*.[3] Although most new masters were not the sons of masters, the number of new entrants was a tiny proportion of the hundreds of journeymen who worked in these trades every year. Many of them, of course, became master artisans elsewhere, but others abandoned the trades entirely. Both the legal entitlements to employment that some journeymen enjoyed and the informal customs that accompanied wage-systems in many trades are best understood in this context. They were not manifestations of an imperfectly monetarised economy – still less an expression of a timeless and custom-bound world – but, instead, were counterpoints to the continuous transfer of resources from one generation to the next and to the diversity, fluidity and impermanence of the working conditions in which that process occurred.

It is usual in the historiography of artisanal production to set wages and customs against one another. Customs were durable and constant in content, while wages were subject to the incessant fluctuations of product and labour markets. Customs belonged to a pre-industrial world and insulated artisans from the vagaries of markets. Even wages, in the eighteenth century, were determined as much by custom as by markets. Gradually, according to this interpretation, money displaced customs, so

largely unexplored problem of changes in the relative prices of manufactured goods, a subject that awaits its historian. See, however, Jean-Yves Grenier, 'Modèles de la demande sous l'ancien régime', *Annales E.S.C.*, 42 (1987), pp. 497–527. On the inverse relationship between rates of pay and periods of employment, see below, p. 189–91. For a comparable analysis of the demographic particularities and inter-generational transfers informing the workshop economy, see Lars Edgren, 'Crafts in Transformation? Masters, Journeymen and Apprentices in a Swedish Town, 1800–1850', *Continuity and Change*, 1 (1986), pp. 363–84.

[3] A.N. XXe 64 (6–8, 11–13, 24, 27, 28, 30, 32–6); Anne-Marie Bruleaux, 'Les Maîtres-Serruriers parisiens et leurs travaux de grande serrurerie', (Thèse de l'Ecole des Chartes, n.d.), pp. 107–8. The annual number of entrants to the Parisian joiners' corporation fluctuated from 119 in 1776–7 (after Turgot's experiment) to 73 (1778–9), 40 (1779–80), 49 (1780–1), 54 (1781–2), 30 (1782–3), 48 (1783–4), 64 (1784–5), 90 (1785–6), 74 (1786–7), 69 (1787–8): A.N. H 2118, *comptes de la communauté des menuisiers–ébénistes–layetiers*.

that working people were obliged to learn the rules of the market-based game.[4] It is a characterisation of the relationship between wages and customs that has been grounded upon two aspects of the world of the eighteenth-century trades: the large number of informal customs that undoubtedly existed in many trades, and the durability of many of the formal rates of pay set by corporations or the courts. These well-attested facts have been reinforced by a more debatable assumption that artisanal workshops belonged to a world of stable divisions between employers and workers, in which continuity of employment was offset mainly by slumps caused by wars, increases in corn prices, deaths at court or other extraneous events. From this perspective, both custom and the customary character of wage-rates were the effects of journeymen's abiding concern to maintain wages at levels appropriate to their skills and to respond to the permanent threat of unemployment caused by the disruption of product markets or the dilution of their crafts.

It is difficult, however, to reconcile this explanation of the importance of custom with some of the other features of the eighteenth-century trades. The terms 'employment' and 'unemployment' do not fit the incessant movement of many journeymen from shop to shop and town to town all that well, nor are they particularly appropriate to the sub-contracted character of many of the arrangements made between master artisans and journeymen. The frequency with which eighteenth-century French corporations sought to establish *bureaux de placement* or require journeymen to carry certificates of previous employment was a measure of the open character of many large urban labour markets and the ease with which journeymen, in ordinary circumstances, were able to move through the network of particular productive units. Customs, moreover, were as much a part of the life of the trades in large cities – where, despite the importance of credit, journeymen still needed money to pay rent or buy their meals – as they were in small towns. Furthermore, and despite the apparent precision of many occupational labels, there was little that distinguished the range of skills associated with one particular trade from those of many others. Joiners, carpenters and wheelwrights, for example, all worked on wood and used similar tools. The small number of materials used in many of the urban trades meant that much of what was produced in eighteenth-century French cities was related only contingently to any one trade rather than another.

These features of the urban trades suggest the possibility of an alternative explanation of both the determinants of wage-rates and the

[4] The *locus classicus* of this interpretation was by E. J. Hobsbawm, 'Custom, Wages and Workload', in *Labouring Men* (Anchor Books edn, New York, 1967), pp. 405–35. See too John Rule, *The Experience of Labour in Eighteenth-Century Industry* (London, 1981), chapter 2; Richard Price, *Labour in British Society* (London, 1986), p. 20.

ubiquity of custom. The repeated reiteration of formal scales of wage-rates over many decades may, perhaps, be most intelligible in the context of rivalries between master artisans. Formal scales of wage-rates were not necessarily the rates that were paid. As the substantial discrepancy (of nearly 100 per cent) between the rates prescribed in the Parisian roofing trade and those felt worthy of complaint suggests, the relationship between formal and real rates was often quite distant. Yet formal scales were sufficiently sticky to be worth reiterating. Their durable character was not, however, the product of custom, however much master artisans might have invoked customary usage to justify their reiteration. Instead, the age and marital status of many journeymen, the relatively centralised character of urban labour markets, the brevity of most periods of employment and the imprecision of many occupational boundaries may be sufficient explanation of the long-term trend in wage-levels, and may also explain the ubiquity of custom. Customs distinguished trades from one another even though many of the materials that they used and many of the products that they made were only contingently associated with one trade rather than another: they were, in other words, a constituent part of the identities associated with particular trades and places. They were a precondition of both labour and product markets because they conferred a quasi-institutional collective identity upon the myriad small enterprises associated with particular trades.

The incessant movement of journeymen from shop to shop and the continuous interdependence of most master artisans as both buyers and sellers of goods and materials and as competitors in the market for labour meant that wage-rates and wage-agreements in the eighteenth-century trades had something of a collective character whether or not they were made between collectivities. Even in the small number of trades in which relatively high levels of integration obtained (among printers or hatters, for example), the trade rather than the firm – the *métier* rather than the *maison*, as journeymen put it – was the usual canvas against which agreements were made or bargains struck. Information about wages and working conditions was easily obtained and widely disseminated. Comparison between trades in different towns, or between different trades in the same town, was a recurrent feature of litigation between masters and journeymen during the eighteenth century.[5] These episodic trials of strength were complemented by more ordinary gossip and rumour. Three journeymen joiners were arrested in Paris in 1751 after one of them had been heard to remark that the painters with whom they were working at the Louvre were better-paid than they were and were also entitled to carry

[5] See above, chapter 3, and Sonenscher, *Hatters*; 'Weavers, Wage-Rates and the Measurement of Work in Eighteenth-Century Rouen', *Textile History*, 17 (1986), pp. 7–18 (p. 9); 'Journeymen, the Courts and the French Trades, 1781–1791', *Past and Present*, 114 (1987), pp. 77–109.

swords and canes. A Parisian toymaker (*compagnon tabletier*) complained in 1764 that one of his workmates had spread a rumour that he had been working at home making caskets at 4 *sous* 6 *deniers* each instead of the usual rate of between 5 and 6 *sous*. He was afraid that he would be assaulted after the journeymen of the trade had met to discuss his case.[6] Information of this kind was an ordinary part of the life of the trades, and its availability was reinforced by the relatively highly centralised markets for labour that existed in most large towns.

The division between the core and periphery of urban labour markets meant that most journeymen (or a very large minority) worked for the quarter or third of master artisans who were regular and relatively substantial employers of labour. Wage-rates and working conditions were therefore set by a relatively small number of large employers. Even in Paris, where the membership of most corporations ran into hundreds, if not thousands, the core of substantial employers of journeymen was very much smaller. In the hatting trade in 1739, ten large concerns accounted for nearly 50 per cent of the total number of journeymen in employment, and similar patterns obtained among locksmiths, joiners, carpenters or coopers and many other trades in which the distance between the core and the periphery was very much less pronounced. In 1785, after a dispute between master painters and decorators and the journeymen of the trade, an inspection to discover how many men had failed to register with the corporate office yielded a total of 300 unregistered journeymen working for 33 masters or widows. For all its obvious limitations, it is a brief, partial image of the structure of the trade. A painter (veuve Thibault) near the Chaussée d'Antin had 35 journeymen on her books; a gilder (Dupré) on the rue de la Verrerie employed 36 journeymen; a workshop on the rue Poissonière belonging to the celebrated sculptor Le Prince had over 40 journeymen at work making marble mantelpieces and furnishings. Between them, these three individuals accounted for over a third of the total number of journeymen who had not registered.[7]

The relatively highly centralised demand for labour in the majority of the urban trades was matched by a concentration of supply. The place de Grève in Paris, frequented by journeymen and labourers in the building trades, was the most substantial of many urban labour markets. According to a police ordinance of 1667, established journeymen expected newcomers to pay a fee (*bienvenu*) and host a meal before they were allowed to occupy a place on the square. Matters had changed little over a hundred years later, when, as a police official explained in 1785, the phrase 'faire grève' meant a decision by building workers 'de ne point

[6] A.N. Y 15 349 (6 December 1751): Y 11 952 (30 July 1764).
[7] Sonenscher, *Hatters*, p. 45; A.N. Y 11 028 (5 October 1785); see also chapter 5, above, for similar patterns among locksmiths and joiners.

travailler pour en faire augmenter de prix leurs journées'. A police ruling in 1787 referred sententiously to 'désordres et excès' perpetrated by journeymen on the place de Grève and, in terms that echoed the regulations applied to the marketing of corn, prohibited anyone from remaining on the square after 7 a.m. in summer or 8 a.m. in winter.[8]

In the baking and tailoring trades, where the range of workshop sizes was more limited and the core of regular employers somewhat more diffuse, the concentration of large numbers of peripatetic journeymen among a small number of lodging houses gave rise to equally centralised labour markets. The strategic position occupied by three lodging houses in the tailoring trade of Rouen was a particular case of a pattern that existed in every large city during the late eighteenth century. Where journeymen in the Parisian building trades invoked the norms of the place de Grève in their transactions with contractors and sub-contractors, journeymen in the victualling and clothing trades referred to the *usage des logis* in their dealings with their employers. Four Parisian journeymen tailors who specialised in making women's clothes complained in 1772 that they had been expected to pay the astonishing sum of 150 *livres* each to participate in an informal association maintained by over 60 journeymen lodging in an inn on the rue des Arcis. Anyone refusing to pay the fee, they said, would be prevented from working in Paris. Some of the inns in which journeymen bakers lodged were of comparable size.[9]

Journeymen were well aware of the significance of decisions made within the core of the trades. In a dispute in the Parisian painting and decorating trade in 1766, a journeyman explained that he and two dozen of his associates had walked out of a shop belonging to one of the Martin brothers, the best-known and most prestigious decorative painters and japanners in the capital, because, as he put it, they were the men 'qui devoient donner le ton; que tous les autres compagnons de la ville avoient les yeux sur eux et que s'ils mollissoient tous les compagnons leur feroient un mauvais parti'. A journeyman farrier voiced the same sentiments during a dispute in the trade in 1769 by refusing to register his name, age and place of birth with the corporate office until 'les compagnons maréchaux travaillant dans les grandes boutiques auroient donné les leurs'.[10] In the shoemaking trade of Marseille, where a small number of manufacturers producing mainly for colonial markets employed upwards of 50 journeymen each, a manufacturer named Paret, with over 80 journeymen on his books in 1769, was at the centre of series of disputes

8 Archives de la Préfecture de police, Fonds Lamoignon, 15, fol. 54 (21 May 1667); N. Delamare, *Traité de police*, vol. 4 (Paris, 1738), p. 121; A.N. Y 9949 (2 May 1785); AD I 25ᵇ (17 August 1787); Sonenscher, 'Journeymen, the Courts and the French Trades', p. 77.

9 A.N. Y 15 379 (6 October 1772); on the baking trade, see A.N. Y 15 375 (11 April 1769) and, on the *usage des logis*, see below, p. 267.

10 A.N. Y 11 007ᵃ (14 May 1766); Y 11 786 (23 December 1769).

in 1769, 1777 and 1781 in which journeymen sought either to bring his shop into line with the trade as a whole, or to extend norms established in his shop to the rest of the trade.[11] The combination of relatively centralised labour markets and the frequency with which most journeymen moved from one employer to another meant that prevailing levels of wage-rates had a very public character and that bargains between particular masters and journeymen were negotiated in relatively open markets.

Despite the scale of migration, regional variations in wage-levels appear to have remained constant for long periods. Piece-rates set by the Parisian shoemakers in 1720 and 1742 (20 *sous* for a pair of ordinary men's shoes) were 25 per cent higher than those set in Marseille in 1724 and 1743 (15–18 *sous*), which, in their turn, were some ten per cent higher than rates in Bordeaux and Nantes. Variations of the same order of magnitude obtained in the piece-rates paid to journeymen working on the felting side of the hatting trades of Paris, Lyon and Marseille between 1726 and 1785.[12] These continuities were both an expression of durable local variations in levels of urban rents and the price of subsistence goods, and, it can be inferred, a measure of the capacity of single men travelling from town to town to adapt their budgets to prevailing conditions in local labour markets.

At the same time, however, the instability of the relationship between the core and periphery of the trades in any one locality meant that in the short term wage-rates fluctuated over a relatively wide range. Only in a very small number of trades (wigmaking and fancy baking are the two most obvious examples) were schedules of orders so closely related to the social and liturgical calendars that the majority of employers were bound to the same cycle of production. Although shoemakers in Bordeaux were not supplied with meals by their masters during Lent, common constraints of this kind were exceptional in character.[13] In most urban trades, seasonal

[11] A.C. Marseille, FF 378 (29 July 1769); FF 387 (8 May and 16 September 1777); FF 391 (10 May 1781).

[12] A.N. Y 9421 (6 July 1720); B.N. Réserve, Grands Folios, Régistre d'affiches (30 December 1719); Archives de la Préfecture de police, Fonds Lamoignon 27, fols. 1 and 76; B.N. F 12.907; Archives de la Préfecture de police, Fonds Lamoignon 35, fol. 220 (5 August 1743); A.C. Marseille, HH 404: A.D. Gironde, C 1804; 12B 342 (1772); B (unclassified) *arrêt* (4 May 1772); A.C. Nantes, HH 123; Sonenscher, *Hatters*, pp. 86, 99, 114–15, 163.

[13] As a journeyman shoemaker explained in 1762 after a fight in a cabaret on the rue d'Enfer 'où ils prennent leurs repas, attendu que pendant la Caresme, les maîtres cordonniers de ladite ville ne sont pas dans l'usage de donner à manger à leurs garçons'. A.D. Gironde, 12B 320 (9 March 1762). Gingerbread-makers in Paris (*maîtres pâtissiers en pain d'épices*) complained of a *cabale* by journeymen in the trade in October 1751. They explained that they sold almost the whole of their output in January every year. The journeymen had walked out as baking got under way, demanding payment of 12 *livres* a month instead of 10 (in addition to meals, lodging and laundry) and a higher commission than the 10 or 15 *sous* for each *écu* of gingerbread they sold either in the city or in nearby towns and villages: A.N. Y 14 195 (30 October 1751).

peaks and troughs, together with longer-term changes in aggregate levels of demand and employment, concealed wide but discordant variations in the rhythm of orders and sharp but asynchronous fluctuations in the number of journeymen employed in particular workshops at different times of the year. Since most master artisans took on the majority of the journeymen they employed to carry out particular pieces of work (so that most periods of employment ranged from a week or two in the tailoring trade to three to six months in the furnishing trades), short-term demand for labour was erratic, relatively unpredictable and governed by considerable pressure to ensure that orders were met in full and on time. In these circumstances, the distinction between day-rates and piece-rates was often more apparent than real, while the prevailing level of the rates themselves was the subject of ceaseless informal negotiation.

Although wage-systems in most branches of the textile trades took the form of payment by the piece, while most journeymen in the building trades were paid by the day, wages in the furnishing, victualling, transport and clothing trades were paid in a variety of different ways. Daily rates co-existed with fortnightly, monthly and annual rates of pay, as well as payment by the piece for sub-contracted work (or the *toise* in work involving measurements of surface areas or volumes), in proportions that expressed the varied composition of the workforce of different trades and the segmented character of particular markets for labour. A corporation like the Parisian locksmiths' corporation was divided into a number of distinct sectors: some journeymen made springs for coaches; others made wrought ironware; others made hinges and brackets for the building trades; some journeymen actually made locks.[14] The composite character of the trade – which was replicated in a wide variety of others – meant that many different modes of wage-payment and periods of employment were subsumed under a single occupational label.

In the short term, wage-rates in many eighteenth-century French trades varied both from season to season and from shop to shop.[15] The best-

---

[14] On the variety of branches within the locksmiths' trade, see A.N. Y 13 751 (7 September 1746); Garrioch and Sonenscher, 'Compagnonnages, Confraternities', p. 36. Journeymen paid by the day or the month might also undertake sub-contracted work. A Parisian master joiner 'ayant des planches en fusée à faire' in 1786, offered them 'en entreprise' to two journeymen who had been working for him for the past six months. The journeyman, 'le voyant pressé de cet ouvrage' agreed to do the work but at an additional 5 *sous* a *toise*. The following day another journeyman came to ask for work. The master decided to give the sub-contracted work to him instead, 'en l'engageant de se chercher un camarade parce qu'il falait absolument deux d'intelligence pour le faire'. The interlopers were subsequently assaulted: A.N. Y 14 576 (23 March 1786).

[15] The fullest and most recent discussion of the question can be found in Jean-Pierre Poussou, *Bordeaux et le Sud-Ouest au xviiie siècle* (Paris, 1983), pp. 320–31. What follows is a substantially modified version of M. Sonenscher, 'Work and Wages in Eighteenth-Century Paris', in Maxine Berg et al., eds. *Manufacture in Town and Country before the Factory* (Cambridge, 1983).

known such variations were the seasonal fluctuations in the daily rates paid to journeymen and labourers in the Parisian building trades, where the difference between the lowest and highest rates in any one year between 1727 and 1786 could be as much as 33 per cent, and, on average, was never less than ten per cent above or below the annual mean.[16] The large number of relatively substantial building projects in eighteenth-century Paris and the highly centralised market for labour on the place de Grève both, however, tended to limit the range of fluctuation of wage-rates paid to journeymen on different sites. The day-rates paid to journeymen masons, stone-cutters, *limousins* and their labourers, whether they were working on the future Panthéon, the Quinze-Vingts, the Colisée or the Hôpital des Incurables, were therefore very much more uniform than those in many other trades in which daily rates obtained.

In the roofing, carpentry, saddlery or joining trades both the short-term character of most periods of employment and the erratic schedules of most master artisans' orders ensured that journeymen were paid at quite substantially different rates. In the Parisian carpentry trade, for example, the rates paid to journeymen working at the same time for the same employer in 1771 and 1772 varied by 20 per cent, from 30 to 36 *sous* a day. Piece-rates, for obvious reasons, showed even more substantial variations, and continued to vary even when the product in question was identical. In the shoemaking trade of Marseille, for example, piece-rates for making a pair of the same type of men's shoes in 1781 varied from 21 to 26 *sous* from one employer to another, despite the existence of a formal *tarif*.[17]

Although short-term differences between minimum and maximum rates were not particularly substantial, they represented very much more considerable differences in income over the course of a whole year. Yet only a small minority of journeymen worked for the same master for a year or more. This was an additional reason why wage-rates in the eighteenth-century French trades remained relatively insensitive to long-term price movements despite the fact that, in the short term, they fluctuated over a relatively broad spectrum. The rates at which journeymen were paid remained constant only for as long as they remained in the same shop or on the same site. Seasonal variations in daily rates or differences in the rates paid to journeymen in the same shop were usually achieved not by changes in the rates paid to the same men but by changes in the composition and size of the workforce. Although climatic

[16] Yves Durand, 'Recherches sur les salaires des maçons à Paris au xviiie siècle', *Revue d'histoire économique et sociale*, 44 (1966), pp. 468–80 (pp. 473–6).

[17] A.D. Ville de Paris, D⁵ B⁶ 2804, *rôle des ouvriers pour Fillion, maître charpentier* (1771–3): D⁵ B⁶ 4140, *livre des ouvriers belonging to an anonymous master mason* (1765–6): A.N. Y 12 460, *rôle des ouvriers des Quinze-Vingts* (1780–1); Durand, 'Recherches sur les salaires', pp. 476–8. A.C. Marseille, FF 391 (2 May 1781).

conditions played some part in determining relative levels of wage-rates, particularly in the building trades, variations in the onset of the annual upward or downward trend from year to year are a clear indication of the secondary effects of the duration of particular projects, and the resultant leads and lags that occurred when agreements made at one time of the year were carried into the following months.

These leads and lags are particularly apparent in the rates paid in the Parisian building trades. Although the Parisian masons' corporation devised seasonally graduated scales of day-rates (*tarifs*), their chronological precision bore little relationship to the timing of changes in seasonal trends. Close examination of the rates at which journeymen were paid indicates that upward or downward movement in the level of wage-rates began at quite widely different intervals from year to year.[18] Similar leads and lags obtained in ancillary trades. A journeyman carpenter taken on at a rate of 36 *sous* a day in July could continue to be paid at that rate in December. Inversely, however, a journeyman taken on in December could remain at the winter rate until he had completed his work, or found work elsewhere.[19] The rates changed as the men changed, and the direction in which they changed was a function of many small-scale calculations and much manoeuvre by both masters and journeymen. The duration of particular kinds of work, and the range of opportunities for employment at different times of the year, superimposed themselves upon purely climatic constraints. The wage was, in this sense, a bargain whose duration was limited by the amount of work that a master needed to be done or that a journeyman could find at different times of the year. Once the work was over, journeymen were forced to strike other bargains with other masters on different terms.

The leads and lags that were an intrinsic part of labour markets in which a high level of movement from shop to shop and a wide variety of dissonant schedules of production were superimposed upon seasonal changes in levels of demand were one effect of the interdependent character of workshop production. The term 'productive network', rather than 'productive unit', is therefore as appropriate to the conditions in which most journeymen worked as it is to the elaborate divisions of labour in which most master artisans participated. Divisions of labour endowed the trades with their coherent form and, at the same time, imparted particular patterns to the timing and duration of specific kinds of work. Just as the production of finished goods was often divided among several

---

[18] Despite the existence of the *tarif*, seasonal downward trends began in October, November and December in different years, while upward trends were distributed even more widely between March and July (Durand, 'Recherches sur les salaires', p. 475). On the *tarif*, see Sonenscher, 'Journeymen, the Courts' pp. 90–3.

[19] A.D. Ville de Paris D⁵ B⁶ 2804.

trades or corporations, so various technical processes were divided both spatially and temporally within particular workshops. The work of making a hat, or a cabinet, or a shoe, was a complex mixture of different activities and processes, some irregular and episodic in character, others more frequent, regular and time-consuming. These differences were reproduced in both the composition of the workforces of most trades, with their small number of relatively sedentary journeymen and their larger number of very much more peripatetic counterparts, and in the multiple forms of wage-payment that co-existed within the same trade.

The terms used by both masters and journeymen in descriptions of the various constituent parts of the workforces of the trades echoed these differences. At one level, there was a core of men who remained in the same shop for months, if not years at a time: *premiers garçons* in the tailoring trade, *gorets* or *maîtres-ouvriers* among shoemakers and hatters, *premiers compagnons* or *maîtres compagnons* in the building and furnishing trades. Many of them performed functions of a supervisory nature and, like the *prôte* Nicolas Contat, took considerable responsibility for the daily management of the shops in which they worked. At another level, however, there was the larger and very much more itinerant population of *compagnons battants la semelle*, or *remue-pieds*, who moved from shop to shop to take on different kinds of work as and when they were needed.[20] Different kinds of work were done by different journeymen as they moved from node to node within each productive network. In the clothing, baking, furnishing and decorative trades, master artisans took on journeymen to work *en premier*, *en second*, *en troisième*, and so on. There were also *aides* and *dispenciers*, just as there were *compagnons* and their *ouvriers* in the building trades, but *ouvriers* and their *compagnons* in the hatting trade.[21]

The composite character of the productive networks that linked artisans

---

[20] On Contat, see above, chapter 1; on the various supervisory activities undertaken by some journeymen, see Sonenscher, 'The *Sans-Culottes* of the Year II: Rethinking the Language of Labour in Revolutionary Paris', *Social History*, 9 (1984), pp. 301–28 (p. 311).

[21] In the tailoring trade of Bordeaux journeymen were taken on *en première ou seconde dispence*, as *journaliers* or as *ferme-boutiques* or as *journaliers*: A.D. Gironde, 3E 15 011 (28 February 1761). In the wigmaking trade of Rouen, 688 (24·2 per cent) of the 2,837 journeymen who registered with the corporate office and whose positions were specified were taken on *en premier*, 986 (34·7 per cent) *en deuxième*, 998 (35·1 per cent) *en troisième*, 164 (5·7 per cent) *en quatrième* and 1 (0·3 per cent) *en cinquième*. The figures refer to a little over half the total number of registrations because the corporate clerk only began to note journeymen's positions in 1785. The terms did not simply apply to the order in which journeymen were taken on, but also referred to specific tasks within the shop, so that a master wigmaker could have employed more than one individual working *en deuxième* or *en troisième* at the same time. Figures have been calculated from A.D. Seine-Maritime 5E 148.

in different trades also affected the relationship between individual master artisans and the journeymen they employed. Since so many master artisans dealt mainly with other master artisans or put work out on a sub-contracted basis, the word 'employment' is often an inappropriate term to apply to the many different individuals for whom particular journeymen worked. Journeymen in the Parisian painting and decorating trades objected to having to register for work with the corporate office in 1784 because, they claimed, it was often the case that they worked for two or more people on the same day.[22] In the building and furnishing trades, where a great deal of work was done by master artisans for private individuals in their own homes or apartments, journeymen working 'à l'entreprise' were often paid by their masters' clients and later settled their accounts with the principal contractors or sub-contractors who had supplied the work. Not all the income that journeymen received, therefore, was supplied by the masters for whom they worked. The treasurer of the painters' Académie de Saint-Luc noted payment of 3 livres 'pour leur vin' to the journeymen printers who produced a revised edition of the corporation's statutes in 1672. The Parisian farriers objected to increasing the rates they paid their journeymen in 1791 on the grounds that journeymen were paid modest fees by the owners of the horses they shod as well as the daily or monthly wages paid by the masters who employed them.[23]

Just as many transactions between master artisans could crystallise into relatively stable patron–client relationships, so certain aspects of the wage-relationship could acquire the same form. Journeymen were often entitled to collect the annual étrennes that master artisans and their clients gave to one another at Christmas. Two Parisian journeymen spurmakers complained that they had been prevented from collecting the customary étrennes from their master's clients at Christmas in 1769 when the journeymen working for a second master made the rounds first.[24] A group of master shoemakers had their dinner in the Tour d'argent on the rue de Seine in Paris interrupted early in 1765 when a dozen journeymen let off a rocket into the cabaret. It transpired that two of the masters had made a point of refusing to give their journeymen any étrennes at Christmas and that the journeymen had decided, as one of them innocently put it, 'de tirer un gâteau entr'eux et s'amuser'.[25]

Entitlements to informal customs of this kind were closely related to

[22] B.N. 4° Fm 20904. Mémoire pour le Sieur Martin, Peintre-Vernisseur du Roi; le Sieur Charny, Peintre, ancien Professeur de l'Académie de Peinture, sous l'invocation de Saint-Luc (Paris, 1786).

[23] B.L. 503 e. 11 Comptes de Jean Vissac maître sculpteur et peintre à Paris, juré et garde dudit art...de la Saint-Luc dernière 1671 jusques à la Saint-Luc de 1672; A.N. AD XI 65 Précis pour les maréchaux de Paris (Paris, 1791).

[24] A.N. Y 12 057 (2 January 1770).

[25] A.N. Y 10 799 (13 January 1765).

continuities of employment within particular productive networks and to the age and seniority of particular journeymen. Yet, although some journeymen were obviously more experienced, older or proficient than others, the rapidity with which most work could be done, and the brevity of most periods of employment, meant that only the division between *premier compagnons*, *gorets* or *prôtes* and the rest of the workforce had a significantly durable character. Differences in age and experience were not matched by durable hierarchies in rates of pay. The overlapping hierarchies of age, seniority and income that were one of the hallmarks of nineteenth-century factories were conspicuously absent from the world of the eighteenth-century trades.[26] Instead, differences in rates of pay – payment by the day, the month or, occasionally, the year – expressed the differences in the length of time that journeymen remained in the same shop. Most journeymen moved too frequently from shop to shop for the hierarchies associated with the firm-specific skills of nineteenth-century factory work to take form.

The high level of labour turnover meant that familiarity with a wide range of products, materials and their uses was the most fundamental measure of skill in the eighteenth-century French trades. The skills that most journeymen acquired, as joiners, locksmiths, carpenters, wheel-wrights or painters were measured most usually by their ability to do different things in different shops. In the wigmaking trade of Rouen, a journeyman taken on *en premier* by one master had less than a 50 per cent chance of continuing to work *en premier* with another.[27] There is little reason to suppose that this pattern did not exist in almost all the urban trades. Flexibility, adaptability and assiduity, rather than a specialised ability to produce high-quality artefacts, were the qualities that most master artisans required of most journeymen.

The apparent clarity of most occupational labels can disguise the very imprecise boundaries separating work in one trade from work in another. Sharp divisions between skilled and unskilled occupations were tempered by more subtle variations in levels of proficiency, while the limited range of materials used in the majority of the urban trades meant that occupational distinctions were often very much more porous than they appear. After a dispute in 1757 between master and journeymen locksmiths in Bordeaux which led to a boycott of the city by itinerant journeymen, masters took on men employed by toolmakers and smiths

26 On hierarchies in nineteenth-century factories, see Michael Huberman, 'Invisible Handshakes in Lancashire: Cotton Spinning in the First Half of the Nineteenth Century', *Journal of Economic History*, 46 (1986), pp. 987–8.
27 Calculated from A.D. Seine-Maritime, 5E 148. As mentioned, the term *en premier* denoted a task or series of tasks as much as it referred to the sequence in which journeymen were engaged.

(*taillandiers et gens de forge*), even though, they noted, skilled workers able to make wrought ironware from designs (*des pièces de dessein et de gout*) were in distinctly short supply. Skills associated with particular materials were, therefore, relatively easily transferable from one occupation to another. Twenty Parisian journeymen spurmakers broke into a shop belonging to the *épronnier des Petites Ecuries du Roy* in 1747 when he took on a number of locksmiths to do their work and dragged one of them into the street, saying that 'il leur avoit coutté cinq années de temps et deux cents livres d'argent pour apprendre l'epronnerie, et qu'il n'étoit pas juste qu'il trouvât de l'ouvrage préférablement à eux'.[28]

If the absence of sharp distinctions in the kinds of proficiency and skill associated with most trades meant that the rates that journeymen were paid were depressed by the range of ancillary (and potentially overlapping) occupations found in most cities, the short-term character of most periods of employment meant that journeymen faced considerable pressure to find ways of working as quickly as possible to earn as much as they could during the time that they were employed. Even in the building trades, where daily rates were the usual mode of payment, the frequency with which journeymen undertook sub-contracted work meant that the amount they earned was often determined as much by their speed and proficiency in particular kinds of work as by the length of time that they spent with particular employers. Delays caused by bad weather were a further and recurrent source of anxiety. Two dozen journeymen stone-cutters threatened to walk out on a Parisian building entrepreneur in 1769 when he refused to allow them to work through their meal breaks to recover lost earnings caused by rain, on the grounds, he said, that 'il fallait du repos à l'homme'.[29]

The tension between different perceptions of the relationship between time, work and income occasionally found its expression in heated arguments over the quality of work. A master locksmith who took it upon himself to advise his journeyman that he would do better to turn his work in a different way received a torrent of abuse and was informed by the irate journeyman 'qu'il se foutait des boutiques et des maîtres'. A journeyman locksmith working in the Hôtel de la Bretèche in Paris was violently arraigned by the master mason responsible for the work and told 'd'un ton brutal et en le tutoyant qu'il étoit un imbécile'. The Parisian joiner André-Jacob Roubo argued that payment by the day was the only way to ensure that journeymen would not spoil materials in their haste to finish their work. The tailors of Marseille prohibited payment by the piece in 1750

[28] A.D. Gironde, B (unclassified) *arrêt* (20 September 1757): A.N. Y 9532 (17 June 1747).
On the imprecision of occupational distinctions, see below, chapter 9.
[29] A.N. Y 11 687 (23 September 1769).

because, they claimed, 'un ouvrier empressé de finir les pièces dont il est chargé ne s'aplique point à leur donner la perfection nééessaire'.[30]

It is improbable, given the multiplicity of different needs and schedules of production, that co-existed in most trades, that hostility towards payment by the piece was translated into durable practice. Piece-rates remained widespread in most trades and ranged over a fairly broad spectrum defined principally by the amount of time needed to make the artefact in question. Yet some kinds of work were clearly easier to do or were more remunerative than others. Attempts to promote flexibility were occasionally a source of bitter conflict between journeymen and their masters. Journeymen shoemakers in Marseille objected to making men's shoes because they were invariably paid at lower rates than women's shoes. Journeymen tailors in Bordeaux refused to make waistcoats and breeches (*gilets et culottes*) and insisted upon their right to cut up materials themselves.[31] Journeymen were well aware of how the use of different materials or the nature of different products generated substantial differences in levels of income. Much of the ceremonial that they maintained, particularly the ritual distribution of that symbol of unity the *pain bénit*, after the mass – which was one of the hallmarks of the collective life of almost every journeyman's association in the eighteenth century – was a sometimes poignant commentary upon material circumstances that were often anything but uniform.[32]

The many different connotations of the passage of time were particularly apparent in wages paid on a temporal basis. Journeymen employed by the month were never paid a simple multiple of the daily rate. The Parisian tailors set the monthly rates they paid their journeymen in 1660 at 2, 3 or 4 *livres*, but paid journeymen engaged by the day at 10 *sous*, excluding the value of the 'pain, pot, lit et maison' they also received. Tailors in Bordeaux set the rates they paid their journeymen in 1785 at 6 *livres* a month, in addition to food and lodging, while the day-rate was fixed at 10 *sous*, exclusive of the meals to which journeymen were also entitled.[33] A corporate decision by the locksmiths of Bordeaux in 1709 set the daily rate paid to journeymen at 6 *sous* over and beyond meals and lodging. Journeymen engaged by the month, however, were to receive 100 *sous*, or

30 A.N. Y 12 461 (12 November 1770); Y 11 981 (9 August 1785); A. J. Roubo, *L'Art du menuisier* (Paris, 1770), vol. 4, pp. 1243–4; A.D. Bouches-du-Rhône, 380E[236] fol. 202 (17 February 1750).

31 A.D. Gironde, B. (unclassified) *arrêt* (26 February 1772).

32 On the *pain bénit*, see below, p. 258.

33 Cited in Alfred Franklin, *La Vie privée d'autrefois* (Paris, 1889) vol. 5, p. 99, and *Dictionnaire historique des arts, métiers et professions exercés dans Paris depuis le treizième siècle* (Paris, 1906), p. 676; A.D. Gironde 13B 242 (13 August 1785); B (unclassified) *arrêt* (3 September 1785).

33 per cent less than the amount a journeyman paid by the day would have earned had he worked continually for a 25-day month. Piece-rates (a maximum of 7/6d 'la fermeture') were higher again.[34]

The relationship between the level of wage-rates and the duration of periods of employment was also apparent in more integrated trades. In the Parisian printing trade, after the conflicts of the second half of the seventeenth century, a minority of compositors working *en conscience* were paid by the day or the month, while the majority were paid for particular pieces of typesetting in a complex scale of piece-rates which varied according to the size of the characters and the format of the page, but were invariably higher than a multiple of the day-rates paid to *ouvriers en conscience*. A Parisian compositor refused to work on Panckoucke's *Encyclopédie méthodique* in 1785 at a rate of 15 *livres* 10 *sous* a sheet because, he said, he would need a full week to set the type in *petit romain* while he needed no more than two and a half to three days to set a sheet of Rollin's *Histoire ancienne* in *caractères philosophes* at a rate of 11 *livres* 10 *sous*. At those rates he would have earned between 806 and 1,196 *livres* a year had he worked regularly. Journeymen working *en conscience* earned substantially less (between 2 and 3 *livres* 10 *sous* a day towards 1770) but remained in the same shop for longer periods than the compositors taken on to carry out particular pieces of typesetting or *labeurs*. In the hatting trade too, journeymen who made felt were paid by the piece while finishers, who were often older, married men, were paid a lower daily rate. Piece-rates were invariably likely to generate higher incomes than day-rates, and day-rates in their turn were invariably higher than monthly or annual rates of pay.[35] Other things being equal, the level of wage-rates varied inversely with the length of periods of employment.

Since so many journeymen worked for such short periods in the same shop, there was a price to be paid for continuity of employment. The longer a journeyman was taken on, the lower the rate was likely to be. Inversely, however, the longer a journeyman remained in the same place, the greater was the range of opportunities to marry and establish himself on his own account. Nearly two thirds (62·3 per cent) of the 196 journeymen who married in Nîmes between 1785 and 1789, but had not been born there, had been living in the city for at least five years, while only 13 (6·6 per

---

34 A.D. Gironde, B (unclassified) *arrêt* (22 June 1709). Even if allowance is made for the (somewhat mythical) 111 Sundays and holidays of the eighteenth-century French working year, and it is assumed that journeymen paid by the month were paid irrespective of whether they worked or not, while those paid by the day were paid for no more than 254 working days, annual day rates were still over 25 per cent higher than monthly rates. See also below, p. 194.

35 A.N. Y 11 428 (28 December 1785); Giles Barber, ed., *Anecdotes typographiques* (Oxford, 1980), p. 146; on the printing trade, see above, chapter 1; on the hatting trade, see Sonenscher, *Hatters*, pp. 133–4.

cent) of them had been living in the city for less than two years.[36] The proportions are a measure of the gulf separating sedentary and itinerant journeymen. Disputes involving journeymen paid by the day, just as journeymen paid by the piece could be ignored by journeymen paid by the day, just as journeymen paid by the month were usually absent from disputes involving journeymen working on day-rates. A journeyman shoemaker who worked as a *maître-ouvrier* in one of the large shoemaking concerns of late eighteenth-century Marseille complained that he had been wrongfully arrested during a dispute over the level of piece-rates in 1785. 'Il ne travaille point à pièce mais bien à journée, ce qui exclut toute idée de cabale et d'attroupement à l'effet de faire augmenter le prix de la façon des souliers,' he claimed.[37]

Masters and journeymen struck their bargains in the light of their capacity to assess how much time a given amount of work would take and how many opportunities for alternative employment existed at different moments during the year. Journeymen were called upon to consider the relative advantages of the generally higher rates, but shorter periods of employment associated with payment by the day or the piece, as against the lower rates, but longer periods of employment associated with payment by the month or, occasionally, the year. Masters were obliged to set the recurrent costs of different forms of wage-payment and the uncertainty that accompanied engaging journeymen whose competence and reliability were unknown against the advantages of higher levels of production and more rapid turnover of assets. The segmented character of the workforce of most trades was a result of these different possibilities, opportunities and calculations.

The variety of considerations that entered into transactions between masters and journeymen was one reason why delay was preferable to an immediate decision. The ubiquity of credit in relations between masters and journeymen in the eighteenth-century French trades was by no means a simple response to recurrent shortages of small coin.[38] Credit was as common in the clothing or victualling trades, with their relatively direct access to final consumers and cash, as it was in the building or furnishing trades, where most master artisans produced, on credit, for members of their own or ancillary trades. Credit made it possible for both masters and

---

36 Figures have been calculated from all the marriage contracts drawn up in Nîmes between 1785 and 1789: see Michael Sonenscher, 'Royalists and Patriots'. They are, if anything, an underestimation, because 13 of the 196 journeymen born outside Nîmes did not specify how long they had lived there. A further 108 journeymen were natives of Nîmes. The figures do not include the very much larger number of workers involved in textile production.

37 A.C. Marseille FF 395 (9 April 1785), petition by Charles Raymond.

38 For discussion of the relationship between cash and access to final consumers, see Sonenscher, '*Sans-Culottes*', pp. 308–9.

journeymen to defer decisions and, where possible, to transfer some of the risks attached to the wrong decision to the other party. An advance on the wage allowed journeymen more time to consider the relationship between the work that they had undertaken and the possibilities of finding work at a better rate elsewhere. Long payment allowed masters the time to carry current costs until income from work that had been done was received. Credit bound masters and journeymen together because it transformed a bargain into a promise and made a simple transaction a more complex dialogue over rights and obligations. In this sense it was a counterpart to the range of considerations that entered into the wage relationship. It allowed decisions to be deferred and enabled both masters and journeymen to maintain uncertainty for as long as possible.

Credit was complemented by the prevalence of sub-contracted modes of wage-payment. The practice was an intrinsic part of the economy of the building trades, where journeymen masons, plasterers, roofers and stone-cutters hired their own labourers and where the apparent simplicity of uniform day-rates sometimes masked elaborate transactions between men who worked in gangs or *bandes* and settled their accounts among themselves when they were paid by their contractors.[39] In the furnishing trades too, journeymen joiners, locksmiths, wheelwrights and coach-makers who undertook sub-contracted work engaged and paid other journeymen before they settled their accounts with principal contractors. Even in the hatting trade, substantial manufacturers would lease the use of their installations and equipment to journeymen working on either their own or their employer's account.[40] Sub-contracted modes of wage-payment were also a form of credit, allowing master artisans to transfer some or all of the costs of materials and wage-payments to journeymen until accounts were settled and balances struck.

Payment in kind was also a form of credit. In some trades many master artisans housed, fed and supplied bedlinen to their journeymen: they were, as the usual phrase went, 'couchés, nourris et blanchis'. The familial or patriarchal connotations of the phrase should not, however, mask the fact that payment in kind was also a way of transferring the current costs of employing journeymen to members of the victualling and laundering trades. Nor, of course, were journeymen who were housed by their masters any more likely to remain there for longer periods of time.[41] Payment in kind made it possible for master artisans to settle their accounts with bakers, butchers, grocers, wine merchants and laundresses in the same

[39] A.N. O¹ 487 fol. 758 (17 October 1776) for a dispute between Parisian builders' labourers and the journeymen who employed them, and Y 11 731 (25 February 1788) for a later dispute.

[40] A.N. Y 11 446 (28 and 31 March, 1722).

[41] As is apparent from the turnover of journeymen in the tailoring trade of Rouen: see above, pp. 164–8.

way as they settled their accounts with their journeymen. Just as credit allowed both masters and journeymen to keep the uncertainties of labour and product markets in abeyance, so payment in kind allowed master artisans to keep the market for subsistence goods at one remove.

The proportion of journeymen who were housed and fed by their employers varied substantially. The Parisian shoemakers claimed in 1719 that they were the only trade in the capital in which the practice existed.[42] Although the statement was a considerable exaggeration, there were obvious reasons why the practice was more widespread in smaller cities. Court rulings indicate that it was widespread in the tailoring trades of Lyon and Paris in the second half of the seventeenth century, as well as in the furnishing trades of many large provincial cities.[43] It was most usual among tailors, shoemakers and wigmakers, where both the small size of the workforce and the ease with which journeymen could set themselves up on their own account were considerable incentives to payment in kind and close surveillance of journeymen's activities. Journeymen wigmakers were almost invariably housed by their masters throughout the eighteenth century, even in Paris. In late eighteenth-century Rouen, nearly half of the total number of journeymen tailors who registered for work between 1778 and 1781 were housed by their masters. The proportion was substantially higher than in the trades of the city as a whole, where under a third of all journeymen were lodged by their masters in 1765. By contrast, almost all the 1,086 journeymen locksmiths who registered for work in the city between 1783 and 1791 lived in furnished rooms or inns of one kind or another.[44]

There were, of course, limits to the number of men that an employer could accommodate. In the building trades, as well as those in which some master artisans employed dozens or scores of journeymen, like printing and hatting, journeymen were rarely accommodated on the premises. The substantial increase in overseas trade and the growing prosperity of urban France in the eighteenth century both favoured increases in the range of workshop sizes and heightened the distance between the core and periphery of many trades. As the dimensions of the bazaar economy grew, the proportion of journeymen who were housed and fed by their masters fell. The process was most marked in the furnishing trades, particularly those of the capital, although sectors of the clothing trades in which production for international markets was considerable also saw the development of a huge gulf between a small number of very substantial

[42] Archives de la Préfecture de police, Fonds Lamoignon 27 fol. 1 (28 December 1719).
[43] B.N. F 26 473, *Reglemens des maistres tailleurs d'habits de la ville et fauxbourgs de Lyon* (Lyon, 1729); A.C. Lyon, Imprimés, S.M. 181: HH 185.
[44] See above, chapter 5; figures on locksmiths have been calculated from A.D. Seine-Maritime, 5E 654 and 649.

employers and a much larger number of small artisanal enterprises. The shoemaking trades of Marseille, Bordeaux, Nantes and the other great port cities came to be structured in this way, so that the proportion of men who were housed and fed by their masters fell considerably. In Marseille, a *tarif* drawn up in 1781 set the piece-rates paid to journeymen who were housed by their masters at only a *sou* less than those who were not.[45] The very small difference was a measure of the unimportance of a practice that had been rendered relatively obsolete by the scale of production of the city's largest shops.

It is very unlikely, however, that there was any simple linear trend away from payment in kind to payment in cash. The two co-existed and were played off against one another as prices, schedules of production and conditions in local labour markets changed. Journeymen locksmiths in Bordeaux in the early eighteenth century were paid for what they made but were housed and fed for as long as they remained with a particular master. A journeyman locksmith in Lyon who was asked to explain why he had only worked for 68 days between August and early November 1764 explained that he had only counted the days for which he had been paid. 'Dans la profession des serruriers,' he pointed out, 'les maîtres ne payent point leurs compagnons les fêtes et dimanches, ny les journées perdues, et qu'ainsy il n'a parlé que de celles qu'il a employées au travail.' He had, none the less, been housed and fed by the three masters for whom he had worked during that time.[46] Three years later, however, there was a dispute in the trade over the journeymen's right to be fed. A note circulated within the trade and among journeymen smiths (*forgeurs*) warned that journeymen taken on at purely monetary rates, or who were seen eating a meal in an inn or *gargotte*, were to be ignored and regarded as 'des misérables qui ne valent rien'.[47]

Food therefore could be as contentious as money. Just as money advanced, retained or deferred could transform bargains into promises and rewards into sanctions, so meals belonged to an equally wide range of interdependent forms of credit. At the most obvious level they allowed journeymen to transfer the costs of price fluctuations to their masters. A large number of itinerant journeymen locksmiths decided to leave Marseille in 1741 'attendu la cherté des vivres et la modicité de leurs salaires'. They called upon their masters to feed them at their tables or increase their wages. Two masters agreed; the rest refused and over two dozen journeymen left the city.[48] Yet the costs of meals were not carried by master artisans alone: it was more usual to include a standard, and

45 A.C. Marseille, HH 404 (8 January 1781).
46 A.D. Rhône, BP 3307 (3 November 1764), interrogation of Marc Tournure.
47 *Ibid.* BP 3338 (18 September 1767).
48 A.C. Marseille, FF 347 (4 September 1741).

occasionally contentious, deduction for the price of meals when accounts were settled. In a dispute in the shoemaking trade of Nantes in 1786, the corporation's officials explained that it was usual to give their journeymen an *ordinaire* of two meals a day, with meat on the five *jours gras* and soup on the remaining *jours maigres*. In return, journeymen were expected to pay 16 *sous* a week when they settled their accounts.[49] A decision to replace this system by a cash payment of 10 *sous* was, it can be inferred, designed to transfer the effects of retail price fluctuations from masters to journeymen.

Meals were also an instrument of competition among master artisans in local labour markets, as the Parisian nailmakers noted in 1751 when they decided to end the practice of feeding and housing their journeymen. In Nantes nailmakers continued to feed their journeymen until the last decade of the Old Regime; in 1787, however, they decided that the *pitance* of two meals a day allowed well-to-do masters to capture a disproportionately large share of the available workforce. Nailmaking, they noted, had none of the seasonal fluctuations in orders found in the majority of trades. Labour shortages or imbalances caused by the indirect effects of the provision of meals were less likely to occur if payment was entirely in cash. In both Paris and Nantes, however, some masters continued to provide their journeymen with meals.[50] The instability of the relationship between the core and periphery of the trades meant that corporate decisions to abolish the provision of meals were never unanimous and frequently gave rise to violent argument among master artisans. Artisans with different needs and schedules of production made very different assessments of the relative costs and advantages of payment in kind.

Meals were also a means of discriminating between employers, as a group of five journeymen locksmiths in Bordeaux explained after they walked out on a master in the *faubourg* Saint-Seurin in 1759. 'A déjeuner,' they complained, 'il ne leur donnoit que du pain avec des raves ou ressorts et une demy bouteille de vin par personne', when they were entitled to 'une fricasée ordinaire comme il l'avoit fait au commencement et comme l'on fait dans les autres boutiques de la ville et du faubourg'. They could not, however, complain about the quality of their other meals.[51] In this sense, meals merged with the range of other considerations that journeymen applied to distinguish between good and bad employers. The qualities that a group of Parisian journeymen cutlers identified with a good master in order to refute a charge that they had walked out to raise wages

[49] A.C. Nantes, HH 123.
[50] Archives de la Préfecture de police, Fonds Lamoignon 40, fol. 135 (2 November 1751):
A.C. Nantes, HH 116.
[51] A.D. Gironde, 13 B 217 (6 February 1759).

in 1748 – 'tous maistres qui travaillent, qui payent et nourissent bien leurs compagnons n'en manquent jamais' – were echoed, in negative form, in an anonymous letter sent to an official of the grocers' corporation during a dispute in the trade in 1786:

Vous voudriez que nous soyons chez vous comme de vrais forcats. Si vous pouriez nous nourrir que d'aricot et de pin bis vous le feriez.

Another letter demanded rhetorically:

combien d'entre nous n'ont pas 12 sous de trop lorsqu'en travaillant comme des chevaux, nourris comme des cochons chez la pluspart, couchés comme des prisonniers, vous nous allouez 100 ou 120 livres qu'il faut manger ou crever.[52]

Good meals were a corollary to, rather than a substitute for, good pay. The precision with which masters and journeymen measured the relative advantages of meals and cash is indicative of the extent to which wage-systems in the eighteenth-century French trades were very much more complex than the vague customary arrangements often associated with artisanal production. In the shoemaking trade of Bordeaux the allowance made in a *tarif* drawn up in 1782 for the *ordinaire* of two meals a day that masters provided varied according to the type of shoe that journeymen made. A journeyman who made an ordinary pair of men's shoes was paid 22 *sous* or 18 *sous* with the *ordinaire*, but a journeyman who made a pair of men's shoes with double seams could expect 24 *sous* or 22 *sous* with the *ordinaire*. The value of meals on one rate was twice as much as the value of meals on the other, a difference that can be explained only by variations in the length of time needed to make different kinds of shoe and in the relative proportions of piece-rates in the final price of finished goods. Since wage-costs represented 20 per cent of the final price of the cheapest men's shoes, but between 21 and 25 per cent of better quality articles, masters were prepared to pay a higher cash differential to journeymen who pro-duced ordinary shoes than to those who made shoes with double seams.[53] Precision of this kind is most usually associated with the very detailed scales of piece-rates that existed in textile production. The relatively highly standardised range of patterns and weaves, the long periods of time needed to weave different pieces of fabric, the technical inseparabilities associated with work by different individuals on the same loom and the continuities of employment in particular urban centres all made graduated scales of piece-rates and sub-contracted forms of wage-payment an almost universal

[52] A.N. Y 12 151 (12 November 1748); B.N. MS. Joly de Fleury 1732 fols. 357 and 364.

[53] A.D. Gironde, C 1804: Figures of the relation between piece-rates and final prices have been calculated from a *tarif* established in Marseille in 1743. Although it is probable that the proportions varied, the general pattern of low costs and higher relative profits on cheaper articles is likely to have been a constant one: A.C. Marseille, HH 404.

form of wage-system on the weaving side of textile production. Relatively highly developed levels of product standardisation were often associated with formal scales of piece-rates. Although none of them was as elaborate or as complex as those established in the silk industry of Lyon, the cotton trades of Rouen or Troyes, the ribbon trades of Paris and St Etienne or the hosiery industries of Lyon or Nîmes, modes of wage payment in a number of non-textile trades were often very similar.[54]

In the hatting trades of Paris, Lyon and Marseille, the nailmaking trades of Bordeaux and Nantes, or the shoemaking trades of the great port cities, a relatively uniform range of products co-existed with considerable local continuities in the composition of the workforce and a relatively regular working year. Levels of employment were affected as much by upswings and downturns emanating from colonial and other non-domestic markets as by the more erratic surges of demand associated with local clienteles. The kin-based character of the workforces of these trades was a result of these continuities, as well, of course, as of the very much greater resources of credit and capital needed to manage the more substantial outlays on materials and the slower returns associated with production for non-domestic markets. At different times, journeymen hatters, nailmakers and turners in Paris, Lyon, Marseille and Nantes all emphasised that they were married and had families to support. Women, many of them the daughters or wives of journeymen, made up a substantial proportion of the workforce and were often paid by their male kin.[55]

In most other urban trades, however, there are few traces of kin-based workforces of this kind. Instead, the workforce of the great majority of urban trades consisted overwhelmingly of young, single men. There were, therefore, very few male breadwinners in the eighteenth-century French trades. As a result, estimates of family budgets and measures of real wages as if they were designed to support a family of five are somewhat anachronistic. Most journeymen simply did not have families to support. A detailed budget drawn up by journeymen in the Parisian building trades in 1785 made no reference to the possibility that any of them had dependent kin, despite the fact that the budget was designed to show that they were entitled to substantially higher rates of pay.[56] This was a further

54 On *tarifs* in textile production, see Sonenscher, 'Weavers, Wage-Rates and the Measurement of Work'.

55 On women in the hatting trade, see Sonenscher, *Hatters*, pp. 23–5; in textiles, see Garden, *Lyon et les lyonnais*, pp. 162, 296. On the number of married men in the nailmaking trade, see A.C. Nantes, HH 120; and, among turners, A.C. Marseille, FF 394 (24 July 1784).

56 The assumption has informed discussions of budgets in late eighteenth-century Paris: see Rudé, *Crowd in the French Revolution*, pp. 21–2, 251–2. Similar assumptions inform Michel Morineau, 'Budgets populaires en France au xviiie siècle', *Revue d'histoire économique et sociale*, 50 (1972), pp. 203–37, 449–81. For a revealing case study of the income of a married, unskilled, labourer, see Anne-Marie Piuz, *A Genève et autour de Genève aux xviie et xviiie siècles* (Lausanne and Paris, 1985), pp. 262–73. More recently,

reason – together with the price that journeymen were prepared (or forced) to pay for continuity of employment, the highly elastic demand for labour in most trades, and the relative abundance of local labour pools caused by the porous boundaries separating one occupation from another – for the failure of long-term wage-movements to match short-term wage-variations. Wage-rates bore little relation to the needs of the household economy, because most journeymen ceased to work for wages when they established households.

Standardised systems of wage-payment, in the form of publicly agreed *tarifs*, were confined to a limited number of the eighteenth-century French trades. Yet a dispute that took place in the baking trade of Bordeaux in 1748 is an indication of how the varied modes of wage-payment that co-existed in a single trade could cohere into a relatively uniform wage-system. It began when the bakers' corporation decided to replace the meals that masters provided with an additional daily payment of 10 *sous*. The journeymen objected and called for the reinstatement of their meals. The masters then pointed out that the journeymen were already paid 10 *sous* a day and a further 40 *sous* a week. The money wage covered a basic working day (or night) of two *journées*. If the ovens were used to bake more than two batches of bread a day, the journeymen received a further payment. A third batch was worth an extra *sol*; a fourth, an extra 2 *sous*; a fifth, an extra 3 *sous*; a sixth, however, was worth 5 *sous* more; while a seventh was worth 10 *sous*. There was also a different rate for bread baked on Sunday, ranging from 1 *sou* for one batch to 20 *sous* for five batches. Finally, journeymen were entitled to eat as much bread as they wished and take a one-pound loaf of *choine* to sell or give to their families.[57] The dispute was resolved when the journeymen agreed to abandon the right to take bread and the masters agreed not only to restore the meals, but to increase the allowance for wine from 3 *sous* 6 *deniers* to 5 *sous*.

The system of wage-payment was therefore closely related to the regular and often intense rhythms involved in making bread. The combination of a basic daily and weekly wage for the minimum of two batches of loaves a day and a graduated scale of payments for each additional batch corresponded to the need to maintain punctuality and regularity on the one hand, and obtain the effort associated with working long hours late into the night on the other. Payment by the day, payment by the piece and the provision of meals all contributed to the income that journeymen

it has been claimed that artisans represented the first group of workers in which the 'patriarchal, bread-winning wage can be seen: Wally Seccombe, 'Patriarchy Stabilized: The Construction of the Male Breadwinner Wage Norm in Nineteenth-Century Britain', *Social History*, 11 (1986), pp. 53–76. The statement is not based upon any historical evidence and conflates journeymen's wages with master artisans' profits in the most confusing way.
[57] A.D. Gironde, C 1806 (1748).

bakers received. Minor changes in the component parts of the system of wage-payments made it possible for master artisans to increase the amount of effort that journeymen were required to make in order to earn as much. Inversely, however, higher levels of productivity unaccompanied by changes in piece-rates made it possible for journeymen to earn as much for considerably less effort. Apparent continuities in levels of piece-rates may, therefore, conceal considerable differences in levels of income.

The relationship between time, effort and wage-rates was a recurrent feature of disputes in the eighteenth-century French trades. It was, most notoriously, the principal feature of the sequence of disputes that occurred in the hatting trades of Paris, Lyon and Marseille during the second half of the century. The hatting trade was not, however, unusual in this respect: during a further series of disputes in the baking trade of Bordeaux, in 1758 and 1768, journeymen argued that they were entitled to a higher rate for their *pratiques* (5 *sous* for the third batch instead of a *sol*), because the number of bakers' shops in the city had fallen although the population had grown very substantially. The amount of bread made in most shops had therefore increased, so that most journeymen could expect to work on more than two *journées* a night. One of them stated emphatically that 'il n'en est aucun garçon qui ne sollicite pas l'augmentation, parce qu'elle est juste, et que les fournées extraordinaires que les maître boulangers font faire les expose [sic] nuit et jour à un travail forcé'.[58] Inversely, however, master artisans could argue that higher productivity was sufficient reason to refuse to change piece-rates. The shoemakers' corporation of Nantes claimed in 1786 that there was no reason to increase the rates they paid their journeymen because shoemaking had become much more productive. 'L'ouvrage s'exécute aujourd'hui plus facilement. L'ouvrier fait presque trois paires de souliers dans le même tems qu'il employait il y a quinze ans à en faire deux.'[59]

The scale and extent of such changes in productivity are one of the least-known aspects of the history of the eighteenth-century trades. In the hatting trade, higher productivity was associated with the introduction of a felting solution that made it possible for journeymen to make felt from hare and rabbit fur in less time than was needed to make felt from beaver fur. Silk floss was also a cheaper, and apparently effective, alternative to animal fur.[60] In other trades too, the substitution of labour-saving for labour-intensive materials, the transfer of work from one side of the division of labour to another to create greater horizontal integration, fewer delays and a fuller working day, or the use of standard designs and moulds

58 A.D. Gironde, 12B 333 (27 June 1768), deposition of Jean Daras.
59 A.C. Nantes, HH 123 (16 September 1786).
60 B.N. 4° fm 201 106, *Précis pour le Sr. Leprévost, chapelier privilégié du Roi* (Paris, 1763); A.N. X¹ᵇ 3794 (7 September 1763).

to reduce the amount of time needed to make certain basic parts, particularly in the furnishing trades, played a significant part in changing the productivity of work of a number of trades. The relatively limited range of materials used in the eighteenth-century trades should not mask the fact that the substitution of one material for another or the integration of one kind of work with another could affect the pace and duration of the working day as significantly as mechanisation itself.

Many of the multifarious objects associated with the eighteenth-century luxury trades, particularly the highly fashionable articles of *chinoiserie* – snuff-boxes, *étuis*, ornamental caskets and the like – sold by mercers, jewellers and japanners from the early eighteenth century onwards, were produced on a growing scale by substituting paper and *papier-mâché* for wood. Paper was also used to produce moulded picture frames and furniture parts and, in this way, to replace the elaborate and time-consuming work of sculpting and engraving on wood. Cane instead of wood was also used to make chairs and armchairs, as the Parisian journeymen joiners complained in 1749 in a dispute over the relationship between piece-rates and the time needed to make furniture from the material.[61] In the building trades, changes in the composition of cementing and plastering solutions were also a source of productivity increases as well as a source of additional income for journeymen with contacts among timber merchants or tanners who supplied the materials that were mixed with chalk and ashes to form a cement. Coach-makers raised productivity by expecting journeymen saddlers to fit mirrors in coaches instead of putting the work out to *miroitiers*.[62] There were also hand-powered machines, whose effects upon the fortunes of different artisanal enterprises and journeymen's incomes was equally contentious. Despite repeated prohibitions, the Dutch loom was widely used in the Parisian ribbon trade. An inspection in the *faubourg* Saint-Martin revealed 27 looms in one large enterprise in 1748. In November 1791, well after the famous Le Chapelier law prohibiting assemblies by workers, a police official in the Gravilliers section of Paris reported that *compagnons rubanniers* had met (with 'prudence', 'sagesse' and 'modération') to demand the suppression of the loom.[63]

Changes in unit output – the number of goods produced in a given amount of time – or, more usually, changes in unit costs – the number of

[61] A.N. AD VIII, 1, *Mémoire pour les directeurs, corps et communauté de l'Académie de Saint-Luc contre Simon Bezancon, André Tramblin et consors* (Paris, n.d., but c. 1737), where, it was stated, the practice would ruin 'plus de cent cinquante maitres sculpteurs en bois'; A.N. Y 15 345 (4 October 1749); Y 9523.[b] Bruno Pons, 'Les Cadres français du xviiie siècle et leurs ornements', *Revue de l'Art*, 76 (1987), pp. 41–50.

[62] Sonenscher, 'Journeymen, the Courts', pp. 98–9.

[62] A.N. Y 12 410 (12 June 1748); F[12] 1430 (10 November 1791). For further examples of technical change and higher productivity see Steven L. Kaplan, *Provisioning Paris: Merchants and Millers in the Grain and Flour Trade during the Eighteenth Century*, (Ithaca, 1984), chapter 11.

goods produced for a given outlay on materials, wages and equipment – were only the most visible form of a more ordinary process of negotiation and manoeuvre over the relative costs of materials, the time and effort that journeymen spent working, and the relationship between wages, prices and profits. In principle, higher productivity meant that master artisans could have paid their journeymen higher wages, as the journeymen bakers of Bordeaux argued in 1758. Master artisans, however, claimed that higher productivity meant that journeymen paid by the piece would earn more, even if they were paid at the same rate. In either case, much depended upon the character of particular product markets and the extent to which competition from other producers affected final prices.

The effects of such argument and manoeuvre are most visible in the few surviving eighteenth-century *tarifs*, where differences in the scale of adjustment of piece-rates sanctioned minor modifications to existing working practices and introduced subtle changes in the range of products produced. A *tarif* drawn up by the nailmakers' corporation of Nantes in 1732 listed changes in the rates paid for 33 different types of nail. In 19 cases the rates were increased by a *sol*; in ten cases by 2 *sous*; in three cases by between 3 and 6 *sous*, while in one case the rate remained the same. By 1759 the names of the nails had changed almost entirely, and an additional six new articles were added to a third *tarif* drawn up in 1763. Underlying these changes were many small variations in the size, content and corresponding production costs of the nails in question.[64]

The many disputes that occurred over the length and content of the working day throughout the eighteenth century were closely related to these subtle changes. So too was the apparently erratic pattern of work followed by some journeymen. The oscillation between periods of intense activity and periods of relative idleness that historians have identified as one of the hallmarks of the pre-industrial economy was not the product of an intrinsic predisposition to a particular pattern of work; it was, rather, the product of continuous negotiation over the relationship between costs, working time and the range of opportunities for alternative employment that occurred at different times of the year. All of them – given the small size of most workshops, the limited range of materials used by most master artisans, and the very public character of prices and wage-rates – were very easy to measure. *Coulage*, or ca'canny, were ways of postponing the need to find work elsewhere. They were the ordinary counterparts to the calculations that master artisans made about the uses to which time might be put.[65]

---

[64] A.C. Nantes, HH 116 (1732, 23 October 1759, 14 July 1763). For similar changes in textile production, see Sonenscher, 'Weavers, Wage-Rates and the Measurement of Work'.

[65] It is likely that there was also a relationship between 'Saint Monday' (or *Lundis*) and variations in periods of employment. In nineteenth-century Birmingham, the practice

It is not very easy, therefore, to find many traces of

ce vieux temps d'artisan, extensible, élastique, fluide comme la lumière, allongé ou réduit suivant les saisons, ce temps du soleil, nonchalant et rêveur qui a maintenu dans nos villes des rythmes paysans...libre, flaneur, musard, bavardeur, insoucieux de productivité

in the trades of eighteenth-century France.[66] The range of trades affected by argument and conflict over the length and form of the working day was, in fact, very extensive. Journeymen joiners and locksmiths, printers and bookbinders, painters and decorators, hatters and coach-makers, woollen-croppers and textile-dyers, carpenters and leather-dressers, in Paris above all, but also in the large provincial cities, were all highly aware of when work and breaks for meals should begin and end, or how long work late into the night, when orders were heavy and time was short, might be expected to last.[67] Even in the baking and paper-making trades, where work at night was the norm rather than the exception, journeymen were well able to object to changes in the number of *journées* or reams that they were expected to prepare in the course of a night. Only in the tailoring trade (and, it is probable, the shoemaking and wigmaking trades as well), where periods of employment were exceptionally short, was the question of the length and shape of the working day not a matter of contention.

Even in the building trades, the phrase *une journée de travail* referred as much to a potentially contentious period of time as it denoted a day itself. A journeyman stone-cutter involved in an argument with a partnership of Parisian master masons over payment for 11 days and two hours of work in 1754 was also acknowledging the very precise sense attached to the

[66] was more usual among gunsmiths than jewellers because, according to D. A. Reid, the latter 'was probably the trade with the most stable employment prospects in the town': Douglas A. Reid, 'The Decline of Saint Monday, 1766–1786', *Past and Present*, 71 (1976), pp. 76–101 (p. 97). Explanations of the erratic work rhythms of unmechanised trades have emphasised workers' control over the allocation of their time rather than the duration of periods of employment. See Alain Cottereau, 'Introduction' to Denis Poulot, *Question sociale: Le sublime* (Paris, 1980), and his 'The Distinctiveness of Working-Class Cultures in France, 1848–1900', in Ira Katznelson and Aristide Zolberg, eds., *Working Class Formation* (Princeton, 1986). On the relatively small number of additional drinkers frequenting eighteenth-century Parisian taverns on Mondays, see Brennan, *Public Drinking*, pp. 159–65. It is, in general, the case that *lundis* appear in the sources as days that were honoured by other people rather than by the deponents themselves.

[66] Michelle Perrot, *Les Ouvriers en grève*, 2 vols. (Paris, 1974), vol. 1, pp. 271, 298.

[67] See *Encyclopédie méthodique: Jurisprudence*, vol. 5 (under 'arquebusier') – gunsmiths (1783); A.N. X¹ᵇ 3582 (31 July 1748) – hatters; X¹ᵇ 3854 (19 December 1766) – wheelwrights; AD XI 18 (18 December 1738) – chisellers; Y 13 350 (27 June 1720) – curriers; AD XI 16 (1776) – roofers; Bibliothèque de l'Arsenal, MS. Bastille 12 127 (1761) – gilders; B.N. MS. fr. 22 180 fol. 149 – printers; AD XI 65 (1791) – farriers; X¹ᵇ 3926 (23 April 1770) – joiners; BL R 379 (1794) – paper-makers; B.N. MS. Joly de Fleury 648 fol. 128 (1765) – plumbers; A.N. Y 12 826 (18 October 1776) – bookbinders; A.N. X¹ᵇ 8716 (11 December 1784) – saddlers; A.N. Y 12 073 (21 July 1785) – carpet-makers; Sonenscher, 'Journeymen, the Courts', pp. 94–5; and below, chapter 7.

notion of a day's work throughout the eighteenth century.[68] Since a day consisted of four, five or six two-hour periods, it was possible for a journeyman to be paid for two *journées* for the same day's work. Journeymen working on Parisian building sites were expected to make themselves known to their foremen at the beginning of each such two hour period, so that wage books occasionally record payments for two *journées* to the same individual on a single day, as well as payments to others of amounts equivalent to between a sixth and five sixths of a *journée*.[69] A day was therefore a multiple (and a potentially contentious multiple) of a number of units of time, just as a piece-rate was a fraction of a well-defined, but equally contentious, working day.[70]

The relationship between wage-rates and the incomes that journeymen actually received is therefore very difficult to ascertain. A journeyman printer owed 13 *livres* 1 *sous* 6 *deniers* for a week's work in Paris in 1768 would have earned over 680 *livres* in a year had he worked every week and printed the same number of sheets, but such uniformity was rare.[71] The wide variety of different forms of wage-payment that co-existed in the same trades, the frequency with which most journeymen moved from one employer to another, and the ambiguous character of even the most apparently unequivocal daily rate mean that measurements of journeymen's income by multiplying an average wage-rate by the hypothetical number of days that they worked are based upon too limited a range of variables to have much significance. The composite character of systems of wage-payment and the probability that journeymen were paid by the piece, the day, the week or the month at different times of the year mean that precise measurement of general trends in real wages in the eighteenth century is almost impossible. To take an extreme case, a journeyman cooper could be engaged to work in Paris at an annual rate of 150 *livres* in 1769. He could also be paid by the piece, and work for many different brewers and wine merchants, as well as on his own account in the *halle aux vins* and quaysides during the peak months of June, July, August and September, only returning, as the master coopers complained in 1766, to work in a shop during the winter.[72] In most trades, journeymen's circumstances fell somewhere between these two possibilities. Allowances for Sundays, or trade and religious holidays, do little to obviate the problem because journeymen in some trades (bakers, farriers and

68 A.N. Y 11 471 (7 June 1754).
69 See for example A.N. Y 12 460, *rôle des ouvriers des Quinze-Vingts* (December 1780–February 1781), where payments for periods of a sixth, a third, a half, two-thirds or five-sixths of a *journée* were all recorded. Some of the *limousins* were paid for two *journées* on Wednesday 14 February.
70 For a clear example of the time-based character of piece-rates, see Sonenscher, *Hatters*, pp. 126–9.
71 A.N. Y 12 768 (27 December 1768).
72 A.N. Y 11 256 (4 July 1769); X¹ᵃ 4554 (3 February 1767).

wigmakers in particular) were paid for Sundays and holidays, while others were not.[73]

Masters and journeymen made their own estimates of annual income and, however partial they may have been, they do at least provide rough orders of magnitude. In a request to the Parlement of Paris in 1785 journeymen in the building trades stated that they would earn some 472 *livres* 10 *sous* for a 225-day working year if the daily rate of 42 *sous* that they were paid in the summer was averaged over a whole year.[74] They also presented a detailed description of their daily expenditure, which consisted of:

measure of spirits: 1 *sou* 6 *deniers*
morning meal of a half *sétier* of wine and 2 *sous* of cheese: 5 *sous*
midday meal of an *ordinaire* for 6s and a half *sétier* of wine: 9 *sous*
evening meal: 9 *sous*
bread, two and a half pounds a day: 6 *sous* 3 *deniers*
wear and tear of tools and clothes: 6 *sous*
rent: 7 *sous*

The figures were clearly based upon an assumption that journeymen in the building trades were single men. Expenditure on bread (some 14 per cent of the total) was, for this reason, significantly lower than the 30 to 60 per cent that it has been assumed that journeymen in the building trades spent. The figure of 472 *livres* 10 *sous* that journeymen masons and stone cutters in late eighteenth-century Paris presented as the most they could earn in a year was also substantially higher than the 320 *livres* that builders' labourers are assumed to have earned.[75] Since many builders' labourers were either very young adolescents hired by journeymen, or seasonal migrants from the Massif Central, the higher figure is more representative of the circumstances of journeymen themselves. The shoemakers of Nantes claimed in 1786 that a journeyman was able to make between six and 12 pairs of shoes a week, depending upon his ability and proficiency. At the prevailing rate of 18 *sous* for a pair of ordinary men's shoes, this would have represented an annual income of between 280 and 560 *livres*.[76] The figures are broadly similar to those presented by master silk-weavers in Lyon in 1744 and 1786. There the *maîtres ouvriers*

---

[73] A.N. Y 12 460 (December 1780–February 1781). A journeyman baker arrested for begging in Paris in 1751 denied the accusation, saying 'qu'il gagne par jour aux environs de trente sols et que cela souffit pour le nourrir et qu'il le gagne les jours de feste et dimanches comme les jours ouvriers': A.N. Y 12 416 (21 January 1751). A.N. AD XI 65 *Précis pour les maréchaux de Paris* (Paris, 1791).

[74] B.N. MS. Joly de Fleury 557 fol. 27.

[75] Rudé, *Crowd in the French Revolution*, pp. 21–2, 251–2; Daniel Roche, *Le Peuple de Paris* (Paris, 1981), pp. 86–7.

[76] A.C. Nantes, HH 123 (16 September 1786).

en soie stated that their annual income stood at 1,800 *livres* in 1744 and 1,944 *livres* in 1786 and their expenditure at 2,050 *livres* and 2,301 *livres*. A journeyman's income was estimated at 161 *livres* in 1744, exclusive of food and linen, and 374 *livres* in 1786.[77]

All these figures were presented in the course of disputes in the particular trades from which they emanated; their relationship to actual income and expenditure is therefore highly debatable. The figures produced by the Parisian journeymen masons and the silk-weavers of Lyon showed a spectacular deficit of income over expenditure. The master shoemakers of Nantes claimed, equally predictably, that journeymen could live comfortably on the wages they earned. Yet, since most journeymen were single men in their late teens or early twenties, the figures of expenditure drawn up by journeymen in the Parisian building trades are particularly significant, since they suggest that there was rather more elasticity in journeymen's expenditure than it has been usual to assume. Unless the price of subsistence goods rose substantially, journeymen were relatively far from penury. Everything, however, depended upon continuity of employment and the combined resources of credit and marriage that employment supplied. Credit enabled journeymen to manage the passage of time from week to week, while marriage allowed them to abandon work for wages altogether. Both, however, depended upon knowing and being known. Anonymity was the most dangerous condition that a journeyman could experience, because it was the surest route to exile from the trades and entry into the world of the hospitals and the poor.

Both the tenacity with which journeymen asserted their rights to work in particular localities and the many informal customs that complemented work in the trades are most intelligible in this context. Customs were constituent parts of the identity of particular trades, shared by masters and journeymen because they supplied a vocabulary of particularity that transcended the uniformity of the wood, metals, stone or leather that were common to so many overlapping occupations. The reiteration of customary festivities and retributions was closely related to the weekly and seasonal movement of journeymen from shop to shop, and the more gradual transmission of resources from one generation to the next, because labour markets themselves were so fluid. Customs conferred a quasi-institutional stability upon trades whose composition and boundaries were anything but permanent or precise. They also distinguished one town from another and, like the meals that some masters supplied to their journeymen, played a part in the choice of localities to which itinerant journeymen travelled. A group of itinerant journeymen joiners explained that they had walked

[77] The two budgets have been printed in *Archives historiques et statistiques du Rhône*, 6, p. 157 and F. Rude, ed. *Doléances des maîtres ouvriers fabricants en étoffes d'or, d'argent et de soie de la ville de Lyon* (Lyon 1976).

out of their shops in Nantes in 1764 because they were no longer given the *vin de six heures* that, they said, 'les maistres de Nantes estoient anciennement dans l'usage de...donner'. The city was the only locality in which the practice appears to have existed, just as, according to the master joiners in 1781, it was the only large town in which journeymen in the trade were customarily housed by their masters.[78]

The customs of the eighteenth-century French trades can be grouped into two broad categories: those that marked the passage of time and those that entitled journeymen to keep some of the materials that they used. The distinction was not, of course, particularly precise and each type of custom had a clear, if sometimes disputed, monetary equivalent. When the joiners' corporation of Bordeaux decided in August 1781 to abolish the meals that masters customarily gave journeymen on the principal religious holidays of the year, the journeymen walked out, demanding payment of 15 *sous* as compensation for the loss of the meals and a reduction of an hour in the length of the working day. They were supported by the local journeymen locksmiths.[79] A month later the master joiners of Nantes decided to follow the example of their counterparts in Bordeaux and abolished the four banquets that they were accustomed to offer their journeymen every year, and replaced the *pâté de veille* – 'un soupe somptueux et à discretion à chaque compagnon avec un pâté', given on the first Sunday after the feast of Notre Dame in September – with a cash payment of 30 *sous* as was the practice in Paris.[80]

Customs like these were oral in character, and journeymen who were domiciled and in regular employment in particular towns were best placed to evaluate and assess their significance. A 42-year-old journeyman locksmith who walked out on his employer during a dispute in Paris in September 1746 explained that when his master gave him a *pâté de veille* (a sum of 30 *sous* in this case) to mark the time when night began to draw in and work by candlelight became necessary, he had expected that his son, who worked for the same master, would be given one as well. He had decided to leave, he said, because the master locksmith had refused, even though his son earned 10 *sous* a day. Inversely, however, a 21-year-old weaver from a village in the Dauphine who came to work in Marseille in 1779 was entirely unaware of the significance of a dispute over what was called *la soupe et le sol* that the master linen-weavers of Marseille had decided to abolish. He had found work through his brother, a journeyman shoemaker domiciled in Marseille, who had introduced him to a weaver

[78] A.C. Nantes, HH 149 (5 October 1764); HH 147 (12 September 1781). On the question of customs, see Richard A. Posner, 'A Theory of Primitive Society, with Special Reference to the Law', *Journal of Law and Economics*, 23 (1980), pp. 1–53, and Sally Falk Moore, *Social Facts and Fabrications, Customary Law on Kilamanjaro, 1880–1980* (Cambridge, 1986).   [79] A.D. Gironde, 12B 367 (20 August 1781).

[80] A.C. Nantes, HH 147 (12 September 1781).

known as *comte d'artichau*. Despite a warning that he would be best advised not to work in Marseille during the dispute, and a gift of 19 *sous* to help him on his way, he had gone to work for one of the priors of the weavers' corporation and, predictably enough, had been assaulted.[81]

The best-known, and most universal, customs were the meals and celebrations that accompanied trade holidays held on patron saints' days. They merged with the wider liturgical calendar of the religious year. A Parisian wine merchant who lodged a complaint against a master butcher for failure to pay him 64 *livres* in 1739 stated that the money had been spent on four days of revelry involving the butcher, his wife and a number of *garçons bouchers* working in the vicinity of the rue Mouffetard after 'la réjouissance et divertissement du boeuf gras' that was customary among butchers before Lent.[82] The *garçons bouchers* had collected the money as they paraded the bull through the streets and entrusted the proceeds to the master butcher for safe keeping. He had ordered the food and wine and promised to pay for the meals. Like the meals that the master joiners of Bordeaux and Nantes abolished in 1781, the custom of the *boeuf gras* was local in character and, as in this instance, was enacted by a group of masters and journeymen living and working in the same neighbourhood.

Most trade holidays involved the celebration of a mass, followed by the distribution of the *pain bénit*, often in a *cabaret*, and, later, a banquet and a dance.[83] The principal protagonists in these festivities were the confraternities to which master artisans belonged. The part played by journeymen themselves was ambiguous. Although they did not belong to master artisans' confraternities and frequently celebrated their own masses in separate churches, journeymen's festivities were closely imbricated with those of master artisans. Journeymen invited masters, as well as their wives and daughters, to their dances and often made the rounds of their shops with bouquets and music. Their presence was a constituent element of the whole festive performance.

Trade holidays belonged both to the formal life of trade confraternities and to the less formal social occasions on which the majority of master artisans who played no active part in corporate affairs encountered those who did. They were also moments at which one generation faced another. The annual cycle of processions, masses and banquets placed the immediate relationship between masters and journeymen within the wider context of the dialogue between established artisans and their potential successors. Disputes between masters' confraternities and journeymen's

[81] A.N. Y 13 751 (19 September 1746), interrogation of Louis Chevalier: A.C. Marseille FF. 389 (10 March 1779), deposition of Joseph Chambart.

[82] A.N. Y 11 302 (7 February 1739).

[83] David Garrioch, *Neighbourhood and Community in Paris, 1740–1790* (Cambridge, 1986), p. 159; Daniel Roche, ed., *Journal de ma vie: Jacques-Louis Ménétra, compagnon vitrier au 18e siècle* (Paris, 1982), pp. 124–8.

associations over participation in processions or the use of ornaments and banners were indicative of the tensions which that relationship could generate. Journeymen excluded from a place in processions replied by asserting their place within the cycle of generations. When they were denied the right to take part in the annual procession in honour of St Catherine of Sienna in 1716 journeymen hatters in Marseille pointed out that their confraternity had supplied many of the priors of the master hatters' confraternity. The officials of the Parisian journeymen shoe-makers' confraternity of Saint Crépin made the same claim during a dispute over the use of a chapel in the Cathedral of Notre Dame in 1757.[84] Trade holidays were both a celebration of an ideal community and a more ambiguous and potentially explosive component of the range of distinguishing signs that allowed journeymen to feel that they were entitled to occupy a place in the chain linking the transmission of patrimonies from one generation to the next.

Disputes over informal rights to materials and claims to the exclusive use of particular tools derived from a similar sense of the significance of the passage of time: they expressed a tension between an ideal world of regular employment and access to the supply of available patrimonies and a real world in which the pool of journeymen and the range of potential candidates for places within particular trades was very much more diverse. Journeymen and apprentices involved in the recurrent disputes in the Parisian roofing trade over the right of masters to employ 'étrangers' made a point of insisting that they alone – rather than labourers or itinerant journeymen – were entitled to take old slates and lead pipes from the building sites where they worked.[85] During a long conflict in the Parisian plumbing trade over a similar issue in the late 1760s, a journeyman plumber refused to return his master's hammer because it had been carried by a labourer. 'De concert avec tous les compagnons plombiers de Paris', he insisted that 'il n'y a que les compagnons plombiers qui aient droit de porter des marteau de plombier'.[86]

The practice of taking pieces of wood, or *copeaux*, which was widespread among wheelwrights, carpenters and joiners, was closely related to the continuities associated with regular employment and the concerns of the minority of sedentary journeymen. There were obvious reasons why wood was valued by married men in relatively settled circumstances and why they, more than other journeymen, were particularly hostile to attempts to prevent them from taking pieces from the sites where they worked. During the seventeenth century, journeymen in the Parisian carpentry

84 Sonenscher, *Hatters*, p. 95; A.N. S 118.
85 A.N. Y 14 523 (8 October 1726); A.N. X^{1a} 3547 fol. 153 (19 August 1729); Y 12 768 (10 October 1768); Y 15 375 (21 October 1769).
86 A.N. Y 13 958 (26 June 1765). On the dispute itself, see above, p. 78.

trade repeatedly walked out on masters who refused to allow them or, significantly, their wives to collect pieces of wood. A journeyman carpenter in Lyon who told his wife to take some wood from the shop where he worked and complained to the police authorities when his employer's wife (who was also his neighbour) intervened to prevent her from doing so was making a point about more than the argument that ensued. The complaint was an expression of surprise and anger that an established component of the household economy of married journeymen had not been recognised. As a police ruling published in Troyes in 1773 noted, the practice meant the loss of three hours from a working day, when journeymen 'souvent avec l'aide de leurs femmes, enfants, voisins, parents et amis' descended upon building sites at meal breaks to take what they could. Journeymen, the ordinance continued, claimed that 'la fouillée est un droit affecté à tous les compagnons pour indemnité duquel il leur est du cinq sols'.[87]

None of these customs, however, were rights in any formal sense – their identity and continuity belonged to an informal oral culture that was as much a part of the life of the trades as the legal prescriptions and formal entitlements whose vocabulary they echoed. Like them, they were most frequently invoked by men who lived and worked in the same town. They were counterparts to, rather than substitutes for, the wages that journeymen earned. They marked the boundaries between trades and identified the places occupied by the many different journeymen who worked in them. Since so many of the materials used in the trades were so similar, and so many of the goods that artisans produced were so contingently associated with one occupation rather than another, customs allowed both masters and journeymen to assert identities that were otherwise less easy to define. They made joiners different from turners or wheelwrights, and locksmiths different from smiths or toolmakers, just as they distinguished men who were employed by the month or the year from men employed by the day or the piece. In this way, they complemented the most significant feature of eighteenth-century systems of wage-payment: the inverse relationship between the amounts that journeymen were paid and the length of time that they remained in the same shop. Both customs and wage-systems were the product of the fact that most journeymen worked for wages for a relatively short part of their lives, but did so in the knowledge that by no means all of them would be able to become master artisans in the great cities in which most of them worked. The wages that journeymen earned, as well as the customs that they maintained, were the price of this process of selection and exclusion.

[87] On disputes in the Parisian carpentry trade over the issue of *copeaux*, see below, pp. 256–66, A.D. Rhône, BP 3431 (27 November 1776); A.C. Troyes, Fonds Boutiot, AA 40 *liasse* 1 (10 September 1773).

CHAPTER 7

The Parisian luxury trades and the workshop economy

Ornate objects occupied a special place in eighteenth-century social commentary. The metaphorical connotations of mirrors, watches, buckles and diamonds formed a widely recognised vocabulary of abbreviated observation, criticism and analysis.[1] They were used to denote luxury and, by extension, to pass judgement upon the tenor of public life; they were used too to evoke the international division of labour and the array of exotic substances that converged upon the ports and capital cities of eighteenth-century Europe as the tribute of the whole world; they were used finally to define the difference between the past and the present, and illustrate the principles of social organisation that distinguished commercial from landed societies. 'L'argent que nous dépensons en tabatières et en étuis, les anciens le dépensaient en bustes et statues,' Algarotti wrote disdainfully. 'Et tandis que pour une victoire nous donnons un feu d'artifice, ils élévaient, eux, un arc de triomphe.' 'Tout le monde donc a cherché à se modeler sur ses accessoires,' commented the marquis de Mirabeau in 1759.

L'homme dont les meubles et les bijoux sont guillochés doit l'être aussi par le corps et par l'esprit. L'homme au vernis gris de lin et couleur de rose porte sa livrée en sa robe de chambre, en sa façon de se mettre.[2]

In eighteenth-century France, one name in particular came to be endowed with almost metaphorical connotations in its own right. This

---

[1] The literature on the topic of luxury in the eighteenth century is vast. See Isaac Kramnick, *Bolingbroke and his Circle: The Politics of Nostalgia in the Age of Walpole* (Cambridge, Mass., 1963); J. G. A. Pocock, *The Machiavellian Moment* (Princeton, 1975) and his *Virtue, Commerce and History* (Cambridge, 1985); Istvan Hont and Michael Ignatieff, eds., *Wealth and Virtue. The Shaping of Political Economy in the Scottish Enlightenment* (Cambridge, 1983); Anthony Pagden, ed., *The Languages of Political Theory in Early-Modern Europe* (Cambridge, 1987); Albert Hirschman, *The Passions and the Interests* (Princeton, 1977); John Sekora, *Luxury: The Concept in Western Thought from Eden to Smollett* (Baltimore, 1977); Ellen Ross, 'The Debate on Luxury in Eighteenth-Century France' (unpublished Ph.D. thesis, University of Chicago, 1975).

[2] Francesco Algarotti, 'Pensieri diversi sopra materie filosofiche e filologiche', in his *Opere* (Cremona, 1782), vol. 8, p. 7, cited by Henri Bédarida, *Parme et la France de 1748 à 1789* (Paris, 1928), p. 292; Mirabeau (père), *L'Ami des hommes* (Paris, 1759), vol. 2, p. 285.

was that of the Martin brothers: japanners, painters and decorators not only to Louis XV but to Frederick the Great of Prussia and the Infanta of Spain in Naples. The term *vernis Martin* came to signify any ornate object painted or engraved with an oriental or floral design on a black, red, gold or green background and finished with a high-gloss transparent varnish. The elaborate closet imagined by the journalist Jean-François Bastide in his not very fictitious *La Petite Maison* (1754) consisted of wall-panelling decorated with images of fruit, flowers and exotic birds by Christophe Huet; medallions and overdoors containing 'de petits sujets galans' by Boucher; silver caskets and *toilettes* by Germain; blue porcelain bowls filled with flowers; furniture covered with fabric of the same colour and finished with gilded lacquer (*aventurine*) supplied by Martin. 'On dit communément,' wrote Mirabeau,

qu'un gentilhomme dans sa terre vit mieux avec 10,000 livres de rente qu'il ne le serait à Paris avec 40,000. Qu'appelle t'on dans ce cas vivre mieux? Ce n'est pas épargner plus aisément de quoi changer tous les six mois de tabatières émaillées, avoir des voitures vernies par les Martin.[3]

Voltaire referred sybaritically to

ces cabinets où Martin
a surpassé les arts de la Chine

and, in his play *Nanine*, described a coach drawn by six fine horses —

elle est bonne et brillante,
tous les panneaux par Martin sont vernis

as a symbol of the wealth of contemporary society.[4]

As these passages indicate, the name Martin was associated with varnished coach panels, lacquered overdoors, screens or wall-panels, mock-enamel snuff-boxes, *toilettes* and decorative objects, brightly coloured cabinets, writing tables, chests, cupboards, armchairs or chairs, and more generally with what, in Britain, has come to be known as japanware, and in France as *chinoiserie*.[5] Historians of the eighteenth-

---

3 *Ibid.*, vol. 1, p. 184. On the literary entrepreneur Jean-François Bastide, see Jean Sgard, ed., *Dictionnaire des journalistes* (Grenoble, 1976).

4 F. M. A. Arouet de Voltaire, *Les Tu et les vous: Nanine*, act III, scene 5: *Premier Discours sur l'inégalité des conditions.*

5 The general literature on the subject is not particularly substantial and, on the Martin brothers themselves, is often flawed by minor errors repeated by one author after another. See Henry Havard, *Dictionnaire de l'ameublement et de la décoration depuis le xviiie siècle à nos jours* (Paris, n.d.), vol. 4 (under 'vernis Martin'); Albert Jacquemart, 'Une Manufacture de laque à Paris en 1767', *Gazette des Beaux-Arts*, 1 (1861), pp. 309–11; *ibid.*, *A History of Furniture* (London, 1878), pp. 72–3; Alfred de Champeaux, *Le Meuble* (Paris, 1885), vol 2, pp. 185–98: Karl Robert, *Les Procédés du vernis Martin* (Paris, 1892); A. Phénal, 'Le Vernis Martin autrefois et aujourd'hui', *Revue des arts décoratifs*, 11 (1890–91), pp. 382–5; Constance Dilke, *French Furniture and Decoration in the Eighteenth Century* (London, 1901), pp. 199–201; Hans Huth, *Europäische Lackarbeiten* (Darmstadt, 1955); F. W. Gibbs, 'A Historical Survey of the Japanning Trade', *Annals of Science*, 7 (1951), pp. 401–6, 9 (1953), pp. 88–95, 197–232; Philippe Jullian, 'Comment identifier

century trades have, perhaps understandably, eschewed examination of these objects. Studies of artisans have tended to dwell upon shoemakers, bakers, printers or hatters, while the history of the luxury trades has fallen largely to students of the decorative arts. This has had some advantages, because the historiography of the decorative arts has developed independently of the somewhat teleological problematic of industrialisation associated with much that has been written about artisans. It has also, however, had certain disadvantages, because the close attention to detail and exaggerated emphasis upon the individual creator that has been one of the characteristics of the tradition of connoisseurship has meant that the economy of luxury production has been somewhat neglected.[6]

The luxury trades were more than an array of ornate objects left to a grateful posterity for careful identification and display: they were one of the most substantial components of the eighteenth-century urban economy. The painters and sculptors' corporation of eighteenth-century Paris, known until 1776 as the *Académie de Saint-Luc*, was one of the largest in the capital, with a membership of 967 in 1723 and 1,140 in 1764. It had grown particularly rapidly during the latter half of the reign of Louis XIV. In 1672 it had no more than 276 members, but by 1697 it had more than doubled in size, to 584, a total that was nearly twice as large again at the beginning of the reign of Louis XV.[7] The many different

le vernis Martin', *Connaissance des Arts*, 119 (1962), pp. 43–9; Hugh Honour, *Chinoiserie* (London, 1964); Museum Bellerive, Zurich, *Europäische Lackkunst vom 18. bis 20. Jahrhundert* (Zurich, 1976).

[6] For some generous, but critical, comments on the limits of enthusiastic (but often ahistorical) erudition in the historiography of ornate objects, see David Landes, *Revolution in Time* (Cambridge, Mass., 1983). The contrast between the approaches followed by historians and art historians is particularly striking in publications on the eighteenth century. See Neil McKendrick, John Brewer and J. H. Plumb, *The Birth of a Consumer Society: The Commercialisation of Eighteenth-Century England* (London, 1982) for an example of the former approach; Svend Eriksen, *Louis Delanois, menuisier en sièges* (Paris, 1968) and his *Early Neo-Classicism in France* (London, 1974); Marianne Roland Michel, *Lajoue et l'art rocaille* (Neuilly-sur-Seine, 1984); Bruno Pons, *De Paris à Versailles 1699–1736: les sculpteurs ornemantistes parisiens et l'art décoratif des Bâtiments du roi* (Strasbourg, 1986) for some of the best examples of the latter. I am particularly indebted to Katie Scott of the Courtauld Institute, London for many suggestions and much help in what, for me, is the unfamiliar world of eighteenth-century French art history.

[7] The standard (and only) history of the corporation is by Jules Joseph Guiffrey, *Histoire de l'Académie de Saint-Luc* (Paris, 1915). He gives figures of 276 (1672); 400 (1682); 584 (1697); 967 (1723); 1,140 (1764) and 1,043 (1786) (p. 17). The sources from which the figures derive are not all that evident. Those of 1672 and 1682 are based upon B.N. F 13 233 and F 1548. The former figure can be checked against B.L. 503 e. 11 (1–7), which contains a manuscript list of members of the corporation in April 1672 (269 names) and the names of those admitted until the end of 1677 (16 between May and December 1672; 24 in 1673; 28 in 1674; 27 in 1675; 18 in 1676 and 23 in 1677). A further 59 individuals from the *faubourgs* Saint-Victor, Saint-Germain, Saint-Michel and Saint-Jacques were admitted in 1675. The figure for 1723 is taken from Jacques Savary des Bruslons, *Dictionnaire universel de commerce*, 6th edn (Paris, 1750), under 'communauté'. To these can be added figures of c. 600 and 900 in two memoranda, both

trades and specialised occupations that it housed belonged to a world of courts and capital cities. They fed upon international circuits of designs and designers, colours and chemicals, styles and fashions. They depended upon elaborate networks of information about materials, implements and manufacturing procedures. They were eclectic both in the range of materials they used and in the variety of techniques that they devised to produce artefacts of different substances, colours and designs. In their different ways, printed textiles and wallpaper were both heirs to many of the small-scale innovations in materials, design and marketing that characterised the production of decorative objects during the eighteenth century.[8]

In the luxury trades, the divisions of labour that were the hallmark of the workshop economy reached unprecedented levels of complexity and interdependence. Just as many of the finishing processes involved in the high-quality textile industries of Rouen, Sedan and Troyes entailed very extensive geographical divisions of labour centred upon Paris, so several of the Parisian luxury trades stretched out in an inverse direction into the towns and villages of the capital's hinterland for supplies of primary components and materials. By 1735 the geographical division of labour involved in making fans had become so elaborate that the Parisian toymakers' corporation could accuse the fanmakers of ruining many of its members by putting out the work of making fan-holders (*bâtons*) to villages in Picardy. Geographical divisions of labour in the production of buttons or buckles were no less extensive, and were complemented by many elaborate specialisations and a multitude of interdependent and overlapping techniques within the capital itself. Many of the women who were taken on to work at the Sèvres porcelain works, for example, were recruited from among the workforce of the Parisian fanmaking trade.[9] The heterogeneous range of goods made to meet particular orders, the

produced in 1742 (Bibliothèque de l'Arsénal, MS Bastille, 10 295) and 1,010 in 1786 (B.N. 4° Fm 20904).

[8] On printed textiles, see Serge Chassagne, *Oberkampf, un entrepreneur capitaliste au siècle des lumières* (Paris, 1980); on wallpaper, see Henri Clouzot and Charles Follot, *Histoire du papier peint en France* (Paris, 1935); Françoise Teynac, Pierre Nolot and Jean-Denis Vivien, *Le monde du papier peint* (Paris, 1981); Charles C. Oman and Jean Hamilton, *Wallpapers: A History and Illustrated Catalogue of the Collection in the Victoria and Albert Museum* (London, 1982); *Trois siècles de papiers peints* (Paris and Rennes, 1967); and the special issue of the *Bulletin de la société industrielle de Mulhouse*, 793 (1984).

[9] On fanmaking, B.N. MS. Joly de Fleury, 2018, *Mémoire pour les maîtres peigniers-tabletiers...contre les maîtres éventaillistes de la ville de Paris* (Paris, 1735). The division of labour was a durable one: see A.N. F¹² 562 and Alain Faure, 'Petit Atelier et modernisme économique: la production en miettes au xixe siècle', *Histoire, économie et société*, 5 (1986), pp. 531–57 (pp. 539–40). On buckles and buttons, see John R. Harris, 'Michael Alcock and the Transfer of Birmingham Technology to France before the Revolution', *Journal of European Economic History*, 15 (1986), pp. 7–57. On Sèvres, see André Sergène, 'La Manufacture de Sèvres sous l'ancien régime' (thèse de doctorat, Université de Nancy, 1972–4). For further bibliographical references, see above, chapter 3.

relatively high costs of stocks of many of the materials used in the production of decorative artefacts, and the long credit usually associated with aristocratic, clerical and rentier markets all tended to ensure that the luxury trades consisted of clusters of separate but interdependent enterprises rather than the integrated proto-factories that came to be associated with the production of porcelain, printed textiles and wall-paper. The production of luxury goods tended therefore to entail a multitude of different but overlapping schedules of credit. Credit was extended by suppliers of materials and designs, as well as by artisans and sub-contractors in ancillary trades, where terms of six, nine or 12 months were the norm, with discounts for cash payments within shorter intervals. It was also made available to final consumers, who rarely settled in full and in cash when work was completed. Credit complemented the divisions of labour associated with luxury production, for none of the elaborately ornate objects produced in eighteenth-century France was made in one place by one pair of hands.

Credit in its turn intersected with cash outlays. Irregular payments to suppliers of goods, materials or specialised techniques were matched by more regular weekly wage-payments, which varied in amount as the size and composition of the workforce changed. At times as many as 40 or 50 journeymen could be employed in large enterprises like those belonging to the Parisian sculptor Leprince or to the cabinet-maker Jacob in the late eighteenth century.[10] A substantial artisanal enterprise was therefore obliged to manage its affairs in a fairly sophisticated way. At the heart of its calculations lay the relationship between inward and outward credit movements on the one hand, and inward and outward cash flows on the other. A viable enterprise in the luxury trades was one that could offer as much credit as possible in order to generate sufficient income to meet its outward cash flows. Luxury production thus entailed close attention to the management of time and the uses to which time was put. Work on a number of concurrent projects was usual. The more rapidly that different undertakings were completed, the larger were the returns needed to pay wages and creditors, and, at the same time, the greater was the probability of establishing or maintaining a master artisan's reputation among creditors and a predominantly aristocratic and clerical clientele.

These clienteles were by no means confined to the capital. Markets for the artefacts produced in eighteenth-century Paris extended well beyond Versailles and the hotels and apartments of the Marais, the *faubourg* Saint-Germain and the expanding suburbs beyond the Roule and the Chaussée d'Antin. Parisian artefacts circulated throughout the guilded diaspora of courts and minor principalities of eighteenth-century Europe,

[10] See above, p. 146, and Isser Woloch, 'From Charity to Welfare in Revolutionary Paris', *Journal of Modern History*, 58 (1986), pp. 779–812 (p. 790, note 20).

from Stockholm to Lisbon and from London to St Petersburg. The scale of this international economy bore little relation to the relatively small number of final consumers that it supplied. In one year alone (1752), the royal household of Parma spent over 200,000 *livres* on Parisian goods dispatched by its agent, the banking house of Jean-Baptiste Bonnet.[11] Almost every court, and many minor princes and ecclesiastical dignitaries, had commercial agents in Paris and, on occasion, in Lyon as well. The reputations that took three members of the Martin family to Stockholm, Vienna, Naples and scores of other painters and designers to Stockholm, Berlin and London, or St Petersburg were grounded upon networks of information that originated in Paris.

These channels of information found their expression in a vast traffic in engraved designs which made works like Robert Sayer's *The Ladies' Delight, or the Whole Art of Japanning Made Easy* (London, 1758) a collage of mainly Parisian designs, and ensured that some Parisian engravers, like François Chéreau, developed networks of correspondents whose international dimensions rivalled those of many textile houses.[12] *Chinoiserie* was only a component of a highly specialised and very adaptable range of forms and figures that were easily transferred from one object or material to another. 'Il se trouve,' the Swedish ambassador in Paris reported in 1694,

que ce que l'on appelle ici peintre d'ornements, c'est en premier lieu, un homme qui invente et dispose des desseins d'ornement. Il y a de ceux-la qui ne font que disposer et dessiner sans peindre, d'autres qui dessignent peu et ne peignent point. Il y a en suitte [*sic*] les parties qui entrent dans l'ornement, comme la figure, l'architecture, la perspective, l'allégorie, la grotesque, les animaux, les oiseaux, les fleurs, les masques etc....et puis ce que l'on appelle l'ornement, qui est la feuille de refend, les rinceaux etc.[13]

The hallmark of Parisian design, from the late seventeenth century onwards, was the ease with which designs could be transposed from two-dimensional to three-dimensional forms, so that much of the appearance of brocaded silks or printed fabrics could be reproduced on, or inversely borrowed from, porcelain, wall-panelling, wrought-iron, or brass, gold and silverware. The ease with which designs could be disseminated throughout the international court economy was matched by an eclecticism that allowed a wide range of materials to be adapted to a common repertoire of forms and figures. A well-known association with a particular artefact or process was often – as the career of that most versatile of designers, Jean Pillement, demonstrated – the basis of a

11 Henri Bédarida, *Parme et la France de 1748 à 1789* (Paris, 1928), p. 290.
12 A.N. MC C 621 (23 April 1755).
13 Cronstrom to Tessin, 2 July 1694, cited by R. A. Weigert in his introduction to the catalogue, *Claude Audran. L'Art décoratif français au Musée de Stockholm* (Paris, 1950), p. xxix.

multiplicity of further associations with different types of materials and products.[14] *Vernis Martin* owed much of its celebrity to the wide range of products and materials with which it was associated.

Reputations had a further significance in the eighteenth-century luxury trades: they were often associated with legal privileges. Most large enterprises in eighteenth-century France sought, and often obtained, the title of *manufacture royale*. Over two dozen privileged manufactories were to be found in Paris on the eve of the Revolution. There were, however, very many more artisans endowed with the privilege of producing for the court. The number of assorted *menuisiers, cordonniers, peintres, tailleurs, selliers* or *serruriers du roi* in eighteenth-century Paris ran to well over 100.[15] The functions of their titles were various. Privilege allowed large-scale enterprises (and, in lesser and often disputed measure, court artisans) to manage their own affairs independently of corporate regulation. This was its main purpose and legal justification. It also enabled some manufacturers to produce expensive goods and carry the risks associated with heavy outlays on wages, materials and space into relatively limited markets. Yet, just as the particularism of corporate statutes can disguise the relative homogeneity of many apparently different trades, so the multitude of exclusive privileges associated with luxury production can conceal a more fluid, market-oriented and opportunistic reality.

Privilege was also, and perhaps equally importantly, a very effective marketing ploy.[16] There is little evidence that many of the materials or techniques used in privileged manufactories were particularly esoteric, or that many of the proprietors of exclusive privileges were doing anything very different from other artisans. In his *L'Art du peintre, doreur, vernisseur* (Paris, 1773), the painter and colour merchant Watin listed ten different types of lacquer known and used for different purposes on various

14 An outline of the long career of Jean Pillement (the author of many of the designs found in Sayer's *Ladies' Amusement*) can be found in Marius Audin and Eugene Vial, *Dictionnaire des artistes et ouvriers d'art de France. Lyonnais*, 2 vols (Paris, 1918). On the dissemination of Parisian designs in the seventeenth century, see Marianne Grivel, *Le Commerce de l'estampe à Paris au xviie siècle* (Geneva, 1986), pp. 203–7. For examples of the adoption of Parisian design in eighteenth-century England (including the collections devised by Pierre-Edmé Babel), see Victoria and Albert Museum, *Art and Design in Hogarth's England* (London, 1984), p. 155.

15 Over 1,500 titles were granted between 1682 and 1789, or an average of 14 a year: Pierre Deyon and Philippe Guignet, 'The Royal Manufactories and Economic and Technological Progress in France before the Industrial Revolution', *Journal of European Economic History*, 10 (1980), pp. 611–32. On Parisian manufactories, see Bertrand Gille, *Documents sur l'état de l'industrie et du commerce de Paris et du departement de la Seine (1778–1810)* (Paris, 1963), and *Almanach du Voyageur à Paris* (Paris, 1786), p. 317. For a sketchy discussion of court artisans, see Michael Stürmer, 'An Economy of Delight: Court Artisans of the Eighteenth Century', *Business History Review*, 53 (1979), pp. 496–528.

16 Christine McCleod, 'The 1690s Patent Boom: Invention or Stock Jobbing', *Economic History Review*, 2nd series, 39 (1986), pp. 549–71.

materials in the Paris of his day.[17] The Martin brothers claimed, however, that their lacquer, the lacquer that has come to be known as *vernis Martin*, was different from the rest. There is no evidence that it was, but privilege ensured that it appeared to be.

Privilege was both a legal title and the basis of a reputation for quality. It invested the activities performed by some artisans or manufacturers with qualities of natural ability (or genius) that exempted them from the ordinary rules of the polity and entitled them to exercise their arts as natural liberty prescribed. Throughout the eighteenth century, the phrase *art libéral* had a range of connotations that were redolent of the natural law tradition. The difference between members of the Académie royale and members of the Académie de Saint-Luc was at once legal and ontological. Painters or sculptors who belong to the former were entitled to those privileges that consecrated their natural ability to produce work that was singularly their own: the privileges bestowed upon court artisans and manufacturers derived from the same premises.[18] Yet, once invested with privilege, a reputation for high-quality goods could be turned to the production of low-cost and more profitable commodities. This was the key to the Martin brothers' success. Not surprisingly, the privileges that they claimed also created tensions among master artisans.

Reputation, credit and legal privilege formed a nexus that was one of the hallmarks of luxury production. They made it possible to combine production of substantial batches of relatively low-cost, high value-added goods with more prestigious, high-cost articles. In this context, the law was often very much more than a protective cover whose detailed provisions separated the members of one trade or corporation from another, or defined the respective rights and obligations of particular groups of masters and journeymen. The law could also be used in a more instrumental way, either to promote and market a particular product, to

17 Xavier Folville, 'Matériaux et techniques du décor polychrome au xviiie siècle', *Bulletin de la Commission royale des monuments et des sites* (Brussels), 10 (1981), pp. 193–219, and Ian Bristow, 'Ready-Mixed Paint in the Eighteenth Century', *Architectural Review*, 161 (1977), pp. 247–8. I am grateful to M. Jean Payen of the Conservatoire National des Arts et Métiers in Paris for information on the composition of *vernis Martin*. Like the *Académie des Sciences* in the eighteenth century, he concludes that the lacquer was a variant upon a number of comparable solutions used in eighteenth-century Paris.

18 The distinction was made particularly emphatically during the series of lawsuits between the two bodies between 1760 and 1770: see A.N. X^{1a} 4697 fol. 69vo (7 September 1770). As the artists of the Louvre put it, 'Le même fond qui avoit produit des hommes illustres dans la Guerre, pouvoit produire des génies célèbres dans les Arts, et la supériorité acquise par les armes, se remplacer par celle que donnent les talens de l'esprit': Bibliothèque de l'Ordre des Avocats (Paris), Collection Chanlaire, vol. 161 (3 and 4). *Mémoires pour les Artistes des Galeries du Louvre contre les Directeurs et Gardes de la Communauté des maîtres peintres et sculpteurs de Paris* (Paris, 1763). See also Dominique Désirat, 'Peinture et pouvoirs de 1699 à 1759' (thèse de troisième cycle, Université François Rabelais, Tours, n.d.).

undermine or eliminate competitors and rivals, or to provoke and magnify conflicts in order to nullify unwelcome corporate decisions. It was, in any of these three senses, more than an external regulator of the bazaar economy – it was one of the range of competitive resources available to those artisans who, as Nicolas Guérard put it, set out to pull the Devil by the tail in their pursuit of wealth and honour.[19] The particular structure of the luxury trades – with their growing size, their highly centralised markets in Paris, Versailles and the other European courts, and, not least, the relatively limited number of very wealthy final consumers who made up these markets – meant that litigation and disputes over rights and obligations could sometimes serve other, more latent purposes than their manifest goals appear to indicate.

Guillaume Martin, the eldest of five brothers, was born in 1689.[20] He belonged to that world of settled, relatively prosperous master artisans which remains one of the least-known components of eighteenth-century Parisian society. Although his father, Etienne Martin, was a tailor and his mother, Claude Blot, a seamstress (*maîtresse couturière*), it is probable that their activities placed them at the highly fashionable end of the trade. There were many different types of tailor in Old-Regime Paris. A master tailor on the rue du Colombier who went bankrupt in 1778 had assets of over 160,000 *livres*, but liabilities of some 170,000 *livres*, including over 37,000 *livres* owed to the merchant draper Jean-Etienne Quatremère on the rue Saint-Denis and nearly 17,000 *livres* to the partnership of Georges Le Roux and Michel Delasalle, silk merchants on the rue Saint-Honoré.[21] One of Guillaume Martin's uncles, Pierre Martin, was a building entrepreneur to the Crown (*entrepreneur des bâtiments du Roi*), while another, Denis Martin, was a master sculptor and painter. His cousins, Laurent, Jacques and Jean-Baptiste Martin, were painters and sculptors, the last of them occupying the post of *premier peintre des conquêtes du Roi* and becoming better known as Martin-des-Batailles (see Figure 7.1). Another cousin, Pierre-Alexandre Martin, was a bookseller on the quai des Augustins, whose assets at the time of his wife's death in 1736 amounted to over 100,000 *livres*, including a stock worth more than 80,000 *livres*.[22]

19 See above, chapter 2.
20 A.N. MC CXXI 345 (21 October 1749), *certificat de notoriété* reproducing his baptismal certificate. His godfather, also a Guillaume Martin, was a tailor. His godmother, Marianne Marie Géneviève Dubercelle, was the daughter of a dancing master, François Dubercelle.
21 A.N. X¹ᵇ 4070 (24 November 1778).
22 An Etienne Martin, who may have been Guillaume's father, was admitted to the Academy of Saint-Luc on 23 September 1677 (B.L. 503 e. 11). On the links between the different branches of the family, se A.N. MC LX 109 (14 July 1686): XLV 306 (2 November 1702); XXVIII 136 (29 September 1715); LXXIII 643 (15 December 1716); I 356 (27 November 1731); CI 303 (3 November 1733); CXXI 315 (24 October 1739); CXXI 319 (18 May 1741); CXXI 321 (25 July 1741); B.N. MS. fr. 21 847 fol. 2ᵛᵒ; B.N. fo fm 5625 and 5626.

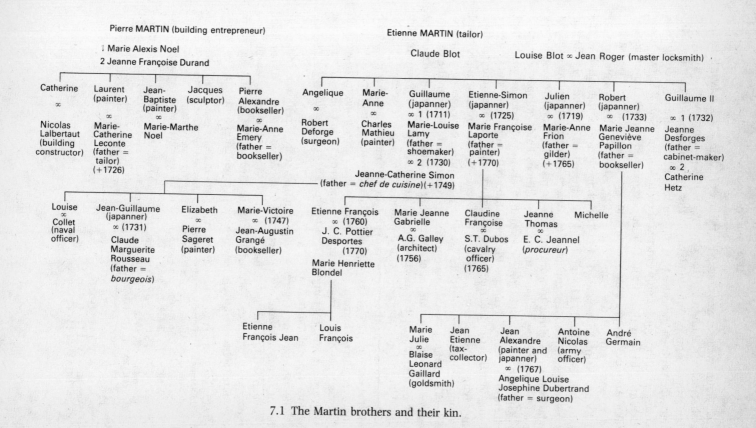

7.1 The Martin brothers and their kin.

Guillaume Martin was married at the age of 22, in 1711, to Marie Lamy, a shoemaker's daughter. Her dowry of 1,000 *livres* was a relatively comfortable sum by the standards of the early eighteenth century. The marriage contract indicates that Martin himself was already known as a *vernisseur*, although he only entered the *Académie de Saint-Luc* two years later, in 1713.[23] By then, he had already established himself in the *faubourg* Saint-Antoine, where, after several changes of address, he leased a six-room apartment at the sign of the *roi de Siam* on the Grande rue du faubourg Saint-Antoine in 1714. The shop sign was indicative of his activities. Between 1711 and 1714 he entered into at least 18 formal agreements with an assortment of engravers, painters and other artisans who undertook either to work for him or place their children under his control to produce, or learn to produce, various kinds of japanware.[24]

The contracts provide some information about the range of goods that Martin was selling. François-Philippe Dubercelle, a painter and designer living on the Grande rue, agreed to work as a painter and produce engravings on lacquer for a period of a year. Martin, in return, promised to supply him with at least 'deux toilettes ou autres ouvrages équivalents' a week.[25] Antoine Bercy, an engraver on copper plate living in the suburb, agreed to produce a number of different pieces, either according to a design that he and Martin had devised or in imitation of three different models that Martin had supplied. He also undertook to engrave scenes from the *Metamorphoses* in the spaces provided in the model designs, for which Martin again was to supply the detailed subject-matter.[26] Another engraver, Pierre Gourdin, also domiciled in the *faubourg*, agreed to work on various types of 'ouvrages de gravure sur verny de la Chine' for a period of two years at rates ranging from between 10 and 22 *livres* for pairs of various types of *toilettes*.[27]

The occupation of *vernisseur* (if not the word itself) was relatively recent in origin. None of the members of the *Académie de Saint-Luc* listed between 1672 and 1677 had the title.[28] The rates that Martin was prepared to pay were, accordingly, indicative of the demand for goods associated with a relatively new branch of production and with conditions

[23] A.N. MC XXVIII 115 (23 November 1711). I owe this, and most of the references to Guillaume Martin's early activities cited in the following note, to the kindness of M. Daniel Alcouffe of the Musée des Arts Décoratifs in Paris. The date of Martin's admission to the Academy is mentioned in the papers listed in the inventory of Marie Lamy's estate: A.N. MC LVII 332 (22 August 1730).

[24] A.N. MC I 257 (15 July 1714) cited in Mireille Rambaud, *Documents du Minutier Central concernant l'histoire de l'art (1700–1750)*, 2 vols (Paris, 1964 and 1971), vol. 2, p. 333. A.N. MC XXVIII 118 (16 May 1712); 119 (10 July 1712); 121 (15 November 1712); 122 (29 January 1713); 123 (1, 2, 6 and 10 May 1713); 124 (11 and 16 July 1713); 125 (9 November 1713); 131 (21 September and 2 October 1714).

[25] A.N. MC XXVIII 118 (16 May 1712); 123 (1 May 1713).

[26] A.N. MC XXVIII 123 (6 May 1713).

[27] A.N. MC XXVIII 131 (2 October 1714).

[28] B.L. 503 e. 11 (1–7).

of considerable labour scarcity. Dubercelle was to receive 4 *livres* for each day's work and a further 100 *livres* every three months. Another engraver, Charles Quéruel, who, like almost all the artisans that Martin engaged, lived in the *faubourg*, was to be paid 3 *livres* a day, while a journeyman engraver living on the rue de Seine in the *faubourg* Saint-Germain was promised an increase in his initial daily rate of 25 *sous* to 3 *livres* if he worked for Martin for more than a year. Adrien Vincent, a painter living in the *faubourg* Saint-Antoine, who agreed in 1714 to work for Martin for two years, was to receive 5 *livres* a day.[29] Both the rates themselves and the premiums paid to journeymen who remained in employment for a year or more had been had they worked regularly throughout the year. Both the rates that Martin was prepared to pay, and the half-dozen children he engaged to train, mainly to engrave on lacquer and, in one case, to design as well, imply that the skills needed to produce *chinoiserie* were in relatively short supply.

There can be little doubt that there was something of a boom for *chinoiserie* in the last years of the reign of Louis XIV. Martin's activities in the *faubourg* Saint-Antoine were complemented by a very much more prestigious undertaking established at the same time in the Gobelins manufactory in the *faubourg* Saint-Marcel. The designs of scenes from the *Metamorphoses* that Martin agreed to supply to one of his engravers echoed a series of 227 master engravings of scenes from the *Metamorphoses* bought for 500 *livres* by the engraver and print-dealer Gérard Audran in 1692. In 1708, Jean Audran, Gérard's nephew and associate, was godfather to one of the children of the battle-painter Jacques Martin.[30] In October 1713, Jean Audran's brother, the painter Claude III Audran, was granted a 20-year royal privilege, beginning in January 1714, to establish une manufacture de verny pour le moins aussy beau que celuy de la Chine, pour être appliqué sur touttes sortes de toilles et étoffes de laine, de soye, de cuir et autres

[29] A.N. MC XXVIII (2 May 1713): 125 (9 November 1713): 131 (21 September 1714). The formal character of the agreements also served a second purpose. As an inhabitant of the *faubourg* Saint-Antoine and one who was not a member of the painters' corporation, Martin was not protected by statutory regulation of the contract of employment. Formal notarial agreements were both a measure of the exceptional price he was prepared to pay to enter the market for *chinoiserie* and, at the same time, an indication of the unusual legal safeguards needed to keep a workforce in conditions of considerable labour scarcity.

[30] A.N. MC XLIX 399 (7 October 1692), cited in Marianne Grivel, *Le Commerce de l'estampe à Paris au xviie siècle* (Geneva, 1986), pp. 276–7; H. Herluison, *Actes d'état civil d'artistes français* (Orléans, 1873), p. 284. On the Audran, see Charles du Peloux, *Répertoire biographique et bibliographique des artistes du xviiie siècle français* (Paris, 1930); G. Duplessis, *Les Audran* (Paris, 1892); and, on Claude III Audran, see R. A. Weigert, *Claude Audran, l'art décoratif français au Musée de Stockholm* (Paris, Bibliothèque nationale, 1950); and 'Claude III Audran, père de l'art décoratif', *Médicine de France*, 115 (1960), pp. 17–32.

matières ployables et de touttes couleurs propres à faire des meubles comme chaises, fauteuils, tabarets, canapez, écrans, paravents, tapisseries, lits, portières, tapis, panneaux de lambris et plat fonds.[31]

The privilege was the basis of a partnership between Audran, an entrepreneur and former inhabitant of Danzig named Pierre Deneumaison, who had been treasurer to Prince Constantine of Poland and had accumulated a string of exotic titles and connections in the course of an already long life, and Jacques Dagly, a native of Liège and the inventor of the lacquer whose clarity, strength and polish were, it was stated, the secret of the process. Audran was to supply ideas for designs 'qui seront mis au net par des personnes qui seront payées aux dépenses de la société'; Dagly was to provide his technical expertise; and Deneumaison was to manage the business from day to day.[32]

Audran's involvement in the partnership appears to have been brief. In 1715 he ceded his share in the venture to Deneumaison and Dagly in return for 6,766 *livres*, representing his part of its outstanding assets. He continued, however, to hold the privilege and, in return for allowing Dagly and Deneumaison to use it, was promised an annual income of 800 *livres* from his former associates until 1 January 1734, when the privilege expired.[33] The partnership continued on this basis for several years. Predictably, payment of the annual fee fell into arrears and, in 1728, Deneumaison ceded Audran an amount of some 4,400 *livres* owed by the Duchesse de Bourbon for 'les ouvrages de la Chine' done for the Château de Saint-Maur under the direction of the architect Aubert, and finished in 1720.[34] Dagly died in 1726 but Deneumaison continued the enterprise for nearly 20 years after Audran's death in 1734. In 1746 he formed a partnership with his son-in-law, the painter Charles-André Tremblin (or Tramblin), himself the son of a very substantial picture-dealer on the quai de Gesvres in Paris whose stock, at his death in 1742, included over 1,000 paintings and an extensive frame-making business sub-contracted out among at least four master gilders. Tremblin had the title of *directeur pour le Roi des ouvrages de la Chine à la manufacture des Gobelins* at the time of Deneumaison's death in 1752.[35]

[31] A.N. O¹* 57 fol. 272 (28 November 1713). The destruction by fire of the minutes of the notary (Dutartre, *étude* LVI) used by Jacques Dagly and, in particular, the inventory of his estate drawn up on 28 December 1728 means that information on the activities of the *manufacture* is limited. For one possible example of the decorative work carried out by the *manufacture*, see Jacques Wilhelm, 'Le Grand Cabinet chinois de l'Hôtel de Richelieu, Place Royale', *Bulletin du Musée Carnavalet*, 1 (1967), pp. 2–14. I have not, however, encountered any reference to the maréchal de Richelieu in notarial transactions involving the Audran–Deneumaison enterprise.

[32] A.N. XLIX 465 (7 December 1713).

[33] A.N. XXVI 291 (1 February 1715).

[34] A.N. XCI 722 (21 May 1728); 743 (10 October 1733); XLIX 553 (1 June 1734).

[35] A.N. MC XXXIII (14 November 1746); CIX 537 (5 July 1742); Jean Gaston, *Une Paroisse parisienne avant la Révolution, Saint-Hippolyte* (Paris, 1908), pp. 27, 103, 179; R. A.

It is probable that the core of the enterprise's activities was made up of painting, decorating and finishing coaches. An inventory drawn up at the time of the death of Deneumaison's first wife in 1733 listed the names of over a dozen nobles, including the prince de Conti, the prince de Bouillon, the duc de Caumont and the comtesse d'Egmont, as well as the Queen of Spain, who owed the enterprise a total of 27,516 *livres* for work on coaches.[36] The inventory drawn up at the time of Deneumaison's own death in 1752 was very similar in content. Work was in progress or had just been completed on ten coaches, carriages or sedan-chairs. Deneumaison had also dealt in pictures in a small way and had two paintings by the Academician Auger Lucas, who also worked for the Martin brothers, among the dozen paintings in his stock. Deneumaison himself had not confined his interests to the decorative arts. In 1740 he had formed a partnership with a Parisian merchant named Jean-Baptiste Gébert to develop and sell a new flour-milling machine, but the venture failed acrimoniously. Other activities were more successful. The partnership with Tremblin also appears to have produced (or sold) lacquered, printed textiles some time before the general prohibition upon the manufacture of calicoes was lifted in 1759. Its stock included 42 pieces of *toile peinte et vernie de façon de la Chine* valued at some 418 *livres*.[37]

The accounts that Tremblin drew up at the time of Deneumaison's death indicate, however, that the enterprise was a relatively modest affair. Between 1746 and 1751 the partnership's total outlay on materials, wages and payment for sub-contracted work was no more than 84,205 *livres*, and it never exceeded 21,000 *livres* in any single year. Even if its sales were double that amount, it was by no means a large enterprise. Deneumaison was an old man, while Tremblin had other interests in hand in addition to the *manufacture des ouvrages de la Chine*. He was responsible for the decorations maintained by the municipality of Paris and later became first painter and decorator of the Opera. In 1760 he went to Vienna, and thence to Russia, where he committed suicide. The agent of the Imperial Court in Vienna who recruited him suggested that he should be employed on the painting and decoration of the court coaches. 'Il a déjà fait plusieurs carosses pour leurs Majestés Imperiales, pour Monseigneur le comte de Könitz etc.,' he reported. 'Il n'y a que lui et le s. Martins [*sic*] qui possèdent ces beaux vernis égaux et supérieurs même à la Chine.'[38]

36 Wiegert, *Claude Audran* p. 25: A.N. MC IV 573 (10 May 1751): XVIII 800 (13 October 1751). Jules-Joseph Guiffrey, 'Scellés et inventaires d'artistes', *Nouvelles archives de l'art français*, 2nd series, 5 (1882), pp. 17, 140. On the Tremblin (or Tramblin), see also Mireille Rambaud, *Documents*, under their name.

37 A.N. MC XCI 741 (3 June 1733): XXXII 499 (8 November 1746).

38 A.N. MC CXXII 684 (13 June 1752): CXXII 692 (23 October and 23 November 1754): LXII 380 (21 November 1740): X^{1a} 4154 fol. 70 (28 March 1752). Tremblin in fact renounced his share of the estate (A.N. MC CXXII 692, 23 November 1754). The letter from Favart to the comte de Durazzo is printed in J. J. Guiffrey, 'Les

The reputations of the two enterprises were indicative of the similarity of their activities. It was probably more than a coincidence, however, that Guillaume Martin obtained a privilege to manufacture and sell 'toutes sortes d'ouvrage en relief dans le gout du Japon ou de la Chine' shortly before Audran's own privilege expired.[39] By 1730, when the Royal Letters Patent announcing the privilege were published, Martin had reached the age of 40 and was a substantial and successful entrepreneur. He had obtained the title of *vernisseur du roi* in 1725 and established a wide range of predominantly aristocratic clients and customers. In 1727 he formed a partnership with his 24-year-old younger brother Etienne-Simon, soon after the latter's marriage to Marie Françoise Delaporte, the daughter of a master painter.[40] The business was organised around a number of workshops and hangars spread around the crown of the northern suburbs of the capital. Guillaume Martin moved from the Grande rue du faubourg Saint-Antoine to rent a house and workshops belonging to the descendants of a distant relative, Antoine Rivet, *menuisier du roi*, on the Grande rue du faubourg Saint-Denis.[41] Etienne-Simon Martin rented another house and workshop on the Grande rue du faubourg Saint-Martin, while a third brother, Julien Martin, who undertook sub-contracted work for the other two, had a further shop and hangar in the *faubourg* Saint-Laurent.

The partnership established in 1727 proved, however, to be a short-lived affair. In 1730, soon after the death of Marie Lamy, Guillaume Martin remarried, the partnership was dissolved and the brothers agreed to go their separate ways.[42] Guillaume took over some 17,668 *livres* worth of debts on goods and wages due to various merchants, sub-contractors and workers and resumed sole control of the shop, hangars, stocks and utensils on the Grande rue du faubourg Saint-Denis, as well as the enterprise in the *faubourg* Saint-Laurent where Julien Martin was based. Etienne-Simon was left in control of the business on the Grande rue du faubourg Saint-Martin. The inventory drawn up in the course of the transaction discloses a wide range of overlapping activities and products.[43] Guillaume Martin's stock in the shop and hangars on the Grande rue du faubourg Saint-Denis was valued at over 10,800 *livres*. The largest item was a pair of cabinets painted green 'a relief et figures', worth 1,600 *livres*. Two other cabinets finished in black lacquer with red drawers were worth 500 *livres*. The 100

Peintres décorateurs du xviiie siècle. Servandoni, Brunetti, Tramblin, etc.', *Revue de l'art français*, 3 (1897), pp. 119–28 (pp. 121–2).

[39] A.N. O¹ 74 fol. 462 (27 November 1730).

[40] A.N. MC LVII 332 (22 August 1730), inventory of the estate left by Marie Lamy. Regrettably the minutes of the notary (Prévost) who drew up the original deed of partnership have not survived. MC XXXV 551 (11 February 1725), marriage between Etienne-Simon Martin and Marie Françoise Laporte (who subsequently entitled herself Delaporte).

[41] A.N. MC LX 109 (14 July 1686) X¹ᵃ 7341 fol. 74 (20 February 1736).

[42] A.N. MC LVII 332 (23 and 28 August 1730); 333 (23 September 1730).   [43] *Ibid.*

items in the stock included a number of small batches of between one and four dozen snuff-boxes or *tabatières*, decanter-holders, ornamental trays and plates, *toilettes* and corner cupboards.

Most of these goods were supplied by sub-contractors, or, from the number of unfinished pieces of furniture in stock, were made up on the premises from parts supplied by cabinet-makers, joiners, and wood- or marble-sculptors, before they were painted or engraved with patterns, oriental designs, birds or flowers and given their lacquer finish. The procedure was applied not only to wooden furniture, but to linen screens (*paravents*), *papier-mâché* trinkets, snuff-boxes and the like, as well as to the sedan-chairs and coaches that were painted and decorated in the hangar. Martin's creditors included three other painters – Dubuisson (1,125 *livres*), Gasselin (392 *livres*) and Remy (600 *livres*) – as well as the fourth of the five brothers, Robert Martin, who was owed 685 *livres* 'pour journées d'ouvrage par luy faittes'. His largest creditors were suppliers of materials: 8,100 *livres* were owed to a merchant named Huet on the rue Saint-Denis; 833 *livres* to a grocer named Delarue, for colours; 858 and 260 *livres* to two *batteurs d'or*, Satin and Bachelier, for supplies of gold leaf; while a variety of smaller sums were owed to some two dozen joiners, turners, carpenters, wheelwrights, masons, goldsmiths, coppersmiths (an Oudry), locksmiths, drapers and merchants for the supply of goods or services related to the enterprise.

The highly dis-integrated character of the enterprise was reflected in the low value (some 1,028 *livres*) of its stock of materials and equipment. Most of it consisted of simple workbenches and ladders, a 'machine à laver les carrosses' (worth 5 *livres*), several jars of varnish and gum, a number of stones and oil to grind and mix colours, 2,000 sheets of gold leaf (worth 160 *livres*), as well as three 'planches de bosqué pour emprimer' (valued at 60 *livres*). Etienne-Simon Martin's shop and hangar on the Grande rue du faubourg Saint-Martin contained a smaller but almost identical range of goods and utensils. In all, their value was set at some 6,482 *livres*. The partnership was also owed a certain amount of money by its clients. A sum of 3,500 *livres* was due from the King, while amounts of 70, 496 and 200 *livres* were outstanding from the duchesse de Tonnerre, the duc de la Tremouille and the duc de Bouillon respectively. The privilege granted to Guillaume Martin after the dissolution of the partnership in 1730 was, it would seem, both the product of an established reputation and confirmation of his place at the apex of the market for luxury goods.

The privilege encountered considerable opposition. Four painters, supported by the *Académie de Saint-Luc*, appealed to the Parlement of Paris to oppose registration of the Letters Patent.[44] The principal opponent of registration was the painter and sculptor Adrien Vincent whom Martin

[44] A.N. X^{1a} 7353 fol. 312 (22 August 1736).

had engaged for two years in 1714. Of the three others – Jean Peinte, Jacques Garnier and Jacques Justice – the last two were *vernisseurs* as well as painters. The Parlement had still not ratified the privilege in February 1736 when the Crown renewed the Letters Patent.[45] In August of that year the Parlement decided to refer the case to the *Académie des Sciences* to establish whether Martin's lacquer was a new invention and whether his products differed from those produced by other painters 'plus par leur nature et qualité que par leur perfection'. The Academy decided that there was nothing intrinsically new or different in the lacquer and registration of the privilege was abandoned. A second set of Letters Patent, issued to Etienne-Simon Martin in 1744, appears to have suffered the same fate. By then, the question of lacquered articles had become part of a second legal battle, between the painters' and toymakers' (*tabletiers*) corporations.[46] The toymakers claimed that they were as much entitled to make and sell japanware as the painters. The case was finally settled by a ruling of the Conseil d'Etat in 1753 which confirmed an earlier ruling by the Parlement of Paris in 1749 allowing members of both corporations to make and sell 'des ouvrages de papier ou toille moulée peints et vernis, vulgairement appellez ouvrages et vernis de Martin'.[47]

The disputed privilege and the litigation that ensued had the effect of establishing *vernis Martin* as a generic term. There is no evidence that the challenge to the exclusive title, or even a detailed description of the technical procedures used to make *vernis Martin* goods (which the toymakers produced in the course of their lawsuit with the painters), had any harmful effect upon the Martin brothers' own activities. When Guillaume Martin died at the age of 60 in 1749, he left a flourishing business and a stock worth some 35,384 *livres*. When the estate was divided the following year, it had a gross value of 64,485 *livres*, including stock, utensils and credit worth a total of 46,254 *livres*.[48] Despite a promise to associate his eldest son, Jean-Guillaume, when the latter married in 1731 – a promise that was briefly honoured in a short-lived and unhappy partnership established with a capital of 41,000 *livres* in 1741 – and repeated references to the need to obtain 'un état plus tranquille' away from 'un établissement aussy considerable' which had affected both his own and his second wife's health, Martin was unable to relinquish control.[49] Like many first-generation entrepreneurs, he died in harness.

Much of the daily management of the concern was, however, transferred to a number of semi-permanent under-managers. In 1737 Julien Martin,

45 B.N. MS. Joly de Fleury 805 fol. 147 (1 February 1736).
46 A.N. X¹ᵃ 7353 fol. 312 (22 August 1736); X¹ᵃ 4060 fol. 70ᵛᵒ (19 July 1749): Y 15 789ᵃ (12 July 1747).
47 A.N. E 1286ᶜ (10 April 1753).   48 A.N. MC CXXI 345 (18 August 1749).
49 A.N. MC LXXII 258 (14 November 1731); CXXI 319 (7 March 1741): 323 (5 April 1742).

his wife and their daughter were engaged for a period of ten years at a rate of 3,000 *livres* a year to undertake 'les ouvrages généralement quelconque tant de peinture que verni de la Chine' that Guillaume would supply to their shop in the *faubourg Saint-Laurent*.[50] A distant relative and *maître-vernisseur*, Louis Pons (his father was one of Guillaume Martin's brothers-in-law by his second marriage; he married one of Martin's second wife's daughters in 1742), was taken on to manage the shop on the Grande rue du faubourg Saint-Denis, also at 3,000 *livres* a year.[51] In 1744, after the failure of the partnership with his son and the death of Louis Pons, Martin engaged a designer and another distant relative, David Durand, for a period of ten years at 900 *livres* a year for the first four years and 5 *livres* a day thereafter, promising at the end of the period 'de donner audit Sieur Durand le secret de son art par écrit de luy certifié véritable'.[52] The emphasis upon a written description with an authentic signature tells its own story – the name, rather than the process itself, was what was of value. Yet despite this appeal to cupidity, the offer appears to have been less than tantalising. By the time of Martin's death, Durand had left and been replaced by a master painter, Charles Lagrange (or Delagrange).[53]

The character of the enterprise remained much as it had been in 1730. The 145 different items listed in the inventory covered the same range of goods, albeit in rather larger quantities, as well as four miniature spinning-wheels or looms.[54] The batches of moulded paper and *papier-mâché* goods were substantially larger in size, frequently running to well over 100 examples of the same type. They were, it is clear, cheap to produce and, when finished, lacquered and polished, highly profitable to sell. The unfinished caskets in Martin's stock were valued at no more than 2 or 3 *livres* each, but by the time that they had been patterned (*guillochés*), decorated, lacquered, gilded and polished they were valued at anything from 15 to 60 *livres* each. It is impossible to know how widely they sold, but the quantity alone suggests that the market for such goods was neither exclusively Parisian nor entirely aristocratic in composition. Substantial decorative projects remained, however, the core of the business. As in 1730, the estate was owed money by the Crown: 5,000 *livres* for work at Versailles and a further unspecified sum by the treasurers of the *Petite Écurie du Roy* for decorating coaches. Martin had also formed a partnership in 1739 with another coach-painter, *vernisseur* and building entrepreneur named Magny, sharing profits and losses on the refurbishment and decoration of aristocratic property. The hangars adjoining the workshops

50 A.N. MC XXX 267 (27 December 1736).
51 A.N. MC CXXI 319 (9 March, 13 and 14 April 1741); 323 (27 January 1742).
52 A.N. MC CXXI 332 (1 November 1744); Martin also engaged a turner, Laurence Copi.
53 *ibid.*, 342 (25 February 1748).
54 A.N. MC CXXI 345 (18 August 1749); XCVIII 521 (6 February 1753).
    A.N. MC CXXI 345 (18 August 1749); MC CXXI 346 (8 February 1750).

contained ten coaches, carriages or portable chairs, whose panels were sumptuously decorated with pictures of flowers, children or other figures, set against backgrounds of gold, *velours*, *aventurine*, red, grey or *chamois*, and finished in gilt.[55]

The range of activities entailed a substantial amount of sub-contracting to other master artisans. Three of the estate's creditors – Huet (2,672 *livres*), Delestre (140 *livres*) and Garcelin (152 *livres*) – were painters (the last of the three was a figure-painter). Two turners, a toymaker (Wolph), a sculptor, a metal-founder and embellisher (*fondeur et garnisseur*), a jeweller and decorator, a gilder and a gold leaf-maker (*batteur d'or*) – all of whom may well have engaged their own journeymen – formed a cluster of regular suppliers of unfinished goods or specialised processes. Beyond them was the larger contingent of suppliers of materials: grocers for colours, oils and varnishes; and goldsmiths or *batteurs d'or* for gold leaf, gold flake or powder. At the same time, however, a substantial amount of work was done on the premises. There were two hangars and four different rooms for making up, painting, varnishing, engraving and polishing the many different objects that fell under the rubric of *vernis Martin*.

Martin's death led to a number of permutations within the family economy. His eldest son, Jean-Guillaume, after ending his association with his father, had established himself on the rue du Bac in the *faubourg Saint-Germain*, where, in 1745, he engaged Antoine Picard, described simply as a *bourgeois de Paris*, to work for three years at rates of 750, 800 and 850 *livres* a year on 'les ouvrages de vernis' that Martin would supply.[56] By 1749, however, he had gone to Parma as official painter to Don Philippe, Infanta of Spain. In 1756 he was in Naples.[57] The enterprise on the Grande rue du faubourg Saint-Denis was accordingly taken over by Robert Martin, who until 1750, had been in Berlin as official painter and *vernisseur* to Frederick the Great. Robert Martin's place in Berlin was taken by his eldest son, Jean-Alexandre.[58] Between 1750 and 1765, when both Robert and Julien Martin died, *vernis Martin* goods were produced from the two shops on the Grande rue du faubourg Saint-Denis and the Grande rue du faubourg Saint-Martin, where Etienne-Simon remained. Julien Martin continued to take on sub-contracted work in his shop in the *faubourg Saint-Laurent*, and also developed a separate business selling decorative plants and miniature fruit-trees.[59] A fifth brother, also named Guillaume, meanwhile moved to Rochefort in an attempt to promote a new hard-wearing mastic, named *vernis Camourlot*, which, it was claimed, would seal

[55] Two belonged to *maîtres selliers*; the remainder were owned by an assortment of nobles, *rentiers* or their wives.   [56] A.N. MC I 423 (22 August 1745).
[57] A.N. MC CXXI 345 (21 October 1749); 365 (24 April 1756).
[58] A.N. MC CXXI 346 (8 and 11 February 1750); XXXIII 563 (27 February 1765); division of Robert Martin's estate.
[59] A.N. MC XXXIII 556 (22 July 1765), inventory of Julien Martin's estate.

ships' hulls more effectively than any other solution. The venture appears to have been singularly unsuccessful, despite an attempt to set up a joint-stock company with a capital of 390,000 *livres* (including contributions by Etienne-Simon and Etienne-François Martin) and branches in Rochefort, Marseille and Dunkirk. When Guillaume Martin died in Rochefort in 1770 he left an estate worth a derisory 90 *livres* to his second wife, Catherine Hetz. [60]

The estate worth 242,738 *livres* (198,637 *livres* after deductions had been made) that Robert Martin left when he died in 1765 was a rather more substantial measure of the success of *vernis Martin* goods. [61] A guide to Paris published in that year, written for the benefit of silk-designers in Lyon, extolled the marvels of the designs painted on the capital's coaches:

Mr. Lucas, excellent peintre d'histoire et académicien est auteur de ces voitures brillantes, dont les panneaux sont autant de tableaux precieux qu'un curieux seroit flatté d'avoir dans son cabinet. Dutour, Huet et Crépin avec leur pinceau sçavant et délicat peignent journellement de ces magnifiques voitures. Dutour peint les animaux. Huet les fleurs et Crépin les paysages. On peut toujours voir de ces équipages précieux, peints par ces artistes et vernis par Martin chez les plus fameux selliers de Paris, et notamment chez Lancry, rue Saint Nicaise. [62]

All these individuals belonged to the same circle. In 1751, the master saddler and coach-maker Antoine Lancry married Jeanne Elisabeth Denise Bourgeon, one of Guillaume Martin's second wife's daughters from her

60   A.N. MC CV 1259 (19 February and 4 March 1757), inventory of the estate of Jeanne Deforges, wife of Guillaume Martin. Martin already owed one of his brothers 12,000 *livres* 'pour pertes et avances qu'il luy a fait dans ses affaires'. The papers listed in the inventory include a reference to an *acte de société* drawn up by the notary Lejay le jeune (whose minutes are not in the Minutier central) on 2 June 1756. See also A.N. F¹² 2237 *dossier vernis Camourlot*. After selling shares in the venture to Jean Villeneuve, the Prince de Condé's concierge, François Payne, *bourgeois de Paris*, André Didier Monmeré Bingeon, *bourgeois de Paris* and Philippe Bonnin de Remirat, *bourgeois de Paris*, Martin sold the privilege to produce the *vernis* in April 1764 to three Parisians: Pierre Millot, *administrateur des hôpitaux des petites maisons et de la Trinité*, Edmé Joseph Leballif and François Fabre, both *bourgeois de Paris*. According to an *acte de société* of 1766, the three established a manufactory to produce the *vernis* in Nantes. The partnership had a capital of 120,000 *livres*: A.N. MC X 587 (11 January 1766): XCIII 632 (10 and 15 September 1760). Martin died at the age of 60 on 15 May 1770 in Rochefort: A.N. MC X 587 (11 January 1766): XCIII 632 (10 and 15 September 1760). Martin died at the age of 60 on 15 May 1770 in Rochefort: parish of Saint-Louis de Rochefort, *registre de décès*, 1770, fol. 9vo. He left his estate to his second wife, Catherine Hetz, the daughter of Joseph Hetz, 'suisse de nation' and Elisabeth Foy, originally of Brie-comte-Robert, whom he had married in Rochefort in 1768: A.D. Charente-Maritime B 1291 (1 February 1768): 2C-2797 fol. 168. I am grateful to Françoise Giteau, archivist of the archives of the Charente-Maritime, for these details.

61   A.N. MC XXXIII 563 (27 February 1767), division of Robert Martin's estate. The minutes of the notary (Lejay le jeune) who drew up the inventory are not in the Minutier central. The enterprise was taken over by Robert's oldest son, Jean-Alexandre Martin. Two months later he married the daughter of Roch Dubertrand, librarian of the Royal Academy of Surgery: A.N. MC XXXIII 564 (11 April and 16 June 1767).

62   Joubert de l'Hiberderie, *Le Dessinateur pour les fabriques d'étoffes d'or, d'argent et de soie* (Paris, 1765), pp. 91–2.

second marriage. Among the signatories to the contract, along with many members of the Martin clan, were the painters Auger Lucas, who had also had some association with the Audran–Deneumaison *manufacture des ouvrages de la Chine*, and Nicolas Huet, one of the royal coat-of-arms' painters (*peintre des armoiries de la cour*). Lucas was also present when one of Martin's own daughters married another painter, Pierre Sageret, in the same year.[63] The ramifications of kin, patronage and clientage formed an environment in which new products could be developed out of a common familiarity with markets and designs and a mutual interest in adapting established designs and techniques to new materials.

The substitution of paper and *papier-mâché* for wood was the most striking of these innovations. The combination of techniques used in japanning – from moulding and turning to painting or engraving on lacquer and block-printing on paper or linen screens – made the trade a seedbed for the expertise and ideas deployed not only in frame-making and furniture but in printed textiles and wallpaper in the latter half of the eighteenth century. Both Oberkampf and Reveillon, the two most successful and celebrated capitalists of the period, made extensive use of the circles of painters and designers, and the materials and techniques, that were initially associated with japanware and *vernis Martin*. Like the Martin brothers too, the success of their enterprises owed much to their capacity to combine high-cost, high quality products with a range of very much lower-priced articles produced and sold in more extensive markets.[64]

Etienne-Simon Martin, the last of the five brothers, died at the age of 67 in 1770. Like his elder brother Guillaume, he left a large and thriving concern, in which he had associated his only son. Etienne-François, in 1767. The balance sheet drawn up by his principal clerk, Antoine Guyot, in 1770 revealed that the enterprise had assets in the form of outstanding book-debts worth an imposing 239,745 *livres* and liabilities of a mere 54,995 *livres*.[65] The stock combined the established range of activities as

[63] A.N. XCV 204 (25 May 1750); CXXI 349 (8 April 1751); CXXI 350 (1 June 1751). On Lucas, see Antoine-Nicolas Dézallier d'Argenville, *Voyage pittoresque de Paris* (Paris, 1778), p. 200. On the painters Crépin and Dutour, see Guiffrey, *Histoire de l'Académie de Saint-Luc*, pp. 239, 282. On Christophe and Nicolas Huet (father of the better-known painter and designer Jean-Baptiste Huet), see R. A. Weigert, 'Un Collaborateur ignoré de Claude III Audran', *Etudes d'art du musée d'Alger*, 1 (1952), pp. 63–76; Louis Dimier, 'Christophe Huet, peintre de chinoiseries et d'animaux', *Gazette des Beaux-Arts*, 3ème periode, 14 (1895), pp. 353–66, 486–96; C. Gabillot, *Les Huet: Jean Baptiste et ses fils* (Paris, 1893), p. 27.

[64] On *papier-mâché* see, most recently, Bruno Pons, 'Les Cadres francais du xviiie siècle et leurs ornements', *Revue de l'art*, 76 (1987), pp. 41–50; John Krill, *English Artists' Paper* (London, 1987), pp. 95–101; and Yvonne Jones, 'The Birmingham Japanning and Papier-Mâché Industries', *Birmingham Museum and Art Gallery. Department of Local History, Information Sheet*, 13 (1981).

[65] A.N. MC CV 1302 (13 June 1770), inventory of the estate of Etienne-Simon Martin; LVII 480 (6 August 1767).

well as a number of new products. A dozen of the 89 items listed in the inventory consisted of small batches of bronze-plated plaster or terracotta medallions and statuettes depicting a range of well-known subjects: the four seasons, a shepherd helping a child from a tree, charity, a horseman, a lion and the King. There was the usual assortment of lacquered vases, decanter-holders, boxes, *toilettes*, miniature spinning-wheels, looms and shuttles, ornate screens, barometer cases, corner cupboards, *écritoires*, tables and furniture parts. Work was in progress on 22 coaches, carriages or portable chairs, including five belonging to the duc d'Orléans. Their panels were decorated with coats of arms, flowers, vases or cherubs floating on clouds, set against grey, gold, green, *chamois* or chestnut backgrounds. Finally, work was also in progress on the decoration of a dozen houses or apartments, including three in the Palais Royal, two belonging to the *curé* and *fabrique* of the parish of Saint-Laurent, and another two belonging to the abbé de Breteuil on the rue Saint-Honoré and in the abbaye de Livré respectively. The largest client of all, however, was the duc d'Orléans. In addition to the work on his coaches, Martin was also owed money for work carried out at his stables on the rue Vivienne and at his château at Saint-Cloud. In all, the estate was owed 40,000 *livres* by the Orléans household.

The origins of the links between the Martin enterprises and their aristocratic or royal clients are particularly obscure. The brothers do not seem to have had any connections with the carpet-makers and upholsterers (*maîtres tapissiers*) who were often the principal contractors in decorative work in eighteenth-century Paris.[66] Aristocratic customers were, however, a feature of the enterprise's activities from the early years of the reign of Louis XV onwards. Both Guillaume and Etienne-Simon Martin undertook work at Versailles, while Robert, Jean-Alexandre and Jean-Guillaume Martin had their own royal patrons in Berlin and Naples. As early as 1711, a noble – Françoise de Bretonvilliers, the widow of Anne d'Hervart, seigneur de Bois-Vicomté – was among the signatories to Guillaume Martin's marriage contract to Marie Lamy.[67]

One possible set of intermediaries between the Martin enterprises and their aristocratic clients may have been the various well-placed minor functionaries and household servants that the clan numbered among its kin and friends. Among those present when Guillaume's cousin, the bookseller Pierre-Alexandre Martin, married in 1716 was the royal confessor Claude Fleury, whose *Histoire ecclésiastique* was to figure

<hr>

[66] For an example of this role, see A.N. Y 13 666 (22 July 1765), describing a dispute between the chevalier de Montigny and a *maître tapissier* named Hérault who had recommended an ornamental painter named Watebled – reputed to be 'le premier ouvrier de Paris en ornements' – over the latter's failure to redecorate de Montigny's apartment.

[67] A.N. MC XXVIII 115 (23 November 1711).

prominently in Martin's own stock.[68] Julien Martin's wife, Marie-Anne Frion, had a niece whose husband was secretary to two magistrates of the Parlement of Paris.[69] Guillaume Martin's second wife, Catherine Simon, had been married twice before her marriage to the japanner in 1730. Her first husband, Gabriel Douru, was responsible for the administration of the landed income of the archbishopric of Paris, was secretary to the Cardinal de Noailles, and later became secretary to one of the treasurers of the royal seal. Her second husband, Jean Bourgeon, was a paper merchant who appears to have had particularly close relations with the Ministry of War. Her father was *chef de cuisine* of the secretary of the Council of the Navy, de la Chapelle.[70] The church supplied a further contingent of cousins, nephews and relatives by marriage, several of whom were curates of Parisian parishes.[71] It was not particularly surprising, therefore, that Etienne-Simon Martin's eldest son, Etienne-François, was married in 1760 to the daughter of the *premier valet de chambre* of the duc d'Orléans, who was herself the duke's daughter's chambermaid.[72] The marriage contract was signed by the duke himself, his son, the duc de Chartres, the abbé de Breteuil and the duke and duchess of Agen.

The market for luxury goods was, in this way, established upon a core of patronage and clientage. Yet the large number of concurrent projects that the network of patronage and clientage generated placed a premium upon the establishment of a reliable cluster of sub-contractors and sources of materials. The business that Etienne-Simon Martin left was, accordingly, the nodal point of a number of other enterprises. Work on coaches was sub-contracted to eight master artisans (three wheelwrights, two farriers, a joiner, a harness-maker and a spurmaker). Painting and decorating involved a dozen master painters, embellishers, gilders, moulders and marble-cutters, including the painters Lecrivain, Bani (or Binet), Chevalier, Dutour, Tardif and Pecquet. Supplies of materials from grocers and gold-

68 A.N. MC LXXIII (15 December 1716); CXXI 315 (29 October 1739).
69 A.N. MC V 309 (13 January 1719).
70 A.N. LVII 302 (29 June 1720); 309 (21 and 30 March 1722); LXX 292 (11 January 1730).
71 Jean-Guillaume Martin's wife, Marguerite Rousseau, had a priest as one of her cousins (A.N. MC LXXII 258, 14 November 1731); Robert Martin's wife, Marie Jeanne Geneviève Papillon, the daughter of a bookseller, had two Jesuits for brothers (A.N. MC CXXI 316, 7 February 1740). The Emery, Durand and Guesnon families, who made up Pierre-Alexandre Martin's relatives by marriage, had several other clerics among their number (A.N. MC CXXI 321, 25 July 1741), as did the family of the bookseller Jean Augustin Grangé, who married Guillaume Martin's daughter in 1747 (MC CXXI 341, 16 November 1747).
72 A.N. MC LVII 442 (28 September 1760). Jeanne Charlotte Pottier Desportes died in 1766 (inventory A.N. MC LVII 476, 12 December 1766). Martin remarried Marie Henriette Blondel, daughter of a *commissaire des poudres et salpêtres du département de Paris*, in 1770 (A.N. MC CV 1302, 27 May 1770).

beaters amounted to 12,142 *livres*, while a larger debt of 50,000 *livres* to the *marchand batteur d'or* Théodore Bachelier had been converted into an annuity.[73] Martin also employed eight journeymen on daily rates, including four *peintres d'impression*, responsible for priming surfaces before they were decorated by floral- or figure-painters, and a further four journeymen gilders who were paid by the piece.

The combination of sub-contracted work, wage-payments and payments for materials generated substantial pressure to maintain the momentum of the various concurrent activities in which the Martin brothers were involved. Etienne-François Martin outlived his father by no more than a year and in 1772, after a six-month interval, the business was taken over by Robert Martin's eldest son, Jean-Alexandre.[74] Between 19 October 1771 and 27 February 1772, when Jean-Alexandre Martin took over, the enterprise was managed by Etienne-François' widow, Marie-Henriette Blondel. During that 19-week period she spent a total of 16,038 *livres*, or an average of 844 *livres* a week, on wages and payments to sub-contractors. A further 315 *livres* were spent on 'étrennes données à différents garçons charrons, selliers et aux différents cochers, frotteurs et garçons des princes, seigneurs et particuliers' at the New Year, and 96 *livres* later went to a designer named Fixon for designs. Four painters (Binet, Chevalier, Dutour and Avoyen) were also paid small amounts for debts due on Etienne-François Martin's estate.[75]

The weekly expenditure on wages was, however, particularly substantial. Some idea of the margins on which the enterprise operated can be reached by comparing the outgoings in 1771–2 with income during an earlier period, between 1749 and 1750. In the 27 weeks between Guillaume Martin's death on 12 August 1749 and the day that Robert Martin took over on 17 February 1750, the enterprise's gross income was 13,656 *livres*, or some 506 *livres* a week. The figure was undoubtedly lower than usual because of the hiatus caused by Guillaume Martin's death. A rough comparison of the figures of monthly income in 1749–50 and monthly expenditure in 1771–2 does, however, suggest the importance of maintaining sufficient momentum on a variety of concurrent projects to generate the cash needed to pay for wages, materials and sub-contracted work. The relatively fine margin between income and expenditure explains a great deal about the recurrent preoccupation with the relationship between time, work and wage-levels

[73] A.N. MC CV 1302 (13 June 1770): CI 443 (3 December 1750), division of the estate of Théodore Bachelier.
[74] A.N. MC CV 1309 (29 October 1771): inventory of the estate of Etienne-François Martin: CV 1310 (20 March 1772): XCVIII 621 (15 April 1777), division of the estate.
[75] A.N. MC XCVIII 621 (15 April 1777). On the Fixon, see Guiffrey, *Histoire de l'Académie de Saint-Luc*, p. 291.

that was one of the features of disputes in the Parisian trades in the eighteenth century. These disputes were by no means confined to the luxury trades: at various times during the eighteenth century, conflict over the length of the working day occurred in at least 16 Parisian trades, including curriers, hatters, wheelwrights, saddlers, joiners, bookbinders, gilders and locksmiths.[76] The disputes in the painting and decorative trades, however, turned upon particularly precise definitions of working time, both because of the pressure to complete a number of concurrent projects and because of the difficulties involved in managing and co-ordinating the variety of related but heterogeneous activities subsumed within the *Académie de Saint-Luc*.

The Martin brothers played a prominent part in all three of the major disputes that occurred in the painting and decorative trades between 1748 and 1786, but their role was an ambiguous one. The difference between their positions and those adopted by the painters' corporation, the *Académie de Saint-Luc*, was an expression of the variety of interests that co-existed among the master artisans who made up the membership of eighteenth-century corporations. Corporate decisions and regulations were often a compromise. Court rulings sanctioning these decisions were therefore by no means a simple reflection of a unanimous opinion – they were often ploys in more elaborate strategies in which considerations of commercial advantage also played a part. The law, in this sense, was not simply an expression of an instinctive corporate consciousness but, instead, a counterpoint to the more obscure arrangements of the bazaar.

The Martin brothers' relationship to the painters' corporation was, it would seem, a distant one. Guillaume, Julien, Etienne-Simon and Robert were all admitted to the *Académie de Saint-Luc* well after they had established themselves as painters and decorators in their own right.[77] The privileges to produce and sell japanware that they obtained from the Crown were opposed by the corporation mainly on the grounds that there were many other painters who also made lacquered goods from *papier-mâché* and other materials. Yet corporate privilege also had its benefits. Between 1741 and 1753 the *Académie de Saint-Luc* went to considerable lengths to prevent members of the toymakers' corporation from entering the market for *chinoiserie*; it also intervened in a dispute that occurred at Versailles in the spring of 1748 when, in early March, it noted that there had been a 'sédition' by journeymen employed by the painters and

[76] For more general discussion of the working day as a source of contention in the Parisian trades, see above, chapter 6.
[77] Guillaume Martin was admitted in 1713; Julien in 1739; Robert in 1736; Etienne-Simon in 1728; Jean-Guillaume, Guillaume's son, in 1736 and Jean-Alexandre, Robert's son, in 1771: Guiffrey. *Histoire de l'Académie de Saint Luc*, p. 382, and the various inventories, cited above.

sculptors who had undertaken work for the King. Both Guillaume and Etienne-Simon Martin were among them.[78] The corporation recorded that the journeymen had sought to impose their own measure of wage-rates and shorten the working day. It decided, therefore, to establish 'une loy stable et inviolable' setting out the details of the working day.

The corporate ruling, ratified by the Parlement on 4 May 1748, prescribed a working day running from 6 a.m. to 7 p.m. with breaks of half an hour from 8 to 8.30 a.m. and an hour between 12 and 1 p.m. Work at night would begin at 7 p.m. and, if it continued until midnight, would be paid as an additional half day. Work that went on after midnight would qualify for an additional day's pay. Journeymen who left their masters were also required to obtain certificates attesting to the satisfactory completion of their work (*billets de sortie*). Predictably, an assorted group of masters and journeymen opposed the ruling and appealed to the Parlement. Four dozen journeymen sculptors on building work claimed that as 'gens à talent' they could not be required to have certificates.[79] They were supported by two groups of master painters: some, who were working as journeymen on sub-contracted work, claimed that the certificates were incompatible with their status; others, who were professors of the Academy, argued that certificates were inappropriate for students of a liberal art which, by nature, was free. Although the Parlement dismissed these claims in a ruling published in March 1749, it did add an additional half hour to each of the two breaks in the working day.[80]

The Martin brothers' own part in the proceedings appears to have been minimal. As entrepreneurs engaged on work for the Crown they had a particularly clear interest in ensuring that work was completed as rapidly as possible. The longer the working day, the more quickly work which did not depend upon natural light could be finished. At the same time, however, their claims to exercise an exclusive privilege and their own close relationship with several members of the Royal Academy, notably the painters Lucas and Huet, made it difficult for them to approve of regulations in which the liberal character of the arts was apparently rejected. There was also a measure of self-interest in this position. A large enterprise involved in a number of synchronous projects needed to take on

78 A.N. X¹ᵃ 4027 fol. 124ᵛᵒ (28 March 1748); 4029 fol. 153ᵛᵒ (4 May 1748); X¹ᵇ 3578 (4 May 1748). Archives de la Préfecture de police, Fonds Lamoignon 38 fol. 596. On the Martin brothers' involvement in decorative work at Versailles, see Pierre de Nolhac, 'La Décoration de Versailles au xviiie siècle', *Gazette des Beaux-Arts*, 3ème période, 17 (1897), pp. 104–14. Thus, 'je vous envoie l'échantillon de vernis que M. le Dauphin a choisi pour Madame la Dauphine, et vous conviendrez avec le sieur Martin pour l'y faire travailler' (Lenormant de Tournehem to D'Etioles, 16 October 1748).

79 A.N. X¹ᵃ 4038 fol. 518 (26 August 1748).

80 B.N. F. 22 812, p. 72 (12 March 1749). I was unable to find the minute of the original ruling in the papers of the Parlement.

and dismiss journeymen as and when it chose, and, given its predominantly aristocratic clientele, was unlikely to attach much importance to the rates that it paid. High wages, but long hours and a rapid turnover of materials and projects, complemented the edifice of credit upon which the enterprise rested.

These tensions were more visible during the two disputes that occurred between 1765–9 and 1784–6. In December 1765 the Academy recorded that there had been a number of conflicts over wages and the length of the working day.[81] Journeymen working at night insisted upon finishing at 10 p.m., rather than midnight, but continued to claim payment for an additional half day's work. The corporation complained that the journeymen's confraternity in the Temple had usurped the functions of its own office over the supply of labour and that assemblies of journeymen in two inns, named the Cadran bleu and the Treize cartons, had become a regular occurrence. It decided to revive the system of registration and, at the same time, established a scale of day-rates set at 30 sous for colour-grinders, 35 sous for finishers (apprêteurs) and ordinary painters (peintres d'impression) and 40 sous for gilders and embellishers. Journeymen working outside Paris were entitled to an extra 10 sous, but painters were to receive 5 sous a day less during the winter months, because they could work only in natural light. Journeymen working at night by artificial light were required to work until midnight during the summer months and until 1 a.m. in winter. Finally, the practice of allowing journeymen to take gold dust and filings known as époustures (which had, it stated, 'occasionné la ruine des maîtres') was prohibited.

The decision was not well received by the journeymen after its ratification by the Parlement in March 1766.[82] Jean-Baptiste Camus, a 52-year-old journeyman painter who was arrested and charged with tearing down a poster bearing the new regulations, explained

qu'il revenait de la paye des peintres et qu'ensuitte il avoit été au cabaret avec ses camarades...Ayant fait ses besoins...il a arraché un petit morceau de papier des affiches.[83]

One of the Academy's directors, the painter Jacques Prudhomme, recalled meeting one of the syndics of the journeymen's confraternity on the

---

81 Bibliothèque de l'Arsénal, MS. Bastille 12 369, copy of the arrêt (24 March 1766); A.N. Y 9534. There is no trace of the original text in the minutes of the Parlement (A.N. X^{1b} 3839 or X^{1a} 4528). Some discussion of journeymen's confraternities in the trade can be found in Anne Lombard-Jourdan, 'Les Confréries parisiennes des peintres', Bulletin de la société de l'histoire de Paris et de l'Ile de France, 107 (1980). pp. 87–103. See also above, chapter 3.

82 The episode was one of a number of concurrent disputes: see, for a dispute among shoemakers, A.N. Y 11 004ᵃ (7 May, 7 and 10 June, 8 and 29 August, 16 September, 9 October 1763), and Arlette Farge, La Vie fragile: violences, pouvoirs et solidarités à Paris au xviiie siècle (Paris, 1986), pp. 300–2.

83 A.N. Y 9525 (26 April 1766).

boulevard Poissonnière early in April. The journeyman reached into his pocket and took out the key to the confraternity's box, saying that it contained enough to fight a lawsuit and keep the journeymen in chicken dinners for some time.[84]

The threat was no idle one. Over 150 journeymen put their names to an appeal to the Parlement in the spring of 1766 and obtained a suspension of the regulations until the case had been heard.[85] In their action, the journeymen called for the preservation of the ruling of 4 May 1748, which had made no reference to rates of pay or the question of *époustures* and had provided for breaks for meals that were longer than those stipulated in 1766. There was widespread stoppages and bitter arguments between groups of journeymen and their employers. Two of the corporation's officials were sent threatening letters: Antoine Vincent, a painter, gilder and *vernisseur*, was warned that unless he continued to pay his painters 40 *sous* a day and allowed his gilders to take *époustures*, 20 journeymen would blow up his house with 20 pounds of dynamite, while Jacques Prudhomme received a placard containing a drawing of a charcoal burner with a pipe in his mouth and a threat of murder.[86]

Some journeymen responded to the requirement to register by walking out during the day, saying that they had to go and register. Others refused to work for less than 45 *sous* a day instead of the 35 fixed by the corporation, and insisted upon finishing their work at night at 9 p.m. rather than midnight. As one of them put it, 'il entend faire les heures comme ses confrères et tout le monde'.[87] Nicolas Sarrasin, a journeyman painter, told one of the *commissaires* of the Châtelet that he would never accept the new regulations even if his head was on the block (*quand même il auroit la tête sur le billot*).[88] He was duly arrested, along with one of his workmates, and was visited every day in prison by the officials of the journeymen's confraternity, which also continued to pay their wages. There were other incidents when journeymen insisted that they were entitled to take *époustures* and spend two hours over the midday meal instead of the hour specified in the regulations. All 13 of the journeymen working in an apartment assigned to the Archbishop of Lyon in the abbey of Saint-Victor walked out when their employer refused to allow them a two-hour break and the rates they demanded.[89]

The journeymen were particularly concerned to ensure that Étienne-Simon Martin did not abide by the new regulations. When he announced

---

84 'Que c'étoient les clefs de la confrairie et qu'il y avoit dans ladite coffre de quoi plaider et faire manger des poulets au compagnons': A.N. Y 11 007⁸ (deposition of Jacques Prudhomme).

85 A.N. X¹ᵃ 8078 fol. 282 (11 June 17:6); 8079 fol. 70 (14 June 1766).

86 A.N. Y 11 007⁸ (17 June 1766): Y 9534.

87 A.N. Y 11 007⁸ (14 May 1766).

88 A.N. Y 11 007⁸ (6 June 1766).

89 A.N. Y 9534.

them, early in June 1766, all 24 of the journeymen working in his shop walked out saying that they had no intention of working longer hours at lower rates and that the trade as a whole expected them to set the tone.[90] Martin himself appears to have had mixed feelings about the regulations. When the officials of the corporation called to inspect his shop on 28 June, they found the journeymen still eating their midday meal, even though it was 2 p.m. Etienne-François Martin explained that his father had work in hand for the duc d'Orléans and could not allow it to be disrupted.[91] He had decided therefore, to maintain the old rates of pay and to allow the journeymen to take two hours over their meal break at midday. The directors of the Academy were not impressed. They pointed out that Martin worked so frequently for the duc d'Orléans that there was never a time when one or other of the prince's coaches was not in his hangar. The work involved only a small number of the journeymen that Martin employed, and there were many others engaged on other tasks. In more conciliatory tone, they added that the regulations applied only to the particular groups of journeymen (ordinary painters, gilders, colour-mixers and embellishers) specified in the wording of the the Parlement's *arrêt*. Ornamental, floral or figure-painters – 'qui sont ceux qui font les principaux et plus précieux travaux dont les voitures sont susceptibles' – were not affected.[92] Martin, however, was not prepared to compromise. He drew up (or had a lawyer draw up) a draft request to the Parlement opposing the provisions of the regulations and began to circulate it among the membership of the corporation. The request accepted the need for registration, but rejected any fixed scale of wage-rates as 'contraire à l'équité et même impracticable'.[93] By late July Martin and a number of other masters had added their names to the appeal that the journeymen had presented to the Parlement.

The legal action effectively destroyed the corporation's attempt to fix the scale of wage-rates. In December 1766 a master painter named Bailly complained that he had been forced to pay his gilders 5 *livres* and his finishers 67 *sous* for 12 hours' work, which, the journeymen insisted, was equivalent to a full day and half. Several members of the Academy were openly contemptuous of the regulations. Charles Robert, a master painter, stated that he thought that the journeymen were right to stop work, while another master, named Leclerc, was reported to have said that

si les compagnons faisoient bien ils chieroient dans la marmitte des…jurés et que ceux qui etoient arrêtés devroient, après leur élargissement, leur donner une volée de coups de baton.[94]

In April 1767 the Parlement produced its ruling on the appeal and upheld Martin's objections to the regulations. Although the journeymen were still

---

[90] See above, p. 180.   [91] A.N. Y 9534.   [92] *Ibid.*

[93] A.N. Y 11 007[b] (7 July 1766).

[94] A.N. Y 9534; Y 11 007[b] (18 December 1766); Y 11010 (13 May 1769).

required to register with the corporate office, the fixed scale of day-rates was abolished.[95] Martin duly proceeded to flout the other regulations as well. An inspection of his shop in July 1769, two months after the corporation had had the officials of the journeymen's confraternity arrested, revealed that none of the men he had working for him had registered their names or addresses with the corporate office.[96] His *commis*, Guyot, informed the Academy's directors somewhat disdainfully that Martin had registered the names of his journeymen in 1766 and, if necessary, would do so again.

Martin had little to gain from corporate regulations of the kind adopted by the *Académie de Saint-Luc* in 1766. At best they were irrelevant; at worst disruptive. This, it may be surmised, is what they were designed to be, for the dispute between the corporation and the journeymen was matched by a second, concurrent dispute within the *Académie de Saint-Luc* itself. In 1766, 39 members of the Academy initiated legal proceedings over what they claimed was the unrepresentative character of the corporation's administration. Corporate decisions, they asserted, had been made by, and in the interests of, masters who had adopted 'un genre de travail purement mechanique'.[97] At least 45 of the men who had held the post of director of the Academy since 1738 (when its new statutes had come into effect) were mere artisans:

des sculpteurs en ornemens et en bois, ou des sculpteurs en bâtimens, ou des doreurs, ou des marbriers, ou des marchands de tableaux, ou des vernisseurs, ou des marchands de couleurs.[98]

Genuine artists, notably the professors who taught anatomy and design, were conspicuously under-represented. The opponents of the *status quo* (who included two members the Martin family among their number) proposed a major revision of the corporation's statutes to exclude all but those recognised as *académiciens* from corporate decision-making. They singled out two of the incumbent directors, the sculptor and ornamental designer Pierre-Edmé Babel and the *vernisseur* Antoine Vincent as evidence of the unrepresentative character of the current system of representation. Most of the animus of their *mémoires* was directed at Vincent, who held the title of *vernisseur pour les équipages du Roi* and, as a director of the Academy, played a major part in the dispute with the journeymen of the trade. His supporters claimed that he was no mere artisan but an excellent coach-decorator. Several of those on the opposing side, they stated, worked under

95 Bibliothèque de l'Arsénal MS. Bastille 12 369 (11 April 1767).
96 A.N. Y 11 101 (24 July 1769).
97 A.N. AD VIII, 1 *Mémoire signifié pour les Directeurs anciens et actuels de l'Académie de Saint-Luc*. The draft of the revised statutes put forward by the opponents of the corporate status quo can be found in A.N. MC CXV 781 (26 November 1766). The dispute is summarised in Guiffrey, *Histoire de l'Académie de Saint-Luc*, pp. 65–92.
98 A.N. AD VIII, 1, cited in Guiffrey, *Histoire de l'Académie de Saint-Luc*, p. 71.

his direction and, despite their claims to artistic prowess, did no more than execute his designs.[99]

The coincidence of occupations and names is striking; nor is there evidence that the distinction between 'artists' and 'artisans' invoked by both supporters and opponents of the *status quo* bore much relation to reality. Both Martin and Vincent were, among other things, substantial coach-painters, the former having the duc d'Orléans as his major client, the latter, the King. A generation earlier, however, both Guillaume and Etienne-Simon Martin had worked for the King. When Vincent died, in 1772, his estate was as substantial as any of those left by the Martin brothers. Work in his hangars was in progress on over 30 coaches or carriages, including six (and a gondola) belonging to the King, as well as on a number of items of furniture, including seven armchairs and two *canapés* 'le tout très riches en sculptures' belonging to the prince de Condé. The estate also owed wages or fees to 30 journeymen or sub-contractors. Vincent also dealt in the same ornate caskets and *toilettes* often associated with *vernis Martin*. Several of them, for example a 'toilette, fond rouge, islets d'aventurine, ornée de coqs chinois en relief', were very similar in appearance to the Martin brothers' goods.[100]

The similarity was probably more than a coincidence. Antoine Vincent was the only surviving son of the painter Adrien Vincent. Guillaume Martin had engaged Adrien Vincent as a painter in 1714, and the same Adrien Vincent had been one of the principal opponents of Martin's exclusive privilege in the legal action brought before the Parlement of Paris in 1736. Antoine Vincent had succeeded his father shortly after the latter's death in 1746. He had inherited an estate that was heavily in debt, but, by 1754, when his first wife (the daughter of a substantial master saddler) died, his business had assets on unpaid work worth over 130,000 *livres*, including some 22,000 *livres* due from the crown.[101] It is possible, therefore, that both the divisions within the *Académie de Saint-Luc* and the dispute between the corporation and the journeymen were precipitated by more obscure commercial rivalries within the core of the trade. In this, the rhetoric of the tradition of natural law performed a number of different functions. It was the basis of the corporation's claim to re-establish 'bon ordre et subordination' among masters and journeymen; it also allowed some members of the corporation, notably Etienne-Simon Martin, to claim that their activities, as practitioners of one of the liberal arts, exempted

[99] *Ibid.*, p. 80.

[100] A.N. MC XXVII 357 (4 February 1772). On Vincent, see Guiffrey, *Histoire de l'Académie de Saint-Luc*, pp. 77, 481; H. Herluison, *Actes d'état civil d'artistes français* (Orléans, 1873), p. 453; Guiffrey, 'Scellés', vol. 3, p. 25.

[101] Vincent's career can be followed from A.N. MC LXXXIV 431 (5 May 1746); XXXVI 456 (19 July 1747); LXXXIV 435 (14 May 1748); LXXXIV 443 (17 November 1751); XXXI 153 (7 June 1753); XXXI 154 (4 April 1754); XXXI 155 (19 July 1754).

them from any need to comply with these regulations. In both cases, it masked more fundamental tensions in the core of the trade.

The multiple connotations of the rhetoric of natural law were also visible in the dispute that began in 1784 and continued during the following two years. The conflict was, essentially, a re-enactment of the dispute of 1765–9. In November 1784 the *lieutenant général de police* Lenoir ratified a decision by the painters and sculptors' corporation to re-establish many of the regulations affecting journeymen introduced in 1765.[102] The revived regulations were designed to fill the legal hiatus left by the abolition and subsequent reorganisation of the corporations in 1776, when, during Turgot's short-lived campaign against the Parisian corporations, much of the mass of court rulings affecting the trades had been abolished.[103] As in 1765, journeymen were required to register with the corporate office and were ordered to take no more than two hours a day for their meals. As in 1765 too, the journeymen appealed to the Parlement, calling for the restoration of the allowance of two hours for meals at midday and an hour for their morning break.[104] They also objected to the fee of 8 *sous* that they were required to pay for their *livrets* and the further 3 *sous* payable each time they notified a change of employment, claiming that both the institution and the fees were unjust and impractical. Although the appeal failed on the majority of counts, the court ruled that the fees were illegal and that the costs of both *livrets* and registration should be born by the corporation.[105]

The journeymen's action was followed by an appeal by a number of master painters. The principal appellant in this second action was Jean-Alexandre Martin, who, after working in Berlin, had taken over the enterprise on the Grande rue du faubourg Saint-Martin in 1772 after the death of Etienne-Simon Martin's eldest son, Etienne-François. The case that Martin and his co-appellants presented was based upon an appeal to natural law.[106] They argued that when the corporations had been

[102] A.N. Y 14 479[b] (3 December 1784); Y 14 480[a] 17 January 1785).
[103] See Kaplan, 'Turgot's "Carnival"', in Kaplan and Koepp, eds., *Work in France*; Sonenscher, 'Journeymen, the Courts', and below, chapter 8.
[104] A.N. X¹ᵇ 8720 (5 February 1785); 8734 (6 August 1785); 4243 (5 September 1785); 4247 (23 November 1785); 4253 (21 December 1785); 4265 (19 July 1786); Y 11 028 (5 October 1785).
[105] A.N. X¹ᵇ 8734 (6 August 1785); 4243 (5 September 1785); 4247 (23 November 1785); 4165 (19 July 1786).
[106] B.N. 4°fm 30091 *A Nosseigneurs de parlement en la Grand'Chambre. Supplient humblement Jean-Alexandre Martin, peintre–vernisseur du roi, Jean Charny, Louis Bunel, Jean Silvain Belloeil de la Vallée, Charles Douveaux, la veuve Girard, la veuve Thibault, tous peintres de l'ancienne Académie et communauté de Saint-Luc appellans, et Claude-Alexandre Sevaux* (Paris, 1786); 4°fm 20904. *Mémoire pour le sieur Martin, peintre vernisseur du roi; le sieur Charny, peintre, ancien professeur de l'Académie et communauté de peinture, sous l'invocation de Saint-Luc...dénommés dans l'arrêt du 23 novembre 1785* (Paris, 1786). Jean-Alexandre Martin was later to become one of the twelve electors of the *section de Bondy* in 1791 and was

abolished in 1776, the trades encompassed by the *Académie de Saint-Luc* had been allowed to revert to their original condition of natural liberty: 'La profession des Arts libéraux de la Peinture et de la Sculpture fut donc rendue libre, comme elle l'avoit été autrefois et comme elle devroit l'être toujours.'[107]

Martin and his co-appellants argued that article 34 of the edict of August 1776 re-establishing the corporations had maintained this condition of natural liberty by specifying that painting and sculpture were liberal arts. The phrase, they argued, meant that journeymen were free – 'affranchis de tout esclavage' – and were subject to no more than 'la subordination la plus honnête et la plus nécessaire'.[108] The new regulations would entail their subjection 'à la tyrannie, à la vexation, à l'inquisition la plus odieuse et la plus prohibée par le Roi'. At most, however, it would affect only those journeymen whose names had appeared in the unsuccessful appeal to the Parlement. Men or women who had recently completed an apprenticeship, or immigrants to the capital, would, given the limited character of the ruling, continue to enjoy their natural liberty, for painting was 'un art qui respire la liberté'. Liberty, Martin emphasised, did not mean 'celle qui pourroit troubler ou la police ou la société', but, instead, referred to that original liberty 'qui affranchit de tout esclavage, de toute inquiétude sur la tranquillité et le repos de l'Artiste'.[109] Neither the master painters and sculptors, nor the journeymen they employed, could be bound by the regulations.

The appeal was, it would seem, lost. Yet the divisions within the painters and sculptors' corporation that precipitated the series of legal actions in which the Martin brothers were involved serve to underline the ambiguity of the different images with which the eighteenth-century luxury trades have been associated. From one point of view, the Martin brothers were practitioners of a liberal art: 'artistes', as Jean-Alexandre Martin put it; from another, they were successful entrepreneurs, whose activities encompassed a multitude of interdependent small businesses. Nor was there any necessary contradiction between these different activities. The ornate world of courts and capital cities that they supplied co-existed with a world in which time and money were matters of intense importance. In this sense, there was no difference between the luxury trades on the one hand, and the ordinary world of artisanal production on the other. As in most urban trades, the multiplicity of different activities in which substantial employers like the Martin brothers were involved generated

elected to a deputation of members of the 'club fraternel des ci-devant représentants provisoires de la Commune' in February 1791: Etienne Charavay, *Assemblée électoral de Paris, 18 novembre 1790–15 juin 1791* (Paris, 1890), pp. 33–4. The subsequent history of the enterprise remains to be discovered.

107 B.N. 4°fm 20904, p. 22.
108 *Ibid.*, p. 22.
109 *Ibid.*, pp. 22, 56–7, 65–6.

tensions, not only between masters and journeymen, but also among master artisans themselves. The relationship between the brothers and the corporation to which they belonged was as charged with potential conflict as was that between those masters who made up the shifting core of urban labour markets and the journeymen they employed.

The triangular relationship between the Martin brothers, the *Académie de Saint-Luc* and the journeymen of the trade during the second half of the eighteenth century is an indication that disputes between journeymen and their masters were an expression of tensions and rivalries that had many different, occasionally contingent, origins. Litigation, in this context, was as much an instrument of commercial and political rivalry as it was an expression of deep-seated grievances determined by the fundamental relationship between journeymen and their masters. Disputes in the eighteenth-century trades had an indeterminate character or, more precisely, a multiplicity of different determinants. The rhetoric of litigation could therefore serve a number of different purposes. Not all of them, however, found unambiguous expression in the legal idiom in which so many disputes were couched. One consequence of this distance between the vocabulary of the law and the circumstances of the trades was that many of the disputes that occurred in the eighteenth-century French trades were somewhat more complex than initial appearances might suggest, and often owed as much to a sophisticated use of the judicial process as they did to the more obvious vagaries of economic circumstances.

CHAPTER 8

Conflict and the courts

The temptation to cast the conflicts and arguments that arose in the trades of urban France into an unfolding pattern of development is difficult to resist, yet conflict in the urban trades of eighteenth-century France had no easily identifiable beginning and no final point of arrival. The disputes in the printing trades of Paris and Lyon in the sixteenth century are well enough known not to need rehearsal here.[1] The protagonists in the many strikes and conflicts that took place in the nineteenth century were similar enough to eighteenth-century masters and journeymen, at least in purely occupational terms, to belie any simple causal relationship between changing material circumstances and changing social and political aspirations.[2] The things that were said and done in the course of disputes – whether in 1650 or in 1850 – owed much to institutional resources and political constraints and, for that reason, followed procedures that were only partly determined by conditions in the trades themselves.

Yet, if disputes cannot be inscribed within an immanent teleology, they were not mere manifestations of an eternally recurrent pattern of conflict. Since no dispute was an entirely isolated event, the outcome of particular conflicts served, by way of precedent and comparison, to alter the wider institutional and legal environment in which subsequent conflict occurred. The character and form of conflict in the French trades changed not because everyday circumstances and material conditions changed (even though they changed as well), but because the institutional and political environment in which conflicts occurred was gradually transformed. By 1789, many of the legal powers of the corporations had been modified, curtailed or transferred to other institutions. Journeymen's

---

[1] Natalie Z. Davies, 'A Trade Union in Sixteenth-Century France', *Economic History Review*, 2nd series, 19 (1966), pp. 48–69; Henri Hauser, *Ouvriers du temps passé* (Paris, 1899); Sewell, *Work and Revolution*, pp. 42–7. See also chapter 1 above.

[2] Charles Tilly and Lynn Lees, 'Le Peuple de juin 1848', *Annales E.S.C.*, 29 (1974), pp. 1062–91; Jacques Rougerie, 'Composition d'une population insurgée: l'exameple de la Commune', *Le Mouvement social*, 48 (1964), pp. 31–48.

confraternities had largely disappeared from public life. So too had many of the formal distinctions that derived from the conventions of natural law. Both the quality of the dialogue between masters and journeymen and the procedures that they followed in the course of disputes in the trades were significantly affected by these changes. Their cumulative effects are best examined from four vantage points. The first is an initial characterisation of conflict in the French trades; the second is a more detailed analysis of the structural origins of conflict; the third is a description of the extremely heterogeneous concerns brought into play in disputes in the trades; the fourth is an examination of the frequency of conflict. Together, they provide the basis of an account of the interplay between conflict and institutional change during the long eighteenth century.

CHARACTERISATIONS OF CONFLICT

It is possible to find traces of over 500 disputes in the French trades between the mid-seventeenth century and the early years of the Revolution (see Appendix). In one sense, the figure is a large one, larger than much of the historiography of the urban trades before the nineteenth century might suggest. Yet the figure is also surprisingly low for so many different trades and localities considered over a period of nearly 150 years. Nor can it be explained entirely as an effect of variations in the rate of survival of archival sources (even though such variations undoubtedly make a nonsense of exaggerated statistical precision). Even in the relatively well-documented trades of Paris, Marseille and Bordeaux, substantial conflicts between masters and journeymen were an infrequent occurrence. Moreover, the protagonists in such disputes were not usually the 'natural' antagonists that one might expect to find. Trades were often divided. Master artisans often aligned themselves with journeymen rather than with other master artisans, while divisions among journeymen were the norm rather than the exception.

None of this would be particularly surprising were it not for the way in which the concepts of class, labour and capital – in either their presence, absence or immanence – have formed a screen that has obscured the divisions of labour, patterns of employment and structured labour markets that meant that master artisans in any large eighteenth-century French town were both rivals and allies, interdependent as well as independent, patrons at one time yet clients at another, while the journeymen they employed were both workers and aspirant master artisans, young men as well as consumers, migrants as well as workers, and, as such, endowed with many different opportunities, resources and legal entitlements to establish themselves on their own account. The eighteenth-century trades were not embryonic forms or negative counterparts of nineteenth-century industry; still less, through their dissolution, were they the sole source of the language of conflict of nineteenth-century society.[3] The dichotomies between morals and markets, or custom and competition that have informed a long historiographical tradition have, to be explicit, little relevance to a world in which transactions between masters and journeymen were both moral and commercial, customary and competitive, exploitative and co-operative, in ways that ensured that questions of domination and subordination were never settled, were always potentially contentious, and were only contingently related to the idiom of class.

The antithesis between conflict whose character was local and particular and conflict whose character was national and universal is at best a simplification and at worst simply false. The teleology that places 'custom' and 'class' at different points within a developing historical continuum leading from the local to the universal is based upon an unwarranted assumption that general conceptions of the social and political order had no place in the culture of eighteenth-century artisans and that, when they did arise, they could be couched only in the language of class.[4] Yet when a painter responsible for managing the painting and gilding work at the Sèvres porcelain manufactory in 1755 objected to new regulations fixing the length of the working day, he called them 'slavery' and said that he had no wish to work there any longer. No one, he said, could force him to stay:

en France il n'y avoit point d'esclavage et...de quelque façon qui l'on s'y prit, l'on ne trouverait jamais en lui un homme qui se laissat mener comme un enfant...On aurait à faire à un homme et non à un morveux.[5]

Words and phrases like these were not drawn from the experience of particular trades; they derived, instead, from eighteenth-century civil jurisprudence and the vocabulary of natural law, even if, as in this instance, they were also coloured by less formal images of virile independence and male power. Conflicts in particular trades were microcosmic crystallisations of images, metaphors and fictions drawn from

[3] For similar viewpoints, see Gareth Stedman Jones, 'Rethinking Chartism', in his *Languages of Class* (Cambridge, 1983); Jonathan Zeitlin, 'From Labour History to the History of Industrial Relations', *Economic History Review*, 2nd series, 40 (1987), pp. 159–84.

[4] See, for example, E. J. Hobsbawm, 'Custom, Wages and Work-Load', in his *Labouring Men* (London, 1964), and, in more muted recent form, Ira Katznelson and Aristide R. Zolberg, eds., *Working Class Formation* (Princeton, New Jersey, 1986), pp. 3–41. For a recent discussion of the problem, see William Reddy, *Money and Liberty in Western Europe: A Critique of Historical Understanding* (Cambridge and New York. 1987). For a suggestive alternative approach, see Roberto Mangabeira Unger, *Social Theory: Its Situation and Task* (New York and Cambridge, 1987).

[5] Archives de la Manufacture Nationale de Sèvres, D1 *liasse* 2, cited by Andre Sergène, 'La Manufacture de Sèvres sous l'ancien régime', (Thèse de doctorat, Université de Nancy, 1972–74), vol. I, pp. 184–5.

the whole repertoire of social transaction of the eighteenth-century French polity. Consequently, what was said and done in the course of a dispute was, in a narrowly functional sense, invariably superfluous to the particular issues in question. Yet that very superfluity of imagery and rhetoric was what served to transform ordinary argument into sharper conflict. A dispute that took place in Bordeaux in August 1783 is a particularly rich illustration of the phenomenon.

It began on the morning of Wednesday 20 August 1783, when, to the sound of a trumpet, a bailiff posted up a placard on the Porte de la Monnaie, ordering master shipbuilders (*maîtres constructeurs*) to issue printed certificates of good conduct to the journeymen carpenters and caulkers they employed.[6] A 14-year-old apprentice later recalled how he had seen one of the journeymen reading the placard, following the words with his finger while a crowd jostled against him, before it was torn to ground. Many of the men refused to leave the quayside to go out to the ships that they were refitting. They jeered at three of the officials of the shipbuilders' corporation, calling one of them a thief and another *un rompu et une jambe de chien*. On the following morning, several hundred ships' carpenters gathered on the quayside and work on at least three ships came to a halt. A foreman who had been out on one of the ships recalled how, when he returned to shore at 10 a.m. he had met another foreman and ships' carpenter who said to him, 'Comment, vieux nègre, vous travaillez.' 'Vous êtes bien blanc', he replied, 'pour appeler les autres nègres', but he did not return to work.

The stoppages continued episodically during the following week. There were arguments among both masters and journeymen. A group of carpenters working on a ship called the *Neptune* was forced to stop work when 15 journeymen sailed out to the ship and threatened to throw their tools into the water. 'Est-ce que vous allez travaillez vous autres?' asked a journeyman of a group of his peers as they set out from the Calle de La Monnaie to work on a ship called the *Deux Amis*. When they said that they were, he rounded on them, telling them 'qu'ils étaient un tas de j.f. et des f. capons'. 'Est-ce que vous avez peur?' he asked. 'Pour moi, je n'ai pas peur. Faites comme moi: Dormez la grasse matinée.' A ships' carpenter who came to talk to a group of journeymen making masts behind Fort Louis was reported to have told them that the author of the dispute was one of the officials of the shipbuilders' corporation, named Pierre Guibert. 'S'il etait garçon,' he said, 'il ferait un exemple sur la personne du Sr Guibert et...lui danserait les pieds sur le ventre.' He added that the shipbuilders were all thieves 'et qu'ils ne seraient pas si riches s'ils n'avaient pas tant volé'. Guibert, described as responsible for 'notre

[6] A.D. Gironde, 12B 371 (21 August 1783). All citations in the following two paragraphs are from this dossier.

malheur' or 'notre divorce' by seeking to 'nous faire travailler par billets', was repeatedly vilified as a thief. One of the carpenters' wives reported with a certain relish that when her son had seen a little boy eating grapes from their trellis, he had said, 'Ah, mon petit voleur, tu me manges mes raisins.' Guibert happened to be passing at the time and assumed that the remark was addressed to him.

Few of these exchanges had much to do with the substance of a dispute which turned upon the fact that, as the *jurats* put it,

les ouvriers voulaient être libres: qu'on n'obtiendrait jamais d'eux de se soumettre à se munir de billets de congé et qu'ils n'étaient pas faits pour être affichés.

Many of the terms in which the conflict was couched – notably the allusions to race (*vieux nègre*), theft (*mon petit voleur*) and community (*notre divorce*) – were superimposed upon the disputed question of *billets de congé*. Nor, of course, was what was manifestly at issue in the dispute a sufficient explanation of why the printed certificates were so contentious. The courts were concerned with matters of law. As a result, no reference was made to the more immediate concerns of the masters and journeymen who worked on refitting ships, to the variegated composition of the workforce, to seasonal cycles of production and changing patterns of employment, or to conditions in Bordeaux in 1783, as merchant shipping resumed its regular activity at the end of a war.[7]

Master artisans (and their lawyers) were as adept in talking of 'tyranny', 'despotism' or 'natural liberty' as the men they employed. The terms themselves are of little assistance in explaining the immediate causes of conflict. Yet if the circumstances that allowed them to be used as cryptic summaries of certain forms of behaviour at specific times and places were explored only rarely in the legal proceedings that accompanied disputes, the law was more than a veil concealing an underlying economic reality. The composite character of the civil law in eighteenth-century France meant that masters and journeymen faced one another as separate legal agents. Many of the ordinary courtesies and conventions that they observed in their everyday transactions were predicated upon assumptions of formal equality that derived from the tradition of natural law. If master artisans expected to be addressed by the formal 'vous' rather than the more intimate 'tu' by the men they employed, journeymen too could take offence at *tutoiement*.[8] Violations of the convention during arguments were

[7] On shipping in Bordeaux, see Paul Butel, 'Le Trafic colonial de Bordeaux de la guerre d'Amérique à la Révolution', *Annales du Midi*, 79 (1967), pp. 17–64, and his *La Croissance commerciale bordelaise dans la deuxième moitié du xviiie siècle* (Lille, 1973).

[8] A Parisian journeyman locksmith complained that a master mason 'dit d'un ton brutal et ne tutoyant qu'il etoit un imbécile': A.N. Y 11 981 (9 August 1785). See also David Garrioch, 'Verbal Insults in Eighteenth-Century Paris', in Peter Burke and Roy Porter, eds., *The Social History of Language* (Cambridge, 1987), pp. 104–19 (pp. 113–14).

sufficiently significant to provoke comment in complaints to the police authorities.[9] The 'natural subordination' of journeymen to their masters emphasised in so many corporate statutes was matched by a recognition that the provisions of the law applied to the workplace rather than the wider social arena. When a group of journeymen hatters in Marseille invited a master with whom they were in dispute to drink with them, they emphasised, after he had sat down, that he was no longer on his own premises ('qu'il n'était plus chez lui') before launching into a violent tirade over his conduct in the dispute.[10]

The phrase indicates an awareness of the special status of a master artisan's workshop and domestic space. Journeymen rarely assaulted their masters, and if they did, did so in *cabarets* or the street, rather than in workshops themselves. During a dispute in the shoemaking trade of Bordeaux in 1772, a journeyman upbraided his master, calling him a glutton and a drunkard who spent all his time in *cabarets* at his journeymen's expense. 'Si tu n'avais pas été dans ta boutique, je t'aurais bien peigné', he added.[11] When a group of journeymen wheelwrights burst into a workshop in Bordeaux in 1783 with the very clear intention of assaulting the men working there, the presence of a master artisan was sufficient to persuade them to leave. 'Les gaillards sont dans leur turne', one of the frustrated assailants was later reported to have said disconsolately.[12] On another occasion, also in Bordeaux, a master joiner who was entertaining some friends found two journeymen in disguise among his company. After dancing a polite *minuette*, the journeymen were escorted to the door and rejoined a group of 20 others waiting outside on the street to assault the master's employees.[13]

Journeymen who insulted their masters within their own workshops directed much of their invective at their masters' wives, daughters or domestic servants rather than their employers themselves. In part this was because many master artisans' wives, in particular, were actively involved in the day-to-day affairs of the enterprise; it was also because women were used as a surrogate for the authority of master artisans themselves. Scatological remarks about master artisans' wives were also an oblique testimony to young men's ambivalent attitudes towards older men's

[9] Affronts could be more elaborate. As a journeyman stone-cutter in Marseille put it, with characteristic panache, ' un chien regardoit un évêque et faisait pi devant lui ': A.D. Bouches-du-Rhône, 2B 2102 (8 November 1785): a journeyman potter in Paris was described by his employer as 'prenant le ton de maître absolu dans son atelier': A.N.Y 13 267 (25 March 1767).

[10] Sonenscher, *Hatters*, pp 122–3: A.C. Marseille, FF 383 (deposition of Louis Ferraud).

[11] A.D. Gironde, 12B 342 (24 April 1772). Another journeyman, accused of hitting his master, denied the charge, saying 'ce n'est pas moy parce que si je l'eusse fait, j'en aurois donné plus d'un'.

[12] A.D. Gironde, 12B 371 (6 October 1783).

[13] A.D. Gironde, 12B 333 (1 February 1768).

authority.[14] Even on the streets, the presence of a master artisan could be sufficient to prevent fights between journeymen from taking place. A group of six journeymen locksmiths were saved from attack by over 20 journeymen joiners on the place Royale in Bordeaux in 1781 by the arrival of two master joiners.[15] The aura of authority that they were able to present was sufficient to outweigh their numerical inferiority.

Yet the authority that master artisans could invoke was matched by recognition of the status of the journeymen they employed. Journeymen were neither slaves nor domestic servants and did not expect to be treated as such. The processions, banquets and dances that they organised on trade or religious holidays were elaborate performances to which master artisans were expected to contribute by both their own and their wives' and daughters' presence, as well as with money, food or drink. The *étrennes*, *pâtes de veille* and other seasonal retributions that master artisans gave to their journeymen complemented relationships in which short-term bargains rather than long-standing ties of domination and subordination were the norm. The brevity of most periods of employment and the high level of movement of journeymen from shop to shop and town to town were powerful pressures upon regular employers of labour to conform to customs and usages that were the basis of local reputations and traditions transmitted from one urban centre to the next by the itinerant journeymen who formed a major segment of the workforce of most large cities.[16]

Meals had a more ordinary significance as moments at which the everyday courtesies of sharing a table formed a counterpoint to the formal hierarchies specified in corporate statutes and the erratic schedules of the workshop economy. Even journeymen who were not housed and fed by their masters were affronted if they were denied the honours of a proper meal on holidays or after taking on additional work.[17] Journeymen who slept and ate on their masters' premises emphasised their separateness from their employers' households and their distance from the world of domestic service. They did not expect to tidy their rooms or make their own beds and made a point of insisting that their masters' domestic servants or apprentices should carry out the work. A Parisian journeyman shoemaker who came in at 11 p.m. to find his bed unmade went to complain to his master because, as he later put it, 'il est d'usage parmi eux que les maîtres les fassent faire'.[18] Many of these household tasks were performed by apprentices, who, in addition to a great deal of fetching, carrying and cleaning, were expected to wake journeymen in the morning and make sure that shops were securely locked in the evenings. A master paper- and

[14] For examples see A.N. Y 14 069 (20 July 1744); Y 12 986a (23 August 1769); Y 13 103 (15 March 1752); Y 12 768 (3 November 1768); Y 12 057 (14 November 1770).

[15] A.D. Gironde, 12B 367 (20 August 1781).

[16] See above, pp. 119–24.

[17] Sonenscher, 'Sans-Culottes', p. 323.

[18] A.N. Y 15 202 (3 April 1775); see too A.N. Y 10 778 (8 August 1764) for another example.

card-maker felt sufficiently strongly about his apprentice's refusal to open the doors for his journeymen in the morning 'ainsi qu'il est d'usage' that he went to complain to one of the *commissaires* of the Châtelet in 1767.[19]

STRUCTURAL TENSIONS

The nuances and subtleties informing interpersonal transactions in the eighteenth-century trades formed a counterpoint to schedules of production whose irregularity and flexibility entailed constant attention to managing the relationship between the supply and competence of a rapidly changing workforce and the ebb and flow of orders from customers, clients, contractors and sub-contractors. The legal rights and formal distinctions embodied in the conventions of natural law supplied both masters and journeymen with a vocabulary that coloured relationships in which both the short-term character of most periods of employment and the impermanent nature of journeywork itself ensured that the contract of employment had an actual as well as a formal similarity to the lease of a coach or a tool. References to custom, usage, rights, laws, despotism, slavery or freedom were the ordinary medium in which bargains were struck and differences defined not only because transactions between masters and journeymen were informed by legal assumptions but also because the fleeting character of so many of their arrangements bore little relation to conditions of stable employment.

Yet the same short-term character of most periods of employment, as well as the transient nature of journeywork itself, were structural sources of tension in the trades. Few of the trades of Paris or any relatively large French city were able to draw exclusively upon an indigenous population of former apprentices to meet their needs for journeymen. Both the ordinary processes of eighteenth-century urban demography and the greater range of opportunities available to natives of large cities to marry and establish themselves on their own account ensured that migrants occupied a disproportionately large part of the workforces of the eighteenth-century trades.[20] Their presence gave rise to tensions not only among journeymen but also among master artisans. For both of them, short-term questions of the supply, price and availability of labour were overlain by longer-term considerations of marriage, inheritance and a place within a stable network of interdependent enterprises.

The structural tension between the relatively limited number of journeymen supplied by local systems of apprenticeship and the potentially huge number of itinerant journeymen endowed with the requisite range of skills needed to work on most of the materials used in the building

[19] A.N. Y 15 373 (14 November 1767); see also Y 10 899ᵇ (30 April 1770).
[20] See above, pp. 119-24.

furnishing, victualling or clothing trades was legal in origin. In principle, regulations governing apprenticeship and membership of the corporations provided for a broad symmetry between the succession of generations and the number of viable enterprises that a particular trade could accommodate. In practice, the large number of apprentices who failed to serve their time, the high rate of turnover of the membership of the corporations themselves and the unstable division of urban labour markets into a core of relatively regular, substantial employers of labour and a periphery of irregular, tiny employers all ensured that the relationship between the formal provisions of corporate statutes and the reality of conditions in the trades was invariably an approximation of the most limited kind.

The legal entitlements that apprenticeship supplied contributed to the structural tensions both between local and external sources of labour and between the core and periphery of particular labour markets in a number of significant ways. Journeymen who had served an apprenticeship in Paris or any large city had fewer of the incentives (and fewer of the pressures) that led men who had learned the rudiments of a trade in a small town or village to leave the localities where they had been born and find work in a large city. Men who had served an apprenticeship in a large city had more opportunity to marry and establish themselves, and a vested interest in remaining in employment in a single locality for long enough to acquire the resources of credit, kin and clients that were the basis of an artisanal enterprise. The labour markets of any large city were therefore made up of a core of the workforce that had served an apprenticeship locally (even though many such former apprentices were themselves migrants) and a larger periphery of peripatetic journeymen who had learned their trades elsewhere.

Most periods of employment were, however, of relatively short duration. Both masters and journeymen were able to negotiate the tension between the brevity of most periods of employment and the claims of men who had served an apprenticeship locally by recognising hierarchies of precedence and seniority within the workforce. It is logical to assume that, faced with a choice, most master artisans would select their *premiers garçons*, *prôtes* or *maîtres compagnons* from among men whom they knew and who were more likely to have served an apprenticeship locally. Recognition by master artisans could take the form of engaging some journeymen by the month, rather than by the day. Journeymen engaged in this way tended to be paid a lower rate than a multiple of a daily rate would have generated, but had the advantage of continuity of employment.[21] Discrimination by master artisans was matched by discrimination by journeymen. Recognition of seniority among journeymen was embodied in informal rules that ensured that the most recent arrival in a shop, or a

[21] See above, pp. 189–90.

town, would be the first to leave. The division between a minority of relatively sedentary journeymen and a larger number of more mobile migrants was, in this way, maintained. Itinerant journeymen were assimilated into the sedentary core as the combined effects of marriage and the transfer of patrimonies from one generation to the next created new niches within the established workforce.

In the short term, the relative immobility of the sedentary core of the workforce meant that new employers, or master artisans with additional orders, were exposed to local shortages of labour. In the medium term, however (and the medium term in this context could be anything from three months to a year or more), the division between sedentary and peripatetic journeymen tended to generate a chronic over-supply of labour. The composition of the core of relatively substantial employers of labour was, in the majority of the urban trades, never stable. Many (but not all) of the master artisans in any trade moved in and out of the core as they took on additional journeymen to meet additional orders and, given the relative immobility of men who had either served their time locally or had reached a certain degree of seniority, employers found it easier to add to their workforces by engaging men from elsewhere. The result was that periods of rising orders were accompanied by a growing disproportion between men who had served an apprenticeship locally and men who were peripatetic migrants. The combined effect of the entitlements that apprenticeship supplied and the unstable relationship between the core and periphery of urban labour markets served, therefore, to create two moments of potential conflict. The first lay where the size of the sedentary core of the workforce was too small to meet a growing volume of orders. The second lay where the size of the mobile periphery of the workforce was too large to allow men who had served their time to work regularly enough to become master artisans themselves.

Disputes in the urban trades of eighteenth-century France were most usual, therefore, when the ordinary uncertainties of the economy of the bazaar were reinforced by unforeseen events which either exacerbated the ever-precarious balance between the limited size of the endogenous supply of labour and the very much more substantial pool of capable migrants, or threatened to undermine the informal distinctions and legal entitlements upon which they rested. That balance could be upset in a wide variety of different ways. A rise in the price of materials, a change in the volume of orders from large colonial customers, the beginning or end of a major building project, a substantial commission for uniforms, muskets or any of the myriad other goods and services ordered by royal, ecclesiastical or military clients could send reverberations through a multitude of different, but interdependent, trades. The beginning and end of wars had a similar potential to promote sharp modifications to established patterns of employment and create tensions among both masters and journeymen; so too, it has often been claimed, had fluctuations in the price of corn and the retail price of bread.

Nor were the effects of changes in the composition and supply of the workforce experienced solely by journeymen and not by master artisans. The composite character of many urban trades meant that different sectors of the same corporate body could be affected in widely divergent ways by changes in levels of orders and the distribution of demand for journeymen. The variety of products and sectors that fell under the rubrics of trades like lockmaking, joining or even shoemaking meant that shortages or gluts of labour in one branch of activity could affect other, ancillary, sectors of the same trade. Members of entirely separate corporations could encounter the same difficulties. Many apparently arcane disputes between corporations over rights to produce particular products often concealed more fundamental conflicts over access to an adequate supply of labour. A claim by the Parisian painters to an exclusive right to paint fans was also a claim to prevent the master fanmakers from employing the men and women who painted them.[22] In conditions in which occupational distinctions were not matched by significant differences in skills or materials, rights to produce particular goods were sometimes the key to access to the available workforce and the only basis of the viability of many artisanal enterprises.

There is no reason to assume that any of the various factors capable of disrupting the balance between the endogenous supply of labour and the larger pool of migrant journeymen should be privileged at the expense of any other. Nor is there any reason to assume that the courses of action followed by either masters or journeymen obeyed a single logic determined by a uniform set of objectives. The character of particular markets and their capacity to accommodate changes in the prices of different products, the places occupied by master artisans within particular networks of interdependent enterprises, the range of legal entitlements that different groups of journeymen could claim, and the extent to which occupational distinctions masked deeper similarities in the materials and skills associated with apparently different trades, all played a part in defining the various courses of action that masters and journeymen were able to follow.

The word 'dispute', in other words, is a particularly blunt instrument to apply to the many different courses of action available to masters and journeymen. What happened when disputes occurred depended not only upon goals and objectives but also upon resources, perceptions, tactics and opportunities. As a result, it is often more difficult to identify a distinct core of contention than appearances suggest. The problem is compounded by the legal origin of most information on disputes in the eighteenth-century French trades. Disputes were often as much an expression of crises within

[22] A.N. X¹ᵃ 3599 fol. 69ᵛᵒ (1 September 1731).

the formal apparatus of corporate regulation as they were a direct outcome of conflict between particular groups of masters and journeymen. Throughout the eighteenth century all the participants in disputes in the trades were able to regard the courts as their usual interlocutors. Recourse to the courts took two main forms. A corporation could appeal to the judicial authorities to enforce the appropriate provisions of its statutes. In some circumstances, however, no such provisions existed and it was necessary to devise new regulations and present them to the courts for ratification. In either case, the character of the surviving record was structured in significant ways.

In legal proceedings designed to enforce existing corporate regulations, the emphasis fell upon matters of fact and the extent to which certain kinds of action could be shown to have infringed the provisions of existing statutory regulation. Not surprisingly, legal proceedings of this kind (which fell under the rubric of the *police des arts et métiers*) favour images of rebellion, insubordination and defiance, for that was what they were designed to establish. In legal actions over additional provisions to an established panoply of corporate regulation, however, the emphasis fell very much more easily upon matters of law, and the extent to which certain proposals were compatible with the established rights, natural rights or customary usages of the various protagonists. Equally unsurprisingly, legal proceedings of this kind (which entailed an appeal to one of the Parlements) favour an imagery of rights that were variously denied, asserted or invoked, for that, too, was what they were designed to establish. Yet neither course of action was the dispute itself. Still less was either course of action a complete expression of the very much wider range of concerns and preoccupations informing the local economies of particular trades. Disputes, in short, were rather more than either the intermittent rebellion or the elaborate argument over rights that too close a dependence upon the records of the courts might suggest. Yet the identity of that additional element, which usually fell outside the sphere of legal argument, is often very difficult to discover.

ENDS AND MEANS

Two conflicts can be used to illustrate the problem: the first occurred in the Parisian carpentry trade in the late seventeenth century, while the second took place in the tailoring trade of Rouen towards the end of the Old Regime. Both of them had their origins in the structural tension between the endogeneous supply of labour and the more substantial pool of peripatetic journeymen, but they were very different in character. The manifest concerns of the protagonists were overlain by several less visible, and very different, considerations, while the courses of action that they followed were shaped as much by the various resources and entitlements that they enjoyed as by the objectives that they set out to achieve. Nor, in the last analysis, is it possible to be sure of all the goals and motives of the masters and journeymen involved in the disputes. As the case of the shipbuilding trade in Bordeaux in 1783 suggests, any particular matter of dispute was overlain by several other, apparently superfluous, sources of conflict. Yet the very superfluity of rhetoric that was so characteristic of disputes in the eighteenth-century trades was indicative of the fragility of the protagonists' positions. Master artisans, and corporate officials in particular, had as much to fear from other master artisans as journeymen had to fear from other journeymen. Ridicule, humiliation, threats and exhortation were ways of playing upon latent tensions within each group and of exposing the leading figures in any conflict to the risks of isolation and defeat.

The dispute in late seventeenth-century Paris has all the hallmarks of a conflict over an informal custom: in this instance the right of journeymen carpenters to take pieces of wood from the building sites where they worked. It was precipitated by a ruling by the Conseil d'Etat in March 1697 prohibiting journeymen from taking what were termed 'fouées, copeaux, bouts de bois et billots' from the building sites and other places where they worked. Several months passed before the decision was made public, but when it was announced early in 1698 there was an immediate reaction from journeymen in the trade. On the morning of 27 February 1698, as a long, cold winter drew to its end, the four *jurés* of the carpenters' corporation made their way to the residence of one of the *commissaires* of the Châtelet near the place de Grève. There they lodged a formal complaint that 'les compagnons...ont quitté le service des maîtres, caballent entre eux et détournent ceux qui de bonne volonté veulent bien travailler'.[23] They reported that work had stopped on a number of building sites. There had been violent scenes when journeymen who had walked out used their metal compasses and rulers to force those still at work to join them; threats to break the arms and legs of anyone found working had been made; 60 or 80 journeymen had assembled on the place de Grève, the large square on the right bank of the Seine which was the occasional site of public executions and, more usually, was the place where workers in the building trades gathered to be hired for the day or the week. On this occasion, however, the journeymen remained there long after the beginning of a normal working day and rejected all offers of employment unless they were allowed to take pieces of wood.

It is clear that both sides perceived the disputed right as a matter of major importance. In May 1698 over 800 journeymen were reported to have assembled in the cloisters of the Augustinian monastery overlooking

[23] A.N. Y 13 046 (27 February 1698).

the Seine to decide upon their future course of action.[24] They decided to organise a levy of 10 *sous* a head to mount a campaign in the courts. The proceedings continued until 6 September 1700, when the Parlement finally issued a ruling which found against the journeymen and reiterated the prohibition upon taking pieces of wood.[25] The legal action was punctuated by a series of stoppages: in March, May, June and November 1698, November 1699 and August 1700.[26] They were precipitated as much by decisions of the courts as by conditions in the trade. Those of the summer of 1698 followed the imprisonment of two journeymen carpenters who were, also masters of one of several confraternities that the journeymen had established in the capital. Those in the autumn of 1698 and 1699 were the result of rumours that the journeymen had won their case. As the rumours spread, journeymen again insisted upon their right to take pieces of wood and walked out on masters who refused.[27]

An incident that occurred in the summer of 1698 is an indication of the strength of feeling with which the issue was invested. On Sunday 15 June a master carpenter named Simon Joseph Caqué, who was one of the officials of the carpenters' corporation, went to mass in the church of Saint-Laurent near his home on the Grande rue du faubourg Saint-Martin, and during his absence a journeyman named Jacques Forget entered his house. Forget was one of the masters of a confraternity established by the journeymen carpenters in the church of Saint-Nicolas des Champs. Two of its other officials had just been arrested. Forget was carrying a piece of *pain bénit*, or bread presented to the offering when the members of the confraternity celebrated mass. He said that he had come to give the bread to one of Caqué's journeymen. The only person in the house was Caqué's wife, a 54-year-old woman who was paralysed with rheumatism and could not move out of her chair in the kitchen. Forget asked her where her husband was, and she told him that he was at mass in the church of Saint-Laurent. He then said, 'd'un ton menaçant', that he would have a word or two to say to Caqué were he there:

Il égorge ses enfants. C'est luy qui nous poursuit. S'il y a quelques compagnons de punis ce seroit lui-même qui tuerait ledit Caqué, et qu'il n'attendroit pas Christ.[28]

The style of the exchange is a measure of the wider drama of the dispute itself. Forget walked, unannounced, into the home of a *juré* of the carpenters' corporation. He used Caqué's wife to voice some of the journeymen's feelings about the dispute. He then sought out one of his

[24] *Ibid.* (25 May 1698), deposition of Roch Leroy.
[25] A.N. X²ᵃ 508 (6 September 1700). See also A.N. AD XI 16 and Archives de la Préfecture de police, Fonds Lamoignon, 20, fol. 1089.
[26] A.N. Y 13 046 (25 May 1698; 5 November 1698); Y 13048 (24 November 1699); Y 13 047 (31 August 1700).
[27] A.N. Y 13 048 (24 November 1699).
[28] A.N. Y 13 046 (15 June 1698).

journeymen to offer him the *pain bénit* of the journeymen's confraternity in a gesture in which provocation and an appeal to fraternity were combined in equal measure. The bread was a symbol of solidarity. As a commentator of the liturgy explained,

le pain bénit...est ainsi appellé parce qu'il est béni par une prière...L'on ne sauroit trouver un symbole plus expressif de l'union de plusieurs choses que le pain qui est fait de plusieurs grains de bled réunis et confondus ensemble.[29]

In the context in which it was offered, however, it was also a gesture of defiance. The whole episode was a bravado demonstration of equality: equality, despite the domestic privacy of a master artisan's house; equality, despite the privileged relationship between husband and wife; equality, despite the equally privileged relationship between master and journeyman. Forget violated all these privileged relationships because he, the master of a journeymen's confraternity, felt entitled to deal with a corporate official as an equal.

This concatenation of violations is an indication of the importance attached to pieces of wood. Yet it is not immediately apparent why they had such significance. Master carpenters bought their timber on the quayside in ways that allowed for some latitude in the measurement of the size and price of pieces of wood. The system was called selling by the *pied avant et le pied arrière*.[30] The length of a piece of timber was measured in terms of units of three feet, and intermediate lengths were allocated to a higher or lower unit if the timber was more or less than half as long again. Thus a piece of timber 7 feet long was sold at the rate for 6 feet; so too was a piece 5 feet long. A piece 8 feet long would sell as if it were 9 feet, as would a piece 10 feet long. In the first instance, the marginal benefit went to the master carpenter; in the second, it went to the timber merchant. Master carpenters charged their clients in a similar way. The units were lower (18 *pouces* by 18 *pouces*) and anything longer the 3 *pouces* was charged as an additional unit. Clients who insisted upon precise measurement of the timber were charged a sixth more. The relationship

[29] Pierre Lebrun, *Explication littérale, historique et dogmatique des prières et des cérémonies de la Messe* 4 vols (Paris, 1777), vol. 2, p. 288.

[30] It is described in J. H. Hassenfratz, *Traité de l'art du charpentier* (Paris, 1804), pp. 211–12. Recent interpretations of disputes over materials in the eighteenth-century English trades have followed the brilliant and still unpublished thesis by Peter Linebaugh, 'Tyburn: Crime and the Labouring Poor in Eighteenth-Century London', (unpublished Ph.D Thesis, University of Warwick 1975). The clearest summary of this approach can be found in John Rule, *The Experience of Labour in Eighteenth-Century Industry* (London, 1981), pp. 124–46. For an example of the large but not very illuminating literature on contemporary perquisites, see Stuart Henry, *The Hidden Economy* (London, 1978). For an alternative interpretation and one that is closer to the one followed here, see John Styles, 'Embezzlement, Industry and the Law in England, 1500–1700', in Maxine Berg, Pat Hudson and Michael Sonenscher eds, *Manufacture in Town and Country before the Factory* (Cambridge, 1983), pp. 173–210.

between the price and the volume of the timber used by master carpenters was therefore always imprecise. This suggests that in ordinary circumstances there was no reason why they could not have accommodated the loss of what were termed 'copeaux, fouées, bouts de bois et billots' or passed on the cost of such losses to their clients and contractors. One master who gave evidence during the dispute mentioned that the pieces of wood in question were less than a foot long.[31]

Little direct reference was made to the monetary value of the pieces of wood. Three journeymen repairing an inn did agree to return to work when the innkeeper offered to pay them an extra 2 *sous* and a *chopine* of wine a day as compensation for the loss of their right.[32] This was the only reference made to a monetary equivalent of the wood during the entire dispute. Nor, despite the ruling by the Parlement in 1700 confirming the earlier decision to prohibit the practice of taking pieces of wood is there any evidence that it came to an end. The ruling by the Parlement in 1700 was merely one of an extended sequence. The practice of taking pieces of wood had already been prohibited on at least two earlier occasions. In 1631 journeymen made an unsuccessful appeal to the Parlement against a ruling by the *prévôt* of Paris prohibiting them from taking pieces of wood.[33] In 1656, seven years after the Parlement had ratified the revised statutes of the carpenters' corporation, but only a few months after it had reissued the ruling of 1631, it was reported that between 500 and 600 journeymen had assembled on the heights of Belleville because they had been denied the right to take wood, and had scoured the building sites of the capital to find and assault anyone still at work.[34]

The effects of the ruling by the Parlement which ended the dispute in 1700 were as ephemeral as its earlier rulings had been. In 1786, a decision by the carpenter's corporation to replace the right to take wood by an extra 5 *sous* a day (or an additional 12.5 per cent of the nominal daily rate of 40 *sous*), in keeping with a revised set of statutes ratified in 1785, led to a general stoppage headed by journeymen working on what was to become the Panthéon.[35] A manual published in 1833 noted that

31 A.N. Y 13 048 (24 November 1698), deposition of Gilles Jamet.
32 A.N. Y 13 046 (27 February 1698), deposition of Jean Froment.
33 A.N. X¹ᵃ 399 (30 August 1631); see also above, p. 78.
34 A.N. X¹ᵃ 2397 (17 May 1656). The statutes of 1649 are reprinted in René de Lespinasse, *Les Métiers et corporations de la ville de Paris* (Paris, 1893), vol. 2.
35 'Mr. le commissaire Crespy vient de m'écrire que les garçons charpentiers employés à Sainte Géneviève se sont attroupés, ont abandonnés leur travail et cherchent à debaucher ceux de leurs camarades qui travaillent chez les maîtres': A.N. Y 11 281ᴬ (De Crosne to the syndics of the commissaires of the Châtelet, 22 March 1786). 'Dans la matinée les compagnons charpentiers se soulèvent contre leurs maîtres à l'occasion de ce que par un nouveau règlement il avoit été stipulé que moyennant *cinq sols* de plus ajoutés par chaque journée à leur paye ordinaire, ils ne pourroient plus emporter à l'avenir chez eux un seul morceau de bois': B.N. MS. fr. 6685 fol. 315 (23 March 1786).

8.1 A Parisian joiners' shop. Source: *Atelier du sieur Jadot menuisier*, engraving by Pierre Chenu (1776).

the practice of taking pieces of wood had been prohibited under the revised statutes of the carpenters' corporation of 1785, but stated that 'au levage (c'est à dire au travail fait en ville) on leur permet d'emporter les copeaux faits naturellement et non exprès'.[36] Clearly, there were circumstances in which master carpenters were prepared to allow journeymen to take pieces of wood. To understand why they did so at some times, but not at others, several additional items of information are needed. Together, they suggest a rather different interpretation of the substance of the conflict over pieces of wood.

An engraving of a Parisian joiner's shop in the middle of the eighteenth century contains a clue to their significance (Figure 8.1). In the foreground of the image is a woman collecting pieces of wood.[37] Although women worked in many of the trades of Paris, there is no evidence that they had anything to do with the carpentry or joining trades. It is impossible to identify the women in the image – she may have been a domestic servant, collecting wood-chippings for her master, or she may have been a journeyman's wife. An incident during the late seventeenth-century

[36] B.N. F 31881. Malepeyre, *Code des ouvriers* (Paris, 1833), p. 10.
[37] The engraving represented the workshop of a master joiner named Jadot. It was engraved by Pierre Chenu and advertised in the *Affiches, annonces et avis divers* of 26 September 1770: see Marcel Roux, *Bibliothèque nationale. Inventaire du fonds français. Graveurs du xviiie siècle* (Paris, 1940). p. 304.

dispute suggests that this latter possibility was one of the reasons why pieces of wood were endowed with such importance by journeymen working in the Parisian carpentry trade. It implies that pieces of wood were more than customary counterparts to the wages that journeymen earned – they were the staples of an economy in which sub-contracted work was exceptionally widespread and in which journeymen, particularly men who were established and long-domiciled in Paris, played as active a part as their masters.

The incident involved a master carpenter named Roch Leroy. It occurred in May 1698, shortly after the arrest of the two officials of the journeymen's confraternity. Leroy was at home on the rue du Vertbois when he was set upon by four of the journeymen's wives, two of whom were married to the imprisoned masters of the confraternity. One of them called Leroy 'un bougre de chien' and warned him that unless the proceedings against the arrested men were suspended, 'toutes les femmes des compagnons se mettroient apres luy'. She then stated that 'ce ne seroit plus les compagnons qui iroient par les chantiers faire sortir leurs camarades, mais les femmes', and told Leroy's journeymen that unless they walked out they would strangle them. Another of the women took off her shoe and used it to attack one of the journeymen still at work. He was one of her imprisoned husband's cousins.[38]

The incident suggests that pieces of wood belonged to an economy in which sub-contracted work, family resources and competition for materials cut across the formal division between masters and journeymen. The Parisian carpenters' corporation was one of the smallest of the capital's corporations. During the eighteenth century it was made up of no more than some 60 to 90 masters and widows.[39] Given the size of the capital, it is inconceivable that so small a number of master carpenters could have been directly involved with the day-to-day management of many of the various projects in which they were simultaneously involved. Half of the two dozen masters who gave evidence to the police authorities during the conflict made explicit reference to the fact that they had work in progress on more than one site. Some of them were relatively large employers of labour. Hubert Jollivet had 14 journeymen working for him, 'ayant plusieurs bâtiments entrepris'. Charles Louret employed 20 journeymen 'qui travailloient pour lui dans ses chantiers'. Pierre Delacroix had 14 journeymen working for him on four different sites.[40] Several masters stated that they had agreed to allow their journeymen to continue to take pieces of wood because, as they put it, they were 'pressés de besogne'.[41]

38 A.N. Y 13 046 (25 May 1698), deposition of Roch Leroy.
39 A.N. Minutier central, 4B: A.N. XXᶜ 65.
40 A.N. Y 13 046 (27 February 1698); Y 13 048 (24 November 1699); Y 13 046 (25 May 1698).
41 *Ibid.*, depositions of Jacques Couturier, Paul Poisson and Philippe Voisin.

One reason why the number of Parisian master carpenters was not very high was that the trade called for relatively substantial resources of capital and credit. The productive network to which it belonged required adequate funds both to meet the costs of timber and to negotiate the uncertain resources of either the principal building contractor or the final client. At the same time, adequate working capital was needed to pay wages and meet the occasional claims of suppliers of nails, gum, resin and other materials. The most usual solution to the problem of recurrent costs was to devolve them upon sub-contractors and engage journeymen to undertake work 'à l'entreprise', only settling accounts when payments were made by the principal contractor or final consumer.[42] It is very probable, therefore, that the distance between the core and the periphery of the carpentry trade was a substantial one. The two dozen master carpenters who gave evidence in the late seventeenth-century dispute in Paris had at least six times as many journeymen (138) working for them.[43] Both the small number of master carpenters and the relatively large number of men that they employed suggest that many journeymen worked as independent sub-contractors outside the framework of corporate regulation for much of their working lives.

The journeymen who played the most prominent part in the dispute were men who were married, and had lived and worked in Paris for many years. Most of the dozen journeymen employed by Roch Leroy had, he said, been working for him for a long time.[44] Jacques Couturier, a 40-year-old master on the rue Montmartre, stated that several of the journeymen who had walked out on him when he announced on their payday that, because of the *arrêt du Conseil*, he was unable to allow them to take any pieces of wood had worked for him for 13 years.[45] Some of the journeymen employed by a 61-year-old master on the rue de Seine had, he said, worked for him for over 20 years. Long-standing relationships like these (even if the word 'work' may not have implied continuous employment) were as unusual in the carpentry trade as in any other. Only five per cent of the 480 journeymen from an assortment of building trades who were employed on repairs to the Abbey of Saint-Germain-des-Prés between

---

[42] See above, chapter 6.

[43] The pattern was a durable one. The 87 Parisian carpenters who applied for small coin during the early years of the Revolution employed 1,694 individuals according to Braesch's not altogether reliable figures. An indication that the formal division between masters and journeymen was not identical to that between employers and workers can be found in the very sharp increase in the number of employers in the nineteenth century. Over 290 employers were involved in the celebrated strike in the Parisian carpentry trade in 1845: Jean-Pierre Aguet, *Les Grèves sous la Monarchie de Juillet (1830–1847)* (Geneva, 1954), p. 305.

[44] A.N. Y 13 046 (15 November 1698), deposition of Roch Leroy.

[45] A.N. Y 13 046 (4 March 1698), deposition of Jacques Couturier; (25 May 1698), deposition of Raoul-Pierre Delaporte.

1644 and 1646 worked there for a year or more. Over half of them (61 per cent) were employed for less than a month.[46] The relatively settled circumstances of the majority of journeymen identified in the dispute in the late seventeenth century found their expression in the regulations of the confraternities to which they belonged. There were no less than four of them, affiliated to the churches of Saint-Nicolas des Champs, Saint-Paul, Saint-Côme and the Premonstarian Abbey of the Holy Cross.

The confraternity mentioned most frequently during the dispute, and of which Jacques Forget was one of the masters, was the one established at Saint-Nicolas des Champs. It was by no means a clandestine association. In 1694 it had been involved in a dispute with the *marguilliers* (lay dignatories) and *curé* of the parish over its right to maintain its own chapel and use its own ornaments (rather than those belonging to the church, for which a fee was required) in funeral processions for deceased members. As evidence of its established status, its officials stated that members of the confraternity attended mass every Sunday and celebrated the annual feast of St Joseph (patron of the carpentry trade)

They stated that the confraternity had been founded in 997 by King Robert, the 37th King of France, and had been granted an indulgence by Pope Alexander VII in 1658.[48] Its liturgical obligations towards its dead were complemented by a duty to Christian charity, 's'il arrive que quelqu'un des confrères devienne pauvre et denué des biens'.[49] Both obligations indicate that the membership of the confraternity was stable and long-standing. The fact that membership of the association was open to 'toutes sortes de personne de l'un ou de l'autre sexe' confirms the impression.[50]

The disputed question of pieces of wood was linked to a second issue: the right of journeymen who had served an apprenticeship and were domiciled in Paris to have preferential access to employment over journeymen from the provinces. In August 1630, when the *prévôté* of Paris prohibited them from taking pieces of wood, the journeymen had appealed to the Parlement, requesting

avec pompe et éclat...Que la veille ils font carillonner et jouer des orgues aux premières vespres, et le lendemain...ils font chanter une messe haute...aussi avec orgues et carillon, tentures de tapisseries au dehors et au dedans de l'église avec des images de la confrérie.[47]

[46] Corinne Beutler, 'Bâtiments et salaires: un chantier à Saint-Germain-des-Prés, de 1644 à 1646', *Annales E.S.C.*, 26 (1971), pp. 484-517.

[47] B.N. Réserve, Fonds Thoisy 9, fol. 281. 'Réponses aux Défenses. Les Maistres en charge et anciens de la confrérie de Saint Joseph des compagnons charpentiers, demandeurs en requeste du 5 mars 1694'. See too *ibid.*, fol. 279. 'Mémoire pour les maîtres en charge et anciens de la confrérie de Saint Joseph des compagnons charpentiers, demandeurs en requeste du 3 décembre 1695'. See also A. N. 634 (8 February 1728).

[48] *Ibid.*

[49] *Ibid.*

[50] *Ibid.*

a ce qu'ils feussent maintenus et conservez en leur droit ordinaire...d'emporter les fouins, coppeaux, bouts de bois et billots de nulle valeur provenant du bois auquel ils auroient travaillé.

They also demanded that master carpenters

seroient tenus d'employer les compagnons charpentiers qui auroient fait leur apprantissage et estoient domiciliez en nostre dicte ville par préférance aux compagnons estrangers du mesme métier.[51]

The same association between pieces of wood and preferential treatment within the labour market was made during the dispute in 1656–7 and was reiterated both in the ruling by the Conseil d'Etat in 1697 and by the Parlement in its final verdict on the dispute in September 1700. Journeymen were denied the right to take pieces of wood and masters were authorised 'de se servir de tels compagnons que bon leur semblent'.[52]

One way of explaining the long legal campaign and the episodic stoppages of work undertaken by journeymen carpenters in late seventeenth-century Paris would be to take the question of 'copeaux, fouées, bouts de bois et billots', as an example of the custom-saturated economy of pre-industrial society. Whatever its descriptive merits (and it is clear that the journeymen did look upon pieces of wood as a right), the phrase begs almost as many questions as it appears to answer. Despite their apparent precision, the terms 'custom' and 'pre-industrial society' are, in fact, abstractions of a very high order. It is possible that the journeymen carpenters inhabited a 'pre-industrial society' governed by the prescriptions of custom. It is, on the contrary, certain that they inhabited Paris rather than Poitiers, or any of the hundreds of other localities in late seventeenth-century France where carpenters practised their trade. There is, moreover, no reason to suppose that the work that journeymen did in Paris was particularly different from the work done by journeymen in Poitiers. There were frames to be raised, beams to be laid, timber to be measured and cut. Yet there were many good reasons why neither group of journeymen would have shared this opinion. When journeymen insisted upon the distinctive qualities of the work they did, there is no reason to follow their account and believe that it was the *work* which was different. The point, in the last analysis, was that *they* were different. This was the point of the right to take pieces of wood. When they insisted upon their distinctive rights, journeymen in Paris were also insisting upon their distinctive place within the local economy of the trade.

It is possible, therefore, to explain the conflict in the Parisian carpentry trade in terms of an economy in which many of the journeymen who had

[51] A.N. X¹ᵃ 399 (30 August 1631).

[52] Nicolas Delamare, *Traité de police* (Paris, 1738), vol. 4, pp. 83–4; A.N. X¹ᵃ 2397 (17 May 1656); Archives de la Préfecture de police, Fonds Lamoignon 13, fol. 673 (17 June 1656); A.N. E 661ᵇ fol. 101 (16 March 1697).

served an apprenticeship in the capital subsequently undertook sub-contracted work as regularly as they worked for wages. Through their confraternities, they were able to mount a series of widespread, if ultimately unsuccessful, campaigns to prevent the carpenters' corporation from opening the Parisian labour market to seasonal migrants whose presence was likely to limit both the amount of work and the available supply of materials to small-scale sub-contractors. In this sense, the conflict between masters and journeymen was an expression of the different legal entitlements available to those artisans who belonged to a corporation and those who did not. It masked a more fundamental tension over access to materials. The formal difference between carpenters who belonged to the corporation and those who did not was not, in other words, identical to the difference between employers and employees. Some carpenters, who, in formal terms, were masters of a corporation, were able to use the courts to undermine the position of other carpenters who, in formal terms, were journeymen, by denying them access to materials.

It is very much more difficult, however, to explain why these tensions developed into open conflict at some times rather than others. Figures of the supply of timber or of trends in building work in seventeenth-century Paris do not exist. Trends in the level of rent are very difficult to interpret. Nominal rents were falling in Paris throughout the decade between 1687 and 1697, just as they were between 1648 and 1656, but not, however, between 1624 and 1632.[53] Falling rents may have been a result of a rising housing stock and a growing number of building projects, with attendant pressure upon the local labour market. They may, more plausibly, have been a result of rising corn prices (as was the case between 1687 and 1698 and in the two earlier periods) and stagnation in the carpentry trade. Either set of circumstances might have induced tension in the housing market.[54] Neither, however, can be a sufficient explanation of the incidence of conflict because high corn prices and fluctuations in the level of nominal rents were not confined to the years in which disputes occurred.

Two further possibilities can be suggested. The first is merely a slightly different approach to the question of the supply of materials. The three disputes in the Parisian carpentry trade during the seventeenth century occurred during, or soon after, periods of domestic conflict and foreign war, and it is possible that these events had reverberations upon both the availability of timber and conditions within the Parisian labour market.[55] It

[53] Emmanuel Le Roy Ladurie and Pierre Couperie, 'Le Mouvement des loyers parisiens de la fin du Moyen-Age au xviiie siècle', *Annales E.S.C.*, 25 (1970), pp. 1002–23.

[54] On the movement of prices in seventeenth-century Paris, see Micheline Baulant, 'Le Prix des grains à Paris de 1431 à 1788'; *Annales E.S.C.*, 23 (1968), pp. 520–40, and Jacques Dupâquier, Marcel Lachiver and Jean Meuvret, *Mercuriales du Pays de France et du Vexin Français (1640–1792)* (Paris, 1968).

[55] Robin Briggs, *Early Modern France 1560–1715* (London, 1977), pp. 128–65.

is equally possible that disputes in ancillary trades gave rise to bottlenecks and disruption in the carpentry trade. In the case that it presented to the Parlement, the carpenters' corporation called upon the court to abolish the journeymen's confraternities under the provisions of a ruling that it had made in March 1698 abolishing the confraternity formed by journeymen in the roofing trade.[56] It is impossible to know, however, whether the request was made because the ruling was a convenient legal precedent or because disputes in the roofing trade had had effects upon schedules within the carpentry trade.

It is, in other words, extremely difficult to identify the circumstances that allowed ordinary argument between masters and journeymen to develop into more widespread conflict. If the immediate occasion precipitating conflict in the seventeenth-century Parisian carpentry trade was a legal decision – a ruling by the *prévôté* in 1630, by the Parlement in 1656 and by the Conseil d'Etat in 1697 – the circumstances informing the decisions themselves are shrouded in mystery. It is very likely, however, that these circumstances included a great deal of discussion and argument within the corporations themselves. The dispute that occurred in the tailoring trade of Rouen in the late eighteenth century contains many hints of such argument and discussion. Both the circumstances of the protagonists and the procedures that they followed meant that it was a very different kind of dispute from the one that occurred in late seventeenth-century Paris.

The dispute in Rouen was very much smaller in scale than that in the Parisian carpentry trade in the late seventeenth century. It was, to all intents and purposes, a very banal argument between a single master tailor and half a dozen journeymen. The master tailor, Pierre Vandercruysse, had a shop on the rue Encrière in Rouen. In November 1782, he informed the officials of his corporation that five of the six journeymen he employed had walked out.[57] The *gardes* of the tailors' corporation duly made a formal complaint to the police authorities. An inspector was sent to an inn on the rue Saint-Lô where the journeymen were lodging. He made a search of their rooms and found a substantial quantity of pieces of cloth. Vandercruysse later identified some of them as scraps from a piece of velvet fabric that had been used to begin making a three-piece suit which a customer had ordered. Yet he did not press any charges against the journeymen for theft; instead he left it to the corporate officials to prosecute them for failure to give proper notice and violation of a corporate regulation prohibiting journeymen tailors from finding work themselves.

The journeymen admitted the offences. They told the *bailliage* court

---

[56] A.N. X²ᵃ 508 (6 September 1700).

[57] The dossier of the case is in A.D. Seine-Maritime, 4BP 5945 (23 November 1782). A copy of the court's verdict is in B.M. Rouen, MS. g 165/207 (4 December 1782).

which heard the case that they had been bound by the informal rules of the inn on the rue Saint-Lô where they were lodging. These rules, described by one of the journeymen as the *usage des logis*, entitled two of their number, known respectively as the *premier garçon* and the *premier journalier*, to find work for anyone lodging in the inn. They were also empowered to order journeymen to move from one master to another, and, if necessary, to leave Rouen altogether to accommodate new arrivals from other towns. This informal system was organised around a hierarchy of seniority which ensured that journeymen who worked regularly in the core of the trade were able to remain in regular employment in Rouen. The most recent arrival was expected to be the first to comply with any instruction to move. One of the five journeymen who had walked out pointed out that these practices were well known, and that the officials of the tailors' corporation were entirely familiar with their requirements. His surprise is an indication that the *usage des logis* was a well-established component of patterns of employment in the trade.

The informal system that the journeymen operated was illegal. It had been prohibited by rulings of the Parlement of Normandy in 1763, 1766 and 1777, and by a sentence of the *bailliage* court in September 1782.[58] The ruling of 1777 also stipulated that journeymen were required to register with the corporate office and find work through its auspices. Yet, as both the sequence of court rulings and the behaviour of the five journeymen working for Vandercruysse imply, a number of journeymen evidently continued to abide by the *usage des logis* and assumed that the officials of the tailors' corporation were willing to accept the fact. They could only have done so if some master tailors were opposed to the system of registration. One of them, in fact, had been the master tailor Vandercruysse himself. He had been one of half a dozen master tailors who, in 1778, had appealed to the Parlement of Normandy against the corporation's decision to establish the system of registration, but the court had dismissed their appeal.[59] Yet, despite his earlier position, Vandercruysse apparently had no difficulty in allowing the *gardes* of the corporation to bring an action against his journeymen in 1782.

This change of attitude suggests that master artisans brought a number of different considerations to bear upon regulations governing the supply of labour. They did so because the structural tension between the inadequate local supply of labour and the larger pool of peripatetic migrants affected master artisans in different ways. Pierre Vander-

---

[58] A.D. Seine-Maritime, 1BP 15 224 (8 August 1777), which cites two earlier *arrêts* of 13 June 1763 and 14 August 1766, and A.D. Seine-Maritime, 4BP 5945.

[59] A.D. Seine-Maritime, 1BP 15 227 (20 November 1777). The register of the corporate employment office also refers to two subsequent rulings by the Parlement, on 20 December 1777 and 3 March 1779. Neither appears to be among the series of *arrêts* contained in the Series 1BP.

was one of the central figures within the core of regular employers of labour in the tailoring trade of Rouen.[60] He was in fact, the largest employer in the trade. At one time or another between July 1778 and November 1781 he employed a total of 263 journeymen, who, together, worked some 3,464 man-days in his shop. He was not always the largest employer, however. The monthly totals of man-days worked in his shop varied substantially, and, at times, were lower than the totals worked in other master tailors' shops (Figure 8.2). The asynchronous schedules of production followed by different master tailors meant that there was no uniform change in the level of demand for additional journeymen. A large employer like Vandercruysse was obliged to compete with other members of the changing core of the trade if he wished to respond to short-term changes in the volume of orders from his clients and customers.

It is easier to understand Vandercruysse's initial hostility to the establishment of a *bureau de placement* in the light of both the erratic schedules of demand for labour in the trade as a whole and the constantly changing number of journeymen that he himself employed. The formalities involved in dealing with a corporate employment office introduced an additional complication into the already complicated business of managing the relationship between orders, schedules of production and the supply of labour. Divisions among master artisans over the question of *placement* were a common occurrence when so many periods of employment were of such short duration and so many journeymen were taken on to perform no more than a particular piece of work. Words like 'despotism' and 'natural liberty' could be used as readily by master artisans as by journeymen when faced with a growing number of orders and an apparently recalcitrant corporate clerk determined to ensure that the provisions of corporate regulations were properly enforced.[61]

It is also clear that the tension between the endogenous supply of labour and the recurrent need to employ journeymen from elsewhere placed considerable pressure on Vandercruysse's relationship with the peripatetic inhabitants of the lodging houses. The registers of registration kept by the tailors' corporation of Rouen reveal that he recruited his journeymen from a succession of different *logis* between 1778 and 1781.[62] Between May 1778 and October 1780, all but one of the men he employed and did not house himself lodged in the largest house of call frequented by journeymen tailors, the inn kept by Naudin on the rue des Bons Enfants, in the other inn which housed the majority of itinerant journeymen who came to work

[60] A.D. Seine-Maritime, 5E 709–710 and above, chapter 4.

[61] For examples, see a *mémoire* by a master joiner responsible for placing journeymen in Marseille in 1765: A.C. Marseille. FF 206; and, in the Parisian painting trade. A.N. Y 11 010 (8 and 13 May 1769) and above, chapter 7.

[62] A.D. Seine Maritime, 5E 709–710.

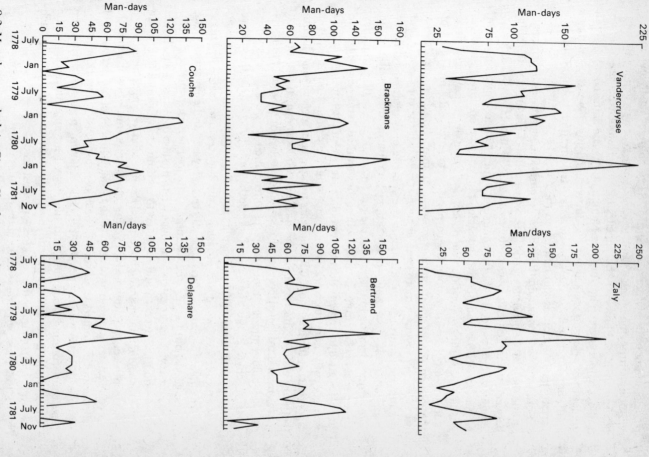

8.2 Man-days worked in Pierre Vandercruysse's shop compared with other leading employers in the tailoring trade of Rouen (1778–81). Source: A.D. Seine-Maritime, 5E 709–10.

in the tailoring trade of Rouen. In April 1781 he changed again and began recruiting journeymen from a small lodging house kept by a widow. By the autumn of 1782, however, he appears to have resumed his practice of employing journeymen lodging *chez* Naudin on the rue Saint-Lô: all five of the journeymen who walked out on him were lodging there. Only at that point, after four years of informal negotiation with the inhabitants of the various lodging houses, did he turn to the courts.

Both the divisions within the tailors' corporation over the establishment of the *bureau de placement* and the constantly changing relationship between the largest employer in the trade and the inhabitants of different lodging houses suggest that the complaint which Vandercruysse made in November 1782 had several possible, but equally obscure, purposes. Despite his earlier opposition, Vandercruysse's complaint may have been a device to put pressure upon the corporation to enforce the provisions of the system of *placement* more rigorously. It may, however, have been intended to provoke a more general conflict between the corporation and the itinerant journeymen, leading to the collapse of the formal system of registration. It may have been designed to harm the reputation of journeymen lodging in the inn on the rue Saint-Lô by revealing that they took pieces of cloth from the shops where they worked. It may equally have been designed to prevent the master tailors for whom the journeymen had subsequently gone to work from completing their orders on time. It is apparent, at the least, that what appears to have been a very banal dispute between a single master tailor and half a dozen journeymen was, in fact, part of a multi-faceted process of negotiation between different groups of master tailors and different groups of journeymen.

It is obvious too that pieces of cloth – or *chiquettes* as they were known – had a very different significance in the tailoring trade of Rouen from the pieces of wood that occasioned the disputes in the carpentry trade of seventeenth-century Paris. The difference lay not in the potential value of the goods, but in the circumstances of the journeymen who took them. The journeymen carpenters who objected to the loss of pieces of wood were men who lived, worked and expected to continue to work in Paris, while the journeymen tailors who frequented the inns and lodging houses of late eighteenth-century Rouen were young, single migrants whose peripatetic circumstances were unconducive to the establishment of the networks of clients and customers that were the basis of sub-contracted work. The two groups of journeymen occupied radically different positions within the spectrum running from men who had served an apprenticeship in the cities in which they worked to the short-term migrants who made up such a large component of the workforce of most trades.

In the most general sense, both disputes were expressions of the structural tension between endogenous and exogenous access to local labour markets, but the issues presented to the courts were very much more varied, and ranged from accusations of assault or breach of contract to charges of using a confraternity for illegal meetings and threats of prosecution for theft. The range of legal resources available to the protagonists in disputes meant that they could exercise considerable discretion in their choice of weapons. Although it is logical to assume that master artisans enjoyed the balance of advantage in the charges that they could press, journeymen were well able to make formal charges themselves. Civil actions over non-payments of wages, or charges of assault brought before the criminal courts, were frequent accompaniments to more wide-ranging conflict. Journeymen domiciled in particular cities were better placed to undertake such actions and, given the size of the sedentary workforce in many of the Parisian trades, legal actions by journeymen were more frequent in the capital than in Lyon, Marseille, Bordeaux, Nantes or Rouen. Although the *compagnonnages* established by itinerant journeymen played some part in disputes in the trades, migrants had fewer of the resources available to men who were settled in large cities. The relationship between sedentary and itinerant journeymen was not always an easy one, and tensions within the workforces of the trades were a frequent accompaniment to conflict between journeymen and their masters.[63]

The varied range of product markets and erratic schedules of most trades were, moreover, rarely conducive to unity among master artisans. Three months of conflict in the Parisian silk and ribbon-weaving trade between a number of masters and an assortment of journeymen or masters working as journeymen resulted in a corporate decision in December 1762 to change the *tarif* of piece-rates. Instead of settling the dispute, however, the new *tarif* precipitated an appeal to the Parlement by 165 master ribbon-weavers, which was still in progress nearly two years later. The venom that such differences could occasion was captured graphically in a remark by a substantial master shoemaker named Paret about two of the officials of the shoemakers' corporation of Marseille during a dispute with the journeymen of the trade in 1769. After complaining that the two officials 'étoient depuis dix ans les perturbateurs', he announced that he and one of his fellows 'scauroient bien les dompter et les rendre plus souples que des gands at des belles filles'. Formal complaints were often the outcome of much manoeuvre among master artisans, occasionally accompanied by attempts to reach an informal settlement, before the officials of a corporation were persuaded, or took it upon themselves, to initiate potentially divisive and costly courses of action by appealing to the judicial and police authorities.[64]

[63] Sonenscher, *Hatters*, chapter 11. See also below, chapter 9.
[64] A.N. X[1b] 3781 (28 February 1763); X[2a] 817 (7 February 1763); X[1a] 7978 fol. 147 (29 March 1763); X[1a] 7987 fol. 22 (2 July 1763); X[1a] 4444 fol. 146[vo] (11 August 1763); X[1a] 8002 fol. 40 (5 January 1764), fol. 327[vo] (14 January 1764); X[1b] 3812 (5 September

Typically, therefore, conflict between masters and journeymen was a diffuse affair in which it is often extremely difficult to isolate the moment at which normal relations broke down and open antagonism occurred. Journeymen were well aware that there were latent tensions among master artisans. Much of the apparently superfluous rhetoric that was so frequent an accompaniment to conflict was designed to humiliate and isolate master artisans (or the journeymen they employed) precisely because decisions made in a small number of workshops or even in a corporate assembly were often fragile compromises between several different interests. Many apparently isolated incidents were, therefore, part of a broader process of testing or undermining often precarious norms.

Thus, early in February 1720 the officials of the Parisian farriers' corporation lodged a complaint that 'almost all' the journeymen of the trade had been leagued together for several months to obtain higher monthly rates of pay. They had refused to work for less than 19 or 20 *livres* a month, exclusive of food and accommodation (but inclusive of a month's pay in advance), instead of the 13 *livres* that was the usual monthly rate.[65] The dispute had taken the form of an earlier series of dispersed conflicts before the *jurés* made their complaint. Jean Caillet, a master farrier on the rue Saint-Benoît, stated that on Sunday 28 January 'après le souper', his four journeymen informed him that 'ils alloient luy apprendre une nouvelle, sçavoir qu'ils ne vouloient point travailler chez luy qu'il n'augmentât leur paye'.[66] Another master farrier reported that his three journeymen had insisted upon settling their accounts and leaving, even though he was extremely busy, and had gone off to a meeting of over 40 journeymen on the Place Maubert. Pierre Houry, another master, stated that he had been walking past a farrier's workshop on the rue de Seine one Tuesday morning when the journeymen working there had shouted at him 'Eh Con, tournez! Parle donc, Hé Monsieur!' When he went up to them, they denied that they had been addressing him. As he went on his way, he saw to his surprise that one of the journeymen was following him, holding his iron tongs in his hand and saying, 'Eh con tourne; qu'est que c'est ce bougre-là; est-ce que je le connois.' When Houry turned upon him to remonstrate, the journeyman threatened him with his tongs, saying 'qui est-ce que, ce bougre-là; si je le foutrez un soufflet et je (le) rajetteray à mes pieds'.[67]

1764): X¹ᵃ 4490 fol. 199ᵛ° (9 February 1765); Y 9525 (20 May 1763); Y 9645 (20 May 1763) Y 11 950 (15 December 1762): on the dispute in the Parisian ribbon-weaving trade. A.C. Marseille, FF 378 (29 July 1769), deposition of Joseph Brun: on the dispute in the shoemaking trade of Marseille. For examples of attempts at settlement during disputes among shoemakers and wheelwrights in Marseille, see A.C. Marseille, FF 378 (26 July 1769), deposition of Jean-Baptiste Barthelémy; *ibid.*, FF 394 (13 September 1784).

65 A.N. Y 9421 (7 February 1720).

66 *Ibid.*

67 *Ibid.*

A similar sequence of small-scale argument in the Parisian shoemaking trade lasted from the spring to the autumn of 1763, and continued intermittently during the following two years. In June 1763 one of the officials of the corporation, responsible for proposing that journeymen should register with a corporate employment office presided over by a police inspector or face imprisonment, complained that three journeymen has staged a mock fight outside his shop, taunting him to intervene and have them sent to prison. 'N'as-tu pas peur d'aller à Bicêtre...Allez prends garde à toy', one of them was heard to say in tones of exaggerated terror. They tried, unsuccessfully, to persuade his own journeymen to walk out, finally concluding that they were 'des f...plats et des jean-foutres'.[68] Parodies of authority, mocking songs and well-publicised anonymous letters, rich in revelations of financial or sexual misconduct, played upon tensions among master artisans and made it easier for the decisions that some of them made to be ignored by others.[69]

THE INCIDENCE OF CONFLICT

It is not easy, however, to identify the circumstances that allowed small-scale arguments and confrontations of this kind to coalesce into the more substantial conflicts that some of them became. It is clear that major conflicts were relatively infrequent occurrences in any single trade. In the Parisian hatting trade, where conflict appears to have been rather more frequent than in many others, major disputes occurred on no more than nine occasions during the eighteenth century, or, on average, once every decade.[70] Major disputes were as infrequent in other trades. In a memorandum written at the time of Turgot's proposal to abolish the Parisian corporations in the spring of 1776, the capital's master silk-weavers (*maîtres et marchands fabricants d'étoffes d'or, d'argent et de soie*) presented a catalogue of occasions when 'l'esprit de révolte et sédition s'est malheureusement emparé de ces âmes mercenaires' (i.e. their workers and journeymen), yet the number of disputes that they listed amounted to only four: in 1718, 1723, 1743 and 1756.[71] There were undoubtedly many other small-scale arguments and conflicts in the trade, but the intervals of five, 20, 13 and 20 years between conflicts that the corporation's officials felt were worthy of note suggests something of the infrequency of major confrontations. During a dispute between master and journeymen farriers

68 A.N. Y 11 004ᵃ (7 May, 7 and 10 June 1763); Y 11004ᵇ (8 August, 29 August, 16 September, 9 October 1763).

69 For examples of anonymous letters and songs, see Garrioch and Sonenscher, 'Compagnonnages, Confraternities', pp. 33–4; Sonenscher, 'Sans-Culottes', p. 319, B.N. MS. fr. 22 118, fols. 275 and 294 (28 December 1763 and 23 October 1765); and above, p. 196.

70 Sonenscher, *Hatters*, p. 30.

71 B.N. MS. Joly de Fleury 596, fol. 80.

over wage-rates in 1791, the journeymen referred to three previous attempts to obtain wage-increases: in 1764, 1769 and 1786.[72] Disputes among printers, carpenters, joiners and roofers followed the same irregular and infrequent rhythm.[73]

Yet despite their relative rarity in any single trade, substantial conflicts tended to occur in clusters. The pattern is particularly evident in eighteenth-century Paris. In the four years from 1697 to 1700, there were conflicts among roofers, farriers, market-gardeners, potters and earthenware-makers, hatters and printers, in addition to the dispute in the carpentry trade.[74] The dispute in the Parisian farriers' corporation in 1720 was one of over a score of conflicts that occurred during the period of rapid inflation, followed by equally rapid deflation, associated with Law's financial system. In February 1720 a police official reported that journeymen in a large number of different trades had combined together (se mettent sur le pied de caballer ensemble) to force their masters to pay 'extraordinary' wages. Disputes among printers, engravers, gunsmiths, tinsmiths, sewermen, cardmakers, bakers, tanners and curriers, hatters, shoemakers and cobblers, upholsterers and carpet-weavers, painters, silk-weavers and framework knitters, as well as farriers, were testimony to the accuracy of the report.[75]

These clusters of disputes were a recurrent feature of the life of the trades throughout the century. In 1751 a wine merchant complained that his four garçons had walked out without notice. His case was taken up by the corporation, in order, it explained, to prevent what had happened among the painters, sculptors, hatters and locksmiths and several other corporations in recent years.[76] Among the other corporations in which disputes occurred between 1748 and 1751 were the wigmakers, joiners, cutlers, tinsmiths, bakers, bookbinders, saddlers, fancy bakers, boxmakers, engravers, roofers, shoemakers, nailmakers and gunsmiths. In 1765, the incumbent lieutenant général de police, de Sartine, authorised a request by the Parisian plumbers' corporation to increase the number of apprentices allowed to each master on the grounds that journeymen and workers in a number of corporations 'sont actuellement dans l'usage abusif de faire la loy aux maîtres des métiers'.[77] In the three years between 1763 and 1765, there had been disputes among glaziers, turners,

[72] A.N. AD XI 65, Précis pour les maréchaux de Paris (Paris, 1791).
[73] Details of conflicts can be found in the Appendix.
[74] B.N. MS fr. 8094 fol. 405 (3 May 1697); MS. fr. 8084 fol. 409 (4 July 1698); A.N. X²ª 508 (6 September 1700); Sonenscher, Hatters, pp. 82–3; A.N. Y 13 047 (27 March 1700); Y 13 888 (11 July 1701); Paul Chauvet, Les Ouvriers du livre en France, des origines à la Revolution de 1789 (Paris, 1959), pp. 142–7; B.N. F 44 776 (21 March 1701).
[75] Bibliothèque de l'Arsénal, MS. Bastille 10 321 (20 February 1720). For archival sources on these and the following conflicts, see Appendix.
[76] A.N. Y 9500 (13 August 1751).
[77] A.N. Y 9500 (13 August 1765).

toolmakers, saddlers, ribbon-weavers, bookbinders, gilders, painters, farriers, roofers, hatters, ropemakers, shoemakers, cardmakers and gunsmiths. The bookseller Hardy adopted a very similar tone in the spring of 1786 when he referred to 'une espèce de fermentation' among journeymen farriers, locksmiths, carpenters, printers, bakers and masons working in the capital. There were also disputes among stone-cutters, hatters, painters, joiners, silk-weavers, grocers, ropemakers, porters, framework knitters and carpet-weavers in 1785 and 1786.[78]

In all, 151 (66 per cent) of the 230 disputes in Paris that have left some surviving record occurred in 24 (17 per cent) of the 140 years between 1650 and 1790. The figure is, of course, no more than an approximation of the real incidence of conflict. It indicates, however, that even in years in which disputes were frequent conflicts occurred, on average, in no more than half a dozen trades. Yet the clustered pattern of conflict also seems to imply some common origin. In some cases, that common origin is relatively easy to identify. Disputes among painters and disputes in the saddlery trade frequently occurred in the same years (in the late 1740s, the 1760s and the early 1780s), because substantial sections of the workforces of both trades were employed in decorating and fitting out coaches.[79] Similar complementarities obtained among joiners and lock-smiths, and, more generally, among the many interdependent trades associated with building and furnishing. It is equally obvious, however, that such complementarities are incapable of supplying a full explanation of the incidence of conflict. Joiners had nothing in common with hatters, or gunsmiths with glaziers. Yet they, and many other groups of masters and journeymen were involved in chronologically synchronous, but occupationally unrelated, disputes on many occasions during the eighteenth century.

Despite many assumptions to the contrary, there is no conclusive evidence that clusters of conflict were closely related to fluctuations in the price of subsistence goods.[80] Although there is clear evidence of such a correlation during the cycle of conflicts between 1719 and 1725, when the inflationary effects of Law's paper currency generated a number of campaigns to raise wage-rates and an equally large number of attempts to cut them again when the system collapsed, that cycle of conflict, like the inflation that precipitated it, was exceptional in character. No other cluster

[78] B.N. MS. fr. 6685 fol. 315.
[79] See above, chapter 7, and Sonenscher, 'Journeymen, the Courts', pp. 87–8, 98–9.
[80] The thesis was formulated most emphatically by George Rudé, *The Crowd in the French Revolution* (Oxford, 1959), pp. 19–22, and in more muted form by Steven L. Kaplan, 'Réflexions sur la police du monde de travail, 1700–1815', *Revue historique*, 261 (1979), pp. 17–77 (especially pp. 33, 72). For a slightly different approach, see Gerard Gayot, 'La Longue Insolence des tondeurs de draps dans la manufacture de Sedan au xviiie siècle', *Revue du Nord*, 63, (1981), pp. 105–34.

of conflict can be explained satisfactorily in terms of pressure by consumers to raise wage-rates to meet higher expenditure on subsistence goods. If the years from 1747 to 1751 were years of relatively high, but stable, wholesale corn prices on the Parisian market, those between 1760 and 1765 were years when prices were falling.[81] They began to rise only in the last three months of 1765. Wholesale prices were falling too in 1785 and 1786, after an increase of some 27 per cent in 1784. Generally, there were as many conflicts in years in which prices were falling as those in which they were rising, and as many years in which prices were rising when there were very few conflicts at all.

If anything, there is a closer chronological fit between disputes in the Parisian trades and the years immediately following the end of wars. The five-year periods 1748–52, 1763–7 and 1783–7 saw a disproportionately large number of conflicts in the trades. It is possible that the rapid growth of credit that was the usual prelude to the end of a war, and the equally sharp restrictions upon credit that accompanied the end of post-war booms, exercised a more powerful effect upon both the volume of means of payment and levels of effective demand for the products of the urban trades than variations in corn prices may have done.[82] The multiplier effect of the revival of commerce, and the colonial trade in particular, even upon many non-textile trades, is a phenomenon that, given the available statistics, can only be deduced rather than measured. It is, at the least, a more promising candidate for a general explanation of conflict than the corn-led recessions that, it has been assumed, were, by way of falling disposable income, the effect of high corn prices upon manufacturing output.

It is probable, too, that variations in corn prices themselves were not entirely unrelated to either the availability of credit or to variations in the social distribution of money and other means of payment. The mechanisms of price formation in eighteenth-century France are still poorly understood, if only because the somewhat circular assumption that agricultural prices were a measure of the size of harvest yields has never (despite David Landes) been subjected to critical scrutiny.[83] Yet there was no significant

[81] Micheline Baulant, 'Le Prix des grains à Paris'; Steven L. Kaplan, *Bread, Politics and Political Economy in the Reign of Louis XV*, 2 vols (The Hague, 1976), vol. 1, pp. 236, 308–18: vol. 2, pp. 484–7.

[82] For a closely argued discussion of the interdependent effects of war and price movements upon theft in eighteenth-century England, see Douglas Hay, 'War, Dearth and Theft in the Eighteenth Century: The Record of the English Courts', *Past and Present*, 95 (1982), pp. 117–60. Hay's argument emphasises the sharp downturns, rather than the equally sharp upturns, that characterised economic life as wars reached their end. As a result, the argument treats prices as an independent variable rather than an effect of the credit inflation that accompanied rumours of peace.

[83] David Landes, 'The Statistical Study of French Crises', *Journal of Economic History*, 10 (1950), pp. 195–211. The whole question of price formation in eighteenth-century

relationship between harvest yields and price levels in early nineteenth-century France and there is no reason to suppose that conditions were any different before 1800. As more comes to be known about the relationship between harvest yields and price formation, it may be possible to replace the traditional corn-led model of the early modern economy by one in which monetary transfers and the availability of credit played a more significant part in the determination of prices.

The incidence of conflict in the trades of Bordeaux and Marseille also indicates an absence of any clear correlation between rising corn prices and disputes between masters and journeymen. In Bordeaux during the 40 years between 1750 and 1790 some 30 conflicts occurred in the 19 years in which wholesale corn prices were rising, while a further 37 conflicts took place in the remaining 21 years when prices were falling.[84] Figures of corn prices in Marseille are available only for the period between 1756 and 1770. Although prices were high in 1764, when there were disputes in the hatting, tailoring, saddlery and baking trades, the first of these disputes began in 1761 and there is no evidence that any of the other three conflicts owed anything to the effects of the rising pressure of prices upon either profits or wages.[85]

Substantial conflicts in the trades of cities like Bordeaux and Marseille (or Lyon, Rouen and Nantes) were too infrequent and too dependent upon the effects of conflict elsewhere for local fluctuations in price levels to have played anything other than a contingent part in determining their incidence. The interdependent character and the mobility of substantial sections of the workforces of trades like hatting, framework-knitting, shoemaking or even tailoring, whose markets were colonial and regional, meant that conflicts were transmitted from city to city as masters and journeymen were forced to redefine their relationship by the outcome of conflict elsewhere. The disputes in the hatting trades of Paris, Lyon and Marseille are a particularly clear example of the phenomenon.[86] Disputes in the shoemaking trades of Bordeaux, Marseille and Nantes, all of which produced for colonial as well as domestic markets, followed a similar pattern. The dispute in Paris that began early in 1763 was echoed in Bordeaux. Further conflict in Paris in 1769 and 1770 was matched by

France is in need of further thought. For the best point of departure, see E. A. Wrigley, 'Some Reflections on Corn-Yields and Prices in Pre-Industrial Economies, in his *People, Cities and Wealth* (Oxford, 1987), pp. 92–130. See too Jean-Yves Grenier, 'Questions sur l'histoire économique: les sociétés pré-industrielles et leurs rythmes', *Revue de synthèse,* 116 (1984), pp. 451–81, and his 'Modèles de la demande sous l'Ancien Régime', *Annales E.S.C.,* 42 (1987), pp. 497–527.

84 For a list of disputes in Bordeaux, see Appendix. On prices in Bordeaux, see Joseph Benzacar, *Le Pain à Bordeaux* (Bordeaux, 1905), pp. 15–23.

85 Corn prices in Marseille are printed in Georges Afanassiev, *Le Commerce des céréales en France au xviiie siècle* (Paris, 1894), p. 546. On disputes in the city's trades, see Appendix.

86 Sonenscher, *Hatters,* chapters 8–11.

conflict in Marseille and Bordeaux. A dispute in Bordeaux in 1775–6 was followed by one in Marseille in 1777. The American War and its aftermath saw conflicts in Nantes (1780, 1784, 1786), Bordeaux (1782) and Marseille (1781, 1783–6). Even if masters and journeymen in any one locality were entirely ignorant of circumstances elsewhere (and there is good evidence that they were not), the common pressures of war and the colonial trade overrode the local effects of changes in corn prices upon the economy of the trade.[87]

The hypothetical relationship between conflict and price fluctuations in urban France in the eighteenth century is, in sum, largely a false problem, not only because the mechanisms of price formation remain largely unknown, because wholesale prices were not retail prices, because most journeymen were not breadwinners, or even because the relationship between prices and conflict is not proven, but primarily because the argument itself is flawed. If it is possible to explain conflict in any particular trade in terms of variations in the wholesale price of corn (and conflict in the bakery trade would be the most obvious candidate), it does not follow that clusters of conflict in a number of trades can be explained in the same way. The frequency with which disputes in the trades tended to occur in parallel was not an effect of a common external cause, but, instead, was symptomatic of the cumulative character of conflict itself.[88] Although it would seem to be a tautology, conflicts were often the outcome of conflict. In Paris, or any other large eighteenth-century city, conflict in any particular trade was more likely to generate conflict in other trades than any independent variable was likely to do. Circular as the argument may seem, it does indicate that conflict, like innovation, was cumulative in character.

It is unnecessary to explain the cumulative character of conflict in purely psychological terms. Although it is perfectly possible that rumour and gossip played a part in sharpening latent tensions across a wide variety of different occupations, the composite character of civil jurisprudence, and the ordinary comparisons and precedents that it engendered, were sufficient in themselves to generate the clustered pattern of conflict that was so regular an occurrence in the eighteenth-century

[87] A.D. Gironde, C 1804: 12B 342 (24 April 1772), 352 (23 August 1775), 354 (19 January 1776); 355 (28 August and 30 September 1776); B (unclassified), arrêts (4 May 1772, 20 November 1775. 7 September 1776); 6E 49; A.C. Bordeaux, HH 83. A.C. Marseille, FF 378 (23 February, 19 and 26 July 1769); FF 387 (8 May 1777); FF 391 (18 May 1781); FF 394 (22 March 1785); FF 395 (25 July 1785); HH 404: A.D. Bouches-du-Rhône, 240E 26. A.C. Nantes HH 123 (7 October 1780, 5 August 1784, 9 September 1786); A.D. Ile-et-Vilaine, 1Bf 1500 (17 November 1780).

[88] I owe the analogy between innovation and conflict to Bernard Lepetit, 'Reseau urbain et diffusion de l'innovation dans la France pré-industrielle: la creation des caisses d'epargne, 1818–1848', in Bernard Lepetit and Jochen Hoock, eds., La Ville et l'innovation en Europe, 14e-19e siècles (Paris, 1987), pp. 131–57.

French trades. Three reasons can be advanced to explain why this was the case. The first was the relatively centralised system of legal decision making; the second was the relatively limited number of decisions that the courts could make; and the third was the way that decisions affecting any particular trade could have unforeseen implications for other trades. Together, they ensured that conflict tended to generate further conflict.

The unforeseen effects of legal decisions were particularly evident when the courts made detailed rulings on working conditions in particular trades. However limited they were intended to be, court rulings affecting any single trade could cause consternation among masters or journeymen in entirely different trades or give an unexpected legal advantage to one or other of the protagonists in disputes that had been simmering for many years. A dispute in the Parisian wheelwrights' trade that began in 1766 was precipitated by a ruling of the Parlement affecting working hours in the saddlery trade. A long drawn out dispute in the hatting trade of Lyon began when the hatters' corporation refused to comply with a ruling by the *consulat* in 1769 ordering it to meet with a deputation of journeymen to establish a new scale of piece-rates in the trade because, they argued, a dispute in the city's hosiery trade had recently ended in a ruling by the Parlement which explicitly prohibited journeymen hosiers from assembling to discuss piece-rates. A further ruling by the Parlement, in 1774, abolishing fixed scales of piece-rates in the hatting trade provoked a wave of alarm among the silk-weavers of Lyon, who began a campaign to maintain (and increase) the *tarif*, or fixed scale of piece-rates, established in the city's largest industry. The weavers' long campaign over the *tarif* was renewed in 1786 in the wake of a decision by the Parlement setting a fixed scale of piece-rates in the Parisian hatting trade. After the weavers' *révolte des deux sous* had been repressed in August 1786, a ruling by the Royal Council prohibiting all fixed scales of piece-rates was seized upon by the master masons of Lyon as a precedent entitling them to abolish a standard daily rate in the city's building trades.[89] Court rulings were as capable of precipitating conflict as they were of ending it.

[89] On the disputes in the Parisian saddlers' and wheelwrights' trades, see above, p. 90, and Sonenscher, 'Journeymen, the Courts', pp. 98–9. On the dispute in the hosiery trade of Lyon and its reverberations in the hatting trade, see A.N. X¹ᵃ 4662 fol. 83: 4674 (10 April 1770): 8200 (29 March 1770): 8213 (8 August 1770): 4695 (6 September 1770): X¹ᵇ 9765 (11 June 1771): A.N. F¹² 768. On subsequent reverberations among the silk-weavers of Lyon, see A.N. F¹² 1440. De Bellaize, *premier président du consulat de Lyon* to Turgot (28 March 1775): F¹² 1441: A.C. Lyon, HH 104. *Imprimés* 703.991. *Ordonnance consulaire* (27 July 1786): Albert Metzger and Joseph Vaesen, *Lyon de 1778 à 1788* (Lyon n.d.), p. 70. B.N. MS. Joly de Fleury 560 fol. 275, 'Lettre de Mgr l'Archeveque de Lyon, en réponse à quelques personnes qui lui avoient demandé des éclaircissements sur ce qui vient de se passer à Lyon' (Lyon, 24 August 1786): J. Beyssac, 'La Sédition ouvrière de 1786', *Revue d'histoire de Lyon*, 7 (1907) pp. 427–58 and in B.N. 4° LI 269. On subsequent conflict in the building trades, see A.D. Rhône, 3E 4727 (3 August 1786): 3E 4727 (27 August 1786): 3E 4728 (13 May 1787): A.N. X¹ᵇ 4271

The relatively centralised system of judicial provision affecting the trades meant that, while the number of sources of conflict in any particular trade was both large and unpredictable, the number of possible solutions was very much more limited. The *chambre de police* of the Châtelet in Paris, the *consulat* in Lyon, the *échevinage* in Marseille, the *capitouls* of Toulouse, or the *jurats* in Bordeaux each dealt in the first instance with disputes in the trades. Their local powers were complemented by the more extensive authority of the Parlements, which heard appeals from the lower courts and ratified any modifications or additions to corporate statutes. Both the lower courts and the Parlements were obliged to conform to their own jurisprudence in the decisions that they reached, while rulings by the Parlements or the Royal Council further restricted the range of decisions available to the lower courts. Even though the limited character of civil rights meant that any particular ruling was, in principle, applicable only to the trade or corporation in question, it was impossible to prevent masters or journeymen in other trades from using court rulings as precedents in arguments of their own.

The tension between the small number of institutions with responsibility for enforcing the provisions of corporate statutes, the institutional inertia engendered by the need to avoid legal innovation and conform to established jurisprudence, and the extremely heterogeneous range of circumstances that could provoke conflict in any particular trade, tended to ensure that no case could be dealt with entirely on its own merits, yet no uniform set of principles could be applied to the different legal entitlements of the various protagonists involved in them. The courts were obliged to negotiate a path between too close an identification with any particular trade and too loose an association with the trades as a whole. Consequently, any decision was often worse than no decision at all, for any particular outcome could become the basis of a chain of comparisons and precedents whose effects extended well beyond the circumstances that had precipitated the original dispute.

Matters were further complicated by the structural divisions that existed in the trades of most large cities. For obvious reasons, substantial conflicts between masters and journeymen centred upon the small number of

(7 September 1786): 4283 (8 April 1787): 4284 (28 April 1787): 3E 5264 (23 June 1787): A.C. Lyon, HH 104. *Imprimés* 703.981. *Mémoire à consulter et consultation pour les ouvriers, compagnons et manoeuvres maçons, platriers et tailleurs de pierre à Lyon* (Lyon, 1787). A full study of these conflicts has yet to be written. See, however, Louis Trénard, 'La Crise sociale lyonnaise à la veille de la Révolution', *Revue d'histoire moderne et contemporaine*, 2 (1955), pp. 5–45; David L. Longfellow, 'Silk Weavers and Social Struggle in Lyon during the French Revolution, 1789–1794', *French Historical Studies*, 12 (1981), pp. 1–40; Antonino De Francesco, *Il Sogno della Repubblica* (Milan, 1983). pp. 29–86; Bill Edmonds, 'A Study in Popular Anti-Jacobinism: The Career of Denis Monnet', *French Historical Studies*, 13 (1983), pp. 215–51; Sonenscher, *Hatters*, pp. 154–7; 'Journeymen, the Courts', pp. 94–6.

relatively large enterprises where the majority (or a large minority) of the workforce was employed. Decisions by employers like the Martin brothers in the painting and gilding trades of Paris, the shoemaker Paret in Marseille, the tailor Vandercruysse in Paris, Lyon and Marseille mattered not only of large hatting firms in Paris, Lyon and Marseille mattered not only because they employed a disproportionately large share of the workforce but also because the conditions of employment that they supplied were the basis of hierarchies of seniority and precedence among journeymen themselves.[90] Modifications to working arrangements, wage-payments, periods of notice or working hours by the small number of relatively substantial employers sent reverberations through whole trades not only because they affected other master artisans but also because they jeopardised the distinctions and informal hierarchies among journeymen that ensured that a sedentary core of the workforce remained in relatively regular employment until it was able to establish itself. Since only a small number of master artisans were regular and substantial employers of labour, the decisions they made were not necessarily those of the trade as a whole, yet their decisions formed a fulcrum around which different groups of master artisans and journeymen were obliged to adopt positions.

In these circumstances, recourse to the courts was capable of generating as many problems as it appeared to solve. Any ruling by the courts was a potential source of further conflict either between different sectors of the same corporate body or between masters and journeymen in quite different corporations. If the legal character of corporate statutes meant that substantial disputes between masters and journeymen tended to be drawn into the judicial system, the composite but centralised character of the system itself meant that magistrates had good reason to seek to avoid adjudicating on conflicts at all. In practice this situation gave rise to a number of attempts to find institutional ways of either preventing conflict from happening altogether or, if this was impossible, to provide corporations with sufficient powers to reduce the need to have recourse to external authority so that no legal precedent could impinge upon other trades.

INSTITUTIONAL SOLUTIONS

There were three possible institutional solutions to the problem of conflict in the trades. The first consisted of transferring almost all the powers of the courts to the corporations themselves. This procedure was followed in only two trades, both of which were markedly different from the majority of

---

[90] On local courts, see Jean-Marie Augustin, 'Les Capitouls, juges des causes criminelles et de police à la fin de l'Ancien Régime', *Annales du Midi*, 84 (1972), pp. 183–211; Jean Cavignac, 'Les Compagnonnages dans les luttes ouvrières au xviiie siècle', *Bibliothèque de l'Ecole des Chartes*, 126 (1968), pp. 377–411.

their urban counterparts. From the seventeenth century onwards, the printers' and barber–surgeon–wigmakers' corporations of Paris and every other substantial city were endowed with their own courts. These *chambres syndicales* were entitled to hear cases that, in other trades, fell within the competence of the local courts. Appeals from a *chambre syndicale*, however, went directly to the Royal Council rather than to one of the Parlements. Consequently the decentralisation of one level of the judicial process was nullified by the very much more considerable centralisation that obtained in the final instance.

The limited number of trades in which this solution was adopted is an indication that only special considerations allowed the Royal Council and the Parlements to contemplate transferring extensive judicial powers to the corporations. Both trades were objects of special concern to the royal government: the printers because they produced books; the wigmakers because their number also included the surgeons, the principal suppliers of medical care in the kingdom. Official control of the size of the printers' corporations ensured that, until 1776, the panoply of legal powers that they enjoyed was limited to no more than 36 employers in Paris and less than a dozen in the largest provincial cities. As the surgeons gradually differentiated themselves from the mass of barbers and wigmakers during the first half of the century, the legal powers that wigmakers had enjoyed were transferred to the surgeons, leaving the wigmakers' corporations with powers that were similar to those of any other corporation.[91] Given the size and the composite character of most corporations, especially in Paris, investing corporate officials with additional legal powers was an invitation to a flood of accusations of despotism from other master artisans which could only magnify the possibility of conflict within the corporations themselves.

One alternative to transferring most of the functions of the courts to the corporations was to abolish the corporations entirely. This was Turgot's solution in 1776 and the solution adopted by the Constituent Assembly in 1791. The Physiocratic attack upon the corporations was, in large measure, grounded upon an assumption that the discrepancy between the relatively small size of most corporations as compared to the large number of journeymen who came to work in big cities, and Paris in particular, was institutional in origin. The Physiocrats identified formal apprenticeship requirements as the chief source of division in the trades.[92] Apprenticeship

91 On the *chambre syndicale de la librairie*, see Paul Chauvet, *Les Ouvriers du livre*; on the surgeons, see Toby Gelfand, 'A "Monarchical Profession" in the Old Regime: Surgeons, Ordinary Practitioners and Medical Professionalization in Eighteenth-Century France', in Gerald L. Geison, ed., *Professions and the French State, 1700–1900* (Philadelphia, 1984), pp. 149–80.

92 Steven L. Kaplan, 'Social Classification and Representation in the Corporate World of Eighteenth-Century Paris: Turgot's "Carnival"', in Steven L. Kaplan and Cynthia Koepp, eds., *Work in France* (Ithaca, 1986), pp. 176–228.

regulations and the requirement that all but the sons of established members of a corporation should submit a *chef d'oeuvre* to qualify for admission were singled out as the principal cause of the restricted output, inflated prices and unnecessary conflict that, it was claimed, were endemic within the trades. The artificial advantages that apprenticeship conferred were symptomatic of the more general way that privilege, and the access to the courts that privilege supplied, created legal imbroglios that were themselves a source of political disorder and economic failure.

The attack upon apprenticeship as a public institution was the most successful and durable of the Physiocrats' achievements. Apprenticeship was abolished in February 1776 and, when the Parisian corporations were re-established in August of that year, the link between apprenticeship and admission to the corporations was all but severed. The new statutes of the Parisian corporations stipulated that anyone under 20 who could show that he had served an apprenticeship of four years was entitled to enter a corporation, while anyone over 25 was entitled to admission whether he had served an apprenticeship or not (provided, of course, that he could pay the other costs of entry).[93] Yet the abolition of the *chef d'oeuvre* and, for adults of 25 or more, of any formal prerequisite for admission to a corporation did not end conflict in the trades. The revised apprenticeship regulations created tensions between old and new members of the reorganised Parisian corporations, while the events of 1785–6 in Paris, Lyon and Marseille revealed that disputes between masters and journeymen were as frequent as they had been before 1776.[94]

The reduction in the number of formal obstacles to admission to the corporations could not eliminate the structural sources of conflict between masters and journeymen. Conflicts originated in the relationship between urban populations, urban labour markets and their effects upon the transfer of resources from one generation to the next, rather than in the public character of apprenticeship itself. Nor could easier entry to the corporations prevent appeals to external authority, for as long as the local

[93] A ruling by the *conseil d'état* of 25 March 1755 had earlier stipulated that anyone who had served an apprenticeship in any of the towns of the kingdom in which corporations existed ('où il y a jurande') was entitled to admission to a corporation anywhere else. It exempted Paris, Lyon, Lille and Rouen from its provisions. After 1776, and a *reglement* of 1 May 1782, apprenticeship was no longer a prerequisite for admission to even the Parisian corporations for men aged over 25: see *Encyclopédie méthodique. Jurisprudence*, vol. 9, under 'apprentissage'. On the effect of this modification to the entitlements that apprenticeship supplied, see, for example, the revised apprenticeship regulations of the Parisian joiners' corporation, or those of the cloth-dyers, fullers and croppers modelled upon those adopted by the engravers, butchers and *traiteurs*: A.N. X1b 4241 (20 August 1785); X1b 4289 (6 July 1787). It is hardly surprising, in the light of the ease of entry, that admissions to the corporations remained at a very high level until 1789: see above, p. 107.

[94] For tensions between old and new members of the Parisian goldsmiths' corporations, see Kaplan, "Turgot's Carnival", pp. 212–14, and, among painters, p. 241 above.

courts and the Parlements remained as interlocutors for masters and journeymen to use in their arguments, conflict in the trades was capable of generating further conflict. Contemporaries were well aware of the problem. Several individuals – all, significantly, master artisans rather than magistrates – made proposals to establish institutions with powers to arbitrate on disputes between masters and journeymen that were analogous to the nineteenth-century *conseils de prud'hommes* in all but name. The fragmented character of these local tribunals would, it was argued, confine argument to limited groups of masters and journeymen so that disputes would not spill over into whole trades and, by way of precedent and comparison, affect other trades as well.[95]

Without a major reorganisation of judicial institutions, the abolition of the corporations was a limited solution to the problem of conflict in the trades. For most of the eighteenth century there were powerful administrative and fiscal reasons for avoiding this course of action. The corporations were an intrinsic part of the highly decentralised system of tax-collection that was the basis of public finance.[96] Abolition of the corporations thus had as its corollary both a reorganisation of fiscal institutions and the creation of a much larger number of local judicial institutions if taxes were to continue to be collected and the established network of relatively centralised judicial provision was not to be swamped. Circumstances, of course, eventually favoured this particular outcome, but, until the Revolution, the difficulties attendant upon implementing this course of action were too great for it to be adopted.

For most of the eighteenth century, therefore, the most widely adopted solution to the problem of conflict in the trades was the establishment of corporate employment offices (*bureaux de placement*). A chronology and a geography of their dissemination would almost replicate the chronology and geography of conflict in the trades. Corporate employment offices were designed both to meet the structural problems of labour supply that lay behind disputes in the trades and, equally importantly, to provide corporations with additional legal powers to prevent journeymen from refusing to work for particular employers. By transferring decisions to find work to corporate institutions and penalising masters and journeymen who failed to meet the obligation to register with the employment office, the courts supplied individual employers and corporate officials with a powerful legal weapon to use against journeymen who refused to work for particular master artisans. Rigorously enforced, the legal obligations that

[95] For examples of such proposals, see Sonenscher, *Hatters*, pp. 147–8, and B.N. MS. Joly de Fleury 557 fol. 20.

[96] One of the best discussions of the relationship between the fiscal system and corporate institutions, in a rural context, can be found in Hilton L. Root, *Peasants and King in Burgundy. Agrarian Foundations of French Absolutism* (Berkeley, California, 1987).

accompanied the creation of corporate employment offices meant that the journeymen were faced with a choice between compliance or migration to another city. Not surprisingly, journeymen could very easily equate the creation of a *bureau de placement* with slavery.

There were some similarities between corporate labour exchanges and the *bureaux d'adresse* established in mid-seventeenth-century Paris on the initiative of the doctor Théophraste Renaudot and the *Compagnie du Saint-Sacrément* to supply work to the able-bodied poor.[97] Just as these charitable institutions required men of no fixed abode to register their names, place of birth and age with the administrators of the *bureaux d'adresse* or face arrest and punishment as vagabonds and *gens sans aveu*, so the regulations governing corporate labour exchanges required journeymen to register their names, ages and place of birth before they were entitled to work. Yet there were intrinsic difficulties in transposing the two-sided relationship between suppliers and recipients of charity to the three-sided relationship between corporations, journeymen and master artisans. Journeymen could well be treated as if they were recipients of charity and denied access to employment if they failed to register, but master artisans needed to employ journeymen as much as journeymen needed to work. There was, in other words, no automatic identity of interest between corporations and master artisans on the operation of corporate labour exchanges.

Corporate labour exchanges were therefore a potent source of division and conflict between corporate officials and master artisans as well as between masters and journeymen. If they were operated according to criteria of strict equity, they threatened to disrupt the unstable relationship between the core and periphery of local labour markets and prevent particular employers from paying higher advances or offering better wage-rates and conditions to the journeymen they needed. Strict adherence to the sequence of registration could disrupt the balance between particular tasks and particular types of ability – a problem that was bound to occur when many trades were made up of many different sectors. The creation of employment offices pushed corporations into areas of the trades in which they were not usually involved and forced their officials into the often unwelcome task of mediating between the rival claims of different employers for the journeymen they needed. Not surprisingly, many *bureaux de placement* were somewhat ephemeral institutions.[98]

[97] Jean-Pierre Gutton, *La Société et les pauvres: l'exemple de la généralité de Lyon, 1534–1789* (Paris, 1971), pp. 321–3; Emmanuel Chill, 'Religion and Mendicity in Seventeenth-Century France', *International Review of Social History*, 7 (1962), pp. 400–25.

[98] In addition to the divisions among the master tailors of Rouen over the creation of a *bureau de placement*, see A.C. Bordeaux HH 83, 'Observations essentielles pour les bayles de la communauté des maîtres cordonniers' (1776); A.C. Marseille, FF 206 (1765); A.C. Nantes, HH 116 (9 January 1770). The falling number of registrations at the office created in Tours in 1782 was probably typical of many others. See above, p. 100.

Above all, however, corporate employment offices threatened established hierarchies of seniority and precedence among journeymen. Even when formal statutory legislation endowing journeymen who had served an apprenticeship locally with precedence in local labour markets had been abolished or abandoned, informal hierarchies remained. Registration and access to employment by way of a corporate office was intrinsically incompatible with the last-in, first-out principle that allowed the core of sedentary journeymen to remain in regular employment in a particular city, and forced the periphery of migrants to continue on its way until local advantage and the gradual succession of generations created a niche within a particular sedentary core. Corporate labour exchanges were threats not only to the short-term advantages that some masters and journeymen could obtain from higher advances and better working arrangements, but to the more fundamental process of acquiring the network of kin, clients and credit that allowed journeymen to establish viable enterprises. At the same time, however, the intensity of the threat varied considerably. Irregular employers of large numbers of journeymen, or recent arrivals in large cities, had fewer reasons to regard labour exchanges with suspicion than regular employers of labour or sedentary journeymen with wives and families.

The care that corporations took in drafting the provisions of regulations establishing employment offices and the many revisions that they were forced to make, either by the courts or in the light of subsequent conflict, was a measure of the difficulty and delicacy of the issue.[99] Innumerable variations on the process of matching masters and journeymen were adopted and discarded. Journeymen were sometimes expected to present themselves at an office and told to go to a particular master's shop; alternatively, they might be allowed to find work themselves, but were required to register at the corporate office after a specified delay. A third possibility allowed journeymen to present themselves to any corporate official, whose responsibility it was to find them work. The question of

[99] As the *procureur général du Roi* at the Parlement of Bordeaux put it in 1757 as the court set about revising a decision by the city's locksmiths to establish a *bureau* in 1752: 'tel set le sort des loix en matière de police: de ne pouvoir prétendre à l'immutabilité des autres loix, étant de la nature de celles qui concernent la police de se proportionner toujours aux circonstances des tems': A.D. Gironde, B (unclassified) *arrêt* (20 September 1757). On other revisions and modifications to the workings of corporate employment offices, see Sonenscher, 'Journeymen, the Courts', pp. 95, 98–9; A.D. Rhône, 3E 6567 (4 January 1699); A.C. Lyon, HH 109 (12 December 1704); Bibliothèque de l'Arsénal, 8° J 4684 (*statuts des menuisiers de Lyon, sentence de police*, 24 March 1729); A.C. Nantes, HH 123 (5 August 1784); and, on variations in the procedures required of Parisian bakers in 1776, 1781 and 1785, Steven L. Kaplan, 'La Lutte pour le controle du marché du travail à Paris pendant le xviiie siècle', *Revue d'histoire moderne et contemporaine* (forthcoming, 1989).

whether journeymen should pay a fee for registration was a further, occasionally bitter, source of argument. The balance between equity and flexibility was as impossible to establish for master artisans. If master artisans were required to engage the men they employed through a corporate office, they ran the risk of having to defer to the claims of other masters, while if they were merely required to register the men they engaged, they ran the equally substantial risk of taking on too large a proportion of the available workforce.

Records of registration and employment presented equally intractable problems. The terms in which they were couched were either an invitation to litigation for defamation of character if they said too much, or an anodyne notation of the passage of time if they said too little.[100] If they remained in the possession of master artisans, they could be wilfully withheld, to a torrent of accusations of slavery and despotism; if they remained with journeymen, they could be equally wilfully lost or forged, reducing the whole exercise to a farce. Nor was it obvious what the penalties for failure to comply with any regulation might be, because it was not at all clear whether responsibility for failure lay with masters, or journeymen, or both, because neither had any inherent material reason for compliance with a regulation established by a third party, a corporation. Finally, since regulations governing the workings of corporate employment offices were necessarily collective in character, but violations were by individuals, any penalties were either superfluous (because breach of contract was already actionable) or of so general a character that they were threats to ordinary civil liberties. It was not easy to argue that a journeyman who failed to register with a corporate office and went to work for a particular master should be denied the right to work for any other master, particularly if he subsequently complied with the regulations and especially if he happened to be married and was domiciled in a city.

It is probable that the difficulties of devising legal formulae that were at once particular in character (because they pertained to a particular corporation) but susceptible to wider application (because the centralised system of judicial provision meant that any legal decision could become an unforeseen precedent) played a part in determining intervention by the royal government in the affairs of the trades. The secrecy with which decisions by the Royal Council were shrouded, and the absence of surviving ministerial papers, make it impossible to know why, early in January 1749, the king issued Letters Patent requiring journeymen and workers in what were termed 'les fabriques et manufactures du royaume'

[100] See the arguments made by Jean-Alexandre Martin and other members of the Parisian painters' corporation in their opposition to the establishment of a *bureau* in 1786: B.N. 4° Fm 20904 (especially pp. 45–54).

to carry a record of previous employment and prohibiting *cabales*.[101] It is possible that the ruling was a response to a number of disputes that had occurred in 1748. Work at Versailles had been disrupted by conflict between masters and journeymen in the Parisian painting and gilding trades. There had been a substantial dispute on the finishing side of the high-quality woollen industry of Sedan, and journeymen shear-croppers were under the impression the Letters Patent were directed specifically at them. There had also been a protracted dispute and a lock-out in the Parisian hatting trade in the autumn of 1748 and at least one master hatter was later convinced that the regulations had been introduced 'pour la police qui doit être observée dans les manufactures des chapeliers'.[102]

The Letters Patent of 1749 were registered by all the Parlements and were widely invoked in subsequent disputes in the French trades, but like all eighteenth-century French law, their studied vagueness allowed for much discretionary interpretation and many opportunities for litigation. Quite apart from the question of the meaning of the term *cabale*, the problem of deciding whether the term *manufactures* referred to the production of any artefact, the production of textiles, or production carried out in one of the *manufactures royales* was inherently impossible to resolve. In this sense, despite their explicitly general aims, the Letters Patent of 1749 belonged to the discretionary tradition of arbitrary authority. Yet although they merely reinforced the practice of particular courts and left them considerable interpretative latitude, the general character of the Letters Patent marked a significant break with the exceptional and limited nature of legal provision as it applied to the trades and ensured that positive law played a greater part in rulings by the courts.[103]

The effects of the Letters Patent upon subsequent jurisprudence were reinforced by the growing reluctance of the courts to recognise formal distinctions among journeymen. From the middle of the eighteenth century at the latest, no court was prepared to rule that journeymen who had served an apprenticeship locally were entitled to preferential access to employment over journeymen from elsewhere. Journeymen's con-

[101] The text is printed, under its date, in Francois André Isambert et al., eds., *Receuil général des anciennes lois françaises*, 29 vols (Paris, 1822–33). Summaries can be found in Emile Levasseur, *Histoire des classes ouvrières et de l'industrie en France avant 1789* (Paris, 1901), vol. 2, pp. 510–11, 669.

[102] There were also disputes among silk-weavers in Tours (A.D. Indre, C 103) and a lockout organised by employers in the linen and fustian trades of Rouen (A.C. Rouen, Tiroir 298, 29 July 1748). On the dispute among painters, see above, chapter 7; on wool-croppers in Sedan, see Gayot, 'La Longue Insolence'; and, on hatters, A.N. Y 11 466 (11 March 1750).

[103] For some examples of interpretative rulings by the courts, see J. B. Denisart, *Collection de decisions nouvelles et de notions relatives à la jurisprudence actuelle*, 7th edn (Paris, 1771), under 'ouvriers'; 9th edn (Paris, 1786), under 'compagnon'; Guyot, *Répertoire universel et raisonné de la jurisprudence civile, criminelle, canonique et bénéficiale* (Paris, 1784–5), under 'compagnon'; *Gazette des Tribunaux*, 11 (Paris, 1781), p. 323.

fraternities were also treated with very much greater circumspection by the civil authorities, partly because of the provisions of the Letters Patent themselves, but equally because of journeymen's confraternities were the (probably unintended) victims of the Jansenist sympathies of the magistracy (especially the magistrates of the Parlement of Paris) and their successful campaign against the Jesuits, culminating in the expulsion of the order from France in 1763. The Parlement's decision in 1760 to order all confraternities to register their titles with the secular authorities or face dissolution appears to have contributed substantially to the gradual disappearance of journeymen's confraternities from public life in Paris and the other cities that fell within the jurisdiction of the court. Although they remained in existence in other parts of France, and in Marseille in particular, confraternities of Parisian journeymen disappeared from the visible life of the trades during the third quarter of the eighteenth century. [104]

The Letters Patent of September 1781, ratified by the Parlement of Paris in January 1782 and by the other Parlements during the following months, marked something of a departure from previous royal legislation. They repeated the earlier prohibition of *cabales* and required all those employed in the trades to carry a *livret*. In itself, there was nothing new in the practice of requiring journeymen to have printed certificates which were both a record of identity and employment – the novelty lay in the Letters Patent's relative precision and range. All journeymen working in towns where there were corporations were required to register with the municipal authorities and masters were given a model certificate to be used to testify to the satisfactory completion of periods of employment. The Letters Patent made no distinction between journeymen of different kinds. Their influence can be gauged from a ruling by the Parlement of Paris in 1784 during a dispute in Blois which centred upon the question of whether journeymen were required to register and carry *livrets*. Four master masons who had been convicted of employing men without certificates appealed to the Parlement on the grounds that the journeymen in question were employed by the month rather than the day, and were not peripatetic migrants but were domiciled in Blois. The court dismissed their appeal because, it stated, there was no distinction between men engaged by the day or the week and what it termed 'ordinary journeymen'. [105]

[104] On the context in which the Parlement's ruling was made, see Dale Van Kley, *The Jansenists and the Expulsion of the Jesuits from France, 1757–1765* (New Haven and London, 1975), pp. 85, 87; and, on the disappearance of confraternities from Parisian public life, Garrioch and Sonenscher, '*Compagnonnages*, Confraternities', pp. 38–41.

[105] *Gazette des Tribunaux*, 22 (Paris, 1786), p. 184. For other examples of the increasingly narrow range of legal intervention, see Sonenscher, 'Journeymen, the Courts', pp. 98–9 and *Hatters*, chapters 10 and 12. On the general decline of litigation during the latter half

The Letters Patent of 1781 confirmed and reinforced the diminished status of the corporations in public affairs. There were a number of reasons for this change of status. The gradual creation of a system of public finance which looked increasingly to landed wealth as its principal source of revenue and the international financial markets as its principal source of credit may have been partly responsible for the process. For the corporations were public institutions, whose existence was intimately related to the financial needs of the royal government (which was why, when they were abolished in March 1791, the process was handled by the National Assembly's *comité des contributions publiques* and its *rapporteur*, Pierre Gilbert Leroy, baron d'Allarde).[106] Their development during the sixteenth and seventeenth centuries was inseparable from the development of a system of public finance which was devolved upon a variety of semi-autonomous institutions and offices. As the financial function of these bodies became less important, the courts and the royal government had less reason to concern themselves with the particularities of corporate regulation and corporate identity.

In a more obvious way, the development of rural industry was a further limitation upon the legal authority of the corporations. This was explicitly recognised by the judicial officials and administrators responsible for preparing the Letters Patent of 1781.[107] From the early 1760s, when the Crown issued a series of edicts positively encouraging the development of industry in the countryside, it was apparent that the jurisdiction of the corporations could not encompass the scores of dispersed localities in which textile production, in particular, had become established.[108] The Letters Patent of 1781 were a recognition of the need to create a simpler,

of the eighteenth century, see Colin Kaiser, 'The Deflation in the Volume of Litigation at Paris in the Eighteenth Century and the Waning of the Old Judicial Order', *European History Review*, 10 (1980), pp. 309–36. .

[106] Elizabeth Fox-Genovese, *The Origins of Physiocracy* (Ithaca, 1976); *René Nigeon, Etat financier des corporations parisiennes d'arts et métiers au xviiie siècle* (Paris, n.d.); J. F. Bosher, *French Finances 1770–1795. From Business to Bureaucracy* (Cambridge, 1970); Herbert Lüthy, *La Banque protestante en France de la Révocation de l'Edit de Nantes à la Révolution*. 2 vols (Paris, 1959–61); B. Chevalier, 'Corporations, conflits politiques et paix sociale en France aux XIVe et XVe siècles', *Revue historique*, 268 (1982), pp. 17–44. David D. Bien, 'Offices, Corps and a System of State Credit: The Uses of Privilege under the Ancien Régime', in Keith M. Baker, ed., *The Political Culture of the Old Régime* (Oxford, 1987), pp. 89–114.

[107] A.N. F[12] 654. 'Observations sur la police à établir entre les fabricans et les ouvriers des manufactures'; Harold T. Parker, *The Bureau of Commerce in 1781 and its Policies with Respect to French Industry* (Durham, North Carolina, 1979).

[108] The *arrêts* in question were on 7 September 1762, 13 February 1765 and 28 February 1766. Printed copies of the texts can be found in the University of Chicago Library, John Crerar Collection (883, 887, 888); see also Archives départementales de la Somme, C 245. The problem had already arisen in the context of rural industry in the vicinity of Rouen (A.N. F[12] 654). On the campaign of liberalisation of the 1760s, see Steven L. Kaplan, *Bread, Politics and Political Economy in the Reign of Louis XV*. 2 vols (The Hague, 1976).

but more extensive, regulatory code than the plethora of corporate regulation was able to supply.

Finally, and most importantly, they were designed to fill the legal hiatus created by Turgot's abolition of the corporations in 1776, and their subsequent resurrection and reorganisation thereafter. In this, the provisions of the Letters Patent were very similar to those of a series of police sentences ratifying deliberations by the reorganised Parisian corporations after 1776. Since both the *procureur général* of the Parlement of Paris and the *lieutenant général de police* were involved in drafting both the Letters Patent and the regulations of the Parisian corporations, their tenor was very similar. Both were designed to establish a framework of legal provision for the trades in the aftermath of Turgot's experiment. The edict re-establishing the corporations in August 1776 explicitly confirmed the abolition of the mass of court rulings that had made up the *police des arts et métiers*. All that remained of the multitude of particular regulatory decisions and legal verdicts were the Letters Patent of 1749.[109] Turgot's reform and its aftermath made it necessary to devise a form of legal regulation that was more precise than the Letters Patent of 1749 and would supply a basis for legal adjudication of rights and obligations in the very much smaller number of corporations created after 1776. In Paris the number of corporations was reduced from over 110 to 44. Their new regulations governing relations between masters and journeymen took the form of a series of police sentences ratifying a number of highly standardised corporate deliberations based upon a uniform model and which invariably included a requirement that journeymen should have *livrets*.[110] The Letters Patent of 1781 merely extended their provisions to the kingdom as a whole.

The amalgamation and reduction of the number of corporations after 1776 also made the need for recognition of particularity in legal rulings less evident. Many corporations were already composite bodies. Even at the best of times, there was no close relationship between a corporation's title and what its members actually did. Once most corporations housed a number of different trades, as they did after 1776, legal provision could do no more than supply a definition of the broad terms of the contract of employment. Anything else was unworkable, unless the full gamut of particular corporations was to be restored. In these circumstances, legislation such as the Letters Patent of 1781 was little more than an acknowledgement of the *status quo*. The step from their broad provisions

[109]　The texts of the edicts are printed in Alfred Franklin, *Dictionnaire historique des arts, métiers et professions* (Paris, 1906), pp. 780–92. See also Steven L. Kaplan, "Turgot's Carnival".

[110]　For examples of printed copies of such rulings ratifying corporate deliberations by the *paulmiers, boulangers, cordonniers, faienciers, gantiers, arquebusiers, serruriers and charcutiers* respectively, see B.N., F 21 210 (40); F 23 717 (463); University of Chicago Library, John Crerar Collection (1398–1401, 1403, 1411).

to the positive law of the Civil Code, and the development of a sphere of jurisprudence concerned with labour in general, was a small one.[111]

The Allarde and Le Chapelier laws of 1791 were therefore extensions of a process that was already underway.[112] They emptied the public domain of the particularities of the law as it pertained to specific trades. The multiple concerns of masters and journeymen in specific trades were consigned to private transaction and, in the nineteenth century, to the adjudication and arbitration of individual cases by the *conseils de prud'hommes*.[113] Yet the reconfiguration of institutions that took place, first in 1776, and then during the Revolution, had one particularly significant effect: it established a much greater distance between the world of the trades and the world of the courts. Until the Revolution, disputes in the trades occurred in a context in which all those involved acted in the knowledge that their interlocutors were not only their immediate opponents but the lawyers and magistrates responsible for the *police des arts et métiers*. After 1789 that situation changed – lawyers and magistrates were no longer interlocutors in conflicts in the trades. The institutional transformation that took place during the Revolution meant that, in conflict of a collective character, masters and journeymen had only each other as their interlocutors, and a wider public of other masters and journeymen as a more distant audience.

It has sometimes been said that during the nineteenth century the customary relationship between masters and journeymen gradually gave way to more finely calculated bargaining over wages and working conditions because journeymen were slow to learn the rules of the market-based game.[114] Yet the difference between conflict in the eighteenth-century trades and their nineteenth-century counterparts was not one in which there was a new game to be learned. By the early nineteenth

[111] Texts of the basic legislation are printed in C. Schmitt, *Industrie: receuil de textes et de notes*, in *Commission de recherche et de publication des documents rélatifs à la vie économique de la Révolution* (Paris, 1910).

[112] The texts of the Allarde and Le Chapelier Laws are printed in J. M. Thompson, *French Revolution Documents* (Oxford, 1948), pp. 82–6. For the implications of these changes, see the Conclusion, below.

[113] On nineteenth-century labour law, see, with reservations, Theodore Zeldin, *France 1848–1945* (Oxford, 1973), vol. 1, pp. 198–209; André Castaldo, 'L'Histoire juridique de l'article 1781 du Code Civil', *Revue historique de droit français et étranger*, 55 (1977), pp. 211–37; and Alain Cottereau, 'Les Réglements d'atelier au cours de la révolution industrielle en France', in Anne Biroleau, *Les Réglements d'ateliers 1798–1936* Bibliothèque nationale, Département des Livres Imprimés, Collection 'Etudes, Guides et Inventaires' (Paris, 1984). On the *conseils de prud'hommes* (the first was established in Lyon in 1806) see Paul Delsalle, 'Le livret ouvrier et les conflits de travail dans la région de Roubaix-Tourcoing', in Paul Delsalle, ed., *L'Industrie textile en Europe du Nord aux XVIIIe et XIXe siècles* (Tourcoing, 1984) and his *La Brouette et la navette* (Dunkerque, 1985). For a revised view of their importance, see the special issue of *Le Mouvement social*, 141 (1987) on 'Les Prud'Hommes XIX–XX Siècle'.

[114] E. J. Hobsbawm, 'Customs, Wages and Work-Load', especially pp. 412–13.

century the rules of the game had changed, not because the game itself was different but because the institutional framework within which it was conducted was no longer the same. Conflict in the nineteenth-century trades took place in an environment in which neither employers nor workers could have recourse to the civil courts to sanction their claims or promote their objectives. This transformation in the formal situation of the actors in conflicts had several implications. The vocabulary of natural law, with its allusions to slavery, tyranny, natural liberty and natural rights, had very much less purchase in either a narrow, legalistic sense, or in the looser, metaphorical sense in which it was used by masters and journeymen in ordinary argument in the eighteenth century. The Revolution was a turning point in the history of the trades because it destroyed the legal institutions that, whether they willed it or not, had supplied masters and journeymen with a vocabulary to articulate their respective positions and a range of procedures to follow in the course of their disputes.

Disputes in the trades of early nineteenth-century France occurred in an environment in which all the protagonists were very much more dependent upon their own resources. One such resource was made up of the claims of corporate solidarity and fraternity. It is not surprising, therefore, that invocations of trade solidarity and an idiom of corporate identity should have come into their own in the nineteenth century.[115] It was not, however, the only rhetorical resource available to the protagonists in conflicts in the trades. In different ways the many ideals of community associated with republicanism, freemasonry, mutual aid and even the *compagnonnages* could be used by employers and workers to invoke solidarities that were the more imperative because external sources of authority were no longer available to impose unacceptable goals upon unwilling opponents and reluctant allies.

In the eighteenth century masters and journeymen conducted their arguments in terms of slavery and liberty rather than solidarity and fraternity because such solidarities as they needed were provided in substantial measure by the common character of the entitlements that they enjoyed and the small number of legal institutions that supplied them. However much the rhetoric of trade solidarity and particularity of the early nineteenth century might appear to echo the language of the eighteenth-century corporate world, the novelty of voluntary association was none the less very much more significant. Nor, of course, were such associations confined to waged workers. Employers formed their own associations in a growing number of trades. Divested of the public character of corporate institutions, they continued to address the structural problems inherent in

115 Sewell, *Work and Revolution*, especially pp. 162–93.

the economy of the bazaar: the relationship between creditors and debtors, the ownership of copyright in design, the maintenance of adequate supplies of materials, and, of course, conflict in the trades.[116] When masters and journeymen could no longer turn to the courts to accuse one another of illegally exceeding formal rights and legal entitlements – *en faisant la loi* despite the provisions of the law itself, as the usual phrase went – they had only their own unity and strength of purpose to fall back upon. The many ideal communities that they invoked were a measure of the importance of a new quest for collective identities and resources.

[116] On employers' associations in nineteenth-century Paris, see Andrew Lincoln, 'Le Syndicalisme patronal à Paris de 1815 à 1848: une étape de la formation d'une classe patronale', *Le Mouvement Social*, 114 (1981), pp. 11–34.

CHAPTER 9

Journeymen's migrations and the mythology of the 'compagnonnages'

Fewer than a fifth of the journeymen employed in the building, furnishing, clothing and victualling trades of eighteenth-century France had been born in the towns in which they worked.[1] Most journeymen, therefore, were migrants of one kind or another. Some of them (perhaps as many as 50 per cent) were men who had been born in small towns or villages and, at the age of 13 or 14, had been sent to larger cities to serve an apprenticeship. The remainder (perhaps a further 30 per cent) were itinerant journeymen who had learned a trade or served an apprenticeship in one locality but had set out to find work elsewhere. Despite the plethora of legislation affecting vagrants, beggars and the poor of early modern France, no formal obstacles (like the English settlement laws) prevented men and women from leaving the towns or villages in which they were domiciled to find work in other localities.[2] The short duration of most periods of employment and the seasonal cycles of the local economies of many trades meant that many migrant journeymen travelled widely over what came to be known as the *tour de France*. Few of them remained in a single locality for long enough to have much reason to belong to established journeymen's confraternities.[3] Yet impermanence did not prevent many of them from creating their own networks of association.

The first and most readily available form of association was supplied by common geographical origin. Towards the end of the nineteenth century,

[1] The proportions are, of course, guesses based upon the information discussed in chapter 4. In none of the trades examined there was the proportion of native journeymen higher than 20 per cent, and in most of them it was well below ten per cent.

[2] On legislation affecting the poor, see Olwen Hufton, *The Poor of Eighteenth-Century France* (Oxford, 1974); Jean-Pierre Gutton, *La Société et les pauvres: l'exemple de la généralité de Lyon, 1534–1789* (Paris, 1971); Colin Jones and Michael Sonenscher, 'The Social Functions of the Hospital in Eighteenth-Century France: The Case of the Hôtel-Dieu of Nîmes', *French Historical Studies*, 13 (1983), pp. 172–214. For a recent survey of English legislation and institutions, see Joanna Innes, 'Prisons for the Poor: English Bridewells, 1555–1800', in Douglas Hay and Francis Snyder, eds, *Law, Labour and Crime in Historical Perspective* (London, 1987).

[3] On journeymen's confraternities, see Garrioch and Sonenscher, '*Compagnonnages*. Confraternities'; Sonenscher, *Hatters*, chapter 7 and above, chapter 3.

Martin Nadaud, who began his long and varied life as a migrant building worker, recalled how migrants from the Creuse (where he had been born) who came to work in Paris were known as either *Brulas* or *Bigaros*. The former were men from the region of La Souterraine, the Grand-Bourg or Dun; the latter were from the area around Vallière, Saint-Sulpice-les-Champs or Pontarion. 'Un maître compagnon ou un appareilleur *Bigaro* se serait bien gardé d'embaucher des *Brulas*,' he noted.[4] Regional loyalties and rivalries of this kind were the basis of well-established patterns of informal association not only among itinerant workers but among all those, who, for one reason or another, were far from their *pays* and the resources that kin, neighbours or local knowledge supplied. Regional origin was the most obvious point of contact among strangers. In eighteenth-century France, the idiom of the *pays* was shared by soldiers, criminals and journeymen alike.[5]

The *compagnonnages* were a very different form of association. Although they were established by journeymen who were often long distances from home, they transcended the particularities of place or region, and subsumed regional origin within a wider idiom of association modelled upon the ceremonies of the church and the courts. They encompassed a large number of trades, but flourished mainly in sectors of the urban economy in which elaborate divisions of labour and extensive geographical migrations meant that itinerant journeymen had access to information about employment and working conditions from many different sources, and were able to use the skills that they had acquired in many overlapping occupations. The distinctive ceremonial of the *compagnonnages* was most ubiquitous in the building, furnishing and clothing trades, and in provincial cities located along the principal axes of geographical migration: from Troyes southwards towards Dijon, Mâcon, Lyon and Marseille, westwards towards Nîmes, Montpellier, Toulouse and Bayonne, northwards to Bordeaux, La Rochelle and Nantes and eastwards along the valley of the Loire towards Angers, Tours and Orléans. The heterogeneous range of occupations encompassed by the *compagnonnages* was, at least in part, an expression of the ease with which information could be transmitted between different branches of the division of labour, particularly in the building and furnishing trades. The many local, or trade-specific, variations upon the cluster of rituals that fell under the rubric of the *compagnonnages* allowed journeymen who were far from

[4]   Martin Nadaud, *Mémoires de Léonard, ancien garçon maçon*, ed. Maurice Agulhon (Paris, 1976), p. 145.

[5]   On soldiers and civilian life, see Colin Jones, 'The Welfare of the French Foot-Soldier', *History*, 214 (1980), pp. 193–213; André Corvisier, *L'Armée française de la fin du xviie siècle au ministère de Choiseul: le soldat*, 2 vols (Paris, 1964), especially the section on *noms de guerre*. On the ubiquity of the idiom of *pays* among criminals see Hufton, *The Poor*, chapter 9.

home to limit access to the information that the division of labour supplied. Ritual served to create a measure of order and difference within the fluid world of the urban trades of eighteenth- and early nineteenth-century France.

The existence of the *compagnonnages* first came to light towards the middle of the seventeenth century, when a Parisian shoemaker named Henri Buch denounced a number of journeymen to the very Catholic Company of the Holy Sacrament for performing blasphemous ceremonies of initiation into a clandestine association known as the *devoir*. The Company initiated criminal proceedings against the journeymen and brought their ceremonies to the attention of the Doctors of the Faculty of Theology of the Sorbonne.[6] In 1655, the Faculty issued a resolution condemning journeymen in five Parisian trades – tailors, hatters, saddlers and cutlers, as well as shoemakers – for practising heretical ceremonies of initiation into the *devoir*. In various forms, the pattern of association by initiation which characterised the *devoir* was a continuous, and increasingly widely reported, part of the life of the French trades between the mid-seventeenth and the mid-nineteenth century.

6 The ruling is printed in Emile Coornaert, *Les Compagnonnages en France du moyen âge à nos jours* (Paris, 1966), pp. 350–4. See also Raoul Allier, *La Cabale des dévots* (Paris, 1902) and Emmanuel S. Chill, 'The Company of the Holy Sacrament: Social Aspects of the French Counter-Reformation', (unpublished Ph. D. thesis, Columbia University, 1960), pp. 126–38. On the *compagnonnages*, see E. J. Hobsbawm, 'Ritual in Social Movements', in his *Primitive Rebels* (London, 1959); Sewell, *Work and Revolution*, and, particularly, Cynthia M. Truant, 'Solidarity and Symbolism among Journeymen Artisans', *Comparative Studies in Society and History*, 21 (1979), pp. 214–26; Jean Lecuir, 'Associations ouvrières de l'époque moderne: clandestinité et culture populaire', *Revue du Vivarais* (special issue on *Histoire et clandestinité du Moyen Age à la Première Guerre Mondiale*, Albi, 1979), pp. 273–90. There are several older accounts of the *compagnonnages*. The fullest, and in many ways the least tendentious, remains E. Martin Saint-Léon, *Le Compagnonnage* (Paris, 1901); Emile Coornaert, *Les Compagnonnages en France*, contains a valuable selection of documents, but its value is limited by its author's neglect of the usual apparatus of notes and bibliography. Coornaert, in particular, assumes that all forms of association created by journeymen were really *compagnonnages*. See too Henri Hauser, *Les Compagnonnages d'arts et métiers à Dijon aux xviie et xviiie siècles* (Paris, 1907); Germain Martin, *Les Associations ouvrières au xviiie siècle (1700–1792)* (Paris, 1900); Emile Levasseur, *Histoire des classes ouvrières et de l'industrie avant 1789*, 2 vols (Paris, 1900). For one attempt to come to terms with their ritual, see Mary Ann Clawson, 'Early Modern Fraternalism and the Patriarchal Family', *Feminist Studies*, 6 (1980), pp. 368–91. See, for comparison, Andreas Griessinger, *Das symbolisches Kapital der Ehre* (Frankfurt, 1981), and, for an attempt at a comparative study (which does not, however, deal with ritual) Ulrich-Christian Pallach, 'Fonctions de la mobilité artisanale et ouvrière – compagnons, ouvriers et manufacturiers en France et aux allemands (17e–19e siecles)', *Francia*, 11 (1983), pp. 365–406. The *compagnonnages* still exist; for an account of their recent history, see Christian Faure, 'Vichy et la "rénovation" de l'artisanat: la réorganisation du compagnonnage', *Bulletin du centre d'histoire économique et sociale de la région lyonnaise*, 3–4 (1984), pp. 103–19. What follows is a modified version of Michael Sonenscher, 'Mythical Work: Workshop Production and the *Compagnonnages* of Eighteenth-Century France', in Patrick Joyce, ed., *The Historical Meanings of Work* (London, 1987). I am greatly indebted to Cynthia Truant for her comments on that paper. Her own study of the *compagnonnages* will be a very much more definitive account.

Much of the ceremony of the *compagnonnages* was very mysterious. This was not, of course, an accident – mystery was one of the hallmarks of the *compagnonnages* from the mid-seventeenth century onwards. Yet the significance of the mystery with which the *compagnonnages* were invested can be approached in several ways. Mystery can be a veil concealing a more substantial reality, or a performance that creates or recreates a reality that might otherwise not exist. The distinction is, of course, one of degree rather than kind, but it is more helpful to approach the ceremonial of the *compagnonnages* from the latter point of view rather than the former. For the significance of mystery for the journeymen initiated into the *compagnonnages* lay in what they sought to create, rather than in what they attempted to conceal. What they created was a complex world of ephemeral distinctions.

There were good reasons why such distinctions mattered greatly in the everyday life of many eighteenth-century trades. There were also good reasons why they should be ephemeral. In a world in which the range of materials used in many trades, and the levels of competence required to manipulate them did not vary greatly, mystery supplied a vocabulary of distinction when legal rights did not. The ceremonial of the *compagnonnages* provided an informal counterpoint to the legal rights enjoyed by some journeymen. As these legal rights gradually disappeared, ritual enabled journeymen to create their own ephemeral hierarchies and distinctions to meet the complex schedules of the workshop economy. The golden age of the *compagnonnages*, which ran from the mid-eighteenth century to the July Monarchy, coincided with the redefinition of the relationship between the law and the trades that took place in the wake of the Royal Letters Patent of 1749 and 1781 and the reorganisation of the corporations in 1776.

The ritual of the *compagnonnages* complemented several of the structural features of the eighteenth-century French trades: the wide diffusion of a relatively limited range of skills in many urban trades; the absence of clear occupational distinctions among many of the journeymen who worked upon the relatively small number of materials used in many trades; the large number of towns (larger than in any other territorial state in Europe at the time) in which many trades were practised; the elaborate divisions of labour and relatively short periods of employment associated with the production of many of the objects and artefacts consumed in eighteenth-century France; and the gradual erosion of the legal provisions that distinguished the formal rights of journeymen in some urban centres from others. The ceremonial of the *compagnonnages* was a commentary upon a world in which the work that people did was often very similar. The point, however, was to make it appear to be different.

The *compagnonnages* emerged from clandestinity in the early nineteenth century. In 1821, Charles Evérat, a member of the *société philanthropique de Paris* recalled how, after the publication of Sir Frederick Morton Eden's *Inquiry into the State and Present Condition of the Poor* (1797), the society had decided to investigate whether the French capital contained any equivalent to the English Friendly Societies upon which Eden had lavished such praise. A sub-committee of the society had been established in 1804 and, after three months' work, its president, the political economist Pierre Samuel Dupont de Nemours, reported the discovery of 28 mutual aid societies, or *sociétés de prévoyance*.[7] He also stated that there were other types of society in existence in the capital, and mentioned that journeymen carpenters and joiners were known to belong to an association known as the *devoir* which could be found all over France.

As Evérat recalled, it had been impossible to discover anything more about the *devoir*.[8] He proceeded none the less to describe the internal organisation of the elusive association. To become what was known as a *compagnon du devoir* an initiate was first required to have been a *gavaud*, a term, Evérat reported, that was equivalent to the masonic word 'apprentice'. One then passed to the rank of what was called a *drille* and, after a further period, to that of *renard*. From this grade one moved to the most prestigious of all ranks, that of *compagnon du devoir*. A *compagnon du devoir* was identified easily, Evérat claimed, by the long stave that he carried on his travels around the country on the celebrated *tour de France*; those on the lower grades of the hierarchy were allowed to bear only short batons. Finally, a *compagnon du devoir*, like the freemasons, was acquainted with a number of secret passwords.

Evérat's presentation of the *compagnonnages* as a monolithic, quasi-masonic association was, of course, completely wrong. In 1839 something of their real identity emerged when the journeyman joiner Agricol Perdiguier published his *Livre du Compagnonnage*.[9] Instead of the quasi-masonic hierarchy of grades that Evérat had imagined, Perdiguier revealed that the *compagnonnages* consisted of three relatively distinct groupings, distinguished from one another by their insignia, their rituals and, most fundamentally, by their different origins in a mythical history that began on the site of Solomon's Temple. The first and, according to Perdiguier, most senior of the associations, or rites, were the *enfants de Salomon*. They were the descendants of the stone-cutters and masons who had

[7] Bibliothèque historique de la ville de Paris 4371, *Rapport de la société philanthropique de Paris*, an xiii (Paris, 1805).

[8] 'On nous avoit parlé des compagnons de devoir, qu'on disait exister dans la classe des menuisiers et autres ouvriers en bois. Les menuisiers eux-mêmes nous ont declaré n'en avoir qu'une connaissance très imparfaite. Nous nous sommes informés dans les autres professions, et personne, jusqu'à present, n'a pu ou n'a voulu nous donner des renseignements sur ce compagnonnage. Il est couvert d'un voile impénétrable. C'est probablement une espèce de franc-maçonnerie qui échappera toujours à nos investiga-tions.' *Ibid*, Report of 1821.

[9] Agricol Perdiguier, *Le Livre du compagnonnage* (Paris, 1839).

constructed Solomon's Temple as described in the *Book of Kings*. They were also called *gavots, compagnons étrangers, loups, renards* or, in the nineteenth century, *compagnons du devoir de liberté*.

The second rite consisted of the *enfants de maître Jacques*, descended, it was said, from a master craftsman who had organised the construction of Solomon's Temple before leaving Judea to sail to France. They were also known as *compagnons du devoir, devoirants, compagnons passants* or *loups garous*. The third association was made up of the followers of another master craftsman, the *père* Soubise. He too had worked upon Solomon's Temple and had sailed to France with *maître* Jacques. After their arrival, there had been a quarrel and Soubise's allies had conspired to murder *maître* Jacques as he meditated, Christ-like, in the wilderness. The *enfants du père* Soubise were also variously entitled *drilles, bons enfants*, or *compagnons passants*.

These, according to Perdiguier, were the three different rites to which journeymen in a number of trades belonged. The characterisation of the *compagnonnages* which he produced has remained largely unchallenged in subsequent historical interpretation, even though much of Perdiguier's description was as redolent of the early nineteenth-century fascination with mystery, clandestinity and secret societies as of anything to do with the trades of early modern France.[10] This has been one reason why historians have had some difficulty in explaining the nature and function of the *compagnonnages*. Perdiguier's description has been taken at its face value and historical interpretation has consisted largely of attempts to graft the corpus of myth that he presented on to earlier, and arguably different, contexts.

Some of the features of the *compagnonnages* that Perdiguier described were relatively constant throughout the eighteenth and early nineteenth centuries.[11] Members of the *devoir* had designated inns, or *cayennes*, where they lodged. The inn-keepers (or, more usually, their wives or widows) who housed and fed them were known as their *père* or *mère*. Journeymen lodging in the inns elected one of their number to the position of *rolleur* or *rouleur*, a word whose ambiguity encompassed the dual functions of keeping a roll of local members of the association and of transferring journeymen from shop to shop to accommodate new arrivals. A second member of the association was designated as the *premier en ville*, or *capitaine*, and was responsible for ensuring that its rules were upheld and its rituals observed, and that correspondence with members of the association in other towns was maintained. Members of the *compagnonnages* wore ornate garlands of ribbons whose colours varied

[10] The subject awaits fuller study. See J. M. Roberts, *The Mythology of the Secret Societies* (London, 1972).

[11] See the works by Martin Saint-Léon and Coornaert cited above, note 6.

according to the trade they practised. They performed elaborate ceremonies to see one another on their way and exchanged ritual greetings when they encountered fellow initiates in the course of their travels. They fought ferocious battles with other journeymen, loyally attended upon those of their number if they were injured or fell foul of the law in these often bloody affrays, and, when necessary, took part in funeral processions to bury their dead.

Many of these activities were by no means confined to journeymen. Much of the emphasis upon physical prowess, often of an explicitly sexual kind, that was a feature of the *compagnonnages* was shared by young, single men in many other circumstances. Members of the *compagnonnages* who referred disparagingly to the sedentary workers employed in textile production as *corrichons*, and to themselves as *drilles*, drew upon an imagery of male virility that was common to soldiers and students as well as young, migrant journeymen. Unlike soldiers or students, however, members of the *compagnonnages* were initiated into a more extensive quasi-organisation. However imprecise their boundaries may have been, the networks of association formed by the *compagnonnages* were distinguished from other forms of informal association by the significance attached to the oath of initiation. A journeyman locksmith who walked out on his master in Troyes in 1788 emphasised the point by stating that although he had called himself a *compagnon du devoir* when he had signed his *livret*, he could not, in fact, be one because he had not been initiated into the rite.[12]

Yet, despite these continuities, many other aspects of the *compagnonnages* that Perdiguier described in 1839 were very different from those proscribed as heretical by the Doctors of the Faculty of Theology in 1655. The ceremony of initiation described by the Sorbonne in 1655 was a very elaborate affair. Perdiguier, in 1839, made no reference to a ceremony of initiation at all.[13] Inversely, however, there is no trace of the legend of Solomon's Temple in any of the surviving evidence related to the *compagnonnages* until Perdiguier published his work. The legendary *maître* Jacques of Solomon's Temple was a very much more clearly defined figure than the rather shadowy *maître* Jacques to whom journeymen made reference during the eighteenth century. Nor, in the eighteenth century, did journeymen make reference to anything other than the *devoir* in their descriptions of the *compagnonnages*. Although they used a large number of terms to describe the non-members of the *devoir* – *compagnons étrangers*, *gavots*,

---

12 A.C. Troyes, FF *supplement* (unclassified, 23 July 1788). The terms *cornichon* and *agrichon* were used in Troyes: see A.C. Troyes, Fonds Boutiot AA 40, *liasse* 1 (10 September 1773). On young men's associations, see Natalie Z. Davis, *Society and Culture in Early-Modern France* (London, 1975), chapter 4–6.

13 Perdiguier was, however, aware of the investigation conducted by the Sorbonne, perhaps by way of J. F. Lebrun, *Histoire des pratiques superstitieuses* (many editions; see the 1751 edition, vol. 4, pp. 60–8).

loups-garous, chiens or renards were the most frequent, while devoirants were also known as compagnons passants, loups or drilles – the terms enfants de Salomon and enfants du père Soubise were never used.

Like so many images of artisans, the corpus of myth and ritual presented by Perdiguier in 1839 was not passed from one generation to the next as an unvarying totality; instead, it was a more loosely structured repertoire used by journeymen in different times and places in ways that were themselves often very different. The mythology of the compagnonnages that Perdiguier described owed a great deal to freemasonry, most obviously in its adaptation of the masonic legends centred upon the Book of Kings and the construction of Solomon's Temple. Yet freemasonry and the trades had little in common until the nineteenth century. Only in the wake of the Revolution, after Barruel had done so much to establish the subversive reputation of the masonic lodges – and Buonarotti, Blanqui and their followers had, in their turn, done so much to confirm his worst suspicions – did the acacia begin to lose its polite following and some assimilation of freemasonry into the culture of the trades begin to occur.[14] During the seventeenth and eighteenth centuries, however, the ritual of the compagnonnages owed nothing to freemasonry. Instead, much of it was modelled upon the ceremonial of the church and the courts. The recurrent re-enactment of ritual, rather than the content of the ritual itself, was the most enduring characteristic of the compagnonnages.

Much of the eighteenth-century ritual of the compagnonnages was an adaptation of the ceremonial of the two institutions that journeymen encountered most regularly before the Revolution: the church and the courts. In its most obvious form, that ceremonial was most visible in the damnations that members of the compagnonnages visited upon particular employers (or towns), or in the charcoal gibbets that journeymen occasionally inscribed on buildings in which their enemies were known to meet.[15] Such adaptations, however, were more extensive than mere words or images. The figure of the pilgrim, and the imagery of unity in diversity symbolised by the offering and the distribution of the pain bénit after the mass, represented an alternative to the emphasis upon property, particularity and stability that played so large a part in the vocabulary of natural law.[16] The unifying imagery of the church lent itself readily to the circumstances of peripatetic journeymen whose origins and expectations were extremely diverse. Initiates into the devoir included men who had been born outside the kingdom and, in Bordeaux in particular, a small

[14] On the changing social composition of freemasonry, see Maurice Agulhon, Pénitents et francs-maçons de l'ancienne Provence (Paris, 1968); Ran Halévi, Les Loges maçonniques dans la France d'Ancien Régime (Paris, 1984).

[15] See, for example, A.N. Y 18 764 (3 June 1789) and Garrioch and Sonenscher, 'Compagnonnages, Confraternities', p. 29.

[16] See above, chapters 2 and 8.

number of black journeymen.[17] Until the nineteenth century, the church was one of the few institutions whose public rhetoric and ceremonial practice acknowledged geographical mobility in a positive manner.

Much of the corpus of ceremony and imagery that the church supplied was readily available to migrant journeymen in the practice of established journeymen's confraternities, which met regularly in cloisters and *cabarets* after the mass. They celebrated saints' days and trade holidays, collected money for their *bourses communes* and expected their members to attend funerals for those who died.[18] They were also vehicles for substantial legal conflicts with master artisans. The *compagnonnages* drew particularly heavily upon the ceremonial of journeymen's confraternities, notably the ritual distribution of the *pain bénit*, in their own ceremonial life. Members of the *compagnonnages* also paid fees to be initiated, and commemorated saints' days and trade holidays. They had written rules that they stored in chests in their *cayennes* and expected initiates who transgressed them to pay fines into a common fund. Members of the *compagnonnages* also imitated the ceremonial of the courts in elaborate trials in which, as a group of journeymen carpenters in Lyon were reported to have done in 1776, they wore women's wigs to impersonate lawyers and magistrates.[19]

Ritual allowed the *devoir* to have an inclusive character that was at variance with almost every other aspect of eighteenth-century public life. Yet ritual was also a powerful mechanism of selection and exclusion. Both Perdiguier in 1839 and the Doctors of the Sorbonne in 1655 emphasised the mysterious and secretive character of the oaths of initiation, concealed papers and clandestine networks of correspondence associated with the *compagnonnages*. Yet despite the aura of clandestinity surrounding the *compagnonnages*, their presence in many of the small towns and larger cities of provincial France was often highly visible and, on many occasions, extremely public.[20] Secrets are exclusive. Yet it is not immediately obvious who was excluded from the secrets of the *compagnonnages*.

17 For black *compagnons du devoir*, see A.D. Gironde, 12B 312 (17 August 1755), in which the son of a slave explained how he had been initiated in Bordeaux at the age of 18 after he had finished his apprenticeship. He added that 'il avoit fait son tour de France et étoit allé à Marseille, à Lyon, à Paris et à Nantes'. See also A.D. Gironde 12B 325 (1 December 1764). On the greater homogeneity of the membership of confraternities, see above, p. 85.

18 See above, chapter 3.

19 'Estant déguisés, ayant des coefures de femme sur la teste, contrefaisant les juges, procureurs et huissiers au grand scandale du public': A.D. Rhone, 134B (Justice d'Ecully, 29 April 1776).

20 The journeyman glazier Jacques-Louis Ménétra described how he and his fellow *compagnons* had celebrated the feast of St Luc in Lyon in 1763: 'Le jour se fait avec pompe. L'on n'a jamais vu une fête pareille. Tout Lyon veut nous voir passer deux à deux au son de la musique moi en tête ayant deux rubans à la troisième boutonnière, le père des compagnons à ma droite. Le pain bénit porté est d'une grande grandeur demesurée par quatre apprentis. La fête se passe et le repas très triomphalement.' Daniel Roche, ed., *Journal de ma vie, Jacques-Louis Ménétra, compagnon vitrier au 18e siècle* (Paris, 1982), p. 128.

The *compagnonnages* were well known to many of the magistrates and municipal authorities of eighteenth-century France, not least because of the many brawls and pitched battles in which they were involved. In 1726, the *jurats* of Bordeaux produced a detailed description of the *devoir* among journeymen locksmiths, to which they appended a list of 15 towns in which the rite was practised and a further ten localities boycotted by members of the association (Figure 9.1). In 1760, the *bailliage* court of Etampes recorded the existence of a *société* among journeymen carpenters known as the *compagnons du devoir* or *bons drilles*.[21] The journeymen met in an inn kept by a man named Jacques Fauvet, whom they called their *mère*. Fauvet had a register containing the names of all those belonging to the *devoir*. Anyone not on the register was known as a *renard* and, if he refused to become a *drille*, was forced to leave Etampes. Information of this kind was not simply the outcome of criminal proceedings. In 1748 a number of journeymen joiners who were *gavots* attempted to persuade a police inspector in Troyes to force a master joiner to dismiss a journeyman who belonged to the *devoir*, because, they claimed, the *devoirant* had stolen one of their member's shirts in Montpellier. Journeymen hatters in Marseille engaged a barrister at the Parlement of Provence in 1784 to advise them on a lawsuit in which they were involved with members of the *devoir*.[22]

Some years earlier, the *bailliage* court of Montereau was given a description of the ceremony of the *conduite*, when a journeyman wheelwright complained that he had been assaulted by two journeymen masons who belonged to the *devoir*.[23] It transpired that the wheelwright was also a member of the *devoir* and had asked the two masons to perform the *conduite* to see him on his way. Normally the ceremony consisted of a ritual farewell, accompanied by songs and wine, before a journeyman set out on his travels. On this occasion, however, the two journeymen had gathered up the *sac* containing the wheelwright's tools, bought some wine and prepared to escort him out on to the road in the prescribed way, only to find, to their disgust, that he had changed his mind and wanted to stay.

In 1767, the *procureur général* of the Parlement of Paris was sent a detailed description of the ceremony of initiation and the ordinary rituals observed among journeymen leather-dressers (*blanchers–chamoiseurs*) in

21 B.N. MS. Joly de Fleury 1730 fol. 266 (9 September 1760). For another example of a man known as the journeymen's *mère* see A.C. Troyes, Fonds Boutiot, AA 40, *liasse* 1 (15 December 1759).

22 A.D. Gironde, C 1814; A.C. Troyes, FF *supplément* (unclassified, 5 August 1748); Sonenscher, *Hatters*, p. 138.

23 A.D. Seine-et-Marne, B (unclassified), *bailliage de Montéreau* (11 September 1763). B.N. Joly de Fleury 1729 fol. 3 (17 June 1765).

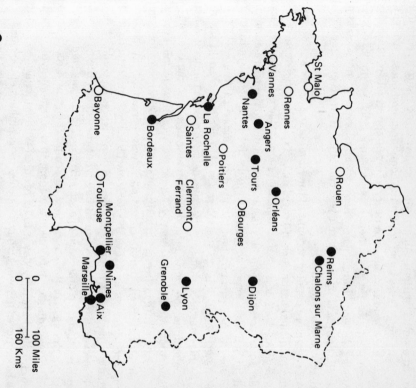

● Towns where the *devoir* was practised

○ Towns boycotted by the *compagnons du devoir*

9.1 Towns associated with the *devoir* of
journeymen locksmiths (1726)
Source: A. D. Gironde C1814

Chalons-sur-Marne.[24] Although the initiation was rather less complex than the ceremony described by the Doctors of the Sorbonne in 1655, it followed a similar pattern. An aspirant member was led into a room in the *cayenne*, where, after a number of ritual commands and questions, he was made to kneel and take an oath never to reveal the secrets of the *devoir* to any non-initiate. He was then baptised and given a name (such as *Languedoc le beau chanteur*) in which an allusion to a (not necessarily flattering) physical or moral trait was combined with an evocation of the initiate's *pays* of origin.

An even more detailed account of the ritual of the *devoir* was presented to the municipal authorities of Troyes in 1782, when a nineteen-year-old journeyman leather-dresser (*mégissier*) named Jacques Minder, acting under some pressure from his master, complained to the police authorities that he had been forced to spend 30 *livres* to be initiated as a *compagnon du devoir*.[25] The ceremony had occurred on Sunday 25 August 1782. On that day, towards four in the afternoon, Minder had been in his room above his master's shop on the rue de la Grande Tannerie when a journeyman named Pierre Briand, known as *le Bordelais*, came to find him. Briand took Minder to a nearby *cabaret*, where they found five other journeymen leather-dressers drinking at a table. After three or four bottles of wine had been consumed, Minder was persuaded to become a *compagnon du devoir* and gave the *Bordelais* 15 *livres* to meet the costs of his initiation, promising to pay a further 15 *livres* when he could.

The seven journeymen went to buy what they called their livery from a milliner and then proceeded to a second *cabaret* in the *faubourg de Croncels* kept by the *mère* of the *compagnons du devoir*. There, in a room upstairs, Minder was initiated into the association, in a ceremony which, he later said, involved kneeling down to be baptised with wine, and swearing on his blood never to reveal what happened in assemblies of the rite. He was then given a name: that chosen for him was *L'Aimable*. The six other journeymen then wrote something on a sheet of paper which he was asked

[24] Paul Bondois, 'Un Compagnonnage au xviiie siècle: le devoir des bons drilles blanchers-chamoiseurs', *Annales historiques de la Révolution française*, 6 (1929), pp. 588–99.

[25] A.C. Troyes, FF *supplément* (unclassified, 30 August 1782). Unless otherwise indicated, all the following citations come from this dossier. The journeymen described the ceremony of initiation into the rite in the following ways: 'La cérémonie consiste à se mettre à genoux et à être baptisé avec du vin et à jurer par son sang qu'on ne révélera jamais rien de ce qui se passe dans les assemblées des associés.' Another of them stated that the rituals 'consistent à faire mettre le récipiendaire à genoux sur une serviette, à lui verser du vin sur la tête en lui disant, "Enfant, je te baptise au nom du Père, du Fils et du Saint Esprit," et à lui faire jurer au récipiendaire qu'il le tiendra toujours dans son compagnonnage et de ne rien dire de ce qui se passe'. A third journeyman described how those already initiated 'le firent entrer seul dans la chambre, le firent mettre à genoux, lui versèrent sur la tête du vin et de l'eau, disant qu'ils le baptisèrent. Ils le firent jurer de rénoncer à tous les Gavots et Espontons, et en dressèrent un acte'.

to sign. When the ceremony was over the journeymen went down and presented a livery, consisting of a long ribbon or sash, to their *mère* to mark the occasion.

Minder spent the night at the inn and on the Monday morning he and the other journeymen went out to buy some more ribbons to prepare for the initiation of two more individuals. Several witnesses later emphasised the very ostentatious character of the journeymen's behaviour. They paraded around the streets with their hats and coats garlanded with brightly coloured ribbons, making a point of passing workshops on the rue de la Grande Tannerie and adjoining alleys to encourage other members of the trade to join them. Ten of them were seen at 10 a.m. in the haberdasher's shop, where they seemed to be a little drunk. They bought 30 ells of ribbon, explaining that it was needed for the purpose of receiving ' un de leurs du devoir ', and that there would be further receptions at the end of the week, for which even more ribbon would be required.

Monday was thus given over to ceremonial, food and wine, so that all the journeymen spent the night in the *cabaret*. On Tuesday morning some of them wanted to return to work, but came under pressure from the others to remain. There was an argument and a brief fight in which a journeyman was slightly injured. Minder, who owed the *compagnons* half the initiation fee, made his way back to work where, perhaps rather naively, he asked his master for an advance of 15 *livres* on his wages. As a result, he was encouraged by his master to complain to the authorities.

The ensuing proceedings served to throw considerable light upon the combination of ritual and improvisation that characterised the *compagnonnages*. When Pierre Briand, the journeyman known as *le Bordelais* who had been the main figure in organising the initiation ceremonies, heard of what had happened he decided to try and avoid criminal proceedings by joining the army. He approached a recruiting sergeant-major of the *régiment de Brie* garrisoned in Troyes and asked to enlist. He explained rather disingenuously that he had been unaware that the *compagnonnages* were illegal in Troyes and hoped that by joining the army a blind eye would be turned to his offence.

According to Briand the initiations into the *compagnonnage* had taken place because the association of *compagnons du devoir* in Troyes had become moribund. He had, he said, only just arrived in the town and had made the acquaintance of two journeymen known as *Vivarais* and *Mâconnais* in order to find work. *Vivarais* asked him whether he was a *compagnon du devoir*, and he replied that he was. Accordingly he and the only other two *compagnons du devoir* in the trade initiated five journeymen into the association. It was a costly procedure because none of the initiates could pay the customary 30 *livres* in full. The three journeymen were owed a total of 54 *livres* by the *aspirants* and were also involved in discussions over the settlement of a sum of 30 *livres* outstanding on the 60 *livres* that they had spent on food and drink in the inn run by their *mère*.

The journeymen's *mère*, a *cabaretière* named Briey, raised difficulties when attempts were made to negotiate over when the outstanding sum would be paid, and also said that she did not wish to be considered to be the *mère des compagnons du devoir* because she had not been given a formal title by the journeymen. It transpired that the formal title consisted of the papers of the *compagnons du devoir*, which were in the possession of another *cabaretière* named Marie Maître, who had an inn on the rue Dauphin. She admitted that she had been the *mère* of the *compagnons tanneurs* several years ago, but had decided to renounce the position in 1776 when, she said, the *campagnonnages* had been prohibited. At that time the journeymen had owed her 60 *livres* and had left their papers with her in a small chest as security. The debt had never been paid and the papers had been left in their chest until April 1782, when a number of journeymen had arrived and asked for a room. When it became evident that they were *compagnons du devoir* they were ordered to leave. This was why they had transferred their activities to the inn in the *faubourg de Croncels*. The new venue was not a random choice. The journeymen's new *mère*, Marie Briey, had worked as a domestic servant for the *cabaretière* Marie Maître, before setting up on her own account when she married. She had, she said, initially suspected that the journeymen who invited her to become their *mère* were not genuine *compagnons du devoir* because, as she put it, they did not have a *maître Jacques*.

The maître Jacques in question was, it was revealed, a figure painted on the chest containing the papers of the *compagnons du devoir*. A search of the *cabaret* on the rue Dauphin led to the discovery of the chest, upon whose cover were the figures of what the police officials described as three saints, with the figure in the middle representing Saint-Jacques Pèllerin, (which was why the journeymen called it a *maître Jacques*). When the chest was opened it was found to contain no more than some cards and an empty notebook cover.

If the *compagnonnages* were relatively well-known to magistrates, they were, it is clear, equally familiar to master artisans. The episode in Troyes is an indication that relations between journeymen and master artisans in the leather-dressing trade of Troyes were hardly in keeping with what might have been expected of a clandestine association. It is particularly apparent that Jacques Minder was unaware of any contradiction between taking an oath to keep the secrets of the *devoir* and approaching his master for an advance of 15 *livres* to meet the costs of his initiation. There was one very obvious reason why he could have behaved with such apparent inconsistency. Master artisans had, in most cases, once been journeymen and, like many journeymen, had been members of the *compagnonnages*. For them, the ceremonies of the *devoir* were no mystery at all.

It is not difficult to find many other examples of master artisans' familiarity and continued involvement with the *compagnonnages*. A journeyman stone cutter described how he had been initiated into the *devoir* in Bordeaux on Ascension Day 1754 by a master architect and two dozen current and former members of the rite.[26] In 1771, a journeyman carpenter from Troyes described how he had been approached by a *compagnon du devoir* in the same trade who asked him for the whereabouts of the association's *cayenne*. He explained that since it was the custom to examine a newcomer on the mysteries of the *devoir*, he had performed various exercises with the newcomer. They had then retired for a meal to a baker's shop where they found two master carpenters with whom they ate sumptuously and resumed their exercises.[27] Master artisans were likely, therefore, to have been entirely conversant with the rituals of the *compagnonnages*. A petition presented by the *compagnons du devoir* of Auxerre after some of them had been arrested in 1786 for assaulting a number of *gavots* explained that only a small minority of masters employed journeymen who were not attached to the *devoir*. Members of the rite had, they claimed, been disgusted by their brutality and would not work for anyone who was not prepared to accept the *devoir*.[28]

Familiarity with the rituals of the *devoir* could not, however, prevent episodic conflict between masters and journeymen. In 1774 the master turners of Bordeaux complained that all their shops had been boycotted by the *compagnons du devoir* when some masters revealed the secrets of the rite in an attempt to put an end to the association.[29] A song confiscated from journeymen basket-makers (*compagnons vanniers*) in Orléans in 1765 tells its own story:

Pour célébrer la gloire
de tous les vanniers d'Orléans.
Digne de mémoire, je vous le dits
Aujourd'hui sans faloire
Sur tous les jolis compagnons.

Je vous direz en peu de mots
ce qui se passera en ville.

26 'Il a ésté reçu par maître Richon, maistre architecte, à l'auberge de la Providence...en présence de plus d'une vingtaine de compagnons tant remerciés qu'autres, parmy lesquels il se rappelle le nomme Jolicoeur d'Agen qui est encore compagnon quoyque marié, cadet Berant de Bordeaux qui est aussi marié, le nommé Roussai qui a remercié.' A.D. Gironde, 13B 212 (25 November 1754).
27 'L'usage étant parmi eux d'éprouver le passant sur le devoir, il s'est exercé à différents exercises...avec ledit compagnon.' A.C. Troyes, FF supplément (29 January 1771).
28 A.D. Yonne, 1B 551 (10 June 1786).
29 A.D. Gironde, 12B 350 (10 August 1774).

C'est du dernier étez passez.
Les maitres sans faintise,
ont fait dans cet évenement,
casser tous leurs réglemens.

Les compagnons ayant
heu touz de la crainte
qu'on les attrape.
Chez maitre Poignard,
ils se sont assemblez
en sept-cent-soixante et quatre,
ou ils se sont dit,
sans nul déguisement,
faute entre nous de nouveaux réglements.[30]

For all its bravado, the song was an expression of the ambivalent relationship between members of the *compagnonnages* and master artisans. Some master artisans (in this case a master named Poignard) were prepared to support members of the *compagnonnages* in conflicts between other masters and their journeymen. The instability of the relationship between the core and periphery of local labour markets, and the strategic significance of migrant journeymen within the workforce as a whole, favoured rivalries among employers as well as conflicts with journeymen, particularly over access to adequate supplies of labour to meet the abrupt changes in demand that occurred from week to week and month to month at the level of the individual shop. Not surprisingly, many provincial corporations were deeply divided in their attitudes towards the *devoir*. At different times, corporate decisions to prohibit the *devoir* in localities as diverse as Chalon-sur-Saône, Lyon and Bordeaux generated angry debate and intense opposition from substantial minorities of master artisans.[31]

The many possible tensions inherent in the local economies of particular trades also left itinerant journeymen initiated into the *devoir* in an

[30] Loosely translated, the song runs, 'To the glory of the worthy basket-makers of Orléans/ I will relate what took place last summer/when the masters overturned their regulations/ The journeymen took fright/and met in 1764 at master Poignards'/where they demanded a new regulation.' The song is printed under A.D. Loiret, B 1988 in the inventory of the series B of the archives of the Loiret (Orléans, 1900). The documents themselves were destroyed during World War II.

[31] A number of master joiners were involved in an assembly of journeymen when the rules of one of the rites of the *compagnonnages* of Chalon-sur-Saône were drawn up in 1666, 'suyvant l'antient coustume que nos predecesseurs nous ont laissés, tant pour le proffit des maistres que celluy des compagnons': A.C. Chalon-sur-Saône, HH 20. Master joiners in Lyon were deeply divided over a police regulation prohibiting the ceremonies of the *compagnons du devoir* in 1735. A majority (67) called for the total suppression of the *devoir*, while a minority (41) claimed that it was beneficial to the trade, 'en ce qu'elle attire en cette ville les compagnons du devoir, lesquels ayant travaillé dans plusieurs villes des différentes provinces...sont bien plus experimentez que les autres compagnons qu'ils appellent gavots': Bibliothèque de l'Arsénal, 8°J 4684. *Statuts des menuisiers de Lyon. Sentence de police* (2 June 1735): A.D. Gironde B (unclassified. 20 September 1757).

ambiguous position. Their concerns were not necessarily the same as those of journeymen who were domiciled or had served apprenticeships in the large towns in which most migrants worked. Nor, however, were all migrant journeymen members of the *devoir* or the circumstances of initiates and non-initiates identical. These differences found one expression in the many different names that journeymen used to describe one another. The profusion of these terms – *devoirants, gavots, droguins, loups, loups garous, renards, chiens, bons enfants, drilles, passants, étrangers, braves, espontons, cornichons, agrichons, jolis compagnons* – makes it difficult to envisage the different rites of the *compagnonnages* as entirely separate entities. They were, instead, local, or trade-specific, variants upon the repertoire of ritual associated with the *devoir*. Yet non-members of the *devoir* also maintained a distinct, if derivative, ceremonial life of their own.

A report sent by the mayor of Orléans to the Prefect of the Department of the Loiret in 1805 referred to associations among journeymen in 30 different trades.[32] All of them were small in size. In most cases journeymen were associated with the *devoir*, which encompassed some 25 to 30 different trades. In some trades, notably the carpenters, joiners and locksmiths, both *gavots* and *devoirants* had their supporters. The pattern was a general one. The division between *devoirants* and *gavots* was, in many respects, a replication of the division between members of established journeymen's confraternities and members of the *devoir*. Just as much of the ceremonial life of the the *devoir* was an adaptation of the ceremonial of journeymen's confraternities to the circumstances of peripatetic migrants, so much of the ritual of the journeymen who came to be known as *compagnons étrangers* or *gavots* was modelled upon that of the *devoir* or *compagnons passants*.

Ritual was not, therefore, confined to the *devoir*. A fight in Bordeaux in 1770 occurred when over 150 *gavots* – some of them joiners, others locksmiths, masons or stone-cutters – who had attended the funeral of one of their number came upon a group of *compagnons du devoir* as they were escorting two other *gavots* about to leave Bordeaux and, as the phrase went, 'battre au champs'.[33] Journeymen known as *compagnons étrangers* (or *gavots* by their enemies) were therefore more than members of the *devoir*. Although the word *gavot* had pejorative connotations of rusticity and was used in southern France to refer to migrants from the remote rural areas of Haute Provence or even Spain, it also referred to a rite as distinct as the *devoir*.[34] Papers confiscated from the *gavots* of Mâcon in the mid-eighteenth century reveal a ceremonial life as elaborate as that of the

32 A.N. F7 4236.
33 A.D. Gironde, 12B 339 (26 September 1770).
34 Its best-known member was, of course, Agricol Perdiguier himself. See his *Mémoires d'un compagnon*, ed. Alain Faure (Paris, 1977).

devoir and a clear sense of the geographical horizons of the association from the vantage point of the Burgundian town:

> Dans Lyon cette grande ville
> Nous avons des compagnons
> tous gavots plain de courrage
> qui soutiendront notre nom
> Vienne, Romans et Vallance
> Avignon faut le nommer
> nos compagnons d'assurance
> ils sont fort bien renommés.[35]

In Lyon joiners and locksmiths belonging to the two rites frequented different inns on virtually the same street.[36] Locksmiths who were *gavots* met in the church of the *Recollets* to celebrate mass and distribute the offering on the first Sunday of every month and the principal trade holidays. Afterwards they adjourned to the nearby cloisters to discuss their affairs and settle their accounts.

If the identity of the *devoir* was a mystery, it was, therefore, a mystery that was most impenetrable to other journeymen. The secrecy of the *compagnonnages* was a very open secret indeed for the many master artisans who employed itinerant journeymen. Migrants, particularly the many young men aged between 15 and 20 who left small towns to find work elsewhere, were in a different situation. The ritual of the *devoir* allowed men from many different places to draw upon a vocabulary that transcended the particularities of *pays*, but was at the same time also a mechanism of selection and exclusion. It belonged to a world in which many people did the same thing, but some did it better than others. This, of course, was the point of the ritual.

Ritual could be conciliatory or provocative, inclusive or exclusive. If it allowed strangers to recognise their common affiliation to the *devoir*, it could also be used to humiliate those outside the circle of the initiate and underscore rivalries between members and non-members of the rite. These

[35] A.C. Mâcon, HH 11 (pièce 18). Loosely translated, the song runs: 'In the great city of Lyon/Are none but courageous *gavots*/Our reputation runs to Vienne, Romans, Valance and Avignon/All those in these towns/are justifiably celebrated.'

[36] *Devoirants* and *gavots* who were locksmiths frequented different *cabarets* on the rue Ecorcheboeuf; among the joiners the *gavots* met at the *Pomme de Paix* also on the rue Ecorcheboeuf, while the *devoirants* met *au Purgatoire*, on the adjacent rue Ferrandière. The *gavots' capitaine*, a 22-year-old native of a village in Provence, explained that 'en sa qualité de capitaine il est à la tête des autres compagnons. C'est luy qui préside aux délibérations qu'ils font, qui fait ranger les comptes, et apaise les difficultés qui peuvent naître entre les compagnons et les maîtres et entres les compagnons les uns avec les autres, qui fait dire la messe tous les premiers dimanches de chaque mois et présente le pain bénit, qui a soin de receuiller et faire payer les amendes imposées aux compagnons lorsqu'ils s'écartent de leurs devoirs et enfin qui a soin de fournir aux besoins des compagnons non du devoir qui passent en cette ville et qui n'ont pas d'argent, et qui entretient une correspondence avec les autres compagnons non du devoir des différentes villes.' A.D. Rhône, BP 3307 (3 November 1764).

rivalries found their most recurrent expression in pitched battles between members of the *devoir* and journeymen who refused to be initiated into the rite or, more usually, between members of the different rites themselves. A 15-year-old boy described how one such battle, between joiners belonging to the *gavots* and the *devoirants*, was organised in Troyes in 1773. The two groups of journeymen gathered near the corn market towards nine in the morning. The *devoirants* approached the *gavots* and, in a formal way, offered to make their peace. The *gavots* rejected the invitation and announced their desire to fight.[37] The two groups then separated and made their way to the appointed place in the suburbs of Troyes where the fight was to take place. Both, of course, took good care to bring their staves.

Fights between *devoirants* and *gavots* involved journeymen from a wide variety of different trades. Joiners assaulted locksmiths; hatters attacked wheelwrights; iron-founders fell upon harness-makers; shoemakers stoned building workers.[38] Brawls among journeymen from so many different occupations were rarely fights over matters directly related to the workplace. They occurred most frequently on Sundays and holidays, after taunts and insults had been traded in *cabarets* and other public places. They were struggles for prestige and, in particular, for prestige among the membership of the same rite or group of itinerant journeymen. Indirectly, however, they were also conflicts to maintain, or establish, the standing of a rite in a particular locality.

Feats of prowess in battle were demonstrations of physical superiority conducted in the mode of mimesis. So too were the less violent trials of proficiency conducted between *gavots* and *devoirants* in a wide variety of different trades. Competitors made the same things, but made them better. They did so either to win sums of money wagered by the rival rites, or to win an exclusive right to work in particular towns. The money was the measure of the challenge rather than the prize to be won. The victor did not keep the often substantial sums wagered on these feats of prowess, but spent the prize on food and drink with other members of the rite. The ultimate challenge was a competition for the right to work in a particular town. Victory became part of the orally transmitted annals of the rite. The great battle between *gavots* and *devoirants* fought at Tournus, near Mâcon, in 1825 was a physical re-enactment of a competition (which, it was said, the *gavots* had lost) held in 1725.[39] The prize had been the right to work in the town for 100 years.

[37] One of them said, 'Messieurs voulez-vous nous rendre la canne et nous arranger? Nous serons amis comme nous l'avons jamais été.' The gesture was met by an invitation to fight. 'Les devoirans ont demandé comment. Les gaveaux ont repondu à coups de poing. Les devoirans ont dit. Messieurs on se fouillera, et ceux qui auront des couteaux ou bastons on le desarmera': A.D. Aube, 1B 1133 (15 March 1773).

[38] See for example A.D. Loire Atlantique, B 8729" (7 November 1782); A.D. Yonne, 1B 579 (11 June 1760); A.C. Marseille, FF 342ª (6 September 1736).

[39] On the famous battle of Tournus, see Coornaert, *Compagnonnages*, pp. 80, 401–12.

The sums of money involved in these trials of proficiency were relatively large. A competition between rival groups of journeymen locksmiths in Chalon-sur-Saône in 1775 ended in acrimony when the *compagnon du devoir* took flight, leaving the *gavots* in possession of the 120 *livres* wagered on the competition.[40] Disaster was narrowly averted during a trial between rival groups of *tailleurs de pierre* over the sum of 720 *livres* in Bordeaux in 1774. The two contestants, one a *compagnon passant*, the other a *compagnon étranger*, challenged one another to execute two projects which each had devised. Each contestant was to work alone in a closely guarded room. The plans were exchanged and the contestants were locked away for almost three months. It was then discovered that one of the journeymen had executed the plan presented by his opponent, while the other had attempted to do them both. The *jurats* of Bordeaux were called upon to adjudicate. Prudently they decided that the competition was a dead heat, returned the sums of money to the journeymen and offered to exhibit each contestant's work as an example to students in the school of architecture.[41] Honour was thus preserved, at least to the satisfaction of the municipal authorities, if not of the journeymen themselves. The rival rites continued to be involved in pitched battles on and around the site of Victor Louis' new theatre throughout the rest of the decade.

Ritual itself could be an object of ridicule. Much, of course, depended upon the situation and cultural resources of the parties involved. The combination of legal advantage, the high opportunity costs that migrants incurred to establish a viable artisanal enterprise, and the greater resources of indigenous journeymen meant that the *compagnonnages* were a minor presence in the life of the Parisian trades throughout the eighteenth century. Journeymen who emigrated from Paris were, of course, able to become members of the *devoir* once outside the capital. Others, however, refused. Two journeymen locksmiths from Paris who had been engaged to work for a master locksmith in the little town of Auxerre in 1760 ostentatiously refused to have anything to do with the local *compagnons du devoir*. They were asked if they were *gavots*, whereupon one of them replied dismissively that he had never heard the term, and the other said haughtily that they had been sent for from Paris and that the customs of the *compagnonnages* were fit only for apprentices. Anyone who resented their presence was free to try and do their work themselves.[42] The equation between apprentices, the *compagnonnages* and shoddy work was plain enough. Not surprisingly, the two journeymen were assaulted.

[40] A.C. Chalon-sur-Saône, FF 39 (9 September 1775).

[41] A.C. Bordeaux, HH 101 (23 February 1774).

[42] 'Ne sachant que vouloit dire ce langage,' he said, 'qu'il ne sçavoit pas ce que c'est que de gavot'. The other said 'qu'ils venoient de Paris parce que l'on les avoit mandé, et qu'il n'y avoit que des apprentifs qu'on embauchoit, et qu'il ne connoissoit pas les règles des compagnons, que s'ils étoient jaloux de l'ouvrage qu'ils faisoient, ils n'avoient qu'à le faire eux mêmes': A.D. Yonne, 1B 579 (11 June 1760).

The difference between the rites of the *compagnonnages* was measured in a similar way. After a brawl between a number of journeymen carpenters in Nantes in 1791, the municipal authorities received a long memorandum on behalf of the *compagnons du devoir* stating that the fight was an expression of 'les haines que les renards charpentiers portent aux vrais artistes compagnons du devoir'. Its author, a member of the National Guard of Richebourg and the cashier of the artillery works there, explained that he had done the *tour de France* on foot himself and (in an evocation of the rhetoric of the Revolution) had come to admire the fraternity displayed by journeymen carpenters affiliated to the *devoir*. He proceeded to define the difference between a *compagnon du devoir* and a *renard*. Members of the former rite had a long practical and theoretical experience of architectural drawing. They were 'vrais artistes'. *Gavots*, on the other hand, were utterly ignorant and only to be found in Nantes, where they were prepared to work for 20 to 24 *sous* a day, instead of the 30 *sous* paid to members of the *devoir*. A *gavot* was incapable of the most elementary building work.[43]

The opposition between *vrais artistes* and a despicable minority of incompetent individuals, willing to accept derisory rates for shoddy work, could not have been more complete. The identity of each rite, as of informal groupings of journeymen outside the *compagnonnages*, was constituted by such comparisons, evaluations and assertions. A near riot by a crowd of 60 journeymen joiners attempting to find a German journeyman employed by a cabinet-maker in Troyes in 1788 was caused, the authorities were told, by 'jalousie d'état' and an argument over whether Germans were better than French journeymen in the finer arts of joinery.[44]

Both *devoirants* and *gavots* shared a repertoire of ritual that expressed the

[43] 'Ayant moi-même fait le tour de France à pied', he explained, 'j'ai eu occasion de connoître les compagnons charpentiers du devoir et j'ai admiré la fraternité qui règne entre eux et les secours mutuels qu'ils se donnent réciproquement. Un compagnon du devoir est celui que a fait preuve de sa probité devant ses camarades et de son savoir faire. Pour y parvenir, il subi nombre d'examens pratiques sur l'art du trait, de charpente et sur la construction des ouvrages les plus difficiles en ce genre ... Un compagnon qu'on nomme renard au contraire est un yndividu qui n'a point voyagé et qui ne sçai point absolument son métier ... Ces compagnons renards vu leur ignorance travaillent pour 20 à 24 sous par jour tandis que les autres en ont 30. Il n'y a qu'à Nantes où est le refuge des compagnons renards ... Dans toutes les autres ville on ne les souffre point ... Faittes interroger des compagnons renards sur l'art du trait de charpente; vous verrez leur ignorance; ou bien faittes leur faire une édifice; vous verrez qu'ils n'en viendront jamais à bout.' A.C. Nantes, I² Carton 3, d.4 (4 August 1791). There is no trace of this pejorative image of the *gavots* in Perdiguier's autobiography. He was, of course, a *gavot* himself.
[44] 'L'almant de Becair [i.e. Becker, a master cabinet-maker] dispute au français de Lange (a master joiner) qu'ils ne sont pas sy adroit que les almans pour ce qui a de delicat à faire dans la menuiserie, de manière que la dispute enflammé et excitée par le boisson, ils sont sorti du cabaret pour abattre': A.C. Troyes, FF *supplément* (24 June 1788). Other witnesses of the incident described 'l'almant' as 'l'italien'.

common, but often antagonistic, situation of peripatetic journeymen. Each rite was the mirror image of the other, so that the differences between them were often difficult to define. Although journeymen occasionally described the distinctions between different rites, and between trades associated with the *compagnonnages* and those that were not, the criteria that they used varied substantially. A stone-cutter arrested in Bordeaux in 1754 after a fight with two *gavots* explained that he had nothing in particular against non-members of the *devoir*, but could not tolerate them wearing the ribbons of the rite. He added that they were to be found usually in Burgundy and the Champagne.[45] The frequency of fights between members of rival rites suggests, however, that geographical affinities of this kind were the outcome, rather than the basis, of conflict between rival groups of itinerant journeymen. The claims made by *gavots* and *devoirants* to exclusive control of particular towns were claims of precedence that embodied more subtle distinctions of definition and counter-definition than mere geographical difference.

A *devoirant*, for example, could be recognised if he was well-mannered, worked well, paid his way and did no harm to anyone, according to a *tailleur de pierre* in Bordeaux in 1754. Membership of the *devoir* implied friendship and mutual pleasure, a journeyman in the same trade explained in 1761.[46] *Gavots* had their own self-definitions. A journeyman joiner arrested in 1737 after a fight with a *compagnon du devoir* in Bordeaux stated that he was a *gavot*, which, he said, meant that he was free to work where he chose. A second journeyman, asked to explain what the term meant, replied that it meant the freedom to find work wherever it could be found without having to pay a *bien-venue*, or customary fee, on entering a shop.[47]

Journeymen also claimed to have a clear sense of the identity of the trades affiliated to the *devoir*. A cabinet-maker charged with membership of the *devoir* in Bordeaux in 1737 explained that he was not entitled to membership of the association, because he was a cabinet-maker rather than a joiner. This, he added, was why journeymen joiners who were

---

45 'Il n'y a jamais eu de ces sortes de compagnons à Bordeaux qu'à présent; qu'ils se tiennent ordinairement dans la Bourgogne et dans la Champagne et autres lieux': A.D. Gironde, 13B 212 (7 December 1754).

46 'Lorsqu'il est sage, qu'il travaille bien, qu'il paye sa dépence et qu'il ne fait tort à personne': A.D. Gironde, 13B 212 (7 December 1754). 'C'est être amy ensemble, de se faire plaisir mutuellement': A.D. Gironde, 12B 318 (15 May 1761).

47 He said 'qu'il est gaveaux, de ceux qui sont libres de travailler où bon leur semble'. 'Que c'est d'être libre de travailler et d'aller travailler où il se peut trouver, sans être obligé de donner aucun argent': A.D. Gironde, 12B 266 (3 June 1737). 'qu'il est censé gaveau, n'étant pas du devoir explained to the *jurats* of Bordeaux in 1762 'qu'il est censé gaveau'. Another joiner, arrested after a fight between members of different rites in the same city, stated 'qu'il est gavau et que par conséquent il ne fait pas de devoir': A.D. Gironde, 12B 321 (31 August 1762); 12B 339 (26 September 1770).

members of the rite had attacked him.[48] A journeyman farrier involved in a dispute with a number of masters in 1776 in the same city also stated that he did not belong to any of the rites because his trade was unattached to the *compagnonnages*. Journeymen farriers in other localities made the same claim, while shoemakers too made a point of emphasising (despite the prominent position of journeymen shoemakers in the condemnation of 1655) that their trade had no connection with the *devoir*.[49]

Journeymen farriers, wigmakers, tailors and shoemakers were among the members of a number of trades that journeymen claimed had no connection with the *compagnonnages*. Yet this was never entirely the case. A master joiner involved in a dispute with members of the *devoir* in Marseille in 1736 complained that, by way of reprisal, the journeymen had supplied him with men who knew nothing about joinery. On one occasion the *devoirants* had presented him with a journeyman hatter and on another a journeyman shoemaker.[50] Journeymen in trades reputed to have no connection with the *devoir* also conducted a ceremonial life that had many similarities to the ritual of *devoirants* or *gavots*. Farriers in Paris in 1696 frequented an inn near the place Maubert kept by their *mère*; ninety years later, in 1786, the same inn remained a meeting place and lodging house for migrant journeymen in the trade.[51] Migrant journeymen wigmakers in Marseille conducted their own trials, complete with a formal *plaidoirie*, and maintained a network of correspondence that was comparable in both form and content to any maintained by the *devoir*. Journeymen wigmakers in Paris were reported to frequent an inn kept by their *père* in 1765. A group of journeymen farriers arrested in Chalon-sur-Saône in 1731 as they marched, singing and carrying a figure of a horse-shoe struck in silver at the end of a stave, explained that they were practising the *devoir*.[52] The peripatetic journeymen tailors known as

48 'Il est ébeniste, qui est d'une communauté différente de celle des menuisiers. C'est pourquoy tous les compagnons menuisiers veulent mal à luy': A.D. Gironde, 12B 266 (3 June 1737).
49 'Qu'il n'est d'aucun devoir, ny ayant pas de compagnon de leur état': A.D. Gironde, 12B 355 (13 August 1776). A journeyman farrier arrested in Troyes in 1786 also stated 'qu'il est du devoir entre les compagnons maréchaux seulement': A.C. Troyes, FF supplément (10 August 1786). A group of shoemakers making their way to the quayside in Bordeaux in the same year '[pour] faire leurs adieux à un compagnon qui partait', encountered two journeymen stone-cutters. 'Taupe,' said one of them, in the ritual greeting used by the *compagnonnages*. One of the shoemakers replied 'qu'ils n'y avaient point de taupe parmy eux'. They were then asked their trade and declared that they were 'de braves garçons cordonniers'. 'Vous n'êtes point des braves mais des jeans foutres,' was the predictable and provocative reply: A.D. Gironde, 12B 355 (7 October 1776).
50 A.C. Marseille, FF 342ᵃ (6 September 1736).
51 B.N. MS. fr. 8084 fol. 405, (3 May 1697); A.N. Y 14 576 (20 February 1786). A.C. Marseille, FF 337 (15 June 1731); Garrioch and Sonenscher, '*Compagnonnages*. Confraternities', p. 29; A.C. Chalon-sur-Saône, FF 10 (11 June 1731). Shoemakers in Le Havre met regularly at the *Banneau de la Ville* and petitioned the municipality for recognition of their society in 1790: A.C. Le Havre, FF 50; HH 39, Shoemakers in

garçons de logis frequently borrowed the idiom of the *devoir*. A journeyman tailor in Nantes revealed his attitude to a requirement to register his name with the corporate authorities by stating that the name he had on the *tour de France* was *Je me fouts de cela*.[53]

Ritual feats of prowess were equally common among journeymen reputed to have no association with the *devoir*. The *fer de gageur* was a competition widely enacted among journeymen farriers. Jean-Baptiste Varin, a Parisian journeyman known as *le petit Champagne* who had been arrested in 1745 for possession of a forged double *louis d'or*, explained that it had been the prize he had won for a *fer de gageur*. He had been in a *cabaret* along with four other journeymen in the *faubourg* Saint-Germain. There had been a discussion of some kind and Varin became embroiled in an argument with a journeyman known as the *Auvergnat*. They traded challenges, and the following morning Varin arranged to have what was called a *lopin* – a small iron bar – sent to where the *Auvergnat* worked. The *lopin* contained a mark indicating how much the wager was to be: in this instance a single *louis d'or*. The *Auvergnat* responded with his own challenge. He had no desire, he said, to take on so small a wager. He had already lost two wagers for that amount during the past year and had no wish to compete for such trivial sums, particularly in Paris. He proposed a wager of 6 *louis* and, some days later, on the eve of Candlemas, sent a further *lopin* increasing the wager to 48 *livres*. His challenge was accepted and the competition took place at Neuilly outside Paris on the following day. Varin, *le petit Champagne*, did not have the money and borrowed two *louis* from a compatriot known as *le grand Champagne*. When the shoes were made, Varin was adjudged the winner and given the stake of 96 *livres*. He spent half his winnings on a dinner for all those who had been present and returned the money he had borrowed, in the form of the forged double *louis*, to the *grand Champagne*.[54]

The presence of the *compagnonnages* in the life of the eighteenth-century French trades was invariably more partial and more fluid than the image of the rites that Perdiguier presented in 1839 might imply. The small number of journeymen involved in the initiations to the *devoir* in Troyes in 1782 was an indication that *compagnons du devoir* accounted for a relatively small proportion of the workforce of the local leather trades. In

Grenoble embarked on legal proceedings against their masters in 1788: A.C. Grenoble, FF 66 fol. 397. Journeymen wigmakers also had their own associations, meeting regularly in Lyon, for example, and celebrating the feast of St Louis, 'jour auquel les garçons perruquiers ont quelques retributions'. In 1772 one of them complained to the municipal authorities that his former master had accused him of the theft of some hair. 'Cette calomnie,' he stated, '[lui] a fait un tort considérable...puisqu'étant sur le point d'être nommé syndic dans la dernière assemblée de ses confrères, sa nomination a été suspendue jusqu'à ce qu'il soit purgé de l'imputation': A.D. Rhone, BP 3304 (5 June 1764); BP 3389 (2 July 1772).

[53] A.C. Nantes, HH 169 (8 July 1762).   [54] A.N. Y 13 750 (6 April 1745).

1787 there were 33 master tanners in the city, a figure that suggests that some 40 to 60 journeymen were employed in the trade.[55] Most of them were not *compagnons du devoir*. The same image emerges from an incident in 1786, when a journeyman tanner from Bonn in Germany reported that half a dozen 'compagnons chamoiseurs se disant du devoir', had demanded 6 *livres* from him if he wanted to work in the town. Another journeyman working in the same trade, but from Burgundy, had been told by nine *compagnons du devoir* seated in an inn that he and his company were not fit to sit at their table because they had refused to join the *devoir*.[56]

Encounters of this kind are indicative of the small scale of the world of informal association in which the rituals of the *devoir* were enacted. There is no reason to suppose that the small number of *compagnons du devoir* working in the tanning and leather trades of Troyes was exceptional. Much of course depended upon the size of towns, and the number of journeymen employed in particular trades, but even in large cities like Lyon, Marseille, Bordeaux or Nantes the surviving evidence reveals that the ordinary life of informal associations was maintained by groups of journeymen who could be counted more usually by the dozen or the score, and only exceptionally by the hundred. In Bordeaux two series of registers confiscated from the *compagnons du devoir* in 1742 and 1761 provide some information about the size of the rite among journeymen locksmiths. The number of new arrivals to the city recorded by the *compagnons du devoir* was never more than half a dozen a month, while at any one time the association appears to have had between 30 and 70 members.[57] In Nantes, 56 journeymen joiners and 22 saddlers took a solemn oath to renounce the *devoir* when it was prohibited by the municipal authorities in 1750.[58]

Reports of the number of individuals present on occasions when the *compagnonnages* encountered the police authorities reveal gatherings of comparable magnitude. A funeral for a journeyman joiner in the parish of Saint-Nizier in Lyon in 1764 was attended by some 50 joiners and a further 30 or 40 journeymen locksmiths who were also *compagnons du devoir*.[59] Other occasions saw larger gatherings: in Bordeaux, over 300 journeymen carpenters were reported to have gathered at the inn kept by their *mère* on St Joseph's Day, their trade holiday, and escorted her in pomp to mass at the Cordeliers church and back again.[60] At least 150 journeymen joiners arrived bearing bouquets of flowers to attend a high mass performed by three priests in honour of their trade patron, St Anne,

55 A.C. Troyes, Fonds Boutiot, AA 41.
56 A.C. Troyes, FF *supplément* (21 July 1786).
57 A.D. Gironde, 12B 280; C 3708.
58 A.C. Nantes FF 69 (28 and 30 April 1750).
59 A.D. Rhône, BP 3303 (14 May 1764); A.C. Lyon, 701.414.
60 A.D. Gironde, 12B 356 (30 July 1777).

in Bordeaux in 1788. The mass was followed by a huge banquet in an inn on the *allée* Boutant.[61]

The figure is substantial, yet there were 126 master joiners or widows employing journeymen in Bordeaux in 1788.[62] If each master or widow employed an average of two individuals, it is likely that there were some 250 journeymen working in the city. There were, therefore, at least as many journeymen in Bordeaux who were not *compagnons du devoir* as those who were. This does not mean that they were not involved in the *compagnonnages* at all. Others undoubtedly belonged to the *gavots*, who had a substantial following among joiners and locksmiths in Bordeaux. Others too were not involved in any of the rites and were known derisively by those who were as *espontons*.

The *compagnonnages* were, therefore, a variant upon the many different forms of association established by eighteenth-century journeymen. Older, more settled journeymen sometimes frequented *chambrées*. A journeyman tailor in Lyon told his master that during the political disturbances there in the summer of 1790, a journeyman hatter had approached him to invite the members of the *chambrée* to which he belonged to join the hatters and other workers in their campaign against the municipality.[63] In Lille, as in many northern French towns, the *compagnonnages* were unknown. Journeymen met in *estaminets* which were open only to those who paid for their upkeep.[64]

If *chambrées* and *estaminets* were the venues of other types of informal association in the trades, the most substantial and widespread alternative to the *compagnonnages* remained the confraternity. Journeymen in centres of textile production like Rouen, Amiens, Troyes and Nîmes all maintained their own separate and semi-legal confraternities for much of the eighteenth century.[65] More importantly, they remained the most usual form of association among journeymen in Paris until the last quarter of the eighteenth century.[66] As the *jurats* of Bordeaux explained in 1726, the *devoir* was not to be found in the capital. The statement was reiterated in

[61] A.D. Gironde, 12B 385 (14 August 1788).

[62] A.C. Bordeaux, HH 70 (*Catalogue des maîtres menuisiers, sculpteurs et ébenistes de la ville et faubourg de Bordeaux*, 1788).

[63] 'Pour lui proposer et ses camarades, réunis dans la chambrée dont il faisait membre, de se joindre aux ouvriers chapeliers et autres': A.D. Rhône, BP 3539 (5 August 1790).

[64] 'Il n'en existe aucune (association) de cette espèce dans cette ville,' the municipal authorities reported in 1783. 'Il y a, à la vérité, comme dans toutes les villes de la Flandre des estaminets qui ne sont ouverts à d'autres particuliers qu'à ceux qui en font les frais': A.C. Lille, AG 38 (2).

[65] On Rouen, see Sonenscher, 'Weavers, Wage-Rates and the Measurement of Work', pp. 7–18; on Amiens, see Pierre Deyon, *Amiens, capitale provinciale* (Paris, 1969); on Troyes, see P. Colommès, *Les Ouvriers textiles de la région troyenne* (Troyes, 1948); on Nîmes, see M. Sonenscher, 'Royalists and Patriots', and A.C. Marseille, FF 391 (14 January 1781).

[66] See above, chapter 3, and Garrioch and Sonenscher, '*Compagnonnages*, Confraternities'.

an anonymous description of the *compagnonnages* sent to the *procureur général* of the Parlement of Paris in 1767.[67] Unlike the *compagnonnages*, confraternities were trade-specific and were made up, in the main, of journeymen who lived and worked in a single city.

In many respects, mimesis was the hallmark of the *compagnonnages*. It was always, of course, more than mimesis. For the imitative ritual of the *compagnonnages* was designed to demonstrate, by a particular feat of prowess, the superiority of a particular rite or individual performer. Like the secret initiation that was not a secret, and the fights in which victory was won on one's own side, whether or not one defeated one's opponents, mimesis also involved meeting a hidden agenda, which was set by the tension between proficiency in a trade and the vagaries of the workshop economy.

It is not difficult to identify the reasons for that tension. There is an initial clue in the occupations of the journeymen involved in the ceremonies of the *compagnons du devoir* in Troyes. Some of them were called *compagnons mégissiers*; others were *compagnons tanneurs*; others still were *compagnons chamoiseurs*. All of them, however, worked on the same materials (leather) and used the same range of implements. Too close an emphasis upon the diversity of the corporate world can lead to too little consideration of the relatively limited range of materials used in the eighteenth-century trades and the very substantial number of localities in which it was possible to work upon many of them.

The range of occupations found in the towns of eighteenth-century France varied substantially, but was rarely unusually narrow. To give one entirely random example, the 1,103 *capitables* listed on the *capitation* roll of Anduze, in the Cévennes, in 1782 included two goldsmiths, nine wigmakers, eight farriers, nine locksmiths, 20 tanners, 15 hatters, six harness- or bridle-makers, three carpenters, 25 masons, 13 tailors, 21 joiners, coopers or casket-makers, 51 shoemakers or cobblers, as well as a mass of peasant proprietors and an assortment of weavers, framework knitters and ancillary textile workers.[68] There is no reason to suppose that this range of occupations was in any way typical, but there is no reason, equally, to suppose that the arts of working with wood, leather and iron were not practised in some way or another in most of the 800 or so localities which qualified as towns (and many more which did not) in France during the eighteenth century. The rudiments of most trades were

[67] 'Le statut que les garçons ouvriers appellent devoir ne se fait pas dans la ville de Paris': A.D. Gironde, C 1814. The author of the memorandum on the *compagnonnages* sent to the *procureur général* of the Parlement of Paris in 1767 stated that if the *devoir* were prohibited in the town in which he lived, 'on jouiroit des mêmes douceurs vis-à-vis du Compagnonnage que jouit la bonne ville de Paris': Paul M Bondois, 'Un Compagnonnage au xviiie siècle' (cited above, note 24), p. 500.

[68] A.C. Anduze, CC 60.

available to a large number of potential practitioners. By any objective criterion, there was a vast pool of labour available for most of the work done in most eighteenth-century trades.

The *compagnonnages* were most ubiquitous in those trades in which the pool of labour was most substantial: among workers on wood, stone, leather and metal, rather than glass, ceramics, gold, bronze, marble or paint. In trades in which journeymen worked regularly in the same place, if not the same shop, like printing or hatting, journeymen formed associations that had little in common with the *compagnonnages*. Paper-makers too had a ceremonial life of their own which, even if it had some similarities to the rituals performed by peripatetic journeymen, owed more to the complex working arrangements and long hours of work at night that were peculiar to the trade.[69] The ceremonial of the *compagnonnages* was confined to trades in which a relatively small number of widely accessible materials were used to make a wide variety of different products and where, as a result, occupational boundaries were particularly blurred. The measure of skill in the eighteenth century was largely a matter of materials and the kinds of familiarity and dexterity which workers could be expected to have with them. There were, for example, hatters who made woollen hats and hatters who made beaver hats. Wool was cheap and widely available, while beaver was not, and was used almost entirely in Paris, Lyon and Marseille.[70] This was why there was a difference between a hatter from Paris and a hatter from Reims or Auxerre.

Not all journeymen could match the elaborate wrought iron produced by Philippe Lamour for the place Stanislas in Nancy, or equal the marquetry and ornate furniture made in the workshops belonging to Jean-Henri Riesener or Louis Delanois.[71] There are, of course, many examples of their interest in the techniques of their trades. A *compagnon du devoir* arrested after a fight in Bordeaux in 1754 produced an account of his leisure activities that was a model of professional propriety. On trade holidays he went to mass in the morning and then to evensong and a sermon in the afternoon. Afterwards he would return home to practise technical drawing.[72] A journeyman carpenter admitted having attended an assembly of over 100 other journeymen in Bordeaux in 1777, but stated that its only object had been for relaxation and instruction in the

[69] See above, chapter 1. On paper-makers, see Leonard N. Rosenband, 'Work and Management in the Montgolfier Paper Mill', (unpublished Ph.D. thesis, Princeton University, 1980).

[70] Sonenscher, *Hatters*, pp. 36–7.

[71] See Pierre Verlet, *L'Art du meuble à Paris au xviiie siècle* (Paris, 1968); Svend Eriksen, *Louis Delanois, menuisier en sièges, 1731–1792* (Paris, 1968).

[72] 'Les jours de festes il va exactement aux offices, les matins à la congrégation des Jésuites...et l'après midi il va exactement aux vespres et au sermon...et ensuitte il se retire chez luy où il travaille à dessigner': A.D. Gironde, 13B 212 (25 November 1754).

arts of their trade.[73] A Parisian journeyman carpenter was outraged when the professor of design whose course he was attending remarked that a book that the journeyman was reading must have been written by some penniless and ignorant worker. The journeyman retorted angrily that his professor had no talent and was incapable of doing anything more than draw pretty pictures.[74] Yet work in many trades did not require rare abilities or esoteric techniques. The rituals of the *compagnonnages* – the initiatory ceremonies, the pitched battles, the feats of prowess in arts which too many of them could master – were an inverted acknowledgement of the wide dissemination of ordinary abilities. They made it possible to transform similarity into difference in a world in which too many people could do the same thing.

The absence of rigid technical and occupational divisions in many sectors of the urban economy of eighteenth-century France was reinforced by the scale of turnover of labour in the trades associated most closely with the *compagnonnages*.[75] The very high levels of labour turnover affected the circumstances of journeymen in a number of ways. They meant that the working environment changed very frequently and that a premium was attached to adaptability and flexibility. The connection between the rhetoric of the *compagnonnages*, the benefits of the *tour de France* and this structural characteristic of workshop production is obvious. 'Vrais artistes', who could claim mastery of a wide range of different types of work in the same trade – from making springs to making railings, for example – were most able to find work.

The high incidence of labour turnover placed a further constraint upon eighteenth-century journeymen. Just as the kind of work expected of them was never entirely the same, so the men with whom they worked changed too. The relationship between a journeyman's age, experience, competence and seniority changed constantly in the passage from *boutique* to *boutique* and, more obviously, from town to town. A man of 30 who had been established for months or years in one *boutique* could find himself working as a newcomer alongside a 17- or 18-year-old in another. The *premier compagnon* in one locality became the *dernier en ville* when he reached the next.

The elaborate but impermanent hierarchies created by the ceremonial of the *compagnonnages* were a symbolic counterpoint to the frequent inversions of age, seniority and precedence attendant upon a high level of labour turnover. Within the *cayenne* journeymen fined one another for virtually anything. Fines were paid into the common box and the funds

73 'Leur motif de cette assemblée n'avoit d'autre object que de divertir et de s'instruire les uns aux autres sur les ouvrages de leur métier': A.D. Gironde, 12B 356 (30 June 1777).
74 A.N. Y 11 024ᵃ (30 May 1782).
75 See above, chapter 5.

were consumed on trade holidays. In this way, real differences were transcended by the equality created by what amounted to joking relationships. The papers of the locksmiths of Bordeaux listed fines imposed during the first six months of 1758 for breaking the furniture, hitting another journeyman, talking about the *devoir* in public, working twice in the same shop, drawing a pistol indoors, taking a bottle of wine at an initiation, failing to collect money, finding work for an aspiring member of the *devoir* without permission, failing to attend an assembly and losing some of the association's property.[76] Although there were rules, it is clear that they were sufficiently imprecise to allow offences to be invented when the need arose. In a world that was turned upside-down all too frequently, the equalities created by offences of which everyone was guilty at one time or another were a counterpoint to the inequalities of age, ability and experience which itinerant journeymen encountered in the course of their peregrinations. To those outside the circle of the initiate, the ritual of the *compagnonnages* created inequalities, in a world where too many men had too much in common. To those within the circle, it created equalities, in which differences of age, ability and geographical origin might be suspended.

The *compagnonnages* emerged when differences between journeymen were sanctioned by the law. Journeymen in all five of the trades singled out by the Doctors of the Sorbonne for their association with the *devoir* in 1655 were among many groups of Parisian journeymen whose confraternities remained in existence until the second half of the eighteenth century. Journeymen who had served an apprenticeship in at least three of the five trades (hatters, cutlers and shoemakers) enjoyed rights of preferential employment over migrants from the provinces. Article 50 of the statutes of the Parisian shoemakers of 1573 made it clear that masters were permitted to employ *étrangers* only when there were no *compagnons de Paris* seeking work.[77] Master cutlers were prohibited, by their statutes of 1565, from employing more than three journeymen at a time. Migrants from the provinces were required to leave the city and find work outside Paris and its suburbs if they were unable to find work under the terms of the provision.[78] In 1700 a ruling by the *chambre de police* ordered master hatters to give preferential employment to Parisian journeymen provided

[76] 'Pour avoir quasé le meuble du père; pour avoir frapé un compagnon; pour avoir raportés les afair des compagnon; pour n'avoir pas aporté le billet d'argent; pour avoir travaillé deux fois de la même boutique; pour avoir tiré son pistollet dans sa chambre; pour avoir mis une bouteille à la récépesion dans sa poche; pour avoir anbauché un aspiran sans la permission du premier compagnon; pour ne pas avoir aporté d'argent à son tour; pour avoir manqué l'assemblée: pour avoir abandoné les afair des compagnon.' A.D. Gironde, C 3708.

[77] René de Lespinasse, *Les Métiers et corporations de la ville de Paris* (Paris, 1897), vol. 3, p. 350.

[78] *Ibid.*, vol. 2 (Paris, 1892), p. 391.

that they did not attempt to raise their wages to levels higher than those paid to provincial journeymen.[79]

The ritual of the *compagnonnages* emerged on the periphery of the corporate world. Its characteristic forms imitated the ceremonial performed by journeymen's confraternities and echoed rights sanctioned by the courts. The *compagnonnages* were created by journeymen from Bolbec and Bapaume, Laval or Largentière, rather than men who were settled in Bordeaux or Lyon, Paris or Toulouse. They were created by men who had little to expect and not much to inherit, but who also needed to work in order to live. As the formal distinctions which separated journeymen from Paris or the other major cities from those of the rest of France were gradually destroyed during the eighteenth century, the *compagnonnages* came into their own. By the last quarter of the eighteenth century, shoemakers or hatters or cutlers in Paris (and journeymen in many other trades and cities) were no longer able to find recognition in the courts for their distinctive legal rights. A ruling by the Conseil d'Etat in 1775, for example, allowed master cutlers in Paris to employ as many journeymen as they saw fit.[80] As a result, differences that had been sanctioned by the courts gave way to differences which journeymen created among themselves. The golden age of the *compagnonnages*, which ran from roughly 1760 to 1830, was the product of this state of affairs. In a world divested of legal rights, symbolic distinction – the distinction created by ceremonies of initiation, physical fights and feats of prowess in particular trades – came into its own.

As the distance between the courts and the trades widened during the latter half of the eighteenth century, the *compagnonnages* became the most ubiquitous of journeymen's associations. Yet, if magistrates became increasingly familiar with 'cette fatale association du devoir...cent fois proscrite par les règlements', as the municipal authorities of Nantes put it in 1787, the legal status of the *devoir* was, as the statement implies, a more intractable problem.[81] Although the church had proscribed quasi-religious ceremonies of initiation, much of the life of the *compagnonnages* continued to centre upon the cloister and the chapel. The ambivalent relationship between the church and the state during the eighteenth century often

79 *Ibid.*, vol. 3, p. 292. See also Sonenscher, *Hatters*, chapter 7.
80 A.N. E 2515, fols. 623–4 (31 May 1775). For a good example of the small-town origins of many of those initiated into the *compagnonnages* and the tension between rudimentary proficiency and specialist skills, see the autobiography of the woollen-weaver (*étaminier*) Louis Simon. Simon was taught how to make *étamines* by his father, a weaver in La-Fontaine-Saint-Martin, near Le Mans. He set out on his *tour de France* at the age of 22 but found, in Nantes, that weaving cotton was beyond his ability. Even in Amiens, where woollen fabrics were produced, he was told that 'puisque vous ete un Etaminier du Mans il n'y a point ici d'ouvrage fine pour vous faur aller a Rhains (Reims)': Anne Fillon, ed., *Louis Simon étaminier 1741–1820 dans son village du Haut-Maine au Siècle des Lumières*, 2 typed vols. Université du Maine. Le Mans, n.d. [1985], vol. 1, MS. 9, p. 13.
81 A.C. Nantes, HH 147 (14 December 1787).

ensured that meetings in cloisters or monastic rooms, particularly after the celebration of mass and the distribution of the *pain bénit*, passed unmolested by the civil authorities.[82]

The peripatetic life of the *compagnonnages* also meant that public gatherings in *cabarets* and inns were difficult to prevent and often impossible to pursue, because the journeymen had left to work elsewhere. The limited character of the law ensured that rulings made by one court did not necessarily apply in regions that fell under the jurisdiction of another authority. After the Parlement of Paris had issued two rulings prohibiting assemblies by members of the *compagnonnages* in the aftermath of criminal proceedings arising from pitched battles in Lyon and the little town of Murat in 1778, the *procureur du roi* of La Rochelle (which also fell within the court's jurisdiction) informed the *procureur général* of the Parlement that the prohibition was pointless. Unless it was reiterated by the Parlements of Britanny and Guyenne, journeymen working in La Rochelle would merely leave the city and travel to Nantes or Bordeaux to continue the *devoir* there.[83]

Faced with these practical difficulties, magistrates responded to the *compagnonnages* with intimidation. The courts prescribed savage penalties for journeymen arrested after fights or found wearing the insignia of the rites. After a number of battles between rival groups of journeymen in Bordeaux, the *procureur général* of the Parlement of Guyenne decided in 1774 that 'il est temps d'arrêter des attentats aussi criminels par la terreur des peines que les loix et les ordonnances prononcent'.[84] Henceforth any gathering by journeymen, whether they were armed with batons or not, and any procession, fight or attempt to provoke a fight, would be punishable by death. The magistrates of the Parlement of Provence adopted the same strategy in May 1787 after several weeks of almost uninterrupted fighting by members of the different rites of the *compagnonnages* on the streets of Marseille.[85] These draconian measures were complemented by threats of severe penalties for journeymen who gathered in numbers as low as three or four, and massive fines for the inn-keepers or *cabaretiers* who allowed their premises to be used by the associations.

Penalties of this degree of severity were consonant with the arbitrary and discretionary character of the eighteenth-century criminal law. There is little evidence, however, that journeymen arrested as members of the *compagnonnages* were ever sentenced to death, even though men convicted

[82] See above, p. 81, and B.N. MS. Joly de Fleury, 510 fol. 303, where the *procureur du roi* in La Rochelle reported on his difficulties in enforcing the edict of April 1777 prohibiting assemblies: 'Nous éprouvons la plus grande résistance de la part des communautés religieuses. Les religieux Recollets ont été les plus obstinés ou les moins adroits à ce cacher. Les garçons menuisiers du *devoir* y font dire une messe chaque premier dimanche du mois. Il est vrai qu'ils ne vont plus à l'offrande et que le pain béni ne paroit plus, mais on assure que ce pain béni se distribue à la sacristie.'
[83] *Ibid.*   [84] A.D. Gironde, B (unclassified, 29 July 1774).
[85] A.D. Bouches-du-Rhône B 5656 (22 May 1787).

of assault after brawls between rival rites were undoubtedly sent to the galleys.[86] The late eighteenth-century campaign against the more draconian aspects of the criminal law added to the uncertainty surrounding the legal status of the *devoir*. The author of the article entitled 'Compagnon' in Panckoucke's *Encyclopédie méthodique* (1791) reproduced the Paris Parlement's ruling of 1778 prohibiting the *compagnonnages* and commented that 'elle a quelque chose d'odieux' in its inquisitorial character and, especially, in its clause prohibiting more than four journeymen from meeting together at once.[87] By then, many magistrates had reached similar conclusions. As the *procureur général* of the Parlement of Bordeaux informed his counterpart in Paris in 1779, 'il est aisé de défendre, mais très difficile de faire exécuter les défenses'. The court had decided therefore not to follow the example of the Parlement of Paris and prohibit the *compagnonnages* yet again. 'A différentes époques,' he wrote, 'on en a fait à peu près de semblables,' but there was little obvious benefit to be gained by reiterating rulings by the Parlements. He suggested that a royal declaration, 'une loy positive et générale', might be a better solution and, in the interim, advised his colleague that 'la voye de la douceur vis à vis des êtres aussi rustiques peut être la meilleure'.[88]

The 'rustic beings' initiated into the rites of the *compagnonnages* undoubtedly saw them in a different light. The echoes of the ceremonial of the church and the courts in the rituals of the *devoir* were indirect testimony to the pervasiveness of the culture of the polity among men who, during the eighteenth century, had learned their trades in little towns that were far from Paris, Toulouse, Bordeaux or Nantes. The echoes of the legends of freemasonry in the rituals of the *compagnonnages* that Perdiguier presented in the early nineteenth century was indirect testimony to how much of that culture was transformed by the Revolution. If the *compagnonnages* were not, as has often been assumed, the organisational form of a highly skilled artisanal elite, the networks of information and association that they supplied were, none the less, the principal resource of single men far from their *pays* of origin. If they were not, as has been equally frequently assumed, primordial forms of the modern labour movement, the *compagnonnages* were, none the less, a counterweight to the resources of corporate power that master artisans could deploy. Above all, however, the *compagnonnages* supplied the journeymen who created them with a symbolic vocabulary of difference and distinction in a world in which too many of them had too much in common to be acknowledged.

86   Andre Zysberg, *Les Galériens au xviiie siècle* (Paris, 1987).
87   For a recent study of the various cases cited by law reformers, see William Doyle, 'Dupaty (1748–1788): A Career in the Late Enlightenment', *Studies on Voltaire and the Eighteenth Century*, 230 (1985), pp. 1–125.
88   B.N. MS. Joly de Fleury 510, fols. 308 and 312.

CHAPTER 10

Artisans, 'sans-culottes' and the politics of republicanism

There were five successful popular insurrections in Paris between 1789 and 1793.[1] By the autumn of 1793 France was a republic and at war with most of the rest of Europe. Political power in Paris lay uneasily among a nebulous cluster of institutions and informal associations located somewhere between the street and the state. Among the many potential rivals and alternative sources of political authority to the republican Convention were the *commune* of Paris and the general assemblies of the 48 sections into which the capital had been divided since 1790. These sectional assemblies were complemented by fluid networks of affiliated popular societies, linked in their turn either to the Cordeliers club or, more usually, to the Jacobins. Many of the men and women who participated in the sectional assemblies and popular societies in 1793 and 1794 were artisans or shopkeepers of one kind or another. Many of them called themselves *sans-culottes*.[2] The *sans-culottes* were more than participants in sectional assemblies and popular societies. Many of them were armed, either because they belonged to the National Guard or because they had enlisted in the republican militia, or *armée révolutionnaire*, created in September 1793. Its 6,000 members made it the largest of over 50 such popular militias established all over France.[3]

Between the autumn of 1793 and the autumn of 1795 the political life of Paris and much of the rest of France was dominated by conflict between

---

[1] Thus for Camille Desmoulins in December 1793, good citizens were those 'vétérans de la révolution, ceux qui ont fait les cinq campagnes depuis 1789...qui, depuis le 12 juillet, ont marché entre les poignards et les poisons des aristocrates et des tyrans': Camille Desmoulins, *Le Vieux Cordelier*, ed. Henri Calvet (Paris, 1936), pp. 42–3. The classic study of the Parisian insurrections is George Rudé, *The Crowd in the French Revolution* (Oxford, 1959).

[2] The point of departure for any study of the *sans-culottes* remains Albert Soboul, *Les Sans-Culottes parisiens en l'an II* (Paris, 1958). For a recent review of the subsequent literature, see Haim Burstin, 'I Sanculotti: Un Dossier da Riaprire', *Passato e Presente*, 10 (1986), pp. 23–52.

[3] Richard Cobb, *Les Armées révolutionnaires: instrument de la terreur dans les départements*, 2 vols (Paris and The Hague, 1961 and 1963).

different groups within the Convention and their various supporters and opponents within the *commune*, the Jacobins, the Cordeliers, the sections, the popular societies, the *armée révolutionnaire* and the National Guard. Gradually, the many alternative sources of political power were eliminated. When elections to replace the Convention by the two Councils that were the legislative arm of the Directory took place in the autumn of 1795, the sections, the popular militias and the *sans-culottes* had all but disappeared from political life.[4] The history of the Convention ended, as it had begun, in insurrection. This time, however, insurrection failed. In May 1795 the army invaded the *faubourg* Saint-Antoine on the eastern side of Paris and disarmed thousands of *sans-culottes*. In October, Bonaparte's 'whiff of grapeshot' put an end to a royalist rising organised within the sections of western Paris. Military intervention finally ensured that political power in revolutionary France passed definitively from the street to the state.

Nothing in the history of the eighteenth-century French trades foreshadowed these developments. The early years of the Revolution were marked by a number of conflicts between masters and journeymen, but their form and content continued to follow well-established patterns. In many cases, journeymen seized the opportunity of the political crisis of 1789 to press claims on disputed issues on which the courts had previously made unfavourable rulings. Journeymen in the hatting trades of Lyon and Marseille made a point of electing men who had figured prominently in disputes in the trade as delegates to the electoral assemblies called in the spring of 1789 to draw up corporate *cahiers de doléances*.[5] Weavers in the textile trades of Lyon, Rouen and Troyes revived their campaigns to obtain legally sanctioned scales of piece-rates and in Lyon, at least, they were successful. A new scale of piece-rates, which came to be known as the *tarif Monnet*, was sanctioned by the Royal Council early in 1790.[6] The booming conditions in the great port cities of Marseille, Bordeaux and Nantes in 1790 and 1791 encouraged journeymen working in trades associated with shipbuilding and dock work to press for higher daily rates and shorter working hours. Workers in the Parisian quarries, the Gobelins manufactory and the Savonnerie revived campaigns over

4 Kare D. Tönnesson, *La Défaite des sans-culottes* (Paris and Oslo, 1959); Isser Woloch, *Jacobin Legacy: The Democratic Movement under The Directory* (Princeton, 1970).

5 Sonenscher, *Hatters*, pp. 161–2.

6 A.D. Rhone 3E 6628 (89) (3 April 1789); A.N. E 1676[b] (1), *arrêt du conseil d'état* (29 November 1789); B.M. Lyon, *Mémoire des électeurs fabricants d'étoffes de soie et tarif dressé en exécution de l'arrêt du 8 août 1789* (Lyon, 1790); *Receuil de mémoires et tarif dressés en exécution de l'arrêt du 8 août 1789, obtenu par Messieurs les députés de la ville et sénéchaussée de Lyon* (Lyon, 1790); David L. Longfellow, 'Silk Weavers and Social Struggle in Lyon during the French Revolution', *French Historical Studies*, 12 (1981), pp. 1–40; Bill Edmonds, 'A Study in Popular Anti-Jacobinism: The Career of Denis Monnet', *French Historical Studies*, 13 (1983), pp. 215–51; M. Sonenscher, 'Weavers, Wage-Rates and the Measurement of Work'; Jean-Jacques Vernier, *Cahiers de doléances du Bailliage de Troyes* (Troyes, 1909), pp. 177–87.

wage-levels or modes of wage-payment. Here too, the campaigns were a success. More generally, there was a widespread and equally successful movement to shorten the working day in the building and furnishing trades of Paris and many other cities.[7]

Many of the forms and ceremonial of journeymen's associations were also carried over into the new revolutionary institutions. In Marseille, journeymen locksmiths who belonged to the *devoir* volunteered to form a company of the National Guard to complement two other companies made up of masters and journeymen domiciled permanently in the city. In Nantes, journeymen continued to celebrate trade holidays and Saints' Days with festivities and high masses until 1792, but headed their processions with men wearing the uniform of the National Guard. In Paris, as in many much smaller localities, journeymen's associations began to meet openly and to adopt the prevailing idiom of patriotism and fraternal goodwill in their proceedings and public statements. Long-standing antagonism between rival rites of the *compagnonnages* also found new expression in the vocabulary of fraternity, patriotism and civic responsibility that gained such wide currency after the fall of the Bastille.[8] Yet none of these activities and pronouncements heralded the politics and rhetoric of the *sans-culottes*.

Nothing, moreover, could be more striking than the difference between the fluidity, diversity and complexity of the local economies of particular trades and the simplicity and uniformity of that symbol of republican integrity and civic conformity, the *sans-culotte*. Nor did the inflexible character of the rhetoric by which the world of the *sans-culottes* was evoked echo many of the different registers in which the dialogue between masters and journeymen was conducted. The didactic portrait of

[7] A.C. Bordeaux, HH 80 (4 September 1788); A.D. Gironde, 12B 385 (29 August and 4 November 1788); 12B 386 (4 September 1788); A.C. Nantes I² carton 3, dossier 4 (21 July 1791; 4 August 1791); *ibid.*, F⁷ carton 9, dossier 2 (11 May 1792); F. J Verger, *Archives curieuses de la ville de Nantes* (Nantes, 1837), vol. 5, p. 229 (24 February 1792); Yannick Guin, *Le Mouvement ouvrier nantais. Essai sur le syndicalisme d'action directe à Nantes et à Saint-Nazaire* (Paris, 1976), pp. 18–19; A.N. F¹³ 1395; AD XI 65, *Requête au Roi et mémoire sur la nécessité de rétablir les corps de marchands* (Paris, 1817); Angela Groppi, '"La classe la plus nombreuse, la plus utile et la plus précieuse". Organizzazione del lavoro e conflitti nella Parigi rivoluzionaria', European University Institute, Working Paper No. 88/325 (Florence 1988); Haim Burstin, 'Travail, entreprise et politique à la manufacture des Gobelins pendant la période révolutionnaire', paper presented to the *colloque on La Révolution française et le développement du capitalisme* (Lille, November 1987).

[8] A.C. Marseille HH 430 (n.d., but probably 1790); *ibid.*, HH 416, *Mémoire présenté à MM les maire et officiers municipaux par les ouvriers ébenistes et menuisiers de Marseille* (n.d. but, from the allusions, probably 1791); A.C. Nantes, I² carton 3, dossier 4 (4 August 1791; 25 June 1792); Sonenscher, 'Journeymen, the Courts', pp. 105–6. For other examples, see A.C. Le Havre, HH 4 (34), for an association of journeymen tailors, and HH 39, 'Adresse à messieurs de la commune de la ville du Havre (par la société des garçons cordonniers)'; Jean Legoy, 'Une Corporation turbulente: les cordonniers havrais au xviiie siècle', *Cahiers Léopold Delisle* 32 (1982–3), pp. 159–65; A.C. Grenoble, HH 45 (4 June 1790).

industrious civic commitment presented by the republican Vingternier in 1793 in response to the 'impertinent question, *mais qu'est-ce qu'un sans-culotte*' was an evocation of moral qualities that had little to do with the trades of eighteenth-century Paris.[9] There was a gulf between the small-scale, self-contained world of manual labour celebrated by the eponymous hero of a thousand speeches, motions and pamphlets and the elaborate divisions of labour, unstable hierarchies of contractors and sub-contractors and fleeting arrangements between masters and journeymen that endowed the trades with their fragile coherence and interdependent vitality. The transformation of artisans into *sans-culottes* was not, in short, a simple transposition of the concerns and preoccupations of the workshop to the popular societies and republican institutions of 1793 and 1794.

It has been usual, however, to argue the contrary. Images of artisanal production embedded in the political rhetoric of republican France have been amalgamated with analyses of the workshop economy itself to explain the emergence of the *sans-culottes* as a political force in 1793 and 1794. Not surprisingly, the descriptions of the artisanal economy informing this social interpretation have been very similar to those produced by the *sans-culottes* themselves. Such additional criteria as have been used to define the social context in which popular republicanism developed derive from highly simplified characterisations of industrial society. Since the average number of journeymen employed by master artisans was very low, it has been easy enough to contrast the small-scale character of the workshop economy with the large-scale character of the factory and argue that the politics of the *sans-culottes* were an expression of the pre-industrial form of the eighteenth-century urban economy. The circularity of the whole procedure needs no emphasis.[10] The workshop economy has come to be seen principally in terms of what it was not, rather than what it was, while the politics of the *sans-culottes* have been explained mainly in terms of features of artisanal production that have been identified principally on the basis of what the *sans-culottes* themselves said and did.

The limitations of this circular explanation of popular republicanism have been exposed still further by two additional assumptions. It has been generally accepted that, until the Revolution, artisans took no part in public life. The logical corollary to this assumption has been that the Revolution was an intensive course of political education, allowing men and women who had no great experience of high politics to acquire a

9 Walter Markov and Albert Soboul, eds. *Die Sansculotten von Paris* (Berlin, 1957), p. 2. What follows is a development of Michael Sonenscher, 'The *Sans-Culottes* of the Year II: Rethinking the Language of Labour in Revolutionary France', *Social History*, 9 (1984), pp. 301–28, and 'Les Sans-Culottes de l'an II: repenser le langage du travail dans la France révolutionnaire', *Annales E.S.C.*, 40 (1985), pp. 1087–1108.
10 Burstin, 'I Sanculotti', p. 31.

political consciousness and a political vocabulary that conformed to their everyday concerns. The Revolution was, from this standpoint, a process of 'politicisation and radicalisation of the common people of Paris' which culminated in the emergence of the *sans-culottes*.[11] The popular republicanism of the Year II, with its emphasis upon material independence, direct democracy and the unlimited sovereignty of the people, translated the ordinary experience of small-scale producers into a political vocabulary that best embodied the vulnerability of artisans to dependence, scarcity and dearth.

Neither of these assumptions is acceptable. There was no great gulf between the cultural world of eighteenth-century artisans and the legal world that supplied many of the terms and propositions used in conflicts in the trades. Artisans did not need to read Rousseau or form popular societies to learn about slavery and freedom, dependence and independence, natural rights and legal obligation. The terms were used in ordinary speech, as well as legal argument, throughout the eighteenth century. The masters and journeymen who found themselves on the threshold of a new political order in the spring of 1789 were as much – or as little – aware of the great conceptual issues informing the conflicts of the day as were the lawyers, administrators and officials who seized the political initiative at Versailles and all over France in the early months of the Revolution. The trades were not isolated from the rest of the eighteenth-century French polity, still less from the aristocratic, administrative and professional circles whose households they built, decorated, furnished and supplied. The artisans who were prominent as *sans-culottes* in 1793 and 1794 were broadly representative of the many different trades that endowed the Parisian economy with its structured form. Many of them were men in their thirties or more.[12] Most of them, either as masters or journeymen, would have experienced at least one major conflict in the trades before 1789. Few of them were likely to have been innocent of the vocabulary of legal argument and everyday political negotiation of the eighteenth century.

Yet, just as the concerns and cultural resources of those associated with the trades cannot be isolated from those of the rest of the polity, neither can those of any particular group be privileged at the expense of any other. At no time between 1788 and 1795 could anyone foresee what would

[11] R. B. Rose, *The Making of the Sans-Culottes, Democratic Ideas and Institutions in Paris 1789–92* (Manchester, 1983). p. 20.

[12] Albert Soboul and Raymonde Monnier, *Répertoire du personnel sectionnaire parisien en l'an II* (Paris, 1985), pp. 8–16. Their places of birth were also characteristic of the population of Paris as a whole: some two-thirds (63 per cent) of a sample of 386 individuals drawn from the biographical details presented by Soboul and Monnier were born outside Paris; only 37 per cent were natives of the capital. The proportions match those calculated by Alain Blum and Jacques Houdaille, '12,000 Parisiens en 1793', *Population*, 46 (1986), pp. 259–302.

happen. All the actors in the revolutionary process were imperfectly informed. All of them were condemned to make use of such cultural and political resources as they had at their disposal to achieve, or prevent others from achieving, goals that could be anticipated in only a limited way. If the Revolution was a process of political education, it was a process in which lawyers, nobles and clergy had as much to learn as master artisans and the journeymen they employed.

There was, therefore, no necessary connection between being an artisan and becoming a *sans-culotte*. The relationship between the two was a contingent one, as was the relationship between artisans and Royalism in Nîmes in 1790, or the relationship between artisans and Federalism in Lyon in 1793.[13] In Paris, however, many artisans came to identify themselves as *sans-culottes*. They did so not because there was anything inherent in the workshop economy that predisposed artisans to become republicans of a certain kind, but because the tensions and ambiguities inherent in late eighteenth-century French republicanism were such that conflict over the aims and purposes of republican government tended to become inherent in the identity of republicanism which began soon after the fall of the Bastille and gathered in intensity after the flight of the King to Varennes in 1791 and the overthrow of the monarchy itself in August 1792.

It is customary to associate the republicanism of the French Revolution with Rousseau and the *Social Contract*. Yet when the deputy to the Convention, Camille Desmoulins, set out, in December 1793, to commemorate 'les fondateurs de la république' as part of the campaign waged by Danton and his associates against the leadership of the Paris *commune* in general and the journalist Jacques-René Hébert in particular, he chose to introduce the first issue of *Le Vieux Cordelier* with an epigraph from Machiavelli's *Discourses on Livy* – 'Dès que ceux qui gouvernent sont haïs, leurs concurrens ne tarderont pas à être admirés' – and proceeded to litter many of following issues with long quotations from the works of Tacitus.[15] Many of these citations were taken not from the classics

---

[13] On Nîmes, see M. Sonenscher, 'Royalists and Patriots'; on Lyon, see Edmonds, 'Denis Monnet'. On Federalism in general, see Bill Edmonds, '"Federalism" and Urban Revolt in France in 1793', *Journal of Modern History*, 55 (1983), pp. 22–53.

[14] The point of departure for any study of the political culture of revolutionary France is François Furet, *Penser la Révolution française* (Paris, 1978); see, for the best subsequent study, Lynn Hunt, *Politics, Culture and Class in the French Revolution* (Berkeley, 1984); and, most recently, Colin Lucas, ed., *The Political Culture of the French Revolution* (Oxford, 1988). The study of eighteenth-century republicanism has been transformed by J. G. A. Pocock, *The Machiavellian Moment* (Princeton, 1975); see too the works cited below, notes 16 and 17.

[15] Desmoulins, *Vieux Cordelier*, ed. Calvet, especially pp. 91–108.

themselves, but from the works of a Scot named Thomas Gordon, whose *Discourses on Tacitus* had been published in England in 1728, and were translated into French by the Huguenot Pierre Daudé in 1742.

Gordon is now relatively well known.[16] Together with Thomas Trenchard, he was the author of a series of pamphlets published in London at the time of the South Sea Bubble in 1719 and 1720 under the titles of *The Independent Whig* and *Cato's Letters*. In them Gordon set out to show how a combination of public credit, political patronage and ecclesiastical bigotry threatened to undermine the political independence and civic commitment that were the basis of English liberty and political stability. Much of the argument in *The Independent Whig* and *Cato's Letters* echoed the earlier work of James Harrington, whose *Oceana* had been edited and published by John Toland in 1700. Together, the works of Harrington, Toland, Trenchard and Gordon formed part of an English republican tradition that has been variously entitled 'Commonwealth', 'Old Whig,' or 'Civic Humanist'.[17] The key point of reference in this tradition was the work of Machiavelli.

Desmoulins' choice of a passage from Machiavelli's *Discourses* as the epigraph to the first issue of *Le Vieux Cordelier* is an indication of the extent to which the republican tradition with which the Florentine was associated had been assimilated into the political culture of revolutionary France. The process owed something to the work of Montesquieu, whose *De l'Esprit des lois* had drawn heavily upon the Machiavellian tradition both in its characterisation of republican virtue and in its portrayal of the English constitution in terms that were close to those adopted by Trenchard and Gordon.[18] Yet in a polity that was a monarchy, Montesquieu's Machiavelli

---

[16] On Gordon, see Caroline Robbins, *The Eighteenth-Century Commonwealthmen* (Cambridge, Mass., 1961); J. G. A. Pocock, *Virtue, Commerce and History* (Cambridge, 1985); and, for a bibliography of Gordon's work, J. M. Bulloch, *Thomas Gordon, The 'Independent Whig'* (Aberdeen, 1918).

[17] The most recent discussions of this tradition can be found in Pocock, *Virtue*; Istvan Hont and Michael Ignatieff, eds., *Wealth and Virtue: Anthony Pagden, ed., The Languages of Political Theory in Early Modern Europe* (Cambridge, 1987). For a valuable discussion of the relative importance of the civic humanist tradition in the recently established United States of America, see Joyce Appleby, 'What is Still American in the Political Philosophy of Thomas Jefferson?', *William and Mary Quarterly*, 3rd series, 39 (1982), pp. 287–309, and her *Capitalism and a New Social Order. The Republican Vision of the 1790s* (New York, 1984); Lance Banning, 'Jeffersonian Ideology Revisited: Liberal and Classical Ideas in the New American Republic', *William and Mary Quarterly*, 3rd series, 43 (1986), pp. 3–19, and the reply by Joyce Appleby, 'Republicanism in Old and New Contexts', *ibid.*, 20–34.

[18] The subject awaits its historian. See, with reservations, Joseph Dédieu, *Montesquieu et la tradition politique anglaise en France* (Paris, 1909), pp. 287–8; Albert Cherel. *La Pensée de Machiavel en France* (Paris, 1935), pp. 239–43. A more recent study questions the extent to which Montesquieu was directly indebted to Gordon, but the objections it raises do not undermine the more general relationship between Montesquieu and the English civic tradition, a tradition that was, of course, present in the works of Bolingbroke as much as in Gordon: see Quentin Skinner, 'The Principles and Practice of Opposition: The Case of

was republican in no more than a figurative sense: a symbol of a different political order, or, at most, a reminder of the importance of civic responsibility in a polity whose vitality and stability depended upon the active involvement of privileged bodies, and the Parlements above all, in the maintenance of civil liberties.

It was in this sense that Machiavelli could be interpreted in the aftermath of the publication of *De l'Esprit des lois*. In his introduction to a translation of Machiavelli's *Discourses* published in 1782, Joseph de Menc, a magistrate at the Parlement of Aix, argued that the common characteristic of monarchies and republics was their commitment to political liberty.[19] Political liberty, he wrote, was the right of every citizen to participate in matters pertaining to the general concerns of society. Once, in simpler societies, that right had been exercised by every citizen. As society had become more complex, social inequalities more pronounced and the flux of disparate events (*revolutions*) more rapid, that original state of political equality could no longer be sustained. Instead, various representative intermediaries had developed to endow monarchical government with its distinctive form. Power had come to be distributed among the various classes of citizens into which the polity was divided in proportion to the service that each class rendered to the state. Political liberty in a monarchy was therefore grounded upon the interdependent, but differently weighted, contribution of each class to the polity as a whole. The circle could thus be squared, and the apparent difference between monarchical and republican government could be shown to mask a deeper similarity.

De Menc's Machiavelli was redolent of Montesquieu. Nevertheless, the assimilation of the republican tradition into an account of monarchical government that was common to both *De l'Esprit des lois* and its later imitation was by no means the only construction that could be put upon Machiavelli's works. In 1786, in an anonymously published *Eloge de Montesquieu*, one of the many inhabitants of the literary netherworld of the

19 Bolingbroke versus Walpole', in Neil McKendrick, ed., *Historical Perspectives* (London, 1974), pp. 93–128, and Isaac Kramnick, *Bolingbroke and His Circle: The Politics of Nostalgia in the Age of Walpole* (London, 1968). If Montesquieu relied upon Tacitus (rather than Gordon) as his chief authority, *De L'Esprit des lois* nonetheless played an important part in rehabilitating the republican Tacitus (as a surrogate for the republican Machiavelli) in the latter half of the eighteenth century, in place of the absolutist and amoral Tacitus (as a surrogate for the even more dangerously amoral Machiavelli) of seventeenth-century French political commentary: see Catherine Volpilhac-Auger, 'Tacite et Montesquieu', *Studies in Voltaire and the Eighteenth Century*, 232 (Oxford, 1985); and, more generally, Jurgen Von Stackelberg, *Tacitus in der Romania* (Tubingen, 1960).

See his introduction to his translation of the *Discorsi*, entitled *Réflexions de Machiavel sur la première décade de Tite Live* (Amsterdam, 1782). On the eighteenth-century use of the word revolution, see Keith Michael Baker, 'Revolution', in Colin Lucas, ed., *The Political Culture of the French Revolution* (Oxford, 1988).

High Enlightenment, a Parisian of Irish Jacobite descent named James Rutledge, set out to present a different Machiavelli.[20] Rutledge's Machiavelli was modelled not upon Montesquieu, but upon the work of the *abbé* Gabriel Bonnot de Mably, whose *Des droits et des devoirs du citoyen* had been written in 1758 and circulated in manuscript form until its publication in 1790. Mably's works represented the most substantial importation of the English Commonwealth tradition into the political culture of eighteenth-century France.[21] Through them, Rutledge was able to present Montesquieu in a very different light.

The true sources of Montesquieu's masterpiece were, Rutledge claimed, Machiavelli and Harrington. Yet, whether through prudence, or through an understandable reluctance to undermine the conceptual basis of the established political order, Montesquieu had been unwilling to acknowledge the parallels between his own work and those of his predecessors. More fundamentally, he had refused to make explicit the difference between his work and that of Harrington. For where Montesquieu had organised his discussion of the various forms of government around three types, Harrington had written of only two. Monarchical government as it was usually defined, Rutledge stated (in a phrase borrowed directly from Mably), was no more than 'un être de raison, une chimère imposante'.[22] As Harrington had shown, all governments were either republican or despotic. Political liberty in a monarchical government was an illusion.

Rutledge's somewhat backhanded eulogy of Montesquieu's achievement is an indication of the divergence between the neo-Harringtonian republican tradition and its more orthodox counterpart. Central to the former tradition was the concept of an agrarian law. As the authors of *Cato's Letters* put it:

It proceeds from a consummate Ignorance in Politicks, to think that a Number of Men agreeing together, can make and hold a Commonwealth, before Nature has

[20] Jacques Rutledge, *Eloge de Montesquieu* (London, 1786). The work, with its allusions to 'ce beau songe de cinq années [qui] s'est évanoui', was probably a coded panegyric of Necker. On Rutledge, see Raymond Las Vergnas, *Le Chevalier Rutlidge* [sic] '*Gentilhomme Anglais*' (Paris, 1932). Robert Darnton's celebrated essay on 'The High Enlightenment and the Low-Life of Literature' now in his *The Literary Underground of the Old Régime* (Cambridge, Mass., 1982), pp. 1–40 would be reinforced by fuller examination of the ideas and concepts manipulated by the many forerunners of the hero of Balzac's *Illusions perdues*. See, more recently, Sara Maza, 'Le Tribunal de la nation: les mémoires judiciaires et l'opinion publique à la fin de l'ancien régime', *Annales E.S.C.*, 42 (1987), pp. 73–90.

[21] On Mably, see Keith Michael Baker, 'A Script for a French Revolution: The Political Consciousness of the abbé Mably', *Eighteenth-Century Studies*, 14 (1981), pp. 235–63, and his 'Memory and Practice: Politics and Representation of the Past in Eighteenth-century France', *Representations*, 11 (1985), pp. 134–64. See also Thomas Schleich, 'Die Verbreitung und Rezeption der Aufklärung in der französischen Gesellschaft am Beispiel Mably', in Hans Ulrich Gumbrecht, Rolf Reichardt and Thomas Schleich, eds., *Sozialgeschichte der Aufklärung in Frankreich*, 2 vols (Munich, 1981), vol. 2, pp. 147–70.

[22] Rutledge, *Eloge*, p. 21; Baker, 'Script', p. 244.

prepared the Way; for she alone must do it. An Equality of Estate will give an Equality of Power; and an Equality of Power is a Commonwealth or Democracy. An *Agrarian* law, or something equivalent to it, must make or find a suitable distribution of Property; and when it comes to be the case, there is no hindering a popular form of Government.[23]

The case against any analogy between a genuine republic and the quasi-republican model of monarchical government that Montesquieu had presented followed logically from the difference between the material independence and social equality that were the basis of true republics on the one hand, and the immense resources of credit and patronage available to modern monarchies to undermine equality and promote despotism on the other. An agrarian law did not, of course, entail any immediate or wholesale redistribution of property. Properly enforced, an upper limit upon the amount of property that any one person could acquire, coupled with a system of partible inheritance, would, in the fullness of time, create the material independence and equality that were the basis of political liberty.

Formulations like these were far removed from the concerns and preoccupations of artisans. The Commonwealth tradition entered late eighteenth-century France by way of anonymous translations and coded messages whose significance was confined to the *cognoscenti* of the *salons* rather than the wider public of the *cabarets*. The *Independent Whig* was published in French by the Baron d'Holbach in 1767 under the title of *L'Esprit du Clergé, ou le Christianisme primitif vengé des entreprises et des excès de nos Prêtres modernes*.[24] An article on Harrington, written by the chevalier de Jaucourt, was published in Diderot's *Encyclopédie* under the discreet heading 'Rutland', the county of Harrington's birth.[25] Other allusions to neo-Harrington political argument, notably Mably's *Des droits et des devoirs du citoyen*, circulated in manuscript form for many years, or appeared in self-conscious echoes of English political debates, like Rutledge's short-lived journal, *Le Babillard*, modelled, as its title indicates, upon the *Tatler*.[26] Yet however restricted the dissemination of Commonwealth arguments may have been during the late eighteenth century,

---

[23] Cited in Robbins, *Commonwealthmen*, p. 125. The concept of an agrarian law has fascinated historians concerned with the origins of socialism. The classic study remains André Lichtenberger, *Le Socialisme et la Révolution française* (Paris, 1899). Regrettably the recent study by R. B. Rose suffers from the same teleological bias (and a marked lack of familiarity with the work of Robbins and Pocock); R. B. Rose, 'The "Red Scare" of the 1790s: the French Revolution and the "Agrarian Law"', *Past and Present*, 103 (1984), pp. 113–30. The same applies to Florence Gauthier, 'Loi agraire', in Institut National de la Langue Française, *Dictionnaire des usages socio-politiques (1770–1815), fascicule 2* (Paris, 1987), pp. 65–98. For a more wide-ranging presentation of late eighteenth-century debates on property, see Gregory Claeys, *Machinery, Money and the Millennium* (London, 1987), pp. 1–33.

[24] Bulloch, Gordon, p. 16.

[25] See also S. B. Liljegren, *A French Draft Constitution of 1792 Modelled on James Harrington's Oceana* (Lund and London, 1932).

[26] Baker, 'Script', pp. 237–8.

their appeal received a powerful impetus from events in the United States after 1776, in Geneva after 1781 and in France itself from 1787 onwards.

The first great wave of French interest in the Commonwealth tradition coincided with, and was stimulated by, the mid-century conflict over the legal status of Jansenism and the wider issues of secular authority, clerical power, civil rights and royal sovereignty that it raised.[27] The second coincided with, and was stimulated by, the Revolution. The unprecedented character of the events of 1789 was a powerful incentive to find models of political conduct among a wide range of sources. As Sénac de Meilhan put it in 1813.

Les ouvrages politiques, tels que ceux de Montesquieu, si profond dans sa légereté apparente, du déclamateur Raynal, le plus dangereux de tous; le livre apocalyptique intitulé *Contrat Social*; les dissertations pesantes de Mably, étoient-ils lus des officiers municipaux, des curés, des magistrats subalternes, des soldats, des bourgeois? Toutes ces classes avoient-ils médité sur les conceptions abstraites qu'ils renferment? Non, certes; mais c'est au moment de la révolution, que pour étayer leurs idées indéfinies de la liberté, ils ont eu recours à ces ouvrages, comme on s'adresse à un avocat pour fournir des motifs à l'appui d'une cause.[28]

New French editions of Gordon's *Discourses on Sallust and Algernon Sydney's Discourses on Civil Government* appeared in 1794, although Harrington himself was translated into French only in 1795.[29]

The best known of this later incarnation of the Commonwealth tradition was the group of writers and political figures associated with the *Cercle Social*. Many of the group's publications alluded confidently to recognised landmarks in the English civic tradition: *The Tatler*, *The Letters of Junius* and that symbol of republican stability, the Venetian *bocca de verita*. Both Nicolas Bonneville and Claude Fauchet, the bishop of Bayeux, drew heavily upon the neo-Harringtonian concept of an agrarian law in their many publications between 1789 and 1793. Much of the masonic imagery upon which the *Cercle Social* also drew was redolent of the anti-clerical deism of Holbach which Holbach had done so much to promote by producing translations of their work a generation before the Revolution.[30] A more peripheral figure within the *Cercle* itself.

---

[27] *Ibid.*, p. 241–2; see too Dale Van Kley, *The Jansenists and the Expulsion of the Jesuits from France, 1757–1765* (New Haven, 1975).

[28] Sénac de Meilhan, *Portraits et caractères des personnages distingués de la fin du xviiie siècle* (Paris, 1813), p. 219. See also J. Q. C. Mackrell, *The Attack on 'Feudalism' in Eighteenth-Century France* (London, 1973), p. 28.

[29] Charles Alfred Rochedieu, *Bibliography of French Translations of English Works 1700–1800* (Chicago, 1948).

[30] On the *Cercle Social*, see Gary Kates, *The Cercle Social, the Girondins and the French Revolution* (Princeton, 1985). On Holbach and his circle, see Alan Charles Kors, *D'Holbach's Coterie. An Enlightenment in Paris* (Princeton, 1976). On freemasonry, see Ran Halévi, *Les loges maçonniques dans la France d'Ancien Régime* (Paris, 1984), and, on the possibility of a deist and masonic underground tradition stretching from late seventeenth-

but a man of considerable standing in Paris between 1789 and 1793, was the future *conventionnel* François Robert, who lectured on public law to the *société philosophique*, and published a work entitled *Le républicanisme adapté à la France* in 1790. His wife, Louise Kéralio-Robert, editor of the *Mercure nationale*, was also part of the same circle. Many of the scores of British supporters of the Revolution who visited Paris between 1789 and 1792 found a familiar political vocabulary in the works of the *Cercle Social*.[31]

Yet familiarity with the neo-Harringtonian republican idiom extended well beyond the Kéralio-Robert *salon* and the circle made up of Bonneville, Fauchet and their associates. Morellet claimed that Sieyès' espousal of the division of the nation into 83 departments in 1789 owed much to Harrington and the territorial divisions imagined in his *Oceana*. At a less exalted level, traces of Harrington's work can be found in the many pamphlets produced by the *lyonnais* silk-designer François-Joseph L'Ange between 1788 and 1793, with their calls for a new core unit of political representation, the *centurie*, made up of 100 households. Mirabeau, along with his many voluntary and involuntary collaborators (including Camille Desmoulins), was entirely conversant with the tenets of the Common-wealth tradition, even if, like his English interlocutors at Bowood House, he found little in it that was congenial to his own complex political stratagems.[32] Others, however, were more enthusiastic. In April 1791, the *abbé* de Cournand, a professor at the *Collège de France*, produced a very Harringtonian work, entitled *De la propriété, ou la cause du pauvre plaidée au tribunal de la Raison, de la Justice et de la Vérité*. In 1792, a Parisian named Théodore Lesueur presented the newly elected Convention with a draft of

century England to late eighteenth-century France, see the (somewhat tendentious) Margaret C. Jacob, *The Radical Enlightenment* (London, 1981). The whole subject of deism, freemasonry and coded political messages in eighteenth-century France awaits an authoritative study that would encompass both the politics, beliefs and culture of the great noble households of Paris and Versailles and the intellectual history of freemasonry. There is no full study of François Robert, Louise Kéralio or the *sociétés fraternelles* that they promoted in Paris in 1791. See, however, A. Kuscinski, *Dictionnaire des conventionnels* (Paris, 1917), p. 530; L. Antheunis, *Le Conventionnel belge, François Robert (1763–1826), et sa femme Louise de Kéralio (1758–1822)* (Wetteren, 1955) and P. Gaffarel, *François Robert, ses travaux scientifiques, son rôle politique, son rôle artistique* (Dijon, 1889). More generally, see Hugh Gough, 'The Radical Press in the French Revolution', in Patrick J. Corish, ed., *Radicals, Rebels and Establishments* (Belfast, 1985). Different, but complementary, information on the politics of the period between 1789 and 1792 can be found in Kates, R. B. Rose, *The Making of the Sans-Culottes* and Maurice Genty, *L'Apprentissage de la citoyenneté: Paris 1789–1795* (Paris, 1987).

31 See most recently David V. Erdman, *Commerce des Lumières, John Oswald and the British in Paris, 1790–1793* (Columbia, Missouri, 1986).

32 On L'Ange see Louis Trénard, 'L'Utopie de François-Joseph L'Ange', paper presented to the *colloque* on *La Révolution française et le développement du capitalisme* (Lille, November 1987). On Mirabeau's English connections, see J. Bénétruy, 'L'Atelier de Mirabeau: quatre proscrits génévois dans la tourmente révolutionnaire', *Mémoires et documents publics par la société d'histoire et d'archéologie de Genève*, 41 (Geneva, 1962) and Albert Goodwin, *The Friends of Liberty* (London, 1979), pp. 104–5.

a constitution that was equally indebted to Harrington's *Oceana*. Like Cournand's work, the proposal included a very moderate agrarian law, limiting the amount of property that any individual could enjoy to land producing an annual income of 120,000 *livres*, an amount that, even making allowance for inflation, only a very small number of ex-noble landowners could ever have received.[33] Like most exponents of the agrarian law, Lesueur left the redistribution of property to the effects of a strictly enforced system of partible inheritance.

However unreal some of these proposals may seem, they were very much in keeping with the political possibilities raised by the events of 1789 and, *a fortiori*, 1792. The confiscation of church property, the abolition of seigneurial titles, the reorganisation of public finance, the recodification of the civil and criminal law, and the uncertain status of *émigré* land were all immense opportunities to translate some of the tenets of the Commonwealth tradition into reality. Yet very little trace of what was a well-established republican doctrine found its way into the mainstream of the political life of revolutionary France. The *Cercle Social* enjoyed a brief heyday in 1791, but by 1793 many of its members had lost their political influence and, in some cases, their lives in the aftermath of the bitter conflict between Brissotins (or Girondins) and the Jacobin Mountain.[34] When, in May 1793, a delegate from the Jacobin club in Lyon told the Parisian Jacobins that 'il faut établir le machiavelisme populaire; il faut faire disparaître de la surface de la France tout ce qu'il y a d'impur', the qualification *populaire* was indicative of the limits of one kind of republicanism.[35] Both the valedictory title of Desmoulin's newspaper *Le Vieux Cordelier*, and its insistent invocation of the neo-Harringtonian republican tradition, were symptomatic of a recognition that the Commonwealth tradition's time had passed or, perhaps, had never come to pass. Its failure is of more than antiquarian interest. Like Sherlock Holmes' dog that did not bark, the silence in which the Commonwealth tradition in the French Revolution was enveloped is at least as significant as the clamour that surrounded the republicanism of Rousseau and the *sans-culottes*.

Republicanism, in short, did not enter the French Revolution ready-made. It was a constellation of very different traditions whose outlines were highly indistinct. Even that most republican of political theorists, Rousseau, had confined his examples of republican constitutions to small, predominantly rural, communities. The impossibility of establishing a republic in a large state with a population of over 25 million inhabitants

---

[33] On these individuals, see Alphonse Aulard, *Histoire politique de la Révolution française* (Paris, 1921), pp. 86–111, and Lilljegren, *A French Draft Constitution*.
[34] Kates, *Cercle*, especially chapters 9 and 10.
[35] *Moniteur* (Paris, 1793), p. 392.

was a truism of political debate in 1789 and 1790. As Robespierre put it in 1789, 'dans une grande monarchie, le peuple ne peut exercer sa toute puissance qu'en nommant des représentants'.[36] François Robert, in his *Républicanisme adapté à la France*, was only one of a number of political figures (Pétion was among the earliest) to recognise that republicanism could be established in a large state only by radically extending the traditional concept of a *mandat impératif*. If the representatives of the nation were subjected to the permanent sanction of the popular will, just as, in a very much more limited way, deputies to the provincial estates had been mandated to represent corporate bodies before the Revolution, republicanism could be adapted to a population of 25 million people. As Robert also recognised, however, there was nothing in Rousseau that was compatible with the idea.[37]

The republicanism of the *sans-culottes* is best envisaged, therefore, as the outcome of several different and competing characterisations of the post-revolutionary political order. The gradual crystallisation of the word *sans-culotte* into a metaphor with a multiplicity of interdependent connotations was the outcome of efforts by large numbers of political actors to develop an imagery and a rhetoric capable of exercising some purchase both within the many different forums of debate of revolutionary Paris and within the many possible constructions that could be placed upon the concept of republicanism itself. In this process, the dialogue between the members of the many political societies established in Paris after 1789 and a largely artisanal public was central. It was the medium through which the word *sans-culotte* established itself, and, as its connotations expanded, the agency by which the term became part of the vocabulary of political rhetoric between 1791 and 1794. Nor, moreover, was the position of Paris within this dialogue an unproblematic one. The ordinary tensions between the capital and the rest of France were reinforced by the ambivalence of both Rousseau and the neo-Harringtonian republican tradition towards urban society and the luxury and potential for political corruption that it housed. Eighteenth-century republicanism looked to the land, and landed property, for all that was positive in a political community. Thus, just as the equation between artisans and *sans-culottes* was not pre-ordained, neither was the prefix 'Parisian' to the word *sans-culotte* a foregone conclusion.

The dialogue between Parisian political societies and a largely artisanal

[36] Maximilien Robespierre, *Œuvres* ed. Marc Bouloiseau, Georges Lefebvre and Albert Soboul (Paris, 1950), vol. 6, p. 77.

[37] According to Robert, 'J. J. a erré d'une manière bien funeste à la liberté' by failing to see how a *mandat impératif* could be adapted to a large state: *Républicanisme*, pp. 89–95 (especially p. 91). On the concept of the *mandat impératif* see Ran Halévi, 'La Révolution constituante: les ambiguités politiques', in Colin Lucas, ed., *The Political Culture of the French Revolution* (Oxford, 1988).

public began almost with the Revolution itself. Artisans were not latecomers to the Parisian political arena. Simply because there were more of them than any other segment of the settled population, they were the largest component of the 77,000 to 97,500 Parisians able to take part in public life from the spring of 1789 onwards.[38] Only a minority, of course, actually did so. Yet, as participants in the electoral assemblies of 1789, as members of the National Guard, as observers of the ordinary affairs of the districts and sections, and, most importantly, as actual or potential members of revolutionary crowds, the political presence of master artisans was a constant in the history of the Revolution. Journeymen were in a rather different position. Yet the difference between active and passive citizens had rather less practical significance in the context of the urban trades than has often been supposed. Most master artisans had incomes that entitled them to active status, while many of the journeymen who worked for wages and were passive citizens were, given the age-composition of the workforce of the trades, young enough to anticipate becoming active citizens themselves. After 1792, of course, the distinction between active and passive citizens no longer applied. Even in 1789, however, over half the membership of the company of the National Guard of the Parisian district of Saint-Merri consisted of master artisans – and it is unlikely that the proportion was unusual.[39] The equation between artisans and *sans-culottes* was not the result of the eruption of a previously excluded sector of society into political life, but, instead, was the effect of a mutation of both the character of republicanism and the concerns and preoccupations of artisans.

Despite the aura of finality surrounding the Revolution, and the massive enthusiasm that followed the fall of the Bastille, the transition from a monarchical institutional order to the representative institutions of post-revolutionary France was a painful and uncertain process. Representative democracy, wrote the *Ideologue* Destutt de Tracy, in his *Commentary and Review of Montesquieu's Spirit of the Laws* (1811) was a 'new invention, unknown in Montesquieu's time'.[40] Hindsight made it possible to give the revolutionary political order a name, but contemporaries themselves were very much less certain as to how to proceed. Arthur Young, who visited the recently self-proclaimed National Assembly in June 1789, noted with some asperity that 'spectators in the galleries are allowed to interfere in the

---

[38] Genty, *Apprentissage*, p. 117.

[39] B.L. R 573 (6). *Liste des volontaires de la garde nationale parisienne du district Saint-Merry* (Paris, 1789). Some 53 per cent of the 418 members were associated with the trades. On artisanal participation in the political life of the districts and sections in the early years of the Revolution, see Genty, *Apprentissage*, pp. 118–19, 122–5.

[40] Antoine Louis Claude Destutt de Tracy, *A Commentary and Review of Montesquieu's Spirit of the Laws* (Philadelphia, 1811), pp. 19–20.

debates by clapping their hands, and other noisy expressions of approbation'. The conduct of deputies in debates was not much better. 'More than once to-day there were an hundred members on their legs at a time', Young complained.

This arises very much from complex motions being admitted; to move a declaration relative to their title, to their powers, to taxes, to a loan etc. etc. all in one proposition, appears to English ears preposterous and certainly is so. Specific motions, founded on single and simple propositions, can alone produce order in debate; for it is endless to have five hundred members declaring their reasons of assent to one part of a complex proposition, and their dissent to another part.[41]

Matters had not changed much when Young visited the Assembly in Paris in January 1790. 'The want of order', he noted, 'and every kind of confusion prevails now almost as much as when the Assembly sat at Versailles.'

Young, of course, had his own prejudices to air, and made a point of advising the Protestant deputy Rabaut Saint-Etienne to consult Hatsell's *Precedents of the House of Commons* to save members of the National Assembly a quarter of their time.[42] Yet the absence of a common vocabulary and common procedures in the public life of post-revolutionary France was also reflected in the large number of English neologisms that entered the language after 1789. A few, like *club* or *vote*, were already well-established. Some, like *ordre du jour*, *ajourner*, *motion*, *bill*, *amendement*, *petition*, *rejection*, *adresse*, *honorable membre* or *parti*, were constitutional and procedural in origin. Others, like *session*, *jury*, *verdict*, *juge de paix* or *incriminer*, derived from the English legal system. Yet others, like *impopulaire* and *impopularité*, or that quintessentially English word *influencer*, were indirect testimony to the local political resonances of that combination of dynastic patronage and appeals to opinion that were hallmarks of eighteenth-century English political life. The pervasive influence of parliamentary models even left that very indigenous word *commune* poised uncertainly between medieval French, classical Roman and contemporary English usage, so that it could mean either a municipal assembly, a municipal administration or the common people. The ambiguity was carried through to the word *section*, which could be used to refer either to an administrative division or to part of the commons. Thus, while a deputy could argue that 'il peut être très utile, même pour les corps administratifs que les communes puissent discuter sur les affaires publiques', one of the clauses of a law passed on 10 May 1791 could stipulate that

[41] Arthur Young, *Travels in France*, Everyman edn (London, 1913), pp. 165–6.
[42] *Ibid.*, pp. 166, 296–7.

dans les villes où la commune se réunit par sections, les assemblées des sections pourront nommer des commissaires pour se rendre à la maison commune et y comparer et constater les resultats des déliberations prise dans chaque section.[43]

Ambiguities of this kind were to have substantial implications.

England was not the only available source of revolutionary neologisms and models of political conduct. The fundamental question of the form of the new legislative assembly provided many opportunities to consider the various constitutional arrangements of the 13 American States, particularly those of Massachussetts and Pennsylvania, before the National Assembly decided to establish its own unicameral legislature.[44] Nor were such models confined to constitutional and legal debate. The word *sans-culotte* itself had an obvious precedent in the Dutch word *beghard* and, in its earliest usage, was associated frequently with references to the *gueux* of the Netherlands', revolt of the sixteenth century.[45] Yet, as it entered the public domain, the term acquired a growing range of connotations and came to be invested with an increasingly large number of meanings. As it did so, it came to serve as a relay, or shifter, that could be linked to a number of very much older and more familiar figures of speech.[46] This was the key to its success.

The word *sans-culotte* was grafted on to several areas of established linguistic usage. The first was the language of natural law, and, in particular, the concept of natural rights. There was, it should be emphasised, no necessary connection between these concepts and the significance with which they came to be endowed during the Revolution. They had been central to the mainstream of jurisprudential thinking about absolutist government from the time of Grotius and Pufendorf onwards. Yet there was a significant difference between the established sense of the concept of natural rights in eighteenth-century jurisprudence and the sense in which it was used during the Revolution. When the

[43] On these neologisms, see Max Frey, *Les Transformations du vocabulaire français à l'époque de la Révolution* (Paris, 1925); on the ambiguities of the words *commune* and *section*, *Moniteur* (Paris, 1791), p. 543.

[44] Joyce Appleby, 'America as a Model for the Radical French Reformers of 1789', *William and Mary Quarterly*, 3rd series, 28 (1971), pp. 267–86.

[45] The etymology of the word has now been reconstructed with great skill by Annie Geffroy, 'Sans-Culotte(s), novembre 1790–juin 1792', in *Institut National de la Langue Française. Dictionnaire des usages socio-politiques (1770–1815)*. *fasc. 1. Designants socio-politiques* (Paris, 1985). I am greatly indebted to this fine piece of historical and linguistic analysis and to its author for making it available to me.

[46] The concept of a shifter (*embrayeur*), which evokes an automobile clutch, or the *derailleur* mechanism on a bicycle gearing system that shifts the chain from one cog to another, is developed in Roman Jakobsen, *Essais de linguistique générale* (Paris, 1963), vol. 1, pp. 176–96 and discussed by Louis Guespin, 'Les Embrayeurs en discours', *Langages*, 41 (1976), pp. 47–77. For examples of its use in historical linguistics, see the special issue of the review *Mots*, 10 (1985) devoted to 'Le Nous politique'.

former members of the corporation of master locksmiths, farriers, nailmakers, tinsmiths and toolmakers of Orléans appealed to the National Assembly in October 1790 to demand that its officials release the guns that they had bought with the corporation's money to all its members, rather than keep them under corporate control, they based their argument entirely upon the terms of the Declaration of the Rights of Man.[47] Since the first article of that document had stated that 'les hommes naissent et demeurent libres et égaux en droit', and the fourth that 'l'exercice des droits naturels de chaque individu n'a de bornes que celles qui assurent aux autres membres de la société la jouissance des ces mêmes droits', there was no possibility, they argued, that the *syndics* of the corporation could claim a right to keep guns bought with common funds. Natural rights, in this form of argument, were the basis of, and were coextensive with, positive law.

Traditionally, however, natural rights were used to evoke a pre-social condition which, in legal argument, formed a comparative counterpoint to the limited civil rights embodied in positive law. Invocations of natural rights during conflicts in the trades during the eighteenth century were carried out in a negative way. A corporate decision could be opposed on the grounds that it was a violation of journeymen's natural rights. It was not the case, however, that a corporate decision could embody natural rights in a positive manner. In the natural law tradition, civil rights were the limited and exceptional counterparts to natural rights that had been surrendered to the sovereign authority of the King and his courts.

The achievement of the host of political and economic thinkers of the latter half of the eighteenth century, from Rousseau to Turgot and Condorcet, was to modify this relationship in such a way that it became usual to argue that natural rights and positive law should complement one another. Others, like Linguet or Bentham, argued that natural rights were a fiction and that positive law grounded upon the principle of utility was the only basis of civil rights. Instead of the negative and limited quality of the titles, privileges and rights of possession that characterised civil rights in the natural law tradition, the political and economic critics of the established monarchical system sought to demonstrate that civil rights should have the same universal character as the naturally harmonious and orderly society posited by physiocracy and political economy. One way of characterising the Enlightenment, in other words, would be to emphasise the extent to which the concept of law acquired a very much wider set of connotations in the latter half of the eighteenth century than

47 A.D. Loiret, 2J 1915. *Mémoire ou pétition adressée à L'Assemblée Nationale pour tous les anciens maîtres agrégés aux corporations des serruriers, taillandiers, maréchaux, ferblantiers, cloutiers...d'Orléans* (Orléans, 1790).

had previously been the case.[48] It had become usual, by the time of the Revolution, to assume that natural rights and positive law were no longer mutually exclusive. This new perspective on the relationship between nature and society found its best-known expression in the Declaration of the Rights of Man.

The complementary relationship between natural rights and positive law was carried very much further during the early years of the Revolution. In a context in which opposition to a properly elected representative authority presented very difficult problems, appeals to natural rights were used increasingly as a justification of political opposition. The process began in Paris almost as soon as the Bastille had fallen. During the summer and autumn of 1789 heated argument developed over the respective rights and powers of the new municipal authority and the 60 electoral districts into which the capital had been divided for the purposes of elections to the Estates General.[49] The conflict continued into the late spring and summer of 1790 when the districts were replaced by 48 sections for the first elections to the new municipal government. Although it was contained by the National Assembly, the conflict between the municipality, the sections and the political clubs flared up again during the spring of 1791 when a number of disputes in the Parisian trades coincided with (and were partly responsible for) a decision by the National Assembly on 10 May 1791 prohibiting collective petitions. The language used by both the supporters and opponents of this decision, whose number included many of those associated with the *Cercle Social*, drew heavily upon both the provisions of the Declaration of the Rights of Man and the broader current of naturalistic legal argument of the Enlightenment. One of the most significant results of the whole episode was a shift in the ground of political argument towards a general acceptance of the equivalence of natural and political rights. By the summer of 1791 even the most determined supporters of the constitutional *status quo* were obliged to defend their positions in terms of the affinity between positive law and natural rights.

The conflicts of the spring of 1791 were the first substantial disputes in the Parisian trades since the fall of the Bastille. Although there had been a number of conflicts in the clothing trades in the autumn of 1789 they had been settled rapidly on terms favourable to the journeymen.[50] The

[48] The point is well known, particularly in the context of discussions of Newtonian models and metaphors in eighteenth-century thought: see, among others, Elizabeth Fox-Genovese, *The Origins of Physiocracy* (Ithaca, 1976); Keith Michael Baker, *Condorcet. From Natural Philosophy to Social Mathematics* (Chicago, 1975).

[49] The conflicts are discussed in slightly different ways in the three studies by Rose, Kates and Genty cited above, note 30.

[50] On the disputes of the autumn of 1789, see Rudé, *Crowd in the French Revolution*, pp. 64–5, and Sonenscher, 'Journeymen, the Courts', pp. 108–9.

conflicts of the spring of 1791 were very much more protracted and followed the clustered pattern that was a recurrent feature of conflict in the trades throughout the eighteenth century. Significantly, they also took place in many of the same Parisian trades (building, carpentry, farriery, hatting and printing) in which disputes had occurred in 1785 and 1786. They began late in 1790, when workers in the Parisian quarries revived a legal action that they had initiated in 1784 to recover money which, they claimed, had been deducted from their wages by the entrepreneurs responsible for managing the quarries. Early in 1791 an association of booksellers and publishers denounced a society of print-workers for maintaining the same restrictive practices that had occasioned a protracted dispute over the production of the *Encyclopédie méthodique* in 1785 and 1786. Soon afterwards, Quatremère de Quincy, the entrepreneur responsible for overseeing work on the church of Sainte-Geneviève (which was shortly to become the Panthéon), reported that

les ouvriers...par une parodie absurde du gouvernement, regardent leurs travaux comme leur propriété, le bâtiment comme une république dont ils sont les concitoyens, et croyent en conséquence qu'il leur appartient de se nommer leurs chefs, leurs inspecteurs et de se distribuer arbitrairement les travaux.[51]

His attempts to impose greater managerial control encountered considerable hostility among the contractors and sub-contractors involved in the project.[52]

The most substantial dispute, however, occurred in the carpentry trade. It began in the second week of April 1791 and lasted for at least eight weeks, although stoppages by journeymen continued to be reported even in August 1791. While it was in progress, conflicts also began among stone-cutters working on the Pont Louis XVI, among hatters making hats for the Parisian National Guard, and in the farriery trade. Early in June, employers in the farriery trade warned that stoppages were about to occur among shoemakers, joiners and locksmiths.[53] The cluster of disputes was not, in itself, particularly unusual. What was unusual, however, was the context in which the conflicts occurred. Mirabeau's death early in April

[51] On the disputes in 1785–6, see Sonenscher, 'Journeymen, the Courts', pp. 108–9; on the dispute in the quarries, see A.N. Y13 693 (28 July 1784); Bibliothèque historique de la ville de Paris, 139 883, *Mémoire pour le sieur Coeffier entrepreneur des bâtiments et maître maçon à Paris* (Paris, n.d., but 1791 from the content); ibid., 953 933, *Mémoire pour le sieur Coeffier* (Paris, 1790); *Gazette des tribunaux et mémorial des corps administratifs et municipaux*, 7 (Paris, 1793), p. 42; B.N. 4° fm 35344 *Petition des ouvriers employés aux carrières de Paris adressée au Conseil d'Etat* (Paris, n.d.); on the printing trade, see B.N. N.A.F. 2654, fol. 118 (7 January 1791); on the Panthéon, see B.N. Lb⁴⁰ 165, Quatremère de Quincy, *Rapport sur l'édifice dit de Sainte-Geneviève* (Paris, 1791).

[52] *Moniteur* (13 April 1791); Marat, *L'Ami du peuple*, 487 (12 June 1791); A.N. F¹³ 1935; F⁷ 4774⁹ dossier Poncet. See also Haim Burstin, *Le Faubourg Saint-Marcel à l'époque révolutionnaire* (Paris, 1983), pp. 185–6.

[53] A.N. AD XI 65, *Précis pour les maréchaux de Paris* (Paris, 1791). See also A.N. DIV 51, 1488 (18).

1791 and the developing controversy over the civil constitution of the clergy and the oath of allegiance to the new political order broke the few remaining links between the court and the National Assembly. On 18 April, Louis XVI was forcibly prevented from leaving Paris, ostensibly to go to Saint-Cloud. The disputes in the trades thus took place during a period of intense discussion of the viability of the constitutional arrangements that the National Assembly had adopted.[54] More importantly, they took place in something of a legal vacuum, since they began six months after the Parlements had been abolished and only a month after the corporations had been consigned to oblivion by the Allarde Law. As was apparent in a concurrent dispute in Bordeaux, the legal hiatus created by these two measures presented the municipal authorities now responsible for matters pertaining to the trades with a considerable problem. The absence of any penal code (the new one was still in draft stage) complicated matters still further.

The dispute in the tailoring trade of Bordeaux in April 1791, when nearly 100 journeymen decided to walk out on their employers and leave the city, led the municipality to approach the departmental administration for advice on its position.[55] The major problem it faced, the municipality stated, was the absence of any clear legal ruling prohibiting assemblies of journeymen. Article 2 of the National Assembly's law establishing municipalities specifically recognised the right of active citizens to meet together to draw up petitions and addresses and present them to municipal authorities. Although many journeymen were not active citizens, it was perfectly possible that some of them were, and it would be difficult to prove that a peaceful meeting was, in fact, a seditious assembly or *attroupement*. Although royal legislation had explicitly prohibited assemblies of journeymen, it was not clear whether its provisions continued to apply, particularly in the light of the newly drafted Constitution. The best course of action, the municipality suggested, might be to use the martial law of 21 October 1789 if circumstances required, although it emphasised that 'ces jeunes gens' were unlikely to pose a threat to public order and were guilty of no more than 'une étourderie dont il nous paroit qu'ils se punissent eux-mêmes par le parti qu'ils ont pris'. The legal hiatus of the spring of 1791 meant that municipalities were forced either to appear to neglect the traditional role played by authorities in disputes in the trades – and incur the wrath of employers for doing so – or to opt for draconian, and potentially counterproductive, intervention.

The conflict in the Parisian carpentry trade presented the same problems to both the municipality of Paris and the National Assembly. All the protagonists in the dispute met openly in large numbers and presented

[54] See especially Genty, *Apprentissage*, pp. 89–102.
[55] A.C. Bordeaux, D 139 (17 April 1791).

long and detailed petitions to both the *commune* of Paris and the National Assembly outlining their cases.[56] The journeymen carpenters met publicly at the *Evêché* alongside delegates from many of the fraternal societies whose establishment had been promoted by François Robert and Louise Kéralio-Robert. The conflict acquired a further dimension when, on 7 May 1791, the municipality of Paris announced that it intended to close the *ateliers de charité* established in the autumn of 1789. The announcement followed a number of petitions by employers in the carpentry trade seeking to prevent journeymen who had stopped work from enrolling in the *ateliers*.[57] It was followed, three days later, by an even more wide-ranging decision by the National Assembly. On 10 May 1791 the Assembly passed a law prohibiting collective petitions and limiting the right to post placards to properly constituted authorities. The move was precipitated by both the dispute in the carpentry trade and the growing campaign by the clubs against the decision to close the *ateliers de charité*. It generated a substantial movement of opposition couched in terms of natural rights and popular sovereignty which went well beyond the immediate concerns of those involved in the disputes in the trades. The question of the right to petition, which was already closely associated with the rights of journeymen, was coupled with the question of the rights of clubs and the rights of workers in the *ateliers* who, almost invariably, were passive citizens. The movement against the ban on petitions broadened into a substantial campaign against the distinction between active and passive citizens in which much of the emphasis fell upon the rights of those affected by the decision to close public workshops.

The campaign against the law prohibiting collective petitions took place both within and outside the National Assembly. The range of issues that it embraced rapidly eclipsed the immediate concerns of the protagonists to the dispute in the carpentry trade because the law prohibiting petitions went to the heart of the status of informal political associations at a time of considerable political uncertainty. If the journeymen carpenters' *société fraternelle* was denied the right to petition under a collective title, there was

[56] On the dispute, see Archives de la Préfecture de police, Aa 83 (19 April 1791): Aa 198 (21 April 1791): Aa 84 (17 May 1791): Aa 224 (6 June 1791): B.N. MS. fr. 11 697. fols. 146–7 (26 April 1791). fol. 254 (11 May 1791): 4° fm 35345. *Petition présentée à la municipalité de Paris par les ci-devant maîtres charpentiers* (30 April 1791): 4° fm 35346. *Précis présenté à l'Assemblée Nationale par les entrepreneurs de la charpente de la ville de Paris* (22 May 1791): 4° fm 35347. *Précis présenté à l'Assemblée nationale par les ouvriers de la charpente de la ville de Paris* (26 May 1791): A.N. AD XI 65, *Réfutation des ouvriers de l'art de la charpente à la réponse des entrepreneurs*: Sigismund Lacroix, *Actes de la commune de Paris pendant la Révolution*, 2nd series (Paris, 1905), vol. 3, pp. 700, 710–11: vol. 4 (Paris, 1905), pp. 84, 123–4, 136–41, 145–7, 152, 169, 221, 231, 264, 318, 336. 346–52, 483–6: vol. 6 (Paris 1908), p. 362.

[57] A.D. Ville de Paris, VD* 1661, *Petition des maîtres charpentiers de la section du Temple* (4 May 1791): B.N. N.A.F. 2654 fol. 142. See also Alan Forrest, *The French Revolution and the Poor* (Oxford, 1981), p. 112.

little to prevent the Parisian sections, the Jacobins or the Cordeliers from suffering the same fate if they called collectively for the destitution of the King. The law itself, however, was precipitated by events in the carpentry trade. It was presented to the Assembly by its Constitutional Committee in response to a request by the directory of the department of Paris. Although neither the terms of the law nor the speech by the deputy Le Chapelier introducing the measure in the name of the Constitutional Committee made any direct reference to events in Paris, much of the ensuing debate was coloured by speakers' awareness of conflict in the carpentry trade. Speeches by several opponents of the prohibition alluded in a general way to disputes in the trades to justify their opposition. Pétion, the future mayor of Paris, invited the Assembly to consider the case of workers faced with a reduction in wages. 'Pourquoi', he argued, 'ne voudriez-vous pas que ces ouvriers vous presentassent des petitions?' The *abbé* Grégoire claimed that the proposal was 'contraire aux droits naturels de l'homme' and cited a deputation of domestic servants who had presented a petition at the bar of the Assembly in 1790 as evidence that the right of petition had been consecrated as 'un droit imprescriptible de tout homme en société'.[58] At the same time, however, all the participants in the debate were aware of the measure's wider implications, although only a lone royalist voice was heard to call for a ban on political clubs as such.

The conjunction between the disputes in the trades and the disputed status of political clubs allowed all those involved to play one off against the other to further their objectives. The key issue, in May and June, as it remained in Le Chapelier's last speech to the National Assembly in September 1791, was the threat to the sovereignty of elected institutions posed by political clubs. Supporters of the constitutional *status quo* could use the disputes in the trades to attack the political clubs by limiting their right to present petitions and post placards. Opponents of the *status quo* were therefore forced to adopt some of the claims of the journeymen involved in the disputes to prevent their opponents in the National Assembly from carrying the day. Implicit in the claim that journeymen, and passive citizens in general, were entitled to petition collectively, was a recognition that the effectiveness of political clubs would be undermined if the right of petition was limited to individuals. Both sides drew extensively upon the language of natural rights to justify their positions. Le Chapelier, the president of the Constitutional Committee and author of the proposed law, argued that since the right to petition was a natural right, it was one that no individual could alienate or delegate to a collectivity. Thus 'nul corps, nulle société, nulle commune ne peut exercer le droit de petition sous nom collectif'. Robespierre placed his own argument against the proposal on exactly the same terrain, but claimed that since the right to

[58] All the citations are taken from the *Moniteur* (Paris, 1791), no. 131 (11 May 1791).

petition was a natural right, the Assembly had no title to 'ôter à une partie des citoyens les droits imprescriptibles qu'ils tiennent de la nature'.[59] The dispute in the carpentry trade was the occasion, if not the cause, of the first moment in Parisian politics in which the related issues of natural rights, political institutions and popular entitlements found their expression in an organised campaign.

This co-ordinated movement – involving members of the *Cercle Social*, the Cordeliers club, the *point central des arts et métiers* and some 30 more obscure fraternal societies grouped together under a *comité centrale des sociétés fraternelles* presided over by François Robert – formed the context in which the Le Chapelier Law of 14 June 1791 was passed.[60] Although the law was prefaced by an appropriately wide-ranging introduction, Le Chapelier's denunciation of assemblies of workers, 'qui se propagent dans le royaume, et qui ont déjà établie entre elles des correspondances', buttressed by an allusion to a letter confiscated by the municipality of Orléans, indicate clearly that the law was a very circumstantial affair. The letter in question had, in fact, been sent by journeymen in the Parisian carpentry trade.[61] The stoppage by journeymen farriers that began in late May and the reports that further stoppages among shoemakers, locksmiths and joiners were about to occur undoubtedly contributed to a decision to reinforce the earlier law on collective petitions by a measure that was more specifically directed at journeymen's associations themselves. Marat, in number 493 of the *Ami du Peuple* (dated 18 June 1791), described it correctly enough as the final instalment of the measures restricting the right to petition and associate. The purpose of the law was not, therefore, to introduce any radically new provisions as far as formal relations in the trades were concerned; nor, since it did not refer to periods of notice or make any provision for journeymen to register and find work with anyone other than the employer of their choice, could it prevent breach of contract and the selective victimisation of employers that were the usual counterparts to conflict in the trades. Employers faced with deserted workshops and hostile workers could find little to use in the Le Chapelier Law, as a legal ruling arising from a dispute in the pottery trade soon demonstrated.[62] The terms of the law were very much more limited than

59 *Ibid.* For the context in which the debate occurred, see Kates, *Cercle*, pp. 141–51.
60 The text of the law is reproduced in J. M. Roberts, ed., *French Revolution Documents* (Oxford, 1966), pp. 242–5.
61 The report of Le Chapelier's speech in the *Moniteur* does not include this passage. It is, however, reproduced in the *Archives parlementaires*, 1st series (Paris, 1887), vol. 27, p. 210 and the *Journal des débats et décrets*, 752 (14 June 1791). The letter in question was sent on 22 April 1791: Georges Lefebvre, *Études Orléanaises* (Paris, 1962), vol. 1, p. 224.
62 B.L. 924 a. 94, *Gazette des tribunaux et mémorial des corps administratifs et municipaux*, 7 (Paris, n.d.), p. 445, citing a case in which four of the workers employed by an Englishman named Potter, who owned a porcelain manufactory, walked out and went

previous royal legislation (legislation whose status was very much open to question in 1791) and did no more than reiterate the emphasis upon private negotiation between individual parties that had been increasingly visible in legal rulings before 1789. In the context in which it was enacted, the Le Chapelier Law was a response to an unforeseen legal hiatus and, more particularly, a detailed reaffirmation of the limits placed upon collective action by the law of 10 May 1791.

The arguments used during the conflicts in the trades and over the right to petition served to change the terms of political debate. The disputes were the occasion, rather than the cause, of a redefinition of the relationship between legitimate opposition, natural rights and popular sovereignty. The bridge formed between the trades and the political clubs of revolutionary Paris over these related issues ensured that subsequent political conflict was conducted on a different conceptual terrain than had hitherto been the case. After 1791, it became usual to claim that natural rights and political institutions should either complement one another or, if they did not, that the political institutions themselves were illegitimate. An elected assembly that denied the natural right to petition collectively was, it could be argued, in violation of the sovereignty of the people and, more practically, a threat to the political vitality of the clubs and societies of the capital. The coincidence of the disputes in the Parisian trades and conflict over the political status of clubs placed the issues of informal association, popular sovereignty and natural rights at the centre of political debate. By the summer of 1791, much of what was distinctive in the *sans-culottes'* emphasis upon direct democracy and the *mandat impératif* was already part of the currency of public debate. In this context, the concerns and preoccupations of artisans were a very secondary consideration in relation to the wider issue of the right of informally constituted collective associations to play a part in both the political life of the nation and the legislative process itself. It was this claim that the majority of the National Assembly resisted so tenaciously in the law of 10 May and, in a less general way, in Le Chapelier's law of 14 June 1791. The Legislative Assembly, however, was to be very much less successful.

The emphasis placed upon natural rights both as the basis of legitimate authority and as a justification for legitimate opposition to an elected

to work for Chevalier *frères*. Potter sought to convict the four under the Le Chapelier Law, but failed. On appeal, the *tribunal d'appel de police municipal* which ruled on the dispute invoked the Royal Letters Patent of 2 January 1749 and 12 September 1781 and convicted both the workers for leaving without notice and their new employers for engaging them without certificates attesting to the satisfactory completion of their previous work. This is the only example I have found of the use of royal legislation between 1791 and 1794. No reference to either the letters patent of 1749 or 1781, or the *Le Chapelier Law*, was made during disputes in the building trades in 1792 and 1793–4; see A.N. F^{13} 1935. For subsequent labour law, see the Conclusion, below.

authority during the disputes in April and May 1791 was reinforced still further after October 1791. The dissolution of the National Assembly, preceded by a decision denying its members any right to present themselves as candidates for election to the new Assembly, left the Parisian political clubs, and the Jacobin club in particular, as the only major public forums available to former members of the National Assembly. Where once the Jacobin club had been an antechamber of the National Assembly itself, and had adopted many of its procedures and forms, it now became a centre of conflict between members of the Legislative Assembly and their predecessors.[63] In these circumstances, it was very easy to legitimate political opposition by emphasising the natural right of the people to exercise sovereign power as an alternative to the rights conferred upon elected members of the Legislative Assembly. The duel between Brissot and Robespierre was the best-known product of this situation. Military defeat during the summer of 1792, and the close relationship between some elected ministers and defeated (or treacherous) military commanders, made the case for political opposition couched in terms of natural rights an even more powerful one.

The equivalence between natural rights and political institutions established during the conflicts in the Parisian trades in the spring of 1791 echoed, but radically extended, the meaning of a term that was a familiar component of legal argument in the eighteenth century. If the word *sans-culotte* came to be associated with a republicanism in which popular sovereignty was a natural right, it did so because the concept of natural rights itself was one of the cultural resources of Parisian artisans. Argument over the relationship between natural rights and political institutions opened a space that could be filled by the figure of the *sans-culotte* because Parisian artisans and shopkeepers were well acquainted with the rhetoric of the law. After 1791, in other words, republicanism began to be assimilated into a Parisian context. As it did so, it began to lose many of its agrarian and Harringtonian connotations and, instead, came to be increasingly coloured by the cultural resources of the capital.

The concept of natural rights did not in itself imply the metaphor of the *sans-culotte*, yet the word *sans-culotte*, and the social resonances with which it came to be endowed, served to identify those entitled to exercise political sovereignty as a natural right. The resonances that the term acquired between 1791 and 1794 allowed the language of natural rights to be anchored to a cluster of well-established images and familiar figures of speech. Together they endowed the republicanism of the *sans-culottes* with its distinctive identity and purchase. Three reservoirs of figures of speech were particularly significant. The first was the language of the theatre, and, in particular, the songs, imagery and rhetoric

[63] Michael Kennedy, *The Jacobin Clubs in the French Revolution* (Princeton, 1981).

associated with the *parades* and *vaudevilles* of the Parisian fairs. The second was the ordinary language of the trades and, in particular, the informal idiom of selection and exclusion used by masters and journeymen in the course of the bargains that they struck. The third, and most important, was the language of the church, and, in particular, the imagery associated with hunger and deprivation used in sermons throughout the eighteenth century. The words and images that these rhetorical reservoirs supplied were used not only in political forums and the revolutionary press, but also in the burgeoning market for republican pottery, Phrygian bonnets and other emblems of revolutionary politics, modelled, like so much in revolutionary Paris, upon the political artefacts associated with Wilkes and the campaign for political reform in England. The variety and sophistication of the Parisian trades meant that the capital's many artisanal enterprises were well able to develop their own political artefacts, or sub-contract work out to enterprises in provincial cities.[64] The combination of local resources and rhetorical traditions meant that, by the autumn of 1793, the word *sans-culotte* had come to be linked to a complex cluster of images and figures of speech that were all well-established in eighteenth-century Paris. By the time that Camille Desmoulins brought out his *Vieux Cordelier*, nothing in the republican traditions associated with Machiavelli and Harrington could match the multiplicity of local resonances that the term had acquired.

The language and conventions of the Parisian theatre were the most assimilable of the various reservoirs of figures of speech with which the word *sans-culotte* was associated. The term itself was Parisian and theatrical in origin. If it was used at all before the Revolution it referred, in the singular, to a condition rather than a group of people. It suggested an impoverished writer or man of letters, a figure like the young Saint-Preux of Rousseau's *Nouvelle Héloïse*, whose aspirations were not in keeping with his appearance and social condition and whose conduct lent itself to sexual ridicule. In his *Nouveau Paris*, the writer Louis-Sébastien Mercier reported that the word was used in this way to refer to a writer named Gilbert in a satirical piece entitled *Le Sans-Culotte*. According to Mercier, 'les riches adoptèrent volontiers cette dénomination contre tous les auteurs qui n'étaient pas élégamment vetus'.[65] During the first few

---

[64] John Brewer, 'Commercialization and Politics', in Neil McKendrick, John Brewer and J. H. Plumb, *The Birth of a Consumer Society* (London, 1982), pp. 197–262. Serge Bianchi, *La Révolution culturelle de l'an II* (Paris, 1982); Michel Vovelle, ed., *La Révolution française. Images et recit*, 5 vols (Paris, 1986). On the Phrygian bonnet, see *Les Révolutions de Paris*, 141 (17–24 March 1792), p. 534, and, more generally, Jennifer Harris, 'The Red Cap of Liberty: A Study of Dress Worn by Revolutionary Parisians 1789–94'. *Eighteenth-Century Studies*, 14 (1981), pp. 283–312. I am grateful to Richard Wrigley for allowing me to read his unpublished study. 'The Liberty Cap in the French Revolution'.

[65] This paragraph is based upon Annie Geffroy. 'Sans-Culotte(s)'. cited above, note 45.

years of the Revolution, the word retained much of its original pejorative sense. It was used mainly by royalist journalists, particularly a pamphleteer named François Marchant, as a term of political abuse larded heavily with disparaging social and sexual connotations. A *Liste des Sans-Culotte* [sic] *de Paris, avec leurs noms, surnoms et demeures* published early in 1792 contained the names of 80 journalists and members of the Jacobin and Cordelier clubs, all of whom were assigned addresses of a predominantly scatological character.[66] By then, however, the word had begun to acquire more positive political connotations. Significantly, the first sign of the kind of enthusiasm that it could evoke occurred during the hotly contested Parisian elections to the Legislative Assembly in September 1791. Divisions among the 965 Parisian electors led to the formation of two rival clubs of electors, meeting respectively in the Evêché and the Sainte-Chapelle, to scrutinise and prepare slates of candidates. Both groups of electors sought to justify their positions by appealing to a wider Parisian audience, and, in the case of the Evêché club, by opening its meetings to the public. At one of its meetings the future republican military strategist and *conventionnel*, Dubois-Crancé, read an address to the citizens of Paris denouncing the 'calomnies' perpetrated by members of the rival club and their allies in the National Assembly who, he said, had used the word *sans-culotte* to besmirch the political reputations of men like Pétion and Robespierre. Instead of merely rejecting the label, however, Dubois-Crancé accepted it. ' Ah! dussions-nous essuyer de nouvelles calomnies, dut-on ajouter encore quelques expressions injurieuses aux designations de *factieux*, de *sans-culotte*, dont les intrigants honorent les patriotes', he asked rhetorically. The final phrase, according to a hostile observer belonging to the rival *club de la Sainte-Chapelle*, provoked a wave of enthusiastic applause. The address, like several other pamphlets produced by Dubois-Crancé in the autumn and winter of 1791–2, was published by the *Cercle Social*.[67]

The word began to be used substantively – as *les sans-culottes* – in the Jacobin club and on the *journée* of 20 June 1792, when a crowd, made up mainly of members of the National Guard, invaded the Tuileries and forced the King to wear the red cap of liberty. Earlier in the day the crowd had paraded theatrically around the Legislative Assembly demanding the reinstatement of the Brissotin ministers whom the King had dismissed a

66 *Ibid.*, p. 166.
67 The address by Dubois-Crancé and various pamphlets describing the rivalries between the two clubs have been reprinted in Etienne Charavay, *Assemblée électorale de Paris, 26 août 1791–12 août 1792* (Paris, 1894), pp. 512–20. See also B.L. R 658 (5) *Compte rendu des séances électorales et de la division du corps électoral en deux sociétés sous les noms de club de l'Evêché, club de la Sainte-Chapelle* (Paris, 1791), by Nau-Deville, one of the electors affiliated to the Sainte-Chapelle. See pp. 15–16 for his report of Dubois-Crancé's speech. No information on Dubois-Crancé's relationship to the *Cercle Social* is to be found in Kates, *Cercle Social*, nor on this particular occurrence of the word *sans-culotte* in Geffroy, 'Sans-Culotte(s)'. The elections of 1791 would undoubtedly repay further study.

week earlier. According to the *Moniteur*, it made its way through the chamber, to the sound of the *Ça Ira* and cries of 'vivent les patriotes, vivent les sans-culottes!' One of the crowd was seen carrying an old *culotte*, bearing the inscription *vivent les sans-culottes*, while a second man brandished a calf's heart under which was inscribed *coeur d'aristocrate*. From that time onwards, the word was used as a substantive, and, by August 1792, it had been adopted by speakers in the Legislative Assembly, often in opposition to the equally charged term *aristocrate*.[68]

The theatrical origin of the word *sans-culotte* was only one of a number of cases in which terms or symbols used in plays or popular songs were assimilated into political discourse by opponents and supporters of the Revolution. The theatre in eighteenth-century Paris was a popular, as well as an aristocratic, institution and was used as a source of images, figures of speech and satirical stereotypes by both royalists and patriots. The *parades* and *vaudevilles* of the fairs of Saint-Germain, Saint-Laurent and the boulevards were part of a wider arena that reached towards the *guinguettes* beyond the customs barriers, merging annually with the display and songs of the Carnival, and echoing and adding to the ever-changing repertoire of popular songs in which so much comment on current events was passed in eighteenth-century Paris. Just as the original sense of the word *sans-culotte* owed a great deal to the satirical conventions of the theatre, so too did the sense of the word *aristocrate* and the *bonnet rouge* that Louis XVI was forced to wear in July 1792. The journalist Prudhomme explained the adoption of the red cap of liberty in terms of the popularity of Louis Archambault-Dorvigny's play *Janot, ou c'est les battus qui paient l'amende*, first performed in 1779, and Voltaire's *Brutus*.[69] The *sans-culotte*, like so many other symbols of Parisian politics, was a theatrical character, and, in one mode, was a foil to the equally theatrical character of the *aristocrate*.

Theatrical performances were occasionally dramatisations of the idiom of the trades. Archambault-Dorvigny's plays were a particularly successful example of the genre. Some trades, cobblers in particular, were

[68] *Moniteur* (22 June 1792), p. 718. Jacques Guilhaumou, 'Aristocrate', in *Dictionnaire des usages*, cited above, note 45. See also Patrice Higonnet, *Class, Ideology and the Rights of Nobles during the French Revolution* (Oxford, 1981).

[69] B.L. 11738 d. 38 (2), *Jannot, ou les Battus payent l'Amende: par M. Dorvigny*. On the vogue for the play and the many decorative objects and artefacts to which it gave rise, see Henri Lavédan, *Volange, comédien de la foire (1756–1808)* (Paris, 1933). According to one commentator, 'Janot devint le John Bull parisien' (p. 70). On the popular character of the Parisian theatre, see Robert M. Isherwood, *Farce and Fantasy: Popular Entertainment in Eighteenth-Century Paris* (New York and Oxford, 1986). See too Michèle Root-Bernstein, *Boulevard Theater and Revolution in Eighteenth-Century Paris* (Ann Arbor, Michigan, 1984). On songs, see Rolf Reichardt and Herbert Schneider, 'Chanson et musique populaires devant l'histoire à la fin de l'Ancien Régime', *XVIIIe Siècle*, 18 (1986), pp. 117–42. See also the works cited in note 64 above.

traditionally associated with the theatrical repertoire, while the idiom of the *compagnonnages* also found its place in the equally stylized (and occasionally dramatized) *bibliothèque bleue*, notably in the frequently reprinted *L'Arrivée du brave Toulousain et le Devoir de braves compagnons de la petite manicle*, the *Fameuse harangue faite en l'assemblée générale de M. M. Messeigneurs les savetiers* and the burlesque poem *La petite varlope*. The genre of the *plainte*, like the well-known *misère des apprentifs imprimeurs* or the lesser-known *misère des garçons perruquiers*, was a further variation upon a form of popular literature that straddled the theatrical performances of the Parisian fairs and the pamphlets produced in Troyes, Rouen and Orléans during the eighteenth century.[70] In 1792 and 1793 much of the style of these semi-theatrical, semi-literary enactments of the ordinary ceremonial of the trades was carried over into that combination of scatological ridicule and social satire that was one of the hallmarks of popular republicanism.

The most effective exponent of the technique of scatological ridicule was the journalist and former *controlleur des contre-marques* of the *théâtre des variétés amusantes*, Jacques-René Hébert. In the *Père Duchesne* Hébert found a well-known theatrical character from the Parisian fairs, which, like the Phrygian bonnet, could be found in two of Louis Archambault-Dorvigny's plays, *Le Père Duchesne ou la mauvaise habitude*, a play performed on 41 occasions at Nicolet's *Théâtre des variétés amusantes* in 1789, and its successor, *Les Noces du Père Duchesne*, performed in the winter of the same year. Like the original *sans-culotte*, the *persona* of the *Père Duchesne* was used first by opponents of the Revolution as a vehicle for disparaging social and political satire.[71] Hébert developed the character by combining the stylised demotic speech of the fairground *parade* with the more ordinary idiom of the trades to divest the aristocracy, the court, and the world of high politics in general of their distance and aura of authority. When the *Père Duchesne* picked his grapes, he went to the *vendange*

non pas comme ces faquins qui vont aux vignes comme au boulevard pour faire les Messieurs et regarder les autres. Foutre! moi, j'aime à travailler partout, la serpette à la main.[72]

When he visited the King, it was to talk frankly with *le gros bourgeois*, a master artisan who happened to exercise *le métier du roi*. When the Parlements were abolished, he could only applaud the fact that 'tous ces bougres de barbouilleurs de papier vont être forcés de travailler à des arts

---

70 For these (and other) pamphlets see Roger Lecotté, 'Essai bibliographique sur les Compagnonnages de tous les devoirs du 'Tour de France', in Raoul Dautry, ed., *Compagnonnage* (Paris, 1951), pp. 271–417.

71 The most recent examination of the character is by Jacques Guilhaumou, 'Les Mille Langues du Père Duchêne', *XVIII Siècle*, 18 (1986), pp. 143–54; see too F. Braesch, ed., *Le Père Duchesne d'Hébert* (Paris, 1938), pp. 1–36 for the origins of the character, and p. 235.

72 Braesch, *Père Duchesne*, pp. 263 and 768.

utiles, à de bons métiers' and drew upon the idiom of the *compagnonnages* to celebrate their demise: 'qu'ils mériteraient bien qu'on leur fît la conduite de Grenoble'.[73] When Hébert began to use the word *sans-culotte* in 1792, he anchored the term to the dialogue of the Parisian theatre.

If the figure of the *Père Duchesne* complemented the theatrical caricature of an *aristocrate* – and, by extension, served as a foil to the original theatrical connotations of the word *sans-culotte* itself – the more positive sense of the latter term depended upon a rhetoric that placed greater weight upon popular entitlements. Here the language of the sermon was a substantial source of the imagery used to designate the social condition and articulate the claims of the politically disinherited. The identity between crowds, dearth and popular sovereignty that was forged during the Revolution owed much to figures of speech evoking hunger and popular entitlements that were assimilated into Parisian republicanism after 1791. Food riots themselves, however, were never intrinsically republican. Yet one of the most distinctive features of politics in revolutionary Paris was the frequency with which images of hunger and fears of dearth mobilised large numbers of people over issues of high political concern. The repertoire of the price fixing riot in revolutionary Paris grew to encompass sugar and candles during the grocery riots of the early spring of 1792, played an important part in argument over the desirability of a *maximum* during much of the following year, and was central to justifications of the extraordinary measures adopted by revolutionary tribunals and the *armées révolutionnaires* in the autumn of 1793.[74] Yet the relationship between the crowds of revolutionary Paris, the claims of the socially dispossessed and the politics of the *sans-culottes* was not pre-determined. It was as much a contingent one as that between artisans and republicanism.

The association between hunger and political entitlements in revolutionary Paris had its origin in well-established religious imagery. Throughout the century it had been usual to organise processions and prayers for the intercession of St Géneviève, patron saint of Paris, during periods of dearth. Mercier gave the cult of the saint a chapter in his *Tableau de Paris*, and even in the spring of 1785 the archbishop of Paris could feel sufficiently confident of the familiarity of the ceremony to order prayers to St Géneviève to end a drought and avert a dearth.[75] Food riots themselves were never solely the product of dearth. During the eighteenth century, price-fixing riots had accompanied decisions to centralise the market for cotton yarn in Rouen in 1752 and move a cemetery away from the centre

[73] *Ibid.*, p. 270.

[74] For a recent reassessment of the politics of revolutionary crowds, see Colin Lucas, 'The Crowd and Politics', in Lucas, ed., *Political Culture*.

[75] Steven L. Kaplan, 'Religion, Subsistence and Social Control: The Uses of Saint Geneviève', *Eighteenth-Century Studies*, 13 (1979–80), pp. 142–68.

of Lille in 1778. Religious images of hunger and deprivation were recurrent figures of speech in eighteenth-century food riots.[76] 'Ah gros cochon; tu ne jeunes pas toy,' a woman involved in a price-fixing riot in Reims in 1770 was reported to have shouted. 'J'ai quatre enfants', another woman was reported to have said. 'Tenez, je les bats de peur qu'ils ne me demandent pas du pain quand ils pleurent.'[77] Figures of speech like these owed much to the imagery of sermons. Misery, according to one exponent,

C'est une mère désolée, environneé de tristes enfants que la faim devore; qui, après leur avoir donné la vie, ne peut plus leur donner que des pleurs, contrainte à toute heure d'essuyer les demandes de ces malheureux, qui tendent vers elle inutilement les mains; et par leurs cris perçants, déchirent le sein dont ils sont sortis.[78]

De tendres enfants, dont les pleurs, dont les cris innocents demandent à leurs mères une nourriture qu'elles ne sont pas en état de leur procurer; des mères éplorées qui...ne peuvent s'empêcher d'appeler heureuses celles qui sont stériles, et les mamelles qui n'ont point allaité.[79]

'Quel lugubre spectacle se présente tous les jours à nos yeux?' demanded a second.

There is little reason to suppose that the imagery of hunger used in sermons was unfamiliar to artisans, however much they may or may not have had religious convictions of their own. The confraternities, the ceremonial distribution of the *pain bénit* after the mass, the high masses on Saints' Days and trade holidays, the funeral processions, the meetings in cloisters and chapels, the long-standing uncertainty that surrounded the extent to which the spiritual domain of the church was independent of the secular domain of the state were all sufficient reason to endow artisans with more than a passing acquaintance with the rhetoric of religion. Nor, of course, was the language of the sermon entirely innocent of, or unresponsive to, popular preoccupations. For all the hostility of many revolutionaries towards the church, religious imagery remained a powerful medium in which to articulate popular entitlements. When Fouché, in 1793, talked of 'une disproportion épouvantable entre les travaux du cultivateur et de l'artisan et le modique salaire qu'il en retiroit', he invited his audience to share a familiar set of images of 'les atteliers, les greniers, les souterrains de l'indigence' where 'les haillons de la misère, la paleur de la faim, les plaintes douleureuses du besoin' and 'les cris aigus de la maladie' could be seen and heard.[80]

76 For the riots at Rouen and Lille, see William M. Reddy, 'The Textile Trade and the Language of the Crowd at Rouen, 1752–1871', *Past and Present*, 74 (1977), pp. 62–89; and Alain Lottin, 'Les Vivants et les morts au xviiie siècle. Les incidents de Lille (1779) et de Cambrai (1786) lors des translations de cimetière', *Actes du xviiie congrès de la Fédération des Sociétés Savantes du Nord de la France* (Lille, 1979).

77 A.D. Marne 17B 1650 (11 and 12 July 1770).

78 A. Bernard, *Le Sermon au xviiie siècle* (Paris, 1901), p. 311.

79 *Ibid.*, p. 345.

80 Markov and Soboul, *Die Sans-Culotten*, p. 222.

In a context in which it had become usual to associate the concept of natural rights with political institutions themselves and assume that there was no necessary obstacle to translating natural rights into positive law, it was not difficult to draw upon the rich imagery of eighteenth-century sermons to articulate the claims of the politically excluded to their natural sovereign entitlements. If all members of society enjoyed the same natural rights (as had traditionally been argued), and political institutions should embody those rights (as the revolutionary political order maintained), the claims of the excluded could be pressed most forcefully in the language of religious entitlement. This was the strength of the republicanism of 1793. Appeals to natural rights and evocations of hunger had little place in the neo-Harringtonian republican tradition. The language of natural rights owed most to the tradition of natural law, modified by its enlightened critics, and widely extended during the political crises of the spring of 1791 and the summer of 1792. Evocations of hunger owed most to the church, with which most exponents of the neo-Harringtonian tradition had little sympathy.

It may be that one of the keys to Robespierre's immense prestige was his mastery of both modes of address and the ease with which he was able to move between the language of natural rights and the imagery of hunger in his speeches and pamphlets. Many of his pronouncements were redolent of the great set-piece sermons of Bossuet, Bourdaloue, Massillon and their many eighteenth-century emulators. In one of his most celebrated speeches, on 5 February 1794, he set out to define the principles of republican government. 'Nous aurions pu croire', he began, in a remark that was aimed clearly at Desmoulins' *Vieux Cordelier*, 'que le plan de la révolution française étoit écrit en toutes lettres dans les livres de Tacite et de Machiavel.' This, as his deliberate use of the conditional tense implied, was not the case. In a republic, he continued:

Nous voulions substituer dans notre pays la morale à l'égoisme, la probité à l'honneur, les principes aux usages, les devoirs aux bienséances, l'empire de la raison à la tyrannie de la mode, le mépris du vice au mépris du malheur, la fierté à l'insolence, la grandeur de l'âme à la vanité, l'amour de la gloire à l'amour de l'argent, les bonnes gens à la bonne compagnie, la mérite à l'éclat, la charme du bonheur aux ennuis de la volupté, la grandeur de l'homme à la petitesse des grands, un peuple magnanime, puissant, heureux à un peuple aimable, frivole et misérable, c'est à dire toutes les vertus et tous les miracles de la république, à tous les vices et à tous les ridicules de la monarchie.[81]

The whole performance was filled with the cadences, enumerations and antitheses of an eighteenth-century sermon. Here, for example, is one by the *abbé* Poulle, on faith:

[81] The speech is printed in *Archives Parlementaires*, 1st series, vol. 84 (Paris, 1962), p. 72.

Homme du temps, il passe tristement à travers l'inépuisable mensonge du monde, ce séjour fabuleux et variable où tout est inconstant ou faux ...où l'on ne trouve de réel que la haine, l'intérêt, l'ambition, la volupté, l'orgueil, passions perpetuelles et souveraines qui ...font de la société un composé monstrueux de palais et de prisons, d'églises et de théâtres, de réjouissances et de calamités, de luxe et de l'indigence, de mariages et de divorces, de luxe et de l'indigence, d'une enveloppe d'agréments superficiels et d'une abîme d'horreurs profondes, Quelle demeure pour un citoyen du ciel.[82]

The antithetical play upon social description and moral qualities in both the sermon and the speech was the medium in which the republicanism of the year II found its expression and the ground upon which the connection between natural rights, political entitlements and popular sovereignty was established. Between 1791 and 1793 the word *sans-culotte* was divested of its association with disreputable sexual conduct and indeterminate social status and was assimilated into a semantic field in which hunger and natural rights complemented one another. The term came to function as a polysemic metaphor linking well-known legal, theatrical and religious figures of speech to a republicanism that, precisely because of its assimilation of these figures of speech, became very different from the republican tradition associated with Machiavelli, Harrington and Mably. This was its strength and the basis of its resonance within the largely artisanal public of the districts and sections of revolutionary Paris.

The local and Parisian inflections with which republicanism came to be endowed was also one of the sources of the political failure of Brissot, Roland and their supporters after 1792. As republicanism became increasingly Parisian in character, the opponents of the Jacobin Mountain had little choice but to draw upon the local resources of provincial cities to promote their own goals and objectives. If the support for Federalism in Lyon, Marseille, Nîmes and Bordeaux in the summer of 1793 was often local and popular in character, that localism was itself an outcome of political battles that had been won and lost in Paris during the preceding two years.[83] The extensive networks of kinship and patronage that characterised eighteenth-century urban society ensured that divisions established in the capital were transmitted widely over the rest of France and embedded deeply within the provincial cities from which so many Parisians had come, for patronage and principle were never mutually exclusive.[84] The localism of the Federalist revolts of the summer of 1793

82 Bernard, *Sermon*, p. 313.
83 This interpretation of Federalism as Parisian, rather than local, in origin echoes that suggested by Edmonds. 'Federalism' (cited above, note 13). See also Michael Sonenscher, 'Note sur le pasteur et conventionnel Rabaut Saint-Etienne', *Bulletin de la Société de l'Histoire du Protestantisme français*, 121 (1975), pp. 370–74.
84 One of the few works to insist upon the complementary relationship between patronage, clientage and principle in eighteenth-century political life is J. C. D. Clark, *English Society 1688–1832* (Cambridge, 1985).

was a measure of the extent to which the identity of republicanism itself had come to be defined in local, but Parisian, terms.

There is little reason, therefore, to assume any fundamental division between Parisian Jacobins and Parisian *sans-culottes*.[85] There is equally little reason to characterise the rhetoric and imagery associated with the *sans-culottes* as particular to a restricted circle of wealthy employers, or indeed to any single section of Parisian society.[86] The rhetoric of the year II was no more instrumental than any other political rhetoric. It was addressed to a public made up mainly of men and women associated with the trades. Some of them were very wealthy; others were not. Yet the rhetoric of the *sans-culottes* did not emanate from the trades themselves – it developed, instead, within the many public forums established in Paris after 1789. Its content, and the figures of speech upon which it drew, were not already inscribed in the proclamation of the sovereignty of the nation made by the revolutionaries of 1789.[87] The rhetoric of the year II was made up of a variety of elements which fell into place during a long process of political improvisation in which many different groups of people played a part. It was the medium in which political actors established their political standing and republican credentials in the eyes of a Parisian public. It drew upon the language of the courts, the theatre and the church to identify or exclude those entitled to exercise their natural rights as political agents. This was the key to its purchase. For the figures of speech that the courts, the theatre and the church supplied were those that artisans had long been accustomed to use in the course of their own activities. Republicanism became Parisian as it assimilated the cultural resources of the city itself.

[85] This, of course, was Soboul's thesis. It is clear, however, as Maurice Genty has acknowledged (*Apprentissage*, pp. 217–18), that it is no longer tenable.

[86] The argument has been expressed most forcefully by Richard M. Andrews, 'Social Structures, Political Elites and Ideology in Revolutionary Paris, 1792–1794: A Critical Evaluation of Albert Soboul's *Les Sans Culottes Parisiens en l'An II*', *Journal of Social History*, 19 (1985), pp. 71–112. The instrumental argument that Andrews develops fails to explain either the specificity of the figures of speech evoked by the rhetoric of the *sans-culottes*, or their resonances within a Parisian public. Like all instrumental interpretations of political (or any other) rhetoric, it assumes an omniscience on the part of producers, and a plasticity on the part of consumers, that reduces discourse to the model of a commercial exchange in which both parties know what they will get because one of the parties has already persuaded the other. What is missing, of course, is the process of persuasion itself.

[87] As suggested by François Furet, *Penser la Révolution française* (Paris, 1978).

It would be something of an exaggeration to claim any major conceptual difference between the terms 'artisanal production' and the 'workshop economy'. Yet the aura with which artisanal production has been invested has made it easy to assign the workshop economy to a pre-industrial world in which a distinctive form of material independence and culture combined to engender a distinctive style of radical politics in the late eighteenth and early nineteenth centuries. Many aspects of the workshop economy in eighteenth or early nineteenth-century France do not, however, match that image of artisanal production all that well. The wide dissemination of ordinary abilities among the towns of eighteenth-century-century France, the limited range of materials used in many urban trades, the imprecision of occupational distinctions and the porosity of the boundaries separating one trade from another all contradict much that has been claimed about craft skill and corporate particularity both during the eighteenth century and thereafter.

The brief periods of employment, rapid movement of journeymen from employer to employer, complex patterns of inward and outward migration from small towns to large cities, and intermittent argument over the length and content of the working day, do not accord all that easily with the intimacy, continuity and generous rhythms of the artisanal ideal. The unstable cores and peripheries of urban labour markets, the widespread networks of sub-contracted work and the elaborate chains of inter-dependent suppliers and clients do little to enhance the idea of artisanal workshops as self-contained units of production. The enduring differences in the ages of journeymen and their masters, and the many possible assessments of the significance of the passage of time that those differences entailed, bear little relation either to the supposedly hereditary character of corporate institutions or to contemporary notions of employment, unemployment or work to support a family. The apprentices who failed to complete their time, or the journeymen who disappeared from the trades to join the ranks of the poor, were the most visible manifestation of a world

363

whose fluidity and fragility stands at odds with the stability and independence with which it has been so frequently associated.

If these features of the eighteenth-century trades have little in common with an image of artisanal production centred upon craft skill, craft pride and craft tradition, they have the merit of explaining much that artisans said and did. The complex patterns of migration from small towns to large cities and the unstable division between the core and periphery of urban labour markets make it easier to understand how sharp short-term variations in wage-rates could, none the less, coexist with longer-term wage stability. The fragility of many artisanal enterprises and the brevity of most periods of employment make it easier to understand the precarious circumstances of many journeymen and the different types of association that they established. The range of overlapping occupations and interdependent enterprises that cut across the particularity of corporate titles makes it easier to understand why informal customs and usages were constituent parts of collective identities and formed the basis of market transactions and regular employment. Above all, the fluid, dangerous and always potentially conflictual world of the eighteenth-century trades makes it easier to understand why, for both masters and journeymen, the law and the formal entitlements that it supplied or denied formed a constant point of reference in the many different activities that they carried out from week to week and year to year.

Yet the law was not immutable. As he looked back upon what, from the vantage point of the third decade of the nineteenth century, had become the *ancien régime*, the Parisian barrister Louis Ferdinand Bonnet commented upon the profound change in the relationship between the law and public life that had occurred since the Revolution. The Civil Code 'et les autres codes modernes' had, he noted, given rise to a substantial reduction in the number and importance of cases in the civil law. The plethora of civil suits that had come before the Parlements during the eighteenth century had disappeared, while the most prestigious and publicly important cases were now to be found in the criminal law.

Quoiqu'on ne soit pas *menacé* de voir tarir ces sources de procès, et même de grands procès en matière civile, c'est particulièrement les procès criminels qui ouvrent à nos successeurs un noble et fécond emploi de leurs talens : c'est là qu'on peut quelquefois, avec mesure, mêler des considérations publiques, que l'on prodigue souvent avec indiscretion dans des matières qui n'en sont pas susceptibles.[1]

Bonnet's recognition of the diminished importance of civil litigation was an oblique acknowledgement of the more general way in which the

---

[1] Louis Ferdinand Bonnet, 'Souvenirs de 1783 sur le barreau de Paris', in his *Discours, Plaidoyers et Mémoires*, 2 vols (Paris, 1839). On legal change before the Revolution, see Colin Kaiser, 'The Deflation in the Volume of Litigation at Paris in the Eighteenth Century and the Waning of the Old Judicial Order', *European Studies Review*, 10 (1980). pp. 309–36.

Revolution had affected the relationship between the law and politics. Neither Bonaparte's *coup d'état*, nor the Restoration of the Bourbons, could resuscitate the legal environment in which the French trades had existed until the Revolution. The trades entered the nineteenth century politically divided and radically transformed by the institutional revolution that followed the collapse of royal absolutism in 1789. The abolition of the Parlements and the place that they occupied in both the formulation of corporate regulation and the wider sphere of legal argument to which that regulation belonged meant that the civil courts were no longer used as interlocutors by employers and workers in the French trades. In addition, the assimilation of republicanism into a Parisian context between 1789 and 1793 and the divisive effects of the civil constitution of the clergy not only ensured that the political complexion of the capital would play a key part in French political conflict until the last years of the Third Republic, but also created an unbridgeable gulf between the church and the trades.[2] The clerical privileges and immunities that had allowed for so close an association between the cloister, the *cabaret* and the trades – even after the Parlements' successful campaign against the Jesuits in the early 1760s – had, by 1794, become very much a part of the *ancien régime*. By 1803, or 1815, both the church and the civil courts were irretrievably subordinated to the sovereignty of the nation.

The abolition of the Parlements, and, with them, of the mass of legal titles of a limited and exceptional kind that was the hallmark of eighteenth-century French jurisprudence, meant that the abolition of the corporations in 1791 was a foregone conclusion. Despite many appeals for their re-establishment, they were never to return. Even those who, like the *lyonnais* silk-weaver Joseph Déglise, campaigned vigorously for a restoration of many of the regulations that had been particular to the city's three great industries of silk-weaving, hatting and hosiery, did so in ways that were predicated upon the metaphorical and political connotations of the sovereignty of the nation proclaimed in 1789.[3] The legal powers embodied in eighteenth-century corporate regulations were too flagrant a violation of all that 1789 represented for any dilution of the sovereignty of the nation – however construed or metaphorically interpreted – to be contemplated.

In this sense, both lobbyists and legislators during the First Empire and

---

[2] On the civil constitution and its effects, see Timothy Tackett, *Religion, Revolution and Regional Culture in Eighteenth-Century France* (Princeton, 1986).

[3] Bibliothèque municipale de Lyon, 354444. J.-C. Déglise, *Observations particulières et générales sur un projet de loi relatif aux manufactures, et aux gens de travail de toutes les professions* (Lyon, 1802). A major reinterpretation of the whole subject of nineteenth-century French industrial relations is in progress in the work of Alain Cottereau. See especially his 'Justice et injustice ordinaire sur les lieux de travail d'après les audiences prud'homales (1806–1866)', *Le Mouvement Social*, 141 (1987), pp. 25–59.

the Restoration remained true to the tradition of natural law, however much it had been modified during the Revolution. Just as the notion of sovereignty underpinning royal absolutism meant that any particular legal title could only exist by virtue of the sanction of the King and his courts, so the notion of sovereignty underpinning the political order established after 1789 could never permit any fracture to the integrity of the nation. In either case, sovereignty, or the power to make laws, was absolute. Until well into the nineteenth century, factory regulations devised by manufacturers and industrialists were, for this reason, regarded with considerable suspicion by the French courts. Corporate regulations presenting obstacles to an individual's choice of occupation or affecting the formally voluntary character of the contract of employment were *a fortiori* utterly incompatible with the sovereign power of the nation to establish its own laws.[4]

Yet if the undiluted character of the sovereignty of the nation left little room for rules that might be interpreted as a violation of the right of publicly constituted bodies to make laws, it also left no space at all for the protracted legal confrontations that had been one of the features of the relationship between masters and journeymen in the eighteenth-century trades. Workers in the early nineteenth century could no longer claim, as eighteenth-century journeymen had been able to do, that a corporate decision affecting working conditions in which they were named entitled them to be heard by the courts. Collectivities of any kind had no formal place in a nation that, figuratively speaking, had appropriated the absolute sovereignty vested in the King. However numerous or varied collective associations in early nineteenth-century France may have been, their existence or identity found little recognition in the formal conventions of public life.

The permanent abolition of the mass of exceptional and particular legal rights with which the corporations had been invested did not, however, enhance the power of employers. The Le Chapelier Law, which clarified and particularised the Constituent Assembly's earlier prohibition of the right of informally constituted collectivities to petition or post placards, was a pale shadow of the detailed regulations that employers who belonged to corporations had been able to invoke during most of the eighteenth century. After 1791 there was little to prevent working people from walking out on their employers when favourable circumstances presented themselves and little that employers could do to prevent their shops from being boycotted if, for one reason or another, they fell foul of workers in the trade. The long period that elapsed before the French word

---

[4] Alain Cottereau. 'Les Règlements d'atelier au cours de la Révolution industrielle en France', in Anne Biroleau and Alain Cottereau, *Les Règlements d'Ateliers, 1798–1936* (Paris, Bibliothèque nationale, 1984).

for strike, *grève*, acquired its current meaning was not a measure of the 'immaturity' of the French labour movement or (perhaps more plausibly) of the persistence of a 'pre-industrial' repertoire of collective action, but was, instead, an indication of how easily working people could bring pressure to bear upon employers without having recourse to collective stoppages of work. Jacques-Étienne Bédé's account of the long dispute in the Parisian furnishing trade in 1820 was eloquent testimony to the transformation of the formal relationship between workers and employers after the Revolution and the practical limitations upon the powers of employers that it engendered.[5]

Contrary to a long-established historiographical tradition, both the law of 22 Germinal XI (10 April 1803) and the provisions of the Civil Code concerned with the contract of employment underscored that trans-formation. Article 1780 of the Civil Code explicitly denied the courts the power to order workers to return to their previous employers if they left without completing their work. All that employers were entitled to do was to bring an action for damages if they were so harmed. Although the following article (1781) stated that an employer's word would be acceptable evidence in disputes over wage-payments, it is clear from subsequent decisions by the courts that the clause was designed primarily to address the long-standing problem of disputes over the valuation of sub-contracted work and, more specifically, to meet the problem of conflicts between landowners and harvesters in rural areas, where time was of the essence. In this sense, the article represented a continuation of the Old Regime practice of dealing with disputes over harvest work as *cas prévôtaux*, subject to the summary jurisdiction of the *maréchaussée*.[6] The National Assembly had already done as much by explicitly extending the provisions of the La Chapelier Law to harvest work on 20 July 1791, a decision reiterated by the Legislative Assembly in articles 19 and 20 of the *Code rural* of 6 October 1791. In disputes over daily and monthly wage-rates in the urban trades, or even the piece-rates that were usual in the textile and clothing trades, the courts expected more than an employer's affirmation before they were satisfied.[7]

Despite the Le Chapelier Law and articles 415 and 416 of the *Code pénal*, collectivities of an informal kind continued to present problems to the courts. The *compagnonnages* in particular were notoriously difficult to place under any of the categories supplied by either the Le Chapelier Law or the

---

5 On the semantic imprecision of the word *grève*, see Maurice Tournier, 'Grève, Cayenne et Gavots: hypothèse de reconstitution des origines', unpublished paper, Centre de Recherche 'Lexicologie et textes politiques', Ecole Normale Supérieure de Saint-Cloud (September 1977), and his 'Les Mots conflits': l'exemple de *grève* au milieu du 19e siècle', *Le Français aujourd'hui*, 58 (1982), pp. 39–48. On Bédé, see above, chapter 1.

6 On the provisions of the Civil Code and the legal status of agricultural labourers before the Revolution, see above, p. 71.

7 Cottereau, 'Justice et injustice', pp. 57–8.

articles of the *Code pénal* concerned with associations among workers. In 1821, the mayor of Rochefort invoked the Royal Letters Patent of 1749, a ruling of 1778 by the Parlement of Paris (within whose jurisdiction the city had fallen) and the Le Chapelier Law itself to prohibit members of the *compagnonnages* from performing the ceremony of the *conduite* after one such ritual farewell had ended in a brawl involving a building entrepreneur and a number of stone-cutters. The court of appeal at Saintes dismissed his ruling, on the grounds that all the legal statutes that he had invoked had been superseded by the penal code, which (despite its prohibition of collective stoppages of work and boycotts of employers by workers) made no reference to the ceremonies of the *compagnonnages*. The case was carried to the *cour de cassation* in Paris, where, despite the intervention of the Minister of Justice in support of the municipality of Rochefort, the ruling by the tribunal of Saintes was upheld and the action against the *compagnons* dismissed.[8]

Even the notorious *livret* was re-established in a form that had more in keeping with the contractual character of the natural law tradition than with the exceptional powers embodied in corporate titles. Employers were denied the right to withhold a *livret*, even if they were in dispute with their workers, and, in a frequently reprinted circular by the Minister of the Interior, Montalivet, in 1809, were expressly prohibited from making any comment about a worker's performance or ability on the *livret* itself. Nor was an employer entitled to prevent a worker from leaving his or her employment until money paid in advance on wages had been repaid. A record of the outstanding debt could be written into the *livret* and the amount deducted from subsequent wage payments up to a maximum of 20 per cent at a time.[9] It was not, in short, particularly easy to be an employer in early nineteenth-century France.

It is not surprising, therefore, that the majority of those who turned to the *conseils de prud'hommes* in the wake of the creation of the first such court in Lyon in 1806, were employers or sub-contractors rather than workers. Only from the mid-nineteenth century in Paris, and from the 1860s elsewhere, did the *prud'hommes* come to acquire their modern form as courts used mainly by working people to obtain some measure of redress from their employers.[10] Before then, they were used mainly to buttress or legitimate the precarious authority of employers or workers employed in a supervisory role. The popularity of the early councils was an indication of how much importance men and women in positions of authority attached

[8] George Bourgin and Hubert Bourgin, *Les Patrons, les ouvriers et l'état. Le Régime de l'industrie en France de 1814 à 1830*, 3 vols (Paris, 1912–41), vol 3, pp. 314–20.

[9] Claude-Anthelme Costaz, *Mémoire sur les moyens qui ont amené le grand développement que l'industrie française a pris depuis vingt ans* (Paris, 1816), p. 100; Jean-Antoine Chaptal, *De l'industrie française*, 2 vols (Paris 1819), vol. 2, pp. 343–4; Cottereau, 'Justice et injustice', pp. 39–41.

[10] Cottereau, 'Justice et injustice', p. 52.

to forums whose normative decisions formed an alternative to the informal and potentially chaotic negotiations of the labour market.

In this sense, it is possible to see the early councils as extensions of the corporations. Unlike eighteenth-century corporations, however, the *conseils de prud'hommes* were not obliged to make decisions on the basis of formally sanctioned corporate deliberations. Nor, unlike the corporate *bureaux de placement*, did they play any part in a worker's choice of employer. Local practice and usage, rather than legal precedents, were the medium in which they made their decisions. The absence of external interlocutors, particularly of any equivalent of the eighteenth-century Parlements, meant that the overwhelming majority of those who presented disputes to the *prud'hommes* were obliged to settle by way of conciliation rather than continue with litigation.

Paradoxically, both the local character of the jurisprudence of the *prud'hommes* and the absence of external judicial authorities with powers commensurate to those that the Parlements had enjoyed, placed a premium upon the importance of trade-specific identities and customary usages. The local character of the *prud'hommes'* jurisdiction was reinforced by the municipalisation of political life in the nineteenth century. The *mairie*, rather than the local Parlement, was the primary point of reference in local affairs after the Restoration. Only exceptionally did the *préfecture*, like the eighteenth-century *intendants*, impinge upon the ordinary affairs of the trades. With the demise of the tradition of jurisprudence centred upon the Parlements, customs and local usage came into their own.

Customs and local usage were, of course, very much more fluid and impermanent than the terms in which they were couched might suggest. In July 1819 a Parisian police official reported that workers in the hatting trade had assembled 'pour une fête d'usage' on St Anne's day. Before the Revolution, however, journeymen in the hatting trade had commemorated St Michel, St Jacques and St Philippe.[11] Usages related to working practices and arrangements were equally impermanent and subject to ceaseless definition and redefinition in the light of both prevailing local circumstances and the flux of national political life. Like disputes in the eighteenth-century trades, industrial conflict in nineteenth-century France served as much to establish norms as it was occasioned by violations of pre-existent codes of practice. Legal precedent, however, was less central to nineteenth-century conflicts. Norms accepted by employers and workers were constituted or denied both in the ordinary proceedings of the *conseils des prud'hommes* and in the increasingly important forums supplied by municipal administrations and the political clienteles that they housed.[12]

[11] Bourgin and Bourgin, *Les Patrons, les ouvriers et l'état*, vol. 1, p. 263
[12] For an excellent example of this process, see Cottereau, 'Justice et injustice', pp. 26–33.

If the absence of legally defined occupational and corporate identities encouraged employers and workers to make frequent reference to the particularities of the trades to which they belonged, and present themselves as members of informally constituted corporate collectivities, they did so because much of the environment in which they lived and worked was not very different from that of the eighteenth century. As legal entitlements disappeared from the world of the trades, informal collectivities acquired a new importance, if only because employers and small-scale entrepreneurs continued to face many of the same issues that master artisans had faced during the eighteenth century, while workers continued to anticipate the possibility of establishing themselves on their own account. The quality of materials, the reliability of suppliers, the capacity of contractors or sub-contractors to honour their debts, the question of the ownership of, and access to, new designs or minor technical innovations, or the creditworthiness of customers and clients, were all different manifestations of the difficulty involved in acquiring reliable sources of information and trustworthy partners in the uncertain world of the bazaar. The need to have *des connoissances*, as the glazier Jacques-Louis Ménétra put it, did not disappear with the elimination of the corporations.[13]

In 1817, the Conseil de Commerce, faced with a campaign to re-establish the corporations, pointed out that associations existed in over 20 Parisian manufacturing or retail trades, although it had been unable to dis-cover much detailed information about their regulations and functions.[14] Some of them were mutual aid societies; others were employers' associations whose main concern, as the suppliers of building-stones to Paris put it in 1830, was to establish a central source of information about the solvency and creditworthiness of their suppliers and customers as a way of reducing the risks of bankruptcy. They pointed out that over 10 per cent of the annual total of over 400 bankruptcies in Paris between 1827 and 1829 had occurred in the building trades. In other trades, notably the silk industry of Lyon and the cluster of occupations associated with *articles de Paris*, matters of quality control and the ownership of design were given as the main reasons for association.[15]

Whatever their purposes, and however varied the interests of those involved in informal associations may have been, the voluntary character of collective association in the early nineteenth century was a significant

[13] On Ménétra, see above, chapter 1.

[14] Bourgin and Bourgin, *Les Patrons, les ouvriers et l'état*, vol. 1, p. 87. According to one contemporary, some 181 mutual aid societies were established in Paris between 1815 and 1825: G. de la Rochefoucauld-Liancourt, *Notice sur les associations des ouvriers à Paris* (Paris, 1834). See also Andrew Lincoln, 'Le Syndicalisme patronal de la classe patronale', *Le Mouvement Social*, 114 (1981), 1848: une étape de la formation de la classe patronale', *Le Mouvement Social*, 114 (1981), pp. 11–34. For a local example of informal association in post-revolutionary France, see Gail Bossenga, 'La Révolution française et les corporations: trois examples lillois', *Annales E.S.C.*, 43 (1988), pp. 405–26.

[15] Bourgin and Bourgin, *Les Patrons, les ouvriers et l'état*, vol 3, pp. 257–60.

departure from the obligatory associations attached to the *métiers jurés* of the Old Regime. Associations established by artisans in the early nineteenth century were obliged to justify their existence both to public authorities and to their potential constituents in ways that were unnecessary in the eighteenth century. Instead of legally sanctioned rights and obligations, nineteenth-century associations were obliged, therefore, to draw upon a different repertoire of images and purposes to establish or maintain their credentials. The advantages of fraternal association and the moral benefits of social co-operation were the most obvious of the resources upon which they could draw. In this context, the antithesis between competitive individualism and collective association that was made so frequently during the early nineteenth century was less a judgement upon the noxious effects of unregulated markets than it was a response to the absence of any formal injunctions compelling artisans to associate as they had done before the Revolution.

The resonances of socialism may, therefore, be more intelligible in a legal and institutional context than one defined principally in terms of unregulated markets and capitalist development. Socialism in early nineteenth-century France was a rhetoric of time, money and freedom that allowed artisans or their political representatives to present their abiding concerns to an audience composed mainly of other artisans rather than the courts of law. It supplied an alternative measure of justice, centred upon the ownership and distribution of property, when rights were no longer measured in terms of the formal entitlements that apprenticeship, residence, marital status or corporate privilege could supply. Matters that had been couched previously in an idiom centred upon slavery, freedom, rights and duties were incorporated into a vocabulary centred upon property, money, social co-operation and independence.

The benefits of co-operative association were not, moreover, incompatible with changes in the size and composition of markets. A Fourierist shoemakers' co-operative established in Paris in 1840 made a point of seeking to sell its products to the large retailers whose growing presence was one of the more marked features of the urban economy of nineteenth-century France.[16] Department stores and large wholesalers provided outlets for larger volumes of production and allowed for greater continuities of employment in many sectors of the clothing and furnishing trades where, during the eighteenth century, journeymen had moved like corks through a sea of small workshops, as one brief period of employment followed another.[17] The large peripheries of many of the urban trades

16 Michael Sibalis, 'Shoemakers and Fourierism in Nineteenth-Century Paris: The *Société Laborieuse des Cordonniers-Bottiers*', *Histoire sociale/Social History*, 20 (1987), pp. 29–49.
17 On department stores, see François Faraut, *Histoire de la Belle Jardinière* (Paris, 1987) and Michael B. Miller, *The Bon Marché. Bourgeois Culture and the Department Store, 1869–1920* (Princeton, 1981).

formed an obvious constituency for co-operative associations. Large wholesalers and retailers in Paris and the other great French cities found a substantial source of suppliers on the periphery of the trades, while the core of relatively substantial employers had rather more durable clienteles and rather fewer reasons for co-operative or socialist experiment.

Large-scale capitalist distribution and small-scale co-operative association tended, therefore, to converge in ways that had little to do with the negative effects of competitive individualism and unregulated markets upon small producers, and very much more to do with the advantages of alternatives to the irregular schedules of production and erratic periods of employment that were usual in so many urban trades.[18] The unstable relationship between the core and periphery of urban product and labour markets until well into the nineteenth century, particularly in the clothing and furnishing trades, formed a fertile ground for experiments and conflicts over marketing arrangements that, in the eighteenth century, had been brought before the courts. Many of the early nineteenth-century fulminations directed at ready-made goods (*confection*) and *marchandage* are more intelligible in this context than in one defined solely in terms of the rise of unregulated capitalist enterprise. So too is the noticeable association between migrants to large cities like nineteenth-century Marseille and republican and *dém-soc* politics.[19] Both were a continued

[18] This approach runs counter to many claims. Thus the history of the tailoring trade in nineteenth-century Paris' amounts to the history of the rise of capitalism within one of the purest artisan crafts of the age': Christopher Johnson, 'Economic Change and Artisan Discontent: The Tailors' History, 1800–48', in Roger Price, ed., *Revolution and Reaction. 1848 and the Second French Republic* (London, 1975), pp. 87–114 (p. 90). 'The impact of capitalist practices on tailoring in the 1830s and 1840s was to expand the number of people engaged in a household mode of production and drive increasing numbers of skilled workers into it. The exploited, marginal part of the trade grew, pulling into its ranks those who had once disdained it': Joan Wallach Scott, 'Men and Women in the Parisian Garment Trades: Discussions of Family and Work in the 1830s and 1840s', in Pat Thane, Geoffrey Crossick and Roderick Floud, eds., *The Power of the Past* (Cambridge 1984) pp. 67–93 (p. 73). 'For most groups of artisans who experienced decline and degradation in the early nineteenth century, the factory was not the direct cause. The anti-capitalist ideas which emerged were those appropriate to artisans facing "merchant capitalism" in the form of monopolistic middle-men reorganising production in garment-making, shoemaking or cabinet-making for the ready-made trade, or in building displacing the autonomy of the craftsman through " general contracting"': John Rule, 'The Property of Skill in the Period of Manufacture', in Patrick Joyce, ed., *The Historical Meanings of Work* (Cambridge, 1987), pp. 99–118 (p. 117). For a different approach, see Sabel and Zeitlin, 'Historical Alternatives to Mass Production'.

[19] The whole question of *confection* in the eighteenth-century Parisian clothing trades would repay further research. In 1760 a ruling by the Parlement ratified a decision by the tailors' corporation prohibiting master tailors from producing printed circulars advertising their prices. Despite this, a tailor named Dartigalongue advertised ready-made men's clothes in 1770: B.N. F 26 137 (10 December 1760): Madeleine Delpierre, 'La Mode et ses métiers à Paris au xviiie siècle', *Bulletin de la société de l'histoire de Paris et de l'Ile de France*, 93 (1966), pp. 46–9. There is little reason to imagine that markets for uniforms (including the liveries of domestic servants or those of the Parisian National Guard) or

expression, in a different rhetorical mode, of the recurrent tension between the core and peripheries of the urban trades.

In the eighteenth century there were small businesses and the *petite bourgeoisie*. The differences between them cannot be assumed. It is now clear that it is impossible to approach the small-scale character of nineteenth-century French industry as a vestige of an archaic past.[20] It is equally clear that much of that nineteenth-century world was common to the eighteenth century. Instead of the survival of traditional trades, or their gradual decomposition during the nineteenth century, it may be more appropriate to emphasise the precocity of modernity in eighteenth-century France. Yet the point would be somewhat spurious. Although small-scale production was a continuous feature of French industry until the twentieth century, several profound changes took place within the world of small-scale enterprise during the course of the nineteenth century. If they do not fit the conventional framework supplied by the concepts of industrialisation or modernisation all that well, they were, none the less, very significant.

The first was a change in the size and variety of markets. Michelet's evocative image of the substitution of polychrome printed cotton fabrics for the monochrome wool or linens of the past – 'tout ce peuple de femmes qui présente sur nos promenades une éblouissante iris de mille couleurs, naguère était en deuil' – was a comment upon a more widespread process of change in internal patterns of consumption whose scale and variety will continue to elude historians until Say's Law has been replaced by a fuller analytical vocabulary centred upon objects, their uses and significance.[21] Markets did not precede products. They were not already there, to be 'captured', 'occupied' or 'filled' by enterprising producers. The history of the nineteenth-century French trades cannot be entirely divorced from notions like luxury or fashion (or even France), for their resonances played some part in the promotion of products made in artisanal workshops or

large institutions like the *Compagnie des Indes* were not, as in eighteenth-century England, important outlets for ready-made clothes produced in Paris; on England see Beverly Lemire, 'Developing Consumerism and the Ready-Made Clothing Trade in Britain 1750–1800', *Textile History*, 15 (1984), pp. 21–44. On the relationship between immigration and political radicalism see William H. Sewell Jnr, 'Social Change and the Rise of Working Class Politics in Nineteenth-Century Marseille', *Past and Present*, 65 (1974), pp. 75–109, and his 'The Working Class of Marseille under the Second Republic: Social Structure and Political Behaviour', in Peter N. Stearns and Daniel J. Walkowitz, eds, *Workers in the Industrial Revolution* (New Brunswick, N.J., 1974).

20 The point is now well established. For two recent contributions, see Robert Aldrich, 'Late Comer or Early Starter: New Views on French Economic History', *Journal of European Economic History*, 16 (1987), pp. 89–100, and John Vincent Nye, 'Firm Size and Economic Backwardness: A New Look at the French Industrialization Debate', *Journal of Economic History*, 47 (1987), pp. 649–69.

21 Jules Michelet, *Le Peuple*, ed. Paul Viallaneix (Paris, 1974), p. 97. For a pioneering study of the variety of objects consumed in eighteenth-century Paris, see Annik Pardailhé-Lebrun, *Naissance de l'intime* (Paris, 1988), pp. 273–401.

urban putting-out systems. Luxury or fashion were not, therefore, intrinsic to the products to which they were attached, but were the way by which needs, markets and objects were brought into play with one another, both in France and elsewhere. By the last quarter of the nineteenth century, many of the artefacts associated with the traditional luxury trades – high-quality textiles, leather goods, pottery, glassware, furniture, *articles de Paris* and *bimbeloterie* – had come to occupy a larger share of the total value of French exports than they had done in the late eighteenth or early nineteenth centuries.[22]

The growth in the size and depth of external and internal markets during the nineteenth century appears to have had substantial repercussions upon patterns of employment and, possibly, upon modes of entry into the trades. By the first decade of the twentieth century fewer than 20 per cent of the workers employed in the French furnishing trades had worked for the same employer for less than a year. Over 40 per cent of the workforce had been employed by the same firm or individual for between one and five years, while well over 30 per cent had worked in the same enterprise for between five and 30 years.[23] At the same time, endogamous recruitment to the trades, at least in Paris, appears, if anything, to have increased. Over three-quarters of entrants to the furnishing, metal-working or building trades in 1869 were following in their father's footsteps.[24] The differences between the demographic characteristics of eighteenth- and nineteenth-century cities, particularly the greater probability that children would live to succeed their parents, together with the greater size and variety of markets, make this apparent paradox relatively easy to understand. Their effects were substantial. Both the continuities in employment and between the generations suggest a more sedentary population than was usual in the eighteenth century. By the late nineteenth century, the rapid mobility of journeymen from shop to shop and city to city that was so characteristic a feature of the world of the eighteenth-century trades had all but disappeared. The magnitude and effects of this transformation in terms of urban demography, housing, relations between men and women, social expectations and urban politics have still to be fully assessed.

Modernity, at least in France, is very much less easy to identify than

---

[22] See Paul Bairoch, *Révolution industrielle et sous-développement*, 3rd edn (Paris, 1969), pp. 334–6. See also Whitney Walton, '"To Triumph before Feminine Taste": Bourgeois Women's Consumption and Hand Methods of Production in Mid-Nineteenth Century Paris', *Business History Review*, 60 (1986), pp. 541–63.

[23] Ministère du Commerce, de l'Industrie, des Postes et des Telegraphes, Office du Travail. *Rapport sur l'apprentissage dans les industries de l'ameublement* (Paris, 1905), pp. 270–1.

[24] Lenard R. Berlanstein, *The Working People of Paris* (Baltimore, 1984), pp. 74–5. On entry into eighteenth-century corporations, see above, pp. 107–8.

appearances suggest. Arguably, much of what was modern in France was already there, many generations before Marx wrote the *Eighteenth Brumaire of Louis Bonaparte*. Much of what has been associated with the dissolution of craft communities – generalised sub-contracting, *marchandage*, the elimination of customary practices, the dilution of skill – were either the subject of intermittent conflict between employers and workers throughout the eighteenth century, or, like skill, wage-systems or customary practices, existed in conditions that were so radically different from those usually associated with artisans that it is impossible to assimilate them into the linear process of material change that, putatively, led from craft production to factory production. What changed in France between 1748 and 1848 was not so much the relationship between workers and employers, or the immediate circumstances in which production was carried out, as the identity of the public to which actors in conflicts appealed and the manner in which those appeals were couched. Instead of lawyers and magistrates, nineteenth-century workers and employers addressed other workers or employers and, increasingly, their own political intermediaries or representatives.

The identity of modernity cannot be found, in other words, by extrapolating from the labour process, or productive relations as such, towards political action or institutional procedures. The history of the French trades has, in this respect, a wider implication. A 30-year-old English journeyman tailor named George Weeks made the point in an indirect way when he was arrested in Marseille in 1731 after a dispute between the tailors' corporation and the journeymen of the trade over the establishment of a corporate *bureau de placement*. 'Il croyoit,' he said,

que ce fut en cette ville comme en Angleterre, où il n'y a aucun embaucheur: les garçons étant libres de se placer chez le maître qu'il [*sic*] trouve à propos. [25]

Weeks' remark may serve as an invitation to more precise comparative analysis not only of legal, institutional and political variations in the circumstances of masters and journeymen, but also of the differences in products, markets and urban systems within which particular trades developed or decayed.[26] Historians of many persuasions have tended to approach artisanal production as a staging post in the rise of capitalism. Yet there were differences in the circumstances of artisans and differences in the ways that capitalism developed and changed. If it is almost impossible to associate capitalism with a necessary configuration of production processes, products, markets, or legal and political institutions, the same applies to the many different contexts in which the trades

25 A.C. Marseille, FF 337 (6 June 1731).
26 An outline of some comparative themes was presented in M. Sonenscher, 'Le Droit du travail en France et en Angleterre à l'époque de la Révolution', *Colloque sur la Révolution française et le développement du capitalisme* (Lille, November 1987).

developed and changed.[27] Those contexts are best understood historically and comparatively. Fuller understanding of their many different constituent parts may reveal more about the diversity and indeterminate character of past societies than it has been usual to assume and, at the same time, may also suggest a wider variety of future possibilities than it has been customary to imagine.

[27] See, for a wide-ranging discussion, Roberto Mangabeira Unger, *Social Theory: Its Situation and Task* (New York and Cambridge, 1987).

Disputes between masters and journeymen were not the only form of conflict in the eighteenth-century French trades; nor were they necessarily the most fundamental. They do, however, have the great merit of revealing many aspects of the ordinary life of the trades, albeit in often distorted, heightened or merely puzzling ways. Yet a catalogue of disputes also has its disadvantages. A summary list is something of an arbitrary exercise, not only because of the vagaries of the survival of archival sources, but also because many conflicts between masters and journeymen were an outcome of more complex divisions among masters or journeymen themselves. Both the character of the sources and the imprecise quality of the phenomenon itself make the term 'dispute' particularly difficult to define.

The following list is therefore no more than an outline of the sources used to identify the clustered pattern of conflict discussed in chapter 8. It is not a comprehensive catalogue of conflict in the eighteenth-century French trades. I have listed disputes in Paris, Bordeaux, Lyon and Marseille but have confined my references to events in Nantes and Troyes to the notes in the text. Nor have I included conflicts in cities or towns like Abbeville, Amiens, Angers, Auxerre, Chalon-sur-Saône, Dijon, Grenoble, Laval, Montpellier, Nîmes, Orange, Orléans, Reims, Rouen, Saint-Quentin, Sedan, Toulouse or Tours, whose archives I have explored but where, for a variety of reasons, disputes between masters and journeymen were either relatively infrequent or have left few traces in the surviving record. My research in the vast archives of the eighteenth-century French courts has, moreover, been far from exhaustive. Subsequent investigation will undoubtedly bring many more conflicts to light – even in Paris, or Lyon and Marseille. I hope to publish a fuller list of my own limited findings elsewhere and to establish a machine-readable data-base of sources on disputes in the eighteenth-century French trades and on the local legislation that frequently preceded or followed their occurrence.

In what follows, I have restricted my references to archival and contemporary printed sources and referred to the secondary literature only if it is the sole reliable source of information. In some instances, the occurrence of a dispute has been identified by a later court ruling. The location of sources has been abbreviated in the following way:

A.C.B. – Archives communales, Bordeaux.
A.C.L. – Archives communales, Lyon.
A.C.M. – Archives communales, Marseille.
A.D. BdR. – Archives départementales des Bouches-du-Rhône.
A.D.G. – Archives départementales de la Gironde.
A.D.R. – Archives départementales du Rhône.
A.N. – Archives nationales (Paris).
A.P.P. – Archives de la Préfecture de police (Paris).
A.V.P. – Archives de la ville de Paris.
B.A. – Bibliothèque de l'Arsénal (Paris).
B.H.V.P. – Bibliothèque historique de la ville de Paris.
B.L. – British Library (London).
B.M. – Bibliothèque municipale.
B.N. – Bibliothèque nationale (Paris).
Coornaert – Emile Coornaert, *Les Compagnonnages en France du moyen age à nos jours* (Paris, 1966).
Sonenscher – Michael Sonenscher, *The Hatters of Eighteenth-Century France* (Berkeley, California, 1987).

PARIS

1630–1   Carpenters: A.N. X^{1a} 399 (30 August 1631).

1641   Printers: B.H.V.P. *Imprimés*, 102 825 (14 October 1641).

1645–51   Roofers: A.N. X^{1a} 455 (4 March 1651).
Printers: A.N. X^{1a} 2282 fol. 30 (7 September 1650); X^{1a} 5742 (7 September 1650).

1653–4   Printers: A.N. X^{1a} 2356 fol. 706vo (14 July 1654).

1656   Carpenters: A.N. X^{1a} 2397 (17 May 1656). A.P.P. Fonds Lamoignon, 13, fol. 673.

1658   Printers: A.N. X^{1a} 2439 fol. 458 (13 April 1658).

1660   Tailors: Alfred Franklin, *La Vie privée d'autrefois* (Paris, 1897), vol. 5, p. 99.
Building workers: Guy Patin, *Lettres* (Paris, 1692), vol. 3, p. 219.

1663–5   Printers: A.N. X^{1a} 2565 fol. 613 (8 May 1665). B.N. MS. fr. 22 064 fol. 83. A.P.P. Fonds Lamoignon, 14, fol. 883 (16 April 1665). B.H.V.P. *Imprimés* 102 825, p. 153 (17 March 1663). University of Chicago Library, John Crerar Collection, 1243.

1667   Building workers: A.P.P. Fonds Lamoignon, 15, fol. 54.

1670–1   Painters: B.H.V.P. *Réserve* 402 524 (16 December 1670: 20 November 1671).

1671   Printers: B.N. MS. fr. 21 741, fol. 105 (28 April 1671).

1680   Joiners: A.N. E 1802, fols. 78 and 256 (9 August and 16 December 1680).

1683   Cutlers: A.P.P. Fonds Lamoignon, 17, fol. 84.

1684–92   Roofers: A.N. X¹ᵃ 3000, fol. 150 (31 March 1692), B.N. MS. fr. 8093 (31 March 1692).

1686–9   Printers: B.N. MS. fr. 21 741, fol. 108; MS. fr. 21 749, fol. 66.

1691   B.H.V.P. *Imprimés*, 102 825, p. 178 (11 August 1689).

Joiners: A.N. X¹ᵃ 8757, fol. 391 (20 August 1751). University of London, Goldsmiths Library, 8611, *Statuts des menuisiers*.

1695–6   Joiners: A.N. X²ᵃ 487 (4 January 1696).

1697   Farriers: B.N. MS. fr. 8084, fol. 405 (3 May 1697).

1697–1700   Carpenters: A.N. E 661ᵇ, fol. 101 (16 March 1697); Y 13 046 (27 February, 25 May, 5 November 1698); Y 13 047 (31 August 1700); 13 048 (24 November 1699); X²ᵃ 508 (6 September 1700). B.N. *Réserve*, Gr. Fol. 15 [283] (1 August 1698). A.N. L 634 (8 February 1728).

1698   Market gardeners: B.N. MS. fr. 8084, fol 409 (4 July 1698). Roofers: A.N. X²ᵃ 508 (6 September 1700).

1699–1700   Hatters: Sonenscher, p. 82.

1700   Potters: A.N. Y 13 047 (27 March 1700).

1700–02   Printers: A.N. Y 13 888 (11 July 1701); B.N. MS. fr. 8084 fol. 421 (7 December 1700), 21 741, fol. 105; 21 749, fol. 66: 22 064, fols. 130, 132, 134. University of Chicago Library, John Crerar Collection. 1260 (19 June 1702).

1701   Tilemakers: B.N. F 44 776 (21 March 1701). Locksmiths: François Husson, *Artisans français. Les serruriers: étude historique* (Paris, 1902), p. 198. Roofers: A.N. X¹ᵃ 3547, fol. 153 (19 August 1729).

1702   Joiners: A.N. Y 14 348 (5 December 1785).

1703   Shoemakers: B.N. F 23 740 (14 August 1703).

1704   Bakers: A.N. Y 9498 (12 December 1704). A.P.P. Fonds Lamoignon, 22, fol. 88. B.N. *Réserve*, Gr. Fol. 15 (12 December 1704).

Roofers: B.A. 4° J 2366 (23 December 1704). Joiners: B.N. F 21 041 (36); 23 617 (741). A.N. AD+ 633 (19 July 1704).

1709   Market gardeners: B.N. F 12 987.

1710–14 Shoemakers: B.N. F 22 871 (13 June 1710; 6 March 1714).

1714 Masons: Bibliothèque de l'Assemblée nationale, MS. 1229 (20 August 1714).
Sculptors on wood: A.N. O¹ 1907 (9 May 1714).

1718 Silk-weavers: B.N. MS. Joly de Fleury 596, fol. 80.
Farriers: B.N. *Réserve*, Gr. fol. 15 (23 July 1718).

1718–19 Bakers: A.N. Y 9532 (12 December 1718); AD XI 14 (24 April 1719).

1719 Building-workers: A.P.P. Fonds Lamoignon, 26, fol. 742 (10 May 1719).

1719–20 Tanners: B.N. MS. fr. 8084, fol. 525 (7 December 1719; 12 December 1720). B.N 8° Z Le Senne, 11 527, p. 238.

1720 Curriers: A.N. Y 13 350 (27 June 1720).
Shoemakers: A.N. Y 9421 (6 July 1720); S 118 (16 October 1720). B.N. MS. fr. 21 793, fol. 402; *Réserve*, Gr. fol. 15; 8° Z Le Senne, 4195 (1). A.P.P. Fonds Lamoignon, 27, fols. 1 and 76.
Cobblers: A.P.P. Fonds Lamoignon, 27, fol. 131. B.N. *Réserve*, Gr. fol. 15, fol. 138.
Farriers: A.N. Y 9421 (22 February 1720). A.P.P. Fonds Lamoignon, 27, fol. 34. B.N. F 44 775 (22 February 1720).
Upholsterers and carpet-weavers: A.N. AD XI 27. A.P.P. Fonds Lamoignon, 27, fol. 749. B.N. F 13 255, 13 256 (23 March 1723).

1720–5 Printers: A.N. Y 12 018 (11 July 1724). B.A. MS. Bastille, 10 858. B.N. MS. fr. 8089, fol. 377; 21 857, fols, 32, 82; 22 062, fol. 175; 21 741, fol. 127; 22 064, fol. 119. A.P.P. Fonds Lamoignon, 28, fol. 270.

1721 Hatters: Sonenscher, p. 83.

1721–22 Painters: A.N. Y 9423 (6 February 1722).

1722 Bakers: A.N. Y 9614 (5 September 1722).
Gunsmiths: A.N. AD XI 12ᵇ

1723 Silkweavers: A.N. Y 9500 (20 March 1756). A.P.P. Fonds Lamoignon, 40, fol. 375. B.N. MS. Joly de Fleury, 596, fol. 80.
Sewermen: A.N. Y 9523ᵃ

1724 Framework knitters: A.P.P. Fonds Lamoignon, 28, fol. 43. B.A. MS. Bastille, 10 846. B.N. MS. fr. 8096, fol. 467.
Printers on copperplate: A.N. Y 12 018 (26 July 1724).
Tinsmiths: B.N. F 26 431 (16 November 1724).

1725 Cardmakers: A.N. Y 9615 (13, 14 December 1725). B.N. F 12 918.
Wigmakers: A.N. Y 9498 (19 June 1725).

1725–6 Hatters: Sonenscher, pp. 86–7.

1726–9 Roofers: A.N. AD+ 802 (6 September 1727). A.N. Y 14 523 (8 October 1726); X¹ª 3547 fol. 153 (19 August 1729); X¹ª 8987 fol. 195 (21 July 1727).

1727 Locksmiths: A.-M. Bruleaux, 'Les maîtres serruriers parisiens et leurs travaux de grande serrurerie', Thèse de l'Ecole des Chartes, Paris, n.d., p. 92.

1728 Bakers: B.N. MS. fr. 21 640 fol. 7; *Réserve*, Gr. fol. 18 (13 February, 23 April, 7 May, 25 September 1728).

1731 Farriers: B.A. MS. Bastille, 11 132.
Printers: A.P.P. Fonds Lamoignon, 30, fol. 377. B.N. MS. fr. 8089, fol. 427; 22 175, fol. 92.

1732 Goldsmiths: B.N. MS. fr. 8089, fol. 193.

1734 Goldsmiths: A.N. Y 9523ª (28 May 1734).

1735 Masons: Bibliothèque de l'Assemblée nationale, MS. 1229 (20 June 1735).

1736 Framework knitters: A.N. Y 9499; Y 13 086 (20 November 1736). A.P.P. Fonds Lamoignon, 32, fol. 221. B.A. MS. Bastille 11 321.

1736–7 Coopers: A.N. X¹ª 4554 (3 February 1767). B.A. MS. Bastille, 11 364.

1737 Farriers: B.A. MS. Bastille, 11 287.
Harvest-workers: B.N. MS. fr. 8097, fol. 252 (17 July 1737).
Painters: B.N. MS. Joly de Fleury, 645, fol. 72ᵛº.

1737–8 Cardmakers: B.N. F 12 918 (27 June 1738.

1738 Goldsmiths: B.N. MS. fr. 21 797. fol. 400 (11 October 1738).
1738).

  Chisellers and gilders: A.N. AD XI (18 December 1738).
A.P.P. Fonds Lamoignon, 33, fol. 49.
Packers: A.N. Y 9618 (27 June 1738).

1738–9 Bakers: A.N. Y 10 986 (15 February, 6 June 1738, 18 June 1739). B.N. V 11 518 (31 July 1749).

1739 Joiners: Coornaert, p. 426.
Locksmiths: A.N. Y 12 922 (9 November 1739). A.P.P. Fonds Lamoignon, 33, fol. 546. B.N. MS. fr. 8097, fol. 293; F 44 761 (20 June 1739).
Silk-weavers: B.N. F 12 963.
Pastrycooks: A.P.P. Fonds Lamoignon, 33, fol. 613. B.N. MS. fr. 8097, fol. 309 (31 October 1739); F 46 609.
Vinegar-makers: B.N. F 22 609 (23 February 1739).

1739–46 Roofers: A.N. E 1210ᵇ (18) (25 February 1744); X¹ª 3959 fol. 170 (20 August 1745); X¹ª 8750 fol. 216ᵛº (4 August 1746); X¹ª 7505 fol. 76 (10 July 1743); Y 11 159 (18 February 1740); *Minutier central* LXXXVI 601 (19 July

1739). A.P.P. Fonds Lamoignon, 35, fol. 318. B.N. MS. Joly de Fleury, 645, fol. 253: 2340, fol. 88: F 21 035 (4). Bibliothèque de l'Ordre des Avocats, Collection Gaultier-Debreil, 35, no. 68.

1740   Building-workers: A.N. Z^{1J} 230 (24 September 1740). Sewermen: A.N. Y 11 303^b (6 October 1740). A.P.P. Fonds Lamoignon, 34, fol. 230.

1741   Dyers: A.N. Y 15 364 (17 September 1741).

1742–3   Shoemakers: A.P.P. Fonds Lamoignon, 35, fol. 220. B.N. F 12 907 (5 August 1743).

1743   Joiners: B.N. MS. Joly de Fleury, 1879, fol. 60 (26 November 1743). Potters: A.N. AD XI 18 (20 July 1743). A.P.P. Fonds Lamoignon, 35, fol. 203. B.N. F 44 776. Sculptors: A.N. Y 14 068 (24 October 1743). Silk-weavers: A.N. Y 14 068 (9 August 1743). B.N. MS. Joly de Fleury, 596, fol. 80.

1744   Harness-makers: A.N. E 1390^c (24 July 1764); X^{1a} 8778, fol. 17 (5 July 1765); X^{2b} 997 (20 October 1745).

1744–6   Wheelwrights: B.N. MS. fr. 8090, fols. 49, 282.

1745–6   Silk-weavers: A.N. Y 9624 (30 April 1745). B.N. F 26 465 (5 April 1746).

1746   Coopers: B.N. V 11 515 (9 August 1746). Locksmiths: A.N. X^{1b} 3557 (23 July 1746): X^{1a} 3974 fol. 153 (28 April 1746); Y 14 391 (7 August 1746); Y 13 751 (13 September 1746). Y 12 151 (28 May 1748); Y 13 103 (12 July 1753). A.P.P. Fonds Lamoignon, 37, fol. 575. B.A. MS. Bastille, 11 590, 11 596. B.N. F. 44 761.

1747   Spurmakers: A.N. Y 9532 (17 June 1747).

1747–8   Button-makers: A.N. AD XI 14. B.N. F 13 217 (24 May 1748).

1748–9   Cutlers: A.N. Y 9533: Y 12 151 (12 November 1748). B.N. V 11 518 (2 January. 18 September 1749); MS. fr. 8090. fol. 385 (4 March 1748). Painters: A.N. X^{1a} 4027. fol. 124vo (28 March 1748); X^{1a} 4029 fol. 153vo (4 May 1748); X^{1a} 4039, fol. 518 (26 August 1748); X^{1b} 3578 (4 May 1748). A.P.P. Fonds Lamoignon, 38, fol. 546. Hatters: Sonenscher, pp. 91–2.

1749   Tinsmiths: B.N. F 26 431 (9 December 1749). Wigmakers: A.N. AD XI 25 (1 July, 12 Dec. 1760): X^{1b} 3740 (12 December 1760). Joiners: A.N. Y 9523^b: Y 15 345 (4 October 1749). Lutemakers: B.N. V 11 518 (18 September 1749). Bakers: A.N. Y 9499. B.N. V 11 518 (31 July 1749).

1750   Shoemakers: A.N. S 118 (6 April 1750).

1750-1   Roofers: A.N. Y 11 167 (2 April 1750).

1750-2   Gunsmiths: A.N. AD XI 12ᵇ (12 December 1750, 17 February 1751); Y 9452ᵃ.

1751   Printers on copper plate: A.N. AD XI 19 (21 April 1752); H 2120 (22 August 1750); Y 11 466 (17 July 1750). A.P.P. Fonds Lamoignon, 39, fol. 389. B.N. F 44 779.

Basket-makers and ironmongers: B.N. 8° Z Le Senne, 4194 (30 June 1751).

Saddlers and harness-makers: A.N. Y 9523ᵇ (27 October 1751); Y 14 311 (7 November 1751).

Bookbinders: A.N. X¹ᵃ 4118 (25 May 1751); X¹ᵇ 3621 (25 May 1751).

Hatters: Sonenscher, pp. 92-3.

Wine-sellers: A.N. Y 9500.

Gingerbread-makers: A.N. Y 14 195 (30 October 1751).

1751-2   Nailmakers: A.N. Y J5 363 (12 June 1751); Y 10 994 (19 January 1752). A.P.P. Fonds Lamoignon, 40, fol. 135.

1752   Coopers: A.N. X¹ᵃ 4554 (26 February 1767).

Farriers: A.N. Y 15 450 (25 January 1752).

1753   Wigmakers: A.N. X¹ᵇ 3740 (12 December 1760). A.P.P. Fonds Lamoignon, 40, fol. 243.

1755   Wigmakers: A.N. Y 9456ᵃ (2 April 1755); X¹ᵇ 3740 (12 December 1760).

1755-6   Joiners: A.N. X¹ᵃ 4193, fol. 5ᵛᵒ (25 March 1755); X¹ᵇ 3657 (25 March 1755); X¹ᵃ 7791, fols. 300ᵛᵒ and 322 (1 October 1755); X¹ᵃ 7795, fol. 298ᵛᵒ (11 December 1755); X¹ᵃ 4239, fol. 289 (4 August 1756); K 1031 (121).

Roofers: A.N. X¹ᵃ 4207, fol. 80ᵛᵒ (27 August 1755); X¹ᵃ 4224, fol. 181 (4 September 1756); Y 9500 (27 September 1755).

1755-8   Shoemakers: A.N. L 551: S 118, fols. 16-17.

1756   Wigmakers: A.N. Y 9524ᵇ: Y 12 964 (6 and 31 May 1756); 12 159 (7 May 1756); Y 11 572ᵃ (7 May 1756).

Silk-weavers: A.N. Y 9500 (20 March 1756), A.P.P. Fonds Lamoignon, 40, fol. 375.

Bakers: A. N. Y 9499 (6 August 1756); Y 14 316; Y 12 604. B.N. F 44 704 (6 August 1756).

1756-7   Bookbinders: B.N. MS. fr. 22 118, fol. 165 (22 May 1757).

1758-9   Wood-floaters: A.N. Z¹ʰ 645 (2 January 1759).

1759   Gunsmiths: Coornaert, p. 426.

1760-1   Wigmakers: A.N. AD XI 25 (1 July 1760); X¹ᵇ 3740 (12 and 23 December 1760); X¹ᵃ 7931, fol. 131 (29 July 1761); B.N. MS. Joly de Fleury, 1839, fol. 375.

1761 Gilders: A.N. Y 11 344ᵇ (1 July 1761); Y 11 345ᵃ (2 July 1761). B.A. MS. Bastille, 12 127.

1762–4 Ribbon-weavers: A.N. X²ᵃ 817 (7 February 1763); X¹ᵃ 7978. fol. 147 (29 March 1763); X¹ᵃ 7987, fol. 22 (2 July 1763); X¹ᵃ 4444, fol. 146ᵛᵒ (11 August 1763); X¹ᵃ 8002, fol. 327ᵛᵒ (14 January 1764); X¹ᵃ 4490, fol. 199ᵛᵒ (9 February 1765); A.N. X¹ᵇ 3781 (28 February 1763); X¹ᵇ 3812 (5 September 1764); X¹ᵃ 8002, fol. 40 (5 January 1764); Y 11 950 (15 December 1762); Y 9645 (20 May 1763); Y 9500; Y 9525.

1763 Toolmakers: A.N. AD XI 26 (16 May 1763).

1763–5 Turners: A.N. X¹ᵇ 3835 (9 January 1766).

1763–6 Shoemakers: A.N. X¹ᵃ 4443, fol. 131ᵛᵒ (6 August 1763); X¹ᵃ 4538, fol. 337 (9 July 1766); Y 11 004ᵃ (7 May, 7 and 10 June 1763); Y 11 004ᵇ (8 and 29 August, 16 September, 9 October 1763) Y 9534 (13 September 1763); Y 15 368 (6 and 12 December 1763); Y 15 369 (28 January 1764); Y 10 799 (13 January 1765); Y 15 370 (25 March 1765); Y 11 082 (21 April 1766).
Glaziers: A.N. X¹ᵇ 3847 (6 August 1766); Y 9500.
Bookbinders: A.N. X¹ᵇ 3835 (22 January 1766). B.N. MS. fr. 22 118, fols. 275, 294.

1763–8 Saddlers and harness-makers: A.N. E 1390ᶜ (24 July 1764); E 1426ᵃ (11 August 1767); X¹ᵃ 4521 (11 January 1766); X¹ᵃ 8778, fol. 17 (5 July 1765); X¹ᵃ 8076 (14 May 1766); X¹ᵃ 8079, fols. 346 and 413 (18 June 1764); X¹ᵃ 8139, fol. 188ᵛᵒ (4 May 1768); X¹ᵃ 8145, fol. 229 (9 July 1768); X¹ᵃ 8785 fol. 193 (16 July 1768); Y 9500; Y 11 583ᵃ (31 January 1766); Y 11 085 (31 July 1769). B.N. MS. Joly de Fleury, 647, fol. 281; 648 fol. 290; F 26 468.

1763–70 Roofers: A.N. AD XI 16; X¹ᵃ 4528 (21 March 1766); X¹ᵃ 4536, fol. 267 (20 June 1766); X¹ᵃ 8087, fol. 30ᵛᵒ (5 August 1766); X¹ᵃ 4611 (1 August 1768); Y 11 682 (26 July 1763); 9466ᵃ (10 February 1764); Y 9500; Y 12 768 (3 and 10 October 1768); Y 15 375 (11, 19 September, 21, 23 October, 7 November, 11, 12 December 1769); Y 10 899ᵇ (30 April 1770).

1764 Gunsmiths: A.N. Y 10 778 (30, 31 January, 8 August 1764). Farriers: A.N. AD XI 65.

1764–5 Hatters: Sonenscher, p. 13.
Cardmakers: A.N. Y 9500; Y 15 463 (20 September 1764); Y 15 372 (12 August 1766); Y 15 373 (14 November 1767). B.N. MS. Joly de Fleury, 648; F. 12 918.

1765 Ropemakers: A.N. Y 11 687 (2 September 1765); B.A. MS. Bastille, 12 245, fol. 22.
Plumbers: B.N. MS. Joly de Fleury 648, fol. 128.
Carpenters: Coornaert, p. 426.

1765–9 Painters: A.N. X¹ᵃ 4528 (24 March 1766); X¹ᵃ 8078, fol. 282 (11 June 1766); X¹ᵃ 8079, fol. 70 (14 June 1766); X¹ᵃ 4548, fol 847 (6 September 1766); X¹ᵃ 4553, fol. 132ᵛᵒ (19 January 1767); X¹ᵃ 8100, fol. 345 (4 February 1767); Y 9534 (14 April 1766); Y 9525 (26 April 1766); Y 11 007ᵇ (16 December 1766, 7 July 1767); 15 375 (1 July 1767); Y 11 010 (8, 13 May 1769); B.A. MS. Bastille, 12 369.

1766 Printers on copper plate: A.N. H 2120 (6 February 1767); Y 11 082 (25 March, 7 May 1766); Y 11 084 (25 August 1768); Y 11 085 (25 July, 11 August, 30 November 1769).

Paulmiers-raquetiers: A.N. X¹ᵇ 3839 (25 March 1766); A.N. X¹ᵃ 4528, fol. 210.

1766–7 Coopers: A.N. X¹ᵃ 4554, fol. 246 (3 February 1767).

1766–8 Wheelwrights: A.N. X¹ᵇ 3854 (19 December 1766); X¹ᵃ 8101, fol. 99 (7 February 1767); X¹ᵃ 8114 (20 June 1767); X¹ᵃ 8121 (29 August 1767); X¹ᵃ 4618 (1 September 1768). B.H.V.P. 402 104.

1767 Harvest-workers: A.N. Y 11 691 (29 July 1767).

1769 Bakers: A.N. Y 15 375 (11 April 1769); B.H.V.P. 412 081; *Encyclopédie méthodique, Jurisprudence*, vol. 9, under 'boulanger'.

Carpenters: A.N. Y 14 332 (29 July 1769).

Joiners: A.N. Y 13 673 (29 April 1769).

1769–70 Farriers: A.N. AD XI 65; Y 11 786 (23 December 1769); Y 15 376 (2, 8 January 1770); Y 15 383 (4 July 1774).

1770 Plumbers: A.N. Y 12 175 (2 February 1770).

1770–1 Wigmakers: A.N. X¹ᵇ 3925 (21 March 1770); X¹ᵃ 4694 (4 September 1770); X¹ᵃ 8795, fol. 194 (14 August 1771); X¹ᵃ 4704 (20 August 1771), B.N. MS. Joly de Fleury, 649, fol. 155 (22 July 1771).

1770–4 Joiners: A.N. X¹ᵇ 3926 (23 April 1770); X¹ᵃ 8213, fol. 206ᵛᵒ (11 August 1770); X¹ᵃ 8221, fols. 249 and 324 (11, 12 January 1770); X¹ᵃ 8220, fol. 332ᵛᵒ (3 December 1771); X¹ᵃ 8241, fol. 150 (15 December 1772); X¹ᵃ 8248, fol. 48 (28 April 1773); X¹ᵃ 4738, fol. 111 (22 January 1774).

1772 Ironmongers and basket-makers: B.N. 8° Z Le Senne, 4194 (19 December 1772).

Printers on copper plate: A.N. H 2120 (27 September 1772).

1773 Wigmakers: A.N. AD XI 25 (6 September 1773).

1774 Farriers: A.N. Y 15 383 (4 April, 1 August 1774).

Silk-weavers: A.N. Y 12 787 (15 June 1774).

Hatters: Coornaert, p. 426.

1775 Printers on copper plate: A.N. H 2120 (22 November 1775). Cutlers: A.N. E 2525, fol. 623.

1776 Bookbinders: A.N. Y 12 826 (18 October 1776); Y 12 793 (11 October 1776). B.N. MS. fr. 6682, fol. 281. Wallpaper workers. A.N. Y 11 193. Builders' labourers: A.N. O¹ 487, fol. 758. Labourers: B.N. MS. Joly de Fleury, 1421, fol. 36. Bakers: A.N. Y 9499.

1777 Carpet-weavers: A.N. Y 12 073 (21 July 1785). Pavers: *Encyclopédie méthodique. Jurisprudence*, vol. 9, under 'ateliers'. Wheelwrights: A.N. 2120 (13 June 1777). Printers: B.N. MS. fr. 22 180, fol. 149. Shoemakers: *Encyclopédie méthodique. Jurisprudence*, vol. 9, under 'cordonnier'.

1778 Locksmiths: University of Chicago, John Crerar Library, 1403.

1779 Farriers: A.N. Y 14 570 (23 September 1781). Léopold Malepeyre, *Code des ouvriers*, pp. 9–10. Roofers: A.N. AD XI 16 (19 June 1779). Toymakers, fanmakers and lutemakers: B.L. 10173 aa. 50 (10 September 1779).

1780 Joiners: A.N. Xᵀᵇ 4118 (7 September 1780); Xᵀᵇ 4261 (27 May 1786); Y 14 348 (5 December 1785). B.N. F 21 201 [39] (2 February 1780).

1781 Hatters: Coornaert, p. 426. Bakers: A.N. Xᵀᵇ 4142 (28 August 1781); Xᵀᵃ 4250 (12 January 1786). Roofers: A.N. Y 13 689 (21 March 1781). Wigmakers: *Encyclopédie méthodique. Jurisprudence*, vol. 9, under 'perruquier'.

1782 Hatters: Coornaert, p. 426.

1783 Gunsmiths: *Encyclopédie méthodique. Jurisprudence*, vol. 9, under 'arquebusier'. Pinmakers, nailmakers and iron-workers: Coornaert, p. 426.

1784 Quarry-workers: A.N. Y 13 693 (28 July 1784).

1784–5 Saddlers and harness-makers: A.N. Xᵀᵇ 8716 (11 December 1784); Y 11 280 (24 December 1785).

1784–6 Painters: A.N. Y 14 479ᵇ (3 December 1784); Y 14 480ᵃ (17 January 1785); Y 11 028 (5 October 1785); Xᵀᵇ 8720 (5 February 1785); 8734 (6 August 1785); 4243 (5 September 1785); Xᵀᵇ 4247 (23 November 1785); 4253 (21 December 1785); Xᵀᵇ 4265 (19 July 1786). B.N. 4° Fm 20904; 4° Fm 30091.

1785 Hatters: Sonenscher, pp. 150–1.

1785–6

Joiners: A.N. Y 14 348 (5 December 1785).

Stone-cutters and masons: A.N. 9949 (2 May 1785); AD XI 20 (15 July 1785); B.N. MS. Joly de Fleury, 557, fols. 7–11, 27: MS. fr. 6685, fol. 149.

Carpet-weavers: A.N. Y 12 073 (21 July 1785 and 6 September 1785); 15 094ᵃ (9 September 1785).

Silk-weavers: A.N. AD XI 11 [164] (13 April 1785).

1786

Porters and *commissionnaires*: A.N. Y 11 280 (17 December 1785); Y 14 601 (18 January 1786); Y 12 816 (18 January 1786); B.N. MS. fr. 6685, fol. 262 (2 January 1786); MS. Joly de Fleury 558, fol. 232 (13 January 1786). Bachaumont, *Mémoires secrets pour servir à l'histoire de la République des lettres*, 31 (2, 3, 12, 20 January 1786).

Printers: A.N. Y 11 428 (28 December 1785); Y 11 429 (14 March 1786 and 4 September 1786); B.N. MS. fr. 6685 fol. 259; MS. Joly de Fleury 1682, fol. 329. B. L. 27 d. 11 [127], (2 September 1786 and 15 September 1786).

Bakers: A.N. Xᴵᵇ 4142 (28 August 1781); Xᴵᵇ 4250 (12 January 1786).

Carpenters: B.N. MS. fr. 6685, fol. 315; A.N. Y 11 281ᵃ (22 March 1786).

Locksmiths: B.N. MS. fr. 6685, fol. 315; A.N. Y 11 281ᵃ (22 March 1786).

Ropemakers: A.N. Y 18 738 (4 April 1786); 10 243 (2 April 1786).

Grocers: B.N. MS. Joly de Fleury, 1322, fol. 227.

Farriers: A.N. Y 14 576 (20 February 1786); 15 013ᵃ (1 March 1786); 12 210 (1 March 1786); 13 012ᵃ (1 March 1786); 11 281ᵃ (24 February 1786); Y 9959 (27 February 1786); AD XI 20; B.N. MS. Joly de Fleury, 558, fol. 226; A.P.P. Ab 383; Bachaumont, *Mémoires secrets* (1, 20 March 1786).

1787

Shoemakers: A.N. Xᴵᵇ 4282 (30 March 1787).

Locksmiths: A.N. Y 14 578 (17 January, 12, 19 March 1787).

Toymakers: A.N. Xᴵᵇ 4285 (1 May 1787).

Stone-cutters and masons: A.N. AD XI 25ᵇ (17 May 1787).

Printers on copper plate: A.N. H 2120 (7 March 1787).

Farriers: Coornaert, p. 426.

1788

Builders' labourers: A.N. Y 11 731 (25 February 1788).

1789

Hatters: Sonenscher, p. 143.

Carpenters: A.N. Y 18 763 (24 May 1789); 18 764 (1 June 1789).

Wigmakers: A.N. T 514¹; *Les Révolutions de Paris* (Paris, 1789) vol. 6, pp. 17–18, 27.

Tailors: *Les Révolutions de Paris*, vol. 6, pp. 15, 27; Sigismund Lacroix, *Actes de la Commune de Paris, Serie 1*, 7 vols (Paris 1894–6), vol. 1, pp. 265, 268, 276.

Shoemakers: *Les Révolutions de Paris*, vol. 6, p. 32; S. Lacroix, *Actes de la Commune de Paris*, Serie I, vol. 1, p. 416.

1791
Hatters: Sonenscher, p. 162.
Carpenters: B.N. MS. fr. 6562; MS. fr. 11 697; 4° Fm 35345, *Petition présentée à la municipalité de Paris par les ci-devant maîtres charpentiers*; 4° Fm 35346, *Précis présenté à l'Assemblée nationale par les entrepreneurs de la charpente de la ville de Paris* (22 May 1791); 4° 35347, *Précis présenté à l'Assemblée nationale par les ouvriers en l'art de la charpente de la ville de Paris* (26 May 1791); A.N. AD XI 65; A.P.P. Aa 83 (19 April 1791); Aa 198 (21 April 1791): Aa 84 (17 May 1791); Aa 224 (6 June 1791).
Printers: A.N. C177.
Farriers: A.N. AD XI 65, *Précis pour les maréchaux de Paris* (4 June 1791); DIV 51, 1488 (18).
Stone-cutters and masons: A.N. F^{13} 1935 (29 July 1791). B.N. Lb^{40} 165, *Rapport sur l'édifice dit de Sainte Geneviève par Mr. Quatremère-Quincey*.
Market gardeners: A.N. Z^{1H} 564 (28 May 1791). A.N. F^{12} 1461.

BORDEAUX

The papers of the *jurats* and the court whose jurisdiction covered the *sauvetats* of Saint-André and Saint-Seurin are the main source of documentation on disputes in Bordeaux (A.D. Gironde, series 12B and 13B). They have been classified and used extensively by Jean Cavignac in his 'Les Compagnonnages dans les luttes ouvrières au xviiᵉ siècle', *Bibliothèque de l'Ecole des Chartes*, 126 (1968), pp. 377–411. In the following list, I have supplemented Cavignac's sources by adding references drawn mainly from the papers of the Parlement (A.D.G. series B, unclassified) or the corporations of Bordeaux (A.D.G. series C and 6E; A.C. Bordeaux, series HH). I have not listed the many fights involving members of the *compagnonnages* that came before the *jurats*, nor have I cited the documents in the series 12B and 13B used by Cavignac (so that the following list makes reference only to sources *not* cited by Cavignac). References to several disputes in the late seventeenth century listed below can be found under their dates in the chronological *Inventaire sommaire des registres de la Jurade, 1520–1783*, 8 vols (Bordeaux, 1896–1947), hereafter, *Inventaire*.

1651   Locksmiths: A.D.G. B. (22 June 1709): C 1814.
1664   Bakers: *Inventaire*.
1670   Joiners: *Inventaire*.
1675   Shoemakers: A.D.G. B (1 February 1675).
        Masons: *Archives historiques du département de la Gironde* (Bordeaux 1900), vol. 41, p. 191.
1695   Bakers: *Inventaire*.
1698   Locksmiths: A.D.G. B (22 June 1709).

1702 Bakers: A.D.G. C 1806.
1703 Gunsmiths: *Inventaire.*
1709 Locksmiths: A.D.G. B (22 June 1709).
1719 Tailors: A.D.G. B (26 February 1772).
1721 Bakers: A.D.G. C 1806.
 Joiners.
1723–4 Joiners: A.D.G. B (24 July 1724).
1733 Locksmiths.
 Tailors.
1737 Joiners.
1742 Locksmiths.
1743 Boatmen.
1748 Bakers: A.D.G. C 909; C 1806.
1749 Joiners.
1751 Joiners: A.D.G. B (9 January, 31 July 1751).
1752 Locksmiths: B.M. Bordeaux J 2891/1.
1754 Stone-cutters.
 Carpenters.
1757 Locksmiths: A.C.B. BB 124.
1758–59 Bakers: A.C.B. HH 21.
1759 Locksmiths.
1760 Locksmiths: A.D.G. 6E 112.
 Masons: A.N. F^{12} 757^a.
1761 Tailors: A.D.G. 3E 15 011 (28 February 1761); A.C.B. BB 126 (7 April 1761).
 Smiths.
1762 Wigmakers: A.D.G. B (27 March 1762).
 Shoemakers.
1762–3 Joiners: A.D.G. B (21 February 1763).
1763 Shoemakers: A.D.G. C 1804.
 Nailmakers: A.D.G. C 1754.
1764 Joiners.
1766 Locksmiths: A.D.G. C 1776.
 Wigmakers: A.D.G. B (16 April 1766).
 Saddlers and harness-makers.
1768 Joiners.
 Bakers.
1770 Shoemakers: A.D.G. C 1804.

1771 Saddlers and harness-makers.

1772 Tailors: A.D.G. B (26 February 1772).
      Shoemakers: A.D.G. B (4 May 1772); C 1804.
      Locksmiths: A.D.G. C 1776.

1772–3 Saddlers and harness-makers: A.D.G. C 1779.

1774 Sailors.
      Stone-cutters: A.C.B. HH 101.
      Saddlers and harness-makers.
      Turners and toymakers.

1775 Stone-cutters: A.D.G. C 1757.

1775–6 Shoemakers: A.D.G. B (20 November 1775, 7 September
        1776); C 1804; 6E 49. A.C.B. HH 83.
        Joiners.
        Farriers.

1776 Saddlers and harness-makers: A.D.G. C 1779.
      Gunsmiths.
      Wigmakers: A.D.G. B (16 July 1784).

1777 Nailmakers: A.D.G. C 1754.
      Carpenters.

1778–9 Saddlers and harness-makers: A.D.G. C 1779.
        Carpenters: A.D.G. C 1791.

1780 Locksmiths.

1781 Joiners.
      Nailmakers: A.D.G. C 1754.

1781–2 Smiths and toolmakers: A.C.B. HH 96.
        Carpenters: A.D.G. C 1791.

1782 Shoemakers: A.D.G. C 1804.

1783 Ships' carpenters.
      Locksmiths.
      Wheelwrights.

1784 Wigmakers: A.D.G. B (16 July 1784).

1785 Carpet weavers: A.D.G. B (3 August 1785).
      Tinsmiths (*ferblantiers*): A.D.G. B (30 June 1785).
      Nailmakers.
      Glaziers A.D.G. B (6 September 1785).

1785–6 Locksmiths: A.D.G. B (26 January 1785); C 1775; 6E 112.

1785–7 Smiths: A.D.G. B (30 August 1785; 31 January 1787).
        A.C.B. HH 96; 119.
        Wheelwrights.
        Tailors: A.D.G. B (3 September 1785; 12 January 1787).

1787 Tinsmiths (*chaudronniers*): A.D.G. B (16 January 1787).
      Joiners.
      Carpenters: A.D.G. C 1791.

1788   Joiners.
Nailmakers: A.D.G. C 1754. A.C.B. HH 80.
Carpenters: A.D.G. C 1791.

1790   Wigmakers: B.M. Bordeaux, D 68 764, D 74 253.

1791   Tailors: A.C.B. (17 January 1791).

LYON

Sources on the disputes that occurred in Lyon in 1785–6 are cited above, pp. 279–80.

1655   Printers: A.N. X¹ᵃ 5798 (14 August 1655); X¹ᵃ 2386 fol. 194 (18 September 1655).

1661   Locksmiths: A.C.L. HH 183; A.D.R. BP 3622.

1662   Printers: A.N. X¹ᵃ 2519 fols. 44ᵛᵒ and 270ᵛᵒ (20, 27 October 1662).

1680   Bakers: A.C.L. HH 24.

1680–1   Printers: A.N. V⁶ 664 (7 November 1681).

1688   Tailors: A.C.L. HH 125.

1698–9   Joiners: B.A. 8° J 4684; A.D.R. 3E 6567 (4 January 1699).

1704   Bakers: A.C.L. HH 24.

1719–25   Printers: A.N. X²ᵃ 649 (10 July 1724); X¹ᵇ 3296 (15 December 1725).

1723   Tailors: B.N. F 26 473.

1729   Joiners: B.A. 8° J 4684.

1735   Joiners: A.D.R. 3E 7601 (25 May 1735); B.A. 8° J 4684.

1743–4   Dyers: A.D.R. 3E 4653 (27 October 1743); A.N. F¹² 1440.
Carpenters: A.D.R. 3E 2804 (27 May 1744); A.N. X¹ᵃ 3928 fol. 327 (27 June 1744).
Silk-weavers: A.N. F¹² 1440.
Framework knitters: A.N. F¹² 1440.

1744–6   Hatters: Sonenscher, p. 90.

1758   Saddlers: A.C.L. HH 181.

1760   Tailors: A.C.L. HH 185.

1761–2   Silk-weavers: A.N. X¹ᵃ 4317 fol. 313ᵛᵒ (7 September 1759); B.N. MS. Joly de Fleury, 360, fol. 368.

1762   Hatters: Sonenscher, pp. 98–101.

1762–4   Framework knitters: B.A. 8° J 4669.

1764   Wigmakers: A.N. X¹ᵇ 3814 (24 October 1764).
Joiners: A.D.R. BP 3303 (14 May 1764).

Appendix

1765   Wigmakers: A.D.R. BP 3304.
        Locksmiths: A.D.R. BP 3307 (3 November 1764).

        Harness-makers: A.D.R. BP 3319 (6 December 1765).

1767   Locksmiths: A.C.L. HH 184; A.D.R. BP 3338.

1769   Silk-weavers: A.D.R. BP 3358.

1769–70 Framework knitters: A.N. X^{1a} 4662 fol. 83; X^{1a} 4674 (10
        April 1770); X^{1a} 8200 (29 March 1770); X^{1a} 8213 (8
        August 1770); X^{1a} 4695 (6 September 1770); X^{1b} 9765
        (11 June 1771).

1769–74 Hatters: Sonenscher, pp. 100–17.

1770   Silk-dyers: A.N. F^{12} 772.

1771   Joiners: A.D.R. BP 3381.

1772   Wigmakers: A.D.R. BP 3389.

1774   Silk-weavers: A.N. F^{12} 1440.

1776   Bakers: A.C.L. HH 24.

1776–8 Hatters: Sonenscher, pp. 132–8.

1780   Locksmiths: A.C.L. HH 184.

1785–6 Hatters: Sonenscher, pp. 154–7.
        Silk-weavers.

1786   Stone-cutters.
        Shoemakers.

MARSEILLE

Sources on the many brawls involving the *compagnonnages* which occurred in
1787 and 1788 are cited in my *Hatters of Eighteenth-Century France* and are not
reproduced here.

1684–5 Locksmiths: A.C.M. HH 430.

1708   Bakers: A.D. BdR. 240E 5.

1718–19 Hatters: Sonenscher, pp. 93–5.

1724   Plasterers: A.C.M. FF 204.

1726   Joiners: A.C.M. FF 331^b (4 September 1726): FF 190 fol. 31
        (6 September 1726).

1729   Toolmakers: A.C.M. FF 335^c; FF 190 fol. 31 (21, 24
        February 1729).
        Locksmiths–joiners: A.C.M. FF 335^a; FF 190 fol. 131 (11
        February 1729).
        Wool-croppers: A.C.M. FF 190 fol. 86 (19 August 1729).

1731   Wigmakers: A.C.M. FF 337 (15 June 1737).
        Tailors: A.C.M. FF 337 (6 June 1737).

Appendix

1734   Cutlers: A.C.M. FF 340 (17 December 1734).
1735   Framework knitters: A.C.M. FF 341.
1736   Toolmakers: A.C.M. FF 342ᵇ (15 February 1736).
        Hatters.
1737   Joiners: A.C.M. FF 342ᵃ (6 September, 14 November 1736).
        Gunsmiths: A.C.M. FF 342ᵃ (21 November 1736).
        Wool-croppers: A.C.M. FF 343.
        Hatters: Sonenscher, pp. 174–5.
1739   Harness-makers: A.C.M. FF 345 (6 March 1739).
        Saddlers: A.C.M. FF 343 (2 May 1739).
1740   *Caissiers*: A.C.M. FF 346 (17 September 1740).
1741   Ships' caulkers: A.N. Marine, C⁴3 fol. 257 (24 August
        1741).
        Locksmiths: A.C.M. FF 347 (4 September 1741)
1743   Shoemakers: A.C.M. HH 403.
1749   Shoemakers: A.C.M. FF 356.
1750   Tailors: A.D. BdR 380E²³⁶ fol. 202; 380E²³⁷ fol. 1108.
1750–2 Hatters: Sonenscher, pp. 93–4.
1755   Wigmakers: A.C.M. FF 362 (28 July 1755).
1761–4 Hatters: Sonenscher, pp. 101–4.
1764   Saddlers and harness-makers: A.C.M. FF 373 (5 February
        1764).
        Bakers: A.C.M. FF 373 (22 August 1764); 240E⁶ fol. 315.
        Tailors: A.C.M. FF 373 (19 September 1764).
1765   Joiners: A.C.M. FF 206.
1769   Shoemakers: A.C.M. FF 378 (23 February, 26, 29 July
        1769).
1769–70 Linen- and fustian-weavers: A.C.M. FF 379 (19 June 1770).
1773–4 Joiners: A.D. BdR B 5643 (26 April 1773); 2B 1167 (2
        November 1773).
1774   Wigmakers: A.C.M. FF 383 (17 January 1774).
1774–7 Hatters: Sonenscher, pp. 118–31.
1776   Wigmakers: A.D. BdR 240E¹¹³ (29 August 1776).
1777   Shoemakers: A.C.M. FF 387 (8 May 1777).
1778   Bakers: A.D. BdR 351E¹¹⁸⁹ fol. 686.
        Joiners: A.D. BdR B 5647 (10 April 1778).
        Hatters: Sonenscher, pp. 130–1.
        Weavers: A.C.M. FF 389 (10 March 1779); A.D. BdR 2B
        1225 (10 April 1779).
1780–1 Framework knitters: A.C.M. FF 391 (14 January 1781).

1783   Shoemakers: A.D. BdR 240E[26] (20 January 1781); A.C.M. FF 391 (18 May 1781); HH 404.

Shoemakers: A.D. BdR 240E[26] (30 July 1783).

1784   Turners: A.C.M. FF 394 (24 July 1784).
Farriers: A.C.M. FF 394 (26 August 1784).
Wheelwrights: A.C.M. FF 394 (13 September 1784).

1784–5   Shoemakers: A.C.M. FF 394 (22 March 1785); FF 395 (25 July 1785).
Hatters: Sonenscher, pp. 151–2.

1785   Locksmiths: A.D. BdR 2B 2102 (11 January 1785).
Stone-cutters: A.D. BdR B 5654 (19 September 1785); 2B 2102 (8 November 1785).

1786   Shoemakers: A.C.M. HH 404: A.D. BdR 240E[26] (1 May 1786).
Hatters: Sonenscher, p. 153–4.
Wigmakers: A.C.M. FF 396 (3 June 1786).
Bakers: A.C.M. FF 396 (17 July 1786); A.D. BdR 351E[1198] fol. 544; 351E[1199] fols. 62vo, 515; B 3707 (19, 21 July 1786).

1787   Hatters: Sonenscher, p. 158.
Tailors: A.D. BdR 240E[125] (12 September 1787. 10 March 1788).
Joiners: A.C.M. HH 416.

Primary and secondary printed material has been listed together. The locations and callmarks of relatively inaccessible pamphlets and legal memoranda are indicated in parentheses. An outline of the procedures followed with the manuscript sources used in this book can be found in my *Hatters of Eighteenth-Century France*.

A Messieurs les Prévôt des Marchands et Echevins juges consulaires des arts et métiers de la ville de Lyon (Lyon, 1777) (University of Toronto Library, T-10/ 7 [21])

A Nosseigneurs de Parlement en la Grand'Chambre. Supplient humblement Jean-Alexandre Martin, peintre-vernisseur du roi, Jean Charny, Louis Bunel, Jean Silvain Belloeil de la Vallée, Charles Douveaux, la veuve Girard, la veuve Thibault, tous peintres de l'ancienne Académie et communauté de Saint-Luc appellans, et Claude-Alexandre Sevaux (Paris, 1786) (B.N. 4° fm 300919)

Afanassiev, Georges, *Le Commerce des céréales en France au xviiie siècle* (Paris, 1894)

Affiches, annonces et avis divers, ou journal général de la France (Paris, 1750–89)

Aguet, Jean-Pierre, *Les Grèves sous la Monarchie de Juillet (1830–1847)* (Geneva, 1954)

Agulhon, Maurice, *Pénitents et francs-maçons de l'ancienne Provence* (Paris, 1968)

'Working Class and Sociability in France before 1848', in Pat Thane, Geoffrey Crossick and Roderick Floud, eds., *The Power of the Past* (Cambridge, 1984), pp. 37–66

Aldrich, Robert, 'Late Comer or Early Starter: New Views on French Economic History', *Journal of European Economic History*, 16 (1987), pp. 89–100

Algarotti, Francesco, 'Pensieri diversi sopra materie filosofiche e filologiche', in his *Opere* (Cremona, 1782), vol. 8

D'Allemagne, Henri-René, *Les Anciens Maîtres serruriers parisiens et leurs meilleurs travaux*, 2 vols. (Paris, 1943)

Allier, Raoul, *La Cabale des dévots* (Paris, 1902)

Almanach de cabinet (Paris, 1765)

Almanach du Voyageur à Paris (Paris, 1786)

Anderson, Michael, 'The Emergence of the Modern Life-Cycle in Britain', *Social History*, 10 (1985), pp. 69–87

Andrews, Richard M. 'Social Structures, Political Elites and Ideology in Revolutionary Paris, 1792–1794: A Critical Evaluation of Albert Soboul's *Les Sans-Culottes Parisiens en l'An II*', *Journal of Social History*, 19 (1985), pp. 71–112

Antheunis, L., *Le Conventionnel belge, François Robert (1763–1826), et sa femme Louise de Kéralio (1758–1822)* (Wetteren, 1955)

Antoine, Michel., *Le Conseil du Roi sous le Règne de Louis XV* (Geneva, 1970)

Appleby, Joyce, 'America as a Model for the Radical French Reformers of 1789', *William and Mary Quarterly*, 3rd series, 28 (1971), pp. 267–86

'What is Still American in the Political Philosophy of Thomas Jefferson?', *William and Mary Quarterly*, 3rd series, 39 (1982), pp. 287–309

Capitalism and a New Social Order. The Republican Vision of the 1790s (New York, 1984)

'Republicanism in Old and New Contexts', *William and Mary Quarterly*, 3rd series, 43 (1986), pp. 20–34

Archives historiques du département de la Gironde (Bordeaux, 1859–1932)

Archives parlementaires, 1st series (Paris, 1887 and 1962), vols. 27 and 84

Aron, Jean-Pierre, Dumont, P. and Le Roy Ladurie, Emmanuel, *Anthropologie du conscrit français* (Paris, 1972)

Aubry, Gérard, *La Jurisprudence criminelle du Châtelet de Paris sous le règne de Louis XVI* (Paris, 1971)

Audin, Marius, and Vial, Eugène, *Dictionnaire des artistes et ouvriers d'art de France. Lyonnais*, 2 vols. (Paris, 1918)

Augeard, Mathieu, *Arrêts notables des différents tribunaux du royaume*, 2nd edn (Paris, 1756)

Augustin, Jean Marie, 'Les Capitouls, juges des causes criminelles et de police', *Annales du midi*, 84 (1972), pp. 183–211

Aulard, Alphonse, *Histoire politique de la Révolution française* (Paris, 1921)

Bairoch, Paul, *Révolution industrielle et sous-développement*, 3rd edn (Paris, 1969)

Baker, Keith Michael, *Condorcet. From Natural Philosophy to Social Mathematics* (Chicago, 1975)

'A Script for a French Revolution: The Political Consciousness of the abbé Mably', *Eighteenth-Century Studies*, 14 (1981), pp. 235–63

'On the Problem of the Ideological Origins of the French Revolution', in Steven L. Kaplan and Dominick LaCapra, eds., *Modern European Intellectual History: Reappraisals and New Perspectives* (Ithaca, 1982)

'Memory and Practice: Politics and Representation of the Past in Eighteenth-Century France', *Representations*, 11 (1985), pp. 134–64

'Politics and Public Opinion Under the Old Regime: Some Reflections', in Jack R. Censer and Jeremy D. Popkin, eds., *Press and Politics in Pre-Revolutionary France* (Berkeley, California, 1987)

'Revolution', in Colin Lucas, ed., *The Political Culture of the French Revolution* (Oxford, 1988)

Banning, Lance, 'Jeffersonian Ideology Revisited: Liberal and Classical Ideas in the New American Republic', *William and Mary Quarterly*, 3rd series, 43 (1986), pp. 3–19

Bardet, Jean-Pierre, *Rouen aux xviie et xviiie siècles*, 2 vols. (Paris, 1983)

Baulant, Micheline, 'Le Prix des grains à Paris de 1431 à 1788', *Annales E.S.C.*, 23 (1968), pp. 520–40

Bédarida, Henri, *Parme et la France de 1748 à 1789* (Paris, 1928)

Behagg, Clive, 'Custom, Class and Change: The Trade Societies of Birmingham', *Social History*, 4 (1979), pp. 455–80

'Masters and Manufacturers: Social Values and the Smaller Unit of Production in Birmingham, 1800–50', in Geoffrey Crossick and Heinz-Gerhard Haupt, eds., *Shopkeepers and Master Artisans in Nineteenth-Century Europe* (London, 1984), pp. 137–54

Bénétruy, J., 'L'Atelier de Mirabeau: quatre proscrits génévois dans la tourmente révolutionnaire', *Mémoires et documents publiés par la société d'histoire et d'archéologie de Genève*, 41 (Geneva, 1962)

Bennet, Jean, *La Mutualité française: des origines à la Révolution de 1789* (Paris, 1981)

Benzacar, Joseph, *Le Pain à Bordeaux* (Bordeaux, 1905)

Berg, Maxine, *The Age of Manufactures 1700–1820* (London, 1985) and Hudson, Pat, Sonenscher, Michael, eds., *Manufacture in Town and Country before the Factory* (Cambridge, 1983)

Bergeron, Louis, *Banquiers, négociants et manufacturiers parisiens du Directoire à l'Empire* (Paris, 1978) ed., *La Statistique en France à l'époque napoléonienne* (Brussels, 1981)

Berlanstein, Lenard R., *The Barristers of Toulouse in the Eighteenth Century (1740–1793)* (Baltimore, 1975)

Bernard, A., *Le Sermon au xviiie siècle* (Paris, 1901) *The Working People of Paris* (Baltimore, 1984)

Berthelé, Joseph, ed., *Montpellier en 1768 et 1836 d'après deux manuscrits inédits* (Montpellier, 1909)

Beutler, Corinne, 'Bâtiment et salaires: un chantier à Saint-Germain-des-Prés de 1644 à 1646', *Annales E.S.C.*, 26 (1971), pp. 484–517

Beyssac, Joseph, 'La Sedition ouvrière de 1786', *Revue d'histoire de Lyon*, 7 (1907), pp. 427–58, and in B.N. 4° Ll 269

Bianchi, Serge, *La Révolution culturelle de l'an II* (Paris, 1982)

Bibliothèque nationale, Département des Estampes, Inventaire du fonds français; graveurs du xviie siècle (Paris, 1968)

Bien, David D., 'Offices, Corps, and a System of State Credit: The Uses of Privilege under the Ancien Regime', in Keith M. Baker, ed., *The Political Culture of the Old Regime* (Oxford, 1987), pp. 89–114

Bigo, R., 'Aux origines du Mont-de-Piété parisien: bienfaisance et crédit', *Annales d'histoire économique et sociale*, 4 (1932), pp. 113–26

Blondel, Jean, 'Plaidoyer pour Jean Louis', *Gazette des tribunaux*, 1 (Paris, 1775)

Blum, Alain and Houdaille, Jacques, '12,000 Parisiens en 1793', *Population*, 46 (1986), pp. 259–302

Bondois, Paul, 'Un Compagnonnage au xviiie siècle: le devoir des bons drilles blanchers-chamoiseurs', *Annales historiques de la Révolution française*, 6 (1929), pp. 588–99

Bosher, J. F., *French Finances 1770–1795, From Business to Bureaucracy* (Cambridge, 1970)

Bossenga, Gail, 'La Révolution français et les corporations: trois exemples lillois', *Annales E.S.C.*, 43 (1988), pp. 405–26

Boudet, Antoine, *Les Affiches de Paris*, 5 vols (Paris, 1746–50)

Bouloiseau, Marc, ed., *Cahiers de doléances du tiers état du bailliage de Rouen*, 2 vols (Paris, 1957)

Bonnet, Louis Ferdinand, 'Souvenirs de 1783 sur le barreau de Paris', in his *Discours, Plaidoyers et Memoires*, 2 vols (Paris, 1839)

Bourdieu, Pierre, *Esquisse d'une théorie de la pratique* (Geneva, 1972) 'Les Stratégies matrimoniales dans le système de reproduction', *Annales, E.S.C.*, 27 (1972), pp. 1105–27 *Le Sens pratique* (Paris, 1983)

Bourgin, Georges and Bourgin, Hubert, *Les Patrons, les ouvriers et l'état. Le Régime de l'industrie en France de 1814 à 1830*, 3 vols (Paris, 1912–41)

Boyer, Marie-Bernadette, 'Nîmes au xviiie siècle' (D.E.S., Université de Montpellier, 1960)

Braesch F., 'Un Essai de statistique de la population ouvrière de Paris vers 1791', La Révolution française, 63 (1912), pp. 289–321

Brennan, Thomas, 'Beyond the Barriers: Popular Culture and Parisian Guinguettes', Eighteenth-Century Studies, 18 (1984–5), pp. 153–69

Bresson-Le Minor, Anne, 'Le Vol domestique au xviiie siècle d'après les arrêts du Parlement de Paris', Thèse de droit, Université de Paris, 1978

Brewer, John, 'Commercialization and Politics', in Neil McKendrick, John Brewer and J. H. Plumb, The Birth of a Consumer Society (London, 1982), pp. 197–262

Briggs, Robin, Early Modern France 1560–1715 (Oxford, 1977)

Brillon Pierre-Jacques, Dictionnaire des arrêts, ou jurisprudence universelle des Parlements de France, 2 vols (Paris, 1727)

Bristow, Ian, 'Ready-Mixed Paint in the Eighteenth Century', Architectural Review, 161 (1977), pp. 247–8

Bruleaux, Anne-Marie, 'Les Maîtres-Serruriers parisiens et leurs travaux de grande serrurerie', Thèse de l'Ecole des Chartes, Paris, n.d.

Bulletin de la société industrielle de Mulhouse, 793 (1984), Special issue on the archives of the firm of Zuber & Cie

Bulloch, J. M., Thomas Gordon, the 'Independent Whig' (Aberdeen, 1918)

Burke, Peter, Popular Culture in Early Modern Europe (London, 1978)

Burlamaqui, Jean Jacques, Principes du droit de la nature et des gens (originally published Yverdon, 1766–8), reprinted in his Œuvres, 5 vols (Paris, 1820–1).

Burstin, Haim, 'Conditionnement économique et conditionnement mental dans le monde du travail parisien à la fin de l'ancien régime', History of European Ideas, 3 (1982), pp. 23–9

Le Faubourg Saint-Marcel à l'époque révolutionnaire (Paris, 1983)

'I Sanculotti: Un Dossier da Riaprire', Passato e Presente, 10 (1986), pp. 23–52

'Travail, entreprise et politique à la manufacture des Gobelins pendant la période révolutionnaire', paper presented to the colloque on La Révolution française et le développement du capitalisme (Lille, November 1987)

Butel, Paul, 'Le Trafic colonial de Bordeaux de la guerre d'Amérique à la Révolution', Annales du Midi, 79 (1967), pp. 17–64

La Croissance commerciale bordelaise dans la deuxième moitié du xviiie siècle (Lille, 1973)

Cameron, Ian, Crime and Repression in the Auvergne and the Guyenne, 1720–1790 (Cambridge, 1981)

Casselle, Pierre, 'Pierre-François Basan, marchand d'estampes à Paris (1723–1797)', Paris et Ile de France, 33 (1982), pp. 99–185

Castaldo, André, 'L'Histoire juridique de l'article 1781 du Code Civil: "Le maître est cru sur son affirmation"', Revue historique de droit français et étranger, 55 (1977), pp. 211–37

Castan, Nicole, Justice et répression en Languedoc à l'époque des Lumières (Paris, 1980)

Catalogue des maîtres menuisiers, sculpteurs et ébénistes de la ville et faubourg de Bordeaux (Bordeaux, 1788) (A.C. Bordeaux, HH.70)

Cavignac, Jean, 'Les Compagnonnages dans les luttes ouvrières au xviiie siècle', Bibliothèque de l'Ecole des Chartes, 126 (1968), pp. 377–411

Cerutti, Simona, 'Du Corps au métier: la corporation des tailleurs à Turin entre xviie et xviiie siècle', *Annales E.S.C.*, 43 (1988), pp. 323–52

Champeaux, Alfred de, *Le Meuble*, 2 vols (Paris, 1885)

Chaplain, Jean-Michel, *La Chambre des tisseurs, Louviers: cité drapière 1680–1840* (Paris, 1984)

Chapman, Stanley, 'The Textile Factory Before Arkwright: A Typology of Factory Development', *Business History Review*, 48 (1974), pp. 451–78

Charavay, Étienne, *Assemblée électoral de Paris, 18 novembre 1790–15 juin 1791* and Chassagne, Serge, *European Textile Printers in the Eighteenth Century* (London, 1981)

Chaptal, Jean-Antoine, *De l'industrie française*, 2 vols (Paris, 1819)

Chartier, Roger, 'Texts, Symbols, and Frenchness', *Journal of Modern History*, 57 (1985), pp. 682–95

Chassagne, Serge, *La Manufacture de toiles imprimées de Tourmemine-les-Angers* (Paris, 1971)

'La Naissance de l'industrie cotonnière en France: 1760–1840. Trois générations d'entrepreneurs', Thèse de doctorat, Ecole des Hautes Etudes en Sciences Sociales, Paris, 1986

Oberkampf, un entrepreneur capitaliste au siècle des lumières (Paris, 1980)

Chauvet, Paul, *Les Ouvriers du livre en France, des origines à la Révolution de 1789* (Paris, 1959)

Cherel, Albert, *La Pensée de Machiavel en France* (Paris, 1935)

Chevalier, Bernard, 'Corporations, conflits politiques et paix sociale en France aux xive et xve siècles', *Revue historique*, 268 (1982), pp. 17–44

Chill, Emmanuel, S., 'The Company of the Holy Sacrament: Social Aspects of the French Counter-Reformation', unpublished Ph. D. thesis, Columbia University, 1960

'Religion and Mendicity in Seventeenth-Century France', *International Review of Social History*, 7 (1962), pp. 400–25

Claeys, Gregory, *Machinery, Money and the Millennium* (London, 1987)

Clark, J. C. D., *English Society 1688–1832* (Cambridge, 1985)

Clawson, Mary Ann, 'Early Modern Fraternalism and the Patriarchal Family', *Feminist Studies*, 6 (1980), pp. 368–91

Clouzot, H. and Follot, C., *Histoire du papier peint en France* (Paris, 1935)

Cobb, Richard, *Les Armées révolutionnaires: instrument de la terreur dans les départements*, 2 vols (Paris and the Hague, 1961 and 1963)

Cochin, Henri, *Œuvres*, 8 vols (Paris, 1821–2)

Colommès, P., *Les Ouvriers textiles de la région troyenne* (Troyes, 1948)

Contat dit Lebrun, Nicolas, *Anecdotes typographiques ou l'on voit la description des coutumes, moeurs et usages singuliers des Compagnons imprimeurs*, ed. Giles Barber (Oxford, 1980)

Coornaert, Emile, *Les Corporations en France* (Paris, 1941)

Les Compagnonnages en France du moyen age à nos jours (Paris, 1966)

Corvisier, André, *L'Armée française de la fin du xviie siècle au ministère de Choiseul: le soldat*, 2 vols (Paris, 1964)

Costaz, Claude-Anthelme, *Mémoire sur les moyens qui ont amené le grand développement que l'industrie française a pris depuis vingt ans* (Paris, 1816)

Cottereau, Alain, 'Introduction' to Denis Poulot, *Question sociale: le sublime* (Paris, 1980)

'Les Règlements d'atelier au cours de la révolution industrielle en France', in Anne Biroleau and Alain Cottereau, *Les Règlements d'ateliers 1798–1936*, (Bibliothèque nationale, Département des Livres Imprimés, Collection 'Études, Guides et Inventaires' Paris, 1984)

'The Distinctiveness of Working-Class Cultures in France, 1848–1900', in Ira Katznelson and Aristide Zolberg, eds., *Working Class Formation* (Princeton. 1986)

'Justice et injustice ordinaire sur les lieux de travail d'après les audiences prud'homales (1806–1866)', *Le Mouvement social*, 141 (1987), pp. 25–59

Cover, Robert M., *Justice Accused: Antislavery and the Judicial Process* (New Haven, 1975)

Daget, Serge, 'Les Mots esclave, nègre, noir et les jugements de valeur sur la traité negrière dans la littérature abolitionniste française de 1770 à 1845', *Revue d'histoire d'outre-mer*, 60 (1973). pp. 511–48

Darnton, Robert, 'The High Enlightenment and the Low-Life of Literature', in his *The Literary Underground of the Old Regime* (Cambridge. Mass.. 1982), pp. 1–40

The Great Cat Massacre and Other Episodes in French Cultural History (New York. 1984)

'Working Class Casanova', *New York Review of Books* (28 June 1984), pp. 32–7

'The Symbolic Element in History', *Journal of Modern History*, 58 (1986), pp. 218–34

Daumard, Adeline, *La Bourgeoisie parisienne de 1815 à 1848* (Paris, 1963)

Daumas, Maurice, *Les Instruments scientifiques aux xviie et xviiie siècles* (Paris, 1953)

and Payen, Jacques, eds., *Evolution de la géographie industrielle de Paris et sa proche banlieue au xixe siècle* (Conservatoire National des Arts et Métiers. Centre de documentation d'histoire des techniques) (Paris, 1976)

Davis, Natalie Z.. 'A Trade Union in Sixteenth-Century France', *Economic History Review*, 2nd Series, 19 (1966), pp. 48–69

Society and Culture in Early-Modern France (London, 1975)

'Women in the Arts Mécaniques in Sixteenth-Century Lyon', in *Lyon et l'Europe. Hommes et Sociétés* (Lyon, 1980), pp. 139–59

Dawley, Alan, *Class and Community: Lynn in the Industrial Revolution* (New York, 1979)

Debbasch, Yvan, *Couleur et liberté. Le Jeu du critère ethnique dans un ordre juridique esclavagiste*, 2 vols (Paris, 1967)

Dédieu, Joseph, *Montesquieu et la tradition politique anglaise en France* (Paris, 1909)

Déglise, J-C., *Observations particulières et générales sur un projet de loi relatif aux manufactures, et aux gens de travail de toutes les professions* (Lyon, 1802) (B.M. Lyon, 354 444)

Delamare, Nicolas, *Traité de police*, 4 vols (Paris, 1705–38)

Delpierre, Madeleine, 'La Mode et ses métiers à Paris au xviiie siècle', *Bulletin de la société de l'histoire de Paris et de l'Ile de France*, 93 (1966), pp. 46–9

Delsalle, Paul, 'Le Livret ouvrier et les conflits de travail dans la région de Roubaix-Tourcoing', in Paul Delsalle, ed., *L'Industrie textile en Europe du Nord aux xviiie et xixe siècles* (Tourcoing, 1984)

La Brouette et la navette (Dunquerque, 1985)

Dénisart, Jean Baptiste, *Collection de decisions nouvelles et de notions relatives à la jurisprudence actuelle*, 9 edns (Paris, 1759–86)

Derathé, Robert, *Jean Jacques Rousseau et la science politique de son temps* (Paris, 1950)

Désessarts, N., *Causes célèbres, curieuses et intéressantes* (Paris, 1775)

Désirat, Dominique, 'Peinture et pouvoirs de 1699 à 1759', Thèse de troisième cycle, Université Francois Rabelais, Tours, n.d.

Desmoulins, Camille, *Le Vieux Cordelier*, ed. Henri Calvet (Paris, 1936)

Destutt de Tracy, Antoine Louis Claude, *A Commentary and Review of Montesquieu's Spirit of the Laws* (Philadelphia, 1811)

Deyon, Pierre, *Amiens, capitale provinciale: étude sur la société urbaine au xviie siècle* (Paris, 1967)

Désaillier, Philippe, 'The Royal Manufactures and Economic and Techno-logical Progress in France before the Industrial Revolution', *Journal of European Economic History*, 9 (1980), pp. 611–32

Dézallier d'Argenville, Antoine-Nicolas, *Voyage pittoresque de Paris* (Paris, 1778)

Dilke, Constance, *French Furniture and Decoration in the Eighteenth Century* (London, 1901)

Dimier, Louis, 'Christophe Huet, peintre de chinoiseries et d'animaux', *Gazette des Beaux-Arts*, 3ème periode, 14 (1895), pp. 353–66, 486–96

Domat, Jean, *Les Lois civiles dans leur ordre naturel*, originally published Paris, 1689–94, reprinted in his *Œuvres complètes*, 4 vols (Paris, 1835)

'Harangue prononcée aux assises de 1679', in his *Œuvres complètes*, (Paris, 1835), vol. 4

Donati, Benvenuto, *Donat e Vico, ossio del Sistema del Diretto Universale* (Macereata, 1923)

Doyle, William, *The Parlement of Bordeaux and the End of the Old Regime 1771–1790* (London, 1974)

'Dupaty (1748–1788): A Career in the Late Enlightenment', *Studies on Voltaire and the Eighteenth Century*, 230 (1985), pp. 1–125

Dumas, F., 'Les Corporations de métiers de la ville de Toulouse', *Annales du Midi*, 12 (1900), pp. 475–93

Dunn, John, *The Political Thought of John Locke* (Cambridge, 1969)

Dunoyer, Luc Henri, *Blackstone et Pothier* (Paris, 1927)

Dupâquier, Jacques, Lachiver, Marcel and Meuvret, Jean, *Mercuriales du Pays de France et du Vexin Français (1640–1792)* (Paris, 1968)

Dupin, C., *Dictionnaire des arrêts modernes en matière civile et criminelle* (Paris, 1814)

Duplessis, G., *Les Audran* (Paris, 1892)

Durand, Yves, 'Recherches sur les salaires des maçons à Paris au xviiie siècle', *Revue d'histoire économique et sociale*, 44 (1966), pp. 468–80

Edgren, Lars, 'Crafts in Transformation? Masters, Journeymen and Apprentices in a Swedish town. 1800–1850', *Continuity and Change*, 1 (1986), pp. 363–83

Edmonds, Bill, 'A Study in Popular Anti-Jacobinism: The Career of Denis Monnet', *French Historical Studies*, 13 (1983), pp. 215–51

Ehmer, Josef, 'Master's Household or Journeyman's Family: The Units of Artisan Outwork Production in Central Europe and England in the Mid-Nineteenth

Century', paper presented to the ESRC Workshop on Proto-Industrial Communities, University of Essex, October 1986

Encyclopédie méthodique: Jurisprudence, Police, 9 vols (Paris, 1782–91)

Erdman, David V., *Commerce des Lumières. John Oswald and the British in Paris, 1790–1793* (Columbia, Missouri, 1986)

Eriksen, Svend, *Louis Delanois, menuisier en sièges (1731–1792)* (Paris, 1968)

Early Neo-Classicism in France (London, 1974)

Expilly, J. J., *Dictionnaire géographique, historique et politique des Gaules et de la France*, 6 vols (Paris, 1762–70)

Fairchilds, Cissie, *Domestic Enemies* (Baltimore, 1983)

Faler, Paul G., *Mechanics and Manufacturers in the Early Industrial Revolution* (New York, 1981)

Faraut, François, *Histoire de la Belle Jardinière* (Paris, 1987)

Farcy, Jean-Claude, 'Rural Artisans in the Beauce during the Nineteenth Century', in Geoffrey Crossick and Heinz-Gerhard Haupt, eds., *Shopkeepers and Master Artisans in Nineteenth-Century Europe* (London, 1984), pp. 219–38

Farge, Arlette, *La Vie fragile: violences, pouvoirs et solidarités à Paris au xviiie siècle* (Paris, 1986)

and Foucault, Michel, *Le Desordre des familles* (Paris, 1982)

Farr, James, '"So Vile and Miserable an Estate", the problem of Slavery in Locke's Political Thought', *Political Theory*, 14 (1986), pp. 263–89

Faucon, L., ed., *Mémoire sur les véxations qu'exercent les libraires et imprimeurs de Paris* (Paris, 1879)

Faure, Alain, 'Petit Atelier et modernisme économique: la production en miettes au xixe siècle', *Histoire, économie et société*, 5 (1986), pp. 531–57

Faure, Christian, 'Vichy et la "rénovation" de l'artisanat: la réorganisation du compagnonnage', *Bulletin du centre d'histoire économique et sociale de la région lyonnaise*, 3–4 (1984), pp. 103–19

Fenet, Pierre Antoine, *Receuil complet des travaux préparatoires du Code Civil*, 15 vols (Paris, 1827–36)

Fernandez, James, 'Historians Tell Tales: of Cartesian Cats and Gallic Cockfights', *Journal of Modern History*, 60 (1988), pp. 113–27

Fillon, Anne, ed., *Louis Simon étaminer 1741–1820 dans son village du Haut-Maine au Siècle des Lumières*, 2 typed vols, Université du Maine, Le Mans, n.d. [1985]

Fitzsimmons, Michael P., *The Parisian Order of Barristers and the French Revolution* (Cambridge, Mass., 1987)

Folville, Xavier, 'Matériaux et techniques du décor polychrome au xviiie siècle', *Bulletin de la Commission royale des monuments et des sites* (Brussels), 10 (1981), pp. 193–219

Forbes, Duncan, *Hume's Philosophical Politics* (Cambridge 1975)

Forrest, Alan, *The French Revolution and the Poor* (Oxford, 1981)

Fox-Genovese, Elizabeth, *The Origins of Physiocracy* (Ithaca, 1976)

Francesco, Antonino De, *Il Sogno della Repubblica: Il Mondo del Lavoro dall' Ancien Régime al 1848* (Milan, 1983)

Franklin, Alfred Louis Auguste, *La Vie privée d'autrefois*, 27 vols (Paris, 1887–1902)

Dictionnaire historique des arts, métiers et professions exercés dans Paris depuis le treizième siècle (Paris, 1906)

Fraser, Steven, 'Combined and Uneven Development in the Men's Clothing Industry', *Business History Review*, 57 (1983), pp. 522–47

Freudenberger, Herman and Redlich, Fritz, 'The Industrial Development of Europe: Reality, Symbols, Images', *Kyklos*, 17 (1964), pp. 372–403

Frey, Max, *Les Transformations du vocabulaire français à l'époque de la Révolution* (Paris, 1925)

Funck-Brentano, F., 'Le Droit naturel au xviiie siècle', *Revue d'histoire diplomatique*, 1 (1887), pp. 491–511

Furet, François, *Penser la Révolution française* (Paris, 1978)

Gabillot, C., *Les Huet: Jean Baptiste et ses fils* (Paris, 1893)

Gaffarel, P., *François Robert, ses travaux scientifiques, son rôle politique, son rôle artistique* (Dijon, 1889)

Garden, Maurice, *Lyon et les lyonnais au xviiie siècle* (Paris, 1970)

'Les Relations familiales dans la France du xviiie siècle: une source, les conseils de tutelle', in Bernard Vogler, ed., *Les Actes notariés* (Strasbourg, 1979), pp. 173–86

Garenc, Paule, *L'Industrie du meuble en France* (Paris, 1958)

Garrioch, David, *Neighbourhood and Community in Paris, 1740–1790* (Cambridge, 1986)

and Sonenscher, Michael, 'Compagnonnages, Confraternities and Associations of Journeymen in Eighteenth-Century Paris', *European History Quarterly*, 16 (1986), pp. 25–45

'Verbal Insults in Eighteenth-Century Paris', in Peter Burke and Roy Porter, eds., *The Social History of Language* (Cambridge, 1987), pp. 104–19

Gaston, Jean, *Une Paroisse parisienne avant la Révolution, Saint-Hippolyte* (Paris, 1910)

Gauthier, Florence, 'Loi agraire', in Institut National de la Langue Française, *Les Images des confréries parisiennes avant la Révolution* (Paris, 1908)

Dictionnaire des usages socio-politiques (1770–1815), fascicule 2 (Paris, 1987), pp. 65–98

Gayot, Gérard, 'La Longue Insolence des tondeurs de draps dans la manufacture de Sedan au xviiie siècle', *Revue du Nord*, 63 (1981), pp. 105–134

Gazette des tribunaux (Paris, 1776–89)

Gazette des tribunaux et mémorial des corps administratifs et municipaux, 12 vols (Paris, 1791–5)

Geertz, Clifford, *Pedlars and Princes* (Chicago, 1963)

The Interpretation of Cultures (New York, 1973)

'Suq: the Bazaar Economy in Sefrou', in Clifford Geertz, Hildred Geertz and Lawrence Rosen, *Meaning and Order in Moroccan Society* (Cambridge 1979)

(with Hildred Geertz and Lawrence Rosen), *Meaning and Order in Moroccan Society* (Cambridge, 1979)

Local Knowledge (New York, 1983)

Geffroy, Annie, 'Sans-Culotte(s), novembre 1790–juin 1792', in Institut National de la Langue Française. *Dictionnaire des usages socio-politiques (1770–1815), fasc. 1. Désignants socio-politiques* (Paris, 1985)

Gelfand, Toby, 'A "Monarchical Profession" in the Old Régime: Surgeons, Ordinary Practitioners and Medical Professionalization in Eighteenth-Century France', in Gerald L. Geison, ed., *Professions and the French State, 1700–1900* (Philadelphia, 1984), pp. 149–80

Genty, Maurice. *L'Apprentissage de la citoyenneté: Paris 1789–1795* (Paris, 1987)

Gibbs, F. W., 'A Historical Survey of the Japanning Trade', *Annals of Science*, 7 (1951), pp. 401–6; 9 (1953), pp. 88–95, 197–232

Gille, Bertrand, *Documents sur l'état de l'industrie et du commerce de Paris et du département de la Seine (1778–1810)* (Paris, 1963)

Ginzburg, Carlo, *The Cheese and the Worms. The Cosmos of a Sixteenth-Century Miller* (London, 1982)

Goodwin, Albert, *The Friends of Liberty* (London, 1979)

Goody, Jack, ed., *Literacy in Traditional Societies* (Cambridge, 1968)

Gossez, Rémi, ed., *Un Ouvrier en 1820, manuscrit inédit de Jacques-Etienne Bédé* (Paris, 1984)

Goubert, Pierre, *L'Ancien Régime: les pouvoirs* (Paris, 1973) and Roche, Daniel, *Les Français et l'Ancien Régime* (Paris, 1984)

Gouesse, Jean-Marie, 'Parenté, famille et mariage en Normandie aux xviie et xviiie siècles. Présentation d'une source et d'une enquête', *Annales E.S.C.*, 27 (1972), pp. 1139–54

Gough, Hugh, 'The Radical Press in the French Revolution', in Patrick J. Corish, ed., *Radicals, Rebels and Establishment* (Belfast, 1985)

Grandjean, Serge, *Catalogue des tabatières, boîtes et étuis des xviiie et xixe siècles du musée du Louvre* (Paris, 1981)

Grenier, Jean-Yves, 'Questions sur l'histoire économique: les sociétés pré-industrielles et leurs rythmes', *Revue de synthèse*, 116 (1984), pp. 451–81

'Modeles de la demande sous l'Ancien Régime', *Annales E.S.C.* 42 (1987), pp. 497–527

Gresset, Maurice, *Gens de justice à Besancon au xviiie siècle* (Paris, 1983)

Griessinger, Andreas, *Das symbolisches Kapital der Ehre* (Frankfurt, 1981)

Grivel, Marianne, *Le Commerce de l'estampe à Paris au xviie siècle* (Geneva, 1986)

Groppi, Angela, '''La classe la plus nombreuse, la plus utile et la plus précieuse''. Organizzazione del lavoro e conflitti nella Parigi rivoluzionaria', *European University Institute, Working Paper No. 88/325* (Florence, 1988)

Guespin, Louis, 'Les Embrayeurs en discours', *Langages*, 41 (1976), pp. 47–77

Guiffrey, Jules-Joseph, 'Scellés et inventaires d'artistes français', *Nouvelles archives de l'art français*, 2nd series, 10–12 (1884–6)

'Les Peintres decorateurs du xviiie siècle. Servandoni, Brunetti, Tramblin, etc.', *Revue de l'art français*, 3 (1897), pp. 119–28

Histoire de l'Académie de Saint-Luc (Paris, 1915)

Guignet, Phillippe, *Mines, manufactures et ouvriers du Valenciennois au xviiie siècle* (New York, 1977)

Guilhaumou, Jacques, 'Aristocrate', in *Institut National de la Langue Française. Dictionnaire des usages socio-politiques (1770–1815), fasc. 1, Désignants socio-politiques* (Paris, 1985)

'Les Mille Langues du Père Duchêne', *XVIIIe Siecle*, 18 (1986), pp. 143–54

Guin, Yannick, *Le Mouvement ouvrier nantais. Essai sur le syndicalisme d'action directe à Nantes et à Saint-Nazaire* (Paris, 1976)

Gutton, Jean-Pierre, *La Société et les pauvres: l'exemple de la généralité de Lyon, 1534–1789* (Paris, 1971)

'Lyon et le crédit populaire sous l'ancien régime: les projets de mont-de-piété', in *Studi in Memoria di Federigo Melis*, 5 vols (Naples, 1978), vol. 4, pp. 147–54

Domestiques et serviteurs dans la France de l'Ancien Régime (Paris, 1981)

Guyot, Pierre Jean Jacques Guilhaume, *Répertoire universel et raisonné de la jurisprudence civile, criminelle, canonique et bénéficiale*, 17 vols (Paris, 1784–5)

Halévi, Ran, *Les Loges maçonniques dans la France d'Ancien Régime* (Paris, 1984)

'La Révolution Constituante: les ambiguités politiques', in Colin Lucas, ed., *The Political Culture of the French Revolution* (Oxford, 1988)

Hamet, Cathérine, 'Les Ebenistes parisiens dans la seconde moitié du xviiie siècle (à partir des inventaires après décès)', *Mémoire de maîtrise*, Université de Paris X (Nanterre), 1973

Hanagan, Michael, *The Logic of Solidarity: Artisans and Industrial Workers in Three French Towns, 1871-1914* (Urbana, Illinois, 1983)

Harris, Jennifer, 'The Red Cap of Liberty: A Study of Dress Worn by Revolutionary Parisians 1789-94', *Eighteenth-Century Studies*, 14 (1981), pp. 283-312

Harris, John R., 'Michael Alcock and the Transfer of Birmingham Technology to France before the Revolution', *Journal of European Economic History*, 15 (1986), pp. 7-57

Hassenfratz, J. H., *Traité de l'art du charpentier* (Paris, 1804)

Hauser, Henri, *Ouvriers du temps passé (xve-xvi siècles)* (Paris, 1899)

Les Compagnonnages d'arts et métiers à Dijon aux xviie et xviiie siècles (Paris, 1907)

'Le Travail dans l'ancienne France', in his *Les Débuts du capitalisme* (Paris, 1931)

Havard, Henry, *Dictionnaire de l'ameublement et de la décoration depuis le xviiie siècle à nos jours*, 4 vols (Paris, 1887)

Hay, Douglas, 'War, Dearth and Theft in the Eighteenth Century: The Record of the English Courts', *Past and Present*, 95 (1982), pp. 117-60

Henrion de Pansey, Pierre Paul Nicolas, 'Plaidoyer pour Roc, nègre', reprinted in *Annales du barreau français*, 6 (Paris, 1825)

Henry, Louis and Blayo, Yves, 'La Population de la France de 1740 à 1860', *Population*, 30 (1975), pp. 71-122

Henry, Stuart, *The Hidden Economy* (London, 1978)

Herluison, H., *Actes d'état civil d'artistes français* (Orléans, 1873)

Higonnet, Patrice, *Class, Ideology and the Rights of Nobles during the French Revolution* (Oxford, 1981)

Hirschman, Albert, *The Passions and the Interests* (Princeton, 1977)

Hobsbawm, E. J., 'Ritual in Social Movements', in his *Primitive Rebels* (London, 1959)

Labouring Men (London, 1964)

'Custom, Wages and Work-Load', in *Labouring Men* (New York, 1967), pp. 405-35

Hodgson, Geoffrey M., *Economics and Institutions* (Oxford, 1988)

Hoffmann-Krayer, E. and Bachtold-Staubli, Hans, *Handwörterbuch des Deutschen Aberglaubens* (Berlin and Leipzig, 1927)

Honour, Hugh, *Chinoiserie* (London, 1964)

Hont, Istvan, 'The Language of Sociability and Commerce', in Anthony Pagden, ed., *The Language of Political Theory in Early-Modern Europe* (Cambridge, 1987)

Hoock, Jochen, 'Réunions de métiers et marché régional: les marchands réunis de la ville de Rouen au début du xviiie siècle', *Annales E.S.C.*, 43 (1988), pp. 301-22

Höpfl, Harro and Thompson, Martyn, P., 'The History of Contract as a Motif in Political Thought', *American Historical Review*, 84 (1979), pp. 919-44

Hoppit, Julian, 'Understanding the Industrial Revolution', *Historical Journal*, 30 (1987), pp. 211-24

Huberman, Michael, 'Invisible Handshakes in Lancashire: Cotton Spinning in the First Half of the Nineteenth Century', *Journal of Economic History*, 46 (1986), pp. 987-8

Hufton, Olwen, *The Poor of Eighteenth-Century France* (Oxford, 1974)

Hunt, Lynn, *Revolution and Urban Politics: Troyes and Reims, 1786–1790* (Stanford, 1978).

— *Politics, Culture and Class in the French Revolution* (Berkeley, California, 1984)

Husson, François, *Artisans français. Les serruriers, étude historique* (Paris, 1902)

Huth, Hans, *Europäische Lackarbeiten* (Darmstadt, 1955)

Innes, Joanna, 'Prisons for the Poor: English Bridewells, 1555–1800', in Douglas Hay and Francis Snyder, eds., *Law, Labour and Crime in Historical Perspective* (London, 1987)

Isambert, François André et al., eds., *Receuil général des anciennes lois françaises*, 29 vols (Paris, 1822–33)

Isherwood, Robert, M., *Farce and Fantasy: Popular Entertainment in Eighteenth-Century Paris* (Oxford and New York, 1986)

Jacob, Margaret, *The Radical Enlightenment* (London, 1981)

Jacquemart, Albert, 'Une Manufacture de lacque à Paris en 1767', *Gazette des Beaux-Arts*, 1 (1861), pp. 309–11

— *A History of Furniture* (London, 1878)

Jacquet, Pierre, 'La Manufacture Zuber & Cie', *Bulletin de la Société Industrielle de Mulhouse*, 793 (1984), pp. 81–6

Jakobsen, Roman, *Essais de linguistique générale*, 2 vols (Paris, 1963)

Johnson, Christopher, 'Economic Change and Artisan Discontent: The Tailors' History, 1800–48', in Roger Price, ed., *Revolution and Reaction. 1848 and the Second French Republic* (London, 1975)

Jones, Colin, 'The Welfare of the French Foot-Soldier', *History*, 214 (1980), pp. 193–213

— and Sonenscher, Michael, 'The Social Functions of the Hospital in Eighteenth-Century France: The Case of the Hôtel-Dieu of Nîmes', *French Historical Studies*, 13 (1983), pp. 172–214

Jones, S. R. H., 'The Organization of Work, A Historical Dimension', *Journal of Economic Behaviour and Organization*, 3 (1982), pp. 117–32

Jones, Yvonne, 'The Birmingham Japanning and Papier-Mâché Industries', *Birmingham Museum and Art Gallery, Department of Local History, Information Sheet* 13 (1981)

Joubert de l'Hiberderie, Antoine Nicolas, *Le Dessinateur pour les fabriques d'étoffes d'or, d'argent et de soie* (Paris, 1765)

Journal des débats et des decrets, nos. 1–862 (Paris, 1789–91)

Jullian, Philippe, 'Comment identifier le vernis Martin', *Connaissance des Arts*, 119 (1962), pp. 43–49

Kahn-Freund, Otto, 'Blackstone's Neglected Child: The Contract of Employment', *Law Quarterly Review*, 93 (1977), pp. 508–28

Kaiser, Colin, 'The Deflation in the Volume of Litigation at Paris in the Eighteenth Century and the Waning of the Old Judicial Order', *European History Review*, 10 (1980), pp. 309–36

Kaplan, Steven, L., *Bread, Politics and Political Economy in the Reign of Louis XV*. 2 vols (The Hague, 1976)

— 'Réflexions sur la police du monde de travail, 1700–1815', *Revue historique*, 261 (1979), pp. 17–77

— 'Religion, Subsistence and Social Control: The Uses of Saint Geneviève', *Eighteenth-Century Studies*. 13 (1979–80), pp. 142–68

— and Dominick LaCapra, eds.. *Modern European Intellectual History: Reappraisals and New Perspectives* (Ithaca, New York, 1982)

— ed., *Understanding Popular Culture* (Berlin and New York, 1984)

Provisioning Paris: Merchants and Millers in the Grain and Flour Trade during the Eighteenth Century (Ithaca, N.Y., 1984)

and Koepp, Cynthia J., eds., Work in France: Representations, Meaning, Organization and Practice (Ithaca, N.Y., 1986)

'The Character and Implications of Strife among the Masters inside the Guilds of Eighteenth-Century Paris', Journal of Social History, 19 (1986), pp. 631–47

'Social Classification and Representation in the Corporate World of Eighteenth-Century Paris: Turgot's "Carnival"', in Steven L. Kaplan and Cynthia J. Koepp, eds., Work in France (Ithaca, N.Y., 1986), pp. 176–228

'Les Corporations, les "faux-ouvriers" et le faubourg Saint-Antoine au xviiie siècle', Annales E.S.C., 43 (1988), pp. 453–78

Kaplow, Jeffry, The Names of Kings: The Parisian Laboring Poor in the Eighteenth Century (New York, 1972)

Kates, Gary, The Cercle Social, the Girondins and the French Revolution (Princeton, 1985)

Katznelson, Ira and Zolberg, Aristide R., eds., Working Class Formation (Princeton, 1986)

Kennedy, Michael, The Jacobin Clubs in the French Revolution (Princeton, 1981)

Kors, Alan Charles, D'Holbach's Coterie. An Enlightenment in Paris (Princeton, 1976)

Kramnick, Isaac, Bolingbroke and his Circle: The Politics of Nostalgia in the Age of Walpole (Cambridge, Mass., 1963)

Krill, John, English Artists' Paper (London, 1987)

Kuscinski, A., Dictionnaire des conventionnels (Paris, 1917)

Labrousse, C. E., Esquisse du mouvement des prix et des revenus en France au xviiie siècle, 2 vols (Paris, 1933)

LaCapra, Dominick, 'Chartier, Darnton and the Great Symbol Massacre', Journal of Modern History, 60 (1988), pp. 95–112

and Steven L. Kaplan, eds., Modern European Intellectual History: Reappraisals and New Perspectives (Ithaca, 1982)

Lacoste-Palisset, J., 'Les Tailleurs bordelais dans la seconde moitié du xviiie siècle', T. E. R. Université de Bordeaux, 1973

Lacroix, Sigismund, Actes de la commune de Paris pendant la Révolution, 1st and 2nd series, 15 vols (Paris, 1894–1914)

Landes, David, 'The Statistical Study of French Crises', Journal of Economic History, 10 (1950), pp. 195–211

'What Do Bosses Really Do?', Journal of Economic History, 46 (1986), pp. 585–623

Las Vergnas, Raymond, Le Chevalier Rutlidge 'Gentilhomme Anglais' (Paris, 1932)

Lavédan, Henri, Volange, comédien de la foire (1756–1808) (Paris, 1933)

Lavoisier, Antoine-Laurent, 'Essai sur la population de la ville de Paris, sur sa richesse et ses consommations', in his Œuvres (Paris, 1893), vol. 6

Lebrun, Pierre, Histoire critique des pratiques superstitieuses qui ont séduit les peuples et embarassé les sçavans (Paris, 1702)

Explication littérale, historique et dogmatique des prières et des cérémonies de la Messe, 8 vols (Paris, 1777–8; original edn, Paris, 1716–26)

Lecotté, Roger, 'Essai bibliographique sur les Compagnonnages de tous les devoirs du Tour de France', in Raoul Dautry, ed., Compagnonnage (Paris, 1951), pp. 271–417

Lecuir, Jean, 'Associations ouvrières de l'époque moderne : clandestinité et culture populaire', *Revue du Vivarais* (special issue on *Histoire et Clandestinité du Moyen Age à la Première Guerre Mondiale*) (Albi, 1979), pp. 273–90.

Lefebvre, Georges, *Etudes Orléanaises*, 2 vols (Paris, 1962)

'Le Meurtre du comte de Dampierre', in his *Etudes sur la Révolution française*, 2nd edn (Paris, 1963)

Lefuel, Hector, *Georges Jacob, ébéniste du xviiie siècle* (Paris, 1923)

Le Goff, T. J. A., *Vannes and its Region: A Study of Town and Country in Eighteenth-Century France* (Oxford, 1981)

Legoy, Jean, 'Une Corporation turbulente : les cordonniers havrais au xviie siècle', *Cahiers Léopold Delisle* 32 (1982–3), pp. 159–65

Le Masson, J. B., *Le Calendrier des confréries de Paris* (Paris, 1621), reprinted edition, introduced and annotated by Valentin Dufour (Paris, 1875)

Le Mée, R., 'Population agglomerée, population dispersée au début du xixe siècle', *Annales de démographie historique*, 7 (1971), pp. 455–510

Lemire, Beverley, 'Developing Consumerism and the Ready-Made Clothing Trade in Britain 1750–1800', *Textile History*, 15 (1984), pp. 21–44

Le Moyne des Essarts, Nicolas Toussaint, *Causes célèbres, curieuses et intéressantes*, 67 vols (Paris, 1772–87)

Lepetit, Bernard, 'La Croissance urbaine dans la France pré-industrielle', *Bulletin de l'Institut d'histoire économique et sociale de l'Université de Paris 1*. 7 (1978), pp. 1–19

and Royer, J. F., 'Croissance et taille des villes : contribution à l'étude de l'urbanisation de la France au début du xixe siècle', *Annales E.S.C.*, 35 (1980), pp. 987–1010

'Réseau urbain et diffusion de l'innovation dans la France pré-industrielle : la création des caisses d'épargne, 1818–1848', in Bernard Lepetit and Jochen Hoock, eds., *La Ville et l'innovation en Europe, 14e–19e siècles* (Paris, 1987), pp. 131–57

Le Roy Ladurie, Emmanuel and Couperie, Pierre, 'Le Mouvement des loyers parisiens de la fin du Moyen-Age au xviiie siècle', *Annales E.S.C.*, 25 (1970), pp. 1002–23

Lespinasse, René de, *Les Métiers et corporations de Paris*, 3 vols (Paris, 1886–94)

Levasseur, Emile, *Histoire des classes ouvrières et de l'industrie en France*, 2 vols (Paris, 1901)

Levi, Giovanni, 'I Pericoli del Geertzismo', *Quaderni Storici*, 58 (1985), pp. 269–77

Levy, Darlene Gay, *The Ideas and Careers of Simon Nicolas Henri Linguet* (Urbana, Illinois, 1980)

Lichtenberger, André, *Le Socialisme et la Révolution française* (Paris, 1899)

Liljegren, S. B., *A French Draft Constitution of 1792 Modelled on James Harrington's Oceana* (Lund and London, 1932)

Lincoln, Andrew, 'Le Syndicalisme patronal à Paris de 1815 à 1848 : une étape de la formation de la classe patronale', *Le Mouvement social*, 114 (1981), pp. 11–34

Linebaugh, Peter, 'Tyburn: Crime and the Labouring Poor in Eighteenth-Century London', unpublished Ph.D thesis, University of Warwick, 1975

Liste des volontaires de la garde nationale parisienne du district Saint-Merry (Paris, 1789) (B.L. R 573 [6])

Lombard-Jourdan, Anne, 'Les Confréries parisiennes des peintres', *Bulletin de la société d'histoire de Paris et de l'Ile-de-France*, 107 (1980), pp. 87–103

Longfellow, David L., 'Silk Weavers and Social Struggle in Lyon during the French Revolution, 1789–1794', *French Historical Studies*, 12 (1981), pp. 1–40

Lottin, Alain, 'Les Vivants et les morts au xviiie siècle, Les incidents de Lille (1779) et de Cambrai (1786) lors des translations de cimetière', *Actes du xviiie congrès de la Fédération des Sociétés Savantes du Nord de la France* (Lille, 1979)

Lucas, Colin, ed., *The Political Culture of the French Revolution* (Oxford, 1988)

'The Crowd and Politics', in Colin Lucas, ed., *The Political Culture of the French Revolution* (Oxford, 1988)

Lüthy, Herbert, *La Banque protestante en France de la Révocation de l'Edit de Nantes à la Révolution*, 2 vols (Paris, 1959–61)

McCleod, Christine, 'The 1690s Patent Boom: Invention or Stock Jobbing', *Economic History Review*, 2nd series, 39 (1986), pp. 549–71

McKendrick, Neil, Brewer, John and Plumb, J. H., *The Birth of a Consumer Society: The Commercialisation of Eighteenth-Century England* (London, 1982)

Mackenzie, D. F., 'Printers of the Mind', *Studies in Bibliography*, 22 (1969), pp. 1–75

Mackrell, J. Q. C., *The Attack on 'Feudalism' in Eighteenth-Century France* (London, 1973)

Macpherson, C. B., *The Political Theory of Possessive Individualism* (Oxford, 1962)

Malepeyre, Léopold, *Code des ouvriers* (Paris, 1833)

Marat, Jean Paul, *L'Ami du peuple* (Paris, 1789–93)

Marglin, Steven, 'What Do Bosses Do?', in Andre Gorz, ed., *The Division of Labour* (London, 1976)

Markov, Walter and Soboul, Albert, eds., *Die Sansculotten von Paris* (Berlin, 1957)

Martin, Germain, *Les Associations ouvrières au xviiie siècle (1700–1792)* (Paris, 1900)

Martin, Henri-Jean, *Livre, pouvoirs et société à Paris au xviie siècle (1598–1701)*, 2 vols (Geneva, 1969)

Marx, Karl, *Capital* (reprinted London, 1965)

Maza, Sara C., *Servants and Masters in Eighteenth-Century France* (Princeton, 1983)

'Le Tribunal de la nation: les mémoires judiciaires et l'opinion publique à la fin de l'ancien régime', *Annales E.S.C.*, 42 (1987), pp. 73–90

Mémoire à consulter et consultation pour les ouvriers, compagnons et manœuvres maçons, platriers et tailleurs de pierre à Lyon (Lyon, 1787) (A.C. Lyon, HH 104, Imprimes 703.981.)

Mémoire en la cause pour Jean Chastel...et autres au nombre de quatre-vingt-six, tous compagnons couvreurs de la ville et fauxbourgs de Paris (Paris, 1743) (Bibliothèque de l'Ordre des Avocats, Paris, Fonds Gaultier-Debreil, 35 [68])

Mémoire des électeurs fabricants d'étoffes de soie et tarif dressé en exécution de l'arrêt du 8 aout 1789 (Lyon, 1790) (B.M. Lyon 354 440)

Mémoire des maîtres gardes de la communauté des maîtres-ouvriers et marchands d'étoffes d'or, d'argent et de soye (de Lyon) (Lyon, 1732) (University of Toronto Library, T–10/7 [11])

Mémoire ou petition adressée à l'Assemblée Nationale pour tous les anciens maîtres agrégés aux corporations des serruriers, taillandiers, maréchaux, ferblantiers, cloutiers...d'Orléans (Orléans, 1790) (A.D. Loiret, 2J 1915)

Mémoire pour le sieur Coeffier (Paris, 1790) (B.H.V.P. 953 933)

Mémoire pour le sieur Coeffier entrepreneur des bâtiments et maître maçon à Paris (Paris, n.d., but 1791 from the content) (B.H.V.P. 139 883)

Mémoire pour le sieur Martin, peintre vernisseur du roi; le sieur Charny, peintre, ancien professeur de l'Académie et communauté de peintre, sous l'invocation de Saint-Luc...denommes dans l'arrêt du 23 novembre 1785 (Paris, 1786) (B.N. 4° fm 20904)

Mémoire pour les directeurs, corps et communauté de l'Académie de Saint-Luc contre Simon Bezançon, André Tramblin et consors (Paris, n.d., but c. 1737) (A.N. AD VIII, 1)

Mémoire pour les syndics, jurés et communauté des maîtres couvreurs de la ville de Paris (Paris, 1743) (B.N. MS. Joly de Fleury, 2340 fol. 93)

Mémoire présenté à MM les maire et officiers municipaux par les ouvriers ébénistes et menuisiers de Marseille (Marseille, n.d. but, from the allusions, probably 1791) (A.C. Marseille, HH 416)

Mémoire signifié pour la communauté des maîtres charrons-carossiers de la ville et faubourgs de Paris (Paris, 1767) (B.H.V.P. 402 104)

Mémoire signifié pour les boulangers-forains du fauxbourg Saint-Antoine...contre les maîtres boulangers de Paris (Paris, 1760) (Bibliothèque de l'Orde des Avocats (Paris), Collection Chanlaire, vol. 102. no. 4)

Mémoire signifié pour les directeurs anciens et actuels de l'Académie de Saint-Luc (Paris, n.d.) (A.N. AD VIII. 1)

Mémoires pour les artistes des galeries du Louvre contre les directeurs et gardes de la communauté des maîtres peintres et sculpteurs de Paris (Paris, 1763) (Bibliothèque de l'Orde des Avocats (Paris), Collection Chanlaire, vol. 161. nos. 3 and 4)

Menc, Joseph de, *Réflexions de Machiavel sur la première décade de Tite Live* (Amsterdam, 1782)

Ménétra, Jacques-Louis, *Journal de ma vie*, ed. Daniel Roche (Paris, 1982)

Merriman, John M., ed., *Consciousness and Class Experience in Nineteenth-Century Europe* (New York, 1981)

Metzger, Albert and Vaesen, Joseph, *Lyon de 1778 à 1788* (Lyon, n.d.)

Michel, Marianne Roland, *Lajoue et l'art rocaille* (Neuilly-sur-Seine, 1984)

Michelet, Jules, *Le Peuple*, ed. Paul Viallaneix (Paris, 1974)

Migne, Jacques Paul, ed.. *Collection intégrale et universelle des orateurs sacrés*, 99 vols (Paris, 1844–66)

Miller, Michael B., *The Bon Marché. Bourgeois Culture and the Department Store, 1869–1920* (Princeton, 1981)

Ministère du Commerce, de l'Industrie, des Postes et des Télégraphes, Office du Travail, *Rapport sur l'apprentissage dans les industries de l'ameublement* (Paris, 1905)

Mirabeau père (*i.e.* Riquetti, Victor, marquis de Mirabeau), *L'Ami des hommes*, 3 vols (The Hague, 1758)

Moch, Leslie Page, *Paths to the City* (London, 1983)

Moniteur (Paris, 1789 onwards)

Monnier, Raymonde, *Le Faubourg Saint-Antoine (1789–1815)* (Paris, 1981)

Montias, J. Michael, 'Cost and Value in Seventeenth-Century Dutch Art', *Art History*, 10 (1987), pp. 455–65

Moore, Sally Falk, *Social Facts and Fabrications, Customary Law on Kilamanjaro, 1880–1980* (Cambridge, 1986)

Moriceau, Jean-Marc, 'Les "Baccanals" ou grèves des moissonneurs en Pays de France (seconde moitié du xviiie siècle)', in Jean Nicolas, ed.. *Mouvements populaires et conscience sociale* (Paris, 1985), pp. 420–33

Morineau, Michel, 'Budgets populaires en France au xviiie siècle', *Revue d'histoire économique et sociale*, 50 (1972), pp. 203–37, 449–81

Mots, 10 (1985), special issue devoted to 'Le Nous Politique'

Mouilleseaux, J. P., 'Recherches sur l'activité du bâtiment à Bordeaux (1769–1790)', T.E.R. Université de Bordeaux, 1970

Moulin, Anne-Marie, *Les Maçons de la Haute-Marche au xviiie siècle* (Clermont-Ferrand, 1986)

Mouvement Social, Le, 141 (1987), special issue on 'Les Prud'Hommes: XIX–XX Siècle'

Museum Bellerive, Zurich, *Catalogue of the exhibition on Europäische Lackkunst vom 18. bis 20. Jahrhundert* (Zurich, 1976)

Nadaud, Martin, *Mémoires de Léonard, ancien garçon maçon*, ed. Maurice Agulhon (Paris, 1976)

Nau-Deville, *Compte rendu des séances électorales et de la division du corps électoral en deux sociétés sous les noms de club de l'Evêché, club de la Sainte-Chapelle* (Paris, 1791) [B.L. R 658 (5)]

Nicolas, Jean, *Mouvements populaires et conscience sociale* (Paris, 1985)

Nigéon, René, *Etat financier des corporations parisiennes d'arts et métiers au xviiie siècle* (Paris, n.d.)

Nolhac, Pierre de, 'La Décoration de Versailles au xviiie siècle', *Gazette des Beaux-Arts, 3ème periode*, 17 (1897), pp. 104–14

Nye, John Vincent, 'Firm Size and Economic Backwardness: A New Look at the French Industrialization Debate', *Journal of Economic History*, 47 (1987), pp. 649–69

Oman, Charles C. and Hamilton, Jean, *Wallpapers: A History and Illustrated Catalogue of the Collection in the Victoria and Albert Museum* (London, 1982)

Pagden, Anthony, ed., *The Languages of Political Theory in Early-Modern Europe* (Cambridge, 1987)

Pallach, Ulrich-Christian, 'Fonctions de la mobilité artisanale et ouvrière – compagnons, ouvriers et manufacturiers en France et aux Allemands (17e–19e Siècles)', *Francia*, 11 (1983), pp. 365–406

Papillon du Rivet, N. G., *Sermons*, in Jacques Paul Migne, *Collection intégrale et universelle des orateurs sacrés* (Paris, 1844), vol. 59

Pardailhé-Lebrun, Annik, *Naissance de l'intime* (Paris, 1988)

Parker, Harold T., *The Bureau of Commerce in 1781 and its Policies with Respect to French Industry* (Durham, North Carolina, 1979)

Peloux, Charles du, *Répertoire biographique et bibliographique des artistes du xviiie siècle français* (Paris, 1930)

Perdiguier, Agricol, *Le Livre du compagnonnage* (Paris, 1839)

Perdiguier, Agricol, *Mémoires d'un compagnon*, ed. Alain Faure (Paris, 1977)

Perrot, Jean-Claude, *Genèse d'une ville moderne: Caen au xviiie siècle*, 2 vols (Paris, 1975)

Perrot, Michelle, *Les Ouvriers en grève*, 2 vols (Paris, 1974)

Petition des maîtres charpentiers de la section du Temple (Paris, 1791) (A.D.V.P. VD* 1661)

Petition des ouvriers employés aux carrières de Paris adressée au Conseil d'Etat (Paris, n.d.) (B.N. 4° fm 35344)

Petition présentée à la municipalité de Paris par les ci-devant maîtres charpentiers (Paris, 1791) (B.N. 4° fm 35345)

Phénal, A., 'Le Vernis Martin autrefois et aujourd'hui', *Revue des arts décoratifs*, 11 (1890–1), pp. 382–5

L'Age d'or de la statistique régionale française (an IV–1804) (Paris, 1977)

Pillement, Jean Nicolas, *The Ladies' Amusement, or Whole Art of Japanning Made Easy*, ed. R. Sayer (London, 1762; reprinted Newport, 1959)

Piore, Michael, ed., *Unemployment and Inflation* (New York, 1979)

and Sabel, Charles, *The Second Industrial Divide* (New York, 1984)

Piret, Armand, *La Rencontre chez Pothier des conceptions romaines et féodales de la propriété foncière* (Paris, 1937)

Piuz, Anne-Marie, *A Genève et autour de Genève aux xviie et xviiie siècles* (Lausanne and Paris, 1985)

Plinval de Guillebon, Régine de, *Paris Porcelain, 1770–1850* (London, 1972)

'La Manufacture de porcelaine de Dihl et Guerhard, rue de Bondy et rue du Temple', *Bulletin de la société de l'histoire de Paris et de l'Ile de France*, 109 (1982), pp. 177–212

La Porcelaine à Paris sous le Consulat et l'Empire (Geneva and Paris, 1985)

Pocock, J. G. A., *Politics, Language and Time* (London, 1972)

The Machiavellian Moment (Princeton, 1975)

Virtue, Commerce and History (Cambridge, 1985)

Pons, Bruno, *De Paris à Versailles 1699–1736: les sculpteurs ornemantistes parisiens et l'art décoratif des Bâtiments du roi* (Strasbourg, 1986)

'Les Cadres français du xviiie siècle et leurs ornements', *Revue de l'Art*, 76 (1987), pp. 41–50

Posner, Richard A., 'A Theory of Primitive Society, with Special Reference to the Law', *Journal of Law and Economics*, 23 (1980), pp. 1–53

Pothier, Robert Joseph, *Traité du contrat de louage* (Paris, 1778), reprinted in his *Œuvres*, ed. M. Bugnet, 10 vols (Paris, 1845–6; 2nd edn 1861)

Poulain, Guy, *La Distinction des contrats de travail à durée déterminée et indéterminée* (Paris, 1971)

Poussou, Jean Pierre, *Bordeaux et le Sud-Ouest au xviiie siècle* (Paris, 1983)

Préaud, Maxime, Casselle, Pierre, Grivel, Marianne and Le Bitouzé, Corinne, *Dictionnaire des éditeurs d'estampes à Paris sous l'Ancien Régime* (Paris, 1987)

Précis pour le Sr. Leprévost, chapelier privilegié du Roi (Paris, 1763) (B.N. 4° fm 201 106)

Précis pour les maréchaux de Paris (Paris, 1791) (A.N. AD XI 65)

Précis presenté à l'Assemblée nationale par les entrepreneurs de la charpente de la ville de Paris (Paris, 1791) (B.N. 4° fm 35346)

Précis presenté à l'Assemblée nationale par les ouvriers de l'art de la charpente de la ville de Paris (Paris, 1791) (B.N. 4° fm 35347)

Prévôt de la Jannès, Michel, *Les Principes de la jurisprudence françoise*, 2nd edn (Paris, 1770)

Price, Jacob M., *Capital and Credit in British Overseas Trade. The view from the Chesapeake, 1700–1776* (Cambridge, Mass., 1980)

Price, Richard, *Labour in British Society* (London, 1986)

Pris, Claude, *Une Grande Entreprise française sous l'Ancien Régime: la manufacture royale des glaces de Saint-Gobain, 1665–1830* (New York, 1981)

Prothero, Iorwerth, *Artisans and Politics in Early Nineteenth-Century London* (London, 1979)

Prude, Jonathan, *The Coming of Industrial Order* (Cambridge and New York, 1983)

Putterman, Louis, ed., *The Economic Nature of the Firm: A Reader* (Cambridge, 1986)

Quatremère de Quincy, Antoine Chrysostome, *Rapport sur l'édifice dit de Sainte-Geneviève* (Paris, 1976)

Raison-Jourde, Françoise, *La Colonie auvergnate de Paris au xixe siècle* (Paris, 1976)

Rambaud, Mireille, *Documents du Minutier Central concernant l'histoire de l'art (1700–1750)*, 2 vols (Paris, 1964 and 1971)

Rancière, Jacques, 'The Myth of the Artisan', in Steven L. Kaplan and Cynthia J. Koepp, eds, *Work in France* (Ithaca, N.Y., 1986) pp. 317–34

Receuil de memoires et tarif dressés en execution de l'arrêt du 8 aout 1789, obtenu par Messieurs les députés de la ville et sénéchaussée de Lyon (Lyon, 1790) (B.M. Lyon 354 440)

Reddy, William M., 'The Textile Trade and the Language of the Crowd at Rouen, 1752–1871', *Past and Present*, 74 (1977), pp. 62–89

The Rise of Market Culture: The Textile Trade and French Society, 1750–1900 (Cambridge, 1984)

Règlements des maistres tailleurs d'habits de la ville et fauxbourgs de Lyon (Lyon, 1729) (B.N. F 26473)

Reichardt, Rolf and Schneider, Herbert, 'Chanson et musique populaires devant l'histoire à la fin de l'Ancien Régime', *XVIIIe Siècle*, 18 (1986), pp. 117–42

Reid, Douglas A., 'The Decline of Saint Monday, 1766–1786', *Past and Present*, 71 (1976), pp. 76–101

Requête au Roi et mémoire sur la nécessité de rétablir les corps de marchands (Paris, 1817) (A.N. AD XI 65)

Révolutions de Paris, Les, (Paris, 1789–93)

Robbins, Caroline, *The Eighteenth-Century Commonwealthmen* (Cambridge, Mass., 1961)

Robert, Karl, *Les Procédés du vernis Martin* (Paris, 1892)

Roberts, J. M., ed., *French Revolution Documents* (Oxford, 1966)

The Mythology of the Secret Societies (London, 1972)

Robespierre, Maximilien François Marie Isidore, *Œuvres*, ed. Marc Bouloiseau, Georges Lefebvre and Albert Soboul, 14 vols (Paris, 1910–86)

Roche, Daniel, *Le Siècle des Lumières en Province*, 2 vols (Paris, 1978)

Le Peuple de Paris (Paris, 1981)

Rochedieu, Charles Alfred, *Bibliography of French translations of English Works 1700–1800* (Chicago, 1948)

Rochefoucauld-Liancourt, G. de la, *Notice sur les associations des ouvriers à Paris* (Paris, 1834)

Root, Hilton, *Peasants and King in Burgundy. Agrarian Foundations of French Absolutism* (Berkeley, California, 1987)

Root-Bernstein, Michèle, *Boulevard Theater and Revolution in Eighteenth-Century Paris* (Ann Arbor, Michigan, 1984)

Rose, R. B., *The Making of the Sans-Culottes. Democratic Ideas and Institutions in Paris 1789–92* (Manchester, 1983)

'The "Red Scare" of the 1790s: The French Revolution and the "Agrarian Law"', *Past and Present*, 103 (1984), pp. 113–30

Rosenband, Leonard N., 'Work and Management in the Montgolfier Paper Mill', unpublished Ph.D. thesis, Princeton University, 1980

Rosenberg, Nathan, ed., *The Economics of Technological Change* (London, 1971)

Ross, Ellen, 'The Debate on Luxury in Eighteenth-Century France', unpublished Ph.D. thesis, University of Chicago, 1975

Rougerie, Jacques, 'Composition d'une population insurgée: l'example de la Commune', *Le Mouvement social*, 48 (1964), pp. 31–48

Roubo, André-Jacob, *L'Art du menuisier*, 4 vols (Paris, 1770)

Roudier, Jacqueline, 'La Situation de l'imprimerie lyonnaise à la fin du xviie siècle', in Henri-Jean Martin, ed., *Cinq Etudes Lyonnaises* (Paris and Geneva, 1966), pp. 77–111

Roux, Marcel, *Bibliothèque nationale. Inventaire du fonds français. Graveurs du xviiie siècle* (Paris, 1940)

Roze de Chantoiseau, *Essai sur l'almanach général d'indication d'advesse personelle et domicile fixe des six corps, arts et métiers* (Paris, 1769)

Rude, F., *Doléances des maîtres ouvriers fabricants en étoffes d'or, d'argent et de soie de la ville de Lyon* (Lyon, 1976)

Rudé, George, *The Crowd in the French Revolution* (Oxford, 1959)

The Crowd in History (New York, 1964)

Paris and London in the Eighteenth Century (London, 1970)

Rule, John, *The Experience of Labour in Eighteenth-Century Industry* (London, 1981)

The Labouring Classes of Early Industrial England 1750–1850 (London, 1986)

'The Property of Skill in the Period of Manufacture', in Patrick Joyce, ed., *The Historical Meanings of Work* (Cambridge, 1987)

Rutledge, Jacques, *Eloge de Montesquieu* (London, 1786)

Sabatier, Jacqueline, *Figaro et son Maitre* (Paris, 1984)

Sabean, David Warren, *Power in the Blood: Popular Culture and Village Discourse in Early Modern Germany* (Cambridge, 1984)

Sabel, Charles, *Work and Politics* (Cambridge and New York, 1982)

and Zeitlin, Jonathan, 'Historical Alternatives to Mass Production: Politics, Markets and Technology in Nineteenth-Century Industrialization', *Past and Present*, 108 (1985). pp. 133–76

Sahlins, Marshall, *Islands of History* (Chicago, 1985)

Saint-Léon, E. Martin, *Le Compagnonnage* (Paris, 1901)

Savary des Bruslons, Jacques, *Dictionnaire universel de commerce*, 2 vols (Paris, 1723; 6th edn 1750)

Schleich, Thomas, 'Die Verbreitung und Rezeption der Aufklärung in der französischen Gesellschaft am Beispiel Mably', in Hans Ulrich Gumbrecht, Rolf Reichardt and Thomas Schleich, eds., *Sozialgeschichte der Aufklärung in Frankreich*, 2 vols (Munich, 1981), pp. 147–70

Schmidt, Charles, *Industrie: receuil de texts et de notes, commission de recherche et de publication des documents rélatifs à la vie économique de la Révolution* (Paris, 1910)

Schmitt, Jean-Marie, *Aux Origines de la révolution industrielle en Alsace* (Strasbourg, 1980)

Scholte, Bob, 'The Charmed Circle of Geertz's Hermeneutics', *Critique of Anthropology*, 6 (1986), pp. 5–15

Scott, Joan Wallach and Hobsbawm, E. J., 'Political Shoemakers', *Past and Present*, 89 (1980), pp. 86–114

'Men and Women in the Parisian Garment Trades: Discussions of Family and Work in the 1830s and 1840s', in Pat Thane, Geoffrey Crossick and Roderick Floud, eds., *The Power of the Past* (Cambridge, 1984), pp. 67–93

Scoville, Warren C., *Capitalism and French Glassmaking* (Berkeley, California, 1950)

Scranton, Philip, *Proprietary Capitalism: The Textile Manufacture at Philadelphia, 1800–1885* (Cambridge and New York, 1983)

Seccombe, Wally, 'Patriarchy Stabilized: The Construction of the Male Bread-winner Wage Norm in Nineteenth-Century Britain', *Social History*, 11 (1986), pp. 53–76

Segalen, Martine, *Les Confréries dans la France contemporaine* (Paris, 1975)

Sekora, John, *Luxury: The Concept in Western Thought from Eden to Smollett* (Baltimore, 1977)

Sénac de Meilhan, Gabriel, *Portraits et caractères des personnages distingués de la fin du xviiie siècle* (Paris, 1813)

Sergène, André, 'La Manufacture de Sèvres sous l'Ancien Régime', Thèse de doctorat, Université de Nancy, 1972–4

Sewell, William H. Jnr., 'Social Change and the Rise of Working Class Politics in Nineteenth-Century Marseille', *Past and Present*, 65 (1974), pp. 75–109

'The Working Class of Marseille under the Second Republic: Social Structure and Political Behaviour', in Peter N. Stearns and Daniel J. Walkowitz, eds., *Workers in the Industrial Revolution* (New Brunswick, N.J., 1974)

Work and Revolution in France: The Language of Labor from the Old Régime to 1848 (Cambridge and New York, 1980)

Structure and Mobility: The Men and Women of Marseille, 1829–1970 (Cambridge and New York, 1985)

'Visions of Labor: Illustrations of the Mechanical Arts before, in, and after, Diderot's *Encyclopédie*', in Steven L. Kaplan and Cynthia J. Koepp, eds., *Work in France* (Ithaca, N.Y., 1986)

Sgard, Jean, ed., *Dictionnaire des journalistes* (Grenoble, 1976)

Shennan, J. H., *The Parlement of Paris* (London, 1968)

Shephard, Edward, 'Social and Geographic Mobility of the Eighteenth-Century Guild Artisan: An Analysis of Guild Receptions in Dijon, 1700–1790', in Steven L. Kaplan and Cynthia J. Koepp, eds., *Work in France* (Ithaca, N.Y., 1986), pp. 97–130

Sibalis, Michael, 'The Workers of Napoleonic Paris, 1800–1814', unpublished Ph.D. Thesis, Concordia University, Montreal, 1979

'Shoemakers and Fourierism in Nineteenth-Century Paris: The *Société Laborieuse des Cordonniers-Bottiers*', *Histoire Sociale/Social History*, 20 (1987), pp. 29–49

Skinner, Quentin, 'The Principles and Practice of Opposition: The Case of Bolingbroke versus Walpole', in Neil McKendrick, ed., *Historical Perspectives* (London, 1974), pp. 93–128

Soboul, Albert, *Les Sans-Culottes parisiens en l'An II* (Paris, 1958)

and Monnier, Raymonde, *Répertoire du personnel sectionnaire parisien en l'an II* (Paris, 1985)

Société philanthropique de Paris, Rapports (Paris, 1801–21)

Sonenscher, Michael, 'Note sur le pasteur et conventional Rabaut Saint-Etienne', *Bulletin de la Société de l'Histoire du Protestantisme français*, 121 (1975), pp. 370–4

'Royalists and Patriots: Nîmes and its Hinterland in the late Eighteenth Century', unpublished Ph.D. thesis, University of Warwick, 1978

'Work and Wages in Eighteenth-Century Paris', in Maxine Berg, Pat Hudson and Michael Sonenscher, eds., *Manufacture in Town and Country before the Factory* (Cambridge, 1983)

'The *Sans-Culottes* of the Year II: Rethinking the Language of Labour in Revolutionary France', *Social History*, 9 (1984), pp. 301–28

'Les Sans-Culottes de l'an II: repenser le langage du travail dans la France révolutionnaire', *Annales E.S.C.*, 40 (1985), pp. 1087–1108

'Journeymen's Migrations and Workshop Organization in Eighteenth-Century France', in Steven L. Kaplan and Cynthia J. Koepp, eds., *Work in France* (Ithaca, N.Y., 1986), pp. 74–96

'Weavers, Wage-Rates and the Measurement of Work in Eighteenth-Century Rouen', *Textile History*, 17 (1986), pp. 7–17

and David Garrioch, '*Compagnonnages*, Confraternities and Associations of Journeymen in Eighteenth-Century Paris', *European History Quarterly*, 16 (1986), pp. 25–45

'Un Ouvrier en 1820', *History Workshop Journal*, 21 (1986), pp. 174–9

'Journeymen, the Courts and the French Trades 1781–1791', *Past and Present*, 114 (1987), pp. 77–109

The Hatters of Eighteenth-Century France (Berkeley, California, 1987)

'Mythical Work: Workshop Production and the *Compagnonnages* of Eighteenth-Century France', in Patrick Joyce, ed., *The Historical Meanings of Work* (London, 1987)

'Le Droit du travail en France et en Angleterre à l'époque de la Révolution', *Colloque sur la Révolution française et le développement du capitalisme* (Lille, November 1987)

Stackelberg, Jurgen von., *Tacitus in der Romania* (Tubingen, 1960)

Statuts des maîtres cartiers, papetiers, faiseurs de cartes, tarots, feuillets et cartons (Paris, 1764)

Statuts des maîtres potiers de terre, carleurs de la ville de Paris (Paris, 1752)

Statuts des menuisiers de Lyon (Bibliothèque de l'Arsénal, 8°J 46849)

Stedman Jones, Gareth, *Languages of Class* (Cambridge, 1983)

'Rethinking Chartism', in *Languages of Class* (Cambridge, 1983)

Stewart-McDougall, Mary Lynn, *The Artisan Republic: Revolution, Reaction and Resistance in Lyon, 1848–1851* (Montreal, 1984)

Stürmer, Michael, 'An Economy of Delight: Court Artisans of the Eighteenth Century', *Business History Review*, 53 (1979), pp. 496–528

Styles, John, 'Embezzlement, Industry and the Law in England, 1500–1700', in Maxine Berg, Pat Hudson and Michael Sonenscher, eds., *Manufacture in Town and Country before the Factory* (Cambridge, 1983), pp. 173–210

Suite du nouveau receuil des édits, déclarations, lettres patentes et règlements de Sa Majesté (Rouen, 1741)

Sutherland, Donald, *France 1789–1815: Revolution and Counterrevolution* (London, 1985)

Tableau de la comptabilité du Mont de Piété (Paris, 1790) (B.H.V.P. 12834)

Tableau de Rouen (Rouen, 1775 and 1788) (University of London Library, Institute of Historical Research)

Tackett, Timothy, *Religion, Revolution and Regional Culture in Eighteenth-Century France* (Princeton, 1986)

Teynac, Françoise, Nolot, Pierre and Vivien, Jean-Denis, *Le Monde du papier peint* (Paris, 1981)

Thoinan, Ernest, *Les Relieurs français (1500–1800)* (Paris, 1893)

Thomas, Yves, 'Note sur la chambre de police du Châtelet de Paris à l'époque de Louis XVI', *Revue historique de droit français et étranger*, 54 (1976), pp. 361–78

Thompson, E. P., *The Making of the English Working Class* (London, 1963)

'The Grid of Inheritance, a Comment', in Jack Goody, Joan Thirsk and E. P. Thompson, eds., *Family and Inheritance* (Cambridge, 1976), pp. 328–60

'Folklore, Anthropology and Social History', *Indian Historical Review*, 3 (1978), pp. 247–66

'Eighteenth-Century English Society: Class Struggle without Class', *Social History*, 3 (1978), pp. 133–65

Thompson, J. M., *French Revolution Documents* (Oxford, 1948)

Thompson, Martyn P., 'The History of Fundamental Law in Political Thought from the French Wars of Religion to the American Revolution', *American Historical Review*, 91 (1986), pp. 1103–28

Thomson, J. K. J., *Clermont-de-Lodève, 1633–1789* (Cambridge, 1982)

Tilly, Charles and Lees, Lynn, 'Le Peuple de juin 1848', *Annales E.S.C.*, 29 (1974), pp. 1062–91

Tomlinson, Jim, 'Democracy inside the Black Box? Neo-Classical Theories of the Firm and Industrial Democracy', *Economy and Society*, 15 (1986), pp. 220–50

Tönnesson, Kare D., *La Défaite des sans-culottes* (Paris and Oslo, 1959)

Tournier, Maurice, 'Grève, Cayenne et gavots: hypothèse de reconstitution des origines', unpublished paper, Centre de Recherches 'Lexicologie et Textes Politiques', École Normale Supérieure de Saint-Cloud, September 1977

'Les Mots conflits: l'exemple de grève au milieu du 19e siècle', *Le Français aujourd'hui*, 58 (1982), pp. 39–48

Trénard, Louis, 'La Crise sociale lyonnaise à la veille de la Révolution', *Revue d'histoire moderne et contemporaine*, 2 (1955), pp. 5–45

'L'Utopie de Francois-Joseph L'Ange', paper presented to the *colloque* on *La Révolution française et le développement du capitalisme* (Lille, November 1987)

Trois siècles de papiers peints (Paris and Rennes, 1967)

Truant, Cynthia. M., 'Solidarity and Symbolism among Journeymen Artisans', *Comparative Studies in Society and History*, 21 (1979), pp. 214–26

Tuck, Richard, *Natural Rights Theories* (Cambridge, 1979)

Tully, James, *A Discourse Concerning Property: John Locke and his Adversaries* (Cambridge, 1980)

Unger, Roberto Mangabeira, *Social Theory: Its Situation and Task* (Cambridge and New York, 1987)

Van Kley, Dale, *The Jansenists and the Expulsion of the Jesuits from France, 1757–65* (New Haven, 1975)

Vattel, Emmerich de, *Le Droit des gens ou principes de la loi naturelle* (Leiden and Neuchâtel, 1758)

Venard, Marc, 'Les Confréries dans l'espace urbaine: l'exemple de Rouen', *Annales de Bretagne*, 90 (1982), pp. 321–2

'Christianiser les ouvriers en France au xviie siècle', *Acts du 109e congrès national des sociétés savantes. Section d'histoire moderne et contemporaine* (Paris, 1984), vol. 1, pp. 19–30

Verger, F. J., *Archives curieuses de la ville de Nantes*, 5 vols (Nantes, 1837)

Verlet, Pierre, 'Le Commerce des objets d'art et les marchands-merciers à Paris au xviie siècle', *Annales E.S.C.*, 14 (1958), pp. 10–29

L'Art du meuble à Paris au xviie siècle (Paris, 1968)

Les Bronzes dorés français du xviie siècle (Paris, 1987)

Vernier, Jean-Jacques, ed., *Cahiers de doléances du Bailliage de Troyes* (Troyes, 1909)

Vial, Jean, *La Coutume chapelière* (Paris, 1941)

Victoria and Albert Museum, *Art and Design in Hogarth's England* (London, 1984)

Vincent, Antoine Jean, *Le Livre des proverbes français*, 2 vols (Paris, 1859)

Voetzel, René Frederic, *Jean Domat (1625–1696), essai de reconstitution de sa philosophie juridique* (Paris, 1936)

Volpilhac-Auger, Catherine, 'Tacite et Montesquieu', *Studies in Voltaire and the Eighteenth Century*, 232 (Oxford, 1985)

Voltaire, François Marie Arouet de, *Les Tu et les vous; Nanine; Premier discours sur l'inégalité des conditions*, in his *Œuvres*, Kehl edn, 70 vols (1785–9)

Volvic, Gilbert Joseph Gaspard Chabrol de, *Recherches statistiques sur la ville de Paris*, 3 vols (Paris, 1823–9)

Vovelle, Michel, *La Chute de la Monarchie* (Paris, 1972)

La Révolution française. Images et récit, 5 vols (Paris, 1986)

Vries, Jan de, *European Urbanization (1500–1800)* (London, 1984)

Wall, Richard, 'Work, Welfare and the Family: An Illustration of the Adaptive Family Economy', in Lloyd Bonfield, Richard Smith and Keith Wrightson, eds., *A World We Have Gained* (Oxford, 1986) pp. 261–94

'Leaving Home and the Process of Household Formation in Pre-Industrial England', *Continuity and Change*, 2 (1987), pp. 77–101

Walton, Whitney, ''To Triumph before Feminine Taste'': Bourgeois Women's Consumption and Hand Methods of Production in Mid-Nineteenth Century Paris', *Business History Review*, 60 (1986), pp. 541–63

Weber, Max, *General Economic History*, Collier Books edn (New York, 1961)

Weigert, R. A., 'Introduction' to the catalogue, *Claude Audran. L'Art décoratif français au Musée de Stockholm* (Paris, Bibliothèque nationale, 1950)

'Un Collaborateur ignoré de Claude III Audran', *Etudes d'art du musée d'Alger*, 1 (1952), pp. 63–76

'Claude III Audran, père de l'art décoratif', *Médecine de France*, 115 (1960), pp. 17–32

Wilentz, Sean, *Chants Democratic. New York City and the Rise of the American Working Class, 1788–1850* (Oxford and New York, 1984)

Wilhelm, Jacques, 'Le Grand Cabinet chinois de l'Hôtel de Richelieu, Place Royale', *Bulletin du Musée Carnavalet*, 1 (1967), pp. 2–14

Wille, Johann-Georg (or Jean-Georges), *Mémoires et journal*, ed. Georges Duplessis, 2 vols (Paris, 1857)

Williamson, O. E., 'The Organization of Work', *Journal of Economic Behaviour and Organization*, 1 (1980), pp. 5–38

Woloch, Isser, *Jacobin Legacy: The Democratic Movement under The Directory* (Princeton, 1970)

'From Charity to Welfare in Revolutionary Paris', *Journal of Modern History*, 58 (1986), pp. 779–812

Wrigley, E. A., 'Some Reflections on Corn-Yields and Prices in Pre-Industrial Economies', in his *People, Cities and Wealth* (Oxford, 1987) pp. 92–130

Wrigley, Richard, 'The Liberty Cap in the French Revolution', unpublished paper, 1987

Yeazell, Stephen C., *From Medieval Group Litigation to the Modern Class Action* (New Haven, 1987)

Young, Arthur, *Travels in France*, Everyman edn (London, 1913)

Zeitlin, Jonathan, 'From Labour History to the History of Industrial Relations', *Economic History Review*, 2nd series, 40 (1987), pp. 159–84

Zeldin, Theodore, *France 1848–1945*, 2 vols (Oxford, 1973–7)

Zysberg, André, *Les Galériens au xviiie siècle* (Paris, 1987)